PATTON: ORDEAL AND TRIUMPH

"The longest, most detailed and wide-ranging study . . . not a Patton eulogy . . . the large hates that were in him, his abuse of position and his grotesqueries are also told fully."   —The New York Times

"One of the most satisfying books I ever read. . . . An objective and penetrating study. . . . It satisfies even the most critical reader . . . it satisfies the soul."   —Gene Smith, author of WHEN THE CHEERING STOPPED

"Vivid . . . affectionate . . . thoroughly frank. . . . Mr. Farago has captured Patton's many-sided character—his lusty exuberance, his flaming anger, his blasphemy, his great qualities as a leader, and his glaring moments of human weakness."   —John Toland, author of BUT NOT IN SHAME

"History at its most compelling sweep, Mr. Farago's breathtaking Patton biography is written with the General's own color and verve, and a deep understanding of the man and events."   —Robert Payne, author of THE LIFE AND DEATH OF LENIN

ABOUT THE AUTHOR: LADISLAS FARAGO is the bestselling co-author of Behind Closed Doors and the author of the widely heralded The War of Wits and The Tenth Fleet. The author's fourteen other books have been principally concerned with the subjects of intelligence and military history. Mr. Farago has served as confidential consultant to Radio Free Europe and during the war was Chief of Research and Planning, Special Welfare Branch, Chief of Naval Operations, U.S. Navy.

PATTON:
ORDEAL AND TRIUMPH

BY LADISLAS FARAGO

A DELL BOOK

Published by **DELL PUBLISHING CO., INC.**
750 Third Avenue, New York, New York 10017

Copyright © 1963 by Faracorn Ltd.

Dell ® TM 681510, Dell Publishing Co., Inc.

All rights reserved.

Reprinted by arrangement with
Ivan Obolensky, Inc., New York, New York

Dedication: For John

First Dell printing—July, 1965

Printed in U.S.A.

CONTENTS

BOOK ONE: THE ORDEAL

BOOK TWO: THE TRIUMPH

BOOK ONE ☆ THE ORDEAL

CHAPTER ONE
ROBERT IS COMING

Shortly after sunset on November 7, 1942, the British Broadcasting Corporation began to sneak into its programs beamed to French North Africa a cryptic message made up of just two words:

"Robert arrive" . . . "Robert is coming!"

All BBC broadcasts to the Axis-occupied countries had been spiked with such laconic signals, and *"Robert arrive"* was but one of a score of coded messages inserted into the programs on this Saturday night. The uninitiated listener, though thrilled or intrigued by the melodrama of such clandestine communications on which he was permitted to eavesdrop, did not know what they portended. Even the growing underground army of men and women fighting the Nazis on the secret fronts of the war could not make head or tail of them unless certain specific messages were directly beamed to them in codes to which only they had the key.

Many of the messages were sheer blinds, concocted and broadcast to befuddle the enemy or send him on wild-goose chases. Others were genuine enough. There were instructions to Allied secret agents behind the Nazi lines to execute prearranged operations.

"Robert arrive" was strictly *bona fide*. It was put on the air at this moment to let a small band of anti-Nazis in Algeria and French Morocco know that "Robert" was coming at last to liberate their countries.

On this quiet and balmy Saturday, French Morocco was enjoying the uneasy peace the men of Vichy had abjectly accepted from Adolf Hitler with the surrender of 1940 at Compiègne. At Rabat, the glittering white holy capital city where Mohamed V, his Shereefian Majesty the Sultan of Morocco, and General Auguste Noguès, Vichy's Resident General, had their seat, there was no apprehension that the war—so remote for the past 28 months—would suddenly encroach upon this old coast of High Barbaree within the next 12 hours.

In Morocco, the conquerors of France chose to be relaxed and inconspicuous. They were represented by a 200-man detachment of the German Armistice Commission under a monocled general named Erich von Wulisch, a suave proconsul of Hitler, who handled his delicate job with diplomatic tact. The General's regime had grown soft and lazy on the infectious lassitude of this exotic assignment. Accustomed as he was to the endless flow of such coded signals broadcast by the BBC, which his radiomen kept picking up at regular intervals but which never before had disturbed his own pleasant routine, General von Wulisch paid no attention to the one that was to uproot him just when he felt so safe and smug in his Moroccan sinecure.

It was different on a rooftop in Casablanca. In a shed resembling a pigeon coop, a sinewy, pale young Frenchman was also monitoring the BBC. He was "Ajax," the best radioman of the underground in Morocco, operating "Lincoln," one in a network of clandestine radios a mysterious group of Americans had set up during the year to be ready, as they put it, for any eventualities. Exactly what those "eventualities" would be they didn't say, probably because they themselves did not know. A dense fog had descended upon the war, and anyway, Morocco seemed sufficiently off its beaten path to become even a way station on the Allies' expected march back to Europe.

For a couple of months, Ajax had handled mostly routine traffic—some intelligence data London and Washington had requested, and information the American agents in Morocco —David King, W. Stafford Reid and Kenneth W. Pendar, masquerading as vice consuls attached to the United States Consulate General at Casablanca—thought would interest their home office in Washington. But in October, King told Ajax to watch out for a special signal announcing the imminent arrival of a certain "Robert." Ajax was not told anything more, but he felt in his restive bones that this "Robert" would be much more than just a wayward traveler.

Now on this Saturday evening he opened up for business at 6 P.M., tuning his radio to the BBC as usual. Fidgety at first when the overdue message again failed to come in, he looked down on the harbor, dark under a starless sky, and out to the sea, as far as he could see beyond the jetties. It was so silent except for the steady murmur of the surf.

What Ajax could make out in the dark was ominous even in its slumbering stillness—the big, but unfinished, battleship *Jean Bart* at her berth alongside the Mole de Commerce, a battery of coast defense guns on the El Hank promontory, the 100-mm. guns of Batterie du Port at the other end of the harbor toward Fedala, the farthest Ajax could see. Behind him on the gray Hallicrafter tuned to a whisper, the BBC program was coming from the loud speaker. Then, exactly 38 minutes after 6 o'clock, Ajax heard the words: "*Robert arrive!*"

It was not the first coded message meant for his friends, the American "vice consuls," he had picked up. He was almost blasé by nature, but the signal coming from the speaker abruptly and clearly galvanized him.

"*Enfin,*" he said. "At last!"

He jumped to his feet and pulled himself up as if trying to grow beyond his height, his shoulders shaking and his curved fingers nervously scratching the moist palms in his balled fists. But his trance lasted only a moment. Then Ajax became all business again.

He sent his partner "Marie," a woman in her early twenties and exquisite in her dark beauty, to fetch Stafford Reid. A member of the hush-hush trio at the Consulate on Place de la Fraternité, Reid was a New York construction engineer turned secret agent, who handled the codes of this surreptitious traffic.

When he arrived at the garage just off the harbor where they usually kept such dates, Ajax told him that the signal had come. Then he said, a bit hesitantly, for it was not his business to probe for the meaning of such messages:

"Excuse me, Monsieur Reid . . ."

"Of course, Ajax," the American said. "What is it?"

"Who is 'Robert'?"

Reid became pensive, for this was a secret he was supposed to share with only three Frenchmen in Morocco, and Ajax was not one of them. Then suddenly overcome by the joy of this moment, he blurted out:

" 'Robert' is Patton, Ajax!"

But he drew a blank.

"Pat-tohn?" the radioman asked, his face drawn with disappointment. "Who is *Pat-tohn*, Monsieur Reid?"

"*Pat-tohn,*" of course, was George Smith Patton Jr., the tall, taut, tense American general of vague fame and growing notoriety, the swashbuckling tank-wizard the tabloids in the States already called "Old Blood and Guts." But Stafford Reid was not quite correct, for "Robert" was much more than just Patton. It was the secret synonym for "Torch," the big and bold operation the Allies had put together in fewer than five months to establish a foothold in French North Africa from which the tedious return to Hitler's *Festung Europa* would be staged.

"Torch" was, among others, the Western Task Force under Major General Patton, now in the process of being ferried across the ocean by "the greatest war fleet sent forth by the United States" to force a landing on the coast of French Morocco. It was the fantastic assembly of 33,845 young Americans in 29 transports, forging ahead on a zigzag course through U-boat infested waters, "to move against the enemy," as Patton put it, "wherever he may be and destroy him."

On this November 7th, less than four days from his 57th birthday, in his 33rd year in the United States Army, George Patton was moving at 14 knots toward what he liked to call his rendezvous with destiny. The day before, he wrote to his wife, in a letter he planned to mail in Casablanca: "It seems that my whole life has been pointed to this moment."

And in his private diary, he entered: "I can't decide logically if I am a man of destiny or a lucky fool, but I think I am destined. Five more days will show . . . This may sound like junk, or prophecy, within a week."

That "Torch" would need a man of destiny blessed with luck, Patton had no doubt. This first major campaign of the United States in World War II was more like a bold adventure than a military operation. Fretting in his small office on the heavy cruiser *Augusta,* flagship of the armada that carried the Western Task Force, he felt like the Dauphin in *King John.* "Well," he kept telling himself in Shakespeare's words, "keep good quarter and good care tonight: The day shall not be up so soon as I, to try the fair adventure of tomorrow."

Patton's assignment was plain and ingenious. He was to

land his forces at 4 A.M. on November 8th at three key points on a 240-mile stretch of this Moroccan coast where a hundred years before the Barbary pirates sought refuge— at Safi in the south, at Port Lyautey in the north, and at Fedala in the center. He was to secure the Protectorate as quickly as possible—without bloodshed if possible or conquer it if need be.

But the plan was also ambiguous, fraught with uncertainty, a gamble. Patton had been told that a secret understanding with certain French officers in Morocco would assure a welcome for his forces and that his landings would not be opposed. But he had his doubts. Even on this last leg of the ocean journey (it took the armada a fortnight to zigzag across), when he was only 20 miles from his destination, he did not know with anything resembling certainty how he would have to carry out his mission.

What if the inscrutable, unpredictable, bitter French decided to resist after all?

Patton had only four divisions in his force, all the United States could spare for him at this early stage of the war, what with fighting it across two oceans simultaneously. None of his men had seen combat before. All of them had to be trained hastily. To complete its complement at the last minute, one division had attached to it 400 men who had not even undergone basic training.

The French had 100,000 troops in Morocco, all of them trained and seasoned, and led by experienced professionals. They included the Goumiers of tough Berber stock who always fought for the sake of fighting and never asked any questions. They could not be expected to be swayed by secret diplomacy.

The day before Patton left Washington, Paul Frederick Culbert, an Annapolis-trained former Consul in French Morocco now acting as his diplomatic adviser, brought him a document the State Department had prepared to fit whatever contingency he might encounter. If Patton needed proof that not even the State Department knew what to expect in Morocco, this treaty supplied it. It was the draft of an armistice agreement he was to sign with the French upon arrival. But it was made out in three versions.

"Treaty A" was nicely worded, presupposing a friendly reception. "Treaty B," written in a sterner tone, was to be used in the event of token resistance. "Treaty C" was a tough one. It contained harsh surrender terms "to be imposed on the French forces in the event of an all-out fight."

Patton had sent for the drafts several times during the journey, and read them again and again, as if trying by some extrasensory perception to divine which one he would need. But they proved of no help. Nor did repeated reviews of the situation in shipboard conferences with Culbert, Commander Leo A. Bachman, the Naval Intelligence officer, and his own G-2, Colonel Percy G. Black.

"If our G-2 estimate of the enemy is correct," Patton wrote to Eisenhower after one of the discussions, "we will have quite a fight. Just how hard it will be will depend upon the amount of earnestness the French put into it.

"It does, however, seem to me very desirable from a political point of view to make this seem a very serious resistance, in order to put them right at home, because if we admitted that they made only a token resistance, we are apt to get their families in metropolitan and occupied France in trouble.

"Perhaps it isn't necessary to worry about this as they may fight like hell anyway."

The doubt continued to plague Patton throughout the crossing. On November 3rd he noted in his diary: "Every once in a while the tremendous responsibility of this job lands on me like a ton of bricks." Three days later he wrote to his wife: "In 40 hours I shall be in battle, with little information, and on the spur of the moment will have to make most momentous decisions. But I believe that one's spirit enlarges with responsibility and that, with God's help, I shall make them and make them right."

Earlier on this Saturday, when the convoy was already deploying for the landings, he sent a message to his troops on the transports, letting them know for the first time what they were up to. Signed simply "G. S. Patton Jr.," without giving his rank or designation, the message began:

"Soldiers, we are to be congratulated because we have been chosen as the units of the U.S. Army best fitted to take part in this great American effort."

Then he took the men into his full confidence and let them share his own gnawing doubts: "It is not known," he told them, "whether the French Army, composed of French and Moroccan troops, will contest our landing. It is regrettable to contemplate the necessity of fighting the gallant French who are at heart sympathetic, but all resistance by whomever offered must be destroyed . . .

"When the great day of battle comes, remember your training, and remember, above all, that speed and vigor of attack are the sure roads to success. And you must succeed, for to retreat is as cowardly as it is fatal. Americans do not surrender."

It was the only time throughout World War II that Patton used the word "surrender" in any of his orders to his troops!

At 7 P.M. he went to dinner, outwardly undismayed by the oppressive ambiguity of his mission. He sat down at the table with a broad grin on his albino face, and told his host, Rear Admiral Henry Kent Hewitt, commander of the naval force:

"Admiral, you have the best Goddamn mess I've ever seen. I'm afraid I've grown fat during the crossing."

At the same time, Adolf Hitler was riding in his bulletproof train from his headquarters in East Prussia to Munich in Bavaria to keep a sentimental date that had nothing to do with the war. Nineteen years before, on November 8, 1923, he had tried to grab power for the first time in a pathetic putsch. It began in a beer hall and ended in front of the Munich War Memorial, where a detachment of the *Reichswehr*, the regular army, fired into his Nazi rabble and put it to flight. Each year afterward Hitler commemorated the event by returning to his old comrades in Munich and addressing them, first in defiant, and then in vainglorious, words.

Now, too, he left the East, despite the gradually growing chaos around Stalingrad, for this year's installment of his annual payment of memories. He was accompanied only by his closest military aides, Field Marshal Wilhelm Keitel and General Alfred Jodl, and a skeleton staff. The Führer was maintaining but tenuous contact with the outside world and the war at large.

At 7 P.M., just as Patton was sitting down to dinner, Hitler moved over to the conference compartment of his private car to attend the regular evening situation meeting and listen to General Jodl's report.

Prior to their departure from Rastenburg at noon, Jodl was given a comprehensive summary of intelligence reports describing an ominous concentration of Allied ships at

Gibraltar. On October 31st Nazi spies at Algeciras, the Axis observation post in Spain west of the Rock, had spotted 21 transports, apparently laden with combat-ready troops. On the morning of this November 7th, a last-minute report handed to Jodl spoke of "four to five Allied divisions on shipboard off Gibraltar."

It was now Jodl's job to draw the conclusions from these reports. As soon as Hitler had seated himself at the head of the conference table, he began his estimate of the situation.

"My Führer," he said, "at this hour we have no clear indication as yet of the enemy's specific intentions. But it is possible to draw up a number of assumptions in the order of their likelihood, based on certain hard intelligence about the movement of the enemy's ships.

"There appears to be no doubt that the Allies are planning to land substantial forces in the south—but where?

"It seems to be most likely that the landings will take place in Cyrenaica, to reinforce the British 8th Army of General Montgomery and expedite the eventual destruction of Field Marshal Rommel's armies. It is possible also that the maneuver has for its collateral aim the recovery of Crete to establish a powerful Allied bastion in the Eastern Mediterranean.

"Last, but not least, the possibilities of landings in Malta or Tripolitania, or even in Sicily, can not be ruled out altogether, but they appear to be less likely."

If he was rather evasive up to this point, Jodl concluded his situation report without equivocation. "An attack on the French territories in North Africa," he said, echoing Hitler's own conclusions based on his famed intuition, "is out of the question."

At 7 P.M., too, Captain de Verthamon picked up the telephone at his home and heard a voice say, *"Robert arrive."* It was David King calling a key member of the local conspiracy, the young aide of General Marie-Emile Béthouart, commander of the Casablanca Division of the French Colonial Army, to alert him with the prearranged password.

De Verthamon rushed to the office where Béthouart was waiting. He scribbled on a scrap of paper, *"Débarquement à 0200 demain,"* and placed it on the general's desk.

Béthouart, a gallant officer who had led the French Expeditionary Force at Narvik in Norway in the spring of 1940, had been chosen by the underground to prepare Morocco for Patton's coming and to insure that the landing of the Western Task Force would be unopposed.

In Rabat, the capital city 55 miles northeast of Casablanca, a detachment of Béthouart's men burst into the office of General Georges Lascroux, commander of all French ground forces in Morocco, and kidnaped him. The Colonial Infantry Regiment of the Casablanca Division was sent to Rabat with orders to surround the compound of the Residency. The telephone lines of the Residency, on which General Noguès could alert his forces, were cut.

Then two minutes after midnight, on what now was D-Day, General Béthouart drove to the capital and moved into the office of Lascroux, designating himself as the abducted general's successor.

The complex apparatus seemed to be working with clockwork precision. For a while it promised to assure a friendly reception for George S. Patton.

After dinner, Patton made himself comfortable in Admiral Hewitt's quarters, enjoying a bit of banter on the eve of his first D-Day in World War II. It now seemed that all the doubts had vanished from his mind. He was in one of his jocular moods when everybody present was a fair target for his barbs.

Patton had had his scraps with the Navy while planning and preparing "Torch." Early during this crossing, ensconced on the *Augusta* with only his closest staff around him, and both he and his Task Force subject to naval authority, he was straining at the leash. Impatient in his temporarily subordinate role, he let off steam by talking to his blue-clad hosts in his usual pugnacious way, mildly disparaging "the Goddamn Navy," with an impish twinkle in his pale blue eyes.

He predicted that the Navy would mess up things "as usual," and leave it to the Army to save the day. "Never in history," he said, "has the Navy landed an army at the planned time and place. But don't worry! If you land us anywhere within 50 miles of Fedala and within one week of D-Day, I'll go ahead and win."

By his fifth day at sea, however, Patton seemed properly

chastened by the spectacle of this vast naval effort that surrounded him as far as he could see. In Admiral Samuel Eliot Morison's colorful description of the convoy, it was a brave sight, from the air or sea, and a tempting one from under the sea.

"In the van, as flagship of Rear Admiral Giffen's Covering Group, steamed the mighty *Massachusetts*," Morison wrote in his account of the crossing. "O.T.C. [Officer in Tactical Command] of the fleet was in heavy cruiser *Augusta*, flying the two-starred flag of Rear Admiral Hewitt, and screened by a semicircle of destroyers. *Brooklyn* acted as liaison vessel between the flagship and the main body of the convoy; 35 big transports, cargo vessels and tankers steaming 1,000 yards apart, in nine columns and five lines, with the veteran battleships *Texas* and *New York* on the two flanks of the front line."

Twelve miles astern of the main convoy steamed the air group, *Ranger* and four escort carriers, accompanied by the cruiser *Cleveland* and nine destroyers. In all, more than 40 destroyers were patrolling assigned stations in the outer and inner antisubmarine screens. The air patrol of cruiser-based and carrier-based planes swooped about, keeping watch for U-boats and intrusive neutral merchantmen. Task Force 34, including the outer screen, covered an area of ocean 20 by 30 miles. Yet so expert had the signalmen become, that a flag hoist made on Admiral Hewitt's flagship could reach the entire fleet in 10 minutes.

This extraordinary show left a deep impression on Patton. "It is remarkable," he wrote in admiration "for its orderly, and apparently faultless, efficiency." Now, as he was chewing the fat with Hewitt and his staff in the Admiral's domain, all was quiet and serene, nothing indicating that a major and risky military operation would take place within the next six or eight hours.

Then suddenly this jovial assembly exploded. In came Colonel Black, Patton's tall, lean, suave Intelligence specialist. A product of the exclusive Groton School, always immaculately groomed and exquisitely courteous, Black was something of a busybody with no sense of humor and little of the savvy an officer needed for his survival on Patton's staff. He came to show Patton the leaflet the Office of War Information had prepared for the invasion, to be dropped on the cities of French Morocco at H-Hour.

Patton prided himself on his knowledge of French. A

great friend of France, he was keenly interested in public relations with the populace of the country he was about to invade. He looked eagerly at the leaflet, a flimsy sheet with the Stars and Stripes printed on its front page, and the facsimile of General Eisenhower's signature on the reverse side. Its brief message was printed in bold black letters under the heading: *"Francais de l'Afrique du Nord!"* ("Frenchmen of North Africa").

Then Patton began to read the opening lines: *"Fidele a l'amitie traditionelle et seculaire du gouvernement et du peuple des Etats Unis pour la France et pour l'Afrique francaise du Nord une grande armee americaine debarque sur votre sol."*

He had hardly gone beyond the first few words when he blew his top.

"Black!" he roared. "What's wrong with this Goddamn leaflet?"

"Wrong, sir?" Black asked in obvious consternation.

"Wrong, Goddamn it!" Patton yelled in the falsetto of his quick anger. "Some Goddamn fool in the States forgot to put the accents in this thing. Here!" He pushed the leaflet under Black's nose. "In *'fidele'* the *acute grâve* is missing from the middle E and the *accent acute* is left off the E in *l'amitie.*"

Suddenly the miserable leaflet looked like the hinge of fate. Patton could not have been angrier if someone had forgotten to bring along the medium tanks he needed for the landings at Safi.

He turned back to the hapless Black. "Don't just stand there, Goddamnit! Do something!"

"Yes, sir," the Colonel said sheepishly.

"Yessir, what? Get a bunch of your men and put them to work! Let them put the accents where they belong or none of these Goddamn leaflets will be dropped. Or do you expect me to land on French soil introduced by such illiterate calling cards—Goddamn it?"

Black vanished without a word to round up proofreaders. Sergeant Joe Rosevich, Patton's secretary, was reading Arthur Koestler's *Darkness at Noon* in the fantail when he was called to the petty officers' wardroom to perform his first operation in the face of the enemy—putting in the accents on that confounded leaflet. Colonel Hobart R. Gay, Patton's Chief of Staff, sent for his secretary, Sergeant Delmont, to help Rosevich.

When seven hours later the troops began to storm the shore, they were still at it. "Goddamn it," Delmont said, his vision blurred and fingers cramped, "if our victory in Morocco depends on these blasted accents, we'd better turn around and go home."

"Oh, hell!" Rosevich shrugged. "It's just like the Old Man —a Goddamn perfectionist!"

☆

In the discreet far corner of the restaurant of the Hotel Miramar in Fedala, where the German Armistice Commission had its headquarters, General von Wulisch was entertaining Theodor Auer, a mercurial millionaire who served as German diplomatic agent in Morocco, and a few local friends. It was all small talk, gradually blurred by the champagne—Bollinger Brut 1934—of which the Miramar kept an enormous supply at von Wulisch's orders.

The dinner celebrated Auer's last night in Morocco. He had been called to Vichy by his friend Otto Abetz, the Nazi Ambassador at Marshal Henri Philippe Pétain's court, for consultation and reassignment. Auer had done a good job in Morocco, keeping on friendly terms with everybody who counted, even those American "vice consuls" whose real mission was hardly a secret to him. He was generally very well informed. But if he had heard the signal on the BBC announcing "Robert's" imminent arrival, he seemed to have missed its significance.

"Herr General," he toasted von Wulisch, "I regret deeply to be leaving this splendid country and the pleasure of working with you. I sincerely hope that our paths will cross again in the not too distant future."

The party broke up around 1 A.M., and von Wulisch, his head heavy with champagne, went to bed in his suite on the second floor of the Miramar. His windows opened on the broad sea, which was covered at this point by the 100-mm. guns of Batterie du Port, affording him a comfortable sense of security.

He did not need the lullaby of the surf to fall asleep. But he was jolted awake a scant hour later by urgent knocking on his door. It was Major Schönau, his aide.

"Herr General," Schönau called through the locked door.

"You are wanted on the office phone, sir. Urgent."

With only his tunic over his pajamas, von Wulisch dashed to the office and picked up the phone.

"*Herr General*," he heard the staccato voice of Colonel Ernest von Schimmel, a member of the Armistice Commission at Algiers. "*Mensch,* you won't believe this! It seems the Americans are landing around Cape Matifou between Surcouf and Wadi Reghaia, barely 20 kilometers from this phone."

"*Das ist unmöglich!*" von Wulisch replied haltingly, his tongue thick with sleep and his hangover.

"It isn't impossible," von Schimmel roared back. "It's a fact! Anything at your end?"

"Nothing," the General said. He looked out of the window at Cape Fedala, blacked out and silent, the 75-mm. guns of the fort of the little peninsula cloaked in darkness. "Absolutely nothing! This place is as quiet as a cemetery."

"Well," von Schimmel said, "you better contact Noguès at once! And keep in touch! I'll try to keep you posted."

General von Wulisch replaced the receiver, then looked at Major Schönau with empty eyes.

"The Americans are landing near Algiers, Schönau," he told his aide. "Maybe it's only a raid, one of those hit-and-run things, you know." He stopped for a moment, then said hoarsely, "But if it is the real thing, I fear the worst."

The major looked at his general, wondering what made the "Old Man" so apprehensive.

"The Führer will have no difficulty in pushing them back into the sea," Schönau said stiffly, but von Wulisch told him:

"No, no Schönau! This is an awfully smart thing, this landing at Algiers! It may even be the turning point of the whole war! If the Americans succeed in making it stick, this will be the greatest setback to German arms since 1918. They will take Rommel in the rear, and we shall be expelled from Africa."

As he said it, tears were rolling down his cheeks.

Patton had gone to bed at 10:30 P.M., fully dressed except for his boots (as was his custom before every operation, even in peacetime), and tried to catch some sleep. "This was

22 THE ORDEAL

hard to do," he later remarked to Rosevich—but somehow he managed to sleep until 1:30 in the morning of what now was his D-Day.

Just as he was putting on his boots, he was jolted by another of his fits of white fury. The ship's radio had opened up with a blast, blaring out a familiar voice that penetrated the entire vessel.

It was President Roosevelt speaking—to "his friends" in North Africa—from a record the BBC had put on at exactly 1:30 A.M.

It was one of a series of grave security violations that were plaguing Patton since he had begun to plan his campaign. First, back in August, page 17 of the operations plan of "Torch" vanished without a trace at General Eisenhower's headquarters in London. This page contained the locations of Patton's landings in Morocco. What if a German spy had gotten hold of that confounded page?

Then another, apparently even more serious, security violation shattered Patton's hope that he would be able to sneak ashore in Morocco without the enemy's knowing it. On September 19th the news editor of the United Press in London cabled Lyle Wilson, the UP's bureau manager in Washington, telling him in plain and specific language to prepare for coverage of American landings in Casablanca "and elsewhere in French Morocco" which were expected to occur early in November. The message slipped through the British censorship. Since it went by radio, the Germans should have had no difficulty in intercepting it.

Patton could not know, of course, whether the Germans possessed the missing page or had gotten hold of the UP's cable. But he knew for certain that another "indiscretion," deliberately plotted in our own camp, would spoil whatever little there seemed to be left in his element of surprise.

The landings of "Torch" were scheduled in two installments—in Algeria by the forces moving over from Gibraltar, and in Morocco by Patton's Western Task Force. The landings inside the Mediterranean were to begin at 1:30 A.M. on November 8th, whereas the Patton landings would not get under way until 4 A.M.

Washington thought it would be wise to proclaim the arrival of the American forces in a special message by the President. It was decided to begin the broadcast at 1:30 A.M. to coincide with the landings at Algiers and Oran.

As soon as Patton heard of this decision, he sent a frantic message to Eisenhower protesting what he regarded as a "breach of faith," certain to compromise the security of his Task Force. But Eisenhower told him the broadcast would go on as planned.

"I do not believe that any loss of surprise for your attack will result if the broadcast precedes your H-Hour," the Commander-in-Chief signaled back. "Word of the action by the Center and Eastern Task Forces will certainly be transmitted to the Casablanca authorities, broadcast or no broadcast."

The President's words, in his correct but heavily accented French, were resounding in the *Augusta* when Patton reached the flag deck at 1:45 A.M. His lips were white with anger as he heard them again and again. For a while he kept pacing the bridge, mimicking the President's voice and repeating *"Mes amis . . . mes amis!"* But then the tense realities of the rapidly developing drama restored his sense of rationality.

As he looked around, sniffing the fragrant air of the pitch-black night, his first thought was the weather. It had been bothering him since November 4th, just when Hewitt's armada reached latitude 31° N on its northeasterly course, crossing the track made by Christopher Columbus' three little ships on their westward voyage in 1492. (The great historian of Columbus' journey, Professor Morison, was with the Task Force in the cruiser *Brooklyn* to gather material for the story of this venture with which, as he put it, "America was at last repaying her debt to the first Admiral of the Oceans and in a sense fulfilling his ambition to deliver Jerusalem.")

Only three days from his destination, it suddenly seemed that nature would double-cross Patton. The sea had made up with a rising northwest wind. For the next two days a brisk Atlantic storm whipped the vessels of the convoy— some of them, like the minesweepers, rolling 42 degrees. By November 6th the weather had become so bad and the prospects so dismal that Captain Robert R.M. Emmett, USN, who commanded the transports, wrote in his log: "Heavy seas reported off Moroccan coast give rise to considerable doubt as to the possibility of success in executing landing attack plan."

Weather forecasts from Washington and London deepened the gloom. According to them, winds were expected to whip the surf 15 feet high and make the landing impossible.

Advance studies of the whimsical weather along the Moroccan coast had created such apprehension in General Eisenhower's mind that he instructed the planners to devise "contingency plans" for landings of the Western Task Force inside the Mediterranean at Phillipville, Bône or Bougie, or any other available Algerian port. Patton was upset by the prospect. He told Ike in no uncertain terms that he intended to defy the weather, whatever it may be on November 8th, and go through with the original plan instead of pushing on to Algiers. In the event of bad weather on the Moroccan coast, he proposed to threaten bombardment of Casablanca from the sea "in an effort to gain entrance to the port without resistance." He suggested that the Navy use at least one battleship for storming the harbor and supporting the ground forces that he planned to put ashore as quickly as possible to gain a foothold.

In the meantime he would issue a 30-minute ultimatum to what he called the "Governor of Casablanca," telling him that "I will accept his surrender and give him all honors and parole his troops; or that I will bombard him from the sea, bomb him from the air, and attack him on the ground."

Patton realized that he would be taking a "helluva chance," because his forces were woefully inferior to those of the "Governor of Casablanca," should he decide to resist. But he had abiding confidence in his luck. When this "contingency plan" was later recorded by him, he added: "It is my belief this bluff will work." Eisenhower seemed to share the belief, for he approved the alternate plan, stipulating only that Patton clear with him before starting the bombardment.

Initially Admiral Hewitt had serious misgivings about involving his forces in a frontal assault on the heavily defended coast; he preferred alternate plans either for landing inside the Mediterranean or awaiting favorable weather offshore. But during the crossings, he and Patton became fast friends. The Admiral had succumbed completely to the General's persuasive charm and infectious enthusiasm. On November 6th, when the weather showed no signs of subsiding, he told Patton that the Navy would go with him all the way and storm the fort whatever the elements, and in the face of the forbidding coastal guns.

Patton was not making these plans out of sheer bravado, with blind reliance on his luck and courting disaster by challenging fate. On the eve of his bold ventures, he would brood about his plans in solitude, mostly at night in bed. Then his brain—far more scientific than generally believed and soaked in the history of war (every incident of which was stored in it tidily like cards in an index file)—worked overtime figuring out the "angles" and evaluating all the possible maneuvers with a keen sense of proportion.

His supreme confidence in himself, on which he let no doubts or fears intrude, was reduced to its basic formula by an injunction he had borrowed from Stonewall Jackson: "Do not take counsel of your fears."

For Patton was no superman impervious to fear. He could be as scared as any man, and he was never ashamed to admit it. Long before Roosevelt told the nation that the only thing it had to fear was fear itself, Patton recognized this as a basic element of his own prowess as a soldier. He had no blind regard for senseless courage. An intricate human being with an intellectual turn of mind, he discovered early in life that although he was brave, he was not altogether unquestioning in the face of danger.

He resolved to condition himself against fear, and set a course of training that seemed as reckless and foolish to the outsider as it was purposeful and systematic to him. During his equestrian exercises and contests, he regularly sought out the most difficult obstacles and the highest hurdles, not to show off—as was actually believed by his audiences—but as part of his training to overcome his fears.

In his last year at West Point, a few weeks before his marriage, Patton suddenly stood up and stuck his head into the line of fire during some sharpshooting exercises. Later he casually recounted the incident to his father.

"Why did you do that, Georgie?" his father asked. "Just to show off how brave you are, you fool?"

"No, sir," Patton said sheepishly. "I just wanted to see how afraid I'd be and train myself not to be scared."

He had long before concluded that chances were there to make the most of. Those who grabbed their opportunities, however hazardous they appeared to be, had a distinct advantage over others limited by their narrow view of the vistas that lay beyond. He had encountered timidity under many other names—patience, moderation, reasonability or logic—all his life, even during the planning of "Torch." He was not congenitally opposed to reason. But he was dead set against letting it ruin a good chance.

In his confrontation with the inscrutable weather, Patton found two allies on the *Augusta* who refused to fall victims to the gloom of the pessimistic meteorologists. One of them was Paul Culbert, his diplomatic adviser. Culbert had lived in Morocco long enough to know something about the caprices of its coastal weather. Now he assured Patton that Eisenhower's weathermen were unduly pessimistic. "I am convinced, sir," he said, "that surf conditions will not be too severe for the landing."

His other ally was a weather expert, Lieutenant Commander R. C. Steere, USN, the Task Force's aerologist. Steere had reported to Patton in October, when they were still in Washington, to give him the results of extensive studies he had made of the weather and surf conditions on the Moroccan coast.

"Well, Commander," Patton asked him, half teasingly, "would you care or dare to take a pot-shot at a long-range weather forecast?"

"Yes, sir," Steere replied, and told him bluntly, "the weather will be good on November 8th."

Impressed with the courage and apparent competence of the aerologist, as well as the evidence he submitted in support of his contention, Patton then and there accepted Steere as his final authority on the weather.

When the storm of November 4-6th seemed to disqualify the expert, Patton instinctively stuck by him, and stated "I still have faith in this meteorologist." By then the gloomy prognostications of Washington and London had piled up in the weather file of the *Augusta*, but they failed to shake Steere's confidence in his own prognosis and Patton's confidence in Steere.

While the convoy battled its way through the heavy weather—even when the battleship *Texas* was so badly battered that she seemed in danger of losing her boats and the guns mounted on her forecastle—Steere kept assuring Patton that all would be well by November 8th. He told the General, "The storm is bad, to be sure, sir—but it's moving too fast to have a dangerous effect on the plan." He predicted with positive assurance, "There will be locally moderating weather off Morocco, making for good landing conditions on the 8th."

When now, under the starless sky, Patton arrived on the

flag deck and was told that the weather was excellent, with tidal waves lowest in months, he sent for Steere and told him, "I want to thank you, Mr. Steere, for getting me this fine weather. How did you do it? You must be Houdini!" Afterward, when he spoke of Steere—and he mentioned him frequently whenever his meterologists baffled or annoyed him with adverse predictions—he always referred to him as "that Navy aerologist, what was his name? Commander Houdini."

The sea was calm with a moderate ground swell. Offshore the air moved gently in a breeze. Though Patton could not see them, he knew that 12 troop transports of the Center Attack Group, with the nearly 20,000 officers and men of the Western Task Force who would land at Fedala with him, had arrived at their stations exactly when and where the plans had stipulated. As a matter of fact, the Group had made Fedala Roads even while Patton was still asleep—at exactly 7 minutes before midnight. Whatever doubts Patton once had of the Navy's ability to take him to war on time, and to land him exactly on target, his opinion had undergone a radical change.

It was a curious sensation for Patton to know he was at his destination, at last, with only two hours left to the landings. But there was nothing he could do except to wait in the wings for his cue. Nor was there much that he could see. As he peered eastward through his binoculars, panning the shore as it curved from north to south, he became somewhat alarmed when he found nothing but darkness where Fedala, his target at dawn, was supposed to be. Was it possible that the French had been alerted and blacked out the town? But he was promptly relieved when he found Casablanca shimmering in the distance.

The lights of the big white city were all ablaze, forming a massive beacon to guide him. From the elevated platform of the *Augusta's* bridge Patton could make out on the shore the old Arab quarter, around whose wall the European section had grown in a semicircle. The broad avenues were marked out for his inspection by their street lights.

But otherwise this strange nocturnal scene was totally shrouded. The night was so dark that the ships were hard put to follow their towing spars to their final unloading positions. No matter how he strained his eyes, Patton could see nothing moving on the sea, not even the water itself. Only the sound of engines and fragments of shouts floating in the air indicated that the Task Force was entering upon the terminal stage of its operations.

Since 1 A.M. the first line of transports had been busy hoisting out boats and loading the troops into them. At 1:45 A.M. four scout boats, commanded by Major James R. Weaver and equipped with powerful infrared flashlights and small radio sets, left for designated points inside Fedala Harbor to locate and mark the beaches—Red One, Two and Three, Blue One and Two—where the troops would be put ashore.

The light wind brought the purring of their engines to Patton on the bridge, but he had to strain to distinguish the noise of the motors muffled with silencers. The scouts had orders to anchor just outside the surf line, and wait for 25 minutes before H-Hour, when they were supposed to commence signaling to the transports with their flashlights. Then, exactly 10 minutes before H-Hour, they were to shoot up flares, indicating by color and number the beach they had marked out: one red light for Red Beach Number One at the southern-most tip of the landing area beneath Fedala Cape and its 75-mm. guns, for instance; two blue flares for Blue Beach Number Two, farthest to the north in the landing area, under the batteries of Pont Blondin.

General Patton was scheduled to land at 8 A.M., yet he followed the muffled sounds of the scout boats as if he himself had been in one of them. He was tense but silent. His exuberance of the night before was completely gone. A professional to his hard core, he now realized that this part of the operation was the Navy's responsibility. He stood aside, without offering any advice, without raising an eyebrow, or even so much as quipping from time to time if only to ease his own tension.

These crucial last hours subdued him and made him sentimental almost to the point of tears. He felt intense pangs of concern for the men in the scout boats on their suicide missions. Trouble had developed on the transports. Trained in special areas on Chesapeake Bay mostly to debark directly onto the beach, the green troops experienced some difficulty in getting off the transports and into the wildly bobbing landing craft. They negotiated the scramble nets with gingerly caution, and were slowed down still further by the heavy equipment they carried. As debarkation was falling behind schedule, Captain Emmett signaled Admiral Hewitt that H-Hour would have to be postponed. Patton was told that it would be 4:45 A.M. instead of 4 when his part of the show could begin. There was no time, however, to let the scouts know of the delay. Their schedule called for action on the old time table. And sure enough, exactly at 3:35 A.M., Patton saw flashes from the shore. The scouts had marked out the beaches and began to operate their blinkers. At 3:50 A.M., red and blue flares shot into the sky. The scouts had accomplished their mission. Now they waited at their precarious outposts to be relieved by the incoming troops. Yet none would come for more than an hour.

This was still another unexpected hitch threatening to betray the invasion. It could have alerted the French around Casablanca and, ignorant as they were of the identity of the force offshore and of the nature of its enterprise, caused them to open up with everything they had. And they had plenty—enough to stop the invasion before it could reach the water's edge.

The State Department had cooperated in this venture by preparing the ground, up to a point, for Patton's arrival and doing what it could through its agents to soften up the defenders for the blow. As a result, a small clique of French officers in Casablanca was set to ease the Americans onto the shore. But the preparations were half-baked and incomplete. Eventually they were completely nullified by secrecy.

Secrecy was an element of war about which Patton could never entirely make up his mind. He realized, of course, that it was essential for surprise. And surprise was one of the short-cuts to victory. But he was far too experienced and sophisticated a soldier to approve the blanket application of secrecy, especially when it tended to impede one's own operations. Frequently he found that it was carried to ludicrous extremes.

During World War I, when he was to board the *Baltic* to accompany General John J. Pershing to France in the van of the AEF, he was instructed to wear mufti during the embarkation and take a round-about way to Hoboken, on the right bank of the Hudson, where the ship was berthed, to fool the German spies. He did as instructed. But when his cab approached the embarkation area, he found signs showing the shortest way to the *Baltic*. Then he came upon big crates on the docks with the marking, "General Pershing's Headquarters, American Expeditionary Force. Consigned to Paris, France."

When he first learned from Culbert of the State Department's efforts to soften up Morocco for his landing, Patton expected some good to come from it. "Anything is welcome," he told Culbert, "that is likely to save American lives." But when he encountered the ironclad secrecy in which the maneuver was cloaked, he discounted the whole effort and made his plans without taking it into consideration.

So closely was the secret of "Torch" guarded from the French (whose cooperation was sought to assure an unopposed landing), that none of our friends in Morocco were given adequate warning to enable them to prepare elements of the French army to cooperate. On October 23, 1942, for example, Major General Mark W. Clark of General Eisenhower's staff was sent to North Africa on a secret mission to discuss "Torch" with a committee of high-ranking Frenchmen, including General René Mast, Chief of Staff to the Commander in Chief of the French Colonial Army. But he had instructions to discuss only the general plan and to refrain from disclosing the exact date and place of the landing.

Secrecy did pay off for Patton in that the Western Task Force had succeeded in sneaking up to the coast, totally unexpected and unobserved. But as Morison put it, "By a curious paradox, the efforts of the Allied armed forces to maintain secrecy probably lost whatever chance there was of an unopposed landing in Morocco."

Patton was a supreme realist in such matters and had the rare gift of thinking through situations from two points of view—his own and that of the foe. Now he sympathized with the French in what he clearly recognized as their predicament. He realized that caught between this mysterious encroachment and the brutal pressure of the Germans, they did not have much choice.

Since they could not know what exactly was in the offing, the emerging clues had left the French with nothing more concrete than conjecture. Maybe this was but another British raid like the one on Dieppe. Maybe it was only another hit-and-run commando assault. If they submitted to it without even going through the motions of an opposition, they could expect the Germans to retaliate, take away what little freedom of action they had left, and perhaps even occupy the Protectorate instead of letting the French maintain their own defensive forces.

General Béthouart, the top-ranking French officer in Morocco who was, even if only at this late hour, privy to the secret of this dawn, had arrived in Rabat shortly after midnight and began to pull the strings from the office from which General Lascroux had been so forcefully evicted a few hours before. At 1 A.M. he sent Captain de Verthamon, his young aide who happened to be the nephew of the Resident General, to General Noguès in the Residency with a politely worded note. "The Americans are about to land in force," it read in part. "You are cordially invited, *mon général,* to join in the liberation of our country."

De Verthamon found the Residency sound asleep. It was evident that Noguès was completely unaware of the impending event, and that not even President Roosevelt's message had alerted him. De Verthamon asked the General's aide to summon his uncle "in a matter of extreme urgency," and Noguès soon appeared—in his dressing robe.

When he read Béthouart's note, he asked de Verthamon in an icy tone, "What force?"

"An American expeditionary force is off the coast at this very moment, *mon général,*" the captain said, "awaiting your decision, sir, on which will depend whether there will be bloodshed or not."

Instead of giving a definite answer, Noguès asked to be excused so that he could dress. Back in his bedroom, he called Admiral Francois Michelier, commanding French naval forces in Morocco, on a private line Béthouart's conspirators had neglected to cut. Michelier had recently arrived from Vichy and was still imbued with the spirit of cooperation with the Nazis which he equated as the honor of a French officer. "Michelier," Noguès asked him, "I am advised by General Béthouart that Americans are landing in force. Do you have anything to report?"

"Nothing, *mon général,*" the Admiral answered firmly. "For a hundred miles out in the Atlantic there is nothing, sir, absolutely nothing."

While Noguès was still dressing, he received a call on the private line. General von Wulisch, head of the German Armistice Commission, was calling from his headquarters in the Hotel Miramar. Von Wulisch told Noguès about the landings in Algiers. He then added that his own radioman had intercepted a broadcast, presumably by the President of the United States, informing the French population of North Africa that an invasion was taking place and urging the civil population to receive the American troops with friendship. At 4 A.M. the telephone again broke into insistent ringing, and when Noguès answered, he heard Michelier's excited voice: *"Mon général,* Pont Blondin reports the sound of high-powered marine engines at an estimated distance of five miles."

Noguès began to pace the floor, trying desperately to fathom the significance of the obscure report and to determine his own action in the face of this challenge. Even if Patton was still on the *Augusta,* it was Noguès who was completely at sea.

At 4:28 A.M., Admiral Michelier reported again: "Pont Blondin has just flashed its searchlights out to sea, and was met by a hail of machine-gun bullets."

For a moment General Noguès stopped dead in his tracks, then he turned to Colonel Alphonse Piatte, head of his military cabinet, his mouth a white line as he issued the fateful order: "Everyone to his post! *S'il se produit quoi que se soit, résistez!"* General Béthouart had his answer at last, and the issue Patton was still debating on the *Augusta* had been resolved.

The die was cast. The order to resist was given.

The beams of the searchlight on Pont Blondin also told Patton that the French would oppose his landing after all. As he looked out toward the Fedala promontory, he saw those searchlights slice a ribbon in the nocturnal sky. At first probing vainly for airplanes whose engines were suspected of causing the mysterious sound Michelier had reported to Noguès, they were then turned on the water in search of ships approaching the harbor. A moment later this visual signal of the pending resistance was followed by the roar of guns. The batteries of Pont Blondin opened up, firing staccato salvos at a foe that, for the moment, remained invisible.

Then machine-gun fire could be heard on the *Augusta.* It provided General Patton with the answer to the question whether the French would resist or welcome him with open arms.

The fight for Morocco was about to begin.

George Patton was a lonely man.

He lived rambunctiously in his self-made world, with arbitrary conventions of his own design, groping desperately all the time to be understood and loved. But he was seized by a strange inner panic and ran away or shied away when he found understanding and love.

For all his apparent strength, and his display of super-abundant energy, he was morbidly afraid that he had some creeping weakness within himself—some brittleness or friability that could ruin his image—like the genius who in his most blessed state of creativity was forever tormented by a fear of insanity.

Except for two persons and only two in the whole world —his wife and his brother-in-law, Frederick Ayer—to whom, in their oft-proven compassion, he dared to reveal himself, he barricaded himself from all the rest with his wild gestures and strong, uncouth words. He dreaded that at closer quarters they might come upon this great and mysterious secret of his life. He thought that with his stubborn temper he would endure like Seneca's man, who could be broken but never bent.

In all his lonesome life Patton had never been lonelier than at this momentous dawn. To the inner solitude he had imposed upon himself was now added that oppressive seclusion all great captains feel when the issue is joined. Napoleon was overcome by this melancholy feeling of exile, not on Elba or St. Helena, but at Austerlitz and Jena, and under the Pyramids. Wellington felt most miserably alone, not in his morose retirement when he would silently watch the drilling of young soldiers in Hyde Park from an iron chair on the roof of his house, but at Rolica and Vimerio, at Vitoria and Waterloo.

Patton had studied their lives, was most deeply stirred by their moments of solitude, and frequently lectured his staff about their oppressive loneliness at junctures of triumphs. Now he also experienced the strain of that loneliness. It was made so much more poignant by the exigency of this awk-

ward campaign that isolated him on a ship, separated by
both water and faulty communications from his fighting
men.

A letter he wrote on that day recounted only minor incidents and engagements—like the quick battles of the Navy
—over which he had no control and in which he himself
played no part.

When the hazy day broke faintly at 6 A.M., Patton knew
only from the absence of any information to the contrary
that his troops were landing according to plan and more or
less on schedule. They were due ashore at Safi, 140 miles to
the south from where he stood; at Mehedia, some 60 miles
to the north, and at Fedala, directly in front of him. But
he did not know how these landings were going, not even
the one at Fedala.

He needed every ounce of his self-control to keep his suspense in check and his curiosity from running away with
him. He felt like jumping overboard and swimming to the
shore. "Goddamnit," he nudged Admiral Hewitt who, at
this stage, was still in tactical command, "can't you get some
news for me from Harmon and Truscott?" But Hewitt was
busy. He passed up the question, if his mind registered it at
all.

"Harmon" was Major General Ernest N. Harmon, Patton's successor in command of the crack 2nd Armored
Division at Fort Benning, Georgia, now landing at Safi with
the medium tanks of the Western Task Force. "Truscott"
was Brigadier General Lucian K. Truscott Jr., an old chum
from their carefree polo-playing days in the Cavalry, now
in charge of the operations at Mehedia.

At Safi, "everything clicked." The landing came off
promptly with only 2 naval casualties, and 10 killed and 75
wounded among the Army's assault troops. Harmon had
Safi before daybreak, both the port and the city, and had
secured the initial beachhead by 10 A.M. But Truscott was
in trouble. The spot for his landing had been ill-chosen to
begin with, but more about that (and why Patton had
picked Mehedia in preference to Rabat) later.

On paper this was supposed to be the easiest of the three
landings. The troops expected to be welcomed "with brass
bands," as Sergeant Jim Webster of the 1st Battalion, 504th
Engineers, put it. But everything went wrong. Instead of the
brass band, they were received with the bullets and bayonets
of the First and Seventh Regiments of Moroccan Tirailleurs,

the Foreign Legion, and the 75-mm. guns of the naval ground units.

To quote General Truscott: "The combination of inexperienced landing craft crews, poor navigation, and desperate hurry, resulting from lateness of hour, finally turned the debarkation into a hit-or-miss affair that would have spelled disaster against a well-armed enemy intent upon resistance."

Now his men of the 9th Division were fighting desperately with mounting casualties to avert that disaster. Virtually the only positive result of the first day's fighting was the "capture" of a cook for Patton under somewhat serio-comic circumstances. While Truscott was giving some orders to Colonel Harry H. Semmes (he had been one of Patton's company commanders in World War I), commanding the 3rd Armored Landing Team, he spotted a shabby-looking bystander, with helmet, navy blouse and army pants, eavesdropping. He could well have been a French spy, hardly in disguise, so Truscott stepped up to the character and shouted "George," the challenge for the landing operations, into his face. The man was supposed to answer "Patton," if he knew what was good for him. But he merely blurted out:

"Me no George! Me Sergeant Lee, best damn cook in whole army." He was in fact, Mess Sergeant Phue P. Lee, who had strayed from his regiment, the 60th Infantry. He wound up cooking for General Patton for the rest of the war.

Events in Patton's own sector at Fedala manifested themselves only by telltale clues from which it was difficult, if not impossible, to piece together a rounded picture of the situation. The fast-developing drama of this tragicomedy of errors (for Morocco could have been secured without bloodshed had the invasion been better prepared) became evident on the *Augusta* mainly by its sound effects. This assault of the Center Attack Group was Patton's main effort in "Torch." It was mounted by 19,870 officers and men of the 3rd Infantry Division, the 1st Battalion of the 2nd Armored Division's 67th Armored Regiment, and special units landed from the 12 transports. Major General Jonathan W. Anderson commanded the assault, under the immediate supervision of Patton.

At 3:55 A.M., a message from one of the control destroyers signaled the commencement of the operation. It was sent by Commander E. R. Durgin, USN, in the *Wilkes*, who told the *Augusta* with understandable exuberance, "The Yanks are coming!"

Wilkes conducted four boats of the first landings wave to their line of departure, but it was only at 5 A.M.—half an hour later than the revised H-Hour—that they could jump off for the beaches. They hit them between 5:15 and 5:25 A.M. By 6 A.M., Blue Beach Two, in a pocket of the estuary of Wadi Neffifikh, the most unpromising of the landing areas, was swarming with the men of the 15th Regiment. At the same time, the advance unit of the 30th Regiment went ashore on Red Beach One under the guns of Cape Fedala.

From where Patton stood on the *Augusta* it seemed for a few tense minutes that the coming of the Yanks would not draw any French resistance. But at 6:04 A.M. heavy machine-gun fire was heard. It was followed four minutes later by the ominous rumble of cannon.

Prior to the landings, the troops were given code phrases to indicate the character of their reception if it was unfriendly. They were to radio the *Augusta* "Batter Up" if they encountered any opposition. "Play Ball" would send the Navy into action in support of the opposed landings.

At 6:10 A.M., Admiral Hewitt received the word. It was "Batter Up." By voice radio from the *Wilkes,* Commander Durgin made it very specific: "Firing," he told the Admiral, "from Fedala and Sherki." This was disheartening news. It meant that Red Beach One was coming under fire from the 75-mm. guns of Cape Fedala, and that the 138.6-mm. guns of Fort Sherki on Pont Blondin were shelling Blue Beach Two.

Admiral Hewitt decided to fight it out. At 6:13 A.M., he signaled Captain Emmett of the Navy, who was in tactical command of the Center Group at this stage, to give the word. Seven minutes later Emmett ordered the fleet by radio telephone to "Play Ball."

At the Admiralty in Casablanca, Admiral Michelier had a visitor. He was Lieutenant Colonel Eugène Mollé, General Béthouart's Chief of Staff. Mollé had come on a desperate mission, the possible futility of which weighed heavily on his mind. He was to persuade the Admiral to abandon his opposition to the inevitable and let the Americans surge ashore without resistance.

But Michelier was not merely a knave tied by his misbegotten allegiance to the Nazis. He was also a fool. And now his professional pride was deeply hurt. When he was first told by General Noguès of the imminence of the landings, he refused bluntly to believe that the Americans, inexperienced newcomers to the war, would be capable of such a major *coup*. Then when the presence of the Western Task Force confronted him with a *fait accompli*, he felt humiliated by the failure of his coastal, air, and submarine patrols to detect the huge armada within cruising distance of the shore.

His humiliation turned into aggression. Even with the convoy poised for the landing, Michelier—now a desperate man grabbing at straws—scouted the possibility that "the Americans could land a force during the night capable of holding any of the forts under my direction." When they did land, nevertheless, captured Safi, and invested Fedala on the outskirts of his own Casablanca, Michelier decided to strike back. Instead of accepting Mollé's invitation, he placed the Colonel under arrest and sent him to Meknes to stand trial for treason.

Michelier directed Brigadier General Raymond Desré, Béthouart's deputy who remained loyal to Vichy, to take the Casablanca Division into action against the Americans. A detachment of Desré's troops was sent to the Place de la Fraternité to throw a cordon of guards around the United States Consulate, where Consul General H. Earl Russell, dismayed by the turn of events and expecting the worst, was burning his papers. As he looked out of the window to the little park across the street, he saw Desré's soldiers setting up an antiaircraft battery. Hostilities had come to Morocco. Soon the port area was blanketed with smoke that rolled in over the city.

Then Michelier signaled the batteries of El Hank, as well as the ships of the French fleet in Casablanca Harbor (including the immobile battleship *Jean Bart*) "open fire when ready."

When the Admiral was thus running amuck, a ¼-ton truck bearing a flag of truce was racing toward the Admiralty. It carried Colonel William H. Wilbur of Patton's staff. During the planning of "Torch" in Washington, Wilbur, a French linguist who had been with Charles de Gaulle at the Ecole

de Guerre at St. Cyr, volunteered to go to Casablanca from
Fedala immediately upon landing to demand the surrender
of the city. Patton, willing to try anything that would save
American lives, gave his blessing. He made Wilbur Chief of
Special Activities of G-2 and provided him with the major
tool for his venture—a large American flag. From a distance, the mission did not seem either too nebulous or too
dangerous. But on the spot it turned out to be both.

The melodrama of this mission left a deep impression on
General Patton. In his innate romanticism, he saw it sym-
bolized, somewhat in the patriotic vein of Francis Scott
key, in the "U.S. Color, silk, infantry, regimental size"
Colonel Wilbur was carrying on his momentous occasion.

"This Color was," he wrote in a special letter to the
Adjutant General in Washington, describing the event
through the fate of the flag, "without question the first U.S.
Color . . . to be landed in North Africa on the landing on
November 8th. It was carried ashore flying, with the first
wave of troops landing in Fedala Bay. During the movement to the shore, the landing boat in which the Colors
were displayed was discovered by a French corvette, was
illuminated by its searchlight, and was fired upon by a .50-
caliber machine gun located near the mouth of Fedala
harbor. This fire was the first fire of action at Fedala."

The flag reached shore in the custody of Colonel Wilbur.
"It was lashed on a ¼-ton truck, driven by Corporal Sanford
M. Forbes, 703396," Patton continued his sentimental narrative, "driving Colonel William H. Wilbur, who was
charged with carrying letters to French high commanders
in the hope that hostilities could be avoided. Passing
through Fedala, the Colors [and, for that matter, Wilbur
and Forbes] were subjected to infantry fire in a melée
which occurred in the gray light just before dawn."

Wilbur was carrying out his prearranged mission, making
his way to Casablanca. "On the road from Fedala to Casablanca," Patton continued, "the Color was carried at high
speed through an area occupied by hostile troops of all
types. The Color was successfully carried to the headquarters of the Casablanca Division. From there to the Admiralty where Admiral Michelier, French Navy, had his headquarters."

It was exactly 8 A.M. when Colonel Wilbur reported to
Admiral Michelier's aide and demanded that he be taken
to the Admiral at once.

"What do you want?" the aide asked stiffly.

"As a comrade-in-arms and a devoted friend of France," Wilbur said in his precise French, "I would like to point out to him the impropriety and futility of resistance that would lead to needless shedding of French and American blood, and propose that he surrender Casablanca to another sincere friend of France, Major General George S. Patton Jr., commanding the Western Task Force off these shores."

"Ah," said the aide. "You need not see the Admiral about that, *mon colonel*. Here is your answer."

He pointed to the open window through which the rumble of the big guns of El Hank drifted to them in the room. The harbor was obscured by a thick smokescreen. Behind it the light cruiser *Primaguet* and seven of Michelier's destroyers sortied for the open sea. They were steaming with their guns ablaze toward Patton on the *Augusta*.

Wilbur's mission failed because of the arrogance and perverted sense of "honor" of a stubborn French admiral. But nothing could dim the glory of the flag in General Patton's eyes, and he decided to preserve it with all the other famed colors in American military history. "Since these Colors have acquired a historic significance," he wrote to the Adjutant General, "and are not the Colors of any particular unit, they are herewith transmitted to the War Department with the recommendation that they be sent to some appropriate place such as West Point where they can serve as a means of heightening the morale of our future soldiers."

General Patton's landing craft was on its davits, with all his belongings in it, to take him ashore as planned at 8 o'clock, only three hours after the initial landings had begun. Standing by to accompany him were Rear Admiral John L. Hall, Jr., Hewitt's Acting Chief of Staff during the crossing and now slated to command the Sea Frontier forces at Casablanca; Colonel Gay, Patton's Chief of Staff; Colonels Johnson and Ely from the staff of the Atlantic Fleet's Amphibious Landing Force; Captain Richard N. Jensen and Lieutenant Alexander L. Stiller, Patton's aides, and Sergeant W. George Meeks, his Negro orderly.

Next to Patton, Stiller was the most picturesque member of this assembly. A daredevil Arizona cowboy and veteran of Patton's tank outfit in World War I, he had hitched a ride to Morocco by imploring Patton to take him on in any capacity. Patton was overjoyed when his friend reported for duty. He made the necessary arrangements in Washington, then sent word to Stiller to join him at Norfolk, Virginia, on October 21st, just prior to the embarkation for "Torch." Stiller arrived, wearing his old World War I uniform with the pancake helmet and the tight-fitting leggings. He had to be hastily outfitted for the new war, then sailed with Patton as his senior aide.

General Patton himself was dressed immaculately as if going to a parade rather than a war. No crease in his uniform showed that he had slept in it the night before. He stood in the group, frowning in his shiny two-star helmet, his 6-foot-2-inch figure in freshly polished cavalry boots towering over the others. But when the battle came close, Patton realized at once that he would not be able to go ashore as scheduled. He was overcome again by the frustration caused by this unexpected intermezzo. The din of the battle flamed him on. His face became grim and pinched. Taking a martial stance, he called out to Sergeant Meeks:

"George, where are my pistols?"

"In the boat, sir," the orderly shot back.

"Get them!" Patton snapped.

Meeks climbed into the landing craft dangling on the davits and returned to Patton with the ivory-handled, silver-plated .45 Colt Peacemaker and the Smith & Wesson .357 Magnum he had stored in the boat for the trip ashore.

Just when Patton was strapping them on, with his chin pulled in and pressed against his chest, buckling them in the Myers holsters and hooking them to his belt, the *Augusta* herself went into action to defend the transports from the cruiser and two destroyers that had managed to break through the screen. The concussion of the first salvo of the *Augusta's* main battery blew out the bottom of Patton's landing craft, and all his belongings fell into the water.

"George, Goddamnit," Patton grinned at Meeks, who was holding a pair of oversize binoculars he had snatched from the boat in the last minute. "It was a close shave, the pistols, I mean. I hope you have a spare toothbrush with you I can use to clean my foul mouth. I don't have a thing left in the world," adding with a snide glance at Admiral Hall, "thanks to the United States Navy."

At noon on D-Day the battle still raged and Patton was still on the *Augusta*. But the delay had its compensations. A signal was picked up from Harmon announcing the capture of Safi. General Anderson reported from Fedala that he controlled both rivers and the high ground, and had captured eight members of the German Armistice Commission.

General von Wulisch was not among them. He had managed to escape to Spanish Morocco with the help of General Noguès. But the special detachment of Patton's G-2, organized in advance by Colonel Black for exactly this mission, had already searched von Wulisch's quarters in the Hotel Miramar and found his abandoned belongings. They included a remarkable headgear—a gleaming white casque emblazoned with the Prussian double eagle. It was the dress uniform helmet of a *Wehrmacht* general. Anderson signaled Patton that pending his arrival he was holding the helmet, a picturesque article of booty he might want to keep as a souvenir.

"Considerate of the sonuvabitch to leave it behind," Patton said. "I shall wear it for our entrance into Berlin."

The impromptu naval battle ended at high noon and the road to Casablanca was open again. A crash boat was provided by Admiral Hewitt as a replacement for Patton's shattered landing craft. He had to descend to it while it was in the water, bobbing in the light waves. It was a sight to behold, the tall, immaculately groomed Commanding General of the Western Task Force negotiating the net nimbly, with a big Havana smoking in his mouth. He was full of vim and fight, and had but one misgiving. He was going to war at last, armed with his faithful pistols, which had accompanied him to Mexico and France. But he had no ammunition for them.

At the time of his departure from the *Augusta*, the situation was still fluid and the issue seemed far from having been decided. But for Patton, the play was not the thing. A few days before, he spoke modestly in his diary of his personal share in the impending campaign: "I really do very little, and have done very little, about this show. I feel that my claim to greatness hangs on an ability to lead and inspire."

Now, at the very moment of the landing, with water splashed all over him, he began to practice what he preached. A highly emotional soldier, as he called himself, he was deeply moved when the first sight he beheld on the shore was a lonely soldier burying his fallen buddy in an improvised grave in the sand.

The mournful little scene drew him close to his troops. If there were any more important tasks awaiting his attention at Fedala, Patton decided to let them wait. He wanted to join his men in their foxholes and at their scattered outposts, undergoing their baptism of fire, before he would condescend to the company of his generals.

At the spot on the beach toward which Patton's crash boat was heading, a small landing craft loaded with ammunition and supplies was struggling in the surf, then hitting a runnel. Its crew, except for the helmsman, leaped into the swirling eddies, looking on as the helmsman tried frantically to free the craft by throwing the engine into reverse. But nothing could make the boat move.

Then Patton's crash boat heaved into sight, and it was an impressive sight at that. Its sides were lined by men holding Tommy guns at the ready. In its center stood Sergeant Meeks, his handsome face serene and impassive, his hands grabbing a mammoth submachine gun. In the bay stood Patton in a tight-fitting trenchcoat with its collar turned up, his helmet strapped, cramping his chin, two Tommy guns and a megaphone at his elbow, shouting his favorite profanities, which sounded gay and lusty to those who heard their sound but could not hear their fury.

The crash boat hit the runnel and shuddered to a halt. Patton vaulted over the side and splashed ashore, running straight to the stranded craft some 20 yards away. Then he waded back into the water and put his shoulder to the beached boat, shouting to the idle crew watching the Old Man with incredulous eyes.

"Come over here!" he roared at the top of his high-pitched voice. "All of you! On the double, Goddamnit!" He was standing waist-deep in the water. "Take hold here," he yelled. "You, too, over at the other side! Wait for the next wave! Lift and push. *Now! Push*, Goddamnit, *push!*"

They pushed like no men ever pushed before. A moment later, the screw of the craft churned and bit the water. She backed away and was on her way to the mother ship.

Now the dripping tall figure turned to the men: "Don't you realize, Goddamnit, that this boat has other trips to make? How in hell do you expect to fight a war without ammunition? Now take the stuff up to the dump on the hill. *On the double*, Goddamnit!"

From the beach, Patton went to a small cabaña under the Casino's sea wall on Red Beach One, where Colonel Elton F. Hammond, his Signal Officer, had a field telephone rigged up for him. Moments later he was listening to the report of the Beachmaster, Commander James W. Jamison, USN, and a liaison officer of the Third Division. The latter complained about the Navy's handling of the unloading, and the former defended himself in vigorous and salty language.

"Goddamnit, Jamison," Patton yelled at the sandy-haired, freckle-faced Beachmaster, who stood before him tensely, his face drawn with fatigue. "I don't give a rap who is right or wrong. I have just seen one of your Goddamn boats abandoned by its crew when it hit a runnel. If you can't handle the job, Goddamnit, I'll get myself another Beachmaster and maybe another Navy."

(Later when he saw things for himself, Patton sent for Jamison and, calling him by his nickname, told him, "I was a bit too harsh with you, Red, but forget it. As a matter of fact I've sent for you because I want you to know what I think of the work you've done here. I think you have saved the whole Goddamn operation.")

Patton was at the cabaña 20 minutes when General Anderson rushed up to him, accompanied by a breathless French colonel and Wilbur, still lugging his white flag of truce. The Frenchman apologized formally to Patton for the resistance, then suggested that he send Wilbur back to Michelier with another demand that he surrender Casablanca.

"What's the use?" Patton fumed. "Wilbur already had his kick of the day in his teeth."

"This is different, *mon général*," the French colonel pleaded. "The first demand was premature. But now Admiral Michelier must be convinced that all further resistance is futile."

"Well, all right," Patton agreed. "Get a jeep, Wilbur, and make the run. But take Hap Gay with you. I want the son-uvabitch to learn a lesson in the futility of diplomacy as opposed to the effectiveness of guns."

Wilbur and Gay went, their jeep flying the Stars and Stripes and Wilbur's white flag. They rode through the French lines into Casablanca, acclaimed by cheering crowds in French, Arabic and Berber. But the Admiral refused even to receive them.

"The French Navy is determined to slug it out with us," Gay told Patton when he reported back.

"What's the matter with the bastard?" Patton asked his Chief of Staff.

"He suffers from the Dreyfus complex, sir," Wilbur answered for Gay. "From my conversation with his aide I gather, sir, that Michelier has an overriding hatred of Jews and strings along with the Nazis because of their Jew-baiting. According to his aide, the *capitaine de frégate,* his boss had it on good authority that the chief objective of our landing was to foment uprisings of the Jews against the Arabs and take Morocco away from the French in the ensuing confusion."

"The poor fool," Patton shook his head.

From the cabaña at the Casino, Patton moved a block north to the Miramar, into General von Wulisch's hastily evacuated suite. He was in high spirits. Except for Mehedia, the news was extremely good, and even in the north, Truscott had taken the crucial airport at Port Lyautey. Michelier was still resisting, but Patton was readying his trump card—that 30-minute ultimatum at the end of which dangled the threat to bombard Casablanca from the sea and bomb it from the air.

"Let's see if Michelier dares to resist that."

The world in Morocco had turned a full cycle in a single day. Exactly 24 hours after his last meal on the *Augusta,* General Patton moved ceremoniously into the *salle à manager* of the swanky Miramar, where the night before General von Wulisch had feted Auer, the Führer's diplomatic agent. Patton was flanked in his triumphant entry into the crowded dining room by Dick Jenson and Al Stiller, his aides, and was followed by Colonel Hap Gay, his laconic Chief of Staff.

His appearance drew cheers and applause, as well as gasps and a gale of laughter. He was wearing von Wulisch's white helmet with the Prussian eagles.

After dinner, Patton sent for Sergeant Rosevich to dictate to him the day's entry for the diary. He received his secretary in his sitting room on the second floor of the Miramar, relaxed in a chair behind a desk. The General seemed in high good humor, but Rosevich recoiled as he entered the room. He found Patton in his shirtsleeves and strangely "beflagged." He was wearing a pair of suspenders. And they were ablaze with red, white and blue.

Patton began the entry for his journal.

"God was exceedingly good to me today . . ."

CHAPTER TWO
ILLITERATE PRODIGY

There is ample evidence that George Patton was born on Wednesday, November 11, 1885, at 6:38 P.M. on the 1,800-acre Wilson-Patton ranch in San Marino, just outside Pasadena in California. The event was duly recorded in his mother's Bible, and in books of the Church of Our Saviour, the oldest Episcopalian Church in Southern California (built by his maternal grandfather).

But Patton regarded his birthdate as merely another link in a historic chain. He believed that his life had spanned the ages. He recalled incidents that had occurred centuries before, yet in which he himself, in earlier incarnations, had had a personal part.

There was, of course, a reasonably rational explanation for this phenomenon. Patton was, like Miguel de Cervantes' Don Quixote, part product of his readings and part of his own imagination. He read avidly whatever books on military history he could lay hands on. As a result his head was, as Cervantes said about Don Quixote, "full of nothing but enchantments, quarrels, battles, challenges, wounds, complaints, amours, torments and abundance of stuff and impossibilities."

Episodes of the past were deposited in Patton's mind like grains of gold in a river ready to be washed out. After a while he identified himself with them and adopted them as, what he once called, his own "subconscious memories."

This psychic phenomenon, the sensation of having been somewhere or seen an event before, is termed *déjà vu* by psychologists. It had a wonderfully positive effect in Patton's case. It enabled him to view war in its broadest panorama, and apply the precedents and lessons of the past to actual situations and current experiences, as well as to future plans. What fascinated him, however, was not this pragmatic value of his highly developed *déjà vu* but the inference that he was a timeless man who would have been fit to live, and would have become a soldier-hero, in any century. He had this in mind when, during the campaign in Sicily in the summer of 1943, he wrote to his wife: "Men live in deeds, not years." And he affirmed his occult notion about "the reincarnation of a fighting man" in no uncertain terms in a Kiplingesque poem he composed in 1918, calling it "Through a Glass, Darkly."

He traced his ageless career as a warrior from prehistoric times (when he "battled for fresh mammoth" and "warred for pastures new") to his days in France at St. Mihiel in World War I (when "with tanks aclatter" he "waddled on the foe"). He saw himself in the phalanx meeting Cyrus the Persian; with Alexander the Great at the walls of Tyre; on Crécy's field in the Hundred Years War; as a general with Murat "when one laughed at death and numbers trusting in the Emperor's star."

He was pleased when General Sir Harold Alexander told him in Africa: "You know, George, you would have made a great marshal for Napoleon if you lived in the eighteenth century."

Patton grinned, said quietly, "But I did," and left it at that.

During World War I, while training a brigade of the newly formed Tank Corps in France in 1918, he was sent on a secret mission to a place he had never been before. His orders were to go to a certain railroad station, "take the first train running west, get off at the third station, and take the next training running south, get off at the second station" where he would be picked up by a waiting staff car.

At the second station he was met by the car with a soldier who drove him at a fast pace to an unknown destination. It was dark, and Patton could not know where he was or where he was going. As the car approached the top of a hill, Patton asked his driver:

"This camp we're going to, Sergeant, isn't it just over the hill to the right?"

"No, sir," the driver replied. "Our camp is further ahead. But there is an old Roman camp over there to the right. I have seen it myself."

Patton finally arrived at the headquarters to which he was ordered to report, and attended to the business on hand. When he was leaving through a side door he turned to a captain in the room and said, "Your theater is over there straight ahead, isn't it?"

"We have no theater here," the captain answered.

But next morning when Patton awoke and surveyed the scene in daylight, he found that there was a Roman amphitheater only about 300 yards away. Patton was somehow convinced that he had been there before, probably as a Roman legionnaire with Caesar in Gaul.

In 1943, in Sicily, which he had just conquered, he asked Signora Marconi, the island's curator of antiquities, to guide him on a tour of the ancient sites. It became quickly apparent that Patton did not need a guide. Indeed, it was he who pointed out to the learned lady the most important historical events connected with the different locations. In one instance, at Agrigento, he even corrected her about something that had occurred in 470 B.C.

He explained to her in vivid detail how the Carthaginian army, which had landed at Agrigento and points west, and numbered 300,000 men, took five years to get to Syracuse, the great port city on the Ionian Sea, and how it then was annihilated.

"The city and harbor of Syracuse," Patton later wrote, "are to me of particular interest because this place probably has been the scene of more amphibious operations than any other harbor in the world. When looking over its water I could almost see the Greek triremes, the Roman galleys, the Vandals, the Arabs, the Crusaders, the French, the English and the Americans, who, to mention only a few, have successively stormed, or attempted to storm, the harbor."

"Have you been here before?" the amazed Signora asked.

"I suppose so," Patton replied, although he was in Sicily for the first time in his life.

Whether it was a psychic phenomenon or the consummate knowledge of the past stored up in his mind, history played an enormously great role in Patton's life. It shaped his body and soul from his early youth to virtually the moment of his death. When he was only 8 years old in San Gabriel, a clergyman named Bliss told him the story of the Parthenon, the magnificent Greek temple Pericles erected on the Acropolis in 432 B.C. in honor of the goddess Athena. The story remained implanted intact in his mind. Then 50 years later he came upon a beautiful Greek temple at Segesta in Sicily and viewed its gently curved lines and columns as familiar sights, for nothing in history was new or strange to him.

It determined him at a tender age to become a soldier, the profession for which he was literally destined by tradition and genetics—ordained, so to speak, by the chromosomes of his ancestors. He was the scion of Southern gentry and the frontier aristocracy of California, the decadence and sophistication of his Virginia heritage balanced by his forebears from Southern California, a simpler and commoner but hardier and more virile stock.

There are many Pattons in the South who are genealogically interwoven but probably only remotely related to George Patton. His connection with the South ceased in the wake of the Civil War, when his roots were transplanted to Southern California to add fascinating new branches to his family tree.

Patton never regarded himself as a Southerner, despite his heritage and the prominent participation of several of his immediate ancestors on the Confederate side in the Civil War. Mostly he thought of himself as a Californian, although he had left that state at the age of 17 and returned only occasionally to visit his family at the ancestral home, and once in triumph upon his return from World War II.

The origins of George Patton can be traced to Scotland of the 18th century. They go back to a mysterious event of some probably violent controversy that forced a strong-willed young man to flee his native Aberdeen and make his way to the Colonies, arriving at Fredericksburg in Virginia during the Revolutionary turmoil of the 1770's. The young man's real name was wiped from the records upon his departure from Scotland. He had reason to obscure it, probably to prevent the authorities from tracking him down in the New World.

He traveled under an assumed name, calling himself Robert Patton. He was a mule-headed, fiery little man with a fondness for ruffled shirts.

Though he arrived in Virginia somewhat under a cloud, it did not take him long to become rich and respectable. He married Anna Gordon Mercer, the only daughter of Dr. Hugh Mercer, a physician who served as Army Surgeon with Colonel George Washington in the Braddock Expedition against Fort Duquesne in 1756, and then enlisted with him as a regular soldier in the War of Independence.

He was the first of George Patton's ancestors who combined erudition and valor in his bloodstream, a legacy that continued through subsequent generations of Pattons. A native of Aberdeen like Robert Patton, he studied medicine at the university there, then served as a surgeon's mate in the Pretender's army. He arrived in America in 1747, settled in Pennsylvania, but found the practice of medicine far too sedate. Originally a surgeon with General Edward Braddock's army, he turned soldier and, in 1758, as a lieutenant colonel of the Provincials, had command of Fort Duquesne.

Mercer returned to medicine at Fredericksburg, also organizing and drilling the militia. He commanded the Minute Men at the outbreak of the Revolution, and was appointed a colonel of the 3rd Virginia Regiment. In June, 1776, at the request of Washington, Congress named him a brigadier general and gave him command of a flying brigade composed of raw militiamen.

He was mortally wounded in the Battle of Princeton under circumstances of valor and cruelty that George Patton, his great-great-great-grandson, was never to forget and forgive. Leading his cold, hungry and weary men on the frosty morning of January 3, 1777, out of the woods toward a bridge, Mercer was halted by the charge of His Majesty's Seventh Regiment under Lieutenant Colonel Charles Mahwood. Although he had his splendid gray horse shot from under him, he tried "with reckless courage" to rally his men on foot.

He was struck by the breech of a musket, then bayoneted on the ground, the British leaving him on the field, unattended. When his aide, Major John Armstrong, rushed up to carry him off, Mercer ordered the young officer to leave him and follow the patriot army. "It needs your services more than I do," he stated. "Suffering intensely with the cold and his terrible wounds," he died nine days later, at the age of 51.

In 1797, the marriage of Robert Patton and Anna Mercer produced a son—John Mercer Patton. The studious young man was so completely dominated by his dictatorial father that he was forced to study medicine at the University of Pennsylvania although he was determined to become a lawyer. As quick-tempered and thick-headed as his father, John wrote him a bitter letter, threatening to kill himself by cutting his throat. A few days later Robert Patton's answer arrived. It was a freshly honed razor, with a note: "Go ahead! Your devoted Father."

In the end, John Patton had his way. He became a lawyer, one of the greatest in Virginia, the acknowledged leader of the Richmond bar. His outstanding legal achievement was the revision of the Virginia Code, both civil and criminal.

A Jacksonian Democrat, he served several terms in Congress, was elected president of the Council of State, and was, for a brief period, Governor of Virginia. Although not so impetuous and quarrelsome as his father, and lacking the martial spirit of his grandfather, he had the stubborn streak and independent mind of a Patton. When the Virginia Assembly voted its disapproval of President Andrew Jackson's withdrawal of deposits from the Bank of the United States in 1833, and a copy of the resolution was transmitted to Congressman Patton in Washington, he remained unyielding in his support of the President and rebuked Governor John Floyd for "officially intimating the desirability of a different course" on his part.

He was just as firm in his patriotism, which bordered on chauvinism. Attracted strongly to the Know-Nothing movement, he was bitterly opposed to "the slightest control over Americans by any foreign power, religious or temporal."

On January 8, 1824, John Patton married Margaret French Williams, daughter of Colonel Isaac Hite Williams. They had six sons. Patton died before the Civil War, but every one of his sons fought in it, none of them escaping unscathed. Four were wounded. Colonel Waller Tazewell Patton was killed at Gettysburg during Pickett's charge. George Smith Patton, a brigadier general at 26, fell in the

Battle of Cedar Creek near Winchester, Virginia, in 1862. He was General Patton's grandfather and namesake. He was also his inspiration, his idol after whom he strove to pattern himself.

The first George Patton was a remarkable young man who crammed a lot of life into his brief span. The family lived at Charleston on the Kanawha at the mouth of the Elk River in the Alleghenies. George was familiarly called "Frenchy," in recognition of his pointed beard, his meticulous attire in the Continental style, and his consummate interest in the ladies. He graduated from the Virginia Military Institute, because by then it was the family tradition (as a tribute to its beginnings in the United States and the memory of the martyred General Mercer) to give the Patton boys a military education.

He read law in his father's office, but he had not much time left to be a lawyer. The slavery issue was coming to a head. The Governor's son was a creed-bound, fiercely patriotic, swash-buckling Virginian, and a fiery debater who never shied from a good fight. In 1859, probably in anticipation of things to come, young Patton became a part-time soldier. He organized his friends up and down the river into what became known as the Kanawha Rifles, a military group of socially prominent men who, on this eve of the War Between the States, danced as hard as they drilled.

Patton was their colonel and the life of the company. He even designed a uniform for his "Rifles" (as his grandson was to do for his tankers some 82 years later). It was smartly tailored with brass buttons on dark green broadcloth, broad gold stripes down the pantaloons, with crossed belts, a fancy headgear, and white gloves. At the outbreak of the Civil War, when young Patton's Rifles became Company H of the 22nd Virginia Infantry, he was given command of the regiment.

A full colonel in 1862, he led his regiment in the second battle of Winchester and was cut down by a Union cavalryman's saber. He was made a brigadier general posthumously and was buried with all honors due a general officer of the Confederate Army.

His death returned the Patton family to the trail of adventure. Brigadier Patton left his young widow, two sons and a daughter in abject poverty. The family was well-to-do before the war, but their fortune was wiped out by the defeat of the South. Mrs. Patton was remarried to one of her husband's friends, Colonel George Hugh Smith, a dashing, full-blooded and thick-headed Confederate cavalry officer.

Lee's surrender was an insufferable blow to Smith. He didn't care to survive the humiliation, certainly not in the ravaged South. He gathered what was left of his regiment and led his bedraggled men in an epic march into exile in Mexico, leaving his young wife with her children destitute in Charleston. In due course he returned to the United States, moving into Southern California to practice law in Los Angeles.

Smith sent for his wife and, as they became settled and their fortune grew, also for the children. In the meantime, George Smith Patton II had entered V.M.I. He was a keen and brilliant young man, but so poor that he had to pay his way through the school by working as a janitor and tutoring several of his classmates. George II inherited his father's good looks and flair, and grew into an attractive young man with a compelling, magnetic personality. But the disillusionment of those dismal post-war years veered his interest from the military profession, although he was at the top of his classes at V.M.I.

At last word came from California. A letter from his mother invited him to join her in Pasadena, suggesting that he read law in his stepfather's office. The boy heeded the invitation eagerly, and developed into one of Southern California's leading young lawyers with a gold-plated clientele. Now it seemed that the military streak in the Patton family had come to an end, for George II, an avid reader, had a decidedly intellectual turn of mind. Seeking an outlet for whatever fight there was in him in local politics, he registered as a Democrat, ran for office, and was elected District Attorney of Los Angeles County.

Among the clients of Smith & Patton was one of the richest and most colorful men of Southern California, the founder of Pasadena, "the dictator of San Gabriel Valley," as he was called. He was Benjamin Davis Wilson, of Scottish descent, who had made his way to the Far West in a most adventurous manner.

Ben Davis was born in Wilson County, Kentucky, in 1811, grew into boyhood in Tennessee, then went West, one of the original people who crossed the continent. He engaged in trapping and trading in New Mexico from 1833 to 1840, then moved on to California the next year with a company of 25 men, the first large group of immigrants to enter the territory in the South by way of Chihuahua City. In 1844 he bought the huge Jurupa Rancho from Juan Bandinin and married Ramona Yorba, daughter of Don Barnardo Yorba, owner of the enormous Rancho Santa Ana, a great portion of which today is Orange County.

Though not a citizen of Mexico, Wilson fought against the Spaniards on the side of the native Californians. After the defeat of Governor Micheltorena, he returned to his ranch to devote himself mostly to raising stock until 1846. He was *alcalde* (Mexican mayor) of Los Angeles when Commodore Sloat raised the American flag at Monterey. Governor Pico of Spain asked him to raise a contingent of residents to drive the American forces from California. "I replied," Wilson wrote in his reminiscences, "that I most respectfully declined, being an American citizen and not a military man. I was then menaced with arrest, if I did not comply. I gathered around me about a dozen Americans who had not left town when it was unpleasant, and even unsafe for them to be there at that time."

He later aided Commodore Robert Field Stockton's capture of Los Angeles, was commissioned by Stockton a captain in the American Army, and appointed the virtual governor of his new frontier before John C. Frémont established civil government there. Wilson spent the later years of his life in Pasadena, which he helped to found, aided its pioneer settlers, and became one of the best-known horticulturists in the Far West. In 1852 he was appointed Indian Agent for the Southern District by President Millard Fillmore, assisted in laying out the reservation at Tejon, and was elected to the State Senate in 1855, and again in 1869.

When his first wife died, Wilson married Margaret S. Hereford, widow of Dr. Thomas Hereford of Los Angeles. The two daughters born of this union, Annie and Ruth, were celebrated belles of the Valley, courted by all its eligible bachelors. Ruth Wilson, the younger daughter, was a charming and keen-witted girl and a lover of the great outdoors. She was celebrated throughout Southern California as an intrepid and courageous horsewoman.

George Patton and Ruth Wilson fell in love and married, then settled on the 1,800-acre ranch near San Gabriel, nine miles east of downtown Los Angeles. The tract was sliced from "Don Benito" Wilson's enormous land holdings in the Valley, which included Los Robles, Oak Knoll and San Marino, on most of which the cities of Pasadena and San Gabriel are situated today.

But by the time George III was born, this fabulous grandfather—remembered in the annals of the Valley as "the foremost pioneer and sterling citizen," for whom Mount Wilson, Wilson Lake, a school and an avenue were named in Pasadena—was no longer around. He died on March 11, 1878, at his Lake Vineyard ranch house, not far from an old mill which Zalvidea had erected in 1812.

His place in the Patton home was taken by Colonel Smith. The old cavalryman-turned-lawyer was extremely fond of his stepson George II and doted on George III, a frisky, tow-headed lad who, under his mother's tutelage, could ride a fast horse virtually before he could walk.

The Pattons lived on the big ranch in a rambling one-story adobe house shaded by tall cedars and fragrant eucalyptus trees. But there was nothing rustic about their life. This was the stylish household of a cultured and affluent family. It was run with an iron hand by Diana Callahan, the stern and tidy housekeeper, who ruled over half a dozen Mexican servants. The cook, a delightful Cockney named Ellen Stevens, was imported from England, where she learned to make the most succulent roast beef and fluffy pudding in the household of Lord Roberts. Young Georgie and his sister, Anne Wilson (Nita) Patton, were in the care of Mary Scally, their governess. She spent her days in frantic but futile efforts to catch up with her rambunctious young charges.

The stables had a dozen blooded horses, including Peach Blossom, young George's Shetland pony, and the chestnut Marmion, Mrs. Patton's favorite mount.

It was an eminently happy and tranquil home, yet the shadow of war was always close at hand. Grandfather Smith never ceased to reminisce about the Confederate glories of the Civil War, and he populated the house with like-minded friends who sustained themselves on their own martial memories. One of them was a retired British officer named Arthur Hutchinson, who had commanded a company of Lancers on the Northwest Frontier Province in India trying to pacify the fierce tribes in the Khyber Pass. But the prize exhibit was Colonel John Singleton Mosby of "Mosby's Confederacy."

Mosby had served brilliantly in the Confederate cavalry under Jeb Stuart until January, 1863, when he turned guerrilla leader in North Virginia. Moving swiftly and stealthily, he and his handful of men routed the Federal cavalry, destroyed communications, seized supplies, and were, in general, a great nuisance to the Army of the Potomac. His most famous exploit was the capture of General Edwin S. Stoughton at Fairfax Courthouse in March, 1863.

Mosby had remained active to the bitter end of the Civil War. But now, in his early sixties, and a Republican, he was condemned, as he put it, to fight the legal battles of the Southern Pacific Railraod, whose attorney he had become. (He lived to see his young friend George Patton grow up into a kind of guerrilla fighter himself in the Mexican Punitive Expedition of 1916.)

Through Hutchinson, Georgie was introduced to Rudyard Kipling, whose lifelong fan he became. And from Mosby he learned the glories of war, engaging the toothless old railroad lawyer in innumerable mock battles, with Georgie, in the saddle of Peach Blossom, usually posing as General Lee.

From a friend of his father, Professor Frederick Holder, the great naturalist, Georgie learned to love nature. The family had a cottage on Catalina Island, and whenever he had time, Professor Holder visited them there to explain to Georgie the marvels of marine life. He also taught him how to sail a fast boat.

It was a fascinatingly rounded life for a lively boy, and Georgie made the most of it with his friends, cousin Jerry Brown, Morris and Ormsby Phillips and Charley Nordhoff (co-author of *Mutiny on the Bounty*), scions of prominent Valley families.

He had plenty of time for the outdoor life because he had yet another privilege few boys of his age and position enjoyed—he did not have to go to school. His father was a cultured man of great erudition, but he didn't believe in formal education for his children. He theorized that young brains were unduly burdened with the strict and stereotyped curriculum of schools, especially the three R's—reading, 'riting and 'rithmetic. He preferred to impart whatever education he thought they needed by reading the classics to them on long evenings in front of their huge fireplace. By the time he was seven years old, Georgie Patton could recite long passages from the *Iliad* in Pope's translation, and knew the Bible by heart.

His games were inspired by his two loves—soldiering and the classics. He would startle his sister Anne, who was two years his junior, by suggesting that they play what he called Hector at Troy. "I'll be the horse and you'll be Hector," he proposed, then dragged her around in the sand.

The extraordinary prodigy of San Gabriel Valley, so erudite yet so illiterate, was 12 years old when, in the fall of 1897, his father decided at last to begin his formal education. He was enrolled in Dr. Stephen Cotter Clark's Classical School for Boys, in a big one-story redwood schoolhouse at the end of the mule-car line in Pasadena. The fact that he could neither read nor write created some problems. On the first day in school he recited a long passage from Johnson's *Rasselas* but he could not put down his words on paper when Dr. Clark told him to write a composition about the work. Yet Georgie quickly managed to learn to read and became an accomplished writer—as shown by the many brilliant articles he contributed to the old *Cavalry Journal;* by the facile style of his diary; the lucid notes in his *"War As I Knew It";* his letters to his wife and his brother-in-law, Fred Ayer, and especially by his crisp and highly professional instruction and orders to his troops. But he never learned to spell, or as he put it, "I have trouble with the A, B, and—what do you call that other letter?"

Arithmetic was another of his weak points. He had passing marks in Dr. Clark's school, but flunked his math test in his plebe year in West Point. Trained by his father to memorize everything verbatim, he found the problems in Smith's *Algebra* hard to tackle.

Called "Georgie" at home, he was "Pat" to his classmates in school. But the latter nickname did not stick. It vanished when he left Pasadena, while the Georgie endured all his life. But men who were permitted to call him Georgie to his face formed a rather select company.

Though he could be disarmingly informal and ingratiatingly friendly, Patton chose his intimates with great care, and kept a distance from his subordinates, including officers of general rank. During World War II, he let nobody on his staff become so familiar that they could call him Georgie. Even his fellow generals had to command an army, at least, to enjoy the privilege of addressing him by his nickname.

George S. Patton Jr. was still at Pasadena when he made the two most important decisions in his life—to become a soldier and to marry Beatrice Ayer.

It had long been arranged that he would stick to the family tradition and go to V.M.I., if only to prepare, so to speak, for West Point. But little Miss Ayer came unexpectedly into his life. The daughter of a Massachusetts textile magnate, she spent the summer of 1902 on Catalina Island, where her mother's brother, Joseph Banning, and his wife had a house not far from the Pattons' cottage. At first she merely watched the Patton boy from the distance, for she did not dare to hope, as she herself later confided, to become friendly with the hard-playing rambunctious youth. But then she took her courage into her hands and made contact.

She was a tiny girl, quite small for her 15 years, while Georgie was getting near the 6-foot mark and was still growing. And she had a habit that seemed at first blush to disqualify her as a companion in Georgie's eyes. At 15 she was still playing with her dolls.

But they also had much in common. Beneath the little-girlish, fastidious exterior of daintily dressed, white-gloved Bea Ayer was a hard-fisted, tough young woman who could ride as well and as hard and fast as Georgie, and participate with plenty of gusto in all his tough and rough sports. She was not especially pretty, but there were sweetness in her blue eyes and a feminine charm that tempered the tomboy and appealed to Georgie.

Patton was never to court another girl, and Bea never had another beau. They went sailing and riding and; before this summer was out, these teenage kids, deeply in love, had their "understanding."

They corresponded but did not meet again for three years, until March 13, 1905. In the meantime, Georgie had graduated from Pasadena High School and spent a year at V.M.I. Then, having passed the entrance examination, he went on to West Point. He was in his plebe year when he was sent to Washington, D.C., with the other cadets to march in President Theodore Roosevelt's Inauguration parade.

Miss Ayer wrote him that she would be in Washington, too, and mentioned, with the modesty becoming a young lady, that she hoped they would renew their acquaintance. Their meeting was described by Patton in a charmingly frank letter to his father:

"When I arrived at the hotel, I was just going to send up my card when Bea grabbed me. She seemed really very glad to see me. Of course I was similarly affected. Pretty soon Mrs. Ayer came and made me go in and get some more dinner while they dressed for the Inaugural Ball. As I was by myself, I ordered all the desserts there were and nothing else.

"Then we went to the ball, or rather, squash, and saw 'Teddy' and the royal family. . . .

"After the dance we went back to the hotel and had supper, and then 12 o'clock came and with it ended my permit, so, like Cinderella I had to go, although if she was having half as good a time as I, I can't blame her if she had lost both her slippers."

During their fleeting reunion in Washington, Georgie told Beatrice that he intended to become a soldier, and that the only thing that could possibly deter him would be what he termed "the Call." It was something he dreaded.

"When my cousin Robbie Patton was a student at the University of Virginia," he told Beatrice, "he had no intention of becoming a clergyman. But then all of a sudden he had 'the Call' and he felt obliged to respond to it. You can't evade 'the Call'," he said with a superstitious shudder.

"Robbie" Patton became a prominent Episcopalian minister, and eventually head of the Church Institute for Negroes. But Georgie, awed by his cousin's "fate," prayed every night that he would not receive "the Call."

CHAPTER THREE
GENTLEMAN SOLDIER

George and Beatrice had Mrs. Ayer on their side. She knew the Pattons well through her brother Joe of California. He assured her that the Patton boy—with an excellent pedigree of his own, plenty of money in the family, a far better than average brain and the firm determination to succeed in his chosen profession—would make an excellent mate for Beatrice. But George was worried that he might not pass the muster of Bea's father, Frederick Ayer.

Though Georgie's ancestry was as splendorous as any in America, he was somewhat apprehensive that it was not quite a match for the Ayers' New England background. The Pattons' aristocracy was the informal, relaxed, unsophisticated kind of nobility that seemed parvenu in proper Bostonian eyes. And Ayer was a Brahmin to the core.

An enormously successful industrialist and financier who parlayed the family's old Connecticut mill into one of the country's largest textile concerns, the patriarchal Ayer was so aloof and grand that he was called "The Governor" and "Sir Frederick"—even in his own family. He kept a big four-story house on Commonwealth Avenue in Boston and spent his summers at "Avalon," his Italian-style Renaissance villa and one of the palatial private houses of Cape Cod. Compared with the Pattons' rambling ranch house in San Marino it was a palace.

A highly civilized person, Ayer surrounded himself with men of great intellectual attainments—prominent clergymen like the Reverend Robert Court, and scientists like Dr. Moses Greeley Parker, the first man to photograph lightning, and the Egyptologist Theodore M. Davis.

Georgie feared that he did not want a soldier for a son-in-law. And sure enough, when he formally asked "Sir Frederick" for Bea's hand, the old gentleman expressed the doubts young Patton suspected he had in mind. He asked Georgie to explain—in a letter, at that—why he chose the military for a career.

Georgie was to graduate from the Military Academy in June, 1909—a year behind schedule because he had been turned back in his first year for having flunked his math test —and he and Bea planned to marry shortly after graduation. On January 18th, he sat down to spell out as best he could in a candid and dignified letter the reasons behind his decision to go into the Army.

"With reference to the profession of a soldier," he wrote to Frederick Ayer, "I think I appreciate most of its drawbacks. As you say, it is very narrowing, but don't you think that a man of only very ordinary capacity, in order to succeed against great competition, must be narrow? That is, have only one motive. I have no experience but from what I have read of successful men, they seem to be of the one-idea sort.

"It is hard to answer intelligently the question: 'Why I want to be a Soldier?' For my own satisfaction I have tried to give myself reasons but have never found any logical ones. I only feel it inside. It is as natural for me to be a soldier as it is to breathe and would be as hard to give up all thought of it as it would be to stop breathing.

"But being a soldier and being a member of the Army in time of peace are two different things. I would only accept the latter as a means to the former."

Sir Frederick was properly impressed. George Patton married Beatrice Ayer on May 26, 1910, in a grand wedding at the Beverly Farms Episcopal Church, near Pride's Crossing in Salem Harbor, the Ayers' church when they were in residence at "Avalon." After honeymooning in England, Second Lieutenant George S. Patton Jr. took his diminutive bride to Fort Sheridan, Illinois, his first Army post. He was the lowest man on the totem pole of Troop K, 15th Cavalry Regiment.

It was not simple for the young Pattons to adjust themselves to the spartan life of the Army, in which Georgie was undoubtedly the richest officer. Although not on Bea's splendid scale, George also had lived in affluent comfort all his life.

Even West Point had had its luxuries, and he could buy whatever he craved on his generous allowance. But now Beatrice was just another Army wife. And George had to reduce his own standard of living, for he could not parade his wealth in a community in which his fellow officers could hardly make ends meet on the pittance of their salaries.

Just when Patton was joining it for better or for worse, as the career to which he was to dedicate the next four decades of his life, the United States Army was at its lowest ebb of prestige and influence. As a career, it offered little but hardships and sacrifices, and total anonymity. A junior officer like Patton, new in the Army, had to sustain his faith with the dedication of a Trappist monk. While undoubtedly many an officer served for whatever security the Army provided, just as many stuck it out from a sense of patriotic duty. No matter how you looked at it, it was not an easy life. In times of peace, the officers of the regular establishment were butts of civilian criticism and condescension, if not contempt; many remained in the grade of lieutenant for 15 years. You would not think that the Army could appeal to a rich young man like Patton, who was somewhat of a playboy besides.

He solved his unique problem of adjustment by simply ignoring it. He thought it would be sheer hypocrisy, completely contrary to his character, to live frugally on his Army pay and to forego the style of life to which he was accustomed. Never actually flaunting his wealth, he nevertheless maintained his standards.

At Fort Sheridan, the Pattons occupied a couple of cell-like rooms in a small house on the reservation, quarters to which a married shavetail was entitled. There hardly was space enough for a dining table in the living room, but the Pattons dressed for dinner every night. This, and their display of other idiosyncrasies that go with inherited wealth, caused tongues to wag at the fort. The other Army wives called them "the Duke and the Duchess."

They never deviated from their stylish regime, no matter how many eyebrows it raised in the military community. Later, whenever it was possible or permitted, they established themselves in more comfortable and even luxurious quarters off base, Patton commuting to his job in his high-priced automobile, which he drove at breakneck speed. While at Fort Myer in Virginia, they lived in a big rented house in Rosslyn, an exclusive residential suburb of Washington. When he was stationed at Fort George G. Meade in Maryland, they lived still more comfortably on Twenty-third Street, Patton racing to and from the fort in his high-powered, expensive gray Pierce Arrow touring car. Once they went all the way and rented "Woodley," one of the capital's showpieces on Cathedral Avenue, just off Rock Creek Park.

In 1912, when Patton competed in the Olympic Games in Sweden, in the then newly introduced category of modern pentathlon, the entire American team lived modestly on S.S. *Finland*, the ship that ferried them to Stockholm and was anchored in the harbor for the duration of the games. But the Pattons, accompanied by George's mother, camped in an expensive suite in the famous Grand Hotel. (Incidentally, George went at his own expense and wound up fifth in a field of 43 competitors.)

When he was transferred to Fort Benning, Georgia, in 1940 to command a newly organized tank brigade, he arrived in his customary grand manner, followed by his train of horses and servants. Then Mrs. Patton arrived to take up residence at Benning, only to find that the quarters assigned to them were far from satisfactory.

Patton especially disliked the house because it was an hour's drive from Tiger Camp, where his men lived and worked. As so often in the past, he dipped into his private purse to remedy the situation. Mrs. Patton designed and had built a delightful house in the Georgia pines. Long and sprawling, it looked like a glorified log cabin from the out-side. It had huge windows, and its inside walls were covered with soft pine panels. A great fireplace built of native stone made the living room especially cozy.

The Pattons lived in their dream house only a short time. In March, 1942, Patton was transferred to Indio in Cali-fornia to organize a tank-training center in the Western Desert. Upon his departure, they donated the house to the Army.

It was natural for Patton to go into the Cavalry, which at that time was the glamour service of the Army. It enabled him to indulge in the most exclusive and expensive sports as part of his regular duties.

He played polo and participated in all forms of eques-trian exercises—cross-country riding, exhibition rides, fox hunting. The Pattons made the most of this opportunity. They maintained their own horses—including thoroughbreds which they raised and raced—and George had his own stable of polo ponies. He took them along whenever he was moved from one post to another. His arrival at every new station always stirred excitement, somewhat like the arrival of a circus in town, with its familiar parade down Main Street. In 1915, shortly after his arrival at Fort Bliss in Texas, on the Mexican frontier, he was summoned to the colonel commanding his new outfit, the 8th Cavalry Regiment.

"Captain Patton," the Colonel pounced upon him. "What is this I hear? You had the temerity and bad taste to move in with four horses and," raising his voice, "twenty-six polo ponies."

"No, sir," Patton replied. "That isn't correct. I have but one horse of my own, a mare called Sylvia Green, and only six polo ponies."

"I don't give a damn, six or twenty-six!" the Colonel said. "Get them off the post or I'll have you court-martialed."

"Yes, sir," said Patton, who usually disagreed but rarely argued with his superior officer—not, at least, face to face. He made prompt arrangements to keep his ponies at a stable in El Paso at his own expense.

The Pattons were always in the whirl of high society, mostly in the horsey set close to the Army post at which George happened to be stationed. As soon as he arrived at Fort Sheridan, he and Mrs. Patton joined the Onwentesia Club at Lake Forest, one of the most exclusive riding clubs in Illinois. In 1933, while stationed at Fort Myer, he was elected Master of the Cobler Hunt near Delaplane, the center of Virginia's fairest fox-hunting country.

He also participated in the hunter trials of the Riding and Hunt Club of Washington, and was a regular star attraction of all the great national horse shows. "Major Patton has had more actual hunting experience than any officer in the service," reported the *Cavalry Journal* at that time. "He was one of the early Masters of the old Mounted Service School Pack, and has hunted with practically every pack on the Atlantic Seaboard."

Although he did not yet make the front pages of the newspapers (the first time he made the New York *Times Index* was 1942), his name popped up regularly in the society and sports columns. "Major George Patton," read a typical item in the Washington *Star*, "hunting with two of the Fort Myer riders, was fourth with a fine performance." Another in the Washington *Post*: "Major Patton accounted for two Blue, two Red, three Yellow and four White ribbons, representing the Office of the Chief of Cavalry." And still another: "The hunter trials at Bradley Farm saw close competition between Major George S. Patton and Major General Guy V. Henry [then the Chief of Cavalry] in the second class, Patton winning the class with 99 to Henry's 97."

"Whenever Patton was stationed at Fort Myer, it was always the center of capital society," recalled Mrs. Hope Ridings Miller, former society editor of the Washington *Post.* "He brought flair and style to the fort and drew like a magnet the best people to Myer."

Patton and his family organized the greatest event of the season at Fort Myer, called the "Society Circus," to raise money for various Army charities. His daughter Ruth Ellen usually wrote the shows under such titles as "The Horse Through the Ages" and "Hoofprints of 1939." Patton himself designed the costumes. At one of them he appeared as King Arthur, with Mrs. Patton as Guinevere.

He was always exquisitely groomed for these occasions, wearing $23.50 boots (the most expensive in those days) made for him by Ugo Ferrini of Rome; his uniform was tailored by Weatheralls of Savile Row, his custom-made "Saumur" saddle by Marquis from Hermes of Faubourg St. Honoré in Paris.

Even then, however, ugly and persistent rumors beclouded his sportsmanship. According to the capital's society gossip, Patton was not really fond of (or, for that matter, good to) his horses, but used them merely as a means for his exhibitionism. It was said that he mercilessly beat them, and even shot them when they had outlived their usefulness.

The charge, preposterous though it sounded, was whispered throughout the horsey set, and the rumors persisted, although those who knew Patton intimately and saw him at close quarters with his horses denied them vigorously. It was repeated to me as late as 1963, when I visited some of the old sites of Patton's equestrian triumphs in Virginia. I tried to track down the ugly rumor and found what I believe was its origin.

Patton spoke of his horses in his usual pugnacious and coarse manner without, it seemed, any of the sentiment and appreciation of the real sportsman. Showing his bulging scrapbook, he would speak deprecatingly about several horses that apparently had not lived up to his expectations.

Pointing to the picture of a mare called Golden Venture, he exclaimed, "This one was just a Goddamn bag of bones. I shot her."

One of the persons to whom he made this remark began to spread the tale that "Patton was shooting the horses he doesn't like," and the rumor snowballed. It seemed to gain confirmation from documented accounts of men who claimed they had actually seen him shooting several horses.

Far from substantiating a cruel streak, the stories of eyewitnesses documented the man's soft, humane side. They originated from an incident early in his career in the Cavalry. In 1913, when Lieutenant Patton was stationed in the Cavalry School at Fort Riley, Kansas, he happened to see the school's veterinarian shoot a horse that had broken its leg. The vet needed two shots to kill the animal, whose agony between shots deeply aroused Patton.

After that, he insisted that he be allowed to fire the *coup de grâce* whenever a doomed horse had to be put away, for he always needed only a single shot for this act of mercy. The incident went far to show how Patton, who rarely knew how to handle his own public relations, and whose thoughtless speech frequently caused him trouble, was himself responsible for at least some of the blemishes that appeared from time to time on his picture.

After World War I Patton developed a liking for yet another sporting hobby. In 1921 he learned to fly and bought a small private plane in which he would keep his dates at distant horse shows and polo tournaments. By 1940 his license had expired. He then needed a plane, but no longer for his pleasure. He was training a new generation of tankmen for another war, and was eager to observe their exercises from the air. The Army had no observation plane to spare, so he renewed his license and bought a Stinson Voyageur.

The Stinson served its purpose as long as he was at Fort Benning, enabling him to get a bird's-eye view of the tanks in various field exercises, and to spot errors. But when he was transferred to the huge Desert Training Center at Indio, it nearly caused his doom.

On going to Indio from Benning in the spring of 1942,

when the United States was already at war, Patton decided to fly in his private plane. The trip required several days, for he had to come down for gas every 200 miles. He reached Tucson, Arizona, at last, and wired the Western Defense Command in the Presidio in San Francisco to let them know that he was flying in. The Commanding Officer was Lieutenant General John L. DeWitt, one of the old-timers among the Army's senior officers, who was not especially fond of Patton, to say the least.

When General deWitt was told that Patton was moving into Indio in his usual grand manner, flying his own plane, he blew his top. "Tell the s.o.b.," he barked at an aide, "that civilian planes will be shot down."

The message was radioed to Patton airbound in the Stinson, and it left him no choice. He had to land and leave the craft at Blyth in California. But when he arrived at the center, he discovered that General DeWitt's petty intervention probably had saved his life. What had been marked out for him as his "landing field" near Indio was a rugged cactus-covered mountainside.

Later at the center he used the Stinson as he pleased. He could be seen every day, cruising over the vast desert, observing the exercises down on the sand. This gave the men he was driving with an iron fist an opportunity to show that they were fond of the Old Man after all, in spite of his martinet regime and strict discipline. They always held their breath whenever Patton came in for a landing, because the field he used was surrounded by rows of telephone poles whose wires made both take-off and landing extremely hazardous.

One morning when he arrived at the field to take up the Stinson, he was startled to find that the poles had disappeared and no wires remained to obstruct the take-off. Where had they gone? The night before, his signalmen, on their own initiative and time, had taken down the poles and buried the wires underground.

"It would be a darned shame," a sergeant said, explaining to Patton the men's decision to get the poles and wires out of his way, "if you broke your neck, sir, *before* you get overseas."

CHAPTER FOUR
ANCIENT MAN IN MODERN ARMOR

George Patton's course in the Army began auspiciously—in fact, the first decade of his career was nothing short of spectacular. When he was still a second lieutenant in 1911, barely three years out of West Point, he moved with perfect aplomb in both the inner sanctums of the Army's high command and the most exclusive drawing rooms of Washington's high society.

The Army was then, as Henry L. Stimson, Secretary of war in the Taft Administration, put it, "slowly awakening after a slumber of nearly 50 years which had been only briefly disturbed by the absurd confusion of the Spanish War."

Those were exhilarating days in the Army, marked by the head-on clash of the progressive and conservative elements. The progressives were in the saddle. Their leader, the flamboyant soldier-surgeon-politician, General Leonard Wood, was the Chief of Staff. The conservatives—mostly deskbound military bureaucrats in the Munitions Building —were headed by General Fred C. Ainsworth, who had powerful Congressional forces to back him up. The clash ended when Stimson decided to side with General Wood, his old buddy in the Spanish War, and forced Ainsworth out of the Army.

Young Patton was close to these exciting events. A man of independent means, married to a New England heiress (Washington society usually referred to him not as Lieutenant Patton but as "Fred Ayer's son-in-law"), he had advantages few second lieutenants enjoyed. He moved almost instantly up to the secluded summit of the high command by becoming aide-de-camp to the Chief of Staff and gaining entrance to the Secretary's own inner circle. He was Stimson's regular companion on his morning rides at Fort

Myer and treated the older man to his ideas about the
Army and war. He left a lasting impression on Stimson,
which benefited Patton during World War II when he sorely
needed the goodwill of the man who was again Secretary of
War, now in Franklin Roosevelt's Administration.

It was perhaps the happiest period of his life. The plush
social climate of the Stimson-Wood regime favored his
fast-stepping ways, which otherwise would have redounded
to his disadvantage in the staid middle-class atmosphere of
the Army. His own colorful boss, a former Army surgeon
like Patton's ancestor Hugh Mercer, whose flair for adventure moved him into the line, not only approved of but also
stimulated Patton's youthful exuberance, and did his best to
pave the way of his buoyant aide. Patton was accepted in
the hierarchy with open arms, for his background and
wealth made him socially eligible, quite aside from his
evident professional competency.

He lived elegantly and flashily. He maintained a lavish
table for his guests and a stable of spirited horses. But professionally, too, he found his assignment most satisfying. It
held out the promise of a dazzling career. He found many
opportunities to gratify his restive spirit and bubbling intellectual curiosity. He did most of the things he liked to do
even when some of them went far beyond the normal routine
and the humdrum duties of a regular Army officer.

In 1912, a military contest called modern pentathlon was
added to the competitions at the Olympic Games. It was, as
General Henry, later the Chief of Cavalry, described it, the
International Olympic Committee's concept of a tournament for modern knights. "This twentieth-century cavalier,"
he wrote, "must be able to overcome all obstacles that may
confront him in carrying out his knightly mission. With the
pistol or dueling sword he engages in personal combat; with
any available horse he swiftly rides across country; the un-
fordable stream he swims; and he finishes the journey on
foot."

The event appealed to Patton, who went to the games at
Stockholm at his own expense, and knocked himself out
to win. He had to be fished from the pool with a boat hook
when he passed out at the end of the 300-meter swim;
then he fainted again from utter exhaustion, in front of the
royal box, on the finish line of the 4,000-meter cross-country run. But he wound up fifth in a field of 32 contestants

with the best showing of any regular Army officer on the United States team.

On his way home, he detoured to Saumur, where the French Army had its famed Cavalry School dating back to the 18th century. Beatrice Patton regarded the trip as their second honeymoon. But her husband used the visit to improve his épée by taking lessons from M. Cléry, the French master, who was adjutant at the school.

Back in the States, he designed a saber that the Cavalry promptly adopted. Patton was named the Army's first Master of the Sword, an honorific then recently created. In the summer of 1913, again paying his own expenses, he returned to Saumur, for he had fallen in love with the place, and with France, on his first brief visit.

The old Anjou town of the Loire in western France, with its 12th-century Church of Notre Dame de Nantilly, 16th-century *hôtel de ville*, and charming Renaissance houses, was in the heart of a region noted for its fine, sparkling wine. Its atmosphere enchanted Patton. But by some prescience, he also recognized that the countryside, in which Fulk Nerra waged his protracted war with Henry I of England for the possession of Maine, would again become a battlefield in some future war.

He had his automobile with him and reconnoitered the whole *bocage* country between Cherbourg and Saumur. He drove down rough watershed backroads on which William the Conqueror once moved his army, and looked in on towns like St. Malo and St. Lô, Falaise and Caen. On his return to the United States, to take up new duties as an instructor at the Cavalry School at Fort Riley, Patton wrote a long report on his "reconnaissance." He stated explicitly his view that the country had distinct military significance, no matter how remote from conflict the times then appeared; and he pointed out, for future reference, that those "watershed roads would always be firm enough to carry military transports no matter how much it rained."

The report was filed and forgotten—until 1944, when Patton returned to the *bocages* of the Loire with the Third Army. This was more than just haphazard *déjà vu*. The phenomenal success of his drive through the region in World War II was definitely facilitated, as he himself put it, by his personal reconnaissance more than 30 years before.

His charmed life continued unabated. In 1916, after a

brief tour of duty with the 8th Cavalry Regiment at Fort Bliss, Patton reached the first high point of his military career and had his initial opportunity to fire a gun in anger. In a rather adventurous excursion to Mexico, chasing the elusive Francisco (Pancho) Villa with more dash than success, he became an aide and favorite of General Pershing, who was to become head of the American Expeditionary Force within a year.

A disciple of the action school in the Army, young Patton appealed to Pershing, whose basic criterion in evaluating an officer was whether he was a "fighter." Patton was a fighter of classic proportions. In Mexico, though, he had to go out of his way to find action because Villa chose to evade his pursuers.

Patton went searching for the elusive foe. He did not find Villa but succeeded in tracking down his bodyguard, "Colonel" Julio Cardenas, hiding in his father's hacienda. He killed him in a quick-triggered fight that far more resembled the pay-off in an adult Western than a military operation.

His unorthodox methods of fighting the Mexican bandits on their own ground and terms both impressed and amused General Pershing. "We have a bandit in our ranks," he would say with a tolerant smile that betrayed his hidden pride, "this Patton boy! He's a *real* fighter." He could bestow no greater praise. Pershing was so impressed with Patton's qualities as an aggressive soldier that he was willing to shut his eyes to his aide's eccentricities.

Up to this point, Patton's wonderful time in the Army was not reflected in any unusually rapid advancement. It took him seven years, until May 26, 1916, to rise from second to first lieutenant. It would have taken even longer—maybe as long as 15 years—to make the modest jump, for promotions were excruciatingly slow in the peacetime Army. But Pershing gave Patton what, under the circumstances, could be euphemistically called a battlefield promotion in Mexico.

Then his career skyrocketed so fast that it amazed even him. He advanced to captain, major and lieutenant colonel in only 22 months between 1916 and 1918. On October 1, 1918, a month and 11 days before his 33rd birthday, Patton was a full colonel commanding a brigade in France. He would have become a brigadier general but for two untoward incidents: He was seriously wounded in the Meuse-

Argonne offensive on September 16, 1918 ("missing half my bottom but otherwise all right"), and World War I ended before he recovered.

After the war he reverted to his permanent rank of captain, and then it took him 18 years to become a colonel again. But those oppressive years of his ordeal were still ahead of him. Now this was 1918 and Patton was on the move. He was making the most of his opportunities in a hectic year that shaped him for his historic role 26 years hence.

Patton arrived in France with Pershing on April 17, 1917, and remained with him as a junior aide and commandant of his Headquarters. He considered it a privilege to serve on the General's staff, but he soon found that his assignment was far different from his association with Pershing during the Mexican Punitive Expedition.

In the vast and intricate machinery of the AEF he was but a tiny cog. And in the enormous Headquarters organization of the Commander in Chief there was no place or time for the informality of their Mexican days. In Mexico he was extremely close to Pershing, but Patton now found that he was becoming remote from him. It never took long for him to start straining at the leash. Early in September, he went to Pershing and asked for a transfer to a combat post. He caught the General at a crucial moment. Preoccupied with the organization of the first American tank unit, Pershing told Patton, "If you want to leave, it's all right with me. I give you two choices. You can have command of a battalion of infantry. Or you can go into the Tank Corps."

What Pershing called "the Tank Corps" was hardly even a gleam in his eyes. On the eve of America's entry into World War I, the Army was a rather backward instrument of power. It remained unaffected by the historic lessons of a monstrous conflict that had been raging since the summer of 1914. In that bloody summer when machine guns were slaughtering thousands at Verdun and on the Somme, the American Tables of Organization and Equipment still allotted only four machine guns to an infantry regiment. Artillery and artillery ammunition were in woefully short supply, even

in the Mexican operation, at a time when Allied and German
guns were being lined up hub to hub, firing barrages of
unparalleled intensity and duration.

By the time the United States was ready to enter it, the
war was no longer what it had set out to be. The precision
clockwork of mass armies had run down and become mixed
in a solid line of trenches and barbed wire. The bankruptcy
of a generation of military thought and planning became
apparent. The British faced up to the crucial problem of this
bloody stalemate with ingenuity. They developed a seemingly utopian weapon that, they hoped, would be an antidote,
as Captain B. H. Liddell Hart called it, to the defensive combination of machine guns and barbed wire.

A colonel named Ernest D. Swinton hit upon the idea of
a "self-propelled vehicle, capable of crossing trenches and
so armored as to be impervious to machine-gun bullets."
Winston S. Churchill, then at the head of the Admiralty, became interested in it. He formed what he called the "Land-
ships Committee" to undertake experiments. Then W. A.
Tritton and Lieutenant Walter G. Wilson were commissioned to design the first machine. To conceal this development from the Germans, a misleading pseudonym was
sought for the new weapon. It came to be called "tank" by
its code name.

When first used, tanks represented a major surprise in
the war. However, whatever was gained by this element of
surprise was dissipated by the fact that, from the outset, the
Allied High Command made very poor tactical use of the
tank. This phase of its spasmodic evolution never ceased to
appall Patton. He later described it succinctly in an article
in the *Cavalry Journal*. He recalled how the tank was
simultaneously developed by both the British and the
French, but along entirely different mechanical and tactical
lines.

"The French," he wrote, "following the lead of Ulysses,
thought of their *chars d' assaut* as armored carriers destined
to transport groups of infantry, unscathed, across No
Man's Land, through the wire and over the trenches and then
disgorge them in the enemy's rear. The British, on the other
hand, followed the Macedonian idea and constructed not
carriers but mechanical fighters whose duty it was to shoot
down resistance, smash wire and bridge trenches so as to
render the infantry assault less possible."

He went on, recalling in a sardonic mood the initial setback of the new weapon: "Unfortunately for the French plan, that mutual esteem and confidence existing between allies prevented either nation from informing the other of its invention so that, when the French had some hundreds of machines almost ready for a surprise attack, the British spilled the beans by jumping off on the Somme on September 15, 1916, with a handful of tanks."

As a matter of fact, British General Headquarters attempted to change the outcome of the Battle of the Somme with only 32 tanks, all that were available for the operation. The Battle of Flanders in the fall of 1917 offered no chance for success as far as the tank was concerned, chiefly because of the unfavorable terrain and the spare use of the new weapon.

By then it seemed that the tank would justify the skepticism of its opponents. However, it redeemed itself in the Battle of Cambrai on November 20, 1917. Without preliminary bombardment, the British launched the battle with a surprise attack, employing 380 tanks. They penetrated the German lines without much trouble and were on the point of breaking through into the open country, but the exhausted troops were unable to take advantage of the situation. Although the Battle of Cambrai ended inconclusively, it did demonstrate that the tank could become an extremely useful weapon.

Ever since General Pershing gave him the choice, Patton was struggling with his dilemma. He was determined not to go into the infantry. And he was queasy about joining the nonexistent Tank Corps. He had observed British tanks deploying for the Battle of Cambrai and was not overly impressed. He could not decide whether he should become involved in the controversial new weapon whose failure, should it prove a dud, would undoubtedly redound to his disadvantage and might even retard his advancement in the Army despite the opportunities the war held out.

In his dilemma he turned to the man whose judgment he trusted implicitly, his father-in-law, old Ayer in Boston. In a carefully worded letter, sent home by a friend to evade the censor, Patton outlined his problem to the patriarch, asking for his advice.

In due course, Mr. Ayer's answer arrived. "I am a man of peace," he wrote. "I know nothing of war. But my advice to you would be to choose the weapon with which you believe you can inflict the most punishment on the enemy while at the same time suffering the fewest casualties yourself."

Immediately Patton went to Pershing and told him, "Sir, I have decided for the Tank Corps. And I accept my new command with particular enthusiasm because with the light tanks I believe I can inflict the greatest number of casualties on the enemy with the smallest expenditure of American life."

He pondered for a moment whether he should ask the question that was foremost on his mind, lest he draw upon himself Pershing's wrath. But he decided to ask it anyway.

"Sir," he said, "I think it's fine that we are going to have a Tank Corps. But if you permit me to ask, what are we going to use for tanks?"

It was not a facetious question. The United States Army was slow in its appreciation of the new weapon.

By the fall of 1917, when the Army decided at long last "to adopt the new weapon," the British and French already had thousands of them. But the United States had only two tanks it could call its own. They were custom built by the Ordnance Department in Washington from French blueprints. But Ordnance had made so many modifications in the original design that the prototypes which resulted from this tinkering proved useless. They were lumbering and gawkish in appearance, and naïve in construction. One of them was propelled by a steam engine, of all things.

Pershing had asked the French and British to supply the tanks he needed, but they told him they had none to spare. "As there was little or no prospect of our obtaining tanks abroad," Pershing noted, "Their manufacture at home was recommended and full details of requirements were accordingly cabled to Washington." The War Department ordered thousands of tanks in the United States, but it took time to get the program rolling. (On Armistice Day there were 23,405 tanks on order. But only 26 had actually been completed when the war ended.)

Patton received his orders on November 19, 1917, and tried to approach his new assignment with an open mind. When he first confronted the tank he disliked it and called it a "coffin on wheels." He even refused to concede that it represented a novel means in warfare. "The appearance of armored fighting vehicles in the World War," he wrote in 1933, when he looked back on his first association with the tanks, "was a striking reaffirmation of the old adage: 'There is nothing new under the sun.'" The idea behind the tank harked back to 1096 B.C. and the Trojan horse, he thought. When "nine years of Hellenic valor had failed to breach the Trojan walls," he wrote in recollection, the wooden horse made its appearance and "by carrying men unscathed within that impregnable circle, destroyed in a night Priam's mighty fort." And he recalled how in 318 B.C. the walls and ditches of Tyre had withstood for a year the furious assault of the best troops of the day, "only to fall in their turn before the moving tower of Alexander."

He did recognize the desperate need for the tank to break the stalemate on the Western Front created by the ascendancy of defense over offense. But even that was nothing new, he thought. "All through history," he wrote, "Victory has oscillated between the spear and the shield, the wall and the charge, tactics and technique." As he saw it in the fall of 1917, the trench was but an inverted wall and the barbed wire an inverted ditch. As they made assaults abortive, they needed the tank—a modern version of the wooden horse and Alexander's moving tower. "The striking circumstance," Patton mused, "that, thousands of years later, necessity has again begat of invention identical solutions for identical problems is truly arresting."

Yet the fact that Patton, soaked as he was in the history of war, could see nothing particularly new in the tank did not dismay or discourage him. If anything, it inflamed his imagination and enthusiasm, while the difficulties of his new job boosted his energy.

At this particular stage, the Tank Corps consisted of Brigadier General Samuel D. Rockenbach, Pershing's choice to command the new service, and of Captain Patton (soon to be upped to major in view of his greater responsibilities).

Rockenbach handled the complicated policy matters, represented Pershing on the Supreme War Council in questions concerning the tank, and fought bitter battles with the British and French to obtain their cooperation for the development of the Tank Corps. Patton worked on creating it against overwhelming odds.

As soon as he made up his mind to become a tanker, he plunged into the task. His specific assignment was to train and command two battalions of tanks, which were to form the first brigade of the Tank Corps. Nothing in his experience and training qualified him for these new duties. Therefore, he started from scratch by going to the British tank school at Bovington in England and the French tank school in Chaplieu to learn the trade before he would teach it.

Patton went to every operation he heard about in which tanks were expected to be used to observe them in action. He was not impressed with the 30-ton British Mark VI heavies; and he rejected out of hand the ponderous French St. Cheumonds and feeble Schneiders in which, as he put it, "many valiant Frenchmen were roasted and from which few Germans were killed."

As it could be expected of an officer whose roots were in the Cavalry, he opted for the light tanks and picked the two-man, six-ton French Renault for his battalions.

Then Patton switched into high gear. He set up a training center near Langres in the Haute Marne, selecting the villages of Bourg and Bren as billets for his troops. They soon began to come in swarms, all of them volunteers. "The tanks have attracted a lot of good men," he wrote to his wife on February 21, 1918, "and I get requests from them to transfer into tanks nearly daily."

Patton's initial skepticism now gave way to unbounded enthusiasm. "It seems to me more and more certain that we cannot punch a hole without tanks," he wrote. "There are too many instruments of death in the way but I believe that tanks well worked up will do the job."

Now he feared only that he would not be able to put all this cramming to practical use. "I hope," he wrote, "the war lasts long enough for us to try our hand."

The French came through with 22 Renaults, which Patton needed for instructional purposes. The tanks arrived at the railroad siding near Bourg on a moonlit night while Patton was sleeping in his quarters after a hard day at the training center. At 10 P.M. Sergeant Joe Angelo, his orderly, burst into the room where he was sleeping.

"The Renaults have just arrived, Major," Joe told him as he shook him awake. "Get up, sir. You are needed at the siding."

Patton dressed and rushed to the station, then spent the next three or four hours working to get the tanks off the flatcars and to the depot. He personally handled every one of them. He had to. He was the only man at the Tank Center who knew how to drive a tank.

This was a slow, uphill job, taxing the best in Patton as a trainer of men.

The tank in particular presented baffling problems. It was exasperatingly primitive. Inside the clumsy machine the two-man crew had to communicate in total darkness by hitting each other—a kick in the driver's back told him to go forward, a kick on his head was the signal to stop. There was no communication among the tanks, much less between them and the infantry they were supposed to support.

At a maximum speed of four miles an hour, they were so slow that often they could not keep up with the marching infantry. Mechanical troubles kept disabling them, and since there were not enough trained mechanics, the majority of the few tanks Patton had in his command were idle most of the time.

Tactics were similarly primitive. Since the tank's true potentialities remained unrecognized in World War I, it was used exactly as Pershing regarded it—merely as an aid to infantry in attack. "As the war progressed," Patton wrote, "a doctrine for the use of tanks was evolved which was officially stated as follows: 'Tanks are an auxiliary arm whose mission it is to facilitate the advance of the assault infantry. To do this they must so act as to bridge the gap between the lifting of the barrage and the arrival of the bayonet.'"

By July, 1918, he had his six companies in shape, and it was generally recognized that they were the smartest in the AEF. Patton became widely known as the Expeditionary Force's "worst Goddamned martinet." A miniature version of the later Patton legend already was springing up about him in World War I, for he insisted on the spit and polish that became synonymous with his name in World War II. He developed the simple gesture of the salute into a high and delicate art. An especially smart salute became known as "a georgepatton" throughout the AEF.

But all this sweat and toil seemed to be for nothing. Patton felt like a man riding a speedboat on a lake, going fast to nowhere. For one thing, his Table of Organization and Equipment allotted 24 tanks to each of his companies, or a total of 144 light Renaults, but he still had only the original

22 with which he began to train his men. Moreover, nothing indicated that his two battalions would be used in action in the forseeable future.

There was no sign, to be sure, that the Germans were faltering or that the war would end abruptly before Patton and his tanks could get into it. In July, General Ferdinand Foch, the Supreme Commander since April 14, suggested that "the Allies give serious consideration to taking the offensive in earnest, looking to a victory over Germany in 1919." But it was merely a suggestion. An Allied offensive that coincided with it ended in defeat. It seemed the Germans still had plenty of fight in them and the war would drag on for months deep into 1919.

Then all of a sudden the entire complexion of the conflict changed. And Patton's period of waiting came to an end.

Foch now had a far greater design in mind—a grand offensive on all fronts—in which the Americans would play an important part at last. As one of the preliminaries to that grand offensive he proposed an operation that was to release the Paris-Arricourt railroad in the region of Commercy. But there was a stumbling block to this plan. The Germans were tenaciously holding a salient at St. Mihiel, an ancient town in the Lorraine on the Meuse built around a Benedictine monastery. It was a 15-square-mile swampy triangle punched into the Allied lines in a heavily wooded country with abrupt bridges over fast streams. They had captured it in September, 1914, thus cutting the strategic railroad line to Verdun and Nancy, and had withstood repeated heavy French attacks during the years.

Foch now planned to evict the Germans from the salient and assigned the job to the Americans. Since July 24th, Lieutenant Colonel George C. Marshall had been working on the operations plans for the offensive at Chaumont, Pershing's headquarters. Toward the end of August, preparations began in earnest for the offensive, which was scheduled to start before the middle of September.

It was, of course, not quite so simple as all this. This first American offensive in World War I was preceded by bitter controversy and was followed by acrimonious debate. Once it seemed that the Americans would be deprived of their opportunity at St. Mihiel because in the meantime Foch had succeeded in eliminating several German salients and no longer thought that the American effort in that sector would be necessary. But Pershing refused to budge. He insisted on going through with the original action. At one point, it was rumored, Black Jack was on the verge of slapping Foch in the face when the Frenchman, irritated by Pershing's refusal to submit to his plans, asked with Gallic irony, "I take it you do not wish to participate in the battle, *mon général?*"

But all the bickerings at Chaumont and Bonbon, headquarters of Pershing and Foch, respectively, had a bearing on Patton only insofar as they threatened to deprive him of the action he had craved for so long and so ardently, and for which he had worked so hard and so arduously.

At 10 A.M. on August 22, 1918, Patton—who had been made a lieutenant colonel the previous March—was told by telephone to report to General Rockenbach with his reconnaissance officer "ready for protracted field service." He was at Army Headquarters at 3 P.M.

"Well, Patton," the General told him, "we have our orders. We will attack the St. Mihiel salient around September 7th, I would say, with three corps. You will command the tanks in V Corps, not only your own six companies but also a company of French tanks."

Patton busied himself at Headquarters the rest of the afternoon, picking up additional details of the plan, but at 8 P.M. he backtracked and sought out Rockenbach. Something had suddenly dawned upon him, something he had overlooked in his initial excitement.

"Goddamnit, General," he told Rockenbach when he found him. "I am wasting my time here with all these Goddamn plans. How in the hell can I command the tanks in the V Corps or in any of the Goddamn other corps, for that matter, when I don't have a single Goddamn one of them?!"

Rockenbach, a no-nonsense man who knew how to handle Patton, snapped, "They are on the way, Patton. You just do as you are told!"

After that, Patton burst into action like a display of fireworks on the Fourth of July. While the other officers slated to command at St. Mihiel prepared for the offensive in close association with their troops, Patton was running off in all directions. He behaved as if victory depended on him alone.

The day after he received his orders somebody told him that the terrain of his approach march to the salient was so marshy that his tanks would not be able to negotiate it. An inveterate optimist who was always skeptical of information that threatened to thwart his designs, Patton decided to see for himself.

He rushed to French Corps Headquarters and coaxed permission to go up to the front. That night he went out with a French patrol to reconnoiter the terrain and was relieved when he found it hard and dry. Upon his return to Bourg next morning, he had another present waiting for him. The tanks had arrived, and he became the busiest man in the AEF.

On September 4th, he was transferred to IV Corps near Toul, to work the 1st Infantry Division into the attack, and had to start all over again. Suddenly he remembered there was a stream in the path of his advance, and started worrying that maybe his tanks would not be able to cross it. He walked down to the river at Xivray, a town in No Man's Land exposed to both German and American fire, and ascertained that the bridge over the Rupt de Mad was intact.

While he was thus busy arranging things and touring the front, the behind-the-scenes battle raged between Foch and Pershing. But in the end everything worked out as originally planned. On September 5th the attack was set for the 12th. The great day for the AEF was on hand at last.

At 1 A.M. on Thursday the 12th, 900 Allied guns opened up and fired for four hours. Then at 5 A.M. the attack began. In the total darkness of this dismal pre-dawn, soaked by a heavy rain and whipped by a brisk wind, some 500,000 Americans and 150,000 Frenchmen went forward. By that evening virtually all the main objectives were reached. The battle was as good as over.

The Germans were overtaken and badly mauled by the swiftness of this American onrush. They lost 15,000 prisoners before they reached the shelter of the Hindenburg Line.

"The bag would have been bigger if the plan had not put a check on the advance," Captain Liddell Hart wrote. "It was an exhilarating result for the first performance of an independent American army, but to many Americans it would leave the sore feeling of a missed opportunity."

Despite its prominence in Legionnaire oratory, St. Mihiel was neither a difficult nor an important engagement. But for Patton it was the fulfillment—his personal Armageddon, the realization of all his dreams. Now in retrospect, when all the facts are in and the Patton story is complete, that relatively insignificant brief battle—insignificant certainly in comparison with those he was later to fight—looms as the microcosm of his military life. It revealed Patton the warrior, as he was constituted for better or for worse, and showed his manner of making war.

He was all over the place throughout the battle, jumping in and out of tanks, walking more than he rode, running more than he walked, now ahead of his tanks, coaxing them on, then behind them when they needed a push, like a frenzied schoolmaster trying frantically to keep in line a flock of unruly pupils on an outing.

Trying to reconstruct Patton's first 24 hours in action is almost impossible, and attempting to keep up with him even more so. The barrage began at 1 o'clock and the attack was due at 5 A.M., but at 3 A.M. his tanks were still not completely detrained. Their hectic trip to points of the jump-off sent him into one monumental rage after another.

His last company detrained at 3:15 A.M., then rolled straight into action. When the attack opened, Patton was on the top of a hill in front of the main line, like a Napoleonic marshal on the *Feldherrnhügel*, his elevated command post, watching his tanks. It was a dismal sight. Of his 174 tanks, only some 70 made it, more than 100 were bogged down in the mud and the trenches, which were 8 feet deep and 14 feet wide. At 7 A.M., through the fog and in knee-deep mud, he moved forward a couple of miles, then went still farther to see how the attack was going. He saw the first dead as he went, not too many because the Boche were not fighting too well or too hard, and our own casualties were absurdly small.

Patton reached the first town—St. Busant—while the Germans were still shelling it. He continued toward Essey, got into the front line, and found the infantry prone on the ground, pinned down by the German shelling.

At Essey he bumped into another American officer who was also walking about under fire. He was Brigadier General Douglas MacArthur, commanding a brigade. "We stood," Patton wrote, "and talked, but neither was much interested in what the other said as we could not get our minds off the shells." He walked on another mile and just when he saw the Germans beyond Essey, a platoon of his tanks, led by a young lieutenant, caught up with him. Patton directed him to advance on the next town, Pannes, but by then four of the platoon's five tanks had run out of gas. Patton went on to Pannes with the remaining tank and told Sergeant Graham, who commanded it, to proceed into the town. Graham hesitated. He seemed nervous to go it alone, so Patton jumped onto the tank and entered the town, then rode on in the direction of Beney. After a while he jumped off, for the tank was too slow for him, and he thought he could make better progress by walking.

In no time Patton was alone facing the Germans. All that he belonged to was miles back of him. He looked around and exclaimed to himself, "I'll be Goddamned!" He was inside the Hindenburg Line!

Suddenly he was overcome by a sensation Moses must have felt when the Lord permitted him to gaze on the Promised Land, or Peary experienced upon reaching the North Pole in 1909. He, indeed, felt like an explorer. He pulled a small silk flag of the Tank Corps from his pocket and dropped it inside the Line. Then he turned back, but he had to crawl toward his own lines, for the Boche were now firing machine guns in his direction. Patton had far greater respect for machine-gun bullets than for the shells.

He bumped into the tank he had left behind and then into four more of his vehicles. With armor around him again, he asked the infantry if they would follow him into Beney. The men said yes, so Patton jumped on the lead tank, directing the advance. When they reached Beney, and his mission was accomplished, he started walking again, this time toward Nonsard, looking for his other battalion. He was tired and hungry. But when he stopped for a snack, he discovered he had lost the sack with his rations. Gone also was the brandy he had taken along in a flask. "Goddamnit!" he said to himself—but loud.

He found Nonsard occupied by 25 of his tanks, but they were out of gas. Patton decided to put them back into action and walked back seven miles to get fuel for the stalled tanks. Now he was *dead* tired. He had not slept for two nights and had had nothing to eat since the night before except a few stale crackers that he took from the knapsack of a dead German.

It began to rain again. Patton could barely make it to Seicheprey in the deepening mud and rapidly descending darkness. As he was getting closer to civilization, he spotted a car driven by what he called a sightseeing officer. He flagged it down and had himself driven to the fuel dump at Seicheprey to arrange for the gas his tanks marooned at Nonsard needed. Then he jumped on a motorcycle and rode to Tank Corps headquarters to make his report.

The grand adventure of George Patton's first day at war refreshed and cheered him, and he was full of vim when he burst into the office of General Rockenbach. But his boss received him with a frown. Rockenbach recognized Patton's unique qualities and did not question his value to the Tank Corps. He was, however, a strict disciplinarian and was becoming increasingly exasperated by his young colonel's penchant for doing as he pleased.

Patton was attracting considerable attention with his dramatics and was drawing upon himself most of the publicity the Tank Corps produced. Besides, Rockenbach was ultimately responsible for everything that happened in his corps and did not cherish the idea of getting himself into hot water for the shenanigans of his iconoclastic brigade commander.

Word had reached him of Patton's irresistible wanderlust during the day and his constant straying from his flock. He was especially irritated by the colonel's excursion into the Hindenburg Line. Now he pounced upon Patton.

"What the heck are you trying to do, Colonel?" he asked angrily. "It's not your business to win the war singlehanded. Your foolish penetration of the German lines is absolutely inexcusable! I'm giving serious thought to relieving you of your command."

Patton was stunned. Then, as was his wont when called on the carpet for something he knew he should not have done, he became contrite. But he always managed to get on the top in bad situations. Exhausted as he was, he waxed eloquent to soothe the General with his profuse and, indeed, humble apologies.

Rockenbach succumbed to this combination of humility and charm. He extracted the promise from Patton that he would stick to his brigade and would never again venture into the German lines. For the time being, he was satisfied to leave things at that. But while Patton was properly penitent during this confrontation, he dismissed the incident from his mind the moment he left the General.

He did not regret anything he had done. "If I had a chance," he told Major Sereno E. Brett, his second in command, "I'd do the same thing again."

But now his first day at war was over. He could go and catch a little sleep.

The battle of St. Mihiel was virtually over the day after it began, but young Colonel Patton, driven by his own momentum, continued to fight on, mostly on his own. Before he knew it, he was in trouble. His problem was minor compared with his later woes, but, minuscule or no, it had lasting significance. First of all, he started a feud that later contributed to his decision to abandon the Tank Corps and return to the Cavalry. Secondly, he exposed his congenital inability to stay within the limits of his assignment—in little as well as big things, in situations involving only him and arrangements on which the fate of entire divisions hinged. He had initiated, above all, the first of a long series of personal clashes which stemmed from his innate propensity to go arbitrarily beyond the essence of his orders, beyond the things which were expected of him, and frequently beyond his rank or the strength of the forces he had at his disposal.

The quickly passing show of St. Mihiel now dismayed Patton. He was hardly in action when he was out again. On September 13th, when he had nothing to do except watch endless columns of German prisoners pouring into the cages, he was already fretting. There was still too much fight in him, and he found it impossible to bridle himself. The next day he returned to Nonsard, where the bulk of his operational tanks were, to see whether there was something he could do with them.

The Germans had retired too far, while the Americans had not advanced far enough. A wide No Man's Land had been left between the adversaries—an ideal terrain for the light tank. Patton decided to send his Renaults into this No Man's Land. He called the operation "reconnaissance in force," but, in reality, it was a hot pursuit—an unheard of deployment of tanks at such a moment. So acute was Patton's vision of the shape of things to come that he had probably made the first non-accidental use of tanks on such a mission.

He led his tanks down the ridge. After half a day, they fanned out into a broad plain, and halted when they were but half a mile from the Hindenburg Line. In the forefield of the Line, Patton spotted some Germans. Eager for action irrespective of risk, he ordered Captain Semmes, who commanded Company A of the brigade's First Battalion, "Go ahead, Semmes! Capture those bastards!" Patton was determined that his command would become the first Allied unit to charge the vaunted Hindenburg Line.

What followed resembled an escapade from Don Quixote. Semmes quickly reached the Boche, only to find that he was too late—those Germans were already prisoners. They were on the march to a nearby prisoner-of-war cage, shepherded by dismounted soldiers of Colonel O. P. N. Hazzard's squadron from the Second Calvalry Regiment. But Patton was not discouraged. He sent Lieutenant Theodore McClure, a daredevil tanker from Richmond, Virginia, directly against the formidable Hindenburg Line—indeed mounting the the first Allied assault upon it—with a total of three tanks.

McClure vanished behind the high ground. Nothing further was heard from him for about an hour. Suddenly the eerie stillness of the countryside was shattered by the din of battle. The sound of gunfire came from the direction in which McClure had disappeared. Then there was silence again—nothing but oppressive, deadly silence. Hopes turned to abject gloom. Patton became nervous. He had just begun to curse himself for the impetuosity that apparently had lost him McClure and three tanks when, an hour and a half later, they came into view, rolling briskly over the top and down into the plain toward him.

McClure had done exactly as he was ordered, hitting the Hindenburg Line in a frontal assault. He had wheeled promptly into the direct fire of a German battery. Instead of turning and running, he charged the guns at full speed and put them out of commission. As an afterthought, he picked up the breech block of one of the pieces to prove his exploit to Patton.

Elated by the victory, Patton stayed in No Man's Land into the later afternoon. By then the German artillery managed to range in on his tanks and took them under fire. This series of bursts gave Patton away: thanks to this, word of his "breakout" reached General Rockenbach, who rushed orders to Patton to break off his private war and report to him.

Abundantly annoyed by the Colonel's solo in the Hindenburg Line only two days before, Rockenbach now chewed

Patton out. He threatened to send him home with the permanent rank of captain. The same Patton who was so cocky the day before in the face of the enemy was now cowering before Rockenbach. Bewailing his "Goddamned impetuosity," he apologized abjectly—and he could be profoundly abject when the occasion required it—promising that it would never happen again.

He weathered the storm with a formal reprimand. Although it went into his record, he resented this far less than another retribution Rockenbach decided to mete out. Knowing that Patton knuckled under to only one person in the world, his wife, Rockenbach wrote a strong note to Beatrice, recounting the two incidents and telling her that he had had to reprimand her wayward husband.

Patton found out about the letter and sent his own confession after it, trying to soften the blow with his own explanation. Mrs. Patton spent years of their marriage in constant agony trembling for her husband, not merely when he went to war, but even when he was driving his car at reckless speed or riding his horses over his chosen obstacles. Patton knew how worried she usually was, and now he told her that he had promised General Rockenbach never to stray from his headquarters again. But if he meant this to reassure her, he spoiled the effect with his next sentence: "But you know, Bea, my headquarters is always under my hat."

CHAPTER FIVE
"JINE THE CAVALRY"

Patton could not know it of course, but now he had only 11 days left in the war and but a few hours in actual combat. The outlook on this Sunday morning after the first all-American battle in World War I was good. His tanks had proved themselves, more or less. They were being scrubbed and refitted for their next assignment. It was expected to be the most ambitious military enterprise in the history of the United States on France's classic strategic soil. This was to become the 47-day Battle of the Argonne Forest, fought incessantly to the bitter end. Though the great men in the high councils of the Allies still expected that the war would last into 1919, this campaign became its grand finale and Pershing's *pièce de résistance*, justifying in a blaze of red, white and blue his stubborn resolve to use the AEF only as an American force.

Close as he was to the granite-faced, tight-lipped, squint-eyed Commanding General of the AEF, Patton had an exceptional opportunity to observe Pershing's stubborn struggle to employ the AEF as "a self-existing entity" instead of doling out his men as replacements in the other Allied ranks, badly depleted in part by the less than adequate competence of the British and sanguine prodigality of the French generals. Until Foch appeared on the scene to make up for all previous blunders, Pershing had no illusions about the generalship of his Allied *confrères*. He was convinced that the AEF would become merely cannon fodder if abandoned to their hands. He formulated his creed in clear and definitive terms, then adhered to them against "the blandishments of Lloyd George, the fulminations of Clemenceau, the explosive reactions of General Ferdinand Foch."

His basic and unalterable policy was spelled out in a ringing directive: "In military operation against the Imperial German Government," he wrote, "you are directed to cooperate with the forces of the other countries employed against the enemy; but in so doing, the underlining idea must be kept in view that the forces of the United States are a separate and distinct component of the combined forces, the identity of which must be preserved."

Patton, who followed Pershing's fight avidly, was thrilled by what he regarded as unabashed chauvinism rather than sound military principle. The controversy made an enduring impression on him. Its memories made him critical in World War II of Eisenhower's masterly implementation of the military coalition, even bitter at times of what he called "too much cooperation" with the British.

Before St. Mihiel, the AEF had participated in 11 enterprises with British and French forces, but they were minor operations so far as the Americans were concerned. St. Mihiel was the first all-American venture on the Pershing pattern, but it was still an operation for a limited objective.

Now the sky became the limit. Almost 1,200,000 Americans were to participate in a grand offensive planned for them by their own operations staff and directed solely by their own commanders.

The plan was bold, brilliantly adapted to the situation, the enemy and the terrain. Since the Germans had no exposed flank, Pershing decided on a powerful frontal attack to effect a breakthrough. He planned his main attack between the Meuse River and the western edge of the Argonne Forest, a zone roughly 20 miles wide, with three corps deployed in line. Each corps was to attack with two divisions in the assault and one in reserve. Three other divisions were held as an army reserve, available as the battle developed.

The country through which the attack was to be made favored the defense. Behind the entire front the Germans had built an elaborate system organized in depth. It contained three complete main lines and a partially completed fourth farther to the rear on ground of great natural strength. In addition, the Germans had converted villages, woods, hills, and other natural obstacles between the lines into strong-points to serve as centers of resistance to break up an attack.

Strong as this defense system was, Pershing hoped the weight of the attack would carry his army through the first three lines without loss of momentum and enable him to open up German flanks to attack. This would effect that state of open warfare for which his army was trained and best suited.

Patton's tanks were assigned to I Corps, to be used on both sides of Buanthe and Aire through Cheppy and Verannes in the direction of Charpentry along the eastern perimeter of the Argonne. He now had only 135 light tanks under him, about one-fifth the total armor earmarked for the offensive.

Again he worked himself into total exhaustion, there being less than two weeks to refit and redeploy his brigade. Preparation for a tank operation in 1918 meant chiefly manual labor and attention to minute detail, almost like the setting up of an intricate acrobatic act on a vaudeville stage. Among other annoying minutiae, the path of the tanks during this approach to the front lines had to be laid out with tapes. This was believed necessary to keep them exactly at their assigned positions in coordination with prearranged artillery barrages and the movement of the troops at the flank.

The tanks were transported to their staging stations by rail, but getting them off the flatcars proved a taxing operation by itself. The trains reached the railroad sidings less than six miles from Cheppy. The village was in enemy-held territory just north of a broad strip of land that had lain undisturbed since the German occupation in 1914. On their arrival the Americans were startled to see German soldiers in this No Man's Land hunting rabbits and squirrels under tall poplars, apparently unaware of the proximity of the enemy.

It was the consensus in Patton's brigade that the unloading of the tanks would have been an "impossible feat" without his personal participation. The cumbersome vehicles had to be unloaded on a totally dark night whose gloom was deepened by steady rain. Then they had to be driven about two miles northward to a small wood whose trees were supposed to conceal them after daybreak. The tanks left telltale tracks in the mud, and Patton worried that they would betray his forces to German reconnaissance planes, which had begun to keep the region under surveillance. The next night he moved his tanks to another small wooded area nearby, leaving the old tracks intact but seeing to it that no new ones were made. He accomplished this by moving the tanks on a carpet of small branches, then strewing another layer of branches on whatever tracks even this maneuver had left.

On September 25th, Patton was alerted for the attack, which was scheduled to begin at 4:25 A.M. the next day after a three-hour bombardment by 75-mm. guns. When it came, it proved so intense and loud that he felt moved to offer up thanks that he was not at the receiving end.

At about 3 A.M. Patton gave the order to move. The brigade, proceeding in two columns to its jump-off point, was suddenly stalled at a bridge that was under heavy fire. Patton had anticipated this. He raced to the bridge ahead of his columns, and by the time the tanks rode up he had the salvos timed and the rhythm of the fire established. He then rushed his tanks across the bridge in groups during the lulls between the salvos without suffering a single casualty.

When the attack erupted, the well-laid plans promptly went up in the smoke of the battle and the fog of the dawn. Before long, the tanks lost the infantry with which they were supposed to cooperate, then rode ahead of them and entered Verannes by themselves.

Patton was doing exactly as he did at St. Mihiel, touring the front on foot, intervening wherever he thought his personal push and flowery swearing could do the most good. Around 9 A.M. he dashed to a company commanded by Captain Matthew English, which had approached to within about 300 yards of the Germans but was then stopped dead by their machine-gun fire. He found the tank crews digging a breach through the German trenches but making little headway because they took shelter whenever the machine guns opened up.

Calling English, he rushed with him to the parapet to persuade the men, with this display of courage and nonchalance, to resume their digging. They actually did. Soon five of his tanks moved through the breach, charged and silenced the machine-gun nest. Patton followed the tanks on foot, running into some 300 badly scared doughboys prone on the slope of a hill that was under very heavy fire.

"Goddamnit," he called out to them, "what are you men waiting for?"

It was imperative, as he saw it, that the infantry follow the tanks to make the most of the breakthrough. Patton called for their commander, but the soldiers were so totally disorganized that nobody in authority came forward. So he took it upon himself to give the order, and yelled "Follow me!"

The men stayed put. He called for volunteers. Five men came forward, one his own orderly, Sergeant Joe Angelo. "Okay, men," he yelled to this small band, just the six of them against the firmly entrenched Germans on the other side, "let's go!"

Patton led the charge and advanced in the hail of bullets. But when he turned around after a few minutes he found that only Angelo was still following him. Three of the doughboys had already been killed and the fourth was wounded. When later he recalled this bold venture, he said, "I looked upon myself during the charge as if I were a small detached figure on the battlefield watched all the time from a cloud by my Confederate kinsmen and my Virginia grandfather."

Now Patton's own time was running out. When only 30 yards from the German lines he was suddenly shaken by a sharp blow that knocked him off his feet and threw him into a shell hole. Angelo jumped after him to see what had happened. Patton was bleeding profusely from a wound in his side that, as he later said, was almost as large as a teacup. Angelo managed to stanch the bleeding; there was not much more he could do except wait for the medics.

Patton was in shock, but, so long as he had even his own orderly for an audience, he kept up a front of nonchalance. But the loss of blood and the novelty of the experience gradually subdued him. He was somehow convinced that his wound was critical and that he would die before the medics found him. When they arrived and told him that his wound was not particularly serious, he insisted that they let him return to the tanks.

This was not just bravado. Patton was sincerely convinced that he had knocked a vital hole into the German defenses at a key point and that a concentration of tanks followed by infantry could develop the breach into a decisive breakthrough. A young doctor, subjected to a barrage of his cuss words, tried to reason with Patton.

"You are in no shape, Colonel," he said, "to stay at the front. As a matter of fact, the sooner we can get you to the nearest evac——"

"Goddamnit, Doc," Patton shouted, "don't tell me what to do!"

He tried to rise but fell back, convinced at last that he was *hors de combat*. But he was not yet ready to quit the war. When they got him into the ambulance, he opened up again and told the driver, as if giving directions to a cabbie:

"Take me to the headquarters of the 35th Division."

"Where?" the driver asked, confounded.

Patton was getting hazy and weak but he kept on shouting.

"Headquarters, 35th Division! And don't you give me any arguments!"

At division HQ, Patton dictated a statement concerning the situation on the front, but the effort proved too much. He lost consciousness and so could not protest when they took him to the evacuation hospital behind the lines for treatment. "The mental hazard," he later wrote, "which is as great as the physical hazard, played its part."

He arrived at the hospital after dark and stayed there for three days. He was then transferred to Base Hospital No. 49, near Dijon, on a slow train that took 20 hours for the 120-mile journey, all in a steady rain. It was an exasperating trip on a makeshift hospital train of boxcars in which the wounded lay in their own stretchers stacked three-high on racks. During the trip Patton was fed but once, and then only coffee, bread, and some molasses.

Patton's sortie was virtually the only effective exploit of the tanks that day. By the time he reached the base hospital, the first phase of the offensive—its seemingly crucial initial assault—had collapsed, partly because tank support proved ineffective. It was not the fault of the tanks but of the arrangements the planners had made for them in the first assault. The terrain was totally unsuited for armor. And the dispersal of the 704 participating tanks among the various corps again proved disastrous. It reduced their impact, whereas a concentration of armor at carefully chosen points could have broken the Germans, who were already bending precariously.

These were important lessons the Battle of the Argonne Forest taught, and their significance was not lost on Patton. His experience in this battle started him thinking of changing tank combat from a static type of warfare to the fluidity that made armor the decisive weapon of World War II.

On October 4th, when his wound was still open, he heard that the First U.S. Army had returned to the offensive and was driving slowly through the deepest of the German lines. Stories of tough fighting, of stubborn enemy resistance and mounting American casualties filtered back to him in the hospital.

Patton became all aflutter, plotting weird schemes to get back to the front. But he had to wait. His wound was still not sufficiently healed to permit it to be sewed up. In the meantime, enough divisions had been committed to action to necessitate the organization of a Second U.S. Army, and now Pershing assumed command of the Army Group, getting set for the third and final phase of the offensive.

It began on November 1st, and by the 7th the heights before Sedan had been seized. The historic town could have been taken by the Americans. But when the news of their opportunity reached General Foch, he quickly changed the boundary of the First Army to permit his own French troops to capture the city, which was the scene of the French capitulation to the Prussians in 1870.

Patton could bear his idleness no longer. He bribed an orderly and got himself a car. Deserting the hospital, he drove to Montmédy, where the American troops were just moving into position for what now promised to be the *coup de grâce*.

Patton drove through Langres, his own headquarters, continued to Montmédy as fast as he could on the crowded roads amid the mounting confusion of this last phase of the conflict, then on to the Meuse, which he reached at Verdun. He arrived in the famous town on his 33rd birthday, ready to celebrate it at the front at last, when the blow fell.

It was November 11, 1918. The Germans had asked for an armistice.

The Meuse-Argonne offensive was one of the greatest battles fought by the United States Army. Nearly 1,250,000 American troops were committed before it ended. The price paid was heavy, some 120,000 casualties, but the military results were decisive. The dogged persistence of the American platoons, companies and battalions, led by young commanders who not many months before had been college students or young business and professional men, met and defeated the best enemy troops and broke the so-called Hindenburg Line.

Now the war was over and he was in trouble again. General Rockenbach took a dim view of his desertion from the hospital and hinted broadly that he had further retribution in store for him. But Pershing was now freed of the pressure and cares of the war, and Patton felt he could enlist his aid to extricate himself from this latest predicament. He asked for an audience with the General, telling his aide, Colonel Carl Boyd, that he had something important to report. Then he told Pershing all about his escapade. He presented the case with his combination of coy diffidence and boyish bluster, and an eloquence and humor that completely won over Pershing. He was forgiven.

But on November 18th, he sent the kind of frantic letter to his wife he usually dispatched in haste and despair whenever he needed her solace. Ever since his "breakthrough" near Cheppy in which he was wounded, Patton expected to get the Distinguished Service Cross, the highest award he could hope for in recognition of his devoted and untiring efforts.

Now the war was over and there seemed to be no DSC forthcoming. Then in the evening of November 17th word was passed through the grapevine that he would not get the DSC. He suspected that Rockenbach was behind this decision and sought out the General, telling him point-blank how chagrined he was.

"You have your colonelcy, George," Rockenbach told him. "That ought to be sufficient compensation at your age."

"Sir," Patton shot back, "I'd rather be a second lieutenant with a DSC than a general without it."

That night he could not sleep. Early in the morning he poured his bitterness into a gloomy letter to his wife:

"I woke up all last night feeling that I was dying, and then it would occur to me what had happened. I cannot realize it yet. It was the whole war to me, all I can ever get out of two years away from you. But I will be God-damned if I am beat yet. I do not know what I will do, but I will do something."

He began to pull strings, buttonholing people who had Pershing's ear, and lobbying openly. The year passed without results, but on New Year's Day in 1919 he received directly from Pershing the DSC he had coveted so much, with a citation that accepted without reservation his own version of the bloody episode at Cheppy:

"Near Cheppy, France, September 26, 1918, he displayed conspicuous courage, coolness, energy and intelligence in directing the advance of his brigade down the valley of the Aire. Later he rallied a force of disorganized infantry and led it forward behind the tanks under the heavy machine-gun and artillery fire until he was wounded. Unable to advance farther, he continued to direct the operations of his unit until all arrangements for turning over the command were completed."

Decorations meant a lot to Patton. "It is vital to good morale," he wrote, "that decorations get out promptly and on an equitable basis." He kept bombarding General Marshall with suggestions about decorations. He once proposed that the G-1 Section of every army and corps staff appoint a member whose specific duty should be to prod divisions and lower units to get out citations. He proposed, therefore, that "when time permits, there should be a citation writer's school attended by officers from corps, army, division G-1 sections."

Patton was as eager to get decorations as he was generous in handing them out. The medal was, as he once put it, the badge of courage, tangible evidence that a soldier had earned his pay and had done his duty to his country. After World War I he was to get still another high honor, the Distinguished Service Medal, for his over-all contribution to the Tank Corps.

"By his energy and sound judgment," this citation read, "he rendered very valuable services in his organization and direction of the Tank Center at the Army School at Langres. In the employment of the Tank Corps troops in combat he displayed high military attainments, zeal and marked adaptability in a form of warfare comparatively new to the American Army."

This was George Patton's last memento of the war. Its award in 1920 ushered in nothing but disappointment.

War may be what Everett Young once called it, a glorious art that gives immortal fame and makes rattling good history. And old Hobbes concluded from his meditation on the conduct of political societies that war was the state of nature. But most of us regard it as a scourge—"the terrible, atrocious thing," as Tolstoi called it. Yet Patton *loved* it, and that was his very own word. He was fascinated by it and he glorified it. How can such an attitude be explained in a normal, humane and intelligent man?

It would be foolish to try to justify this streak in Patton's character, as some of his apologists have tried to do, or to explain, or explain it away, with rationalizations. His love of war was bare of metaphysical or geopolitical scaffoldings. It had no intellectual foundations, none of the Machiavellian or Hegelian philosophers' acceptance of the inevitable in the cycles of history. It was an irrational and maybe absurd idea to which he was totally dedicated, even addicted, with a fervor he did not care to control. In this he was almost alone among military men. For few of them, even the greatest and most successful, ever glorified war, while many of them held with Sherman that war was hell and its glory sheer moonshine.

But then Patton was not a man in any Aristotelian mold. His was a medieval personality in which such anachronisms as feudalism and chivalry were rampant. His Americanism was not of the democratic variety, and was strangely alien to the pacifistic traditions of his nation.

But when all this is said, it must be remembered, too, that Patton, for all his devotion to war and feudalistic traits, never did anything in his life or career either to promote or propagandize war, question the ultimate good of democracy or to set himself up against it. He was no "war hawk." Early in the century when two of his idols, Leonard Wood and Theodore Roosevelt, were beating the drums for preparedness, he stayed out of the debate, even in the privacy of his home.

In the final analysis, I think, George Patton loved war primarily because he thought he was destined for it by his special and limited talents. He was not imbued with false modesty by any means and regarded himself rather highly— but only in his profession as a soldier. Back in 1909 he told his father-in-law that he thought of himself as a man of only limited abilities. His belief that he could do well in life only in a narrow profession was his avowed reason for having chosen the career of soldiering.

He liked to write and could write well, but he also realized that he would make only a mediocre professional writer. He rode well and played excellent polo, but there was no profession in those pursuits. He could never visualize himself as a *good* lawyer, or a *proficient* doctor, as some of his forebears were, and he recoiled at the thought of becoming a clergyman.

Patton hated and dreaded mediocrity. A few days before his death he wrote to Robert P. Patterson, who had succeeded Mr. Stimson as Secretary of War: "Anyone in any walk of life who is content with mediocrity is untrue to himself and to American tradition."

He was firmly convinced that he was best as a soldier, that his special genius was in making war, and that he could rise to greatness only in the military profession. So he chose it and pursued it with ardor, fervor and a singleminded dedication.

He saw no traumatic conflict in being a war-oriented soldier in a peace-oriented America. "The soldier is also a citizen," he declared, supplying the equation. "In fact the highest obligation and privilege of citizenship is that of bearing arms for one's country. Hence," he concluded, "it is a proud privilege to be a soldier—a good soldier."

Patton saw therein his value as a citizen and his usefulness to his country.

In the late fall of 1945, when he had premonitions of death, he ransacked his memories and took stock of his life. He put his thoughts down on paper in a kind of professional memoir he called "Retrospect." He prefaced it by musing that "war is an ancient subject and I, an ancient man, have studied and practiced it for over 40 years."

It gave him the satisfaction and reward he sought from life. It was the golden path he trod and the time supreme, to paraphrase Mary Townsend's sonnet about opportunity, the freighted hour through which his sublime fulfillment gleamed.

Now all was quiet on the Western Front—perhaps a bit too quiet. In the abrupt end of this savage war, its set patterns suddenly disappeared. They were replaced by the agonizing uncertainties of a future for which the world, let down by its fumbling, mediocre statesmen, found itself totally unprepared.

General Pershing was liquidating the war in Europe, upset that he was not allowed to march to Berlin, but compensating for the disappointment in a round of celebrations in Paris and London, Brussels and Longwy. The Big Parade dissolved like the climactic scene of an overlong motion picture. Every day the Paris edition of the *Chicago Tribune* was publishing a banner line on its front page reading, *"Get the boys home toot sweet."* And in New York they were singing, *"We don't want the bacon, all we want is a piece of the Rhine."*

Patton found it hard to adjust. Like a featured actor in a hit show after a long run, he was looking apprehensively to a future that would have no more curtain calls, only an empty stage. But he was reassured. General Rockenbach called him to Chaumont and told him that the Tank Corps would be preserved as the nucleus of an armored force and that, on General Pershing's personal orders, Patton would be retained in it if he so desired. When he told the General, "I can wish for no greater privilege, sir," he was given his parting gift—his own war-seasoned brigade.

"You will take it to Camp Meade," Rockenbach told him, "and maintain it intact until further orders."

A full colonel at the age of 33, commanding officer of a tank brigade, what more could he expect? He was determined to make the most of his opportunity. He would have preferred somebody else over him, but if Rockenbach was to be the Allah of the new armored force, Patton decided that, by God, he would become its Prophet.

Patton arrived back in the United States on May 17, 1919. Although he had been away only a little more than two years, he found enormous changes in America. The nation was restive and impatient. It was becoming industrialized, mechanized and urbanized. Automobiles had taken over the roads. Labor was growing stronger. Women were given the vote and men had their drinks taken away. The country retreated into isolationism when the Senate refused to ratify the Treaty of Versailles and join the League of Nations. But through its recent involvement in ancient European feuds, the United States had irrevocably committed itself to the responsibilities of a world power, even though it took almost two decades for this reality to dawn upon the nation.

With his own focus on the Army, and his private life set comfortably in its affluent grooves, Patton was not too much concerned with the wider world around him. He was interested chiefly in the future of the Army, his own future in it, and, since he could be exasperatingly parochial at times, the future of armor. He was inclined, of course, to exaggerate the contribution tanks in general and his tanks in particular had made to the victory. But he was not completely blinded by his enthusiasm to the woeful limitations of his chosen weapon. He recognized with visionary fervor and the clarity of the expert the potentialities of the weapon, and was now determined to devote his career to the realization of those possibilities.

He had recently read an article by General Marshall in which he attempted to restore a sense of proportion to the thinking of officers who indulged somewhat smugly in the belief that the Army had proven itself fully in a difficult war and was as good as it needed to be.

Patton wrote to Marshall congratulating him on the

paper. It made a tremendous impression on him and was influential in shaping his own attitude toward the tank, not merely in this immediate wake of the war, but throughout the period between the two World Wars. He threw himself into the task, maintaining his brigade spic and span in its peacetime *status quo* and preparing it for future needs.

He carried over to his new assignment at Meade the bubling enthusiasm and unbounded energy that characterized his work in France in 1917-18. Taking his cue from Marshall, Patton now wrote in the *Infantry Journal:* "Only those of us who doctored and nursed the grotesque war babies of 1918 through innumerable inherent ills of premature birth know how bad they really were and, by virtue of that same intimate association, are capable of judging how much better they are now, and how surely they will continue to improve."

He regarded his mission at Meade as laying the foundations for that improvement by promoting as vigorously as possible a program embracing the three main activities he considered essential for the betterment of the tanks beyond the sheer housekeeping job of maintenance—research, development, and training.

Soon after his arrival at Meade, however, he was made to realize that several forces had combined to thwart his efforts at their germinal stage. General Rockenbach was now quite content with the *status quo* and peacetime hibernation. He viewed Patton's eagerness with the misgivings with which he had followed his gyrations in France. Patton had to realize quite early in this game that he would hardly be able to carry out his program so long as General Rockenbach remained at the helm.

But Rockenbach merely represented the general trend, and not only in the United States. "We made war to the end," Clemenceau had said, "to the very end of the end." And now the world turned away from its ecstatic memories with something akin to disgust. The soldier who even a few months before was subject to dithyrambic praise now became the butt of jokes, even contempt. Pacifist sentiments rose to the surface. Preparations were being made everywhere to limit armaments. Naval constructions were radically curtailed. The huge armies were disbanded. It was a kind of reverse binge, like Prohibition.

The United States confronted its own vexatious problems

in a squeamish mood, disillusioned with the costly luxuries of war. The Army was the first to suffer from the hangover. The question of what kind of an army the United States should now have had triggered an acrimonious debate. Congress, reflecting the mood of the nation, resolved it by concluding that the best kind of army was the smallest, cheapest, and least conspicuous.

The Army was swept by a purge. A wave of reductions in rank hit the officers' corps. Even General Peyton C. March, the Chief of Staff, was cut back to major general. Colonel Patton was returned to his permanent rank of captain, but only for a day. He was reduced on June 30, 1919, and promoted to major on July 1st. (He regarded it as a "battlefield promotion," considering the fight he had to put up for it in his own behalf.) But others were not so lucky. Some 2,500 regular officers resigned in disgust, complaining loudly and bitterly about the ingratitude of the nation.

Patton neither complained nor quit. The momentum of the war was still in his brain and limbs. He had a big job ahead of him, and otherwise, too, things were working out fine. Meade was only a few miles from Washington, so he could enjoy fully the capital's social amenities. He had bought himself a Pierce Arrow touring car and was driving it on long trips, and fast. He was close again to his wife and daughters, so peace had its compensations after all. But then the realities of his peacetime Army began to gain on him. Suddenly he found that he could barely solve even the daily housekeeping problems of his brigade with what he was getting. He was not given enough gasoline even for the minimal daily exercises his men and tanks needed to stay in trim. Only a few months before in France, he was allotted 30,000 gallons for the Argonne battle. But now his allotment was reduced to 500 gallons a day, which his tanks burned up in a few hours. Then even that meager quota was cut, and he could operate his tanks only a few minutes each day. He had to park them in their enclosure at Meade, the crews spending their time on building a fence to protect them from the curious and painting their steel hulls. Of paint, Patton found, there was plenty. He had no trouble in getting as much as he wanted.

He kept himself busy by concentrating on solving whatever technical problems he could finance out of his own pocket and for which he needed no outside help. He recognized that an inadequate communications system was primarily responsible for limiting the tank's effectiveness in combat. In France, he had to walk about under fire and run from vehicle to vehicle to keep in touch with his units. His individual tanks had no equipment to communicate with one another, with their supporting infantry on the ground, or the planes above.

He sought the solution in the radio, and began experiments by installing standard Signal Corps equipment in his tanks, using a fishing pole for an antenna. Then he teamed up with Colonel Ralph I. Sasse and developed a coaxial mount for cannon and machine gun to enable the gunners to train the weapon on the target. But his radio did not work because the metal hull of the tanks made reception impossible. And the Ordnance people in Washington turned down his coaxial mount (which, however, became standard in the medium tanks of World War II).

There was but one bright spot in this discouraging situation. Just when Patton arrived at Meade in the spring of 1919, a New Jersey mechanic and racing driver named Walter Christie appeared on the scene with what seemed to be a revolutionary tank design promising a vastly increased operational mobility. It was called the M.1919. As soon as he heard of Christie's "tank," Patton went to Elizabeth, New Jersey, where Christie was working on his invention at a small firm called U.S. Front Drive Motor Company, of which he was president. He found Christie a tall, erect, scholarly looking man of profound technological competence and abundant enthusiasm, and his tank the best armored vehicle he had yet encountered. Its engine was in the rear and it had wheels as well as removable caterpillar track chains, enabling it to move on either wheels or tracks. Although the M.1919 was rather primitive in its experimental model and difficult to maneuver on tracks, Patton recognized in it the features the tank desperately needed to become an efficient combat vehicle—speed and mobility.

He kept close to Christie, even loaned him money, then arranged a demonstration of the M.1919 at Fort Meade. The model they used for the demonstration rode to the fort on its own power over some 250 miles at an average speed of 30 miles an hour. It was an unprecedented feat by itself. It demonstrated that tanks could be made independent of rail transportation and roll into battle on their own.

Patton persuaded seven general officers from the War Department to attend the demonstration. In a short lecture on the proving ground, he told them that the tank was capable of cruising at 30 miles an hour even through sand, knocking down trees, breaking through buildings. It needed Patton's eloquence and then some imagination to recognize Christie's innovation as a tank. It had no armor and little superstructure. It was merely a platform mounted on the sprocket wheels.

"It is so simple to handle," Patton said, "that even a child can drive it." He invited the generals to take it on a trial run. None responded, so Patton repeated his offer. "Well, gentlemen," he asked, "who would like to take the first ride?" There was no answer.

Mrs. Patton had come out with him to the muddy proving ground to watch the test, and Patton now, with more eagerness than tact, turned to her. "All right, Bea," he said, "you demonstrate it!"

She lost her hat on the ride and her flimsy dress became soiled, but the little lady handled the vehicle with perfect aplomb and skill. When she brought it back to the distinguished group, her proud husband turned to the generals. "You see, gentlemen," he exclaimed, "how easy it is to handle? Now, who would like to make a try?"

There was embarrassed silence, then one of the generals spoke up: "Thanks, Major Patton, we have seen enough."

The Ordnance Department turned down the Christie with the explanation that it was too difficult to maneuver. Although later model Christies were adopted, the Army never came around to share Patton's virgin enthusiasm for the epochal invention. However, the Red Army went all out for them. The Soviet Union stepped into the breach and saved Christie from bankruptcy by buying his tank, and making it the backbone of its armored force in the 1930's.

The hopelessness of the situation was now encroaching upon Patton. In 1920 Congress passed the National Defense Act, providing for an army of 280,000 men in nine divisions. (Two years later Congress ordered a cutback to 125,000 men.)

For Patton, the act spelled disaster. It outlawed the Tank Corps, and the War Department ordered that the tanks be dispersed to the other arms. In 1920 total appropriations for tanks amounted to exactly $500.

Patton tried to enlist support for his aborted tank-development program among his influential friends in the Army, but was dismayed to discover that none of them shared his enthusiasm for the new weapon. Even Pershing refused to aid. The General of the Armies would have done anything else for Patton, whom he regarded as his protégé, but he declined firmly to support his tank program. By then Patton himself had come to the conclusion that it was foredoomed, for several reasons. He realized that armor was, next to aircraft, the costliest part of the war machine. All he heard now was preachings of economy and more economy. He still believed that the armies of the future would move on tracks and wheels, but he was now reaching the conclusion that economically tanks were not feasible.

He began to talk about the "economic impossibility of building enough tanks to constitute a mechanical army," at a time when the price of the Christies, for example, was still under $50,000. For all his prophetic powers, he could not see the day when the United States, as William Mellor said, "would open its purses to the tune of billions of dollars to equip not only our own armies but also those of our Allies with trucks and tanks and jeeps and mobile artillery."

The man who only a few months before was outspoken in his advocacy of armor could now be heard deprecating the tank in forceful and graphic language. In 1920, Patton had gone to bat for the Tank Corps by writing in the *Infantry Journal*: "The tank is new and, for the fulfillment of its destiny, it must remain independent. Not desiring or attempting to supplant infantry, cavalry or artillery, it has no appetite to be absorbed by any of them." But now he was reversing himself and began to disparage armor by extolling the ageless and superior virtues of cavalry.

The conflict thus raging within him brought into focus a puzzling contradiction of his character. Patton was given to manic changes in his moods. His euphoric enthusiasm often turned abruptly into deep depression when things did not work out as he had hoped or expected. He was no Billy Mitchell, prepared to sacrifice everything dear to him for a conviction or idea. He was no champion of lost causes if they threatened to ruin his career. A man of considerable zeal but no zealot, he had adopted Disraeli's maxim, "The greatness of England resulted from her ability to compromise," to guide him in such situations and reassure him whenever he opted for the safer solution.

Patton expressed his own creed in his review of Major B. C. Dening's book, *The Future of The British Army:*

"There are probably as many ways of winning a war as

there are of skinning a cat. Some of us pin our faith on an accurate use of commas, others on grease or gas, on foot ease or saddle soap, and in the ardor of our enthusiasm for our especial panacea forget that the way to skin a cat is to remove his hide, and the way to win a war is to beat the enemy."

Now Patton reached the turning point.

He was convinced that he had done his best, and since there was nothing more he could do, it would only "break his heart" if he remained with the tanks—under the circumstances.

He made the break complete in the summer of 1920 by returning to the horse cavalry. "I have never felt more confident of our arm than I do today," he quoted Field Marshal Lord Allenby in his explanation of the move. "It has retained the good, rejected the bad, and has not shrunk from the new." In a strange about-face he now became its defender against undue mechanization—not because he had lost faith in armor by any means. As a matter of fact, he continued to work with Christie behind the scenes, and remained on the Tank Board of the Army for several years. He decided on his course because he thought that, under the circumstances, it was the more politic thing to do.

His real motivation for this return from the future to the past was plainly implied when he concluded a rather weasel-worded paper on the mechanization and motorization of cavalry with the words of the old song, "If you want to have a good time, jine the cavalry."

Major Patton was determined not to burn his fingers in the controversy raging over armor. As far as he was concerned, he was going to have a good time, if he could help it.

CHAPTER SIX
IN THE LIMBO OF PEACE

Drifting aimlessly and subsisting on a shoestring, the Army of the Roaring Twenties had little to roar about or roar with. Probably the most quiescent element in the country, all it had in common with Scott Fitzgerald's fervid world was that it, too, was the haven of a lost generation.

While the United States cavorted in prosperity and caroused in Prohibition, the Army just dawdled, its officers whiling away their time in what Thackeray called a life of dignified otiosity. The word "soldiering" became a synonym for loafing. In this torpid interregnum virtually the only motion seemed to be the constant moving of officers from one post to another, none being allowed to let down roots or do anything lasting. Deprived of a useful purpose, even the best of men succumbed to apathy and relaxed with the sad fatigue of idleness.

George Patton, of course, also had his quota of transfers, about the only interruption in the stifling monotony of his Army life. Between his departure from Fort Meade in 1920 and his return to armor at Fort Benning in 1940, he was moved 10 times and functioned in a dozen different capacities, some of which had nothing to do with his specialties. He studied at every institution of higher learning the Army maintained for its brainier and more promising officers—at the Cavalry School at Fort Riley, the Command and General Staff School at Fort Leavenworth, and the Army War College in Washington. He served in the office of the Chief of Cavalry. During tours of duty in Boston and in Hawaii he was assigned to whatever jobs that needed to be filled, whether he liked them or not, whether he was qualified for them or not.

Patton infused every one of his assignments with his boisterous energy—he conducted his drills snappily and briskly, worked at his desk job with compulsive industry, and studied at the various schools with the sedulous curiosity of a tyro. Although he was not too happy with his *métier* during these indolent years, neither was he too distressed by its routine. He compensated for the vapidity of his vocation with increased vigor in his private life, especially in his sporting pursuits. He remained a major from 1919 to 1934, but rose spectacularly in polo from a three-point to a seven-point player, and gained the coveted captaincy of the Army team.

And he lived in his grand style. When in 1928 he took the Army Polo Squad to Mitchel Field on Long Island for that year's tournament to defend the junior championship title his team had won the year before, the *Cavalry Journal* noted: "Major Patton's string of private mounts will enable him to be well mounted." He was the only member of the nine-man squad who rode his own ponies.

He amassed 400 ribbons and 200 cups in various horse shows from coast to coast, and did considerable steeple-chasing and fox-hunting besides. He still had time for skeet-shooting, tennis, squash and handball. He also took up flying as a hobby.

Once, on Long Island, he had an opportunity to combine pleasure with a little heroics when his attendance at a horse show led to an act of chivalry. On a summer night in 1922, while driving his roadster from the show to his hotel in Garden City, he spotted three rough-looking hombres with a damsel in apparent distress. They seemed to be pushing the girl into the back of a truck. Patton stopped his car, jumped out and forced the men at gun point to release the young woman. Then it developed that the girl was the fiancée of one of the men, who merely were helping her to climb into the truck.

The incident was reminiscent of Don Quixote's encounter with the six merchants of Toledo on the road to Murcia and his spirited defense of Dulcinea's unquestioned virtue. When later Patton laughingly related the story of his gratuitous intervention to a spellbound lady of Long Island society, he was asked, "How come, Georgie, that you go armed to a civilian horse show?"

"I believe in being prepared," he told her. "I always carry a pistol, even when I'm dressed in white tie and tails."

While he thus put up a brawny front of bravado, he also engaged in an entirely different sort of quest, which he

was somewhat shy to advertise lest it distort his picture of
a man of action. He bought a whole library of books, mostly on history and the military arts, and read them all from
cover to cover with an eager and critical mind. He also
began to write, producing some of the best papers by an
officer of the regular Army. He also composed poetry with
a pen obviously plundered from Kipling. But though he
himself thought highly of his verse, it did not really match
his prose.

Patton did most of his writing for his own amusement,
but he had a score of his papers published in the *Cavalry
Journal* (and a few also in the *Infantry Journal,* toward
which he felt only an *intellectual* affinity). Written in his
pugnacious manner, they attracted considerable attention,
not simply for their unorthodox views, but also for their
author's exciting literary style.

"Since that far distant day," he said in a typical piece,
"when the transcendent genius of an unknown savage devised the wheel as an aid to locomotion, the road in all its
forms from marble to chicken wire has played the predomi-
nant role in the bellicose meandering of mankind."

He found similarly attractive words for a description of
the constant interplay of weapons and counterweapons that
has made for permanent revolution in warfare. "When
Samson took the fresh jawbone of an ass," Patton wrote in a
paper about mechanized forces, "and slew a thousand men
therewith, he probably started such a vogue for the weapon,
especially among the Philistines, that for years no prudent
donkey dared to bray. Yet, despite its initial popularity, it
was discarded and now appears only as a barrage instrument for acrimonious debate.

"History is replete with countless other instances of military implements each in its day heralded as the last word—
the key to victory—yet each in its turn subsiding to its useful but inconspicuous niche," he went on. "New weapons
are useful in that they add to the repertoire of killing, but,
be they tank or tomahawk, weapons are only weapons
after all. Wars may be fought with weapons, but they are
won by men. It is the spirit of the men who follow and of the
man who leads that gains the victory. In biblical times this
spirit was ascribed, and probably with some justice, to the
Lord. It was the spirit of the Lord, *courage,* that came
mightily upon Samson at Lehi which gained the victory—
not the jawbone of an ass."

He combined his reading and writing by producing a number of stimulating book reviews for the *Cavalry Journal* (on whose board of editors he served). Especially attractive was his review of Lord Rawlinson's published diary, probably because that great soldier-sportsman-artist appealed to him with the variety of his talents and interests. "All during his life," Patton wrote, "he balanced work and play so justly that he never lost his zest for either . . . True to his principles while Commandant [of the Staff College], he paid as much attention to the hounds as to the students and set a pace in the office and in the saddle such as vastly to benefit both the school and the pack." It read almost like a close-up of himself.

The monotony of Patton's professional life of those days was alleviated from time to time by special assignments which helped to refresh his soldierly ardor for brief periods. On several occasions, he was sent to umpire maneuvers of the Cavalry. He enjoyed the function immensely because it gave some latitude for an exercise of his quizzical mind and tongue.

Once he said that umpiring at a maneuver was far more difficult and personally more perilous than judging a horse show because "in horse shows one secures a friend with each blue ribbon; in maneuvers there are no blue ribbons."

Patton's high professional standards and critical turn of mind made him an exacting judge at the exercises. His critiques, written in a saucy, spleeny style that smacked of smart-alecky hauteur, were not exactly calculated to gain any friends for him. Thus in October, 1929, when he was on temporary duty at the Office of the Chief of Cavalry in Washington, he was sent to umpire cavalry division maneuvers at Fort Bliss. Patton savored the job because the maneuvers were steeped in history, and ancient history, at that.

Eleven years after a World War with all its unfinished business and unresolved problems, the maneuvers at El Paso were arranged to "follow the probable course of a campaign in which the Browns were the invading Etruscans and the Whites the defending Romans." The exercise harked back to the sixth and fifth centuries B.C. when the Etruscans crossed the Apennines and established themselves in the Po Valley, and simulated situations that were unlikely to confront the United States Army in this the 20th century. But Patton did not mind the anachronism. In preparation for the job, he read *The Etruscans* by David MacIver and

R. A. L. Fell's *Etruria and Rome,* then dazzled the assembled senior officers—and there was an overabundance of them present, including Generals W. C. Short, E. L. King, C. J. Simmons and H. W. Harkness—with his erudition. His brash and outspoken critique then turned them against him. He described the maneuvers as "horrid" and, as he put it, "I had the temerity to deduce . . . many defects." As was frequently the offshoot of such events, the assignment earned for him nothing in the end except the animosity of some of his conventionbound superiors.

In all his perambulations, however, there was a firm spot in Patton's life which he could call his professional home—Fort Myer, the hub toward which the spokes of his career invariably led.

The old Fort Whipple, renamed in 1881 for General Albert J. Myer, Grant's chief signal officer in the Civil War, was a microcosm of garrison life in the United States. Covering 304 acres of the former Custis-Lee estate confiscated in 1860, it was garrisoned by some 50 officers and 1,000 enlisted men, usually a squadron or two of the 3rd Cavalry Regiment, a battalion of field artillery, and some machine-gun units. The troops were kept in shipshape condition of preparedness, not to defend the capital by any means, but to provide military extras for Washington's recurring pageants. They were housed in neat brick barracks, trimly aligned, amid well-kept lawns set off by trees and shrubbery. Patton particularly liked the post because it had the best equestrian facilities of the Army anywhere in the United States, including an enormous riding hall that permitted hard exercises throughout the year in perfect comfort.

To Fort Myer's symmetric rows of Victorian houses, the brass of the Army repaired from the Munitions Building every evening to resume the nocturnal routine of their humdrum life—to tend little backyard gardens, listen to the radio, read an occasional book, take in a movie now and then, call on one another to talk shop or barter gossip, and especially to play endless games of bridge, the officers' favorite antidote to boredom.

Patton was tied to Fort Myer by memories of success

and mischief. It was there that his career began so auspiciously in the late winter of 1911. And it was to Fort Myer that he "escaped" after his disillusionment at Meade in the Indian summer of 1920, when he turned his back on armor and assumed command of a squadron of the Army's most spectacular cavalry regiment, the 3rd. His new job was hardly more than a sinecure during the blue period of the Army. He had opportunity to "earn his pay" only on ceremonial occasions, when his squadron was called upon to provide details for funerals, escorting deceased veterans of past wars brought to Washington from all over the country to be interred in Arlington's hallowed soil. The cavalry detachment would pick up the caisson with the flag-decked coffin at Union Station and escort it at a slow trot through the city to the cemetery.

Patton had to bridle himself to put up with this painfully slow ritual. One day he could stand it no longer. On May 23, 1922, he was ordered to lead the detail at the funeral of a veteran of the Spanish-American War. Spring fever suddenly seized Major Patton. He led his detail in a decorous trot through the city and across Memorial Bridge. But when he reached the deserted, unpaved road leading to the cemetery, he ordered the gallop.

The pace proved too much for the staid funeral horses pulling the caisson. They ran away, with Patton chasing after them hell-bent to recover both the corpse and the decorum.

After humdrum tours of duty in Boston and Hawaii, Patton returned to Washington in 1928—first to a desk job in the Office of the Chief of Cavalry (where, recognized as the Cavalry's best pistol shot, he busied himself writing new pistol regulations); then for a year at the Army War College studying advanced tactics in a postgraduate course arranged for hand-picked officers; and finally—in 1932—to his old regiment at Fort Myer, now as its Executive Officer. This was a somewhat more auspicious return, holding out the promise of at least some excitement in his peacetime rut.

His old friend and mentor, Henry L. Stimson, was also back in Washington, this time as Secretary of State in the Hoover Administration. They renewed their friendship in great cordiality, the Pattons dining at "Woodley," the spacious colonial estate they had occupied during the major's earlier assignment at the fort and which now was the home of the Stimsons; or the Secretary and his wife going to the

Pattons at their rented house. They were fancy black-tie affairs, strictly social. It was the way the Pattons lived, their excursions into the best society alternating with their contrived middle-class life in the Army.

Out in the world, the march of events began to quicken. Japan had overrun Manchuria the year before. Then, in February, 1932, she landed marines in Shanghai and started a war against China. For a fleeting moment it seemed that the United States, prodded by Secretary Stimson (whose moral sense was outraged not only by the fact but also by the manners of Japanese aggression), would intervene in the Far East and give the Army a more rigorous part in world affairs.

But Stimson's efforts to impress upon Japan the dangers inherent in her maneuvers foundered on President Hoover's Quaker convictions. "Mr. Hoover was a profoundly peaceable man," Stimson wrote. "Outraged as he was by Japanese aggression, he was opposed, in every fiber of his being, to any action which might lead to American participation in the struggles of the Far East."

All Stimson could do under the circumstances was to stage what he himself called "a bluff." He hoped to restrain Japan by persuading the President to order the fleet to remain in Hawaii instead of returning to its bases on the West Coast after the conclusion of its regular exercises. The Army, however, was left untouched by the events. It was not used even to put some teeth into the Secretary's futile bluff.

The Army's Chief of Staff was another friend of Patton and, like General Wood, a dynamic and colorful soldier. He was General Douglas MacArthur. But the personal distinction that the dramatic MacArthur was bringing to his own job was in sharp contrast to the Army's actual state, which lacked anything even remotely resembling grandeur. Its prestige was at an ebb. MacArthur's predecessor, General Charles P. Summerall, had conceded that "developments in the international situation in the past 10 years have been so favorable that the state of readiness implied in the maintenance of the Regular Army of 280,000 men as provided in the National Defense Act of June 4, 1920, is no longer necessary." MacArthur violently disagreed with his predecessor's assessment of the world situation. When he found that the Army he had inherited consisted of only 12,000 officers and 180,750 men (of whom 54,000 were mobile troops) he pleaded with Congress for a modest increase. But MacArthur not only was turned down but also vigorously criticized as a "militarist" out of step with the national realities, a power-hungry officer trying to build his own empire.

During those vacant days, Patton met with his good friend Major Eisenhower, in whom, during his frustrating tour at Fort Meade, he had found virtually the only ally for his struggle for armor. Patton was Ike's senior in age and service. During the war Eisenhower served as an instructor in a stateside tank school and did not have the practical combat experience of Patton. But he was just as enthusiastic about armor as the Army's pioneer tanker. The two men formed a fast friendship that survived "heated," as Eisenhower said, "sometimes almost screaming arguments over matters that more often than not were doctrinal and academic rather than personal and material."

Now, in 1931, Eisenhower had just written a thoughtful paper about the international situation, and Patton, who disagreed with some of his conclusions, sought him out for one of their old-fashioned bull sessions. They spoke of peace and war, and their conversation then inspired Patton to put down on paper one of the best articles he was ever to write.

Peace was all around him, and oh, it was wonderful.

But the article he now submitted to the *Cavalry Journal* was entitled "Success in War."

CHAPTER SEVEN
A DARK DECISIVE CRISIS

In January, 1928, Major George S. Patton Jr. was beginning the third year of his tour of duty with the General Staff of the Army's Hawaiian Department in Honolulu when his commanding officer was abruptly recalled. He was Major General William Ruthven Smith, a scholarly disciplinarian from Tennessee whose broad competence was somehow indicated in the fact that he had once taught gunnery and ordnance, as well as experimental and natural philosophy, at the War College. Now he was appointed Superintendent of the United States Military Academy and ordered to report to West Point forthwith. Under Army regulations it was General Smith's duty to prepare efficiency reports on the officers he was leaving behind and to read them personally to those who did not, in his eyes, measure up and who rated derogatory remarks. He called Major Patton to his office in the Schofield Barracks for this embarrassing personal confrontation. "This man," Smith recited in his booming voice what he regarded as the most unflattering passage of the report, "would be invaluable in time of war but is a disturbing element in time of peace."

Patton listened stiffly, with tight, thin lips from which the blood seemed to be siphoned off, then snapped to attention and told the General:

"Thank you, sir. I regard your opinion as a great compliment."

Patton was a past master of collecting enemies wherever he served. And Hawaii, for all its soothing, pleasant climate, appeared to be an especially propitious place for him to make lasting ones among the high and mighty whose influence upon his career could have been decisive. It was there in 1935 that his professional life took a melodramatic turn, leaving him to fight doggedly, and even desperately, for his very future in the Army.

At that time it did not seem to matter much one way or another whether a 50-year-old lieutenant colonel would win or lose his personal battle for survival. But in the retrospect of history the stakes now appear in their proper magnitude. For on the outcome of this struggle of two strong and stubborn personalities actually depended whether the Army's greatest tactical genius—"Number One as a combat commander," as General Bradley characterized him in another efficiency report—would be preserved for the vital part he would play in a war yet to come.

It was a bitter clash between Patton and his most influential and resolute personal enemy, Major General Hugh Aloysius Drum.

The son of a captain from Michigan (who was killed in the Battle of San Juan), Drum was the Army's most successful self-made man. With his exceptional military skills and consummate talent for Army politics, he carved a fabulous career for himself without ever having attended West Point or any of the breeding grounds of the regular professional officers' corps. He was 38 years old and a major in 1917 when Pershing, impressed with his precise staff work and organizational ability, picked him for his staff, of which Patton was a junior member.

In France, Drum became a brigadier general and Chief of Staff of the First Army, where a quiet, sandy-haired young Pennsylvanian lieutenant colonel named George C. Marshall, was his Operations Officer. During the closing days of the war Drum became the center of an embarrassing controversy. An ambiguous sentence he added to an order Marshall had drawn up at Pershing's instructions started a disgraceful race for Sedan, the honor of whose capture Foch had reserved for French troops in a gesture to erase the bitter memories of the Prussian victory there in 1870.

However, the scandal did not interfere with Drum's meteoric rise in the postwar Army. Made a permanent major general in 1931, he was appointed Deputy Chief of Staff two years later, and was slated to become Chief of Staff at the end of MacArthur's term. But though Pershing strongly backed him for the job, Drum was bypassed. General Malin Craig was appointed and Drum was sent to command the Hawaiian Department pending (as everybody, and especially Drum, expected) his eventual elevation to the Army's most exalted post.

It was there that Patton stumbled into his orbit. In a somewhat bizarre, if not perverse, move, he was sent to Hawaii in 1935 as Drum's G-2. Surrounding General Drum even at that distant Pacific outpost was an aura of intrigue. The ambitious general was working behind the scenes to assure for himself the coveted Chief of Staff appointment the next time it became available. He was lining up his forces inside the Army and also mobilizing support on Capitol Hill, enlisting influential people in Washington to bear upon the President's decision at the psychological moment.

The titanic fight for the Army's choicest plum split the officers' corps into pro-Drum and anti-Drum cliques, and sharpened the political atmosphere inside the service. Although Patton was not particularly happy with Drum, he was loyal to his chief and did not participate in this palace conspiracy. Yet his destiny suddenly became coupled with

Drum's own fate in a strange sideshow of the greater struggle.

Although the Intelligence assignment was not to his liking, Patton performed with his customary diligence and brilliance. He wrote a couple of bright essays on amphibious operations, including one entitled "Defense of Gallipoli," which was an incisive analysis of defense against seaborne attacks, demonstrating his ability to view a situation from two angles.

He also composed a prophetic paper on the American position in the Pacific, already fraught with considerable perils visible only to discerning observers. Examining Hawaii's possible role in a Pacific war, Patton concluded that a Japanese attack on Pearl Harbor was both possible and probable, and predicted that it would be disastrous to the United States. The date of his report was April 26, 1935.

But he was playing as hard as he was working. He arrived in Hawaii in his customary grand manner, sailing to Honolulu in his yacht, followed later by his stable of saddle horses and polo ponies. It did not take long for him to antagonize Drum with his lavish private parties and his hobnobbing with Honolulu's highest society—the Dillinghams, the Castles, and the Baldwins.

It was inevitable for their dormant enmity to explode in an open clash. It came on schedule, over a relatively trivial matter, in full view of Hawaiian society. Each year, the week of the Inter-Island Polo Championship tournament marked the high point of the social season. The games, which attracted the *créme de créme* of Hawaii's upper crust, were followed by glittering parties each night, among which the Patton's was one of the most stylish.

In the fourth game of the tournament in 1936, the Army team, which Patton captained, was pitted against the Oahu four, whose players were scions of Hawaii's best families. In the heat of the encounter, while Patton was riding off Walter Dillingham, he called out at the top of his piping voice:

"Goddamnit, Walter, you old sonuvabitch, I'll run you right down Front Street."

General Drum was in his seat of honor in the front row of the grandstand. From the look on his face it was obvious that he was pained and embarrassed by the obscenities with which Patton was seasoning the game. When the chukker was over, Drum rose and summoned Patton to him. Then he told him in an icy voice, in front of this select audience:

"I'm relieving you of the captaincy of the Army team, Colonel Patton, for using offensive language in front of the ladies and insulting your competitors. You will leave the field at once."

Patton was stunned, but he merely said, "Yes, sir." He saluted and started to lead his pony off the field. Dillingham, still on his pony, rode up to Drum and asked angrily:

"Is it correct, General, that you have just relieved Colonel Patton?"

"It is," Drum said. "I am not going to have any such language as the Colonel used."

Dillingham threw his mallet to the ground, dismounted, gave the reins of his pony to a groom, and called out to Frank Baldwin, captain of the Maui team, who was on the sidelines waiting to play the next match:

"Well, Frank, that's the end of the tournament for this year."

"It certainly is, Walter," Baldwin shot back. "I have never heard Georgie Patton use foul language of any kind."

He, too, dismounted and walked off the field with Dillingham, trying to catch up with Patton.

General Drum was on the spot. He hated to reverse himself and let Patton's inexcusable conduct go unpunished. But he could not very well cut short the championship week and let the tournament go down the drain. Pale with evident anger, he recalled Patton and restored him to the captaincy of the team. But he never forgave him.

As a first down payment of the retribution Drum planned for Patton, he virtually devastated him in his efficiency report. The second installment he reserved for the day when he would take over the Army as Chief of Staff. Since it seemed a foregone conclusion that Drum would now get what he so ardently sought, Patton's career in the Army appeared to be moving rapidly toward its end.

But his tour in the Islands had its compensations. He could spend more time with his family—his wife, his daughters Beatrice and Ruth Ellen, and his son and namesake, a quiet boy in his early teens with none of his father's flair and exuberance. The carefree, leisurely atmosphere of Hawaii drew the Pattons close to each other. Mrs. Patton found time to write *"Blood of the Shark,"* a romance set in the culture of Hawaii, which gained a modicum of fame for her. The family went on extended anthropological expeditions to remote spots all over the Islands, probing for the picturesque past of Hawaii and the hidden story of its fascinating inhabitants.

But professionally, George Patton's career was both stagnant and precarious.

Patton was, for the first time, beginning to think seriously of retiring from the Army. Though he was in excellent health and kept in perfect trim with his vigorous outdoor life and exercises, he was not getting any younger. He was 50, and a lieutenant colonel after 27 years in the Army. Behind him was a World War in which he had already risen to the rank of full colonel.

The Army had given him a lot and he had given all he had in return, but it was not an entirely cloudless affair. He had accomplished nothing remarkable in the 16 years since his departure from Fort Meade, and his personal relations left much to be desired. As William Mellor put it, Patton was either hated or loved, "there could be no middle ground for so dominant a personality."

This would not have been too bad by itself. But those who loved him were mostly his juniors—younger officers who had served under him and came to know his complex character at close quarters—and though they found much in him to dislike, they found still more to inspire respect, admiration and loyalty. On the other hand, most of the senior officers of the Army, on whose goodwill and friendship his progress depended, hated him. As a general once said feelingly when talking of Patton, "I don't dislike him. I loathe that s.o.b.!"

A supreme realist when the chips were down, Patton began to think that perhaps his usefulness in the Army was at an end, and looked around for a place of his own where he could retire. He found an old farm in South Hamilton near Boston, with a big old house and broad acres, ideal for retirement into an active civilian life. He bought the place while he was still in Hawaii, and Mrs. Patton prepared it for their residence in her exquisite style, calling it "Green Meadows."

It was to "Green Meadows" that the Pattons went from Hawaii when his tour of duty expired, there to contemplate the future while waiting reassignment.

Shortly after their arrival at their handsome estate,

Colonel Patton was kicked in the leg by Mrs. Patton's horse. The mishap did not worry him at first. He had been kicked by horses many times before. He was what could be called "accident prone" but had never suffered serious consequences from any of his mishaps.

Once on a vacation at "Avalon" on Cape Cod, while racing his roadster from Pride's Crossing to a polo match at Topsfield, the car overturned in a ditch and buried him. In Mexico, in 1916, a gas stove exploded in his quarters, giving him a painful time with serious burns.

When he was stationed at Fort Bliss in Texas, Patton socialized with the big cattlemen of the neighborhood, making formal calls on them splendidly attired and wearing his two guns. On one visit his gun went off in its holster while he and a cow baron were standing around sipping their drinks. Conforming to the strict etiquette of the frontier, his host ignored the accident, went on with the chit-chat and pouring of the drinks, politely refraining from asking the embarrassing question whether Patton had hurt himself. As a matter of fact, he had not. The bullet missed his left foot by a fraction of an inch.

But shortly afterward on a patrol, his regulation Army automatic discharged and creased his right thigh. Eager to hairtrigger his guns, Patton had filed a sear to lessen the pull. The mere jolt of his foot had jarred the hammer and snapped it against a cartridge. The wound turned out to be slight, his rage monumental. After that, Patton kept an empty shell in the chamber under the hammer to make sure he would not fire the gun by just stamping his foot.

He continued to live dangerously, courting different hazards. Only a few weeks before his arrival at "Green Meadows," he almost drowned in a mid-Pacific gale on his journey from Hawaii, coming as he went, on his own yacht, the *Arcturus*.

And now this blasted kick! Before long a clot formed in the vein and began to travel upward to his heart. He was rushed to the hospital in critical condition. The doctors worked feverishly for days to dissolve the clot before it could reach the aorta and kill him. Patton spent those days thinking not of death, because he, in his indestructible fatalism, was certain he would pull through, but of his retirement. When he was out of danger but still in the hospital, he worked on the blueprints of a 63-foot Maroni-rigged schooner he had ordered, again with his future in mind. He called it *When-and-If*.

When he recovered he returned to the Army after all, and avidly at that, for he was given his first command, the 9th Cavalry Regiment at Fort Riley. Simultaneously he was made Director of Instruction and taught tactics at the Cavalry School. It was like old times.

For a while at Riley it seemed that the Drum jinx was not working. But just when Patton was convicing himself that his *faux pas* at Hawaii had apparently been forgotten and forgiven, his career took a turn for the worse—with a kick upstairs. He was made a full colonel on schedule—on July 1, 1938. But the command that went with the promotion turned out to be the 5th Cavalry at Fort Clark. Situated near Bracketville in the Texas Panhandle, it was the country's most somnambulant Cavalry post, where superannuated officers, given their colonelcy as a parting gesture, were usually allowed a pleasant last fling before retirement.

A busy outpost after the Civil War for forays against the Comanches, the warlike Indians who made the vast Panhandle unsafe for the white man, Fort Clark subsisted solely on the memories of its past glories. So effective were the punitive interventions of the 5th Cavalry that when the Comanches were pacified at last in 1904 there were only 1,500 left, too few and far too well chastised to cause any more trouble.

After that, the fort's importance began to dwindle until it vanished altogether. By the time Patton took command, it was the forgotten station of the Army in the Texan dustbin.

The 5th Cavalry was an old regiment, but not so old as the 3rd, for example, or so celebrated. Activated in Kentucky in 1855, it was renamed in 1861 during the Cavalry's big reorganization in the Civil War, after which it was moved to Clark to fight the Comanches. In due course *laisser aller-laisser faire* became tradition to the regiment, and it was adhered to by Patton's conservative and relaxed predecessor, Colonel Robert C. Richardson, who, in another tradition connected with Clark, went straight into retirement from the fort.

Patton's customary energy fought obscurity and the stifling sand of the Panhandle. He tried to make the most of his stay, and his brisk regime did breathe some new life into the sleepy reservation. But it was a monotonous, frustrating tour, dulling the edge of his martial fervor while sharpening his nervous temperament.

The year 1937, when Patton went into partial eclipse through his transfer to the Cavalry School, brought a sharpening of crises in Europe and Asia, where Hitler, Mussolini and Japan's military clique were rapidly gaining control over the march of events. War already raged in China, civil war in Spain. Japanese shells sank the United States gunboat *Panay* and several American ore carriers on the Yangtze River above Nanking. Italy withdrew from the League of Nations and Germany repudiated what little there was left of the Versailles Treaty, and as the world moved closer to war, new doctrines and new weapons appeared.

In England and France, hidebound conservative military factions in power remained blind to this fantastic evolution gaining speed at a breath-taking rate. Reports from Germany described in tantalizing detail the rapid spread of mechanization in a vastly growing all-new *Wehrmacht*, representing, by a partial unification of the armed forces at the top, the triumph of a novel concept.

Emphasis shifted to the very two arms the old-timers continued to dismiss, deprecate and neglect—airpower and that controversial weapon which once broke Patton's heart, the tank. In England and France, visionaries like General J. F. C. Fuller and Colonel Charles de Gaulle, who dared to set themselves up as proponents of armor, were still ignored or damned. It was different in Germany. The names Heinz Guderian and Erwin Rommel became increasingly familiar in military circles, even in Washington, thanks to the reports of Colonel Truman Smith, the Military Attaché in Berlin, a keen and intelligent observer of the Nazi military revolution, and especially to the eyewitness account of a young officer, a mere major named Albert C. Wedemeyer. He had studied at the Military Academy at Gatow near Berlin and made many interesting friends—like Walter Warlimont, Guderian and Rommel—among a new generation of German officers. Warlimont represented brand-new operational principles which stood somewhere between strategy and tactics. Guderian in a sense personified the new

spirit of mechanization in the army, while Rommel became
known to a limited circle as the proponent of new and ingenious concepts in infantry tactics.

There were several straws in the wind from which the direction of this development could be determined. On
October 15th, the official journal of the Reich Federation of
German Officers published an article by Guderian entitled
"Armored Attack in Mobility and Fire," in which he dealt
harshly with skeptics and the reactionary opponents of
armor in modern war and placed the tank squarely in the
center of all military considerations and plans. Then he published a slim book called *Achtung! Panzer!*, in which he
described with defiant candor the evolution of the new
armored troops of the Germans and outlined the contours
of a doctrine for their employment in action.

Almost simultaneously Rommel also published a book.
Called *Infantry in Angriff*, it sketched a revolutionary principle for the war of movement in which the infantry was
given unheard-of momentum and striking power through
close cooperation with armored units.

Patton at Fort Riley was electrified by these obscure
events, whose significance was either ignored or rejected
outright by the men in Washington who molded the policies
of the United States Army. Only a handful of utopian seers
envisaged armor as a major tool of war, and Patton was a
charter member of this fraternity. But the man who usually
shouted his advocacy of unpopular causes from the rooftops
now thought it advisable to speak softly in slyly camouflaged terms of his unbounded enthusiasm for the tank, lest
he jeopardize still further his precarious career.

For almost two decades, from the haven of the Cavalry,
Patton had gone to bat for armor in lectures and a series of
brilliant articles. They were written cautiously, in an
Aesopian language he had devised in which he would speak
up for mechanization. He made his point persuasively, to be
sure, but only between the lines, still paying lip service to
ingrained concepts and traditions which predominated in
the minds of those who determined the course of the Army
and tolerated no contradictions.

In a lecture to officers at Fort Myer in 1933, he outlined
the overwhelming advantages armies could derive from
mechanized forces; how armored cars excelled in strategic
reconnaissance; how they could be used effectively for the
pursuit of the enemy; how tanks could decide the issue in an

offensive by being held as an offensive reserve, then brought
forth in the proper moment to deliver the main blow.

But in conclusion, Patton thought it wise to retreat to
safer ground. He went so far as to deprecate in so many
words the very weapon whose tremendous potentialities he
had just praised. He ended the lecture by saying in effect that
there would always be a Cavalry—exactly what his audience
of cavalry officers wanted to hear—and by describing the
tank as just another weapon.

"In closing," he said, "let me remind you of just one more
thing . . . Today machines hold the place formerly occupied by the jawbone, the elephant, armor, long-bow, gun-
powder, and, latterly, the submarine. They, too, shall pass.
To me it seems that any person who would scrap the age-old
tried arms for this new ism is as foolish as the poor man who,
on seeing an overcoat, pawned his shirt and pants to buy
it."

Yet he followed the development avidly, keeping himself
posted on everything printed on the subject in Germany,
Britain and France, where the controversy raged with growing momentum. He spent nights poring over the books of
Liddell Hart and J. F. C. Fuller, British apostles of the "new
war," and Charles de Gaulle, the little-known French
colonel who fought in the front line for the mechanization
of the French Army. When the writings of Guderian and
Rommel were translated by G-2, Patton immediately sent
for copies and devoured them, reading them again and
again until he knew them by heart.

But if he hoped that he would be called to Washington to
participate in an American effort to mechanize the Army,
he was bitterly disappointed. George Patton, for all his
acknowledged competence and creative vision, was in the
doghouse. Although he was sorely needed, he was not
wanted. From the relative importance of his job at Riley,
where he could keep in touch with at least part of this evolution, and even work with armor, of which the Cavalry
School was getting samples for educational purposes, he was
sent somewhat peremptorily into what was tantamount to
exile—to Fort Clark, where the horse was still trump and
the Cavalry was God's own arm.

In the meantime, on that parallel track, General Drum's career was moving, apparently inexorably and safely, toward its gratifying climax. By this strange intertwining of their professional lives, what now was expected to be Drum's meat seemed certain to be Patton's poison.

But then a new plot was unexpectedly injected into the play. In a *dénouement* that had some of the trimmings of a Greek melodrama, Patton's destiny came to be hinged to the fortune of yet another great soldier, General George C. Marshall. It was the forceful intervention of something akin to fate which skyrocketed Marshall to a position of dominant influence in the Army and, simultaneously as its direct result, saved Patton for his great future service. It is probably no exaggeration to say that without Marshall's phenomenal and rapid rise after years of neglect and ostracism, Patton would have vanished through some trap door into the oblivion of a retired colonel.

General Drum left Hawaii in 1937 to move closer to the central plot. In the spring of 1938, General Craig was completing the third of his four-year term as Chief of Staff, and now both the White House and the War Department began to explore the problem of succession. Drum assumed command of the Second Army and the VI Corps Area in Chicago, whence he could commute to Washington and exert his influence more effectively than from distant Honolulu.

He was no longer satisfied with standing idly in the wings while Craig's successor was being chosen. He intensified his campaign in his own behalf only to run into his first stunning disappointment. He went to see Pershing in Washington to insure his old mentor's support, but the General of the Armies now told him bluntly:

"I did my best in 1935, Drum, to get the job for you. But this time I cannot be of any help. The situation has changed in the meantime and now I have another candidate." The other candidate was Marshall.

So eager was Drum to assure Pershing's support that he even prompted Patton, in spite of their badly strained relations, to intercede on his behalf with the old General of the Armies. Patton could not refuse the request and so, on

December 30th, 1937, he wrote to Pershing to sound him out on the matter. By then, however, his mentor had become fully committed to George Marshall.

This was not the only new hurdle Drum now had to surmount. At about the same time, Secretary of War Harry H. Woodring called in Major General Stanley D. Embick, the Deputy Chief of Staff, who was his confidant, and asked him plaintively, "Do I have to select Drum as Chief of Staff?"

"No," Embick replied, "any general in the Army is eligible for the appointment. Moreover," he added, "there will be several vacancies on the list of general officers. You, Mr. Secretary, can select any colonel on the list, promote him to brigadier general, and make him eligible for the job."

By that time, Woodring, too, had his own candidate. It was George Marshall.

Then Marshall was recommended to the President by Louis A. Johnson, the Assistant Secretary of War, whose influence as a former American Legion commander was paramount in the White House in matters affecting the Army. The Marshall boom was on. Drum's chances began to wane.

Although their careers, qualifications and personalities were entirely different, Marshall's and Patton's courses in the Army showed startling similarities. They both reached their first peaks spectacularly in World War I, in which Marshall, who was Patton's senior by only five years, wound up as a temporary brigadier general.

At the age of 38, George Catlett Marshall, scion of a prominent Pennsylvania family but no West Pointer (he graduated from VMI), planner of the Battle of St. Mihiel and the Meuse-Argonne offensive, emerged from World War I as the Army's most promising staff officer with Pershing's friendship and professional support. He became the General's aide and companion during the postwar years, but upon Pershing's retirement in 1924, his career took a nosedive. After years of routine service in China, he enjoyed a brief period of importance when, as commandant of the Infantry School at Fort Benning, he trained a new generation of brilliant young officers. After that he endured nothing but disappointments.

The quietly plodding officer with a passion for anonymity irritated, rather than impressed, General MacArthur. The

Chief of Staff had no use for Marshall and virtually exiled him to Chicago, where he spent three stultifying years as senior instructor of the Illinois National Guard. In 1936, efforts to bring him to Washington in a more important job failed. Instead he was transferred to command the Fifth Infantry Brigade at Vancouver, as remote a post for him as Fort Clark was for Patton. Out in the West at the far end of the Army's line of communications, an officer could easily forfeit his entire future by the simple process of being forgotten.

But now Marshall's time had come. Nothing could stop him from getting to the top. By this capricious gambit of fate, Patton's own career also had reached its turning point. While only a short time before it seemed that he was heading for oblivion, now he suddenly loomed as one of the Army's coming senior officers.

CHAPTER EIGHT
IN THE SHADOW OF MARSHALL

George Patton, the supreme fatalist, once described himself as "a chip floating on the river of destiny." And in another moment of stress and strain, he wrote: "It has been my experience through life that every disappointment I have had has eventually proved a blessing in disguise, and worked to my advantage, although at the time I could not see it."

The year 1938 was such a time.

Though he was shifted to Fort Clark amid indications that he was being considered expendable, other events that seemed to have no bearing on his "destiny" quickly straightened out this slight deviation on his course. Just when he received his orders to move to Bracketville and be damned, Brigadier General Marshall received his at Vancouver to move to Washington and take over the War Plans Division of the General Staff.

General Drum, heir presumptive to Chief of Staff Craig,

was then ordered from Chicago to Governors Island in New York Harbor to assume command of the First Army and the Second Corps Area. It was more than just a straw in the wind. Drum's new command held some military responsibilities, but it was primarily a social plum. The New York assignment usually meant the end of the road for senior generals to permit them to retire in a blaze of publicity, even if not of glory. The top-ranking Army representative in New York was chosen for his social graces and decorative value rather than martial qualities. He had to be a kind of glad-handing, back-patting "ward boss" in uniform in the fast social and political currents of the big town.

In Drum's case the transfer indicated beyond the shadow of a doubt that he was to be bypassed again and that his dream of becoming Chief of Staff of the Army was definitely over.

At the same time, Marshall began to climb straight toward the job. As soon as he arrived in Washington and took over his new duties, General Embick, the Deputy Chief of Staff, began to arrange to remove himself from the General Staff. Only two years from retirement at the statutory age of 64, Embick asked for command of the Fourth Corps Area with headquarters at Atlanta because, as he put it, he felt "old and tired" for the growing burdens of the Deputy's job.

Embick then suggested that Marshall be named his successor, but it needed a veritable *coup d'état* to bring this about. In September, Secretary Woodring was absent from Washington and Assistant Secretary Johnson was Acting Secretary of War. He called a meeting of the War Council and immediately turned to General Craig.

"What about a Deputy Chief of Staff to succeed General Embick?" Johnson asked.

"We'll get that worked out in due course, Mr. Secretary," the Chief of Staff replied.

"What about George Marshall?" Johnson insisted.

"We'll work that out, Mr. Secretary," said the General.

"There is not going to be any War Council until that thing is worked out," Johnson announced.

General Craig left the room. When he returned a few minutes later, he smiled a little and said, "The orders have been issued."

If Patton recognized the significance of these obscure

events to his own career, little, if anything, in his conduct at Fort Clark showed it. He took over from Colonel Richardson on July 1, 1938, and plunged into his job with his usual energy and ruthless reform. There was only one difference from his former methods. This time he was not doing these things just according to the manuals, in their pretty order but essentially in a vacuum. He was preparing in earnest—for war.

Patton did not know more than what he was reading in the newspapers. Nothing in his communications from the War Department or the Office of the Chief of Cavalry hinted at a deterioration of the world situation and a need to adjust the Army to it. But he watched the international scene with quizzical eyes and concluded that Europe was moving inexorably toward the showdown.

The year saw the climactic end of what was later called the dress rehearsal of World War II, the Spanish Civil War, with the daily bombing of Barcelona by German planes. With members of Hitler's new *Luftwaffe* manning their cockpits and bomb bays, an air raid on March 7th killed 1,000 persons in the Catalonian capital. On the 11th, Hitler marched into Austria and annexed it to his Greater German Reich. And on October 1st he occupied the Sudetenland, with another chunk of Czechoslovakia going to Hungary a few weeks later.

These events produced blazing headlines in the American newspapers, but they did little to shake the Army out of its equanimity. Yet the picture began to brighten, if only imperceptibly, for the time being. The taciturn new chief of the War Plans Division recognized what these distant events meant for the United States. A man of long-range vision who rarely lost sight of the trees no matter how dense the forest, General Marshall followed developments in Europe with calm analytical precision. He had already recognized that two crucial issues in particular were gradually emerging from these developments thousands of miles from his desk. For one thing, he realized that Hitler's new military machine was unleashing an unprecedented revolution in warfare, making obsolete all the weapons of World War I and revising its strategy and tactics. For another, he was convinced, at a time when American involvement in a war seemed as remote as a trip to the moon, that Britain and France, whether or not they liked it and realized it, were moving closer to war with Germany and that the United States would be drawn into the conflict sooner or later.

Patton was a very different man from Marshall, yet he was like the quiet Pennsylvanian in that he, too, was quick to recognize the impact of the new German war machine on the future of warfare. He was convinced that, despite all the isolationist and noninterventionist sentiments of the country, the United States would become involved in a war when it came.

Now at Fort Clark he intensified his study of the writings of the new generation of German generals. He began to conduct sand-table exercises, reconstructing from the articles in various service journals German maneuvers in which he recognized preparations for certain specific operations in a coming war.

Colonel Patton baffled and annoyed his officers by daily sending them on "war" games at a time when they could not see war in their own future. He worked ceaselessly to devise new methods of dismounted attack, telling the muscle-bound staff at Clark, "No matter what the old-timers say about the future of horse cavalry in tomorrow's war, I am telling you there will be few horses in the United States Army when that war comes."

His subordinates thought of him as a maniac crazed by his love of war. But he scoffed at his critics. He organized his cavalrymen into machine-gun complements. The troops continued to ride to the exercises in the desert, but then he made them go through the simulated battles on foot. "That's the way you'll have to fight in the next war," he said.

There was plenty of bellyaching at the fort about Patton's stiff regime, about his insistence on spit and polish, his "ridiculous war games," and especially his blasphemous depreciation of Holy Calvary. Word of these strange doings reached Washington and proved grist for the mills of his enemies. They began to refer to him as "the madman of Fort Clark" and said:

"The damn fool! Doesn't he see that he's cutting his own throat?"

Patton was, indeed, being watched from Washington, by someone who was neither friend nor foe, but merely was interested in him. If there was a slant in this interest, it was far different from the malicious expectation of Patton's enemies.

While Marshall was still in War Plans, he began secret preparations for a "purge" at the top, where too many "old fogeys"—as President Roosevelt called the superannuated senior officers infesting key positions—impeded the work of the Army's woefully overdue modernization and reorganization. The problem of armor—the vast and difficult issue of mechanization—was foremost in his mind. He was quietly combing the officers' corps for men who could be entrusted with the task when the time became ripe.

Marshall was not misled by Patton's pussyfooting approach to armor and his opportunistic defense of the Cavalry. He knew that Patton was completely devoted to mechanization and was muting his enthusiasm only to avoid censure from its influential opponents. Shortly after his arrival in Washington, he told Lieutenant Colonel Leonard T. Gerow, his Executive Officer in the War Plans Division, "Patton is by far the best tank man in the Army. I know this from the First World War. I watched him closely when he commanded the first tanks we ever had. I realize that he is a difficult man but I know how to handle him."

Then he said the magic words: "I want him nearer to Washington to be available when needed."

On October 16th, Marshall became Deputy Chief of Staff. One of the first things he did in his new and powerful assignment was to arrange Patton's transfer to Fort Myer, to be closer at hand. The great interest Marshall had in Patton was evidenced by the fact that Patton was already 53 years old, at a time when Marshall had made up his mind not to give any important commands in his new Army to officers above the age of 50. He was impressed with Patton's youthful energy and creative vigor, and was willing to make an exception to his rule.

Marshall had first met Patton in France in 1917, when he was methodically preparing the campaigns of the First Army of the AEF in its Operations Section. Although they had neither reason nor occasion to become close, Marshall developed a personal interest in Patton, whose flamboyance and boisterous conduct, strange as it may seem, neither repelled nor deceived him.

The two men appeared to bear no resemblance to each other, for Marshall was calm, serene and reserved, consistent and pedantic, a man of set principles, whereas Patton was a showman—impetuous and loud—and inconsistent and expeditious, and rather opportunistic. Yet within them existed an intellectual affinity that more than bridged the gulf of their contrasting personalities. Both were highly unorthodox military thinkers and progressive in their appreciation of the art and science of war. They both were skeptical of the glib solution, were unwilling to accept military dogma, and distrusted established patterns and the rule book. They shared a passion for complete and accurate knowledge and a deep concern with the realities of their profession.

George Marshall had many extraordinary qualities as one of the great captains of history, but probably he was best as a judge of men. It did not take him long to recognize that behind Patton's eccentricities and ostentatious mannerisms was a profound military scientist who drew, as he himself did, his conclusions from history.

The consonance of their outlook and the symmetry of their progressive approach to the ever-changing problems of war drew Marshall to Patton, who accepted his proffered friendship with alacrity, and cherished it all his life. In his volatile moods, Patton was apt to deprecate all his colleagues at one time or another. He spared virtually none of them with his barbs. He frequently spoke of his contemporaries in abusive language he was occasionally quick to regret. But nobody ever heard him speak disparagingly of General Marshall.

Marshall's lasting friendship served him exceedingly well throughout World War II. As we shall see, it was this unwavering goodwill and abiding faith in the man's redeeming qualities that preserved Patton in his commands. Marshall forever speaking up for him and saving his neck when *everybody* else was ready to throw him to the wolves.

It was Marshall's firm belief that Patton was the Army's greatest human asset in the field to score decisive victories over the fast-moving Germans. He came to regard him as absolutely indispensable for the triumph of American arms in the Second World War. There was an ample sense of proportion in Marshall's assessment of Patton, because he was fully aware of his limitations. He recognized clearly Patton's proper place in the command structure and knew exactly how much authority and responsibility he could give him.

When the question of the ground command of "Overlord" came up for the initial phase of the Normandy invasion, Marshall remarked to General John Edwin Hull, "Patton would be the best man, of course, to lead the invasion, but he is too impetuous. He needs a brake to slow him down because he is apt to coast at breakneck speed, propelled by his enthusiasm and exuberance. He always needs someone just above him, and that is why I am giving the command to Bradley. . . . And don't feel too bad about this," he reassured Hull, who was one of Patton's chief boosters in the War Department. "Patton himself understands this. This is what makes it so easy to deal with the man." He said the last sentence at a time when everybody else—including General Eisenhower—thought that it was exasperatingly difficult to deal with Patton.

What made this relationship so remarkable was the fact that Marshall's admiration of Patton was based almost solely on their joint experience in World War I. Their paths did not cross between 1920 and 1939, when Patton's performance in the peacetime Army was quite undistinguished and he himself was what General Smith had called him, a disturbing element. Marshall now chose him instinctively or intuitively, mostly on the strength of memories.

Patton qualified for Marshall's confidence (and the later high commands it yielded) solely by his performance in France in 1917-18, over a period of only 10 months, with an off-beat unit of the huge American war machine whose contribution to victory was glamorous and romantic, to be sure, but ephemeral. He remained implanted in Marshall's mind, nevertheless, exactly as he was in France in 1918— *the very first tank officer in the United States Army who stamped a brigade out of the ground with a handful of borrowed tanks, trained his men with unflagging energy and great skill, then led them in battle with courage.*

On the basis of that performance, Patton was to General Marshall the ideal of an American officer—organizer, trainer, combat leader. Marshall knew only too well that there were not many officers like that in the United States Army or, for that matter, in any man's army anywhere in the world.

On November 27th, when he had been at Fort Clark for less than five months, Patton was in the field watching one of his "war games" when his orders arrived. This was the end, it seemed at first blush. He had carried things too far and Washington was giving him the boot. The message designated Colonel Cuthbert P. Stearns to replace him in command of the 5th Cavalry and instructed him to report to Washington forthwith—"to be retired, let's hope." Fort Clark sighed with relief.

But the scuttlebutt reaching the fort told a different story. Colonel Jonathan M. "Skinny" Wainwright, who commanded the 3rd Cavalry and was post commander at Fort Myer, had been made a brigadier general pending his transfer to the Philippines. Patton was slated to replace him in both jobs. It still appeared to be only a routine transfer. Nobody, not even Patton, recognized General Marshall's fine hand behind the order.

No matter what, Fort Clark was glad to see Patton go, and gave him a rousing send-off. On December 5, 1938, the day of his departure, the troops were lined along the drive from the Commanding Officer's quarters to the main gate, the officers of the regiment and the scout car platoon forming the escort.

Back at Fort Myer on his fifth tour of duty in 26 years, Patton moved into the Post Commander's big three-storied red brick home on Jackson Avenue and settled down at once to do to Myer exactly what he had done to Clark. He drove his men unsparingly and trained them to a razor's edge.

Abrupt though his transfer was, its significance was not immediately apparent. The United States was not participating in Europe's race to war. While the country was preoccupied with peace at virtually any price, Fort Myer lingered on in its traditional role as a "social post" where Patton could exercise his fine horses, play polo, ride after foxes, and give his fancy parties. There were, however, a few changes after his arrival.

His strict regime with the added work program of his famous curriculum produced widespread moaning and complaining, for the chichi post was not accustomed to so harsh a grind. Yet Colonel Patton was not altogether disliked. Two of his innovations even made him moderately popular.

For one thing, he turned the annual "Society Circus" into a noisy pageant. His troopers staged the ride of the Valkyries, posed as Don Quixote and Sancho Panza, re-enacted Jeb Stuart's ride, Custer's last stand, and even Lady Godiva's famed tour of Coventry. During the brash finale of the show, a battery of horse artillery dashed into the startled audience. The Patton family staged the whole show, and it was a big hit.

The Colonel made an even bigger hit with his other innovation. He had been at the fort hardly a fortnight when he called in the post chaplain and instructed him to cut his sermons to the bone.

"I don't yield to any man in my reverence of the Lord," he said. "But, Goddamnit, no sermon needs to take longer than 10 minutes. I'm sure you can make your point in that time."

Next Sunday in the chapel, with spurs clinking, he strutted down the aisle and took his seat in the front pew facing the padre. As soon as the sermon began, Patton took out his watch. After eight minutes, he looked up to the chaplain with a portentous glance.

Two minutes later the sermon ended on the dot.

CHAPTER NINE
REHEARSALS FOR WAR

Colonel Patton had been at Fort Myer for a little more than eight months when Europe erupted in war. It began with the stentorian rumble of the German military machine through Poland and a brief but breath-taking demonstration of the *Wehrmacht's* unprecedented mechanized power. But then it petered out in what Senator William E. Borah dubbed the "phony war." The belligerents were sitting tight and tense like chess masters on a floodlit stage, waiting for the other to make the next move.

The United States reacted to the holocaust with a scrap of paper called the Neutrality Law, reflecting the widespread belief in this country that we could stay out of the war simply by outlawing it. To Americans in their splendid isolation, Europe—with its absurd martial stance—seemed as quaint and remote as Tibet, where a frantic search was on for the incarnated successor to the old Dalai Lama, who had recently died. Harry L. Hopkins expressed the sentiment of most Americans in a letter to his brother in California: "The only interest here, as everywhere, is the war, and I believe that we really can keep out of it. Fortunately there is no great sentiment in this country for getting into it, although I think almost everyone wants to see England and France win."

If a visitor from outer space had landed at Fort Myer during those days, he would have thought that this earth was the most equable of planets, possessed of abundant goodwill, not only to men, but even to horses. At the height of the Czechoslovak crisis in the spring, the fort was celebrating gayly its traditional winter season with lavish horse shows and splendid exhibition drills. The season ended on April 16th with the best "Society Circus" in years. After that, Patton took the 3rd Cavalry into spring training, and was kept busy for the rest of the year with the routine curricula of his regiment—exercises at the Engineer School, minor maneuvers in New Jersey and Pennsylvania, and the usual ceremonial functions. On May 5th, he sent a detachment to escort the President of Nicaragua to the White House. On June 10th he personally commanded a squadron in the parade for King George VI and Queen Elizabeth of Britain. While the *Wehrmacht* was gobbling up Poland, Patton was getting ready to lead his regiment on its annual march, then to take it to autumn maneuvers around Fort Meade. When it was over and the regiment returned to the post, it was winter again and time for another social season.

In May, 1940, the war exploded. The Germans broke into the Low Countries, then overran France with an air-tank blitz for which the Polish campaign was but a pale preview. They used new devices which completely upset all standard concepts of tactics and, with the tremendous increase in speed and mobility with which fire power could be brought to bear, burst the confines of the battlefield.

Ever since the Polish campaign, Patton had been following the war in Europe with keen interest. He reread Guderian's book and devoured a series of shrewd papers G-2 had prepared about the novel elements of this war from reports of observers on both sides of the fence. Patton was fascinated. These were the tactics he himself had visualized for the tank two decades before. This was the fluidity of the battle he dared only to dream of during the action he led in the Argonne Forest and which he had developed in his mind while a patient in the hospital at Dijon. Now he abandoned his caution and reverted to his youthful advocacy of the tank, maybe somewhat more sanguinely than the situation warranted. He joined wholeheartedly a fast-growing school both within and outside the armed services which believed that "modern war required a profusion of machines and that personnel employing the machines must receive daily specialized training in their use."

In his restive enthusiasm Patton could no longer bear the quiet routine of his command at Fort Myer. He stumped the War Department in search of an assignment closer to the war. When no such job could be found for him, he decided to go to war anyway, via Canada. He wrote to his old friend, General A. G. L. McNaughton, Commander in Chief of the First Canadian Army in England, asking for a commission. McNaughton answered promptly, offering him command of a unit overseas—with the rank of major.

Patton was seriously considering this when events in France ended all hesitation in the United States and pushed the Army onto the path of modernization General Marshall had envisaged.

As far as the Army was concerned, the calm and inertia of Patton's sheltered outpost at Fort Myer was deceptive. The Army was undergoing a subtle and hardly visible, but enormous, metamorphosis, thanks solely to a single man, the new Chief of Staff. When Marshall was appointed the nation's first soldier only two months before the outbreak of the European war, he found confusion and indecision in the cavernous Munitions Building. The Army's civilian leadership was hopelessly split at the top, Secretary Woodring, an avowed isolationist, feuding openly and bitterly with Assistant Secretary Johnson, who advocated all-out preparedness. Their violent personal struggle then deepened conflicts rampant in the military leadership.

The General Staff in particular was in a sad state of confusion and disorganization. Although it had been established in 1903, it was still not functioning with anything resembling effectiveness or efficiency, and was especially remiss in meeting its responsibility to train the Army. The situation was aggravated by fiery controversies raging in the officers' corps. Like the nation itself, it was split down the middle not only between isolationists and interventionists, but also between diehard conservatives who stuck to the time-honored doctrines and implements of warfare and a new generation of officers who recognized that a fantastic revolution was afoot.

While the old-timers closed their eyes to the *Wehrmacht's* demonstration of that revolution, the progressives appeared to be mesmerized by it. As a result, the military establishment was permeated by a creeping pessimism, if not defeatism, an attitude which even President Roosevelt seemed to share.

"This was a period of impotence," Robert E. Sherwood wrote, "when, with all of civilization imperiled, the leader of the most powerful nation on earth had to wait, day after anxious day, for his own course of action to be shaped by events over which he had no control. It was particularly agonizing for one of his venturesome spirit to be unable to act boldly or even cautiously to plan action in the face of impending calamity, of which the Blitzkrieg in Poland had given a suggestion."

Roosevelt was, for once in his life, deedless and speechless. Early in January, 1940, he told Sumner Welles, the Under Secretary of State, frankly that "the chances seemed to be one in a thousand that anything could be done to change the course of events."

General Marshall was not afflicted with or paralyzed by this impotence. He viewed the situation in its broadest historic sweep, and was looking far ahead. Nothing in what had happened now surprised him, not even the *Wehrmacht's* new methods and means of waging war. Since he was, in his own mind, prepared for them, he also had definite ideas for the solution of the problems they posed.

Although Marshall was not a firebrand who ignited controversies around the things in which he believed, he now became suspect in Washington because he was speaking a strange language for those days. Official thinking in the

United States, influenced mostly by Germany's seemingly irresistible show of power, considered plans only to strengthen the country's defenses to stem the tide should it spill across the ocean to the Panama Canal, for example. But Marshall was talking of armored divisions and long-range bombers, and this seemed to suggest that he might be thinking of the offensive.

His chance to accomplish at once what he thought necessary came in June with the collapse of French resistance in the face of Germany's enormous mechanized and motorized onslaught. In the immediate wake of France's surrender, General Marshall began the mobilization of the country within its own crucial area with a lightning-like reorganization of the Army. He thus embarked upon the rapid establishment of all the elements which the Army needed to change from a hibernating peacetime force into a vast organization of well-trained and well-equipped soldiers, not only capable of waging war, but also fully prepared for it with an excellent prospect of victory even over the "invincible" Germans.

Marshall moved quickly to bring the units of the regular Army to full strength and induct the National Guard into Federal service. He arranged for the activation of the Organized Reserve when and as needed. He separated the Field Armies from the Corps Areas. And he activated a General Headquarters as the high command of the field forces as a first step toward concentrating on the training of the new Army.

On July 10th a tremendous stride was made to catch up not only with the German war machine, but also with the military realities of the times. On that day Marshall resolved the long-simmering problem of armor in the United States Army, virtually with the stroke of a pen, by establishing the Armored Force and creating the first two armored divisions.

That was the day at last for which the Chief of Staff had saved Patton.

Within 48 hours of the establishment of the 2nd Armored Division, Marshall personally arranged that he be lifted from his command at Fort Myer and shifted to Fort Benning to organize a brigade of the division.

A few weeks later Marshall made Patton a brigadier general.

For George Patton, the change represented a tremendous emotional upheaval. He was leaving behind for good not only the reflected glitter of Washington at Fort Myer, but also the whole glamorous world of the Cavalry in which, except for two years whose events had receded from his mind, he had spent his professional life. A somewhat anachronistic soldier and, in the harsh light of those days, a military arm whose time was running out, Patton and the Cavalry were made for each other. He frequently wrapped up his love of the Cavalry by quoting Field Marshal Douglas Haig's felicitous phrase, "Infantry and artillery can win battles—but only Cavalry can make them worth winning."

He had deep pride in the arm and a sentimental attachment to it in his heart even when his mind was telling him that the Cavalry was rapidly losing not its glory (which he regarded as eternal), but its usefulness. Patton himself repeatedly conceded in his writings that the Cavalry was no longer either what it was cracked up to be or used to be— what Cromwell called a happy haven of honest men and free horses. It could not have endured in its pristine stage without inevitable changes after World War I. Its fire power was vastly increased with new automatic weapons; its supply train was motorized, and it was given an increasing quantity of armor of its own.

Even dedicated cavalrymen like General George K. Herr, the last pre-war Chief of Cavalry, thought that it was the ideal and natural foundation of an armored force if only because it had the tradition and experience of mobility. Moreover, the cavalry retained its atmosphere of chivalry in which a gentleman soldier could wave a bloody shirt with knightly magnanimity and decorum.

Benning was for Patton a long step down the social ladder, for the old trading post of the Creek Indians in Georgia's Muscogee County on the Chattahoochee River was the vast domain of the "matchless" Infantry, the Army's pedestrian proletariat. With none of the Cavalry's inherent aristocracy, Benning was a haven of the military *petit bourgeois* for which Patton could never work up anything more than tolerance.

However, he had neither regrets nor qualms on leaving

the Cavalry for the second time. He was getting his opportunity at last and his predestined chance to move again with the razzle-dazzle of his first association with armor 22 years before.

During these days Benning was one of the busiest hubs in the Army—a kind of proving ground for all that was new. At the Infantry School, a completely revised curriculum—inspired by the lessons of the European war—was being hammered into a new generation of officers. Aside from the tanks at the fort, Benning now also housed a brand-new élite emerging from this brand-new war overseas— the paratroopers, commanded by another cocky iconoclast, Major General William C. Lee, called "Bulldog" by his men.

At Benning, the new Brigadier General quickly found that things were not quite so simple as he had expected. He began by running into all sorts of difficulties, some of his own making, others imposed on him by the conditions of the day. For one thing, he was completely bewildered by his sudden return to his old *métier* and did not know at first how to apply the memories and experiences of the past to the new realities of *modern* armor.

In France, Patton had built his tank brigade as a personal and highly individualistic project, taking care of most of the things that had to be done by himself, often putting his own shoulder to the wheel. A commander who strongly believed in personal contact with his men, he started out at Benning by running off in all directions, exploding with energy, and trying to do everything by himself. He was forever touring his units, in a jeep or command car, or flying low over them in his private plane, breathing down the soldiers' necks and telling them not only what to do, but also how to do it.

In 1918, with the small force he had, this was possible, and maybe even effective. But now at Benning, Patton had a vast organization of hundreds of tanks, trucks, half-tracks, jeeps, motorcycles, and thousands of men, and it was plainly impossible to run this complex apparatus by means of a personal regime. Instead of whipping these men and vehicles into an efficient organization along the lines of the plans he himself had drafted, he confused and disorganized everything with his constant intervention.

Patton appeared to be floundering, and even muffing the job for which he suddenly seemed as outdated as the old tanks he once commanded. His transfer to Benning had

been viewed with considerable misgivings. When now his
colleagues at the fort looked at the blustering and energetic,
but haphazard, ways in which Patton was handling his
job, they shook their heads and asked, "Is this really that
much-vaunted Georgie Patton?" and said:

"Well, this is how a legend dies!"

Patton was given the men and the tanks he needed, but
the men were too new and the tanks were too old. Peacetime conscription was adopted in September, during the
war's blackest days in Europe, and only then did the citizen-
soldiers begin to pour in. They were promising young men
so far as appearances went, but quite different from the
rookies of the First World War. The Quartermaster Corps
reported that their bodies were smaller and their feet bigger
than those of the doughboys, but Patton thought it did not
make much difference how big or small their bodies and
feet were. What mattered was the spirit in which they
joined the Army. To his initial dismay, he found that these
boys had none of the eager enthusiasm of the men with
whom he went to war in 1917.

These were the boys of whom Meyer Berger wrote,
"Some stumbled into draft boards with farewell hangovers,
some with their womenfolk's tears still damp on their suit-
ing. Glumly they marched, broken steps, to the troop
trains." The soldiers Patton was supposed to mold into hell-
for-leather tankers were, as Hanson W. Baldwin put in in
the *New York Times,* "a partly organized rabble of khaki-
wearing civilians."

And the tanks! Most of them were ripe for the junk-
yard, with paint peeling off their steel hulls, and their in-
nards in advanced stages of decay. How in hell, Patton wondered, will he be able to build a fighting brigade with such
impossible raw material?

Then abruptly he found himself. It happened dramatically during a staff meeting that Major General Charles L.
Scott, the weather-beaten, rumpled old commander of the
2nd Armored, had called to review the problems of his
division. It was at that meeting, too, that Patton presumably acquired the sobriquet by which he came to be called
in his lifetime and is still best remembered today. He was
drifting, but he did not entirely waste his time at Benning.
He did a lot of hard thinking and planning, and he was
coming around to seeing more clearly the problems confronting him and also their solutions. He listened patiently to

the discussion, which did not seem to lead anywhere for a long time, then suddenly the inspiration hit him. Getting up, he made a rousing speech, defining concisely in his forceful language, the aims of the division and, indeed, of the Armored Force. He said that an armored division needed "blood and brains" to be effective in combat; the alliterative sound of the two "b's" appealed to him. The speech made an enormous impression on the assembled officers who later discussed it widely until the story reached the newspapermen covering Fort Benning. The reporters not only wrote up the speech itself but also sent the Patton legend off to a good start by describing how he had electrified his command with this outstanding and inspiring address. By the time the speech appeared in print, the reference to "blood and brains" came out as "blood and guts"—probably because it was more characteristic of so forceful and colorful an officer.

This, at least, is one of the several versions of the origin of Patton's famous nickname. Actually the birth of that grossly misleading "tag" is lost in the thick mist of the Patton legend. According to Rosevich (who, incidentally, never refers to the General by that nickname), it originated at Benning in the wake of that staff conference. But Robert S. Allen, the syndicated columnist who served on Patton's staff in World War II as an Intelligence officer, wrote in an article after the war that the epithet had been invented by a newspaper reporter covering tank training maneuvers in the desert around Needles, Arizona, in the spring of 1942.

Patton became a magnet that drew reporters to Benning, providing excellent copy with his brash and picturesque conduct, which he quickly recognized as a double-edged asset. It made for excellent publicity and assured write-ups for himself and his units, and filled his men with what he thought they needed most—a masculine attitude toward war, a fighting spirit, an *esprit de corps*. As far as that nickname was concerned, he was not especially fond of it but tolerated it—and never discouraged its use in print—because he thought "blood and guts" epitomized him to his troops and summarized for them the basic ingredients of their own martial spirit. The name spread quickly throughout the nation, and the general's little grandson, Pat Waters, who was then five years old adopted it for his evening prayer, asking the Lord to "take good care of old Blood and Guts."

While the "guts" part of the nickname fitted Patton, its

coupling with "blood" conveyed an implication that misrepresented him as a sanguine commander to whom the lives of soldiers did not really matter and who was willing to sacrifice them recklessly to gain glory for himself. It was a patently unfair and blatantly unjust implication. Far from being callous, Patton was actually second only to General MacArthur in his determination to conduct his operations with a stringent economy of lives. "Duty in combat," Secretary of War Robert P. Patterson said in this connection, "for general as well as for private, means disregard for personal danger; it also means an unlimited capacity for hard work. George Patton's attitude toward both was never in question. He once said: 'A pint of American sweat saves a gallon of American blood.' "

At the dedication of Patton Hall at Fort Riley, Kansas, in 1946, Judge Patterson tried to eliminate the odious nickname from Patton's memory when he said: "His personality was singularly suited to the leadership of combat troops. His picturesque quality appealed to the imagination of his men. They loved to talk about him. They did *not* call him 'Blood and Guts.' That was a reporter's invention. To the Third Army he was 'Georgie.' "

Only once did Patton take formal notice of his dubious nickname. It occurred during an improvised staff conference in a naval warehouse in Norfolk, Virginia, on the eve of the departure of his Western Task Force for North Africa, in the fall of 1942. "The newspapers," he said, "call me 'Old Blood and Guts.' That's all right. It serves its purpose. It makes good reading. But it takes more than blood and guts to win battles. It takes *brains* and guts.

"Remember that—*brains* and guts! No military leader or force ever won a battle through brains alone, or through guts alone. Each is essential for successful military operations. but not just alone. Alone they are not enough. Both qualities must be present. I expect you to use both to your utmost capacity at all times. That's all, gentlemen."

Patton returned to the theme two years later during the Battle of the Bulge. Inside Bastogne a handful of Americans were trying desperately to withstand the onslaught of a German Panzer army. "The Third Army was rushing furiously to the north from its positions in the Moselle Valley," Colonel Allen recalled, "but its full strength had not yet arrived. Patton's staff was worried and gloomy. But he was cheerful and buoyant."

Again Patton held an improvised staff conference, trying to transfuse his own confidence and determination into the bloodstream of his associates. He conceded that the situation was very tense, and perhaps even critical. But it was not hopeless by any means! "All you've got to use," he told his staff, "is *brains* and guts. That wins polo games and it wins battles. We've got plenty of brains and we've got plenty of guts. There's nothing to it. We'll lick those Germans hands down."

Behind that glib nickname fashioned for tabloid headlines was a man somewhat in the mold of John Bright, the British patriot who dared speak out against the Crimean War in the House of Commons, emboldened by the knowledge that no word or deed of his had contributed to a squandering of his country's precious blood. It was, indeed, Patton's "priceless consolation to the end of his existence" that his casualties were among the lowest, even when the going became rough and the opposition stiff during "the terrific battles" of 1944, for example, as his Third Army struggled to breach the outer defenses of Metz.

But that was still years away—seemingly light years in the circumstances of this exasperating, ambiguous year of unpreparedness. Yet Patton was sharpening his "brains and guts" for exactly that sort of future.

Now it suddenly dawned on him how to remedy the situation and whip his brigade into the best "Goddamn tankers in the Army." He also found means to patch up the old tanks, at least temporarily, pending the arrival of the new armor which Ordnance was rushing off the blueprints. One of his mechanics who despaired when he could not get spare parts for the tanks once announced casually that most of them were ordinary parts he used to order from Sears, Roebuck. Patton seized upon the remark. When it proved impossible to obtain the parts through regular channels—partly because of the red tape and partly because the Army simply did not have any at that stage—he ordered them from Sears, Roebuck and paid the bill out of his own pocket. Since most of his 325 tanks were in woeful state of disrepair and needed parts (not to mention the 800 trucks, 500 motorcycles, 500 half-tracks, 360 jeeps, and hundreds of other vehicles of his car park), it came to a tidy sum. Once he had to send an $800 check for a single order, and in the end only Patton knew how much it had cost him to keep his vehicles rolling. It was a secret he took to the grave.

Patton used the indirect approach, which he found the best while training his brigade in France in World War I, to mold these men into fighting tankers. "To be a good soldier," he wrote, "a man must have discipline, self-respect, pride in his unit and in his country, a high sense of duty and obligation to his comrades and his superiors, and self-confidence born of demonstrated ability." He viewed the men who now poured in daily to serve under him and learn to become soldiers with the quizzical eyes of the psychologist. Patton soon came to certain conclusions which not only explained to him what made these men tick but also suggested how he could instill the discipline and pride, the sense of duty and self-confidence he thought they needed.

Last but not least, he decided that his tankers needed a uniform of their own to distinguish them from the other soldiers. He remembered how his grandfather had designed a uniform for his regiment in the Civil War. He even had a faded photograph of the second George Patton in his gaudy Confederate outfit to guide him. What emerged was a combination of Winston Churchill's famous "siren suit"— a glorified version of the Army fatigues—and the picturesque costume of those circus performers who are shot out of cannons. It was all green with red stripes, topped by a gold football helmet Patton obtained from the Green Bay Packers.

Always the first to undertake anything dangerous he expected his men to do, he was the first to wear the suit, too. When he showed up in it at Tiger Camp in Benning, one of the tankers who was up to date on his comic strips exclaimed:

"Look! The Green Hornet!"

The name spread from Benning to Washington, and though his own men did not pick it up and continued to call him the "Old Man," Patton came to be called the "Green Hornet" in the War Department. He never succeeded in persuading the Army to adopt the uniform for the Armored Force—or even to let him issue it to his own men—but he himself continued to wear it for some time. During that period inspection trips to the 2nd Armored became increasingly urgent and frequent, and Tiger Camp was swamped by visiting brass. The generals flew down from Washington on one pretense or another, but really to see with their own eyes Patton as the "Green Hornet."

In his uniform, with his contorted ferocious fighting face and his ivory-handled pistols around his midriff, Patton had to be seen to be believed.

While Brigadier General Patton was preoccupied with the organization of the units entrusted to his care, a titanic struggle was taking place behind the scenes in the War Department on whose outcome depended the entire future of armor in the Army. The National Defense Act of 1920 explicitly prohibited the Tank Corps and stipulated that armor must be distributed throughout the Army. Therefore, when General Marshall decided to create an Armored Force he had to set it up "provisionally, for purposes of service test," pending a final determination of its status.

The establishment of the Force as a quasi-autonomous organization brought into the open all the simmering old controversies and differences of outlook. This was indeed a radical organic change, reaching deeply into virtually every unit. The tank units of Infantry and Cavalry now came under the control of the new Force. Even certain Field Artillery and service units were handed over to it. Moreover, it was to include "all armored corps and divisions, and all GHQ Reserve tank units."

Major General Adna R. Chaffee, former Commanding Officer of the 1st Cavalry Regiment at Fort Knox (within which mechanization and modernization had progressed furthest), was made Chief of the Armored Force. Although his roots were in the Cavalry, General Chaffee was an enthusiastic proponent of armor. He gathered around himself a loyal and articulate group of armor enthusiasts who envisaged the Armored Force somewhat along the lines of the Air Corps, which was then gaining increasing autonomy inside the Army. Although these officers could not, of course, evade the provisions of the law, they were looking forward to creating a force that would have its own autonomous organization as an "arm" in fact, although not in name, with its own supply organization and everything else that was assigned to an independent arm.

However, they met with violent opposition, especially from the G-3 Division of the General Staff, headed by Brigadier General Frank M. Andrews. It was determined to prevent the establishment of an Armored Army as a permanent organization. Despite the demonstration of the German armor's tremendous effectiveness in France, a powerful group of influential officers still refused to see in it a new power source of what came to be called the strategic onslaught. In their pessimism and defeatism, they argued that the tank would be an effective weapon only so long as it was new, but would come a cropper as soon as adequate counterweapons could be devised.

Instead of promoting the development of armor, these men concentrated on the development of antitank weapons while pulling the strings to thwart the success of the Armored Force and throwing monkey wrenches into its rapid and useful evolution.

Patton was following the controversy from the sidelines. Although he was far too busy at Benning, and did not participate in the great debate, there was no doubt where he stood on an issue in which, as he saw it, history was repeating itself and was now forcing a belated decision. He had already been through all these arguments in 1920, when Congress was considering the future of the Tank Corps and he spoke up in its defense. "Tanks are a new and special weapon," Patton then wrote, "newer than, as special, and certainly as valuable as the airplane. Can one imagine infantry airplanes manned by detailed doughboys; or artillery airplanes manned by wagon soldiers or cosmoline kids; or yet cavalry airplanes ridden by sturdy troops with the use of 'lateral aid'? Hardly!

"The tank is a special, technical, and vastly powerful weapon. It certainly is neither a cavalryman nor an infantryman. Yet, give it half a chance, over suitable terrain and on proper missions, and it will mean the difference between defeat and victory to the infantry or cavalry with which it is cooperating.

"What is wanted, then, is neither infantry tanks nor cavalry tanks, but a Tank Corps—a special mobile general headquarters reserve, to be detailed, as circumstances demand, with whichever arm it can best cooperate."

The controversy came to a head in March, 1941. A G-3 memorandum rejected the need for an armored army, while the Armored Force—on the basis of a study made at Fort

Knox of armored organizations in Europe—was pushing its campaign for autonomy of command. Its proponents received powerful aid from G-2 which, on March 1st, issued a memorandum entitled "Evaluation of Modern Battle Forces," an analysis of armored warfare in Poland and France in 1939-40. It was inclined to accept armor as the decisive factor in the lightning-like victories of the *Wehrmacht*.

The memorandum was submitted to General Marshall, who forwarded it to General Lesley J. McNair, a wiry little genius masterminding the organization of the new Army at the head of General Headquarters.

General McNair was broadminded and unburdened by ingrained prejudices. Only recently he had expressed his respect for armor when he wrote in his comments on the G-3 memorandum, "In my view, the essential element of armored action is a powerful blow delivered by surprise. While the armored units may be broken up and attached to division and army corps, it is readily conceivable, and indeed probable, that the entire force, under a single command, may be thrown against a decisive point." It is interesting to note that this was exactly—and well-nigh verbatim—Patton's conclusion, not in 1941, but in 1918, when he recognized how the dispersal of the tanks at St. Mihiel and in the Meuse-Argonne offensive dissipated their effectiveness.

McNair, however, was still not convinced of the continued viability of armor, for he, too, believed that its effectiveness in German hands was at least partly due to the absence or ineffectiveness of Polish and French defenses. And he was certainly opposed to the establishment of the Armored Force along the extreme lines proposed by its exponents.

The burning issue was decided a few days later—against the Armored Force. On March 25th the Office of the Chief of Staff issued instructions which gave it less autonomy than G-3 had recommended and even less than it had had up to that date. G-3 was now directed to make the decision binding with a final directive to be ready "within two days."

Although the instructions were issued by his office, General Marshall had apparently not been consulted about them or else was misled in their interpretation. On March 27th, before the definitive directive was completed, General Chaffee took his case directly to the Chief of Staff, and

Marshall immediately reversed the decision of his own office. Acting upon his oral instructions, G-3 now prepared a directive under which the Armored Force came into its own as part of a balanced army with ample autonomy and latitude for expansion. General Marshall wrote "O.K., GCM" on the G-3 paper, and it was issued on April 3rd. Although the directive was as significant for its omissions as for its positive statements, it established the Armored Force as a more or less permanent organization along the lines of General Marshall's own ideas.

Out of the storm and stress, out of these trials and errors developed the force which was to score so triumphantly in the Second World War. It was an ideal organization for the immediate task ahead. The Armored Force came into existence through shameful bickerings and backstabbings, but somehow the political infighting was not wasted. An independent armored "arm" operating on its own could never have achieved what armor in the hands of virtuosos like General Patton succeeded in accomplishing in World War II, in close cooperation with the other arms within the Army.

But the battle was still far from won. This became abundantly evident in the next few months when the Army left its training grounds and moved into the field to test its mettle in maneuvers.

Patton's own blue period of trials and errors was also at an end. He had learned his lessons. He gave up the intimate and informal management system that hung over in his mind from his service in France and abandoned the impulsive, but impractical, ways of his Cavalry regime. Virtually overnight after that remarkable performance at General Scott's staff conference, he became a hard-headed, strictly utilitarian tank boss down to the Georgian earth.

It was evident from the rapid development of his brigade that the initial misgivings had been exaggerated and premature. During those dark days pressure was put on General Marshall to replace him with someone who was, as Patton's detractors put it, better attuned to the times. But the Chief of Staff refused to throw his protégé to the wolves. Now he was fully vindicated. When Marshall set up I

Armored Corps and named General Scott to its command, Patton was made a major general and given the 2nd Armored Division to do with as he pleased.

It had taken him almost two decades to advance from major to colonel. Even in 1940 his chances of becoming a general appeared remote. Now he went up two notches in only five months, and the end was not in sight. *"C'est la guerre,"* he said with a grin, not giving a damn, of course, that the United States was not yet actually and officially in the fighting war.

He was turning the 2nd Armored into a precision combat instrument in his own new image. Still as gaudy and demonstrative as ever, Patton continued to maintain personal contact with his men, but he had to find different ways to do it. He introduced a method of exercising his influence mostly through his staff and commanders (to whom he was forever writing lucid and detailed directives) while retaining for himself what he, with almost religious fervor, called spiritual leadership. He could no longer deal with his men as individuals, his organization was becoming far too vast; now he had to sustain his contact with the troops collectively. He ordered an amphitheater built at Benning and assembled his men for a series of rip-roaring lectures. They were fun. His pep talks were highly spiced with the bluntest four-letter words soldiers rarely heard from superiors above the rank of drill sergeant.

"War is a killing business," he told his tankers, clearly identifying Germany as the enemy, although the United States was still months away from war with the Third Reich. "You've got to spill their blood, or they'll spill yours. Rip 'em up the belly, or shoot 'em in the guts."

The men did not know what to make of a commanding officer who looked like a general but talked like a top kick. Their bafflement gave birth to the Patton legend, establishing their general as a mysterious figure in their minds. Patton's personality did present many perplexing contradictions to confuse far more sophisticated people than these raw recruits. He was everything his men thought he was and, then, a lot of different things besides.

It was during these days that Corporal Joe Rosevich, a shy young teacher from Wilmington, Delaware (who was serving time, as he regarded it, in Patton's brigade at Benning), suddenly found himself the object of considerable sympathy wherever he went on the post. He could not

explain why everybody he knew—or even hardly knew—
became so kind and considerate. Clerks in the office of the
68th Armored Regiment where he worked as a stenogra-
pher greeted him with a "Hello, Joe" that had a definite tone
of compassion, if not commiseration. Sergeants came up to
him, patted him on the back without the slightest provocation, and told him, "Don't worry, kid, everything'll be all
right"—at a time when Rosevich was *not* worrying at all
and thought that everything *was* all right.

Then a sergeant named Monroe T. Buels who worked in
the big office took him for a drink, picked up the tab,
and invited him to "Have another, Joe," as if trying to
fortify Rosevich for something he was about to tell him.
Buels came out with it after the third round, Scotch, straight
on the rocks.

"Well, Joe, you'll have to find out sooner or later. So
you better get it from me first and gently before Lieutenant
Jenson tells you officially."

"Tells me what?" Rosevich asked, not unduly excited, because he was a stolid man by nature and nothing ever
unduly excited him.

"Joe, old boy, they've picked you to be private secretary
to the Old Man."

"Gee!" That was all Rosevich said.

Rosevich received his orders that afternoon. Next morning he was in the outer office where Patton's personal staff
was working under Colonel Gay, the Chief of Staff, and
Lieutenant Richard N. Jenson, the General's aide. Hardly
had he settled behind his new desk when he was called by
the buzzer into the General's inner sanctum. He picked up
his steno pad and went, by now amply awed by all those
commiserations and warnings—and by what he had heard
of the fate of his predecessor, a hapless boy named Benny
Hall who had become the victim of one of Patton's monumental rages only the day before.

Rosevich entered the General's office, a spacious room at
whose far end stood Patton's desk flanked by the Stars and
Stripes and the flag of the 2nd Armored. He stopped in front
of the desk, and stood there stiffly at attention, waiting like
an ancient gladiator for the lion to pounce. But nothing in
this quiet scene portended anything like that.

The General was sitting at his desk, scribbling with a
rapid hand on a yellow pad. He was in shirtsleeves, wearing
a pair of red suspenders. As Rosevich waited, his curious

eyes surveyed the man from top to bottom, and came to rest on his feet under the desk. "I'll be darned," Rosevich thought. The Old Man was wearing bedroom slippers.

Suddenly Patton looked up. "I'm General Patton, corporal," he said in his high-pitched voice. "What's your name?"

Rosevich introduced himself with as much snap as he was capable of.

"Fine, corporal," Patton said. "Sit down—right there, on that chair." Now Rosevich was jolted by another surprise. Patton had a pince-nez on the bridge of his nose, one of those old-fashioned eyeglasses held in place by a spring. Whatever apprehension there was left in Corporal Rosevich now vanished without a trace. How the hell can you be scared of an old man, he thought, who wears bedroom slippers to the office on an army post and looks at you from behind nosepinchers?

From this day in January, 1942, to June, 1945, from Fort Benning in Georgia to Pilsen in Czechoslovakia, Rosevich remained with Patton as his private secretary. He served him—as did every member of his staff—in a state of ceaseless animation, never knowing when the Old Man might hit him with one of his outbursts.

"On my very first day as Patton's secretary," Rosevich recalls, "I had occasion to see that I was serving two men rather than one. General Patton was the fusion of two men who lived in different worlds. One was his own world of calm efficiency, discipline and order. The other was the world of his immediate environment—our world of extreme tension and nervous strain."

Joe's introduction to Patton's two worlds was abrupt. It came with the first dictation. Patton leaned back in his upholstered swivel chair, puffed on his cigar, and looked at a few notes he had made. Then he started to dictate.

"For a while I was too preoccupied with my own good fortune (or misfortune, I didn't know)," Rosevich said, "that elevated me to this enviable (or unenviable) position. I wasn't actually aware of the meaning of his words. I was just taking them down mechanically in my shorthand book. But gradually it dawned on me that the General was dictating to me a draft of one of his widely quoted fire-eating speeches which earned for him the nickname 'Blood-and-Guts.' But," Rosevich added, "you would never have recognized it as such from the way Patton dictated it."

He spoke in a voice that was fit for the pulpit. Yet what

he said in that quiet voice of his was hardly printable. He spoke of the two most important elements in battle—the need of "guts" and "the desire to spill the enemy's blood." Yet not once did he raise his voice while he dictated these words.

Rosevich was completely dazed by the contrast between the rip-roaring contents of the speech and the cultured, quiet voice of the man who was creating it. However, he was soon launched out of his daze. As soon as he returned to Patton's office with a transcribed copy of the speech, the General called in a couple of his aides to rehearse it in front of an audience. He worked up to a fury. Those purple passages erupted like hot lava from a volcano.

"I was standing there," Rosevich said, "watching the spectacle in speechless awe. Then he came to the end of the speech. Without the slightest pause of warning, Patton made a complete reconversion to his calm self. He sat down and in almost scientific terms, explained the theory behind his speech to us.

"He said that the performance we had just watched was exactly that—merely a performance, a put-up show, a calculated and rehearsed act of bravado. He was convinced, he said, that the young men of America needed such a toughening because they had grown soft and careless in the good life."

Patton said with emphasis: "The whole situation is perfectly ridiculous. You cannot change the mental habits of these boys overnight. You have to shock them out of their ordinary habits and thinking with the kind of language you've just heard in the speech.

"Here," he said, "where I said, 'Rip your bayonets into the bloody bowels of the enemy,' this is one of the best! I see it again and again. It's intended for its shock effect. It's a boisterous method of training and commanding men. But it's certain to pay dividends in ground gained and blood saved."

It was during this quaint rehearsal that Joe Rosevich heard Pattons' famous high-pitched voice raised in apparent anger for the first time. He did not hear it raised again until June, 1942, when they moved into the California desert to train a new generation of tankers for imminent service overseas.

Shortly after their arrival in the desert Rosevich heard what he thought was the genuine article: a real Patton outburst and not merely a rehearsal. The General had a visitor in his tent while Rosevich was typing something for him outside. The visitor was Major General Charles L. Scott who had just returned from North Africa where he had watched Montgomery's epic battle with Rommel. Scott went on to California to relate to Patton everything he had seen.

Soon enough, Rosevich remembers, a raucous voice filled the air and shook the tent. It was booming and menacing, rough, tough and profane. But it wasn't the voice of Patton. It was General Scott. "Listening to them," Rosevich said, "I found myself thinking of Patton and of the cockeyed legend that was then beginning to spring up about him. Scott was closer to the common picture of Patton than Patton himself.

"I don't mean to say that Patton's temper didn't exist or that it was only a temporary expedient—as if someone could turn Niagara Falls on and off like a kitchen faucet. Patton's temper was real, all right," his former secretary concluded. "But it was a tremendous fire burning in an inner furnace under his delicate skin. He knew how to regulate that fire with the thermostat of his complex character."

The backbreaking work to which Patton was subjecting his men produced some of the usual bellyaching to begin with. But gradually the griping dissolved into ready submission inspired by that enlightened form of obedience the psychologists call will-to-cooperate. After a while, Patton the ordinary mortal disappeared from their minds, to be replaced by someone who resembled one of the more rambunctious members of the hierarchy on Mount Olympus. He was, in the eyes of his men, a strange mixture of man and superman. "Like God," Staff Sergeant Aeuhl E. Pullen said of Patton while they were still at Benning, "he has the damndest way of showing up when things go wrong. Unlike God, he dashes leg-long into a creek, gets a stalled tank and its wretched crew out of the water and back into the line of march practically by the power of his curses. You are all right as long as you're doing exactly what you're supposed to do and you don't have to be too brilliant in doing it. But you better don't lay an egg before the Old Man. He doesn't like it."

On February 17th Patton ordered his men to put on the

division's first review. "I want to see," he said, "how men, officers and matériel show up in a big exercise." Now the whole division felt like Sergeant Pullen. Everybody literally prayed that none of the tanks—on this day of all days—should lay an egg before the Old Man.

It was a kind of graduation-day parade, for the 2nd Armored had been perfected as far as it was possible in this short span of time. It was also the parting of the ways for many officers and men about to be shifted to tank schools to train the rookies, to new companies, or to form the cadres of the 3rd and 4th Armored Divisions in the process of being organized.

This was the last day, for example, for tall Major Leo F. Kengla Jr. in command of Company D of the 68th Armored Regiment. He had been shifted to duty as a battalion executive. His replacement, a young first lieutenant, was getting command of the company and his promotion to captain simultaneously. The turnover was rapid through the division. Patton was using the pressure-cooker method to produce the officers and men needed for this breath-taking expansion of the Armored Force.

On the day of the review, a cold, damp wind swept Fort Benning. The tents were streaked after an all-night rain. The tanks, the scout cars, the trucks, the jeeps rumbled into position on water-soaked streets. The 1,200 vehicles of the division were drawn up in a vast square before a reviewing stand on which Patton and a group of visiting dignitaries appeared as undistinguishable blotches to the men lined up in front of their vehicles.

Suddenly a shiny tank, its turret ringed with red, white and blue, jumped away from the reviewing stand and jounced around the field. It was Patton's personal tank. A barely visible projection above the turret, with helmet screwed tightly to his head, the Old Man roared past a regiment of truck-borne infantry, past the motorcyclists, past the mounted antitank guns. Finally he veered toward the tank regiments, then whirled back to the stand.

Orders were barked and the tanks were buttoned up. They rumbled past the Old Man at 20 miles per hour, the odor of warm oil and the steady rhythmic sound of the motors filling the wet air. The tanks, driven with virtuoso skill, passed the reviewing stand in perfect formation.

When it was all over and the vehicles had returned to their park, the men were given sandwiches and hot coffee

and waited in their orderly tents for officers to bring word
from Patton. It took a while, but finally the word came, and
as the officers raced back to their units with the message,
the good news was passed from mouth to mouth, from tank
to tank:

"The Old Man liked the show!"

The division relaxed. The men whistled merrily. It was
worth-while—all this sweat and toil, the blasting they got
from Patton—everything.

"The Old Man liked the show!"

That day Patton, too, had his reward. Like a debutante,
his division was ready to be presented to the world at the
Army's own grand coming-out party—the maneuvers of
1941.

On January 28, 1941, General Marshall had announced that
the Army would have a million men by March and that the
four field armies would be tested for the first time in the
biggest maneuvers in American military history. Exercises
on a substantial scale had been held in August, 1940, in the
immediate wake of France's fall and while Hitler was preparing the so-called "Operation Sea Lion," his invasion of
Britain, but they were disappointing. The Army was too
fresh and the lessons the German campaigns had taught
were not yet completely absorbed. But what made the 1940
maneuvers a total failure was the breakdown of umpiring.
A new umpire's manual had been prepared and arrangements were being made to place umpires in the field with
moving units.

General McNair, who organized the 1941 maneuvers and
was to direct them, insisted that they be conducted in an
atmosphere of brutal impartiality with all the realism of
actual warfare except physical destruction and casualties.
"The truth is sought," he wrote in a letter of May 15th to
the various commanding generals, "regardless of whether
pleasant or unpleasant, or whether it supports or con-
demns our present organization and tactics." The shadow
of the German victories was hanging over the maneuvers,
which were designed to reconstruct the recent campaigns
as closely as possible. When, in preparation for maneuvers
in Louisiana, the signal officers of General Krueger's Third

Army proposed to erect a line of telephone poles, McNair canceled the project as unrealistic, suggesting that Krueger ask his staff "how the German army [had] made such preparations for their campaign in Poland."

The 2nd Armored Division was scheduled to participate heavily in the huge field tests. Its maneuvers were to begin in June with relatively minor tactical exercises in Tennessee, continue with elaborate maneuvers in Louisiana in September, and end with the biggest test of them all in the Carolinas in November.

Patton was looking forward eagerly to the maneuvers because he had some accounts to settle and decided that this was the time. The school within the War Department that was pushing the antitank idea had by no means been silenced by the appearance of the April 3rd directive. It was, in fact, gaining the upper hand. A conspiracy was developing in the War Department to take the wind out of the sails of the "armor boys" and once and for all discredit the tank as a panacea. It was no longer a secret in the inner circles of the Army that the big maneuvers—which General McNair hoped to stage in "an atmosphere of complete impartiality"—were being deliberately rigged against armor.

This was the cue for Patton! As soon as he learned of the conspiracy through the grapevine, he took his division through special exercises in a remote part of the Fort Benning reservation to prepare it secretly for a "mission," on the success of which, he ardently believed, depended the survival of armor in the Army.

Patton's doctrinal concepts of tank tactics jumped prefabricated from his fertile brain in 1918. But then they underwent a painful evolution between the two wars. In their final form they were influenced by the Germans, whose tank warfare in 1940 did not inspire but merely confirmed his own theoretical ideas. He was especially impressed with Guderian's handling of armor in Western Europe and Rommel's shrewd coordination of infantry and armor on the operational level.

Superimposed on this synthesis were Patton's innate contributions to tactics springing from his personality—dash, daring, speed, the willingness to take *calculated* risks. His own combat principles, as he himself called them, were spelled out in a classic paper, his "Letter of Instructions Number 2" to the Third Army. Composed in April, 1944, while waiting in England for the cross-Channel invasion, it presented the final distillation of ideas that had developed slowly through the years and matured and crystallized at Benning while the General was working with the 2nd Armored.

This, then, was Patton's creed of combat that the maneuvers of 1941 were to test and prove:

"There is no approved solution to any tactical situation.

"There is only one tactical principle which is not subject to change. It is: 'To use the means at hand to inflict the maximum amount of wounds, death, and destruction on the enemy in the minimum time.'

"In battle, casualties vary directly with the time you are exposed to effective fire. Your own fire reduces the effectiveness and volume of the enemy's fire, while rapidity of attack shortens the time of exposure. A pint of sweat will save a gallon of blood!

"Battles are won by frightening the enemy. Fear is induced by inflicting death and wounds on him. Death and wounds are produced by fire. Fire from the rear is more deadly and three times more effective than fire from the front, but to get fire behind the enemy, you must hold him by frontal fire and move rapidly around his flank. Frontal attacks against prepared positions should be avoided if possible.

" 'Catch the enemy by the nose with fire and kick him in the pants with fire emplaced through movement.'

"Hit hard soon . . .

"You can never be too strong . . .

"The larger the force and the more violence you use in the attack, whether it be men, tanks, or ammunition, the smaller will be your proportional losses.

"Never yield ground. It is cheaper to hold what you have than retake what you have lost . . .

"Our mortars and artillery are superb weapons when they are firing. When silent they are junk—see that they keep firing.

"Use roads to march on; fields to fight on . . .

"Never permit a unit to dig in until the final objective is reached; then dig, wire, and mine.

"Take plenty of time to set up an attack . . .

"The primary mission of armored units is the attacking of infantry and artillery. The enemy's rear is the happy hunting ground for armor. Use every means to get it there.

"There is no such thing as 'tank country' in a restrictive

sense. Some types of country are better than others, but tanks have and can operate anywhere."

The maxim about holding the enemy by the nose with fire and kicking him in the pants with movement, which was the backbone of the whole "Letter," was first developed by Patton in 1925. He held on to it throughout his life and it became the basic principle of his generalship in World War II.

At the same time, while emphasizing the overwhelming importance of the rapidity of attack, he made the crucial distinction between haste and speed. This more than anything else demonstrates that Patton was, for all his impetuosity and dash, a cautious and sensible general whose dominant thought in battle was to gain the most at the least cost in blood.

"Reconnaissance" had an intimately personal meaning for Patton. He felt safe only when he saw things for himself.

And last but not least, though he is remembered primarily as a "tank general," he held to a strict and wise balance between infantry and armor.

Now on the eve of the maneuvers, his "battle plan" was clear in his mind. If those damned fools in Washington rigged the exercises to prove their point about the superiority of antitank weapons and show up the tank as "junk," he would show them that armor was trump. The nation never learned about this because its highly technical and professional aspects were neither comprehensible nor appealing to the civilian. And yet, riding on this showdown was the crucial issue of victory or defeat, with one group gambling on antitank weapons and the other betting on the tanks. It was fortunate that, thanks largely to Patton's demonstrations in the maneuvers, the latter group won out in 1941, and, consequently, the United States was on the right road when it had to march to war.

On June 12, 1941, the 2nd Armored Division, as proud and polished an organization as the United States Army would ever produce, left Fort Benning on the first leg of what became a 10,000-mile excursion trip, to take part in maneuvers of General Ben Lear's Second Army around

Manchester in Tennessee. Patton's armor rolled into the exercises just when a British disaster in the Western Desert appeared to strengthen the hands of the antitankers. The Germans of Field Marshal Rommel had destroyed 200 British tanks on the Egyptian-Libyan frontier virtually on the eve of the Tennessee maneuvers.

With this strike against him, Patton joined the issue, more than ever determined to expose the fateful fallacy of the antitank crowd. The maneuvers jumped off on June 20th, and Patton immediately took his division into the kind of hell-raising action he had devised for the exercises, hoping to upset the carefully laid plans of General McNair, who directed the maneuvers, as well as the calculations of the antitank advocates.

Right off the bat, he cut behind the lines of the 5th Infantry Division, "decimated" it, then captured its command post. The "hell buggies" of the 2nd Armored continued to run wild, and were winning hands down when McNair ordered the umpires to cut Patton down to size. After that, every decision went against him. But so devastating were his tactics that in the end McNair was forced to call off the exercises 12 hours ahead of their allotted period because Patton had wrapped them up and left nothing more to do.

Nevertheless the antitank crowd presented the experience as a tremendous victory for them. In a letter from the maneuvers, McNair wrote to a friend that he had gained "considerable encouragement" for his advocacy of antitank units. "It can be expected," he added, "that the location of hostile armored elements will be known practically constantly, thus permitting antitank opposition to be moved correspondingly, and massed at the proper point"—a conclusion that was unsupported by the exercises.

"The lessons to be learned from this debut of American armor," wrote Colonel Semmes, "were apparently lost to much of the 'high command.' Instead of seeking to 'harness the tide' to our own advantage, every effort seemed bent on 'stemming the tide.' For example, the epidemic of antitank measures, the doctrine of tank destroyers, and the accentuation of the technical and mechanical weaknesses of tanks and armor were exploited rather than the devastating shock action inherent in armor."

Now that Patton had showed his hand, the opposition was ready for him when next he took his division into the

Louisiana maneuvers in which General Lear's Second Army was to clash with General Walter E. Krueger's Third Army (whose Chief of staff was an obscure young colonel variously described in the press as Eisenborn and Eisenberg). In the light of Tennessee, General McNair reorganized his umpire system and told the 2,000 hand-picked judges during a special briefing: "These exercises are designed to test tank warfare in the face of intelligent antitank defenses. We are definitely out to see if and how we can crush a modern tank offensive."

Then off the record he admonished them: "I want armor used properly in these maneuvers, and Patton must not be allowed to run all over the countryside as he did in the Tennessee maneuvers."

The two great armies gathered in the tough pine country of East Texas and West Louisiana, on the Red, Sabine and Calcasieu Rivers. The terrain was broken up by rice fields, scum-covered stagnant waters, thick forests of pine, poplar, cypress, willow and live oak festooned with Spanish moss. It was decidedly not what some people called "tank country."

Patton entered this one in a sporting spirit, for now he was not only eager to show up the antitankers but, perhaps even more, to win a bet. On the eve of the maneuvers, Major General John A. Greeley, commanding the 2nd Infantry Division in General Krueger's Blue Force, offered a $50 reward for the capture of Patton "dead or alive." Not a man to be outdone in any betting, Patton promptly raised the ante, and offered $100 for the capture of Greeley.

Zero Hour was 5:30 A.M., September 15th.

Jumping off and rolling on through cypress swamps and pine thickets, Patton's tankers went hell-bent looking for Greeley. Outflanking the whole Blue Force arrayed against them, they came upon his CP near Lake Charles, and that was that. Greeley was "scalped" on the first morning of the exercises by a team of Patton's "hell buggies."

The maneuvers went on beneath lowering gray skies and intermittent downpours, which canalized the terrain and were supposed to confine the tanks. But Patton's armor was rolling on in open defiance of the elements. On the 16th it threw the whole Third Army into a panic when the division retired northwest across the Sabine River into Texas, spinning somewhere on a mysterious wide flanking move—until stopped by the umpires. The decision went against Lear and Patton's tanks. At the halfway mark of the exercises, the umpires ruled that the Second Army had been "almost completely annihilated."

Patton returned to the second phase with vengeance. Despite worsening weather, including a hurricane scare, and growing terrain difficulties, he threw his armor into a vast enveloping movement. He was now determined to show what the purposeful use of armor could accomplish under vigorous leadership. His division was now with Blue. Its puzzling moves were followed with fascinated interest by General Krueger's Chief of Staff who, of course, was Colonel Dwight D. Eisenhower.

The climactic problem of this second phase, which started at noon on September 24th, was the defense of Shreveport, Louisiana, against a tank assault. Everything seemed to favor the defenders. In the wake of a veritable deluge, the streams became muddy torrents and the rivers raging floods. The bayous were swollen and mottled with dead branches, silt and mud. Then the rains returned and fell in wind-driven sheets all over the 30,000-square-mile maneuver area, the gale tearing down tents and buffeting the troops. The roads, slick with water, turned into quagmires.

Now Patton had an added special reason to show what he could do, even under these impossible circumstances. General Marshall had arrived to observe the maneuvers. If until now Patton was playing to the grandstand, from now on he was putting on his show exclusively for the Chief of Staff.

"The "Battle of Shreveport" began on September 27th. Patton had issued verbal orders: "We'll take the city no matter what, and we'll take it from the rear." With that he led his division on a fantastic 380-mile encircling move which took him as deep as Glade Water into Texas; then he drove east again, pushing 18 miles down defiles between marshy land from Caddo Lake, reaching the northern suburbs of Shreveport and breaking through the Second Army's massed antitank defenses.

It was 4:45 P.M. on the 28th. The umpires were waving their flags frantically. Shreveport was ringed, its fall imminent. Patton's tanks were occupying the water works at the end of Cross Bayou Bridge. What now?

Orders were quickly issued at Monroe, Louisiana, where

General McNair had his headquarters. "Cease fire!"

Twenty-four hours ahead of schedule! Patton had done it again!

British observers at the exercises expressed amazement at the speed and mobility of the tanks. But McNair thought differently. In his critique he said pointedly: "The Army has not yet learned how to handle armored divisions." Patton was criticized for a few stray tanks which, because of mechanical failures, he had left "marking the path" of his decisive flank march.

Next came the Carolina maneuvers in which the First Army was pitted against IV Corps reinforced by I Armored Corps. This was something Patton looked forward to with particular glee and relish.

The First Army was commanded by Lieutenant General Hugh A. Drum!

It promised to be an encounter he would not have missed for anything.

Drum personally commanded II and VI Corps of his First Army, some 130,000 men arrayed in a vast area east of the Pee Dee River, between Candor and Chesterfield, South Carolina. He sided with the antitank crowd, and was determined to prove once and for all that armor was *not* the wave of the future.

The newspapers of November 15th appeared with banner headlines.

"Answer to Tanks Put to Test Today," one of them read. "Secret Defense Developed by Drum."

He did, indeed, have in his Blue Force a formidable assembly of antitank units, including tanks, armored cars mounting AT guns, planes, and three whole antitank battalions taken over from the Louisiana maneuvers. His forces had been training "secretly" at Fort Bragg for weeks —"for the Big Test."

Lined up against him was what the papers called "the strongest mechanized and motorized force the United States Army ever assembled"—two armored divisions.

Back of it all was General McNair, with his headquarters at Wingate, North Carolina. Again 2,000 umpires were out with their lethal flags all over in the maneuver area.

But Patton had his attention focused on a single objective —Drum.

He deployed his forces during the cold, rainy night until he was moving toward the jump-off in a column 20 miles long. The attack began at 6:30 A.M. on November 16th. Less than an hour later McNair's headquarters were electrified by a signal from the field. It read:

"Lieutenant General Drum captured in Chester, S.C., by elements of Company D of 82nd Reconnaissance Battalion, 2nd Armored Division."

Patton's behavior at these maneuvers may seem adolescent. War is the ultimate in teamwork. The battle turns on cogwheels. No individual unit can arrogate to itself tactical missions without doing some harm to the over-all operations plan. Patton knew this, of course, and did not tolerate any free-wheeling departures from his own set plans when his subordinates tried to get away with them.

However, he did in the Tennessee-Louisiana-Carolina maneuvers exactly what later, when the tables were turned, he censured others for. He set up his 2nd Armored Division as a wheel within the wheel and conducted his campaign with arbitrary and, indeed, opportunistic strokes, instead of being a cog in the wheel and contributing his best to the advantage of the whole.

His *coups de main,* such as the prankish capture of General Drum, were definitely damaging to the efficient prosecution of the exercises. The capture of an enemy's commanding general may be a great, and even decisive, *coup.* But this was no real war. By taking Drum from his headquarters at Chester, Patton disorganized the entire maneuver, which was essentially an experiment to produce certain clues the Army urgently sought.

With Drum removed, the First Army was rendered temporarily incapable of performing its assigned function. McNair was, therefore, properly scandalized. His annoyance was aggravated when Patton vanished with Drum and could not be found for some time; McNair, meanwhile, was looking for him all over the maneuver area to order him to release Drum at once.

Patton was the *enfant terrible* of these exercises. There was, however, a certain factor in these war games that places the events and Patton's part in them in a different light.

As Patton perceived it, his job was to prove the fallacy

of the notion and prove it by whatever means he had at his
disposal. He was, of course, impulsive and boisterous by
nature, and so he went about proving his point impulsively
and boisterously. Yet he succeeded in proving it conclusively—a clear case of the end justifying the means.

His success was not immediately apparent. Those who listened to McNair's critique on November 29th had the
definite impression that armor had lost its case, even though
the two armored divisions had scooped out deep scallops of
Drum's line on a 60-mile front. They virtually annihilated
the First Army with pincer attacks that were tactically similar to the enormously effective wedge and *Kessel* methods
the Germans were using in Russia. McNair did criticize
Drum for "not showing greater preponderance of strength
in the face of the enemy's armor," but he gave the First
Army the decision nevertheless, going out of his way to
praise its "antitank work." When the umpire reports were
all in and the tally completed, 983 tanks were ruled put out
of action, 91 per cent of them supposedly by guns. And
the 1st Armored Division of General Bruce Magruder was
ruled "destroyed."

Patton was singled out for criticism, the principal complaint now being that his staff work had been spotty and
faulty, and he had wasted his strength on "too many piecemeal attacks" far too widely scattered over the combat
area. This was, as McNair put it, "no way to fight a war."
According to him, the terrain was ideal for tanks, yet they
were "pretty nearly stopped by the AT guns."

There was in McNair's criticism, and in the "high command's" censure of Patton, the kind of contradiction that
used to set Coleridge to prolonged sneezing. In effect, Patton was criticized for his demonstration of personal leadership at a time when the lack of it was recognized by Marshall
and McNair as their primary "officer problem."

Writing about the maneuvers, Captain F. H. Weston
shrewdly remarked that although they could not supply
dynamic leadership, they had been useful if only because
they had exposed its absence. Earlier in the year, McNair
had written to a friend that "many officers neither have nor
deserve the confidence of their men." The deficient leadership of a majority of officers was the subject of a special
memorandum General Marshall had prepared for the
Secretary of War. And on June 18, 1941, McNair told
Marshall bluntly, "The principal obstacle now is that com-

manders lack either the guts or the discernment to act."

Yet the discerning commander of the gutsy 2nd Armored Division was censured for exactly these qualities of leadership he had so abundantly displayed during the maneuvers.

But at least Patton made the *New York Times*. A brief feature item described an experiment of his with cloud writing instead of radio communications in emergencies. He had designed an electric signal lamp, operated by hand with a trigger grip which flashed dot-and-dash signals on the sky up to a distance of five miles. The intensity of the light could be regulated by a plastic filter that reduced visibility and eliminated the danger of detection.

The piece in the *Times* was a fine tribute to Patton's ingenuity except for a minor blemish. It spelled his name "Patten."

While the forces of the antitank plot were thus winning one battle after another, they were in fact losing their war against armor. No matter how much it was resented and criticized, Patton's fantastic performance did impress General Marshall and, in due course, even General McNair. Suddenly his resuscitated career as the Army's best and boldest tankman began to sky-rocket.

It was aided, to be sure, by another event over which he himself had absolutely no control.

He had marched the division back to Benning, and wrote out an order complimenting his officers and men on their fine performance.

The order was published on December 6, 1941.

Next morning the Japanese attacked Pearl Harbor and the United States was at war.

CHAPTER TEN
THE CALL

The "call" came at 10:45 A.M. on July 30, 1942, to the Desert Training Center at Indio, Calif. It had that drama of suddenness and unexpectedness which George Patton usually regarded as collateral proof that he was indeed a child of destiny. It was not *the* "Call" he dreaded, the great spiritual command that had summoned Cousin "Robbie" Patton into the ministry. It was a simple telephone call from Washington, with Colonel John Edwin Hull at the other end of the direct line. A cerebral soldier who went into the Army with a Bachelor of Arts degree from Miami University of Oxford, Ohio, and became a full general without a West Point diploma, Hull was a member of the brain trust General Marshall had set up in the Operations Division. Totally unbeknown to Patton, who was his senior by 10 years, Colonel Hull was his friend and booster in the Pentagon.

When he got Patton on the line he told him, "General, I am calling you by order of General Marshall. He wants to see you here in Washington as soon as you can leave the Center."

Patton had been in the desert near Indio, a date-growing town in southeast California's Coachella Valley, since March 27th, in command of a newly created Desert Training Center. His job, in this vast maneuver area that included parts of California, Nevada and Arizona, was to prepare the nucleus of an American "Panzer Army" for action in the war.

Chosen by Secretary of War Stimson, who continued to take a personal interest in his friend's career, Patton was not quite sure whether to like this assignment. On the one hand, it gave him an opportunity to train men for war in armor, as he had done in 1918, and to create a special force the Army urgently needed but woefully lacked. But on the other, his transfer to the Great American Desert, remote from the East where things were popping, filled him with some apprehension that he might be left behind in the sand when the commanders of the combat forces were chosen. His doubts made him doubly eager to make the most of this opportunity and to create an impression that would assure his eventual selection for combat command.

The area—180 miles long and 90 miles wide, covering some 162,000 square miles—was Patton's own choice. Accompanied by Lieutenant Colonel Riley F. Ennis, he had spent four days reconnoitering the region, sometimes flying over it, at other times driving through it, frequently tracking across it on foot. He made the survey under simulated combat conditions, allowing himself and his companion minimum rations, including but one gallon of water a day for each. During this exploration, Patton and Ennis did not meet one individual in all the vast region. This was one reason Patton had decided on the area. Another was that its contours made possible marches up to 400 miles without opposing troops sighting each other.

Now he was firmly settled at the Center, in temporary frame buildings after weeks of camping in tents, commanding a force that comprised some 8,000 officers and men made up of units of I Armored Corps and of elements of the Second and Third Armies.

It was the hottest day of the year in the desert, the thermometer hitting 120°. Patton was alone in his big office, its stillness on this routine morning, when nothing extraordinary was expected to happen, mellowed by the monotonous purring of the air conditioner. With his acute sense of destiny, he recognized immediately that that call was the turning point in his life. But for once he did not respond to it in his usual breezy fashion. When he hung up, and before he did anything else, he went through the ritual he invariably performed upon receipt of momentous messages which signaled upward turns in his fortune. George Patton went down on his knees and prayed.

He had no doubt in his innermost mind, where he let hope forever triumph over reason, that the summons would come sooner or later. Only the day before he had told Rosevich that he considered himself basically blessed with what Alexander Pope called the "eighth beatitude," citing one of his favorite mottoes from Pope's *Odyssey of Homer*:

"Blessed is he who expects nothing, for he shall never be disappointed." Patton believed with mystic fervor that everything good that had happened to him was predetermined by the Lord, no matter how difficult he had made it for his Maker to stick by him.

This, in fact, was his second call, but the first had petered out in disappointment. Earlier in that spring of 1942, shortly after Patton's arrival at Indio, Lieutenant Colonel Allen F. Kingman, representative of the Armored Force at General McNair's GHQ, suggested that the Army send one of its armored divisions to reinforce the British Eighth Army in Egypt, to gain "practical battlefield experience for portions of the Army before the whole of it should be finally thrown into a life and death struggle." The suggestion was avidly accepted, and the project was worked out by the Operations and Plans Division.

The idea was to ship the entire division. Then, when need arose for it elsewhere, bring out only its personnel, leaving the equipment for the British. "The proposition seemed all the more attractive," General Eisenhower wrote, "because we were then engaged in producing an improved tank, and by the time we should be ready to use the division ourself, we counted on having the new equipment for issue."

The question of who should be sent to command this phantom armor was raised by General Marshall, and Ike immediately thought that Georgie Patton would be ideal. He was available on short notice for the assignment, which would have combined training and actual combat. Marshall was convinced that Patton was eminently suited for both tasks.

He told Eisenhower, who headed OPD, to send for Patton, but then the first snag developed. When Eisenhower mentioned the plan in the War Department, the choice of commander met with violent opposition. There was a certain amount of blunt name-calling. Even those who refrained from referring to Patton as an s.o.b. voiced the opinion that he would never do, if only because he could not fit even into an American team, much less into an inter-Allied organization. But the objections did not deter Eisenhower, probably because he knew Patton as an accomplished pro from their old Fort Meade days and was not deceived by his "rather bizarre mannerisms and his sometimes unpredictable actions." He sent for Patton.

"Georgie," he asked him when they met, "would you be

willing to step down from command of your training corps
to take a division into actual battle?"

Patton appeared to be stunned, but only for a moment.
His corps meant a lot to him. When he was given its command only a few weeks before, he had even vowed to
reform by abstaining from his ribald language. During the
speeches which accompanied his ceremonial ascent to the
corps' command, General Jacob L. Devers, chief of the
Armored Force, distinctly outswore him. Patton coyly
explained his abstinence to Colonel Waters, his son-in-law:
"I guess, John, I'll have to quit cussing from now on—
you've got to be dignified when you are a corps commander."

But now the prospect of "real" action overshadowed
everything else. "Ike," he exclaimed, "I'll go as a second
lieutenant if I can get into combat."

Though Eisenhower expected the answer with all its
typical effusiveness, he was gratified nevertheless. Only a
short time before, he had occasion to ask another corps
commander to take over an American combat corps in the
Pacific. But the general declined. He could not visualize
himself, he said, a senior corps commander, serving under
an Australian general he called an "amateur soldier."

Patton's first big chance to get into action, barely three
months after Pearl Harbor—and start his war career by
fighting Rommel—came to nothing. It had nothing to do
with his personality troubles. At that early stage, the United
States did not have the 45 transports and cargo ships the
division would have needed to get to Egypt by the long
route around the Cape of Good Hope.

But Patton had to wait only three months more to get
what he really wanted. And this time nobody in the
Pentagon objected to his selection. In the meantime, on
June 11th, Eisenhower had been named to command the
European Theater, and he had left for London on the 23rd.
Now Patton was summoned by General Marshall himself,
and you did not object to his decisions if you knew what
was good for you.

Colonel Hull told Patton to prepare for a long absence
from Indio, and even for the possibility that he might never
return to the Desert Training Center. That was all he could
tell him safely on the telephone.

Patton arrived in Washington the same day and was
taken straight to General Marshall. "Patton," the Chief of

Staff told him, "I have just returned from London with what we must regard as the second-best solution we can expect under the circumstances to take the offensive against the Axis this year."

Marshall's hope for a limited-objective attack across the Channel in 1942, either to take advantage of a crack in German morale or as a sacrifice operation to aid the Russians, had to be shelved in the face of determined British opposition. It was to be replaced by an operation for which Churchill was even then busy coining a secret name. He picked the code word "Torch," and that was how it became known—the Anglo-American invasion of French North Africa. It was scheduled for "not later than October 30th"—as President Roosevelt then stipulated—exactly three months from this date of Patton's interview with Marshall.

The Chief of Staff told Patton something about the clashes and controversies that led to the "Torch" plan, and they seemed to have been massive even in Marshall's capsule presentation. He was determined to take the direct route to the Continent and had already proposed in March, 1942, only three months after Pearl Harbor, to establish a bridgehead in Europe by seizing Brest or Cherbourg during the early fall of 1942. He had the all-out support of Secretary Stimson, who regarded "a steady, rapid and unrelenting prosecution" of Marshall's plan as "the surest road . . . the easiest road to the center of our chief enemy's heart," the ultimate defeat of Hitler's armies and "the victorious termination of the war." For a while, Marshall was also supported by President Roosevelt, who told Prime Minister Churchill on April 2nd, "As I have completed survey of the immediate and long-range problems of the military situations facing the United Nations, I have come to certain conclusions which are so vital that I want you to know the whole picture and to ask your approval."

The President spelled out his "conclusions" in a memorandum dated April 8th, in which he wrote: "Western Europe is favored as the theater in which to stage the first major offensive by the United States and Great Britain. Only there could their combined land and air resources be fully developed and the maximum support given to Russia. The decision to launch this offensive must be made at once, because of the immense preparation necessary in many directions."

As Roosevelt envisaged it, undoubtedly upon General Marshall's recommendations, the combined invasion forces were to consist of 48 divisions, of which 18 were to be contributed by the British. However, the initial assault scheduled for 1942, whose objective was the establishment of a beachhead in the area around Cherbourg, presupposed the employment of only five divisions. But since no United States divisions would be available by then, the British were told that they would have to supply all five.

A code word, "Sledgehammer," was devised for this chimerical operation, and that was, more or less, how far the project progressed. The British were violently opposed to the plan partly because, as they saw it, its initial phase converging on Brest or Cherbourg was designed as an exclusively British effort, and mostly because, as they knew it, they lacked the resources for even such a limited venture. "Accustomed, with their vast pioneer and expanding economy," wrote Sir Arthur Bryant, "to setting themselves impossible targets and then going all out to achieve them, [the Americans] could not understand the hesitation of their Allies."

General Sir Alan Brooke, Chief of the Imperial General Staff, was most determined in his opposition to "Sledgehammer." "In my mind," he wrote in his diary on July 17th, "1942 is dead off and without the slightest hope. 1943 must depend on what happens to Russia. If she breaks and is overrun, there can be no invasion and we shall then be prepared to go into North Africa instead. But Marshall seems to want some rigid form of plan which we are bound to adhere to in any case."

The British sent the suave and popular Lord Mountbatten to Washington to talk the Americans out of "Sledgehammer." His visit, during which he concentrated on President Roosevelt, served only to annoy Marshall without shaking his determination to mount the offensive as he saw it. The Chief of Staff tried to prevent the British from wheedling his political superior from the "straight and narrow path of frontal attack" into what Stimson, with a Churchillian phrase, called "the wildest kind of diversionist debauch."

It was in this highly charged atmosphere of Allied dis-

unity that Marshall, "very stirred up and emphatic," went
to London for the showdown. He arrived on July 18th,
accompanied by Harry Hopkins and Admiral Ernest J.
King, which caused General Brooke to note in his diary:
"It will be a queer party, as Harry Hopkins is for operating
in Africa, Marshall wants to operate in Europe, and King
is determined to stick to the Pacific."

It started out as a very queer party, indeed, the grand
strategic issue deteriorating into acrimonious debate and
personal vilification. Brooke seized upon a gossipy remark
of the Prime Minister that "Marshall was trying to assume
powers of the Commander in Chief, which was the President's prerogative," and viewed his American opposite with
suspicion and thinly concealed hostility. Marshall, quite
exasperated by what he regarded as British evasiveness and
procrastination, turned on Brooke with a bluntless that was
rare for him. "Well," he asked at one of their meetings,
"how do you expect to *win* the war? You cannot win it by
defensive action!"

By then, President Roosevelt had been "wheedled" to
Churchill's alternative, and that settled the issue for Marshall, a firm disciple of the American system of civilian
paramountcy in such matters. Invoking his constitutional
prerogative in a memo which he signed "Franklin D.
Roosevelt, Commander in Chief," the President told Marshall to stop the bickering and reach "total agreement
within one week of your arrival"—by July 25th, that is.

Three days before, with the conference still deadlocked,
Marshall sought Eisenhower's opinion. The young general
he had hand-picked to command the American forces in
whatever enterprise would be decided upon told him that
he, too, regarded a cross-Channel invasion as hazardous in
1942. On the same day, the President ordered his negotia-
tors to agree on "some other operation [than Sledgeham-
mer] against the European enemy that would involve
American troops in 1942."

When Marshall and his colleagues met with Brooke and
his associates at noon on July 24th and again at 3 P.M.,
complete agreement was reached and goodwill, Hopkins
called it, was restored to the alliance. Marshall agreed to
give up the idea of an immediate encroachment upon the
Continent and begin preparations for an attack on North
Africa instead. Brooke did a bit of crowing in his diary
that night, remarking that "we have got just what we

wanted out of U.S. chiefs." Marshall tried valiantly to swallow his disappointment. It was not easy. Even on July 28th he was still unconvinced of the virtue of the "compromise," as was implied in the President's letter of that date to Churchill. "The Three Musketeers arrived safely this afternoon," he wrote, "and the wedding is still scheduled."

It was a shotgun wedding when it came, but the decision it produced satisfied and elated the President. "I cannot help feeling," Roosevelt wrote to Churchill, "that the past week represented a turning point in the whole war and that now we are on our way shoulder to shoulder." (Incidentally, he proved right in the end.) The President then went on to Hyde Park, New York, but before leaving Washington he issued orders to Marshall for "full steam ahead 'Torch' at earliest possible moment." He asked the Combined Chiefs in Washington (General Marshall, in effect, in collaboration with his British colleague, Field Marshal Sir John Dill) to tell him by August 4th "the earliest date when landings in North Africa would take place."

This was the chain of events that resulted in Marshall's urgent summons to Patton, in a drama behind the scenes over which Patton did not have any influence but which had such a momentous bearing upon his "destiny." This prelude in 1942 somehow reminded him of Pershing's table-banging debate with Foch in 1918, which had preceded his own first call to war. Though Patton attributed Pershing's and Marshall's influence upon his professional fate to Divine intervention on his behalf, the Lord actually worked through Marshall in both cases. In 1918, it was Colonel Marshall, Operations Officer of the First Army in France, who proposed that Patton's tanks be used at St. Mihiel. In 1942, it was General Marshall, the Chief of Staff, who decided to give the major American command in "Torch" to that "s.o.b. nobody wanted"—George Patton.

Everything was still vague about "Torch" on this July 30th, with only the most perfunctory plans on hand, when Marshall broke the news to Patton. His confidence in Patton was supreme. At this point "Torch" was expected to have but one American task force, and for its command he chose Patton, the first American general to lead American troops in action in World War II, the highest honor Patton could imagine.

"You must understand," Marshall told him in a deliberately brusque voice, "that the job will have to be done with the troops and equipment the planning staff will allot you."

Patton nodded his agreement. "Report to the War College," Marshall closed the interview, "where Colonel Hull will show you the detailed plans and brief you."

Patton rushed to the War College, read the plans as far as they went, listened to Hull, then put in a call to Marshall. When told that the Chief of Staff was not available, he asked to be connected with General Joseph T. McNarney, Marshall's deputy, who was even then burdened with the logistic problems of "Torch."

Patton told McNarney bluntly that the plans he had just seen were for the birds. "I need a great many more men," he blustered, "and a lot more ships to do the job."

"All right, Georgie," McNarney said, "I'll tell General Marshall about your misgivings and we'll see what he can do for you." Then he took the message to the Chief of Staff. Marshall listened quietly, even if a bit grimly, then merely said:

"Order him back to Indio."

Patton got his orders immediately, and back he went to the Desert Training Center as abruptly as he had come, badly shaken by the experience. He spent the next two days brooding, chiefly about how to coax himself back into the good graces of Marshall. Then, on August 2nd, he picked up the telephone and called the Chief of Staff.

"General Marshall is in conference," he was told. He called again, only to be told that the Chief of Staff was still not available. Patton called several times more, with the same results. Finally he was willing to settle for McNarney again.

"Hello, Joe," he told the Deputy Chief of Staff, "I did a lot of thinking in the meantime, and I came to the conclusion that maybe I could do the job after all with the forces your stupid staff is willing to give me." There was that self-conscious boyish grin in his voice, as if he were saying, "Well, can't you see? I'm eating crow—so what do you say? Can I have the job after all?"

McNarney went to Marshall with the report of the conversation.

"Order him back to the War College," the Chief of Staff

said, glumly to begin with, but then his face broke into a
smile.

"You see, McNarney," he told his deputy, "that's the way
to handle Patton."

Upon his return to Washington on August 3rd, Patton was
given a loft on the third floor of the old Munitions Building
on Constitution Avenue in Washington, where he was to
plan "Torch." He sent for Colonel Gay; then a colonel
named Kent C. Lambert was assigned to him as his Operations Officer. Patton went to work at once. By the end of
his first day in Washington he submitted a plan of his own.
It proposed the landing at Casablanca.

But his own enthusiasm was not matched by the other
planners either in Washington or in London. Eisenhower
was working on the plans with a special staff under General
Mark W. Clark, but his reports to Washington were far
from reassuring. Now that "Torch" had been agreed upon
at last, nobody appeared to be able to work up enough
confidence in its eventual success.

On July 31st, Eisenhower had discussed "Torch" for an
hour and a half with his top planners, but all he could
elicit were misgivings. Brigadier C. M. Stewart, the British
War Office's Director of Plans, estimated that 11 divisions
would be needed to accomplish the mission (which he saw
as the conquest of Tunisia in 28 days)—a feat necessitating
two assaults. Captain C. E. Lambe of the Royal Navy, the
Admiralty's Director of Plans, promptly voiced the opinion
that the Allied navies did not have enough escorts to move
11 divisions simultaneously to both points, namely to
Casablanca and a point inside the Mediterranean. "The
biggest defects for the entire attack," the conference concluded, "are shortage of naval support and landing craft,
and the surf conditions on the west coast, when heavy
swells from the Atlantic make landing difficult, if not impossible, in the late fall."

The discouraging conclusion of the meeting was duly
cabled to General Marshall. Then other snags were hit.
General Sir Harold Alexander, originally slated to command the British forces in "Torch," had to be shifted to

Cairo. He was replaced by General Sir Bernard Law Montgomery, then an enigmatic figure highly regarded by his superiors, especially Brooke. Then Montgomery, too, had to be shifted to Egypt, to take command of the hard-pressed British Eighth Army. His place was taken by "a Scotsman named Anderson"—Lieutenant General Sir Kenneth A. N. Anderson. The rapid-fire changes in the British command disturbed Eisenhower. He asked General Hastings L. Ismay, who had been seconded to tell him gently about the successive changes, "You seem to have a lot of Wellingtons in your army. Tell me, frankly, are the British serious about 'Torch'?"

At this point General Marshall decided to send Patton to London to explore the situation on the spot and to report his personal findings to him directly and frankly. After the war, Eisenhower wrote in his memoirs that he had been the source of this decision: "I notified General Marshall of my desire to have General Patton command the Casablanca expedition, and within a short time George reported to me in London."

On August 9th, Commander Harry C. Butcher, Eisenhower's Naval aide and diarist, had this notation in the journal he was keeping for Eisenhower: "The C.G. [Eisenhower] had hoped to get Patton for this task, but because of the difference in rank hesitated to ask for him."

Actually, Eisenhower was surprised—even if pleasantly —when in the evening of August 9th he received a phone call at his apartment, just when he was planning to settle down for the night with a bowl of chicken soup and no plans.

"Ike," he heard a familiar voice, "Goddamnit, I've just arrived in this blasted town. I'm holed up in Claridge's and don't know what to do with myself."

"Georgie!" Eisenhower exclaimed, for, of course, Patton was the caller. "Oh, boy, am I glad to hear your voice! Come right over and have some Godawful dehydrated chicken soup with me."

Patton arrived shortly for drink and dinner, then plunged into the discussion of "Torch." He himself was loaded down with apprehensions—the enemy forces he expected to encounter upon landing were supposed to be superior to those assigned to him by those "Goddamn fools in Washington." He feared heavy swells, and worried about a scarcity of landing beaches. But he was supremely confident at the same time, trusting in his own ability to pull through by inspiring his men to a superhuman performance. "I may be stupid on many particulars," he told Eisenhower, "but I can spur any outfit within a week to a high state of morale."

The impromptu party broke up shortly after dinner, Patton returning to Claridge's uncertain in his own mind whether Eisenhower was for or against "Torch," and even whether he himself really liked it or not. That night he wrote in his diary: "We both feel that the operation is bad and mostly political. However, we are told to do it and intend to succeed or die in the attempt. If the worst we can see occurs, it is an impossible show, but, with a little luck, it can be done at a high price; and it might be a cinch."

During his 10 days in London, Patton met nothing but what he called "defeatism"—and that made him come out for "Torch" with all the vigor and eloquence at his command. He exerted what, in the end, became the decisive influence on the eventual acquiescence of Ike and the men around him in the operation. It may be no exaggeration to say that without Patton's contagious enthusiasm and optimism, without his many constructive suggestions during his visit, and especially without his intuitive faith in the enterprise, "Torch" would have been shelved as an operation that, according to the consensus, had a far too fragile chance for success. This was a little-known but enormously significant contribution of Patton to eventual victory in the war. It was, indeed, a contribution on the strategic level because, in the end, "Torch" became exactly what Roosevelt predicted—the turning point in the war against the Nazis.

Patton spent August 10th probing for opinions and estimates, and examining the plans already prepared in London. In the afternoon, on his perambulations, he bumped into his friend, Brigadier General Lucian K. Truscott Jr., an old Cavalry buddy now representing the United States Army at Lord Mountbatten's Commando headquarters. The widespread British objection to "Torch" was especially articulate in Mountbatten's influential circle, and Truscott appeared to share their pessimism. But Patton quickly disabused him. "This may not be the best Goddamn show," he told Truscott, "but it's much better than nothing. As for myself, I am determined to see it through." Then assuming that he had convinced his friend, he told Truscott:

"As far as you are concerned, you old horse-thief—damn it, Lucian, you don't want to stay in London on any staff job with a war going on. Why don't you come with me? I'll give you a command."

Winning Truscott to his side did not prove difficult. But the next day Patton had a tough job when he had to convince the United States Navy's representatives in London that "Torch" was just "what the doctor had ordered." Eisenhower had called a conference at which Admiral Harold L. Stark, the studious and plodding Navy commander in Europe, appeared with a bevy of admirals and a captain named Frank P. Thomas who represented Admiral Royal E. Ingersoll's Atlantic Fleet. Captain Thomas did most of the talking, emphasizing nothing but difficulties. Painting the picture as gloomily as he could, he even brought in the possible threat from one or two German aircraft carriers—vessels which, so far as the *Kriegsmarine* was concerned, were conspicuous solely by their total absence, because the German Navy actually had no carriers. The more Thomas argued against "Torch" the more Patton found himself liking it. He spoke up sparingly and cautiously, but it was evident from what he did say that he was becoming increasingly exasperated. It was due only to Eisenhower's intervention that an open and venomous clash between Patton and Captain Thomas was avoided.

" 'Torch'," Eisenhower concluded the discussion firmly and unequivocally while Patton vigorously nodded his agreement, "is an order from the Commander in Chief, the President of the United States, and the Prime Minister. Whether we like it or not, it has to be carried out, despite any obstacles. If there isn't a single protective warship, my orders call for moving into West and North Africa and I am going to do it, warships or not—and if I have to go alone in a rowboat."

Patton was now touring the "key spots" in London doing missionary work for "Torch." His first and most influential convert became Lord Mountbatten himself, to whom Truscott had introduced him with exactly this ulterior motive in mind. A dinner party was arranged at Claridge's to which Mountbatten came with his top brass—General Joseph C. Hayden, his Chief of Staff, Group Captain Basil R. Willets of the RAF, and Colonel Edmund H. Neville. Patton and Truscott were accompanied by Colonel Lambert,

Patton's Operations Officer, and Colonel Alfred M. Gruenther, who had just arrived from the United States to become Eisenhower's Deputy Chief of Staff in charge of planning "Torch."

Patton was in rare good form at the dinner. By the time the party broke up, "Dicky" Mountbatten and his fellow top-Commandoes appeared to be wholeheartedly "on the side of the angels," as Patton said to Lambert on their way up to their rooms. This party then gave birth to another, which afforded Patton an opportunity to do some more missionary work, but totally unrelated to "Torch."

When the basic problem that inspired the dinner was settled to Patton's satisfaction, and "Torch" receded from the conversation, he singled out Group Captain Willets for some after-dinner small talk—to take his mind off "Torch," as he put it. Before long, he was embroiled in a lively argument with the hero of the famous Commando raid on Crete, about the British nobility, of all things. Pontificating as was his wont, and letting the Group Captain know in no uncertain terms exactly where he stood, Patton said, "My dear Group Captain, there ain't no such thing as typical English aristocracy."

Willets took this for a challenge and arranged a party for Patton at the home of a prominent English lady, with the guest list carefully chosen to prove Patton wrong. None of these guests seemed to shake him out of his conviction, however—until the high point of the evening, which Willets had shrewdly stage-managed. "There was a commotion at the door, which Willets opened," General Truscott described the scene. "And into the room sailed—there is no other fitting word—a majestic presence followed by another of lesser mien, like a battleship trailed by a destroyer. The first was Lady ———, a dowager of sixty-five or thereabouts with several chins resting on a more than ample bosom. Her towering coiffure quivered with her every movement. Divested of her furs, with trailing skirts, strings and strings of pearls, soft hands sparkling with numerous rings, a lorgnette through which she looked down on us lesser creatures, she was a picture from a page in history."

Patton was completely smitten. He sneaked up to Willets and whispered into his ear, "Goddamnit—you win!" Then he proceeded to reduce the formidable lady to size and recapture the scene for the United States.

"After dinner he [Patton] held them spellbound," Truscott recalled, "for that night he was in rare form. He told of the notches on his guns and how he came by them. He talked of Mexico and Pershing and outlaws of the great Southwest. He told of the rare murders he had known and where and why. Of the rare California vintage he sampled and enjoyed only to discover, when the great cask was cleaned, it contained the body of a drowned Mexican."

His audience was duly appreciative and registered the appropriate degrees of horror and astonishment. But mostly doubt.

From social detours into minor conquests, Patton returned to the big job of selling "Torch" on both sides of the Atlantic. It was not an easy job! "Trying to follow the evolution of 'Torch'," Commander Butcher noted on August 12th, "is like trying to find the peas in a three-shell game."

Next day, Patton helped Eisenhower draft a three-page cable about "Torch" to General Marshall, elaborating on the objections of the two navies. If possible, the Royal Navy was even more pessimistic than Captain Thomas of the United States Atlantic Fleet, Admiral Sir Bertram H. Ramsay painted a picture of utter gloom. He told Eisenhower dolefully that he expected to lose a battleship, a couple of aircraft carriers, two or three cruisers, and "God knows what else" in the effort to land the troops in French North Africa. Then came a general named R. H. Dewing, Ike's British liaison officer, to picture the weakness and vulnerability of Gibraltar. He made his case with great eloquence and opposed "Torch" because it meant, as he put it, a depletion of reserves in the British Isles. Patton could hardly keep his peace while Dewing was talking

But "Torch" was not out of the woods yet. The crisis— for a crisis it indeed had become—reached its climax on Saturday, August 15th. It was precipitated by a long cable from General Marshall answering Eisenhower's message of two days before. The Chief of Staff conceded that his own planners were viewing "Torch" as "hazardous, with less than 50 per cent chances of success." But he added that, in his own opinion, this was "an immediate and superficial view." He in turn now asked for Eisenhower's completely frank opinion. At the same time, in a significant gesture, he called for "similar frank expression from General Patton."

By now Patton was for "Torch" without reservations. When Eisenhower called a top-level conference of his own planners to discuss the answer to General Marshall's query, Patton took the floor. Puffing on Butcher's big Havanas one after another, his thin, intense face shrouded in white smoke, he made the plea *for* "Torch" that carried the day and settled the matter once and for all. It was a performance that elicited unanimous admiration from his skeptical audience. He did not have to write a separate message to Marshall stating his own frank view. The one General Eisenhower sent after the meeting—now recommending the operation without any further reservations or qualifications—fully reflected his own opinion—for the simple reason that Ike's note was but a paraphrase of Patton's arguments.

The crisis was over. "Torch" was safe. After the meeting Patton had the feeling that he "was the only true gambler in the whole outfit."

Now Patton had only a few days left—to "mop up," as he put it. He appointed General Truscott to represent him in London and spent a day briefing him for the job and imbuing him with his own enthusiasm and determination. When he went to see Eisenhower to take his leave, he amused the Commander in Chief by pulling a sheet of paper from his pocket and reading it to him. It was the draft of his proposed demand for the surrender of Casablanca. "I just want you to know, Ike," he said in parting, "that after studying my job in Africa my mind is at ease."

"No wonder," Commander Butcher noted, "Ike is so pleased to have him."

CHAPTER ELEVEN

"TORCH"

Just before leaving London, George Patton made a final commitment. A moderate drinker and abstemious in all the usual vices of men, he was a passionate cigar smoker. Since his nicotine tolerance was unusually low, and tobacco was quick to irritate his throat, he usually kept his consumption to three or four cigars a day unless some excitement or exertion increased the quota. The tough debates in London had made him a chain smoker, and he depleted Commander Butcher's jealousy hoarded supply of Havana Caballeros. When Butcher saw him off, Patton—who was always conscious of his obligations and a generous debtor—told him:

"Thanks for the stogies, Butch, and don't worry. I'll send you some as soon as I get back to Washington."

He was no sooner at his desk in the Munitions Building the next day than he called the tobacco stand at the Army and Navy Club and ordered a huge shipment of cigars for Butcher. They reached the Commander in London on September 5th, with a note from Patton, "Partial payment." Butcher, who had never expected Patton to remember his promise amid his more important cares, was deeply moved and told Eisenhower with some feeling, "Georgie is a man one can trust."

Patton arrived in Washington on August 21st, with fewer than seven weeks left to plan and organize "Torch," which was then scheduled for October 7th. He now had the green light all the way from General Marshall, whom he had succeeded in convincing of the feasibility of the operation. The venture was slowly shaping up.

It was now decided that Patton would command the Western Task Force, one of three task forces in the complex operation and the most complex of the lot. It was to be the only all-American force, taken to its destination either at Oran (as Eisenhower planned it) or Casablanca (as Patton preferred it) entirely by the United States Navy without any help from the British. The Royal Navy would take care of the other two task forces going to Algeria.

The naval phase of the enterprise was enough to take one's breath away. Never in history had such a major invasion been mounted from 3,000 miles away. No navy ever had to transport and protect such a great force across an entire ocean infested with the enemy's extremely able and effective submarines.

It was a magnificent pageant even on paper—not quite so dazzling as Captain Thomas had visualized it in London, "the greatest armada of all times—from 200 to 400 transports and 200 warships," a force no Navy in the world would then have been capable of supplying—but still a formidable assembly of ships and men, certainly the greatest overseas enterprise the United States had ever undertaken. The task staggered the imagination. The troops "those stupid staffers" were allotting Patton were to total more than 40,000 officers and men. They were to be shipped on 36 transports, cargo vessels and tankers, escorted by 68 warships—from the battleship *Texas* to the tug *Cherokee*— all the way from Norfolk in Virginia to the Atlantic beaches in French Morocco. It was not surprising that the United States Navy was overawed by the task assigned to it.

Patton, who tended to dismiss lightly collateral difficulties and underestimate the problems other services had to solve in aiding his efforts, regarded the Navy's proper apprehension as something akin to sabotage. He said so, in forceful language, when Rear Admiral Henry K. Hewitt visited him in his makeshift office in the Munitions Building to discuss and coordinate their plans.

There seemed to be abundant prospect for a clash between the two men. Where Patton was dynamic and quick-triggered, Hewitt appeared to be unduly deliberate, somewhat dronish, even comatose at times. The Admiral was given to weighing the pros and cons rather slowly, then was inclined to give the cons greater weight than the pros.

Their very first meeting began with a semblance of interservice cooperation and ended with a major explosion. Patton, who was immediately irritated by Hewitt's leisurely way of doing business, became enraged by the constant interjections of his staff who, like Thomas of the Atlantic Fleet, seemed to overstate the case against the enterprise. Losing his patience after a while, he inundated the startled and shocked Navy delegation of strait-laced, soft-spoken gentlemen with a torrent of his most Rabelaisian abuse.

The Navy people fled from the conference in virtual panic, convinced that they could never work with a general so crude and rude as Patton. Hewitt went straight to Admiral King, the Navy's big boss, to suggest that the Navy bow out of the operation unless the Army removed Patton.

Admiral King was impressed with Hewitt's plight but not surprised. He knew Patton well and had expected some such difficulty all along. He took the matter to General Marshall and formally demanded that Patton be removed from command of the Task Force.

For a moment it seemed that Patton would be sacrificed to save "Torch." But Marshall held on to him. He soothed King and explained his combustible general to Hewitt. He advised him how to handle Patton and pleaded with him to take him as he was, for better or for worse, accepting his rage as professional hazards of the operation. He assured him, however, that Patton's mannerisms would be most unlikely to jeopardize the enterprise.

"On the contrary," Marshall said. "They are more likely to assure its success. And anyway, Patton is indispensable to 'Torch.' "

Admiral Hewitt was not fully convinced that everything would work out as well as Marshall expected, but he returned to the battlefield and continued to work with Patton. As Patton himself was the first to concede later, Hewitt was the ideal man to organize and lead this unprecedented armada. He proved just as ideal to pacify his impetuous Army colleague and, after the initial outburst, to work with him in perfect harmony. As so often happened with Patton, familiarity bred respect.

Hewitt was, in this Indian summer of 1942, 55 years old, exactly 35 years out of Annapolis, a gallant man who had amply earned his Navy Cross in World War I. "A man of impressive port and massive character," Morison wrote about him, "never self-seeking but always generous in giving credit to others, firm but just to his subordinates, tactful and conciliatory with compeers in other armed services— Admiral Hewitt inspired loyalty, confidence, and affection."

He was not remarkable for any of the rugged individualism and dazzling brilliance that characterized Patton. He was rather imbued, as Morison put it with his felicitous choice of words when describing high-ranking Naval officers, "with the Navy tradition of doing one's best with the human and physical material available. He augmented the staff, not by an intensive combing of the Navy for great brains and organizing genius, but by accepting the men assigned to him by the Bureau of Naval Personnel."

In other words, Hewitt was, so far as appearances went, a humdrum, plodding Naval officer, probably the least likely to succeed with a dynamic plotter and planner like Patton. As it turned out, this was the perfect combination. For Hewitt's rather deliberate procedure perfectly implemented Patton's impetuosity. It was due exclusively to his careful and cautious planning that the convoy arrived at its destination on the dot after a gratifyingly dull crossing, probably the most remarkable feat ever accomplished by any Navy at any time in the history of war.

While Hewitt was planning the magnificent journey at his improvised headquarters in the Nansemond Hotel at Ocean View near Norfolk, Virginia, Patton was plotting the mysterious campaign in the dismal loft in which his own inner sanctum was separated from his staff by only a flimsy partition. It hid a mysterious personage who, to his associates, at times resembled the great Wizard of Oz more than a modern major general. Behind the door guarded by a Marine sentry, the staff of the Western Task Force sweated out the stifling Washington summer.

"Out in the open bullpen," Major Charles R. Codman, then a newcomer to Patton's entourage, described the scene, "the staff sections, about whom swirled a never-ending stream of Navy opposite numbers, meteorologists, Air liaison officers, North African consuls, French tugboat captains, and Arab interpreters, struggled with the joint and several problems posed by the first amphibious landings to be launched eastward across the Atlantic Ocean."

And General Patton? "To date just an awesome presence beyond that partition in the Munitions Building," Codman wrote. "At times when it got noisy in the bullpen the partition would vibrate as to a short burst of machine-gun fire.

" 'Tell 'em to stop that Goddamn racket. I can't hear myself think.'

"Out would come Colonel Hap Gay, Chief of Staff.

" 'The General wants QUIET.' That would do it."

Preoccupied with his great responsibility, beset by the extraordinary difficulties of this rather peculiar operation, exasperated by enormous gaps in Intelligence data, Patton isolated himself behind that thin wall. He communed with himself from time to time, especially when visitors, supposed to advise or enlighten him, left him more bewildered with their contradictory information or confusing advice. At this stage he was still inclined to underestimate the important bearing logistics had on his plans, and to dismiss from his mind such problems as replacements and supplies or at least leave them for officers on other or lower echelons to tackle and solve.

Patton was interested in the big picture with its many colorful ramifications—what the Germans called "operational problems," which are not quite strategy but considerably more than just tactics. This resulted in rather impressionistic and fragmentary planning on his part, leaving gaps in the broad tactical design. This inevitably led to some unpleasant surprises in the battle itself, added to the difficulties of his commanders and troops ashore, and eventually rendered the Moroccan venture somewhat less than perfect. But, then, it was only the first step of the United States Army in World War II—and what infant knows how to walk before it learns to crawl?

It was not until September 5th that Patton was given his explicit instructions and objectives. His original design was to mount a frontal attack on Casablanca and capture the big city with a bluff wrapped in a bombastic ultimatum, which the Navy was supposed to implement in the pinch. An estimate of the situation then found that such a frontal attack would be far too costly. And the Navy's doubt in its own ability to take two separate task forces to two destinations threatened to discard the Moroccan plan altogether.

Thus, upon his return from London, Patton had carried with him a directive to prepare an attack against Oran instead of Casablanca. On August 24th, only three days after his arrival in Washington, that directive was superseded by another from the War Department, and so the situation continued in a flux until the objective was permanently established at last, only a little more than two months —64 days to be exact—prior to D-Day.

According to this directive, Patton's mission was to "secure the port at Casablanca and adjacent airfields and, in conjunction with the Center Task Force at Oran, to establish and maintain communications between Casablanca and Oran. It was also to build up land and air striking forces capable of securing Spanish Morocco, if that action should become necessary."

It was a big order. Intelligence estimated that there were between 60,000 and 100,000 French troops in Morocco, about three times the force Patton had at his disposal. The Spaniards were believed to have well over 100,000 men in their part of the Protectorate. By then, his own forces had been whittled down from the original allotment of 40,000 to about 36,000 at first, and eventually to fewer than 34,000. How he could deal in a showdown with 200,000 enemy troops while his own forces were so numerically inferior was a problem Patton did not wish to contemplate at this time or, he thought, he would begin to doubt the wisdom of his eagerness to become involved in this mess.

Though he had learned planning at Leavenworth, Patton was now preparing an actual major operation for the first time—and one, at that, which refused to be fitted into any of Leavenworth's pat formulas or the prefabricated patterns of the textbooks.

Baffled by the task and awed by his responsibility, he thought of Siegfried Sassoon's general—

"He's a cheery old card," grunted Harry to Jack
As they slogged up to Arras with rifle and pack . . .
But he did for them both by his plan for attack."

The planning of "Torch" was a hodgepodge affair, done separately at several places. Though the over-all plan was being drafted in London under Eisenhower, most of the planning for the Western Task Force was done in the United States, at three locations—in the Operations Division under General Thomas T. Handy; in Patton's loft in the Munitions Building by Colonel Lambert under Patton's personal supervision, and by Admiral Hewitt at Ocean View.

What eventually emerged from this patchwork was really no formal plan at all but a mishmash of designs with all sorts of strings attached to them. There was but a single firm and final arrangement in the plan—Patton was to take his task force ashore in three installments. A force, called *Blackstone* by its code name, would land at Safi in the south; another called *Brushwood,* in the center at Fedala, and a third, named *Goalpost,* at Mehedia. What would happen after the landings the planners did not presume to know with anything resembling certainty. Accordingly, they could not make any binding arrangements for the operations ashore.

The final plan was a far cry from Patton's own first design, which he already had hit upon more or less intuitively on August 3rd. He had studied the configuration of the Moroccan coastline and chose Casablanca for his major effort. When it was decided not to put all his eggs in one basket, he chose Safi in the south, Casablanca in the center, and

Rabat in the north. Rabat also figured prominently in General Eisenhower's original plans. It appeared to be the ideal place for decisive action because its capture at the outset would place the capital of Morocco immediately in United States possession. A landing at Rabat also seemed desirable because it would secure the major airport at Sale and leave the French tank regiment stationed there no time to deploy.

But Patton was talked out of Casablanca. The big city was far too heavily defended, he was told, by the crack Casablanca Division under General Béthouart (whose prearranged cooperation with our forces the planners chose to ignore) and by a good portion of the French fleet. A frontal attack upon the city would overtax his own meager resources.

Then he was talked out of Rabat as well. These arguments were only partly military, though Admiral Hewitt did object to it because his planners thought its beach was not too good. "The approach is so silted-up," Hewitt told Patton, "that the landing boats would be stranded well off-shore."

Important though the Navy's objection was, Patton's eventual decision to bypass Rabat and land at Mehedia was the result of other than military considerations. By then he was besieged in his loft by a buzzing swarm of advisers and consultants. These so-called experts professed to know the intricate political, social and religious currents of the country he was heading for and were now telling him how to avoid possible pitfalls in the political sphere, in which he was but an innocent at large.

This was, to be sure, a delicate operation for, after all, French North Africa was not exactly enemy territory and the forces awaiting Patton were not necessarily hostile to his coming. So gradually all kinds of political and diplomatic designs were superimposed on Patton's strictly military plans by the State Department. Then the new Office of Strategic Services, Colonel William "Wild Bill" Donovan's hush-hush secret intelligence service, rushed breathlessly into the breach with operations plans of its own. Such outside help held out the possibility that the invasion would be a pushover. But it also confused planning and tied the hands of the planners. Moreover, it befuddled Patton, who was shrewd and sharp in military matters but lacked sophistication and savvy in politics and diplomacy.

As events later proved, the political experts' own knowledge of the situation and their ability to assess it properly left much to be desired. There was, in particular, a rather spectacular display of ignorance on the part of the State Department officials. How little they really knew of conditions Patton was to encounter was evident in the instructions the State Department had prepared for him. No distinction was made between the political status of Algeria, which was an overseas province of France directly ruled by Vichy, and that of Morocco, which was a protectorate. The latter was ruled nominally by its own sovereign, the Sultan of Morocco, even if *de facto* power was vested in the hands of the French Resident General.

In addition, Patton was treated to intelligence that was not much better than the narrative of popular travelogues. As a result, he gained a distorted picture of the situation and was trapped into arriving at decisions which were to plague him during the campaign and for months to come. Thus he was literally scared away from Rabat by Colonel Black, his G-2, and an Annapolis-bred former naval officer, Paul Frederick Culbert, who was designated his political adviser.

Culbert arrived in Washington from Morocco via London in September and, in close cooperation with Black, whose intellectual resources were by then overtaxed by the complexities of his job, began to unload his own strong personal views in the guise of political advice. He counseled Patton in particular to be careful not to step on the sensitive toes of the Moslems and to avoid "the sacred cities, Rabat and Sale."

Culbert explained that Rabat was a holy city by virtue of being the seat of the Sultan, whose authority was more spiritual than temporal. As *Shereef*—head of a princely Mohammedan family claiming descent from the Prophet through his daughter Fatima—His Majesty Mohamed V exerted great influence on the Moslems throughout Africa and, Culbert warned, they would never forgive Patton if he soiled such a sacred spot as Rabat. Moreover, he said, "the Axis would propagandize our violation of Moslem customs," and that would be certain to redound to our ultimate disadvantage in all Islamic countries.

Culbert went on to paint a grim picture of a dormant ethnic strife in Morocco, a country about the size of California whose 8,000,000 inhabitants were predominantly

Moorish Moslems of Berber strain. They traditionally hated the 200,000 Jews who resided in Morocco and were, therefore, favorably disposed toward the Nazis, who had made Jew-baiting respectable. The Moroccan Jews, according to Culbert, thirsted for revenge and could be expected to seize upon the arrival of the Americans to attack the Moslems. This would lead to riots with religious and racial overtones, and would create complications Patton might find more difficult to overcome than whatever resistance the French might put up.

This was the gist of Culbert's "advice," and it fell on fertile soil in Patton's politically untutored mind. He knew nothing of Morocco except that it was supposed to be ancient Mauretania and had produced some of the best horses in the world at Meknes. ("Barb," the ancestor of our thoroughbreds, had come from the royal stables there.) He remembered the Philippine Insurrection and did not wish to stir up any trouble with the "natives" in Morocco. He succumbed to Culbert and Black, and rearranged his military plans in line with their suggestions.

On September 19th he cabled General Eisenhower that he had decided to bypass Rabat "on religious grounds," and asked that Mehedia be substituted for *Goalpost*. It proved a fateful and, as we shall see, nearly fatal decision, one of the main reasons why Morocco came to be the toughest nut to crack in the whole of "Torch."

In the meantime Patton's forces were assembled and trained in the brief time left for the preparations. From General Anderson's 3rd Infantry Division, one regiment at a time was sent to the Solomon Island training area in Chesapeake Bay and put through day and night landing exercises. Elements of Patton's own 2nd Armored Division, now commanded by General Harmon, also received special training for their duties in the operation.

While Patton put up an impressive and reassuring front of enthusiasm, he was sustaining his confidence only by repeating to himself again and again his favorite motto, "Do not take counsel of your fears." How bewildered he became in the cross-currents of conflicting counsels was evident in his cable to Eisenhower on October 3rd, when he confessed to "gloom" but wrote, whistling in the dark:

"You can rest assured that when we start for the beach we shall stay there, whether dead or alive, and if alive, we will not surrender. When I have made everyone else share this opinion, as I shall certainly do before we start, I shall have complete confidence in the success of the operation."

It was in a defiant rather than confident mood that George Patton went to war. He was scheduled to depart from Norfolk at 2:30 A.M. on October 24th, spending his last night in the United States aboard the *Augusta,* Admiral Hewitt's flagship, which was to be his home for the fortnight of the crossing.

On the 20th he wrote his will and composed a letter to his wife to be opened only "when and if I am definitely reported dead." He enclosed it in a note to Frederick Ayer, his brother-in-law and friend, in which he candidly revealed his innermost thoughts:

"The job I am going on is about as desperate a venture as has ever been undertaken by any force in the world's history." He asked Ayer to look out for his wife and children, and take care of them if anything should happen to him.

That day, accompanied by Admiral Hewitt, he went to the White House to report to President Roosevelt, receive his final instructions, and bid him farewell. Though the Pattons were Democrats all the way back, of the Jacksonian persuasion in their past, Patton himself had no fixed political allegiance but inclined toward the conservatism and respectability of the Republican Party, in which his Bostonian relatives on his wife's side were prominent. He never gave much thought to the New Deal except that he was instinctively against it. But he had a sneaking liking for Roosevelt, and anyway, he was seeing him not as a politician but as his Commander in Chief.

The President gave them a splendid reception but could not impart any useful last-minute intelligence about conditions in Morocco. He was as much in the dark as anybody in Washington and London. He told Patton:

"Our policy is simply the defeat of the Axis powers and the preservation of French administration in their territories overseas. I want the Nazis kicked out of the area with the assurance that the colonies will be continued to be governed by the French."

Roosevelt said nothing to indicate whether his own attitude was either favorable or unfavorable toward the government at Vichy. Patton, with his best bombast, reassured the President:

"Sir, all I want to tell you is this—I will leave the beaches either a conqueror or a corpse." He repeated the statement to General Marshall when he saw him at the Pentagon later that day.

Next morning he went to Walter Reed Hospital to bid good-bye to General Pershing. He left a sentimental account of that memorable visit in a diary note dated October 21, 1942:

"Called on General Pershing. He did not recognize me until I spoke. Then his mind seemed quite clear. He looks very old. It is probably the last time I shall see him but he may outlive me. I said that when he took me to Mexico in 1916 he gave me my start. He replied, 'I can always pick a fighting man and God knows there are few of them. I am happy they are sending you to the front at once. I like Generals so bold that they are dangerous. I hope they give you a free hand.'

"He recalled my killing the Mexicans and when I told him I was taking the same pistol he said, 'I hope you kill some Germans with it.' He also said that he hoped I got a chance to kill someone with my sword whip. He said that at the start of the war he was hurt because no one consulted him, but he was now resigned to sit on the sidelines with his feet hanging over.

"He almost cried. It is pathetic how little he knows of the war."

When Patton was ready to leave, he kissed Pershing's hand, then asked for his blessing. Pershing made him kneel down, squeezed his hand and whispered, "Good-bye, George. God bless you and keep you, and give you victory."

Patton put on his hat and saluted. Pershing rose and returned the salute smartly. "Twenty-five years seemed to drop from him," Patton remarked.

He then went to the War Department to bid farewell to a small group of women secretaries who had handled his classified paper work.

Shortly after lunch Mrs. Patton drove her husband to Bolling Air Field, where a C-47 plane was to take him and his staff to Norfolk. The eight men closest to him during the planning of "Torch" were waiting: General Geoffrey Keyes, slated to be his Deputy Commander; Colonel Gay;

Lieutenant Colonel Paul D. Harkins, his Deputy Chief of Staff; Colonels Black and Lambert; his G-4, Colonel Walter J. Muller; his Signals Officer, Colonel Elton F. Hammond, and his aide, Captain Richard Jenson, a young officer from Patton's hometown of Pasadena.

Within six months Dick Jenson was dead—killed in Tunisia. Lambert and Black did not measure up to expectations and faded from his staff. But Gay, Harkins, Muller and Hammond remained with him all the way—from Bolling Field on this balmy autumn day in 1942 to Czechoslovakia in the spring of 1945.

Patton boarded the C-47—and then, in the rays of the setting sun of October 23rd, he motored from Norfolk to Hampton Roads, where the *Augusta* was waiting to take him to the wars.

It was a day he would never forget—not so much for its glory as for the misery caused by his doubts. The Navy was ready. The huge armada was moved with the precision of clockwork. Nothing was overlooked in Hewitt's planning. A pack of U-boats which Naval Intelligence had discovered in the path of the convoy was ingeniously drawn off in this last minute to a decoy of ships sent to Sierra Leone. The convoy was a glorious and reassuring sight. The embarkation proceeded without a single hitch.

CHAPTER TWELVE
PROCONSUL IN MOROCCO

The battle for Morocco lasted exactly 74 hours, but they were not George Patton's finest hours. What he avowed to crave, but hoped *in petto* to avoid, was now upon him. The Western Task Force had to fight for Morocco after all, and it became quickly evident that this young American expeditionary force was ill-prepared even for this haphazard campaign against a befuddled foe.

The dilettantism of the Intelligence effort and the snap

judgments of the planners came home to roost. Now the
consequences of the decision to substitute Mehedia for
Rabat became abundantly and painfully evident.

During his brief interregnum in the night of November
7-8, General Marie-Emile Béthouart, the top military man
among our friends in the Protectorate, had stationed his
forces at the water's edge in Rabat to welcome the Americans because he naturally assumed that they would land in
the capital. He entertained none of the qualms about the
inviolability of the "sacred city" that had persuaded Patton's oracles to counsel against the landing there.

Even after Béthouart's fall from influence, a landing at
Rabat could have precluded the battle. He told General
Noguès that the Americans were coming in force, but he
could not prove it. When nothing happened in his own back
yard, the shifty Resident General was confronted with the
dilemma of his life. "He had been deeply impressed,"
Morison wrote, "both by German power and by the
propensity of the United Nations to muff every operation,
like Norway, Crete and Dieppe, that they attempted overseas." If the American force of which Béthouart spoke was
but a commando affair, and he failed to oppose it, the Germans would have found the excuse they needed to take
over North Africa, and that was the last thing Noguès
wanted. But an American landing at Rabat, where he could
judge for himself the magnitude of the effort and justify his
surrender, to both the Germans and his own shifty conscience, would have decided the question.

"Those who know General Noguès," Morison speculated,
"think that in the face of *force majeure* he would have
joined the Allies promptly and decisively." Thus, the
decision to bypass Rabat probably lost for Patton whatever
chance there was of an unopposed landing.

Patton was keenly aware of the shortcomings and
hazards which the rapidly developing Battle of Morocco
now revealed. Delayed on the *Augusta* by the unexpected
naval engagement, he could land only about six hours
behind his schedule, his staff reaching the shore even later.
When he was on the beach at last, he found to his dismay
that there was little he could do to influence the course of
the battle.

His own contribution to the operation was virtually nil on
D-Day. Next morning he awoke chipper and eager, looking

his sharpest in his elegant war gear, only to find that he had
no place to go.

The issue was very far from decided. In his own Fedala
sector the day broke ominously. It was expected that the
French under General Desré, who had succeeded the
deposed Béthouart in command of the crack Casablanca
Division, would come out in force to defend Casablanca,
which General Anderson's 3rd Division was approaching
rather cautiously. Although the French failed to show up,
Anderson's advance was stopped nevertheless—"as completely as if by a pitched battle"—by a woeful lack of supporting weapons, vehicles, and communications equipment,
most of which was held up by heartbreaking delays in
unloading.

Patton decided that this was the crux of the matter and
began to intervene in this seemingly subordinate sphere of
the operation. He summoned Lieutenant Stiller, his cowboy-
aide, and went down to the beach to see what they could
do. "The situation we found was very bad" he later wrote.
"Boats were coming in and not being pushed off after
unloading. There was shellfire, and French aviators were
strafing the beach. Although they missed it by a considerable
distance whenever they strafed, our men would take cover
and delay unloading operations, and particularly the
unloading of ammunition, which was vitally necessary, as
we were fighting a major engagement not more than 1,500
yards to the south."

General Patton remained on the beach for about 18 hours,
getting thoroughly wet all of that time, knocking himself out
to speed the unloading at this one area, personally helping
to push off the boats and trying to quiet the nerves of his
men, who kept faltering whenever a French plane flew
over.

"People say," he conceded, "that Army commanders
should not indulge in such practices." But he added, "My
theory is that an Army commander does what is necessary
to accomplish his mission and that nearly 80 per cent of his
mission is to arouse morale in his men." He was quite satisfied that his day was well spent. "I believe," he wrote after
the war when recalling the day, "I had considerable
influence . . . on making the initial landing a success." It
was the only episode in the entire Moroccan battle he felt
worthy of mention to prove that his "personal intervention
had some value."

In the meantime, at the Mehedia beachhead, General Truscott's *Goalpost* force was having considerable difficulties with the agile French forces commanded by General Maurice Mathenet. At daybreak on November 9th his situation was "insecure and precarious." The utter confusion of the campaign was epitomized by the very character of Truscott's troubles. According to the Army's history of the campaign, he "had come ashore in the early afternoon [on November 8th] after a morning during which, because of his inadequate communications, he could gain little exact information and could exercise insufficient control. There he found his battalion and company commanders in similar difficulties with their subordinate units. In a half-track carrying a radio (SCR-193) he ranged over the beachhead attempting to meet the most immediate problems and to improve coordination. As the afternoon gave way to darkness, the unsatisfactory conditions at the beaches were deteriorating still further."

The radios of his tanks, for example, had gone out of order during their passage at sea. The tankers had had no time to reset the sights on their guns before contact with the French. United States Navy planes dropped some of their bombs on our troops, who were also hit by artillery fire that seemed to come from their own batteries.

Truscott's means of communications broke down and he was out of touch for a day. When he finally succeeded in getting through to Patton, who was only 50 miles away at Fedala (still at the beach pushing off those boats), and asked for help, there was none to give. All of our forces had been committed. Moreover, Patton knew far too little of the situation to offer even gratuitous advice.

General Eisenhower was in Gibraltar, waiting in the putrid air of an underground nerve center for news from his commander. At 2:45 A.M. on the 8th, only 75 minutes after its H-Hour, the Eastern Task Force reported: *"Landing successful, A., B. and C. beaches."*

At 5:45 A.M. General Lloyd R. Fredendall, commanding the Eastern Task Force, radioed: *"Landing continues unopposed."* At 8:30 A.M. Fredendall reported again, but there was no word from Patton, four hours after the Western Task Force had been due to go in.

Signals continued to tumble in . . . *Oran airport on fire* . . . *Blida airdrome captured* . . . *French destroyer on fire.*

But Patton was keeping mum.

In the signal center on the Rock, Colonel Darryl F. Zanuck was helping with the traffic while waiting for transportation to Algiers, where he was to supervise the Signal Corps photographic activities. Eisenhower would call him from time to time:

"Anything from Patton?"

"Not a word," Zanuck would report back.

"Battles are raging," he jotted in his personal log, "and we seem to be in control of most of Algiers and Oran, but the Casablanca theater is ominously silent."

Then word came at last about Patton's Western Task Force, but in a roundabout way and from a strange and unexpected source. Pro-Allied French officers at Safi, hard-pressed by Harmon's *Blackstone* sub-task force, radioed Gibraltar that they were losing out, *plut à Dieu,* God grant it. On November 9th the silence was broken, but only once, with a brief signal from Patton in which he reported merely that resistance to the assault had been overcome "at the beaches." Eisenhower radioed back for details. But there was no answer.

That same day, the decisions of the "Torch" operation began to cast their long shadows. Behind "Torch" was a sweeping bold plan. Patton was to hold the Atlantic flank while the Anglo-American forces turned eastward, took over Tunisia in a blitz campaign, and pushed into Tripolitania, pressing Rommel's Afrika Korps flat against the British Eighth Army.

But as early as the third day of the operation it was becoming evident that nothing would come of this ambitious design. The first straw in the wind was the arrival in Algiers of a French colonel named René G. Cerardot. He flew in from El Aouina airfield in Tunisia with word that 40 bombers had landed German troops there, with more coming in by the hour. Admiral Jean-Pierre Esteva, General Noguès' counterpart in Tunisia, was giving them a "friendly reception."

Otherwise, though, good news was reaching Eisenhower

on the Rock. Oran surrendered. A British submarine hit an Italian cruiser. General Fredendall promised to clean up Algiers by nightfall.

But there was still no definitive word from Patton.

What was keeping him from letting Eisenhower know the progress of his invasion? Three things.

First of all, he himself did not really know what was going on.

Secondly, his line of communications broke down in a tragic series of mishaps which went far to show how ill-prepared the Army was almost a year after the United States' entry into the war, and at the time of its first major invasion.

The clandestine radio network (of which "Ajax" at Casablanca was a key station) the OSS had prepared throughout Morocco for exactly this eventuality was frustrated and thwarted by Gibraltar's refusal to deal with it on its own terms. "Ajax" was at his post all through this crucial time, but "unwillingness of the operator at Gibraltar to adopt the procedures which the operator at Casablanca deemed necessary in the light of experience rendered contact imperfect." Impossible would have been a better word.

Patton's own signal arrangements collapsed completely and, indeed, dismally. As the official critique of "Torch" put it, this was the "glaring deficiency" of the whole operation.

General Patton's message center, which was supposed to handle all his communications, was on the *Augusta*. It was set up in three locations spread over the crowded ship. Its nerve center, "Radio One," was so crammed with 25 radiomen operating eleven radio receivers, three cipher machines and other equipment that it simply could not function with anything approaching efficiency.

One mishap followed another. The tactical radio net operated through a control center on the *Augusta,* but the nine men who were supposed to be handling the traffic turned out to be so green that they had to be relieved at noon on November 8th. Then the *Augusta's* heavy guns fighting off the French ships knocked out the transmitter and rendered all circuits inoperative. When repairs restored the transmitter and traffic began to flow over the tactical net, the messages were found to be worthless because they had been improperly enciphered.

"Accomplishments on D-Day were next to nil," wrote the

Army's official history of the Signal Corps. "The operators did keep a log, which revealed upon subsequent examination that, while the subordinate stations in the net had called in periodically, the headquarters had failed to answer."

The operators once intercepted a French message in plain text, describing the damage done to Casablanca and recounting French battery counterfire. But though they recorded it, they failed to pass it on.

Communications on the beachheads were only a little better. The planners had pinned much hope upon the large SC-299 radios. But only one of them was landed, and that one not until November 10th, the third day of the operation. Smaller sets became inoperative in various mishaps. Doused in sea water during landing, the power-supply cords and contacts shorted, and the radios died. Signal operations were smothered by adverse circumstances—signalmen without equipment; equipment inaccessible under layers of other supplies still aboard the ships; the cipher machines scattered at landings far removed from the units to which they belonged.

Without aerial reconnaissance and signal communications equipment, Patton was like Samson at Gaza. At no time during the operation did the situation improve sufficiently to give him the ears and eyes he needed to be able to exercise his command effectively. For once, the United States Army's most loquacious general had lost his voice.

By November 10th, another factor entered the picture, the *third* reason for Patton's protracted silence. But this was one of his own making. While planning his share in "Torch," he obtained Eisenhower's permission to force the surrender of Casablanca, if all other means failed, by threatening to bomb the city from the air and bombard it from the sea, and to carry out the threat should it become necessary. Patton tried to get Ike's consent to such a grave and desperate measure without any strings attached—authority to execute the plan at his own discretion. However, Eisenhower explicitly stipulated that Patton must clear it with him and obtain his unequivocal approval before resorting to this extreme maneuver.

In the afternoon of the 10th, Patton was handed a message from Eisenhower. "Dear Georgie," it read, "Algiers has been ours for two days. Oran defenses are crumbling rapidly with navy shore batteries surrendering. Only tough nut left to crack is in your hands. Crack it open quickly. Ike."

The message left Patton bewildered. He did not know what to make of it—whether to take it as a friendly gesture or a harsh prodding. He decided that Ike did not mean to hustle or taunt him, and that the cable was but an expression of the Commander in Chief's sympathy in his predicament.

Patton was hard-pressed on all sides, and the end was not in sight. Ike's cable made up his mind. There was but one short cut to a quick victory, as he saw it—the full-scale attack on Casablanca to *force* the city into submission.

He gave the order—to Hewitt on the *Augusta* to make his ships ready for bombardment, to Admiral Ernest D. McWhorter on the *Ranger* to prepare his carrier-based planes for the bombing, and to Anderson for the attack on the ground.

But Patton was worried. If he told Eisenhower about the plan, Ike might say no at the last moment. So he decided to go ahead with the operation without calling for his superior's endorsement—in fact, without so much as telling him what he had in mind. The *fait accompli* would take care of everything. Now the collapse of Patton's signal system came in handy. He would be able to blame his failure to clear "this thing" with Eisenhower on the breakdown of communications.

For the first time in the battle he was on the top of events. He was drawing up the plan and giving orders to attack Casablanca in his best, brisk style. "It took some nerve," he wrote the morning after the operation, "as both Truscott and Harmon seemed in a bad way, but I felt we should maintain the initiative." This aside went far to show how little he knew of the total situation. Truscott had captured the airport at Port Lyautey, and Colonel Lauris Norstad's P-40's were already deploying on it for the attack; Harmon had the situation at Safi firmly in hand and was now sending his tanks up from Mazagan to invest Casablanca from the south.

In the evening, Admiral Hall came ashore to make the last-minute arrangements for naval gunfire and the *Ranger's* planes. During the conference, General Anderson asked to be allowed to jump off at dawn, but Patton made it 7:30 A.M. "I don't want any mistakes in the dark," he said firmly.

Then he went to bed.

At 3:30 A.M. on November 11th he was awakened by Colonel Harkins. A French officer had come down from Rabat with what looked like an order for Michelier to surrender.

It developed that at 2 A.M. "a French car, heralded by the blowing of a bugle, its lights on, and white flags flying, [had] appeared at an outpost of Company G, 30th Infantry, northeast of Fedala, carrying two French officers and two enlisted men from Rabat." The group was taken first to the regimental CP and was then directed to Patton's headquarters in the Miramar. Colonel Gay was summoned and told that the Frenchmen were "bearing orders from General Lascroux to General Desré that the Casablanca Division cease firing." Gay then sent Harkins to awaken the General.

Patton dressed quickly and went down to the smoking room of the Miramar to see one of the Frenchmen. It was an eerie scene, illuminated by a single candle stuck in a champagne bottle. Patton sat down at a small table and the Frenchman, his grimy pale face lit up below a black leather helmet, stepped forward. "Commandant Philippe Lebel, Third Moroccan Spahis, *mon général,*" he introduced himself and handed Patton the message he was carrying. Scribbled in a soft pencil on tissue-thin paper, it was from General Georges Lascroux, commander of all ground forces in Morocco, instructing his unnamed addressee crisply and somewhat vaguely that "on receipt of this order French troops will cease hostilities with American troops. French commanders will take immediate steps to notify American outposts."

Patton waved Lebel to the side and, in a low voice, began to discuss the situation with General Keyes, his Deputy Commander, and Colonel Gay. They suggested that he call off the attack at once, but Patton shook his head.

"No, it must go on. Don't you remember what happened in 1918 when we stopped too soon?"

He called Lebel back and told him in a voice that sounded thoughtful, a little tired, and almost kind:

"You're a staff officer, Lebel, aren't you? So you naturally appreciate my problem. If I accept this order at its face value and call off a highly coordinated attack, what is my guarantee that it will be obeyed by the French Navy?"

"Mon général," Lebel said eagerly, "will you allow me to make a suggestion?"

"Go ahead," Patton said.

"I am personally known to Admiral Pierre Jean Ronarc'h, Chief of Staff to Admiral Michelier. If you will permit me to go to the Admiralty now I will personally guarantee that the French Navy will obey the order."

Patton vanished in thought, holding, as Pascal used to, an inward talk with himself alone, his fingers drumming the table nervously as he brooded. Then he turned to the French officer.

"Lebel," he said slowly, "I accept your word and let you go. Tell Admiral Michelier that if he doesn't want to be destroyed he better quit at once because," raising his voice, "I will attack"—but he did not say when.

He called over Colonel John P. Ratay, his deputy G-2, and told him:

"Ratay, you'll accompany Commandant Lebel to Casablanca. Unless the French Navy immediately signifies that it is bound by this cease-fire order, the attack jumps off as scheduled." He paused for a moment, then said, "And Ratay!"

"Yes, sir."

"Don't get yourself shot!"

When Ratay and Lebel dashed out of the room, Patton asked for a piece of paper and scribbled on it: "If you receive message from me in clear 'Play ball' cease all hostilities at once." He handed it to Colonel Elton F. Hammond, his Signals Officer. "Send it to Admiral Hewitt in code," he said, then rose and looked at his wristwatch. It was 4:15 A.M. He called out to Colonel Gay, "Come on, Hap. Let's go to Anderson's forward C.P. It's too sticky in here to sweat out this Goddamn thing."

There was nothing for a whole hour—then another.

At 6:25 A.M. Colonel Norstad's P-40's flew directly overhead on their way to their targets at Casablanca. Outside the breakwater, Hewitt's covering group, with its big guns elevated for action, came into clear sight. Planes from the *Ranger* had reached the city and were circling it with ominous monotony.

At the Miramar, Colonel Hammond was standing at the radio with a walkie-talkie in hand, waiting for the word. Suddenly at 6:48 A.M. his receiver came to life. Patton was calling from the 3rd Division's command post.

"Hammond," his voice came in crackling, "are you in touch with Hewitt?"

"Yes, sir," the colonel said.

"Good. Call it off. The French Navy has capitulated. But you'll have to work fast." There was brief static, then Patton's voice was clear again.

"Thank God," he merely said, and signed off.

"It was a near thing," Patton wrote to his wife, "for the bombers were over the targets and the battleships were in position to fire. I ordered Anderson to move into the town, and if anyone stopped him, to attack. No one stopped him, but [these] hours . . . were the longest in my life so far."

Now the battle was over! And all of a sudden Patton had recovered his voice. At 7:38 A.M. General Eisenhower was handed a slip of paper with just 12 words on it, printed in capital letters: "WORD JUST RECEIVED FROM GENERAL PATTON OF SURRENDER OF FRENCH AT CASA." It had taken Patton only five minutes to let Ike know what was happening. The message required only 48 minutes to travel from him to the *Augusta* and then on to the Rock.

This was but a miniature campaign. Only some 30,000 American soldiers were involved in it. The troops were green and so were their generals, including Patton. Hampered by the cockeyed uncertainties of the situation, the blatant unreliability of whatever advance intelligence he had, the tergiversations of the foe, faulty communications, and, last—but not least—by his own inexperience, he was very far from his top form.

The great plan—produced in what Eisenhower called the "trans-Atlantic essay contest"—was of no help.

The astounding victories were scored by Generals Anderson, Harmon and Truscott in scattered, free-wheeling actions. With rare gallantry and initiative, they seized their own opportunities, made their own decisions, and subsisted entirely on their own meager resources. They had to. Confronted as they were at every step with exigencies for which they were unprepared, and without guidance and tangible help from Patton, they had to improvise.

In a way, it was fortunate that the French had made them fight. The green troops were blooded, their generals gained *savoir-faire*. And Patton was made to realize that war was much more than just dash and fierce intentions. In his *post mortem* to Eisenhower, he was able to point out many lessons the experience had taught him, seemingly minor, but useful in their tactical details and long-range significance.

Patton demonstrated that he was aware of the inadequacies of the desultory campaign when he closed it formally with the customary order to his troops making their victory official and final. He got around to issuing it only on November 15th, four days after the termination of hostilities, but predated it to the 11th. It was short and crisp.

He began and ended the four-paragraph order with praise that was unusually subdued for him. "Soldiers of the Western Task Force," he wrote, "aided by the Navy, you have accomplished the impossible and on the anniversary of Armistice Day have added another armistice which, too, will live in history—at 0700 the enemy ceased firing." The fourth paragraph read: "With complete confidence for our continued success, I congratulate you on what you have already achieved."

But then, in the face of the bitter experience of those crazy 74 hours, George Patton turned realistic and admonished his men: "Do not let your joy in the present victory slacken your efforts to achieve greater fame in the glorious battles which are to come.

"In solemn loyalty to our country and our heroic dead, we must bend every effort to perfect ourselves, not only in tactics, but also in deportment and soldierly appearance."

He went on to spell out what he meant by "soldierly appearance" in a separate order read to all troops: "I fully appreciate the danger and hardships you have been through and the lack of conveniences and clothing which you face. On the other hand you, each one of you, is a representative of a great and victorious army. To be respected you must inspire respect. Stand up, keep your clothes buttoned, and your chin straps fastened. Salute your officers and the French officers, now our allies. Keep your weapons clean and with you."

He concluded with a characteristically Pattonesque flourish: "Your deeds have proven that you are fine soldiers. *Look the part!*"

In a humbler mood, on this same November 15th, he issued another order which, too, was typical, of the man. "It is my firm conviction," he wrote to all commanding officers, "that the great success attending the hazardous operations carried out on sea and on land by the Western Task Force could only have been possible through the intervention of Divine Providence manifested in many ways.

"Therefore, I shall be pleased if in so far as circumstances and conditions permit, our grateful thanks be expressed today in appropriate religious services."

But no matter what went before and how much hard work was still ahead, now his "longest hours" were over. He was a conquering hero and master of Morocco.

It proved a heady part so early in the war.

In his pre-battle order to his troops still on the transports, General Patton had the purpose of this war clearly before him. "The eyes of the world are watching us," he wrote. "The heart of America beats for us. God is with us. On our victory depends the freedom or slavery of the human race."

Then he suddenly seemed to have lost sight of his noble purpose. Indeed, he somehow lost sight of the war. Although the United States had been in it for less than a year, the world had been at war since the fall of 1939, for three long years and two months. England and the Netherlands had been left in partial ruins by the Nazis; Poland and Russia had been despoiled and plundered; France, Norway and other European countries raped, humiliated and chained.

At the side of the Nazi conqueror appeared a despicable character named Major Vidkun Quisling, Hitler's Norwegian vassal.

France, in particular, was ruled by members of this contemptible new caste of traitors tied to their Nazi masters by sheer corruption and odious prejudices—their bitter hatred of the Jews, for example, or their fancy dreams of a latterday despotism.

In Northwest Africa, the preposterous blackguards of Vichy were well entrenched in the military organizations, rationalizing their adherence to the regime of Marshal Pétain, that "antique defeatist," as Churchill called the old man.

The peculiar mentality that produced their warped allegiance was explained by the Prime Minister during those confusing days in a masterful speech to a secret session of the House of Commons.

"In a state like France," he said, "which has experienced

so many convulsions—monarchy, convention, directory, consulate, empire, monarchy, empire, and finally republic— there has grown up a principle founded on the *droit administratif* which undoubtedly governs the actions of many French officers and officials in times of revolution and change. It is a highly legalistic habit of mind, and it arises from a subconscious sense of national self-preservation against the danger of sheer anarchy. For instance, any officer who obeys the command of his lawful superior or of one who he believes to be his lawful superior is absolutely immune from subsequent punishment.

"Much, therefore, turns in the minds of French officers upon whether there is a direct, unbroken chain of lawful command, and this is held by many Frenchmen to be more important than moral, national, or international consideration."

When now the British and Americans arrived in Northwest Africa at last, these men (whose lineal predecessors had tormented Captain Dreyfus with forged evidence and faked charges) exclaimed that they were "honor bound" to resist the Allies.

So often was the word "honor" invoked those days to explain and justify the refusal of French officers to join forces with the Allies that General Clark, whose unhappy task it then was to conduct negotiations with them, finally exclaimed, "If I hear the word 'honor' mentioned again by any of these guys, I'll slug the fellow."

There were, of course, noble and towering exceptions. The real soul of France continued to live, her real heartbeat continued to pulsate in men like de Gaulle, Giraud, Juin, Weygand, and many other officers on the lower levels of the French military hierarchy. But if there were such exceptions, General Auguste Paul Charles Albert Noguès was not one of them, neither was Admiral Michelier, and their haughty, pokerfaced henchmen like Lascroux, Mathenet and Desré.

Noguès, an unhappy figure shaped in the bastard mold of Hamlet and Torquemada, preserved his loyalty to the decrepit marshal at Vichy as long as he could. He did even more than that—he remained true to Pétain's German masters and did his best to delay, if not thwart, this first faltering Allied step toward the liberation of his country. Cooped up in his ivory tower at Rabat, he used the telephone with his intriguer's skill to make Patton's task as difficult as possible. He personally aided General von Wulisch, chief of the German Armistice Commission, and most of his associates to escape to Spanish Morocco.

If these men were not rotten to the core, they were woefully weak. And Noguès moved them like puppets on a string. Even General Béthouart recoiled from his higher duty when he was required to arrest Noguès and remove the fountainhead of resistance to the American landings. This he was not prepared to do. He did not want to be accused of supplanting his chief. He submitted to arrest meekly when he held all the trump cards while Noguès had but a thin line of secret wire to give him power. Captain Philippe Mercier of the *Primaguet* longed in his inner heart for the victory of the Allies. But he obeyed orders from Admiral Michelier and took his cruiser against the Americans.

The tight-lipped, stern-faced nervous Admiral at Casablanca was a faithful servant of Vichy. Michelier threw the French forces in Morocco against the Americans with something worse than mere adherence to what he regarded as his honorable duty—with venom, hatred and contempt. His resolution to resist the landing cost the United States Army and Navy well over a thousand casualties—337 killed, 637 wounded, 122 missing, and 71 captured. The French losses were much heavier.

The senseless treachery and futile conspiracy of Vichyite officers like Noguès and Michelier threw the Allied timetable out of kilter. Their delaying action enabled the Germans, caught by surprise as they were, to move substantial forces to Tunisia, and put off the liberation of the whole of Northwest Africa until the spring of 1943.

Their resistance undoubtedly prolonged the war. The difficulties encountered in North Africa made decisive action against the Continent, as General Marshall had visualized it, impossible in 1943. Yet these were the men General Patton now accepted as honorable adversaries vanquished in a cavalier encounter.

The startling chain of events, which returned to Noguès the victory Patton had won, began at 10 A.M. on November 11th with a "peace conference" between the American and French commanders at Fedala. Even while gravediggers were busy burying the American and French casualties in lime-coated holes on the beach, the generals and admirals of the opposing forces assembled at the Hotel Miramar to bury the hatchet.

Michelier came, fidgeting nervously, wry and pinched, prepared to be difficult. He thawed out somewhat when he realized that the Americans chose to apologize to him, virtually in so many words, for meeting his force with force. Admiral Hewitt held out his hand, but even then Michelier hesitated before he shook it. Hewitt expressed his regret that he had to fire on the French ships which had attacked him, and Michelier replied with a contorted smile as if condescending to put the American at ease.

"I had my orders," he said, "and did my duty. You had yours and did your duty."

In a few seconds, while smoke of the defunct battle was still hovering over the scene, the strange campaign was reduced to the simplest of all formulas from which military men nourish their troubled souls. The gentlemen could look into each others eyes in perfect and harmonious comradeship.

The "peace conference" had to be adjourned because Noguès failed to show up. While waiting for him, the gentlemen repaired to the *Augusta* for lunch, with Admiral Hewitt playing the genial host. Sitting at the head of the table, he had General Patton at his left and Admiral Michelier at his right. Three bottles of vintage French wine were opened, and the conversation quickly took a jovial turn.

Patton was in top form. He was talking to Michelier all the time in his rusty French, regaling him with anecdotes, and treating the man he had called "that bastard" only a day before with circumspect drawing-room courtesy. The luncheon dissolved over brandy, with Hewitt's cigars the traditional peace-pipe. Then they returned to Fedala to meet with Noguès.

General Patton had ordered an honor guard drawn up before the main entrance of the Hotel Miramar to await the arrival of Noguès. ("No use knocking a man when he is down," he wrote to his wife that day.) At exactly 3 P.M. a big black limousine drove up, escorted by a flock of motorcycle outriders. Trim and erect, General Noguès walked up the steps, followed by Lascroux and General

Lahoulle, chief of the French air forces in Morocco. They were formally greeted by General Keyes, who took them to Patton waiting in the smoking room. Seated around a long table were Hewitt, Keyes, Admiral Hall, Colonel Gay, and Colonel Wilbur, who acted as interpreter. At the opposite side were Noguès at Patton's right, Michelier, Lahoulle. Also present was General Desré, whose own immediate superior, the pathetic Béthouart, was conspicuous by his absence. He was in prison, awaiting trial for treason because he had tried valiantly to prevent the bloodshed and, indeed, make such a conference unnecessary.

Patton opened the meeting with an expression of his admiration for "the courage and skill shown by the French Armed Forces during the three-day battle just concluded." Noguès' face remained cold and blank, his posture stiff. Michelier fidgeted in his seat, his pat smile frozen on his face, his fingers playing with a pencil.

Patton then said, "We are here to arrange the terms of the armistice, and here they are."

He nodded to Colonel Wilbur, who rose and read the tough treaty—"Treaty C"—the State Department had prepared for this eventuality. As the severity of its terms became apparent to the Frenchmen, their faces grew even more somber. When Wilbur finished, a strained silence settled on the room. Then Admiral Michelier, the recent guest of honor on the *Augusta,* scribbled a single word—"Inacceptable"—on a piece of paper and handed it to Noguès. The Resident General glanced at it, seemed to hesitate for a moment, then rose to his feet. "Allow me to point out," he said in an icy voice, "that if these terms are enforced, the French Protectorate in Morocco will cease to exist."

This was his trump card on which he pinned his hopes to get the most out of this seemingly uneven bargain. At face value it appeared to be a powerful argument.

"We French might no longer be able to challenge American strength," the Resident General's cold and crisp words were designed to mean, "but that will only be the beginning of your troubles. If you impose this cruel treaty on us, it will fall to you the entire task, not only of preserving order among Arabs, Berbers and Jews, but of securing the Spanish part of the Moroccan protectorate from here, and maintain the long and vulnerable lines of communications with Algiers and Tunisia. We French represent tranquility and stability here. But you Americans, naïve newcomers to this supercharged scene, bring disorder and maybe anarchy."

The situation that confronted Patton on this afternoon of his triumph was ambiguous and precarious. He was sitting at the head of the table, to be sure, and was dictating his terms. But, as George F. Howe, the Army's historian of the campaign, put it, "any appearance of overwhelming superiority was superficial." The force Patton commanded had been barely sufficient for the amphibious assault. It was but incompletely established on shore and depended on subsequent increments of men and matériel to renew the power of attack. Patton was, moreover, "intruded among a population of great political complexity at a distance of 4,000 miles from the United States," and his communications link with General Eisenhower was tenuous, at best.

Noguès' shrewd threat hit a sensitive nerve in Patton. His own political advisers had briefed him exactly on what the Resident General had just implied. He accepted the picture they had painted for him on the face of it because, lacking the political sophistication the situation needed and accurate knowledge of conditions in Morocco, he could not perceive its basic fallacy. The crux of the matter was not what Noguès and his counselors had told him. The choice was not between Noguès or chaos. The issue was not the removal of the French from Morocco, but the replacement of the discredited Vichy crowd by a reputable group of French patriots who were untainted by collaboration with the Nazis and fully committed to the Allied cause, and who now waited in the wings to take over.

The dramatic success of the powerful "argument" Patton had prepared to force Noguès' surrender now faded from his mind. All he saw were the difficulties of the days ahead. He had come to the meeting with his mind made up—to preserve the *status quo*, although it meant that he had to do business with characters like Noguès and Michelier.

When Noguès sat down, Patton rose quickly. This was his cue, a moment for exquisite drama, the emotional spectacular in living color of which he was the unsurpassed master.

Standing stiffly, he asked for the treaty. Colonel Wilbur handed it to him. He held it in his hands for a few seconds, looked grimly at his audience, and tore the paper slowly and ceremoniously into strips. Then he began to speak.

"Gentlemen," he said, "I have known most of you French officers before when I was a student in your Army schools in France, as also has General Keyes. We all belong to the same profession, that of arms. Your word is as good as your written signature. Such has always been true of men of our profession."

"I propose, until final terms are arranged by higher headquarters, that you return all your men with arms to your proper stations, that you take your sick and wounded with you and your dead. I propose the prisoners of yours which we have, we will turn over to you; that you will give me your word that you will not bear arms against these forces, that you will turn over to us without delay any prisoners of war which you have and any of our dead which are within your lines; but you will make every effort to maintain good order and discipline in Morocco to include the guarding of the railroad bridges and the railroads through the Taza Gap."

The tension vanished and, as he spoke, the faces of the Frenchmen brightened with every sentence. Even Noguès managed to put on a faint smile. But Patton raised his voice again and, with an impish twinkle in his eyes (the meaning of which his French audience could not anticipate), he said:

"There is, however, an additional condition upon which I must insist."

The French delegation looked at him with apprehensive eyes. Before they could lapse into another spell of gloom, Patton said, signaling to Major Codman:

"It is this—that you join me in a glass of champagne."

The spell was broken. An unsavory chapter in the history of World War II was about to begin.

Fortune, said George Chapman in *All Fools*, is the great commander of the world and has diverse ways of promoting her followers—"to some she gives honor without deserving, to other some, deserving without honor." Though Morocco was at Patton's feet and it was for him alone to decide how and to whom to dispense favors and honors, he suddenly found himself somewhat like Sterne's Didius, hung up on one of the horns of his dilemma.

Cooperation with the French in the land Noguès and his

henchmen had forced him to *conquer* baffled Patton from the very outset. He felt intuitively the embarrassment of working with people described bluntly by their own compatriots as "traitors." Yet pragmatic considerations tended to impel him to swallow such embarrassment and work and even "fraternize" with them. It was a difficult decision to make but it took him only four days to make it.

In the wake of the surrender, Patton did seek to "prevent and mitigate," for example, the persecution of those Frenchmen who were now prisoners of Noguès for the "crime" of having aided the Allies. The case of General Béthouart in particular filled him with compassion, suggesting a policy, the contours of which he incorporated in a memo to Eisenhower on November 14th.

"Major General Béthouard [sic] of the French Army," he wrote, "and a group of French officers took steps before the arrival of American Forces to insure that our forces would be received in a friendly manner and that no opposition would be made to the landing. General Béthouard and his adherents are now held in close arrest by General Noguès."

Patton then went on to describe Noguès' argument and advise Eisenhower of his own opinion.

"The French point of view is as follows," he wrote. "General Béthouard took action in direct disobedience of orders received from higher authority. The French feel that such action must be punished if discipline is to be maintained and the provisions of any agreement which may be signed be carried out promptly and completely. If one officer is permitted to disobey orders, others may do likewise.

"My point of view is as follows: General Béthouard and the officers who worked with him are our friends. They have acted in a courageous manner and exposed themselves to great hazard in our interests. From the point of view of standing by our friends and in order that we shall not lose face, it must be assured that he and his adherents are protected."

This, however, was something of an afterthought. The proposed "treaty" of November 11th included Article 20, which bore directly on the problem and stated that "The authorities in French Morocco will immediately furnish the United States authorities with a list of all persons of whatsoever nationality who have been placed under restriction, detention or sentence (including persons sentenced in absentia) on account of their dealings or sympathies with the United Nations. Those still under restriction or detention will be released forthwith if the United States authorities so direct."

However, Patton had scrapped the "treaty." In its place, he concluded what he called a "gentlemen's agreement" with Noguès and explicity permitted the Resident General to "proceed with an investigation and trial of General Béthouard," stipulating only that "no action whatsoever would be taken against General Béthouard and his adherents except upon the final approval of General Eisenhower."

The Noguès crowd interpreted this as implicit permission to try and sentence Béthouart and his associates at a secret trial arranged as quickly as possible, and even to execute them, forestalling General Eisenhower's intervention with a *fait accompli*. But Patton now showed signs that he regretted his hasty acquiescence to the fate Noguès had carved for the Béthouart group. So he concluded his memo to Eisenhower with the unequivocal sentence:

"I believe it to be of the greatest importance that any officer who has acted to assist this expedition shall be protected and upheld."

He acted promptly upon his belief by instructing Noguès to release Béthouart and a handful of his adherents held at Meknes and arranging their immediate departure from Morocco, virtually a step ahead of their executioners. Even so, his "belief" covered only Béthouart and a few of his friends. Patton did nothing to "protect and uphold" the other pro-Allied victims of General Noguès' vindictive wrath.

On November 15th, in another memo to Eisenhower at Gibraltar, he outlined in detail the prospects of "cooperation" with the "French authorities." It was written in the wake of a visit by General Gruenther of Eisenhower's staff to Western Task Force Headquarters to ascertain how Patton proposed to proceed in this delicate matter. The day before, Patton had sent General Keyes and Colonel Gay to Noguès at Rabat "to take up questions pertaining to the cooperation to be expected of the French." Patton's memorandum to Eisenhower, describing the conference, now went far to show how well Noguès had succeeded in both scaring and ensnaring the man who had just vanquished him.

"At this conference," Patton wrote, "General Noguès gave the general impression that he is most anxious to cooperate in every way possible. General Noguès agreed in principle to all proposals made in my name; in fact, he agreed too readily. I am convinced," he added, still sustaining some of his doubts, "that he is a man who agrees readily but may not always carry out his agreement."

Patton then went on, however, to present the situation in Morocco in the light in which Noguès wanted him to see it.

"General Noguès . . . volunteered the information," he wrote, "that if the Spaniards threatened Morocco from the North he would immediately take military steps to oppose any Spanish invasion. He also agreed to defend Casablanca against German air attack, using French personnel to man antiaircraft defenses." But the next paragraph relayed to Eisenhower without any qualifications on Patton's part one of the *canards* Noguès was peddling, also revealing misinformation he had received from his own advisers.

"My representatives informed him," Patton wrote, "that reports had been received that there was considerable unrest in Morocco, and that pro-American activities were being suppressed. General Noguès stated that that was not correct and that the country was completely calm *except for a stirring of the Jewish population.* General Noguès stated that the Jews in Morocco are of the lowest order, that they expected to take over the country when and if an American Expeditionary Force would arrive, and that they are now agitating against French authorities. He stated that they were being controlled without difficulty."

The question of General Béthouart was also raised at the meeting, and Noguès conceded that "he had intended to have [him] tried a day or two after November 11." But, Patton told Eisenhower, Noguès "had reconsidered and felt that some delay might be advisable."

After discussing matters of press censorship and the rate of exchange, Patton's representatives raised the issue "of the arrest of civilians who have shown pro-American tendencies." Noguès promised that any individuals detained for their pro-Allied activities would be "immediately released" upon Patton's specific request "in each case." However, Noguès qualified the promise by adding, as Patton put it, "The situation in this matter cannot be considered satisfactory as yet, as some time must elapse before American authorities can be properly informed as to the individuals who have been arrested."

This was the turning point. Noguès began to collect on the price of his "cooperation." As Howe expressed it in his study of "political conditions" after the surrender, "Screening those who merited release as purely political prisoners from others was a process bound to take time, since it would be necessary to depend upon the counsel of reliable men who knew French Moroccan politics." But those "reliable men," French, Moroccan and American, were becoming rapidly displaced in Patton's entourage in favor of the "cooperating" Vichyites. "With the invasion," Howe wrote, "an entirely new group of Americans was substituted for those who had previously served the interests of the United States in Morocco. Although Mr. Frederick P. Culbert was selected from the Office of Strategic Services representatives among the consular staff to be General Patton's deputy adviser on civil affairs with broad authority, the staff as a whole was not used effectively to protect the preinvasion friends of the Allies."

By November 19th Patton had his problem solved. He decided to leave the Noguès gang in power, and so advised General Eisenhower in a letter, asserting that "the anti-Darlan-Noguès group does not have the personnel nor is it in a position to control Morocco if given that mission."

Between November 15, 1942, and February 15, 1943, General Patton's letters from the wars read like the travelogues of a starry-eyed tourist rather than a conquering hero and commanding general of an army that had most of the war still ahead of it.

In a sense, they reflected a kind of escapism from the harsh realities of problems which he neither quite grasped nor felt quite qualified or strong enough to solve. Confronted with all the modern inconveniences of his job as the American proconsul in a complex country mixed of feudalism, colonialism and a bustling mercantile civilization that was as up-to-date as the other two were anachronous, Patton sought refuge in a never-never land that was, as he himself put it, "half-Hollywood and half-Bible." This tour of duty then became a Cook's tour, mostly misguided. It was an excellent *divertissement* to take his mind off the pressing problems of his conquest and, indeed, of the war.

Patton's grand tour began on November 16, 1942. Five days after the conclusion of the armistice in the Miramar to the accompaniment of clinking champagne glasses, he visited General Noguès at Rabat and paid a formal call on the Sultan. He started out for the meeting with an escort consisting of scout cars and tanks. But he changed his mind en route. He decided that such a show of force would appear boastful, so he dismissed his escort before reaching Rabat.

Patton's arrival was quite modest for a conqueror, but Noguès outdid himself with the pageantry of his reception. Lined up in front of the Residency was a battalion of Moroccan cavalry. Next in the line stood Noguès' own bodyguard, resplendent in freshly starched white uniforms with equipment made of red Moroccan leather. Two bands supplied musical accompaniment for the pageant, their trumpets blaring harshly, their drums pounding out the oriental rhythm of the marching song, men twirling brass umbrellas, with bells fastened to them, over their heads.

On November 22nd Patton helped to celebrate the Sultan's anniversary in a tremendous parade. On December 8th he again lunched with Noguès in Rabat and had a private talk with the Sultan's Grand Vizier, a "very smart old gentleman of ninety-two." The ancient courtier seemed to be troubled about the future, but Patton put him at ease.

His mischievous little eyes twinkled as he was bamboozling the old Arab, assuring him that, as a profound student of history who had familiarized himself since childhood with the special problems of Morocco, he intended to maintain peace in the Protectorate by consulting His Majesty the Sultan and His Excellency the Resident General.

On December 19th he participated in an enormous *fête des moutons* (festival of sheep) held at Rabat and was met at the Palace with the usual ceremony of the red-robed, white-gaitered guard of giant Senegalese.

On January 12, 1943, Patton again paid a ceremonial call on the Sultan, and on February 1st he went on that boar hunt with the Pasha of Marrakesh. These were the high points in an endless succession of parades and celebrations.

It seemed that the war he had barely begun had already

ended for him. He was content with playing a role in this exotic land reminiscent of the Ottoman pashas who ruled a good part of the world of the 16th century with their special Oriental brand of *laissez-faire*.

His troops had gone into bivouac in a forest of cork trees between Casablanca and Rabat. Patton moved his office into the ultramodern Shell Building in downtown Casablanca, more than adequate even by the keenest American standards. He transferred his private residence from the Miramar to an elegant villa in an exclusive suburb of Casablánca. He moved about in a massive Packard limousine equipped with all the accessories of his rank and position, and a special horn whose basso blast proclaimed his coming for miles.

It was a strange and well-nigh inexplicable interlude in his career. There was so much to be done, yet so little time to do it. Patton, who had craved militant action all his life, now appeared to be satisfied with resting on the laurels of his first and incomplete victory.

His headquarters worked hard and well in the aftermath of the conquest to clear up the rubble of the brief battle, open the ports, turn Morocco into a firm Allied base for future operations, train the troops. Various armed inspection trips were made to check on the situation in the interior. Systematic air reconnaissances were flown from points 20 miles offshore to 100 miles inland. Efforts were made to integrate the French forces into the Allied war machine for what now became the common struggle against the Nazis.

Patton's emphasis was on what, in his wrap-up order, he called "deportment and soldierly appearance." The troops were ordered to wear their helmets at all times, to appear impeccably groomed on all occasions with leggings and all. For the first time in this war, Patton was introducing the regime that made the absence of a button from a soldier's tunic seem as grave a disaster as the torpedoing of a cargo ship by a U-boat in Casablanca harbor.

The war seemed to recede into the background. Patton's headquarters blossomed out as a social center resembling Marshal Murat's lavish court at Turin after his conquest of Piedmont. It was an incongruous spectacle. The battle of Stalingrad was at its height. In Tripolitania, Alexander and Montgomery were locked in a desperate campaign with Rommel. The Battle of the Atlantic was raging unabated.

In Tunisia, American forces fought the growing strength of German and Italian troops flown in to stem the Allied tide.

Yet in Morocco everywhing was serene and gay. Every conqueror is supposed to create a muse. But this conquest produced a hedonistic enclave in the war, with breakfasts in bed, champagne parties, dazzling social fetes, and lavish parades.

When France fell in June, 1940, Kenneth W. Pendar, a student of Romance languages working at the Harvard Library in Cambridge, Massachusetts, felt frightfully useless. He had lived in France a long time, and the impress of her eternity was stamped on his soul. But now he thought, somewhat like Napoleon in 1814, that France had more need of him than he of France.

While most of his countrymen in America looked on the sudden collapse of a free civilization with complacency and equanimity, Pendar tried to do something to help France in her hour of shame—but what? Just then a Navy friend asked him if he would be interested in going to North Africa to work at the American Consulate in Casablanca. The United States was continuing diplomatic relations with Vichy and had agreed to send aid to Morocco and Algeria. The State Department, it seemed, now needed a handful of French-speaking people to supervise the distribution of the aid and insure that none of it fell into Nazi hands.

It was a strange assignment. Recruited by the Army and the Navy, but chaperoned by the State Department, these men were made vice consuls and posted to the various American consulates in the area. In July, 1941, Pendar was summoned to Tangiers and told by Colonel William Bentley, the Military Attaché, that he was really a glorified spy. Bentley gave Pendar and his colleagues a "shopping list" of what the Army and Navy expected to get from them—military maps and intelligence about the ports, the beaches, the movement of ships, the size of the armed units, condition of roads, the location of bridges, tunnels and roads. They were told to set up a secret communication and courier system, and organize local patriots into underground resistance groups for any eventualities.

Pendar was assigned to Morocco with a small group of his fellow "vice consuls"—including the mysterious David King, "a sophisticated yet sincere, witty and rather Elizabethan adventurer." King became the generalissimo of a band of French and Moroccan freedom fighters who performed great services for the Allies for a year and a half, only to be pushed aside after the victory when Patton decided for the *status quo*. Pendar pulled political strings and succeeded in putting together a shadow cabinet of prominent anti-Vichyites—for the Day.

The "vice consuls" had endured a tough time even before. The regular personnel of the consulates viewed them with jealous eyes and hampered their work with petty bureaucratic machinations. The Vichyites and the Nazis tried hard but could not get rid of Pendar. He was eventually forced out of Morocco by the backstabbings and intrigues of his own colleagues at the Consulate in Casablanca. He had to be shifted to Algiers, where he became an assistant to Robert D. Murphy, himself a career diplomat but operating as chief of this strange adventure in diplomacy.

Now, in the immediate wake of Patton's conquest, Ken Pendar was back in Casablanca as Murphy's personal agent to clear up the mystery of a letter President Roosevelt had sent to the Sultan of Morocco, but which apparently had never reached His Majesty.

The letter had been sent in a sealed envelope to H. Earl Russell, the Consul General at Casablanca, with instructions to deliver it to Mohamed V as soon as word was received of Patton's approach. It was written in friendly terms, advising the Sultan of our coming and asking for his cooperation.

In the evening of November 7th, as soon as "Ajax" picked up the password *"Robert arrive"* on the radio, Consul General Russell took the envelope from his safe and handed it to Vice Consul Renè Mayer, who rushed it to Rabat during the night.

Mayer arrived in Rabat when confusion was already rampant in the Residency. He was stopped by the palace guards and prevented from delivering the letter to the Sultan, who was sleeping peacefully in his white marble harem. When Mayer then asked for an audience with Noguès to give him the letter for delivery to the Sultan, he was refused. He thought he had no alternative but to leave the letter with an official at the Residency, hoping that it would be forwarded to the Sultan in the morning.

Several days had passed since the landing, but President Roosevelt had received no answer to his friendly and courteous note. He queried the State Department, which in turn sent a note to Ambassador Murphy in Algiers, and Murphy dispatched Pendar to Casablanca to see what had happened to the letter. Pendar found out that it had been pigeonholed by Noguès. Inquiries at the Residency produced no results. He was told brusquely that General Noguès had no recollection of the President's letter, and would not authorize a search for it.

Pendar had no choice but to take the matter up with the highest ranking American in Morocco—the man, indeed, who was supposed to be in charge—General Patton. The General received the Vice Consul in his spacious office in the Shell Building, listened somewhat impatiently to his presentation, then asked him in a piqued voice:

"What are you trying to do, Pendar, make trouble?"

"No, sir," the Vice Consul said. "But I have my orders, sir, to see to it that the letter reaches His Majesty."

"There is no need for that Goddamn letter," Patton told him. "I have written one myself to the Sultan and that ought to be enough."

"I am afraid you don't see the point, General," Pendar said patiently. "This is a letter from the President of the United States to the Sultan of Morocco, a communication on the highest level of state, and the President is anxious that it reaches the Sultan. I have my orders to see to it. . . ."

Patton interrupted him. "Do you have a copy of the letter?"

"Yes, sir." Pendar handed him the copy and waited silently while Patton, in evident irritation, read it through. When he finished, the General looked up at Pendar over his spectacles and told him with a scowl:

"I don't like it, do you?"

"I think it is an excellent letter, sir," Pendar said.

"There is not enough mention of the French in it," Patton objected.

"You see, General," Pendar explained, "this letter originally was accompanied by a letter for General Noguès and a request that he hand this one to the Sultan. There was no need to mention the French, for we were asking their own Resident General to deliver the letter."

Patton leaned back in his chair and commanded Pendar, "Read it to me!" Pendar read the letter aloud.

"No," Patton said pensively, "I still don't like it." He took the letter and worked it over, inserting additions, then read the rewritten letter to the Vice Consul. "Now, doesn't it sound better?" he asked.

"I don't think, sir," Pendar replied, "any of us has the right to edit the President's letter without his knowledge."

Patton was working up a rage. "Goddamnit, Pendar," he exploded, "I'll take full responsibility for this letter."

"Very well, sir," Pendar said, "I shall tell Mr. Murphy when we telephone tonight."

Patton blew his top. "Goddamnit, I won't have you or any other Goddamn fool talking about this letter on the telephone. Don't you know the wires are tapped?"

"Yes, sir," Pendar said quietly, "I do. They have been tapped for the last year and a half." This gentle reference to the yeomen work the Vice Consul had done in Morocco prior to the arrival of the Western Task Force mollified Patton somewhat, but he was still in a fighting mood.

"General Noguès and I have a perfect understanding," he said, "and I have left all these problems of personnel up to him. Morocco is an extremely difficult country to manage. Now, the Jewish problem. . . ."

He plunged into a long lecture about the Jews in Morocco. Noguès had introduced the Nazi racial laws in the Protectorate and persuaded Patton to continue them in force or else, he told the American general whose victory was supposed to end all oppression in Morocco, the Jews would start an uprising to avenge their humiliation, the Arabs would retaliate with riots, and the whole country would be thrown into a turmoil. It was a patently false issue. There were only 200,000 Jews in the whole of Morocco. They had looked forward to the coming of the Americans and worked splendidly in the anti-Nazi underground with King and Pendar. Though they were now shocked by Patton's fraternization with the Vichyites and angered by their own continued humiliation, they planned no uprising to end their oppression.

Pendar was shocked when he realized how far Noguès had succeeded in poisoning Patton's untutored mind, but he endured the lecture in silence. He was neither high enough nor sufficiently in Patton's good graces at this moment to set him right.

Later that night Ambassador Murphy called Pendar from Algiers and told him that a cable had just been received from Washington demanding an immediate explanation about the letter. Next morning, the Vice Consul returned to Patton in the Shell Building and reported on the talk with Murphy, provoking a prompt outburst in Patton's most violent language.

"Goddamnit," he roared, "I told you I didn't want this letter discussed on the phone. I'll take the full responsibility."

"Then communicate with my superior, Ambassador Murphy," Pendar told him, "and tell him as much."

Patton suddenly reversed himself. "You know, Pendar," he said, "my bark is worse than my bite."

He replaced the frown on his face with a charming smile, buzzed for an aide and ordered him to inquire about the letter. It was quickly learned that it had been "mislaid" at the Residency but was then duly delivered. The mystery was solved and the case closed, but the incident exposed to Pendar the seriousness of the situation. "I was to learn," he wrote, "that the Vichyites were in favor at the moment, and that they had more or less discredited our true friends to the recently arrived American soldiers. One Frenchman who had been most loyal and useful to us in the pre-landing days appeared very depressed and upset when I met him. 'I seem to have been on the wrong side before landing. Everyone agrees that the former collaborationists are the only people your military men get on with or apparently like to see.' "

Patton not only left the Noguès gang of French fascists and pro-Nazis in full power to do as they pleased, but also permitted them to continue the persecution of patriotic Frenchmen who sided with the United States and had worked underground for the common cause, and were now fully prepared and able to cooperate with us in making our occupation of the Protectorate tranquil and safe.

"The Frenchmen of authoritarian sympathies," George F. Howe wrote, "some of them members of fascistic societies like the *Service d'Ordre Légionnaire des Anciens Combattants* and the *Parti Populaire Francaise* and others in less formal associations, seemed prepared even to assist an Axis counter-invasion. They propagandized against the Allies. Frenchmen of pro-Allied views, whether Giraudist or Gaullist, were the object of their surveillance and open hostility. Specific denunciations of these anti-American individuals to American civilian officials were of little or no avail, for their hands were tied by military control . . . General Patton became, in effect, a defender of General Noguès as an indispensable agent who could keep the native population in hand while the French in Morocco were in general kept friendly or neutral."

The Moroccan radio, left in the hands of its Vichyite operators by order of Colonel Black, continued to broadcast blatantly pro-Axis propaganda. Intercepts revealed that Noguès himself was in touch with Vichy, discussing with Hitler's henchmen in metropolitan France anti-Allied measures, and even the possibility of ousting the Americans from Morocco.

Conditions in Morocco and Patton's pro-Noguès administration had been reported to Winston Churchill by British agents (some of whom worked furiously against Noguès but chiefly because they hoped to replace him by their own man, the Count of Paris, pretender to the French throne of the Bourbons, who was awaiting the call in nearby Tangier). Churchill was "grieved to find the success of our immense operation . . . overshadowed in the minds of many of my best friends by what seemed to them a base and squalid deal with one of our most bitter enemies." As early as November 17th he had voiced his shock that "we are ready to make deals with the local Quislings" to President Roosevelt. But the President dismissed his concern with a jocular reference to what he called an old Orthodox Church proverb used in the Balkans: "My children, it is permitted you in time of grave danger to walk with the Devil until you have crossed the bridge."

This fraternization with the devil in Morocco persisted and grew, and on December 9th, Churchill again wrote to the President, this time referring directly to conditions in Morocco under General Patton.

"I have been disturbed by reports received during the last few days from North Africa about conditions in French Morocco and Algeria," he said. "These reports, which come from independent and reliable sources, all paint the same picture of the results which follow from our inability in existing circumstances to exercise a proper control over the local French authorities in internal administrative matters. You are, I am sure, fully aware of this state of affairs, but I think it my duty to let you know the position as it appears in the light of our own report.

"These reports show that the *S.O.L.* [a Vichy organization of ex-servicemen] and kindred fascist organizations continue their activities and victimize our former French sympathizers, some of whom have not yet been released from prison. The first reaction of these organizations to the Allied landing was, rightly, one of fear. But it seems that they have now taken courage to regroup themselves and continue their activities. Well-known German sympathizers who had been ousted have been reinstated. Not only have our enemies been thus encouraged, but our friends have been correspondingly confused and cast down. There have been cases of French soldiers being punished for desertion because they tried to support the Allied forces during their landing."

In the meantime, the conquerors paraded and danced. "The whole Moroccan situation had an Alice in Wonderland quality," Vice Consul Pendar wrote after his visit to Casablanca. He had worked more than 18 months for the liberation of Morocco and participated at Ambassador Murphy's side in the liberation of Algiers. From his ringside seat at the bout with the Vichyites he regarded Patton's fraternization with them as a betrayal of our trust.

"Noguès," he wrote, "having finally decided to cooperate with us, was being utterly charming to the American generals, and had won their hearts with dazzling displays of French military style and gold braid, Arab horsemanship, French cooking and general colonial razzle-dazzle. French and American officers began to mingle happily at marvelous parties given by Patton's political adviser, Vice Consul Culbert, in his magnificently modern apartment in Casablanca. There was a great deal of gaiety, which seemed incongruous with men fighting in Tunisia . . .

"At the top, strode Patton, rattling his great pistols and thoroughly enjoying his own rages."

General Patton had succumbed completely to the military pageant Noguès was producing for him. Whenever he dined at the Residency, he was received by the fanfare of Moroccan trumpeters, a welcoming escort of Spahi guards. He came away dazed and dazzled. Part of this fraternization, Pendar thought, was due to the *esprit de corps* that binds all officers of whatever nationality, whether friend or foe. Part of it was Patton's curious love of pomp, ceremony and imperial glitter.

I cannot rationally account for Patton's sudden relaxation of his martial ardor and strange time-out of the war to play the role of an American pasha hell-bent on out-pashaing the local holders of that title. However, I believe I have an explanation for his alliance with the Vichyites and his indirect persecution of our own best friends in Morocco.

Patton was blessed with many talents, but diplomacy was not one of them. What sometimes passed for tact in his conduct was, in fact, flattery, which he would use unabashedly when he thought it might serve his purpose. "He is a master of flattery," Commander Butcher wrote in his diary when he came to know Patton closely, "and succeeds in turning any difference of views with Ike into a deferential acquiescence to the views of the Supreme Commander. For instance, he told Ike during a lively discussion of history that anyone would be foolish to contest the rightness of the Supreme Commander's views, particularly as he is now— in Patton's words—'the most powerful person in the world.'"

Although he made convenient use of the device, he was by no means immune when it was applied to him. He was, moreover, a thoroughly romantic character who appreciated pomp in its barest exterior appeal and who was imbued with what Poe called "a quixotic sense of the honorable—of the chivalrous." It was Poe, too, who wrote, "Glitter, and in that one word how much of all that is detestable do we express," but to Patton glitter never seemed to be detestable at all.

These streaks of his inner soul were superimposed on his admirable American trait of giving the vanquished a fair shake, whether in a political contest, in a sporting tournament, or in war. He was completely devoid of political savvy. And though exceptionally well read in his own field, he rarely read newspapers or any books on *contemporary* political affairs. He was, therefore, hopelessly ignorant of the violent political cross-currents and grave issues which were at the bottom of this war.

Patton was not what is called a reactionary in politics even if only because he was so innocent in those matters;

but neither was he a liberal by temperament or convictions. Used to his own regimented society in the Army and the absolute finality of the decisions of superiors, however unreasonable or wrong, he applied the system in which he grew up to his new civilian-oriented task. Even his partisan biographer, the late General Semmes, candidly conceded that Patton's methods of boosting the fighting spirit of his men were "peculiar, and perhaps undemocratic." The last man qualified by outlook, disposition and training to play the part of an American proconsul in a conquered land, he was bound to fail, and fail at that, despite his humane instincts and best intentions.

That his instincts and intentions were good, stands beyond doubt. There were many deeds in his life that would have, had they been publicized, endeared him even to the most starry-eyed liberals who became so suspicious and critical of him. In 1944, undeceived by Patton's appearance and manners—"paternal, gruff, a bit diffident, with a warm smile flashing every now and then"—Dwight Macdonald regarded his utterances as "atrocities of the mind," and wrote of him in a bitter blast:

"My favorite general is George S. Patton Jr. Some of our generals, like Stilwell, have developed a sly ability to simulate human beings. But Patton always behaves as a general should. His side arms (a brace of pearl-handled revolvers) are as clean as his tongue is foul. He wears special uniforms, which like Goering, he designs himself and which are calculated, like the ox horns worn by ancient Gothic chieftains, to strike terror into the enemy (and into any rational person, for that matter)."

Undoubtedly Macdonald was right when he ascribed Patton's toughness to theatricalism and neuroticism. Yet behind both was the man himself—an instinctively decent human being even if occasionally he was embarrassed by his own decency which, in moments of challenge and stress, he was inclined to equate with weakness.

He was modest to the point of prudishness in sexual matters, and frowned upon illicit relations. "Patton had very strict moral principles," Field Marshal Alexander wrote, "and he once told me how wrong and unwise it was for a soldier of high standing to have any intimate association with women during wartime." But when Patton was once told that one of the unmarried Red Cross girls attached to his army had become a casualty of the war, so to speak, by becoming pregnant and needed financial help, he wrote out a check for her, worrying only afterward that his prompt generosity might be misunderstood under the circumstances.

Patton was emotionally drawn to the underdog. Now in Morocco the trouble was that, as he saw it, General Noguès was the "underdog."

A man as artless as Patton in matters like these needed strong-minded and judicious political and diplomatic advisers. Unfortunately this was not recognized by the War Department when it selected his Intelligence Officer and Political Adviser before the Moroccan venture. He was burdened with a G-2 (Black) and a political adviser (Culbert) whose leanings were right of center and who preferred to deal with what later came to be called "the Establishment"—people already in authority and *socially* acceptable to them—the "right people," in other words. Patton himself leaned in that direction. He was strongly caste-conscious (he even went so far as to claim that his own kind of "gentlemen" behaved better under stress and strain than ordinary people), and accepted authority as he found it, whatever its political coloration or past sins. During negotiations for the Italian surrender, he attended conferences at Mostaganem in Algeria at which the problems of military government were discussed. Eisenhower asked for Patton's suggestions on the basis of his experience in Sicily. But his only recommendation was "to seek quickly the cooperation of the leading Italian—the mayor or ex-mayor in any captured town—because," he said, "they were most helpful in many ways." The fact that such persons might be disqualified by their fascist past or war crimes did not seem to occur to him or influence his opinion.

It was, therefore, due partly to some of his own personal inclinations, but partly to the advice he was receiving from his accredited political, diplomatic and Intelligence advisers that Patton decided to act as he did in his relations with Noguès and the Vichyites during his four-month reign in French Morocco. In fairness to him and to place the picture in its proper perspective, we must also examine the situation confronting him and his Western Task Force in the immediate wake of the capitulation of the French.

The French could no longer resist him, Howe conceded, but it remained to be seen, he speculated, how genuine their cooperation would be. "Between the French and the natives, the imperialist relations of the Protectorate rested on the French military and the French police," he wrote. "Allied propaganda had encouraged among the Moslem and native Jewish population the hope of liberation from the French. Between Moslems and Jews, endless animosity threatened to boil over unless firmly suppressed. In the native situation, therefore, was the basis for a dangerous diversion from complete concentration on the major military objectives of the Allies."

There were other local problems confronting Patton, which he had to face squarely and solve promptly if he wanted to avoid difficulties. The French and the Spanish governments shared the role of protectors over the realm of the Sultan of Morocco. The boundary between the two areas under their respective control was one the Spanish desired to see much farther south. Should the Spanish forces stationed north of the boundary succumb to the temptation to strike while the French were weakened, American forces would almost certainly become embroiled. If the Axis used Spanish bases for air or ground attacks upon the supply lines across northern Morocco, the Western Task Force would be required to join in countermeasures.

"Thus the force," Howe concluded, "commanded by General Patton felt obliged to move with circumspection, to cooperate rather than to command."

Patton's glittering sinecure reached its climax with his visit to the Pasha of Marrakesh and the ceremonial boar hunt amid the almond trees. But this was destined to be his last pastime. Only a few days later, he received an urgent call from General Eisenhower that was to return him promptly to what he liked to call his inexorable destiny.

CHAPTER THIRTEEN
DETOUR TO TUNISIA

The Casablanca Conference of January 14-24, at which Patton played host to President Roosevelt and Prime Minister Churchill, had broken the ice. Until then, the Allies could hope only that defeat might be averted. Now the certainty of victory began to dominate their thoughts. At Casablanca they planned in cheerful, sweeping strokes and, looking defiantly to the future, proclaimed that nothing less than "unconditional surrender" could buy peace for the Axis.

It was an insolent gesture at this stage of the war. Only a relatively small expeditionary force of the United States Army had had its baptism of fire; and for the time being it had the limited objective of wresting Tunisia from the Axis. Important though this goal seemed, it was hardly more than a stepping stone on the road to Berlin and Rome. And the Allies were not doing any too well even at this minor campaign in which they had all the initial advantages.

It was largely a British show, stage-managed by Major General Kenneth A. N. Anderson, a gallant 52-year-old Scotsman who had a brigade in Flanders and a division at Dunkirk during the dark days of 1940. He was now commanding the First British Army, in which Major General Lloyd R. Fredendall's Eastern Task Force—renamed II U.S. Corps—was learning to fight. It was not exactly what the British call a "good show."

On November 15, 1942, barely a week after the impact of "Torch," General Anderson's First Army touched Tunisia at Tabarka. On November 24th it was ordered to make for Tunis, some 80 miles away. For a few days the advance progressed with the promise of victory. On November 28th the 1st U.S. Armored Division reached the outskirts of Djedeida, and came almost within sight of the offensive's strategic goal.

Three days before, General Eisenhower had arrived in Algiers to take personal charge, and proceeded immediately to the front in his armor-plated Cadillac. But he had a hard time finding General Anderson and then, when he found him at last, he had an even harder time getting from him a coherent and accurate picture of the situation. Encouraged by Anderson's ill-informed optimism, Eisenhower returned to Algiers and—exhilarated by the heady wine of his recent triumph—sent General Marshall a message that was bombastic under the circumstances.

"My immediate aim is," he wrote, "to keep pushing hard, with a first intention of pinning the enemy back in the Fortress of Bizerte and confining him so closely that the danger of a breakout or a heavy counteroffensive will be minimized. Then I expect to put everything we have . . .

on him and to pound him so hard that the way for a final and decisive blow can be adequately prepared."

By the time the message reached Marshall on December 1st, nothing in the situation justified Eisenhower's sanguine words. As a matter of fact, only four days later they sounded as hollow as a shout in an empty barrel. The 10th Panzer Division had sneaked into Tunisia; and in General Walther Nehring the Germans had an ingenious and daring commander on the spot. He was all set to open a counter-push which Hitler had designed, not merely to keep the Allies out of Tunisia, but also to evict them altogether from their newly won foothold in French North Africa.

At 9:15 P.M. on December 3rd General Anderson burst into Eisenhower's office in the St. Georges Hotel in Algiers to give him a picture of the situation as it really was and not as he had painted it only a few days before. He now shocked Eisenhower by telling him in unvarnished terms that his army in Tunisia had reached what seemed to be its "point of diminishing power." After only about two weeks and before they clashed with any major forces of the enemy, his troops had "worked themselves into a state of exhaustion," while the Germans and Italians had not yet even begun to fight.

Incapable of grasping the true situation, Eisenhower ordered Anderson to mount "an all-out attack to take Tunis and isolate Bizerte." He set the D-Day of the offensive for December 9th. But three days before it was to jump off, Ike had to reconcile himself to the inexorable realities of the situation and concede that he had lost "the first race for Tunis."

Then everything bogged down in the mud of the wet and cold North African winter. On December 26th Anderson told Eisenhower that "discretion ruled against attempting an attack for probably six weeks." Just then, Alexander and Montgomery were pushing Rommel westward, adding a complicating factor to Eisenhower's plight. By the time Anderson would be ready to attack, it seemed, he would no longer face only the Axis newcomers in Tunisia but Rommel and the Afrika Korps as well.

This was the situation when the Casablanca Conference convened and Roosevelt told the Axis that only "unconditional surrender" would take it off the hook. Yet grim though the situation appeared to be, nothing could dim the Allies' optimism. Roosevelt, Churchill and their advisers looked at the big strategic picture in which this Tunisian intermezzo was but a tiny background dot. The war was beyond it and they knew that with resources rapidly building up, nothing could stop their forward march.

So they ordered Eisenhower to begin preparations for the next objective after Tunisia. With Churchill plugging his "soft underbelly" strategy with undiminished vigor and eloquence, attention remained focused on the Mediterranean—Sardinia or Sicily. Sicily was chosen in the end, and instructions were issued to start planning for the operation, for which Churchill picked the code name "Husky."

All that remained to be done in Africa was discounted. It was boldly assumed that Tunisia would be secured before long and that Alexander and Montgomery, busy with Rommel in Tripolitania, would be free for "Husky." An army group under Alexander was created on paper to include Montgomery's fabulous Eighth Army and the first American army to participate as an entity in the European war. It was to be called the Seventh Army. And General Patton was to command it.

On Feburary 2, 1943, Eisenhower sent for Patton to give him his orders, and he came over from nearby Oujda, where he happened to be visiting Mark Clark. He went straight to Eisenhower's villa and over lunch was told of his new assignment. Later that day he was off for Rabat by air without even having touched Ike's headquarters at the St. Georges, carrying all his instructions in his head and knowing exactly what he would have to do, and also how he would go about doing it.

In Rabat, Patton reorganized the Western Task Force overnight into what came to be called I Armored Corps, and started his staff on planning for "Husky." At this stage all this was mostly paper work, for he would get his new army only piecemeal, and its training would have to wait until the plans had been agreed upon.

Then the dam burst.

Rommel had arrived in Tunisia, surveyed the situation and concluded that his opportunities were all in the west. Eisenhower had been briefed by Brigadier Eric Edward Mockler-Ferryman, an unmarried, blimpish 47-year-old artilleryman who was serving as his Intelligence chief, that

Rommel was massing his forces and that "bits and pieces of information" indicated he would "lash out" at Pichon via Fondouk in the north.

Colonel Benjamin A. Dickson, a tall Philadelphia mainliner out of West Point with the Class of 1918, called "the Monk," had more than just "bits and pieces." He was G-2 of II Corps, and recognized clearly that Pichon was not the direction of Rommel's intentions. He warned that the main Axis attack would be on Gafsa, on positions thinly held by the American troops, and that the Germans would come through the Faid Pass.

Mockler-Ferryman dismissed "the Monk's" warnings, and when the brigadier assured Eisenhower that the attack would converge on Pichon, dispositions were made accordingly. The attack came on Gafsa and then proceeded toward the Kasserine Pass, exactly as Dickson had predicted. The result was the near-collapse of the Allied front in Tunisia and a defeat which remained the worst such Anglo-American debacle *vis-à-vis* the Germans until the Battle of the Bulge pushed it into second place.

It was a major setback and, at first blush, it seemed that it would place the Allies' chance of winning Tunisia in the balance. Fredendall's II Corps had been badly dispersed by Anderson's dispositions based on Mockler-Ferryman's wrong estimate. Yet when the attack came through the Faid Pass, II Corps was the one hit by its full force. Although Rommel highly praised the green American troops who, as he put it, *"haben sich vorzüglich geschlagen"* ("gave a splendid account of themselves"), when General Alexander inspected the front on February 19th, he absolved Anderson of any blame and left him in command of his battered army, but recommended that Fredendall be relieved. Eisenhower was also told by Major General Omar N. Bradley, who was at large with II Corps as Ike's personal representative, that Fredendall had failed to get the most out of his corps—so Fredendall had to go.

This was the cue for Patton.

He was away from his headquarters when the front exploded, visiting Alexander and Montgomery in Tripoli to review with them his plans for "Husky." He immediately left, for every slight sign that he might be needed always put him in a highly personal "Condition Red." Sometimes a bit of gossip that one or another of his fellow generals had ptomaine poisoning or a death in the family was enough to alert him with great expectations. Every military set-back, no matter how inconsequential, filled him with hope that he would be called to replace somebody.

This time, too, he did not return to Rabat but flew to Algiers to be near Eisenhower in case he might be needed. But Ike was at the front, sweating out Rommel's attack, and Commander Butcher put Patton up in Ike's empty house. Smoking their cigars and sipping a bit of wine, they stayed up late that night while Patton confided to Butcher one of the great disappointments of his recent career which the fiasco in Tunisia had made extremely à-propos.

"As soon as we arrived in North Africa I expected that Rommel would wind up in Tunisia," he said, "and was look-ing forward to hitting up with that brilliant bastard. I had spent years preparing myself for him, had read his God-damn book a myriad times, studied every one of his cam-paigns, and thought I had him pretty well sized up. It was the ambition of my life to chase him a bit, then seek him out personally in battle, and shoot him dead with my own hands.

"I hoped Ike would send me against him in Tunisia. I was the *logical* choice, not only because I had the spirit that went with the job but for simple military reasons. Everything indicated that when Rommel came he would come with armor, and you can say anything you want to, but I think I'm the best Goddamn armor man in the U.S. Army. So you see, Butch," he said plaintively, puffing his cigar, "I cried my heart out when Ike gave the job to Lloyd Fredendall. And besides," he added, "those mealy-mouthed Limies couldn't have pushed *me* around. I'd have stood up to that sonuvabitch Anderson."

It was not until March 4th that Eisenhower decided to take Fredendall out of II Corps and send Patton into the breach. Even then he needed some soul-searching and prodding. Still astounded by his own meteoric rise and lacking the ruthlessness that his top command needed, he was somewhat soft in his relations with his contemporaries he had left behind. He would tell himself to be "cold-blooded about removal of inefficient officers." But when it came to replace a general, he hesitated to act upon his own resolve.

By the end of February the tide had been stemmed and the situation appeared to be stabilized, even if only pre-cariously. Even in that Patton had a distant and indirect part. He had loaned to Fredendall Major General Ernest N. Harmon, the recent hero of Safi, who had the 2nd Armored Division under him in Morocco, to back up Major General Orlando Ward in command of the 1st Armored Division and help him reoccupy the Kasserine Pass.

On February 28th, his mission accomplished, Harmon stopped at Algiers on his way back to Morocco because he thought Eisenhower might be interested in his observations. Though it was a Sunday, Ike went to his office to get this first-hand report. Harmon told Eisenhower that he thought Rommel would leave the great plain west of the Grand Dorsal, from which he had evicted II Corps, as a no-man's-land; at the same time he would move troops from the north to reinforce his units in the south in preparation for Montgomery's attack, which he seemed to be expecting through the Gabes gap. Harmon cautioned Ike that the German had "a few tricks left up his sleeve" and doubted that Fredendall would be capable of coping with them.

"This is Rommel, Ike, and tank warfare at its latest," he said, "way above poor Fredendall's head. 'Pinky' Ward is all bushed, and besides he is hopping mad at Fredendall for letting Anderson disperse his division."

Harmon urged Eisenhower to send Patton to Tunisia or else, he said, II Corps might actually disintegrate.

Still troubled in the goodness of his heart, Eisenhower could not make up his mind. "I had no intention of recommending Fredendall for reduction or of placing the blame for the initial defeats in the Kasserine battle on his shoulders," he wrote in his memoirs, "and so informed him. Several others, including myself, shared responsibility for our week of reverses."

On March 4th, however, he went back to the front to see for himself, and especially to hear from Bradley, whose judgment he trusted implicitly, just how bad the command situation really was. He met Fredendall at Tebessa, but Bradley—who had no status at II Corps and was looked upon as a kind of informer for Eisenhower—was not notified of Ike's visit and was away with Major General Manton S. Eddy at the 9th Division. When Bradley arrived in answer to an urgent summons, Eisenhower was closeted with Fredendall in a small stucco house, but went out to the porch to have a few moments alone with his confidant.

"What do you think of the command here?" he asked.

"It's pretty bad," Bradley replied. "I've talked to all

division commanders. To a man they've lost confidence in Fredendall as the corps commander."

"Thanks, Brad," Eisenhower said, "you've confirmed what I thought was wrong."

That settled it at last, and Eisenhower told Captain Ernest W. "Tex" Lee, an aide, to have Major General Walter Bedell Smith, his Chief of Staff, alert Patton. At 10 P.M. "Beetle" Smith called Patton at Rabat and told him "to report by air to Maison Blanche airfield at Algiers," not later than the next afternoon, March 5th. He was to take along an acting chief of staff, and two or three staff officers, "prepared for extended field service."

On this Friday afternoon, Ike flew into Algiers from Tebessa, Patton from Rabat, and they had their conference then and there, at the Maison Blanche airport, standing up. General Smith and Commander Butcher had come to meet Eisenhower, and they, too, were on hand. Patton had with him Brigadier General Hugh J. Gaffey, a handsome, genteel-faced, impeccably groomed but tough tank expert for whose agile brain and daring he had high regard. Gaffey had come as his Chief of Staff *pro tem.*

Eisenhower began the impromptu briefing by impressing upon Patton the overwhelming importance of smooth cooperation with the British. "There must be created in our Army" he said, "a feeling of partnership between ourselves and the British. Your Corps, George, will take orders as an American unit directly from the 18th Army Group, which is commanded by General Alexander."

Then he explained the plan Alexander had worked out, and Patton thought he would need all the self-restraint he could muster to preserve that "feeling of partnership." Not that the plan was bad or illogical. It was brilliant, in fact, ideally adapted to the situation and sure to force Rommel into a nutcracker. But it restricted II Corps to playing second fiddle to Montgomery's Eighth Army, and that, Patton feared, would cramp his own free-wheeling style.

"Your first big task, George," Eisenhower said, "will be to assist the Eighth Army to get through the Mareth Line. Your corps is to tie up as much German strength as possible and secure Gafsa as a forward supply base for Montgomery.

You must exercise great care in so moving toward the sea as to avoid cutting across Montgomery's line of advance."

The plan had been conceived weeks before, when Beetle Smith visited Alexander and Montgomery in Tripoli during Rommel's attack on the First British Army. General Smith asked how soon the Eighth Army could join up with the First Army north of Gabes, and Montgomery said he expected to be in Sfax by April 15th.

"If you could do that," Smith exclaimed, "you could have anything you want from General Eisenhower."

"In that case," Montgomery said, "I would like an American airplane for my personal use."

He got his chance to expedite collection of the plane even while Patton was flying to his new command. Rommel did exactly as Harmon had predicted. He regrouped in the south, deploying three Panzer divisions against the Eighth Army at Medenine in Tripolitania. On the night of March 5-6 he unleashed a vicious spoiling attack from the Mareth Line, the fortifications the French had built to protect Tunisia from the Italians.

Rommel hoped to disorganize the Eighth Army and decimate Monty's armor by forcing it into the scrap. But Montgomery staved off the attack in his top form. He repulsed the first assault, and when Rommel renewed his attack on the afternoon of March 6th, he drove him back into the line. While Rommel lost 52 tanks, most of them to antitank guns, Montgomery lost none. Resisting the temptation of a pursuit, the Eighth Army remained firm. It continued its preparations for the big job, the capture of the Mareth Line, for which Montgomery needed II Corps' passive assistance.

Patton had left Algiers for the front on March 5th and stopped at Constantine to check in at 18th Army Group Headquarters. He arrived at 4:30 in the afternoon and immediately went to see General Alexander for a discussion that was to last until 1 o'clock the next morning. According to Alexander, they had first met in Tripoli in 1942, when Patton paid a surprise visit to the Eighth Army. "No one could fail," Alexander wrote of that occasion, "to recognize him as a colorful character, this fine-looking man who carried a pearl-handled pistol on each hip. He was, like many Americans, friendly and forthcoming but not in the least aggressive."

This time, however, Alexander was impressed with

Patton's aggressiveness. He spoke of "the Hun" in such violent and emotional terms that tears came to his eyes several times. It was an altogether happy encounter, and Patton felt much better about the prospects of the partnership.

Patton spent the night at Constantine and arrived at II Corps Headquarters in Djebel Kouif at 10 A.M. on March 6th, even as the Battle of Medenine was raging some 250 miles to the southeast. He stormed into the wretched village of mud huts standing like a charioteer in his armored vehicle, wearing his most formidable scowl, his jaw jutted against the web strap of his highly polished helmet with its two stars.

He was leading a procession of scout cars and half-tracks bristling with machine guns, their tall antennas whipping crazily overhead. The shrieking sirens of the cortege drove the frightened Arabs from the muddy street. Even the GI's scurried for cover into the nearest doorways.

Patton came with his own entourage—with young General Gaffey; his aides, Jenson and Stiller; his G-2, Colonel Oscar W. Koch; his G-3, Colonel Kent Lambert; and George Meeks, his faithful orderly. He carried a letter to Fredendall that Eisenhower had written in longhand at the Maison Blanche airfield, making the change in the command of II Corps official and final. This small piece of paper would be the first to let Fredendall know that he was through in Tunisia.

Without warning, the corps found itself in the eye of a hurricane. "In the words of Eisenhower," Bradley wrote, "Patton was to rejuvenate the jaded II Corps and bring it to a 'fighting pitch.' By the third day after his arrival, the II Corps staff was fighting mad—but at Patton, not at the German."

This was more or less what Patton expected and, indeed, wanted. During his conference in Constantine, Alexander told him frankly his views of II Corps and of the "frightful mess" he had found it in during his inspection trip a few weeks before. He spoke candidly of the American troops, whom he had found "disappointing," to say the least, "mentally and physically soft, and very green." He told Patton that they desperately needed toughening and discipline, and that was exactly what Patton determined to give them.

He did it with what to both officers and enlisted men seemed "trivial chicaneries of a crazed martinet" and were, in the words of the scandalized correspondents attached to II Corps, "undemocratic and un-American methods." He put a quick end to the staff's late arrival at their desks in the morning by closing the mess at 7:30 A.M. Then he introduced the most stringent uniform regulations. Helmets had to be worn by everyone (including nurses) at all times. When the corps—incredulous that Patton meant the order seriously—proved tardy in complying, the General himself went out and rounded up officers and enlisted men he found without their helmets, lined them up and told them:

"I will not tolerate any sonuvabitch who fails to carry out my orders promptly and properly. For the last time, I give you the choice—you either pay a $25 fine or face a court-martial. And I need not tell you that the court-martial would show on your records."

The men all coughed up the $25, and cursed their new commanding general.

Trivial or not, Patton's reforms electrified the corps and fast made it lose its softness. "Each time a soldier knotted his necktie," Bradley wrote (somewhat dubiously, not quite knowing whether to laud or censure Patton's spit-and-polish reign), "threaded his leggings, and buckled on his heavy steel helmet, he was forcibly reminded that Patton had come to command the II Corps, that the pre-Kasserine days had ended, and that a tough new era had begun . . . And while [these reforms] did little to increase his popularity, they left no doubt in anyone's mind that Patton was to be the boss."

Now Patton quickly terminated Bradley's own nebulous existence at II Corps.

Bradley had come to North Africa on February 24th, in the immediate wake of the debacle in Tunisia, to help Eisenhower with his chores, but with no explicit duties. The Commander in Chief, however, regarded his coming as a godsend. He was confused by the chaotic events of that horrid week in February and felt badly in need of someone who could size up the situation and act as a top-ranking liaison officer at the front—his "eyes and ears," as he put it. Bradley seemed ideal for the job. He had a clockwork mind capable of thorough attention to detail; he was the perfect pro with a consummate knowledge of his art; and he was discreet, honest and loyal.

"Just as quickly as you can," Eisenhower told him on the afternoon of his arrival, "I want you to get up to the front and look for the things I would want to see myself if I only had the time."

Bradley was to report directly to Eisenhower, offering what he called "suggestive corrections" both to the commanders at the front and the Commander in Chief at Algiers. Fredendall was not a bit enchanted by Bradley's mission. He regarded him as "Eisenhower's agent on the front carrying tales home to the boss outside the chain of command." When Patton inherited Bradley, he was quick to terminate the ambiguity of his assignment.

"I'm not going to have any Goddamn spies running around my headquarters," he said, and phoned Algiers to eradicate the problem. He himself regarded Bradley highly, admiring his competence as much as he valued his discretion and decency. He did not want to get rid of him. Rather he wanted him to join his headquarters in a more formal relationship in which Bradley would be directly under him instead of "snooping for Eisenhower."

Patton got Eisenhower to appoint Bradley II Corps Deputy Commander. Ike was only too pleased to comply, for he had greater things in mind for Bradley when Patton would move on to greener pastures.

As it turned out, this was a brief and strange interlude in Patton's wartime career. It was not properly calculated either to reveal the greatness that was in him or to establish him in the public mind as the invaluable and incomparable combat leader Generals Marshall and Eisenhower were firmly convinced he was. His primary job was not to win any great campaigns, but to reorganize a badly mauled and discredited corps of green soldiers, to instill in them ironclad discipline and fighting spirit, to make them battleworthy. Yet his assignment to Tunisia by the accident of a humiliating defeat had a significance far beyond the importance of his immediate mission. Tunisia thus brought together the legendary American triumvirate which became instrumental in winning the war in Europe—the three great soldiers Marshall had picked with sure eyes.

From there on, they stayed together in perfect harmony with an ideal distribution of labor—Eisenhower the coordinator, Bradley the thinking-machine, Patton the fighter.

The emergence of a trio like this in any army would have been remarkable even if it had come by the sheer exigencies of the war. It was extraordinary in that it was deliberately compounded by Marshall and kept together through all the vicissitudes of the three generals' professional and personal relationship.

Patton was so eager to get into the war that he was now in danger of bursting a vein while waiting for orders from General Alexander for his first combat venture.

"Why are we just sitting down doing nothing?" he said to Bradley during this apparent lull. "Goddamnit, Omar, we must do *something*!"

"Wait a minute, General," Bradley tried to soothe him. "What do you propose to do?"

"*Anything*," Patton exclaimed, "rather than just sit on our butts!"

He was not exactly idle. From the morning after his arrival to the afternoon of March 13th, he had devoted himself to restoring discipline to the badly shaken, listless II Corps. A single week, that was all the time he had! Orders had already been issued to return the corps to the war with an ambiguous offensive scheduled for March 17th. Patton tried to make the most of every minute.

He visited every battalion of the four divisions and delivered to each a different profanity-studded pep talk. In between, he pricked and pushed the staff to stick to its last and complete the plans for the pending operation. What time he had left he spent hunting for officers and men who failed to wear their helmets, leggings, and neckties. So thorough was his inspection that he even peeped into the latrines and fined the men who neglected to wear their helmets while engaged in one of nature's most pristine pursuits.

At the end of the week, Patton was satisfied, more or less, that he had "restored discipline" although he realized that only combat could complete his job. He did subject his troops to a high-voltage shock treatment and *did* drive the fear-of-Patton into their hearts, but it was debatable whether "discipline" was the right term to define their reactions. The soldiers were awed by his calculated despotism but also mad and defiant; they were baffled by his uncouth ways but also disgusted; they laughed at the elaborate pornography of his pep talks but also blushed. These boys were awfully raw, too close to their recent civilian past. The veneer of their civilization had not scraped off sufficiently for them to appreciate Patton's bizarre approach. And, he, in his eagerness to galvanize the men into soldiers, overstressed his theatricals and seemed quite comic at times.

On March 15th General Eisenhower dropped in to see how things were going. He had been told confidentially (not by Bradley) that II Corps staff was not too happy with its new commanding general, but Eisenhower expected that. On his part he now liked what he saw. The staff was working like beavers 20 hours a day and, indeed, so well, that Patton refrained from replacing it with the officers he had brought along. The troops were smart in appearance and at least looked tough. It was obvious that Patton had performed a miracle with the corps in just nine days.

Patton's bounce and sputter, and his blustering display of energy masked some disappointments. Since his arrival at Djebel Kouif he had suffered two blows he regarded as highly personal setbacks. One came from the other side of the fence and, as far as he was concerned, took much of the fun out of the war. His great adversary had vanished from the scene. Field Marshal Erwin Rommel, a broken and sick man, had relinquished his command in Africa, and Patton would now face a mere Italian, Marshal Giovanni Messe. He was an able and dedicated soldier—but no Rommel.

The other blow came from Constantine in the form of an order by General Alexander. It conformed to the strategic plan, which provided for the employment of II Corps merely to ease Montgomery's break through the Mareth Line by diverting as many German and Italian divisions as possible to a make-believe offensive in the direction of the Gabes road. This was the elaboration of orders Alexander had issued on March 2nd, four days before Patton's arrival, which Eisenhower had explained to him at the briefing session in Algiers.

Although Patton recognized the reasons for thus limiting his mission, he hoped that his appearance would persuade Alexander to give II Corps a somewhat bigger part. But no. In a policy directive issued on March 14th, Alexander held the corps to its original assignment. Patton was told explicitly to go slow, and warned not to go too far.

But he was not through hoping. His ambitions went well beyond the part of an extra he was supposed to play in the background while Montgomery would be singing his big aria at the center of the stage. He expected that the battle would create opportunities for him to burst out of his boundaries, and thought it likely that in the heat of a breakthrough he would not be held to the master plan.

Now the battle was upon him and suddenly Patton perked up, throwing all his misgivings to the wind (which, incidentally, was blowing at gale force with torrential rains, whipping the prospective battlegrounds, turning the clay and sand of this exotic terrain into impassable mud).

On the evening of March 16th Patton was overcome by a classic feeling, like Scipio Africanus on the eve of Zama. He called his staff to his dimly lit office at Djebel Kouif and told them with his fiercest martial frown (which he had practiced in the mirror for the occasion):

"Gentlemen, tomorrow we attack. If we are not victorious, let no one come back alive."

It was sheer unadulterated corn. Just when the staff decided that it had the world's worst ham for a commanding general, it had to reserve final judgment by something Patton did in the wake of his bombastic address. He retired to his dingy room and prayed.

"What do you make of this guy?" Captain Leonard M. Bessman, a former Marine now serving in 'the Monk's' G-2 Section, asked Lieutenant Colonel Russell F. Akers Jr., the corps' assistant G-3.

"I'll be damned if I know," Akers answered. "He's certainly a character."

"He sure is," Colonel Robert W. Wilson, the G-4, chimed in.

"Maybe this is the way to win this war," Bessman said, remembering Fredendall's leisurely, colorless regime.

"Or maybe it's the way to make a fool of ourselves," Akers said.

Baffled, they then went off to the war, totally undecided how to estimate Patton as a general and what to make of him as a man. They were still undecided when he left them less than a month later.

D-Day had originally been set for March 15th, but Alexander postponed it to the 17th, to be "closer to the Eighth Army's scheduled attack." Patton was becoming restive. When Alexander's order arrived on the 13th, he recorded in the diary his apprehension that the delay might enable the enemy to strike first. And he was becoming increasingly exasperated with the subsidiary role Alexander's burgeoning plans were assigning to II Corps. On March 15th he noted with evident tongue in cheek that the purpose of the operation was "capturing and securing Gafsa with a view to using it as a forward supply base for resupplying the [British] 8th Army on its move to the north."

But Patton's disappointment did not dim his skill in drawing up his own tactical designs. On March 14th, in another diary entry, he described his plans for II Corps as being patterned after Stonewall Jackson's operation in the Second Battle of Manassas. Just as Jackson had helped General James Longstreet's corps at Bull Run, he would aid Montgomery to break through by conducting a dazzling flank battle.

The offensive was unfurled on the morning of March 17th, and Gafsa was occupied on the first day. Then on the 18th Major General Terry de la Mesa Allen's 1st Infantry Division, fighting for the first time as a division, took El Guettar; and General Ward's 1st Armored Division was getting ready in the mud to open the drive on Maknassy.

Suddenly the opportunity Patton expected would turn up was there. The Italian garrison that held Gafsa had withdrawn without a fight down the Gabes road to the hills beyond El Guettar, there to await the arrival of German reinforcements on a line to protect the rear of the Afrika Korps, dug in on the Mareth Line facing Montgomery's Eighth Army.

Since the Italians were on the run and there were no Germans ahead of him yet, Patton immediately recognized his chance to push straight through Gafsa and El Guettar, and take up positions on the second phase line before the Germans would arrive. He began making his plans for the dash.

But when he awoke on March 19th, General Gaffey

handed him a sealed envelope from General Alexander that had come in during the night. It contained "Outline Instructions for Future Operations," signed by Major General Richard McCreery, Chief of Staff of the 18th Army Group. These instructions dashed Patton's hopes and filled him with foreboding. They ordered him to "(1) hold Gafsa; (2) secure and hold heights east of Maknassy; and (3) send light armored raiding party to airfield at Mezzouna, to destroy installations and return."

What really disheartened him was the fourth item: "Large forces," it read, *"not to be passed beyond the line Gafsa-Maknassy-Faid-Fondouk."* His chance to break through to the sea and bag the Afrika Korps from the rear was gone. All he was allowed to do was "to make noises" in the direction of the Axis forces. He could not even venture out far enough to prevent the German reinforcements from linking up with the Italians.

Patton saw the future rather dark—with two Axis divisions against him, one probably a Panzer division, and he did not expect them to sit tight awaiting their doom with folded hands. And he was angered by Alexander's arrangements that put II Corps in a strait jacket just when it needed all the freedom of action it could have to forestall the Axis threat and make the most of his rapidly vanishing opportunities. On March 19th he wrote: "The . . . plan seems to envision pinching out the II Corps after the capture of the heights in the vicinity of Fondouk."

With characteristic indiscretion (that in his special world was often tantamount to insubordination), Patton hoped to annul Alexander's restrictive order, and prevent II Corps from being pinched out, by making his own arrangements to advance *beyond* Fondouk. He instructed General Ward to prepare the 1st Armored Division for aggressive action near Maharès, totally unauthorized, yet hoping that he would gain Alexander's *post festa* approval with the accomplished fact of the operation's success. Patton was so "mad" about the plan of pinching him out that he decided to resort to something he very rarely did—take the matter directly to Eisenhower over the head of his immediate superior, General Alexander.

On March 22nd the 1st Armored Division made Maknassy at last. But it was then pinned down before Djebel Naemia by the 10th Panzer Division, which had arrived in the meantime, as Patton expected it to, and was to make life difficult for him from then on.

As he had clearly anticipated, the Axis did not dare risk a penetration into its rear that would threaten the lines across which the Afrika Korps was being supplied in the Mareth Line, and had no choice but to attack. It came with savage force on March 23rd.

The night before, Patton went to bed in full pack except for shoes and coat, having ordered General Allen to push on with his 1st Division on the Gafsa-Gabes road and secure heights on the north side. But at 6 A.M. the division was attacked by elements of the 10th Panzer Division with some 50 tanks.

"G-2, II Corps, had surmised the arrival of the 10th Panzer in the vicinity," he wrote with some heat. "G-2, 18th Army Group, disagreed. In this operation we lost six 155-mm guns, six 105-mm guns (overrun by tanks), 24 TD half-tracks and 7 TD M-10's. We put 30 German tanks out of action, 15 of which were later recovered by the Germans and the other 15 blown up by us."

The attack was stopped shortly before noon, after having penetrated to within two miles of Allen's command post.

In the afternoon, Signal Intelligence handed Patton an intercept that the Germans would make a second attack at 4 P.M. Then a second intercept indicated that one of the German artillery regiments could not get up in time, and the attack would be postponed until 4:45 P.M.

In the second attack infantry preceded tanks and got to within 300 yards of our position, where they were stopped by our artillery and air bursts. The battle proved to his complete satisfaction that this II Corps was different from the formless, listless group of green soldiers he had found on his arrival only 17 days before. "When the smoke cleared away," he noted proudly, "we found that not a single American soldier had given any ground."

Now there appeared still another factor in the situation that made Patton even madder. He had argued in vain in 1941 against General McNair's emphasis on tank destroyers, warning that it was an illusion to expect them to cope with tanks in a determined assault. He now saw his fears confirmed in the scattered wreckage of his tank destroyers after a clash with the 10th Panzer Division on March 23-24th—he had lost 24 half-tracks out of 34 engaged, and

7 tank-destroyer M-10's out of 12. "In the heat of battle," Patton wrote, "our tank destroyers reverted to the teachings of the Tank Destroyer School, that is the pursuit of tanks, which in this type of country is impossible." On March 26th he wrote a personal letter to General McNair, describing how disappointing the tank destroyers had proved. Their usefulness was further undermined by the manual prepared by the Tank Destroyer Center—the controversial FM 18-15—prescribing the tactical employment of the tank destroyers in accordance with their misguided enthusiasts who had pinned their hopes on them in their blind opposition to armor. He also informed General Eisenhower of his experience, and Allied Force Headquarters in Algiers promptly issued a training memorandum to clarify the use of tank destroyers in the light of Patton's observations.

By March 25th, Patton's ardor was somewhat dampened by the limitations Alexander had imposed upon him, and their consequences he now had to suffer.

If Patton was disappointed, so were the people in the United States, led by President Roosevelt himself. When he saw Commander Butcher in Washington on March 26th, he remarked that Patton should have been able to "get through soon to a point where he could shell the coastal road." And the people, encouraged by the apparent breakthrough at Gafsa and El Guettar, expected Patton to crash through to the sea behind the Mareth Line, and were keenly disappointed when he failed to do so.

On March 28th, II Corps opened a major attack toward Gabes from positions near El Guettar, employing General Allen's 1st Division on the left and General Eddy's 9th Division on the right, in an effort to force a gap in the enemy positions through which the 1st Armored Division of General Ward could attack. But Patton was making only negligible progress, and the week's fighting brought a virtual stalemate. He was undaunted by his difficulties, but he became somewhat fidgety, and his notes of those days reflected his irritation and confusion.

On the day of the jump-off, after noting that enemy resistance was very severe and the terrain extremely difficult, he became bitterly critical of the 1st Armored and its commander, and also of his troops in general.

By March 29th Patton felt so "futile," as he liked to put it, that he poured out his heart in a letter to General

Marshall, disguised, so to speak, as an informal report about his progress in Tunisia. "We are trying to be simple," he wrote, "not change our plans when made, and keep on fighting." There was merely a subtle undertone of complaint in the letter, Patton telling Marshall that even if and when his armor would be in a position "to gain access to the enemy's rear area," he had to submit to General Alexander's decision whether such an operation would be advisable or, in other words, helpful to the main purpose of his operations, which was to draw off enemy reserves from Montgomery's path. "All I have," he told Marshall, "is the actual conduct of operations prescribed."

Frustrated though he felt, Patton did not really blame Alexander, for he realized that his Group Commander had a bigger job to do, namely to ease the Eighth Army's path to the north. He even went out of his way to praise Alexander to Marshall, describing him as wise and fair-minded.

But on April 3rd he became embroiled with another of his British bosses, Air Vice Marshal Sir Arthur Coningham. In his situation report of April 1st, Patton's G-3 had complained about "total lack of air cover for our units" which allowed the *Luftwaffe* to "operate almost at will." Coningham immediately shot back, now complaining in turn about Patton's nerve to complain, and hinting rather broadly that Patton was using the air force "as an alibi for lack of success on ground." He went on to hurt Patton where he was the most sensitive, questioning the quality of his troops. "If sitrep [situation report] is earnest," Coningham wrote, "it can only be assumed that II Corps personnel concerned are not battleworthy in terms of present operation."

Patton found it difficult to reconcile Coningham's insulting communication with Eisenhower's good feeling of partnership. He protested to Algiers in his most vigorous language, and by noon, Air Chief Marshal Tedder and Lieutenant General Carl Spaatz arrived at his headquarters to smooth ruffled feelings.

The next day Coningham tried to patch up the controversy by radioing Patton: "Signal relating to air operations on II Corps front Number Spec 40 of 2 April from this HQ to above addressees is to be withdrawn and cancelled." Copies were forwarded to "Freedom" (Eisenhower), Spaatz, Alexander, and a few others to whom the original message had been sent. When Patton refused to accept the cancellation of Coningham's offending signal as an amend, the chastised Air Vice Marshal sent another round robin, now offering straight apologies.

"I should like recipient to know," Coningham wrote, "that I visited Commanding General II Corps to express regret that Spec 40 might be interpreted as a slight to American forces. No such thing was intended." He went on to explain that a mistake in transmission had caused the signal to read "II Corps personnel concerned" instead of "few corps personnel concerned."

Patton was now ready to bury the hatchet. "My dear Coningham," he replied immediately upon receipt of the message on April 5th, "Please accept on the part of myself and the officers and men of II Corps our most sincere appreciation of your more than generous signal. Personally, while I regret the misunderstanding, for which I was partially responsible, I cannot but take comfort and satisfaction from the fact that it gave me an opportunity of becoming better acquainted with you, because to me you exemplify in their most perfect form all the characteristics of the fighting gentlemen."

Then on April 6th Patton received orders to take Hill 369 "regardless of losses," and he relayed the order immediately to General Eddy. But he canceled it just as promptly when he learned that "the 47th Infantry, which would have to make the attack, has already lost 23 per cent of its enlisted men and 26 per cent of its officers in 11 days of battle." In situations like this, orders with the callous phrase "regardless of losses" did not carry any weight with him.

However, only 24 hours later, Patton was again forced to remind his superiors that indiscriminate expenditure of blood did not buy victories. At 7:45 on the morning of April 7th, a Colonel Martin, liaison officer of 18th Army Group, appeared at his headquarters with a message from General McCreery, Alexander's Chief of Staff. "General Alexander is convinced," it read, "that the big moment has now arrived for us to give a maximum of aid to the efforts of the British Eighth Army. We must push our armor out into El Guettar section and *must be prepared to accept casualties*. Everything must be done to push forward."

Patton let Gaffey handle the case because on two scores the message upset him to the point of rage. First, he did not cherish the idea of reckless bloodletting in II Corps just to make life easy for Monty. More important, he disliked the message's callous reference to the forward push irrespective of casualties. Coached by Patton, Gaffey told Martin testily, "Orders have already been given for the push. And as far as casualties are concerned, we're prepared to accept them, and have been accepting them throughout the campaign."

Colonel Martin got the message. He assured Gaffey that McCreery had meant "casualties in *armor* and not *infantry* casualties."

Somehow the message drew Patton closer to his men and, in his special brand of sentimental attachment, induced him, as if to make amends for their losses, to issue a General Order praising them in effusive terms and in his best literary style for their performance during the recent exacting weeks.

"After 22 days of relentless combat in mountains whose ruggedness beggars description, you have won the battle of El Guettar. Each one of you in his sphere has done his duty magnificently. Not alone on the front line, where death never ended his gruesome harvest, but everywhere else all of you have demonstrated your valor and constancy."

Patton went on to pay special tribute to the supply services, the maintenance units, the Signal Corps, the Engineers, the airmen of the 12th Air Support Command, the medics, and ended it by saying, "Due to your united efforts and to the manifest assistance of Almighty God, the splendid record of the American Army has attained added luster."

He sent special commendations to the 1st and 9th Infantry Divisions and the 13th Field Artillery Brigade. It always gave him a thrill of satisfaction to let his men know he was proud of them and pleased with their performance.

Then another controversy developed in the wake of an order from Alexander in which Patton thought he recognized a calculated effort to take from him whatever little glory this campaign held out for his corps. On the evening of April 10th McCreery telephoned to tell him that Alexander wanted to shift II Corps from his control in 18th Army Group to General Anderson's First Army. Patton immediately went to Group Headquarters and pleaded with Alexander to reconsider his decision. But his protest fell on deaf ears. Back at his own headquarters he fired off a letter to Alexander that deserves to be reproduced here in full because it demonstrates Patton's application of his patriotism to his manner of making war, and his unrelenting Americanism.

"All the way home," he wrote on April 11th, "I thought over your decision to place the II Corps in the First Army. Frankly, I am not happy about it, and I feel that I should be lacking in candor if I failed to again bring the matter to your attention.

"As I see it, the question is neither one of command nor of signal communication, but of prestige. Should it eventuate that in the last scene of the opening act of our Allied effort, elements of the United States Army appear, however erroneously, to be acting in a minor role, the repercussions might be unfortunate. In my opinion, this danger would not exist if the II Corps appeared in a co-equal role under the 18th Army Group. I feel that you know me well enough to realize that I am impersonal in my remarks. So far as I am concerned, the question of command is immaterial as long as we have the opportunity to fight."

This was something like Patton's swan song at II Corps.

On April 14th Eisenhower arrived unexpectedly at El Guettar and surprised him with the proposition: "I feel, George, that you should now let Bradley carry on and go back to work on 'Husky'."

Behind Ike's decision to send Patton back to Morocco was a combination of motivations. He was sincerely convinced that Patton had accomplished what he had been sent to II Corps to do—to breathe life into the lethargic corps. He also thought that Patton would be more useful henceforth in the planning of "Husky," which was badly lagging behind while the date of the invasion, June 10, was rapidly approaching.

But there was another motive, even if only in the back of Eisenhower's mind. He was eager to give Bradley a chance in top command, for he was grooming his West Point classmate for greater things in this war. He was looking forward to when Bradley would be his *alter ego* in the field, and was deliberately preparing him for that position, just as he was husbanding Patton as his thruster. Ike needed Bradley for still another mission in which Patton figured prominently. He was not only aware of but, indeed, fearful of Patton's combustible personality, and resolved to keep

Bradley in his background to apply the brakes whenever he showed signs of running away with an assignment. It was undoubtedly this felicitous arrangement for which he was now laying the groundwork in Tunisia. It was to become a decisive factor later in the war.

Eisenhower was working quietly but assiduously in the background to build up Bradley for the role. On the eve of Ike's departure to the front to make the change, Ernie Pyle, the war correspondent, had visited in Algiers, and Eisenhower told him, "Next time you're up front, go and discover Bradley."

Pyle did. The nation first heard of Bradley from a series of six columns in which the popular reporter introduced Bradley as the "GI's' general," starting a legend—or was it a myth?—that was to establish Bradley not only as the most democratic general in the Army but also as the brain behind the American high command. It soon reached the point where Bradley would be given credit for Patton's ideas and accomplishments (a practice supported ingenuously by Bradley himself in his memoirs). By the time they reached Sicily, the quip went around among the GI's that "Patton conquered the island in 38 days because he had a secret weapon—Bradley."

Relations between the two in Tunisia were good but ambiguous. Patton admired Bradley's talents as an all-round foot soldier—his professorial approach to tactics; his masterly synchronization of intelligence, operations and logistics; his thorough execution of plans. And he, who was so boisterous and profane, respected Bradley's saintly personality. In Tunisia he found his Deputy Corps Commander self-effacing, impeccably honest, loyal, and industrious.

But although Patton regarded Bradley as a good general, he did not think yet that he was a great one. He considered him eminently qualified to go high in command but not to the top. Rightly or wrongly, Patton thought that his vistas were limited by a creeping timidity: although Bradley could clearly see his opportunities and had the intellectual resources to plan for them, an innate caution restrained him from going all the way. Patton also thought that Bradley, in his modesty and contentment with the slow escalation of an army career, was unduly awed and impressed by his meteoric rise and was, therefore, not quite sure of himself and forceful in his relations with higher-ups.

Bradley, on the other hand, admired Patton's dazzling tactical genius but did not really think—certainly not in Tunisia as yet or later in Sicily—that he had much beyond that. The son of a country school teacher and a seamstress from Missouri, he felt far removed from Patton's aristocratic caste, and could never completely overcome a slight complex which their divergent social backgrounds had implanted in him during their first association.

In strictly professional matters, Bradley was appalled by George Patton's oddly impressionistic conduct of the war—especially by his apparent indifference to logistics. In Bradley's eyes Patton was like Moses, whose supply problems had been solved by the Lord—all he had to do to get water was to hit a rock with a rod while an urgent appeal sent skyward would bring him manna from heaven.

He was scandalized by Patton's vulgar demeanor—his calculatedly rough approach to his officers and men, his deluge of profanities, and his gluttonous hunger for advancement and recognition. In fact, Bradley thought that Patton was somewhat of a maniac—his strong ungovernable desires, his excessive activity alternating with depression, his lust for power and publicity, his foolish, impractical, extravagant deeds appeared to this sane and sound man as clear signs of irrationality, if not insanity. In North Africa, in their first close association, Bradley thus thought that Patton, "however successful he was as a corps commander, had not yet learned to command himself."

A strangely ambivalent relationship developed between the two men. Patton leaned on Bradley heavily but treated him with some condescension, and Bradley accepted Patton's superiority but craved to free himself of this bond. In his congenital loyalty and decency, Bradley would not intrigue against Patton or stab him in the back. But when an opportunity arose spontaneously to free himself, both of his spell and presence—he seized it.

Such an opportunity offered itself on March 22nd, while Patton was preparing the plans of the Gafsa-Gabes attack, and Bradley had to go to "Freedom," Ike's headquarters in Algiers, to make some of the arrangements.

Bradley found Eisenhower badly upset by the way "Husky" was developing. He had just completed a teletype exchange with General Marshall in Washington, and could not tell the Chief of Staff anything positive about the plans for the invasion. When he saw Bradley coming into the office, he asked him whether he thought he could handle II Corps so that Patton might go back to planning at Rabat. On the other hand, he said, if Patton should be indispensable in Tunisia, Bradley would have to take charge of the planning.

"Well," Bradley said, "I would think George ought to go back and resume his Sicilian planning. After all, the I Armored staff is his baby. He could get much more out of them."

"That's just the way I feel about it, too," Eisenhower said.

And that is exactly what happened. Patton returned to Rabat and Bradley got his corps.

Incidentally, this visit of March 22nd brings into focus a kind of "professional rivalry" that developed between the two men only *after* Patton's death. In his memoirs, *A Soldier's Story,* General Bradley frequently claims credit for ideas and plans in the war which Patton on his part represented as his brainstorms and designs. Thus, angered by Alexander's order of March 19th forbidding him to advance beyond Fondouk el Aouareb, Patton decided to appeal the order to General Eisenhower and, according to the diary entry of March 22nd, sent Bradley to Algiers on this mission.

However, Bradley says in his memoirs that it was he who became alarmed by the directive (because it "meant that II Corps would be pinched out of its fair share in the final victory campaign") and, therefore, asked Patton's permission to fly to Algiers "to point out my objections" to Eisenhower. Similar rival claims to the same ideas recur frequently, first in Patton's notes and then in Bradley's memoirs.

In a team set-up like a military command, it is usually difficult, if not impossible, to pinpoint just who thought first of what. Yet the fact remains that Patton's plans and ideas are fully documented in his contemporary papers while Bradley's claims to those same thoughts were published later, in 1951, when Patton was no longer around to contest or reclaim them.

Patton was extremely generous in giving credit where it was due; he also was rather sophisticated in his views about the so-called creative spirit which is supposed to induce original ideas for given situations and which is considered the mark of genius.

Once during the Battle of the Bulge, in December, 1944, he called Rosevich to his office in Luxembourg at 4 A.M. His secretary found him but partly dressed, wearing a combination of his swank uniform and pajamas, indicating that he must have jumped straight from bed for this dictation. Rosevich was used to such summonses at all hours of the day and night, to act immediately upon whatever inspiration his mercurial boss might have had, often, it seemed, in his dreams.

It developed then that Patton was expecting the Germans to mount an attack at a certain spot on Christmas Day. Acting apparently on hunch, he had decided to anticipate the move by mounting an attack of his own. He called Joe in to dictate the order for the operation.

When it was out of the way and the transcript was given to the staff, Patton relaxed again and went back to bed. "In the morning we attacked, almost at the very moment the Germans were jumping off," Rosevich recalled. "They were stopped cold in their frozen tracks. Patton thus averted what could have become a serious threat to his flank."

A day or two later, during another one of his sessions with Rosevich, Patton recalled his nocturnal inspiration and said with a smug smile: "To tell you the truth, I didn't know at all that the German attack was coming. In the future some people will call it luck and some will call it genius."

"What would you call it, General?" Rosevich asked. Patton looked at him, as if astonished by the question. He paused, then said:

"Determination."

The Third Army was still slugging its way out of the Bulge when Patton decided to launch a large-scale attack over the Saur River. It developed into a very successful operation. The morning after its success Patton could be seen moving about like a peacock.

But by the time he got around to Rosevich in the privacy of his inner sanctum, his boastful pride had run its course. He seemed to feel the urge to discuss it with someone, and since Joe was the only one within hearing distance, he decided to discuss it with him. He told Rosevich that the idea of the maneuver was another one of his *sudden* inspirations. He had thought of it abruptly when, for no apparent reason, he woke up with a start at 3 o'clock in the morning.

"Whether ideas like this," he said, "are the result of inspiration or insomnia, I do not profess to know. Nearly every tactical idea I ever had popped into my head in this manner and not in a consciously laborious process."

He looked at Rosevich and said in a dry tone: "Remember this, Sergeant, when you read the history of this war!"

It was unfair to remove Patton from command of II Corps at this particular moment of history, if only because the big victory that seemed to have eluded the Allies was now beginning to shape up, and he should have been permitted to be in on the kill. Patton actually felt in his bones that victory was near, but he could not yet articulate that feeling in action, and it needed another great push, designed brilliantly by General Alexander, to ring the curtain down on the tough Tunisian campaign. Even so, it needed less than a month after Patton's departure. On May 12th Axis resistance collapsed spectacularly. The Germans and Italians outdid one another in surrendering. The parade into the prisoner-of-war cages was led in person by Colonel General Jürgen von Arnim, Commander in Chief of the vaunted Army Group Africa that had thus reached the end of its glory road.

While a certain critical cloud continued to hover over Patton's command of II Corps in Tunisia—his apparent failure at the outset to "crash through to the sea and there bag the Afrika Korps in the Mareth Line"—Bradley was now getting all the praise for this successful end run for which, in fact, Patton had laid the groundwork.

It was somehow characteristic of him that he never grumbled about his removal from II Corps and did not begrudge the glory Bradley inherited. He was always apt to create controversies with some issues whose bearing on the war was accidental and insignificant. And he was inclined to raise a hue and cry over minor matters with which he himself was but indirectly connected. But he let the big things which frequently redounded to his grave disadvantage pass without remonstrance and rancor—with a shrug and a grin.

Eisenhower did invite Patton to attend the celebration of the victory held on May 20th in Tunis, and Patton corrected

an omission by taking Bradley with him. In the end he was
sorry he went. The celebration turned out to be a Franco-
British show dedicated to the glory of Montgomery and the
rebirth of the French army. The United States Army was
represented by a token force, a battalion of the 34th Division.

To add insult to injury, Eisenhower neglected to invite
Patton and Bradley to the reviewing platform, crowded
with Allied commanders, many of whom had watched the
campaign from Algiers, and even from London or Washington. Patton was disgusted.

"A Goddamn waste of time," he told Bradley, and went
back to Mostaganem to resume work on "Husky," from
which he expected the rewards the Tunisian campaign had
failed to produce for him.

It happened to him so often. He was not allowed to follow up his victory in Sicily with a much greater triumph in
Italy. And when in 1944 he opened a path to Paris, another
army was given the honor of entering the liberated city.

Glory was to Patton that bright tragic thing which
meant dominion, warming his name again and again. He
had so much of it, and expected so much more of it, that
he had some to spare for others who would have otherwise
but rarely felt the sun.

CHAPTER FOURTEEN
THE SHADOW OF MONTGOMERY

Patton was rash and indiscreet. Only too often he tempted
Providence in his hot pursuit of destiny. But not now, when
he was given his first big opportunity. In Morocco he had
but a task force to begin with and an armored corps that
was mostly deskbound—all the United States could then
spare for him. And even in Tunisia he commanded merely
a makeshift corps of green soldiers, under the close tutelage
of the British.

This was different.

"Husky" would see the first American army in action. And though it would still be under General Alexander and operate in association with the British Eighth Army of General Montgomery, Patton expected to do more or less as he pleased. It was a fantastic opportunity for a man of war, and it staggered even his imagination. It flattered him, too, to be the general given the honor of taking the first fully developed all-American army into major action in World War II. Not even Pershing had more to begin with 25 years before.

Patton wrote in his diary on April 15th, the morning after his departure from II Corps: "War is very simple, direct and ruthless. It takes a simple, direct and ruthless man to wage war." He had no doubt that he was such a man. And "Husky" appeared to be such a war—simple, direct, and ruthless. Its aim was plain—the eviction of the Axis from Sicily; and it had a reasonable strategic objective —the Straits of Messina dividing the island from the Italian mainland.

Yet "Husky" was not so simple as Patton saw it. The project was loaded with a series of perplexing side issues of policy and command, of strategy and tactics. For one thing, it represented the continuity of Churchill's "tactical opportunism," the safer and cheaper attack on Europe's "soft underbelly" and the protracted evasion of confronting Hitler at the decisive point in northwestern France. Second, it brought into the coalition war Bernard Law Montgomery in person, with all the super-charged possibilities of trouble with that brilliant but high-strung and inordinately vain general.

With proper and prudent recognition of their limited war potential, the British hoped to avoid a frontal attack on the Continent. They preferred a roundabout way to victory, having convinced themselves that German power could be worn down by attrition to the point of collapse, whereupon "the Anglo-American forces in the United Kingdom could perform a triumphal march from the Channel to Berlin with no more than a few snipers' bullets to annoy them."

Even for this panacea something had to be done, if only to keep the war going. And something had to be done to expedite German attrition. Churchill, therefore, developed his own grand design, frequently taxing the patience of his American friends with his constant and tireless advocacy of his strategic concepts. The United States Joint Chiefs of Staff, for example, had "no doubt in their own minds . . . that whenever the persistent Prime Minister started talking about . . . veering toward the 'right' . . . he was resuming the advocacy of strategic diversions to Southeastern Europe and away from Northern France."

Patton was not really interested in these conflicting strategies—they seemed far too esoteric or, indeed, silly for his personal and pragmatic approach to war. He was essentially interested in fighting the war; where he had to fight it—in Italy or France or in the Pacific—was not material to him.

He was always keenly interested in the tactical issues and the problems of command. "Husky" was fraught with both elements, a clear recognition of which had put Patton on his guard. He recalled how only Eisenhower's forceful intervention and Marshall's support had secured the "Torch" command for him; and how even then he had almost lost his opportunity by becoming embroiled in a foolish row with the Navy. Now he had no desire to become involved in the controversial strategic issues or to jeopardize his part in "Husky" by antagonizing Montgomery. At this moment Patton was merely a promise, while Montgomery was riding the crest.

He made up his mind to bide his time and keep quiet, even pliant, for the time being. He had waited this long, he could wait a little longer.

After the decision at El Guettar on April 14th to put Bradley in Patton's place at the head of II Corps, General Eisenhower lingered on for some small talk and a little serious conversation, the latter mostly about cooperation with the British in North Africa. He had some misgivings and a few complaints, but on the whole he was satisfied with the way things were going. He told Patton how absolutely determined he was to make this coalition the smoothest and most successful in the history of war, then added solemnly:

"I have reached a place where I do not look upon myself as an American but as an Ally."

This was a remarkably lucid way of expressing his

philosophy, but Patton recoiled when he heard those succinct words. He remembered, though, how Ike had lectured him on the importance of cooperation with the British, and thought it wise not to make an issue over Eisenhower's statement.

Patton was no xenophobic bigot. We have seen how he loved the French and took to other foreigners as well, including such quaint people as the Berbers, for example. And we shall see how smoothly and snugly he fitted himself into the Anglo-American fraternity of "Overlord." But he was an American, first, foremost, all the way, to the last, in the virgin sense of Daniel Webster's claim. He had none of the qualifying sentiment of Patrick Henry, whose "I am not a Virginian but an American" probably inspired Eisenhower's words. Patton was neither prepared nor ready to haul down the flag. His passionate Americanism was part of his emotional make-up. But like many of his seemingly irrational and bias-ridden beliefs, it also had a practical side.

He was convinced that character is bestowed by nature; that there are certain and permanent character traits; and that people do things exactly as they are constituted—Americans in their fashion, the British in their own ingrained ways. And he was firm in his belief that people wage war according to their national characters. He considered this truism especially important in planning for war, yet he was mortified to see that Eisenhower had abandoned much, if not most, of the planning to British hands. As a result, plans were being made for Americans by aliens, without proper recognition of their national character.

Patton had an opportunity to observe the detrimental results of this in some of the troubles II Corps had with its supplies in Tunisia. When the logistics design was drawn up for the campaign, General Anderson's planners estimated that existing facilities on the front would be capable of supplying only 38,000 troops. The estimate was made from a British point of view, with British capabilities in mind, assuming the limits of British productivity and efficiency. It failed to take into consideration the American way of doing these things and did not anticipate "either the ingenuity of U.S. railroaders or the astonishing capacity of U.S. forces to sustain field armies on trucking operations." In the end, II Corps managed to put in 92,000 troops, and supply them rather liberally throughout the offensive, where the British estimate assumed only 38,000 could be sustained.

The inclination of British planners to project their own capabilities (as shaped by their own national character traits) and to underestimate United States efficiency (molded by the American national character) caused considerable trouble for Patton. Logistics is the critical determinant in any tactical design. An Army can do only as much as its logistics support enables it to do. Since his logistics support had been arranged for him by British planners within their own narrower frame of reference, Patton, caught short in supplies, could never actually accomplish as much as he was capable of doing.

This was a tangible disadvantage of having Britons planning for Americans. There was, however, an intangible side to the problem as well, in which the divergence of national character traits figured probably even more prominently. He was, therefore, rather glad when, on June 23rd in Oran during an inspection tour of troops slated for Sicily, General Alexander brought up the problem by saying that it was "foolish to consider the British and Americans as one."

Alexander appreciated that Patton's "boisterous method" of commanding troops was at least in part due to the fact that he was a red-blooded American with a Wild West background. But he recognized it also as indigenous to Patton, and to him alone, because he missed the "method" (and sometimes sorely) in other American generals. He was, in fact, so impressed with what he called "the Patton prescription" that he asked General Eisenhower to loan the American general out to some of his British troops to train them for a while. He was convinced that Patton would instill in them some of his "boisterousness," no matter how typically and exclusively "American" it was.

Otherwise, though, Alexander accepted the validity of Patton's theory and, therefore, never interfered with certain of his methods—and, for that matter, with the idiosyncrasies of other American generals serving under him—which proved thoroughly alien and maybe even repugnant to him. This recognition of the "American way of doing things" endeared Alexander to Patton and assured his wholehearted cooperation resulting in a smooth and efficient prosecution of the war under Alexander's leadership.

It was an entirely different story with General Montgomery, and this became evident as soon as the victorious general of the Eighth Army had time to devote himself to plans for the Sicilian campaign.

Every war produces its own especial brand of heroes, and every army its own memorable generals. These conspicuous leaders are essential, for victory hinges on more than just the proficiency of arms. In World War II the British people had to wait a long time for their hero to emerge, but when he appeared on the scene, abruptly and unexpectedly, even somewhat accidentally, he came with a bang and put the imprint of his personality indelibly on the war.

He was, of course, General Sir Bernard Law Montgomery, son of an Anglican missionary bishop, whose prodigious generalship may well interest—and baffle—both the student of military history and of psychoanalysis. Military writers still argue over his merits—Alan Moorehead called him "one of the greatest leaders of our time;" but Martin Blumenson regarded him as "the war's most overrated general." The psychoanalyst might say that Montgomery's special brand of generalship was but a string of compensations—for his small stature and physical frailty, for his unhappy childhood—and a subconscious urge to disavow and show up a stern mother for whom he could never do the right thing at the right time. As Montgomery himself put it in his memoirs, "My upbringing as a child has taught me to have resource within myself. . . . I was also taught to count my blessings, and this I certainly did."

Montgomery was a perfectionist with an authoritarian streak who drove himself with a tight rein and applied his own personal regime and ascetic habits to all his human relations. He made himself thoroughly disliked in the British services except for his own army, within which he was idolized. When he emerged from his strictly British environment into the Anglo-American coalition, he came to be regarded with mixed feelings by the American generals whose close associate he was now to become and several of whom he was slated to command. He was "acceptable" to General Eisenhower, who understood him better than did any other American. But he irritated the other United States generals, including those who had unstinted professional respect for him.

"To them," Chester Wilmot wrote, "his methods were the more objectionable because he was so clearly born to command and, even in his most tactful moments, he exercised his authority almost as a matter of right. Moreover, he was not as other men. He revealed no traits of ordinary human frailty, however. He shunned the company of women; he did not smoke or drink or play poker with 'the boys.' He could never be 'slapped on the back.' Because he lived in a small tactical H.Q. with a few aides and liaison officers, he was looked upon as setting himself apart from (and therefore above) his fellows. This impression seems to be confirmed by his practice, resented as much by other British services as it was by the Americans, of sending his Chief of Staff, de Guingand, to represent him at conferences."

Among the generals of World War II, Monty was a lineal descendant of the German Rommel, especially in his fantastic sex appeal to his own troops and to popular imagination, while Patton was, in many minds, the counterpart of both in the American camp. In his comparison of Montgomery and Patton, however, Wilmot made clear the distinction that rendered them as fundamentally different as they appeared to be superficially similar:

"The American attitude toward Montgomery," he wrote, "cannot be accounted for on the ground of national prejudice alone, although this was a contributing factor. His manner and methods would have been equally distasteful in an American."

On the other hand, Wilmot thought, Patton, whose eccentricities were as marked as MacArthur's or Montgomery's and who was far more flamboyant, did not provoke the same resentment. "His behavior made him unpopular in high places, but he was not suspect as an autocrat. The 'tough guy' pose which he adopted in public (complete with pearl-handled revolvers in open holsters) was worn and familiar in the best tradition of the 'Wild West.' Although he liked to pretend that he was hard-boiled, he was intensely emotional and soft-hearted. When deeply moved, he readily gave way to tears. Moreover, in all his posturing he conveyed the impression that he was showing off his personal toughness rather than his professional authority. Highhanded though his behavior often was, he commanded in the American manner, debating his plans with his staff in daily conference as a 'democratic' general should, and abiding by the principle, 'never tell people how to do things, tell them what to do and they will surprise you with their ingenuity.' " Implied in this remarkable character sketch of Patton was Wilmot's opinion that everything Patton was, Montgomery was not.

Montgomery was aware of his personality quirks. He knew they irritated his superiors and equals. But he was thoroughly convinced of the fitness and the probity, as well as, indeed, the virtue of his conduct and methods. One of the private soldiers serving under him in the desert, wholly devoted to his commanding general and enthralled by his management of his men, once called the Eighth Army a "brotherhood," and afterward Montgomery himself liked to refer to it as such. "We were a brotherhood in arms," he wrote. "We did what we liked. We dressed as we liked. What mattered was success, and to win our battles with a minimum of casualties. I was the head of the brotherhood. I was pretty tough about mistakes and especially mistakes which cost lives; I would allow no departure from the fundamentals of the master plan. But I let subordinate commanders do as they liked about details and didn't fuss about the wrong thing."

Until the spring of 1943, the careers of Montgomery and Patton ran on separate tracks. Now they converged. In Sicily, Alexander was to continue his over-all command, but serving under him as equals would be Montgomery with his seasoned and glory-crowned Eighth Army, and Patton with his Seventh Army, as yet to be born.

After the frustrations of Tunisia, Patton was looking forward to the Sicilian campaign as if it were a championship bout. He was perfectly certain in his own mind that even though he might not destroy Montgomery's image or show him up as something of a fraud, he would establish himself in Monty's league by beating the champ. But that was still to come. Monty was the holder of the title. It was his prerogative, therefore, to dictate the terms of the fight. Patton shrewdly recognized that it would have been impolitic at this stage to assert himself and demand attention for his own views and aspirations. Let the facts speak for themselves, he thought. Let Monty set his own trap. In the meantime, let him have all the rope he needed to hang himself in "Husky."

Planning of "Husky," begun in London in January, 1943, progressed so fitfully that it held out little promise the Allies would be ready for the invasion by June 10, the date for which it had initially been scheduled. Then planning was shifted to North Africa under General Eisenhower's personal supervision. Even there it began modestly enough in the St. Georges Hotel in Algiers—in room 141, after which the planning staff was named "Force 141." When it outgrew the confines of the old hotel suite, the staff moved to the Ecole Normale at Bouzerea, a suburb of Algiers, and it was there that some progress was made.

Chief of Staff of "Force 141" was a British major general named Charles Henry Gairdner. A 45-year-old polo-playing and yachting enthusiast who served with the Royal Hussars, he had made a name for himself as a planner in the Middle East in 1941 and had gained practical experience in command of the 6th Armored Division. Under him, the staff produced a series of plans—"Husky 1" to "Husky 7" in rapid succession—but none seemed to be acceptable to all concerned. Time was getting shorter. Days and weeks passed. D-Day for Sicily grew steadily nearer, and still the war against the Afrika Korps dragged on. "Force 141" fidgeted and produced plans four, five, six, seven—and discarded each in turn. It was too late now for a June invasion; so the entire operation was rescheduled for July 10.

In mid-April Gairdner's "Force 141" completed "Husky Eight," and to the top brass connected with the venture— Eisenhower, Admiral Cunningham and Air Chief Marshal Tedder—it seemed to be a superior plan. Sicily presented many problems. This was to be the first large-scale amphibious operation against beaches firmly held by a strong enemy, and the planners had no precedents to draw upon. The assault itself had to overcome a number of vexing obstacles, such as beach gradients and tides. Sicily's terrain was anything but uniform or placid. Its plains were relatively few, its mountains many and rugged. All this the planners had to take into account, and so they came to the conclusion that it was essential for success to secure at least two major ports at the outset to supply the troops fighting inland.

Messina was not just the major port of Sicily. It now loomed also as the strategic plum of the operation, for it was virtually adjacent to the Italian mainland. It was only two miles across the strait at the apex of this misshapen triangular island at which the Germans either could be bottled up or through which they could escape.

Yet Messina had to be ruled out because it was too heavily guarded by fixed defenses, it was too close to the mainland, from which it could obtain quick and ample support, and too far for Allied fighter planes. Two alternative ports were chosen—Syracuse in the east, to be captured by Monty's Eighth Army, and Palermo in the northwest corner, assigned to Patton's Seventh Army.

They were natural choices. History itself vouched for the importance of Syracuse. The city had baffled the greatest amphibious operation of antiquity. In 415 B.C., Alcibiades remarked during the Peloponnesian War: "If Syracuse falls, all Sicily falls also, and Italy immediately afterwards." Within its harbors Athenian and Sicilian triremes had fought each other to a standstill. Although its harbor was relatively small, it provided ample opportunities for enlargement.

Palermo offered a long waterfront with excellent harbor facilities, it was vulnerable to our fighter planes and was lightly defended. It was an important goal for psychological reasons as well, because it was the seat of the Sicilian kings of olden times and the capital of the island.

This, then, was the plan when Patton left Tunisia to resume planning for "Husky" and prepare his move against Palermo. According to General Alexander, this was the *soundest* plan. Yet it was scrapped even before Patton could begin his tactical planning. Why? Because Montgomery disliked it.

Montgomery had only an inkling of "Husky Eight," but an inkling was enough for him to notify Alexander that "from what little [he] could learn about it" the plan did not impress him as a good one. No plan ever made for him by outsiders met with his approval, and not only because he had a strong contrary streak. He was a highly individualistic general who could operate only along lines of his own concepts and was, to put it another way, incapable of adapting himself to strange plans drafted by others. But he was, as Alexander recognized clearly and said so bluntly, also disturbed by the comparative publicity value inherent in the plan. Palermo was a glittering gem, and its capture would have detracted from Montgomery's own deeds at the eastern end of the island. The Seventh Army was, therefore, to be deprived of its dazzling destination, redirected to land on the open beaches of the south, while, as General Alexander himself put it, "the more spectacular assignment of taking Syracuse, Augusta and possibly Messina was to be assigned to General Montgomery's Eighth Army."

It was not yet expressed in such blunt terms of sheer opportunism, of course. At that time Montgomery advanced strong tactical reservations, masking apprehensions motivated partly by his vanity. On April 19th—the very day his Army began a carefully laid offensive against the strong position at Enfidaville in Tunisia—Monty dropped everything and flew to Algiers for a conference with Eisenhower and Alexander. He was anxious to impress upon them the shortcomings of a plan which he, Montgomery, had never yet seen in any detailed form. As a result, he could talk only in generalities, such as "Possibly some sort of compromise will be necessary in order to get ourselves out of the mess we are now in"; and "The preparation for the operation must be gripped firmly, and be handled in a sensible way."

Nothing specific was done at the conference to devise a final plan, only 81 days from the new D-Day, but Montgomery accomplished his purpose. First, he succeeded in discrediting "Husky Eight," and, second, he intimidated Eisenhower and Alexander. While he was away from the front, his offensive bogged down. By the time he got back on April 21st, the attack was so badly off that he decided late in the day to regroup his army and confine the offensive to the coastal region. But it did not help. The offensive was never renewed. However, the loss was more than compensated for by his victory at General Eisenhower's headquarters.

The ground thus prepared, Montgomery flew to Cairo to listen *for the first time to* "Husky Eight" presented to him by General Gairdner. His mind already made up, he sent a signal to Alexander that he could not accept the proposed plan and would put forward his own instead. He then had his staff draw up the counterplan along the lines of his preconceived notions—but confining his proposal to the part his own Eighth Army would play in the invasion. "I had my own ideas about the American landings," he later wrote, "but did not think the moment was yet opportune to put them forward."

Patton had left Gafsa on April 14th, spent the night at Constantine, then, accompanied by General Spaatz, flew to Algiers for a conference with Eisenhower. "Husky Eight" was being firmed up. Palermo was still his destination. All the tactical planning at Rabat which he was to supervise henceforth would have to be made for landings in northwestern Sicily to capture the major port through which he would be supplied promptly for the end run to link up with Montgomery at Messina.

He arrived in Rabat on April 16th and took charge. The planners, euphemistically called Headquarters I Armored Corps (Task Force 343), had made only perfunctory progress in his absence. But now with Patton breathing down their necks, things picked up. On April 26th he moved the headquarters from Rabat to Mostaganem, a town on the Algerian coast some 30 miles east of Oran. He established headquarters in a French battalion compound. It made a very suitable place in that it was completely walled in and there was only one entrance, which could be guarded easily.

Patton had been at his new headquarters but a day when at 10 P.M. Alexander phoned to invite him to an urgent top-level conference about "Husky" to be held at noon the next day at the St. Georges in Algiers. He wanted Patton to attend especially because Montgomery would also be present. This, at least, was what Alexander thought 14 hours before the meeting. Patton was there on time, only to be told that Montgomery was having one of his brilliantly timed influenza attacks and could not make it. He had wired that Major General Francis W. de Guingand would be coming in his place, an arrangement that surprised no one because "Freddy" was invariably standing in for his boss, who liked to play his part unseen from the background. Then came a wire that de Guingand's plane had had a forced landing at El Adam, and General Sir Oliver Leese would be coming in his place. When Leese was held up by fog, Alexander adjourned the meeting until the next morning.

When at 10 A.M. on April 29th Alexander called the meeting to order, he had around him one of the most glittering assortments of top brass ever to fill a room in the Mediterranean. This was clearly a do-or-die conference. It had to settle the burning issue of "Husky" one way or another, or else the whole invasion would be in jeopardy.

Aside from Alexander, Leese and Patton, present were Admiral Sir Andrew B. Cunningham of the Royal Navy, who was to command "Husky" at sea; Air Chief Marshal Tedder of the RAF; Vice Admiral Sir Bertram Ramsey of the Royal Navy, who was to command the naval task force in the east taking the Eighth Army to its destination; Air Vice Marshal Coningham of the RAF, Eisenhower's air chief at AFHQ; Air Vice Marshal Horace Ernest Philip Wigglesworth of the RAF; Commodore Royer M. Dick of the Royal Navy, Admiral Cunningham's Chief of Staff; Major General Frederick Browning, husband of the famous novelist Daphne du Maurier and airborne adviser to General Eisenhower; General Gairdner, Chief of Staff of "Force 141"; Brigadier Arthur A. Richardson, Gairdner's deputy; and Brigadier General Arthur S. Nevins of Eisenhower's staff.

Patton later remarked with some acidity that he and Nevins were "the only foreigners" present. Especially conspicuous by their absence, because they had not been invited, were Admiral Hewitt, who was to command the American naval forces in the operation, and General Spaatz, Commanding General of the United States Army Air Forces in the Mediterranean.

The conference pushed Patton to the brink of despair. Immediately upon his return to his own headquarters, he assembled his staff and brought them up-to-date on the developments—the deadlock after almost three hours of heated debate.

From what he then told them it seemed that he expected the conference to be momentous in its consequences. "It is even possible," he said in effect, "that it will result in a complete change at the top." He sounded like a man who was convinced that the sooner such a change took place, the better it would be for the war effort.

What happened at the meeting to impel Patton to use such strong words? Nothing, according to Montgomery. "The conference produced no result," he wrote. "Tedder said that if the initial bridgehead did not include the airfields at Comiso and Gela, then his air forces could not operate effectively. This led Cunningham to say that unless the air forces could keep enemy aircraft away, the convoys could not operate. Alexander was unable to get inter-Service agreement, and the conference broke up without coming to any decision."

What so upset Patton was the hidden purpose of the meeting, which he recognized clearly from the outset. It appeared to him that General Alexander had called it to rig "Husky" in Montgomery's favor, in accordance with Monty's demands, and to prepare the ground for giving him everything he asked—for on a silver platter. Patton was appalled by the conspiratorial character of what he regarded as an all-British conference designed too obviously to give all the advantages in "Husky" to the Eighth Army, and leave the American army precariously at the mercy of Montgomery as well as the enemy.

He was especially upset by General Eisenhower's absence, which he considered the Commander in Chief's tacit acquiescence in Alexander's surrender to Montgomery and the betrayal of Patton's cause, which he equated with the American cause. He thought that General Marshall, when he heard of the proceedings, would not be a party to the sell-out and either would order Eisenhower to insist upon the original provisions of "Husky Eight" or relieve him of his part in these shenanigans, evidently designed not for any valid military reasons but merely to cater to Montgomery's ego.

Although Patton was right in his assumption that the conference had been called to rig "Husky," he was wrong in calling it a "British plot." Actually, more of those who attended sided with him than with Montgomery. If anything, it was a Montgomery-Alexander assault on "Husky Eight," and Eisenhower's support of the "plot" was implied by the presence of General Nevins, his representative. Nevins indicated that Ike had changed his mind about "Husky Eight" and was more or less committed to Montgomery's "Easter Plan," so named because he had made his staff prepare it in Cairo over the Easter weekend.

If Patton was outraged, he was not the only one by any means. Air Chief Marshal Tedder protested vehemently the adoption of Monty's plan because, as he stressed it, "it would leave 13 airfields in enemy hands, far too many for effective neutralization by air action." Tedder told Alexander point-blank that "unless the airfields could be captured for our use at the earliest opportunity, he would be opposed to the whole operation."

Admiral Cunningham was the next to speak up. Voicing his opposition in even stronger terms, he insisted that it was "essential to secure the use of the airfields at the earliest possible moment to safeguard the mass of shipping lined off the beaches." More important, Cunningham pointed out that the new plan proposed by Alexander and Montgomery would throw the Americans to the wolves and endanger their operation by depriving them of recourse to a port.

Immediately after the conference, Cunningham sent a dispatch to his superior, Admiral Sir Dudley Pound, the First Sea Lord in London, trying to enlist his aid. "Personally I think this plan is unsound," he wrote. "But the seriousness of it all is that here we are with no fixed agreed plan, just over two months off D-Day and the commanders all at sixes and sevens, and even if we do get final agreement, someone will be operating a plan he doesn't fully agree with. Not the way to make a success of a difficult operation."

But there were no repercussions either from London or Washington. Alexander remained adamant and Montgomery's campaign was gaining momentum. Alexander went all the way to Monty's headquarters in Tunisia to post him on what had happened at the conference. The two generals reached complete agreement, not only on "Husky" as Monty wanted it, but also on their tactics of how to force it down American throats.

Another conference was called for May 2nd. Monty showed up, but this time Alexander could not make it. Montgomery utilized his superior's absence to lobby in Algiers in behalf of his plan. He tried to take his case personally to Eisenhower to obtain a direct commitment from him, but he could not find Ike anywhere. He then went through Headquarters looking for General Smith, Eisenhower's Chief of Staff, and tracked him down in the men's room. As Montgomery later described the absurd scene: "So we discussed the problem then and there . . . I said the American landing up near Palermo should be canceled and the whole American effort put in on the south coast . . . The Eighth Army and the Seventh Army would then land side by side, giving cohesion to the whole invasion."

Bedell Smith assured Montgomery that there would be no difficulty whatever in doing what he suggested. "We then left the lavatory," Monty said, "and he went off to consult Eisenhower, who liked the plan." Among the several things the Commander in Chief was *not* told was where his Chief of Staff had been buttonholed and sold on the idea. Much later, in Sicily, Ike visited Monty at Taormina. "We had much fun that night," Monty recalled. "I remember asking Ike, to his great amusement, if he had ever been told that the final plan for Sicily had been put forward in an Algerian lavatory!"

Not quite. Monty had persuaded Smith to call a "staff conference" in Alexander's absence so he could present his case. At no time during these developments did either Smith or Eisenhower consult Patton. And now Smith did not think it necessary to go even as far as Alexander had gone and invite Patton to the meeting. Montgomery dominated it completely with a grandiose presentation, feeling confident and safe to spell out everything, and leaving nothing more— not even his ideas about the American landings—to the imagination. He began humbly, in a conciliatory tone: "I know well," he said, "that I am regarded by many people as being a tiresome person. I think this is very probably true. I try hard not to be tiresome; but I have seen so many mistakes made in this war, and so many disasters happen, that I am desperately anxious to try and see that we have no more; and this often means being very tiresome. If we have a disaster in Sicily it would be dreadful."

But then he bristled and presented the conference with a virtual ultimatum: "I must state here very clearly, and beyond any possibility of doubt, that I will never operate my Army 'dispersed' in this operation." (By "dispersed" he meant if he landed in Syracuse while Patton went to Palermo.)

He presented his plan on a take-it-or-leave-it basis.

"The best place for the Eighth Army to be put ashore," he said, "is between Syracuse and Pachino." Recognizing Tedder's and Cunningham's objections and anxious to win them to his side, he said: "This would meet every requirement . . . except one and that one is very important. It does not secure sufficient airfields . . . in the general area of Comiso and Gela."

Now he felt the moment was ripe to put Patton in his place.

"I consider that the answer to the problem is," he said, *"to shift the U.S. effort from the Palermo area and to use it in the Gulf of Gela, to land on either side of Gela."*

As soon as the conference broke up, Montgomery returned to his headquarters in Tunisia "to await events." At midnight of May 3-4 Alexander notified him that he had won. Tedder and Cunningham had caved in, Eisenhower approved. Palermo was taken away from Patton, the Seventh Army was deprived of the benefit of a port. Moreover, it was ordered to land—exactly as Monty had suggested—on the open beaches east and west of Gela.

Eisenhower and Alexander went along with Montgomery even though they realized clearly and fully that they were confronting the Seventh Army with a well-nigh impossible task that held in it the seeds of disaster. Alexander in particular was quite frank on this score. "The risk," he wrote in his report of the operation, "was unevenly divided and *almost the whole of it would fall on the Seventh Army."* He then went on to say: "In other ways also it might well seem that the *American troops were being given the tougher and less spectacular task:* their beaches were more exposed than the Eighth Army's and on some of them there were open sand bars, they would have only one small port for maintenance and the Eighth Army would have the glory of capturing the more obviously attractive objectives of Syracuse, Catania and Messina, names which would bulk larger in press headlines than Gela or Licata or the obscure townships of central Sicily. Both I and my staff felt that this division of tasks might possibly, on this understandable ground, cause some feeling of resentment."

It now became Alexander's unpleasant task to tell Patton about the changes. "Since it might appear that an American commander was being required to scrap the results of difficult and tedious planning," he mused, "and undertake a heavier burden than he had expected at the order of a British superior, I felt a natural anxiety about American reactions."

But Alexander knew from personal experience that Patton was no Montgomery. "General Alexander was aware," Admiral Cunningham remarked wryly, "from the Tunisian campaign of General Patton's punctilious and scrupulous sense of duty, and knew that his orders would not be questioned."

With self-confessed anxiety and embarrassment, Alexander gave Patton his new orders. The American general reacted exactly as his "British superior" expected he would. "Well, George," Alexander asked when it was over and Patton seemed to be in full control of his emotions, "you might as well tell me—are you satisfied with the new plans for your Seventh Army?"

Patton clicked his heels, saluted, and merely said, "General, I don't plan—I only obey orders."

Actually, Patton was furious. When he got back to his headquarters in Mostaganem, he told his staff, "This is what you get when your Commander in Chief ceases to be an American and becomes an Ally."

Alexander could not help knowing how Patton felt about the blow. The whole St. Georges was abuzz with the story of a meeting Cunningham had with Hewitt and Patton at which the British admiral castigated Montgomery in the most outspoken terms and told his American colleagues to protest against the changes in "Husky." But Patton said:

"No, Goddamnit, I've been in this Army 30 years and when my superior gives me an order I say, 'Yes, Sir!' and then do my Goddamndest to carry it out."

This was very different from the British attitude, by which a general's objections could break up a strategic disposition so as to favor him and harm his associate commander. Admiral Cunningham was convinced to the day of his death that the initial plan was the better, and as Admiral Morison remarked, "so do many others."

Alexander tried to take the heat out of the controversy by giving the events a friendly touching up. "I wish to place on record here," he wrote in his wrap-up dispatch which appeared in the London *Gazette* five years later, "that General Patton at once fell in with my new plan, the military advantages of which were as clear to him as to me, and neither he nor anyone in the Seventh Army raised any form of objection. It is an impressive example of the spirit of complete loyalty and inter-allied cooperation which inspired all operations with which I was associated in the Mediterranean."

Alexander's statement, sugar-coated for the benefit of posterity, was not completely true. Patton did not voice any objection, to be sure, but it was completely untrue that he agreed with him as far as the so-called "military advantages" of the plan were concerned.

The situation was described with far greater historical accuracy by Admiral Cunningham. He also spelled out the possible difficulties and dangers with which the Eisenhower-Alexander-Montgomery plan confronted the Seventh Army and placed its success in the balance. In his rueful report of the outcome of the conference to the First Sea Lord in London, Cunningham wrote:

"I think it is well that you should know of the atmosphere here after the acceptance of the final 'Husky' plan. The Admiral [Hewitt] and General [Patton] of the Western Task Force are very sore about it . . . There is no doubt that the maintenance of three American divisions is a very tricky problem involving the supply over beaches and perhaps one small port for some weeks, 3,000 tons a day and no one really knows whether he [Hewitt] can do it or not.

"Hewitt has told Patton definitely that he does not think he can, but Patton has taken up the attitude that he has been ordered to land there and he will do it.

"I think myself that, barring accidents, it can be done, and I have assured them of all the assistance we can give them."

This, indeed, showed that "feeling of partnership" of which General Eisenhower spoke in his farewell address to Patton at the Maison Blanche airport only a few weeks before. It went amazingly far in Patton's case. Virtually the entire British contingent at AFHQ in the old St. Georges sided with and rooted for him. But his American friends kept mum.

Nobody, though, had any doubt that Patton would prevail. At the height of the controversy, when Montgomery's success in virtually dooming the Seventh Army in "Husky" was widely discussed, a British brigadier named Cecil Stanway Sugden, one of Eisenhower's planners, remarked to an American friend with tongue in cheek:

"I say, you don't need to worry, old chap. With the dispositions as they are, old Patton will soon have poor Monty bloody well surrounded!"

Brigadier Sugden was so distressed by Montgomery's machinations that he took to chewing gum and adopted American idiom for his Oxford-accented speech.

"That Patton bloke," he said. "He's sure cooking with gas—on all burners!"

CHAPTER FIFTEEN
BORN AT SEA, BAPTIZED IN BLOOD

A stooped, khaki-clad figure was walking in the soft sand, away from the nasty sea toward the road whose narrow fluorescent ribbon was glimmering in this lightless pre-dawn, making his way toward a low lime-coated house atop the beach. It seemed deserted, but over the rush of the water the man heard the shrill echo of a telephone's persistent ringing, apparently summoning someone who was not there.

He entered the house, lifted the receiver and asked a bit uncertainly:

"*Che e?* Who is there?"

"Ah, it's you!" he heard a querulous voice. "It's all well then, I presume? I have a report here that the Americans have landed in your sector."

"Oh, no, no," the man said, his sturdy face creased with fatigue but now brightening and his voice gaining a persuasive tone. "It's all quiet here. No landing anywhere."

"No wonder," the distant voice said, "in weather like this." Then they hung up.

The time was 4:37, July 10, 1943. The place a Sicilian beach near Licata, the lively sulphur seaport fronting on the Mediterranean, its good citizens sound asleep with no thought of trouble.

The caller was an Italian general named Achile de Havet, commandant of the 206th Coastal Division. The man who answered wás Michael Chinigo. A war correspondent working for International News Service and covering the Seventh

U.S. Army, he had shipped out with the 3rd Division and stowed away to the shore with the 3rd Battalion of the 15th Infantry. He enjoyed the quaint accident of his experience thanks to his fluent knowledge of Italian.

It was still dark outside, but all around him the invasion was on. "Tiny infantry landing craft were coming in all up and down the sea front," Jack Belden wrote in his eyewitness report, "and other larger boats were edging toward the shore to swell the monstrous and ever-growing heap of beached material. There was an endless, confused mass of men, of tiny jeeps, huge, high-sided ducks, and war jeeps and heavily loaded trucks, stuck and straining in the thick sand or moving clumsily on the wire netting that the engineers had already laid down in some places as a road."

"Husky" had arrived at its destination. General Patton's Seventh Army, established from the stone tower of Gaffe on a rocky cliff in the east all the way westward to Scoglitti on 69 miles of beach, began to push inland with the dash of its commanding general.

According to the dictionary a "bigot" is an "intolerant adherent of a religious creed"—and in the late spring of 1943, General Patton was among "the Bigots." So were Generals Eisenhower, Alexander and Bradley, as well as their staffs, and a few hundred other persons in the Allied camp. But their "intolerance" had nothing to do with any religious creeds.

They were "bigoted" because they knew the details of "Husky." So secret was the upcoming operation that even the highest security classifications—British *Most Secret* or United States *Top Secret*—were not considered safe enough to protect it from eavesdroppers. "Husky's" planners invented a super-secret classification and named it "Bigot." And that made the relative handful of chosen people a very exclusive and distinguished community, called "the Bigoted."

This was a reasonable precaution. "Husky" was history's most ambitious amphibious operation, and the element of surprise was considered essential for its success. If, however, precautions went beyond the usual melodrama of military secrecy, it was because of General Montgomery.

When the jaunty bereted commanding general of the Eighth Army "peddled" his private operations plan in lieu of "Husky Eight," he used as his trump the bugaboo of Axis strength in Sicily. "Planning to date has been on the assumption," he signaled Alexander on April 24th, "that resistance will be slight and Sicily will be captured easily. Never was there a greater error . . . If we work on the assumption of little resistance, and disperse our effort as is being done in all planning to date, we will merely have a disaster."

During the hush-hush conference of May 3rd, when he swayed the Allied brass, he said, "Enemy resistance will be very great; it will be a hard and bitter fight; we must go prepared for a real killing match."

Frightened by Montgomery's warning, "Force 141" made exceptional efforts to ascertain the Axis order of battle in Sicily. The intelligence thus procured appeared to bear out Montgomery. At 9:30 A.M. on June 22nd, Eisenhower and his commanding generals, accompanied by their super-staffs, went to the Ecole Normale at Bouzarea to hear what Patton called "a very secret G-2 estimate" by an anonymous British lieutenant colonel. Patton was usually skeptical of strange G-2 estimates (which, in his experience, rarely conformed to the facts he found); and this time, too, he remained unshocked. "The man," he said afterward, "unquestionably knew a great deal but he succeeded in keeping it to himself."

But what the young lieutenant colonel deemed proper to divulge was enough to fill his audience with apprehension. According to his estimate, the Axis had 14 divisions either on the island or nearby, one of them the crack "Hermann Goering" Panzer Division of the *Wehrmacht*. All told he said, the enemy was believed to have some 400,000 combat-ready troops in Sicily. The air forces showed up even more formidably. The "appreciation" spoke of up to 4,000 German and Italian planes on 32 airports, including the cluster of fields at Comiso, Biscari and Ponte Olivo in the southeast. It was their proximity to his landing area that had induced Montgomery to push through the shifting of the American effort from Palermo to his left flank.

Elaborate measures were naturally needed to mislead the enemy and conceal the pending operation from this awesome conglomeration of Axis power or else the landings could very likely fail under the guns of an alerted foe. The screening of "Husky" became a classic. "Bigot" was introduced as a special security classification. British Intelligence floated "Operation Mincemeat"—dropping into the waters off Spain the corpse of a British officer-courier—"the man who never was"—with "secret" documents on his body. They were faked to persuade the enemy, into whose hands the pro-Axis Spaniards could be expected to deliver the scoop, that Sardinia and Greece, rather than Sicily, would be the next Allied targets in the Mediterranean.

All the components of the invasion were given cover names. Patton's budding Seventh Army became "Task Force 343"; its II Corps "Speedy." Even Montgomery's world-famed Eighth Army had to give up its identity for the time being and masquerade as a phantom force called the Twelfth British Army.

Late in June, II Corps counter intelligence chief Horace Miner, a quiet-spoken, pipe-smoking major who taught anthropology at the University of Michigan, briefed Patton and Bradley, and assured them that the operation was secure from enemy penetration.

In Algiers on July 5th, Patton surreptitiously boarded the *Monrovia* for the journey to Sicily, satisfied that the curtain was tightly drawn around "Husky." Then all this wonderful security blew up in his face.

The French pilot who took the *Monrovia* from its berth to the outer anchorage was the first to give him a shock. Taking leave of Commander T. B. Brittain, her skipper, he said with a knowing smile:

"Bon voyage, mon commandant, pour Sicile!"

Patton expected to tell his men on the transports and landing ships their destination only when they were well out at sea. But he found to his dismay that on the *Monrovia*, at least, there was not a man in need of being told. The day before, it developed, while the transports were still at Algiers and Oran along the spy-infested docks, the solicitous Special Services had distributed pamphlets entitled *Soldier's Guide to Sicily*.

Did the Axis know that "Husky" was on the way?

And how did the enemy's actual order of battle compare with the estimate of "Force 141"?

"Eisenhower was wrongly informed," wrote Field Marshal Albert Kesselring, the German Commander in Chief in Italy, "when he claimed that the invasion of Sicily was unexpected. The Axis powers were clear about it, except for the exact locations of the assault areas."

As a matter of fact, Hitler was the only one at the top who was deceived by the late "Major Martin," the bogus courier with the fake documents, and believed that Sardinia would be the goal of the imminent Allied effort. The Italian Naval Staff in Rome knew about the approach of "Husky" and expected it to hit Sicily. Italian and German planes sighted several Allied convoys on July 8th and 9th—one only 33 miles northwest of Gozo—and reported them promptly. Contact reports tumbled into the Admiralty and Air Force headquarters in Rome every 20 to 30 minutes.

At 6:30 P.M., on July 9th, the Germans alerted their forces in Italy.

And at 1 A.M. on July 10th—less than two hours before H-Hour on D-Day, when no landing craft had left any of the American transports—General Alfredo Guzzoni, who commanded all the Axis forces in Sicily, declared a state of emergency and ordered the harbor obstructions at Porto Empedocle and Licata be blown. "And before D-Day was many hours old," wrote Admiral Morison, "he had correctly estimated that there would be no landings west of Licata, and ordered his mobile units in Western Sicily to make best speed east."

Fortunately for Patton, the concern and the alert did not spread to the first lines of defense on the 69-mile coast he was about to storm. And even more fortunately, there was little real similarity between the actual Axis strength in Sicily and the estimate of "Force 141." The two combined to assure the success of the landings and, incidentally, to prove Montgomery wrong. Events were soon to show that had he been right, the Seventh Army would have met certain disaster by being put down on the open beaches at General Montgomery's insistence.

Seventh Army, in fact, remained thoroughly skeptical of the British estimates. Colonel Koch, Patton's level-headed G-2, dismissed them as nonsense. He had the enemy order of battle laid out clearly on a huge map in the War Room at Mostaganem. In his last briefing on July 1st, just before "I Armored Corps" headquarters closed shop in the French battalion compound, Koch told Patton:

"We estimate that the German and Italian garrison in Sicily consists of 200,000 men. The Italians have six static divisions stretched out along about 500 miles of coast, and four field divisions in reserve further inland. The coast defense divisions are understrength, underequipped and of low combat quality. The field divisions may be better but they are short on equipment. What is more, only one of them is posted in our assault area.

"As far as the Germans are concerned, they have two divisions, one of them Panzer. They are 'hot mustard' but short on tanks. We believe they have only 85 between them. However, they are both pointed toward the invasion area, the 'Hermann Goering' Division just above Gela.

"Air is a question mark," Koch said. "But we do not believe that the enemy has more than 800 planes."

In actual fact, the situation was better than the British estimate and worse than Koch's. The coastal defense divisions were negligible; and the air force on Sicily proper—dispersed on 12 rather than 32 permanent airfields—consisted of only 350 fighter planes, of which only 209 were operational.

However, the Germans had two major forces, the 15th Panzer Grenadiers in the west and the Hermann Goering Panzer Division in the east. The Italians had two corps, one charged with the defense of western Sicily, the other—with two field divisions—hoping to defend the eastern part of the island. The Italians had only 50 light tanks, but the Hermann Goering Division had 100 medium and heavy tanks, and 60 guns. There were about 300,000 men under arms in Sicily, of whom, on July 10th, only about 23,000 were Germans. But before the campaign was over, the Germans would commit a total of 60,000 to the defense of the island.

This, then, was the enemy toward which Patton was now sailing.

Though he discounted the higher estimate of "Force 141," he was not reassured by Koch's lower figures. In his last conference with Bradley, who was going along in command of II Corps, they agreed that under the circumstances imposed upon them by the final plan, their chances of success were only fifty-fifty.

The *Monrovia* was a new ship, built the year before for the Delta Line and converted by the Navy into an attack transport. She reminded Patton of his fortnight on the *Augusta* when he was en route to Casablanca with "Torch." The *Monrovia* was the command ship of the Western Naval Task Force and flagship of Admiral Hewitt, carrying the commanding general of the Seventh Army—which did not officially exist.

Hewitt, on his part, was playing the host in his innate genial style. And he had a special gift for Patton, a memorable souvenir that would forever link the Seventh Army with the Navy.

Now "Husky" was at sea and it was clearly making history. "No amphibious operation on so broad a front—practically eight reinforced divisions landing abreast—had ever been tried before," wrote Morison, "nor was it ever tried again, *even in Normandy,* where the initial assault force was less than this strength."

Patton was sailing with 80,000 men. His forces consisted of the 1st, 3rd and 45th Infantry Divisions, the 2nd Armored Division now commanded by General Gaffey, the 82nd Airborne Division of Major General Matthew B. Ridgway, and Lieutenant Colonel William Orlando Darby's Ranger battalions. The 9th Infantry Division was held in reserve. The complexity of the invasion force was shown in a II Corps troop list that had 151 different units ranging from infantry regiments to engineer well-drilling sections, MP prisoner-escort companies, and graves-registration companies.

The troops were carried in three naval attack forces called *Joss, Dime* and *Cent.* The scheme of landing covered the 69-mile beach front, *Joss* shipping the reinforced 3rd Division of General Truscott to Licata; *Dime* taking Allen's 1st Division to Gela and three points south; *Cent* landing the 45th Division of Major General Troy H. Middleton to five points north and south of Scoglitti.

Patton was going with *Dime* to Gela, and had strategic control of the 82nd Airborne. His forces faced the 18th Coastal Brigade at the beaches, the Hermann Goering Division about 15 to 20 miles north of Gela, the Livorno Division in the hills over Licata, and the Napoli Division to the northeast, its closest position about 25 miles from Scoglitti.

July 6th dawned calm and peaceful, and nothing occurred until the evening of July 8th to mar, as Admiral Cunningham put it, the precision of this remarkable concentration. But that evening the sun set blood red and the light wind dropped to a whisper. On the morning of the 9th, as the great armadas were converging south of Malta to steam for the beaches, a stiff wind blew in. It was Boreas, the north wind of Greek legend, which keeps sweeping down from the Alps and whips the Mediterranean to foam. By the afternoon it was blowing a full gale and the invasion was in trouble. On the *Monrovia,* Admiral Hewitt went looking for General Patton. "George," he said, "this shows every sign of becoming more intense. I think I'll signal Ike and Cunningham to delay the landings."

But Patton had a talisman on the ship—Lieutenant Commander Steere, the aerologist who had restored his faith in meteorology in the Atlantic when the storm blew up on his way to Morocco.

"Wait a minute, Henry," Patton said. "Have you spoken to Steere?"

"Yes."

"Did he say how long this Goddamn storm will last?"

"Well," Hewitt said, "he thinks it will calm down by D-Day."

Patton sent for Steere.

"Well, Houdini," he called him by the nickname he had given Steere, "what do you say?"

"This is a mistral, sir," the aerologist said, "violent but abrupt. I would say it will moderate by 2200, and the weather will be fine by H-Hour, General."

"It had better," Patton said.

"I'm positive, sir," Steere said crisply.

Eisenhower was in Malta with Cunningham, trying to figure out an answer to a signal from General Marshall in Washington, "Is the attack on or off?" Then another signal came in, from Admiral Sir Dudley Pound in London, with the same question. They hoped to hear from Hewitt, but Eisenhower told Cunningham:

"Don't expect a postponement, A.B.C. Georgie is breathing down Hewitt's neck and he won't let him delay. Patton would land in the eye of a hurricane."

At 8 P.M., with no word from the *Monrovia,* the answers went off to Washington and London: "Weather not favorable, but operation proceeding."

At 10:30 P.M. came the break, only 30 minutes behind Steere's schedule. The wind moderated, and continued to ease during the night.

By midnight—just when the *Monrovia's* radar picked up the coastline of Sicily—it almost died away.

This was Patton's witching hour.

His staff assembled on the bridge deck and the Commanding General of the first full-fledged American army in Europe in World War II made a little speech. "Gentlemen," he said, "it's now one minute past midnight 9-10 July 1943, and I have the honor and the privilege to activate the Seventh United States Army. This is the first army in history to be activated after midnight and baptized in blood before daylight."

Admiral Hewitt signaled to his aide, and in marched an honor guard carrying the Navy's gift for Patton—a brand-new flag for a brand-new army. Patton was crying.

"But I could see the fire of pride in his eyes," Commander Brittain said. "It was to him not a ship's deck he stood upon but a peak of glory."

Patton suddenly felt the need of being alone to pray a little and maybe think a little. But he concluded that no amount of thinking was likely to do any good at this late hour. His thoughts went back to a day in May when he was told that he could have the 9th Division on call. It was a new experience for him because until then the United States Army never had enough trained troops to provide for reserves. Then General Keyes, his friend who was to command a provisional corps in Sicily, suggested that an infantry combat team and part of the 2nd Armored Division be held in reserve, and Patton now remembered all the decisions he had made for the venture. He was proud of some of them, for he had had to sweat them out in a cerebral effort, but most of them just popped into his mind ready-made as if an invisible conductor had orchestrated his thoughts.

As he was walking toward his cabin, Patton heard a message of Admiral Cunningham coming from the loudspeakers: "We are about to embark on the most momentous enterprise of the war," the great admiral said, "striking for the first time at the enemy in his own land."

For the first time! His thoughts went out to the green soldiers of the 45th Division floating at his right in the direction of Scoglitti to their baptism of fire. They had come straight from the United States, stopping only at a staging area at Oran for last-minute amphibious training. Patton was concerned about their capability, and went to see them on June 25th, getting up at 3 A.M. to observe a landing exercise at Arzeu. The division amazed him.

Yet now he worried about them. Exercise is one thing but the battle is the pay-off.

Just ahead of him were the transports with Terry Allen's 1st Division. The cocky bastards! Patton did not like Allen, a rebel in his own right and difficult to handle. He had watched his landing exercises, too, on June 24th, and met Allen in the Observation Post near Oran.

The 1st Division had been a problem baby since back in Tunisia. It was a magnificent group of bold men, led flamboyantly by their iconoclastic commanders, Allen and Roosevelt. They both had their drawbacks—Allen was too independent and moody, Roosevelt had a bad case of arthritis and was drinking heavily. And they loved each other all the time. But as leaders of men in combat they had no peers. Their relation with their troops was charismatic. The whole 1st Division was just one big mutual admiration society with Allen's own stubborn and rebellious personality and Roosevelt's raw human touch imprinted on it.

Although Patton found it difficult to live with Allen, he found it impossible to live without him. It seemed that the 1st Division had had it when it returned from Tunisia. It showed too much individualism and too little discipline, and it was insubordinate at times, as was Allen. General Eisenhower, however, decided to put the division on ice for a while and give Patton the fresh but untested 36th Division for "Husky." As soon as he heard of the decision, Patton stormed into Ike's office in the St. Georges and roared:

"I want those sons of bitches! I won't go on without them!" He got them.

It was one of his smartest decisions in the entire war.

"... *striking for the first time at the enemy in his own land* ..." The words of Admiral Cunningham, coming again from the speaker.

Patton was in his cabin, lying on his bunk, just staring at the bulkhead, tense. Will his soldiers fight? He thought they would! These men were different from the boys he had arrived with in Morocco eight months before.

A couple of GI's were standing outside near his window, listening to the Admiral's message, and Patton was monitoring their small talk. All of a sudden he heard one tell his buddy:

"Well, when we go ashore in the morning, I reckon we'll hear the Marines have landed."

Patton knew he did not have to worry any more.

His boys had become men. Even more, they had become soldiers.

Now it was H-Hour—2:45 A.M. on July 10, 1943. D-Day in Sicily.

Invasions are grandiose ventures, but they are terrifying personal experiences for those who take part in them, from the commanding general sweating it out on his flagship to the GI squatting in a landing craft.

The soldiers who were now landing in Sicily did not charge off the boats firing from the hip. Some of them had to be coaxed to go ashore; and when they were on the beach, they had to be told, step by step, what to do next. It was a good thing Patton could not see them from the *Monrovia*.

When a landing craft of the 1st Division in charge of Major Walter Grant grounded on the beach east of Gela and dropped the bow ramp, not a single man moved to step ashore. Grant yelled at them to get off. Still no one moved.

"Jump off," he shouted. "You want to get killed here? Get on the beach!"

Then he himself leaped ashore, a soldier followed, but the rest held back waiting to see what would happen to Grant and the GI beyond the comparative safety of their craft. Nothing happened, so they followed.

Once ashore, nobody seemed to know what to do, what was going on, where the Krauts and the Eyeties were. Not a shot was fired at Grant's little band and there was no enemy on the beach to put up a fight. There was nothing to do, it seemed, so the men just milled around until Grant's sharp voice commanded:

"Get inland! Keep moving! On the double!"

And so inland they went, all in a bunch. The major and his second in command had to keep cutting back and forth across the front, separating knots of men, getting them to spread out.

The invasion had hardly begun and Italian resistance was collapsing all along this Sicilian coast. The Rangers at Gela reported the town secured at 8 A.M. Licata was taken so fast that the enemy inland did not even know it had gone. In the Seventh Army's sector, the Italians either surrendered or beat a hasty retreat across the coastal plain toward the first ring of hills. The fight for the beaches seemed over before it had begun.

But the worst was still to come and it would decide the fate of this invasion.

General Guzzoni was at his desk in his headquarters in Enna, and the 66-year-old veteran of Mussolini's wars now reacted swiftly. Even before dawn he sent orders to Niscemi and Caltagirone for Italian tanks and German Panzers to counter-attack the growing beachhead at Gela. The Germans took their time. But the first Italian tanks came clanking toward the town at 8:30 in the morning.

In Gela, Colonel Darby's Rangers had just gotten the town crier to announce that all danger was past when the first tanks roared in. They were hardly up to date—the light tanks the Italians had taken from the French in 1940 —but they were more than a match for the Americans, who did not have a single antitank gun in town.

The streets were cleared of Rangers in seconds. They rushed into buildings and fired down, with little effect, from second-story windows. Darby himself fired 300 rounds of .30 caliber ammunition at one tank and failed to stop it. Then, as he said, he "ran like hell." But the Italians could do little once the Rangers were indoors because their machine guns, their only armament, could not be elevated.

Darby got into his jeep, raced down to the pier, unmounted a gun that had just been brought ashore, and lifted it into the vehicle. Then he drove his improvised tank-destroyer back to Gela and started shooting. "Every time we slammed a shell in that demounted gun," he said, "she recoiled on the captain and knocked him ass over teakettle into the back seat." But it did the trick, and the Italians soon retreated.

The counterattack might have succeeded had the Hermann Goering Division been with the Italians as ordered by Guzzoni. But Marshal Kesselring radioed Major General Conrath, a former Nazi police officer in command of the Panzer division, to wait until the intentions of the Americans became clear, then prepare a counterattack to start no later than midnight, July 10-11th. As a result, the Italian armored group was cut to pieces even before its tanks reached the Ranger positions.

Satisfied that the main Allied effort was going to be made where landings had already been effected, Guzzoni repeated his original order to attack Gela. Before noon, as Licata and Scoglitti fell, he signaled the 15th Panzer Grenadiers, a motorized infantry division, and the Assietta Division to move east and bolster the two coastal units fleeing Gela and Licata. It was obvious to the Italian general that these two divisions would no longer be needed in the west, where Marshal Kesselring had predicted the main Allied thrust would come.

This was but one threat in a rapidly developing situation to endanger Patton's victory despite the easy conquest of the beaches. Air support proved either nonexistent or, indeed, cruelly harmful, Allied planes bombing our own units both afloat and ashore. On June 21st, after conferences with Air Vice Marshal Wigglesworth, who was in over-all charge of air arrangements for "Husky," and Major General Browning, Eisenhower's airborne adviser, Patton told his staff that he had "enumerated what he regarded as the minimum requirements of air support, but doubted that he would get in fact what he had asked for."

The events of D-Day bore out his fears and doubts. The air forces insisted on conducting their part in "Husky" independently of the other services, and the result was disaster.

Certainly Patton found that the contribution Air was making harmed rather than helped him, and that virtually none of the assistance he had asked from Wigglesworth was given him when the time came.

But Patton was powerless, and so was Hewitt. The situation was so bad that Hewitt, in his wrap-up report, felt compelled to write about air cover, "Close support of aircraft in amphibious operations, as understood by the Navy, did not exist in this theater."

To these problems were added difficulties with the 45th Division. Assigned to clear material off the beaches, the green engineers got completely out of hand. Some even rifled personal luggage stored nearby. Patton later had their commanding officer court-martialed, but in the meantime conditions on some of the division's beaches became so congested that operations had to be suspended and the shore parties had to move to unclogged areas elsewhere.

On this D-Day, in fact, only one element prevented the efforts to supply American beaches from collapsing completely, as Cunningham and Hewitt had feared they would when Montgomery insisted that the Seventh Army be put down on the open beach without recourse to a port. Hewitt's force was the first to use and "Husky" the first amphibious operation to get the new 2½-ton amphibious truck in combat. Called DUKW by General Motors, for no pertinent reason, and "Ducks" by the GI's, they were not stopped by false beaches as were the LST's (landing ship tanks); they did not depend on causeways but could ferry their cargo direct from freighters to any section of the beach, or even to dumps set up inland. The hectic course of the invasion completely confirmed Patton's suspicion that landings on open beaches would jeopardize the success of the operation, and now he told Hewitt with a sigh of relief:

"Without the DUKWs we would have been licked."

By sunset of this Saturday in Sicily, the battle had moved well inland. It seemed that if Montgomery's "killing match" were to take place, it would not come on the beaches. The situation was pretty much under control—except at Gela. General Allen at his CP ashore had word that General Conrath was concentrating his 100 medium and heavy tanks only a few miles from the 1st Division positions.

Everything now depended on where the blow would fall and how powerful the attack would be. Its moment of truth was upon the Seventh Army.

Now everything depended on those cocky bastards of the Big Red One!

Early Sunday morning—D plus 1—General Roosevelt and his aide, Lieutenant Marcus O. Stevenson, drove from Division Headquarters to the command post of the 26th Infantry Regiment a short distance from Gela. They arrived at 6:25 A.M., went in, and started a routine confab with Colonel John W. Bowen, the regiment's commander.

Everything seemed quiet, but only for 10 minutes.

At 6:35 Italian dive bombers began to attack the Gela roadstead.

At 6:40 a phone call from his 3rd Battalion told Bowen that German medium tanks had just broken into its lines.

The Panzer counterattack Patton and Bradley feared had begun. The Hermann Goering Division had quit Caltagirone shortly after midnight, split into two groups, and lunged down the Gela road in a desperate effort to throw Allen's division back into the sea. The tanks overrunning the 3rd Battalion belonged to Conrath's *Kampfgruppe Rechts* (Combat Group Right) coming down from Niscemi like the Italians the day before. Now they were ready to pick up where the light Italian tanks had left off.

The 26th Regiment was not ready to meet the onslaught. All of Bowen's antitank guns had been lost the day before when the LST that carried them had exploded. The Germans came with more than 60 tanks. Bowen had two. What division artillery had been brought ashore was still back on the beaches.

At 6:59 A.M. General Roosevelt put in a call to Allen. At the Division CP, Colonel Charles Stone picked up the phone.

"Charlie," Roosevelt told him, "the 26th on our left is having a tank attack. Don't know how bad as yet. What I want to know is when are they going to get the medium tanks ashore. Let me talk to General Allen."

Allen came on the phone.

"Terry, look," Roosevelt said, "the situation is not very comfortable out here. The 3rd Battalion has been attacked by tanks and has been penetrated. The 2nd Battalion is in support, but that is not enough. We haven't got any antitank protection. If we could get that company of medium tanks it sure would help. Is there any possibility of hurrying those medium tanks? If we are to take the Ponte Olivo airport we must have them."

The tanks had been promised Bowen by 12:15 A.M. but at 7:30 the engineers phoned him that he would not get them—the beach was still too heavily mined to permit vehicles to move. At 7:31 Allen called to verify the engineers' report.

At 8:19 A.M. Roosevelt was talking to Allen again. "Situation not so good," he said hoarsely. "Out of communication with our 3rd Battalion. Terry, any news of what's to be expected? Now what about those medium tanks? Goddamnit, I'll come back and pull 'em out myself. I'll return as soon as situation becomes clarified."

Something had to be done before the 1st Division was torn to pieces.

On the *Monrovia*, General Patton was blissfully ignorant of the 1st Division's plight. This is what happens in an invasion before the situation is stabilized. The commanding general may be just around the corner. For a unit with its line of communications knocked out by an attack, he might just as well be on the moon.

Patton was straining at the leash, but he was so busy with the chaotic air situation and with coordinating the assault forces that he could not leave the ship. Now he was going ashore for the first time, to visit Allen.

It was 9 A.M. on July 11th when he was ready, and it was a sight to behold as he descended to Admiral Hewitt's barge bobbing in the swell. He was groomed immaculately from toe to top, in his best high boots, tight-fitting breeches, smart woolen shirt with only three ribbons, his necktie firmly knotted and stuck into the shirt below the second button, his pistol in the open holster, a pair of oversized binoculars and a map case dangling from his neck, helmet strapped—and a huge cigar between his pale lips. He climbed unaided over the chains of the railing, turned nimbly around, and descended the net into the barge.

His arrival was another treat in Pattonesque nonchalance. The barge could not make it all the way to the beach, so the General went over the side and waded ashore. The procession was led by Stiller and a soldier with Tommy guns at the ready. Patton followed in the water, the gentle surf lapping his thighs. The rear was brought up by General Gay with a carbine.

Patton was walking briskly in the surf, straight toward a Signal Corps movie cameraman, himself perfectly groomed, necktie and all, carbine hanging loosely from his shoulder, his camera covering his face under the helmet—shooting the memorable scene by backing all the way into Sicily.

It was exactly 9:30 A.M. when Patton set foot on the island and looked at the Hamilton chronometer on his right wrist. He stopped momentarily to survey the wreckage on the beach—a couple of DUKWs shattered by mines and half a dozen beached landing craft—then bang! Shells began to hit the water only 30 yards behind him.

"It's all right, Hap," he said to General Gay. "The bastards can't hit us on account of the defilade afforded by the town."

He waited while the soldiers de-waterproofed his scout car for the three-mile trip to General Allen's CP. Then, driving into Gela, he noticed a flag on a three-story house.

"Who's that?" he inquired.

"Colonel Darby, sir," a soldier told him. "It's CP of the Rangers."

Patton jumped out and climbed the three flights to join Darby, one of his favorite soldiers, at his OP on the top floor of the building. The colonel was somewhere in Gela firing a German 77 he had captured the day before, and from his vantage point Patton could see what he was firing at—a horizon filled with Panzers. A moment later he himself was in action. Seven tanks were coming at him.

He looked down to the street and spotted a Navy ensign with a walkie-talkie.

"Hey, you with the radio," Patton yelled down.

"Can I help you, sir?" the ensign asked smartly.

"Sure as hell," Patton said. "If you can connect with your Goddamn Navy tell them for God's sake to drop some shellfire on the road." He pointed to the tanks approaching along the Ponte Olivo.

The ensign was from a shore fire-control party. By a miracle he succeeded in contacting the *Boise,* and shortly the cruiser's 6-inch shells began falling on the tanks. From then on, the Army and the Navy worked together until

Americans and Germans became so closely joined that the shelling risked hitting our own men.

The Germans were getting very close now.

At 10:30 A.M. Colonel Bowen signaled that he was dispersing his CP while his headquarters company and part of the 1st Battalion were getting ready to meet the tanks. Now 1st Division artillery lined up every gun it had on the dunes. Brigadier General Clift Andrus, Allen's artillery commander, dashed from battery to battery, smoking his pipe and laying the guns himself. They fired at ranges down to 500 yards and until their ammunition was expended.

By then the division's other two regiments were also hard-pressed. Late in the morning, 40 tanks of Conrath's *Kampfgruppe Links* broke the 18th Infantry's front. The 16th Infantry seemed to be disintegrating on the Niscemi road, with a signal to Colonel James Taylor, its commander, at his CP: "We are being overrun by tanks!"

Taylor signaled back at 11:05 A.M.: "Everybody stays just where he is! Under no circumstances will anyone be pulled back. Take cover from tanks! Don't let anything else get through! The Cannon Company is on the way! Everyone to hold present positions!"

Cannon Company did not come, and the tanks did get through. Conrath's Panzers were almost on the beaches. But the regiment held fast.

General Roosevelt, now on the division's left flank, saw the armored spearhead cut toward the road near Allen's headquarters, jumped into his jeep with Lieutenant Stevenson, and just barely got through before the first Panzers crossed the highway. At headquarters he found the captain commanding the guns Taylor wanted and persuaded him to wheel his pieces into position on a hill less than 400 yards from the lead tank.

In Gela, Patton ordered all naval personnel to come up and help. And now the tide began to turn. Firing on targets radioed by the ensign, the *Boise's* guns were getting one after another of Conrath's Panzers. The division artillery was getting more. And the guns Roosevelt had commandeered destroyed five Panzers within 1,000 yards of the beach, turned back others.

By 11 o'clock, although the battle still raged on, Patton was satisfied that the worst was over. Each new burning Panzer gave him the message that the beachhead at Gela would be saved after all.

Patton had gone from Darby's CP to an observation post about 100 yards behind the front where he could watch the Panzers moving across the plain 800 yards away. At 11:50 A.M. he returned to the CP, and just when he got there two British planes began bombing the town. Then a battery of German 88-mm. all-purpose guns opened fire. Twice they hit the building in which he was and made a hole in the roof of a house across the street.

At noon, 10 tanks arrived from the 3rd Division in Licata, and Combat Command B sent two more. Patton then reached General Gaffey at the 2nd Armored and ordered him to close the gap between Gela and the 1st Division. He also called for tanks to help Darby, who was patrolling the roads with groups of three half-tracks originally intended, not for combat, but to carry engineers' equipment.

After a conference with Roosevelt, Patton drove toward Allen's CP but met him on the road coming in. The general was dog-tired, looking at Patton with bloodshot eyes.

"Do you think you have it in hand, Terry?" Patton asked.

"I hope so," Allen said, "but we need antitank stuff."

The conference was interrupted by a fight between 14 German bombers and the antiaircraft guns. Patton climbed back into the scout car and drove to Headquarters of the 2nd Armored for a conference with Gaffey.

Now it was 6 P.M. He had been in action nine hours. "We then drove back to Gela without incident," he wrote that night, "except that I think it is quite unusual for an Army Commander and his Chief of Staff to travel some six miles on a road parallel to the fronts of two armies and about equally distant from the two . . . We got back to the *Monrovia* at 1900, completely wet. This is the first day in this campaign that I think I earned my pay."

The landing had been saved by the skin of the 1st Division's teeth. "Only the perverse Big Red One," wrote General Bradley, in whose II Corps area all this happened, "with its no less perverse commander was both hard and experienced enough to take that assault in stride."

By insisting on the 1st Division for "Husky," instead of the 36th Eisenhower wanted to give him, Patton, in Bradley's opinion, saved II Corps "from a major disaster."

Patton was ready to get on with the campaign when he was hit by what seemed to be an even bigger blow than Conrath's attack with a hundred Panzers.

General Montgomery was making trouble again.

When Montgomery snared Eisenhower and Alexander into acceptance of "a plan that suited no one but Montgomery," he tried to go for the whole of "Husky" and establish himself as its sole master. It was his habit to equate his rampaging ambition with obvious military necessities until it appeared that what was good for Montgomery was good for the Allies. Thus the shift of Patton's Seventh Army from Palermo to Montgomery's own left flank was justified by what he called the basic need of the campaign "to secure the island quickly and prevent the escape of its garrison back to Italy."

This was the strategic goal of "Husky," of course—the destruction of the enemy forces on the island and not merely the occupation of a piece of Italian real estate. To this end, Montgomery had devised his master plan. "The two armies," he wrote, "landing side by side on the south coast, should push quickly northwards and cut the island in half. A defensive flank should then be formed facing west, and the combined efforts of *both* armies be concentrated on getting rapidly to Messina to prevent the get-away across the straits."

Montgomery was always masterly in drawing up logical designs with optimum opportunities. But his method of waging war was not adapted to his logic. He was always talking of "quick" actions, yet he was a slow-motion general. He was always planning the entrapment and destruction of the enemy but repeatedly permitted him to escape by failing to close the traps.

Montgomery was not satisfied with the adoption of his "master plan." He also wanted to be the top man on this totem pole, the over-all ground commander with sole jurisdiction over his own as well as Patton's Seventh Army. "It is clear," he pressured Alexander, "that coordination, direction and control should be undertaken by one Army commander and a joint staff."

Alexander agreed, but at last Eisenhower balked. "There will be two armies," he told the Commanding General of the 15th Army Group, who was all prepared to abdicate his *de facto* command, "one American and one British. And they will be under you, Alex, and not under Monty."

It was a fortunate decision because Montgomery's "master plan" turned out far different in practice from what it portended to be on paper. Contrary to his expectations, Montgomery landed with exceptional ease. "All our initial objectives had been secured without enemy counterattacks or indeed serious opposition," he wrote. "None of the German battle groups had been able to intervene against Eighth Army and even the Italian division located near Siracusa had failed to oppose us."

His 5th Division occupied Syracuse, a major and completely undamaged port, at 9 P.M. on D-Day, by marching into it on the main highway. Then the Royal Navy sailed into the harbor of Augusta even before the troops had arrived in town. Now Montgomery had two ports to supply him while Patton had none and was dependent on support over the open beaches, at least one of which was strongly contested by the Germans.

Montgomery bogged down nevertheless. Having failed to move northward with the lightning speed he himself had advocated, he permitted the enemy to "crystallize" his opposition. By July 15th his path to Messina was "blocked by an outnumbered but by no means outclassed [German] regiment, which held up Montgomery's far superior forces."

This was clearly a matter of halting generalship, for his troops had plenty of pluck. The momentum of their own initial spirit could have carried them forward. At least this was how they impressed the men of the 45th Division when they established contact with a mixed bag of Canadians and Britons of the Eighth Army in the Ragusa area on July 11th. But their general's disposition slowed them down. The capture of Enna, military capital of Sicily by virtue of being the seat of General Guzzoni's headquarters, was assigned to Montgomery's Canadians. A group of Canadian war correspondents arrived to record its occupation only to find that their own objective had been taken by the 1st U.S. Division coming up from Gela.

Now Montgomery's master plan was off schedule and out of kilter. The general who craved to be the master of the entire Sicilian campaign obviously had lost control over his own share of the operation. He not only failed to move as fast as had been expected, but worse, he seemed unable to find a way of bursting out of his confinement.

When he now found the coast road to Messina blocked around the eastern side of Mount Etna, Montgomery decided to try the other side. He picked Road 117 on his left flank to which he intended to shift the weight of his advance. But there was a hitch. That road had been assigned to the Americans, and the 45th U.S. Division was already moving northward on it.

Montgomery demanded that Alexander stop the Americans, evict them from the road, and permit his Eighth Army to take it over for what Monty now began to call his "left hook." Alexander acquiesced promptly. He let Patton know about the change in an Army Group directive without any previous consultation, in spite of the inconvenience the abrupt shift would cause the Seventh Army.

This was July 14th, D plus 4. Patton was at his headquarters at Gela when Alexander's directive arrived. Under different circumstances, the arbitrary order—clearly designed to take Montgomery off the hook at his expense—would have thrown him into a rage. But now he appeared to be welcoming the order. He was not impressed with Montgomery's showing in the campaign and recognized in his colleague's slow progress on the road to Messina unexpected opportunities for himself.

"Since the initial successful assault on the beaches before daylight on the 10th," Patton wrote, "we have continued to push along several days ahead of our assumed schedule. This has been due to the fact that having once got the enemy started, we have not let him stop, but have, so to speak, kept on his heels . . . The tally of prisoners, guns, etc., speak more forcefully than words as to the success of the operation. While comparisons are odious, I believe that up to yesterday, the Eighth Army had not taken over 5,000 prisoners."

Now Patton's response to Alexander's directive was to light one of his big cigars, the sign that he was embarking on a plot of his own. Then he sent for Bradley, to whose II Corps the 45th Division was assigned.

"We've received a directive from Army Group, Brad," he said with a resignation that escaped Bradley. "Monty is to get the Vizzini-Caltagirone road in his drive to flank Catania and Mount Etna by going up through Enna. This means you'll have to sideslip to the west with your 45th."

Bradley replied with a torrent of objections.

He had already come to within 1,000 yards of the main road to Enna, but now the 1st Canadian Division would take that highway instead of Middleton's 45th. This meant that he would have to pull the whole division back to where it had come in—actually all the way to the beach—and then squeeze it back into the line on the left flank of the 1st Division. The operation would delay the advance of II Corps several days.

But Patton did not seem to care, not even when Bradley protested, "The enemy is falling back in disorganization. I don't want him to regain his balance."

"Sorry, Brad," Patton said quietly, "but the change-over takes place immediately. Monty wants the road right away."

There was, of course, a reason for Patton's eager acquiescence, but for the time being he was not talking about it. Quite obviously, he figured, there was the possibility of a *quid pro quo* in the arrangement. By giving with the *quid* he saw clearly what the *quo* would be.

The road to the north was thus lost to him, leaving only the west for him to advance. Even there, Alexander's directive had limited the Seventh Army. Patton was free to do as he pleased only as long as he did not impinge upon the principal task assigned to him—to act as bodyguard for the British. In other words, he was not free to commit himself to a major engagement in the west. Specifically, Alexander told him, he was not to attack Agrigento, which was the pivot of Italian resistance in this sector.

The limitation was infuriating because Lucian Truscott, who had his eyes on the town, knew that the enemy there was much weaker than Army Group thought. Immediately after Bradley had left Seventh Army CP to start the withdrawal of the 45th Division, Patton motored to the 3rd Division CP to see Truscott, who was urging him to authorize an immediate attack.

Alexander's directive forced Patton to say no, but he said it with a grin. "Can't you see a way, Lucian," he seemed to be egging Truscott on, "to get around Army Group?"

Truscott was ready with a suggestion. When he presented it, Patton's grin broadened until he looked, in Truscott's words, like the cat that had swallowed a whole flock of canaries.

"We cannot mount a major attack without your permission," Truscott said, "and obviously you cannot give such permission in the light of the Army Group directive. But I could—on my own initiative, mind you—mount a *reconnaissance in force*." According to the book, "reconnaissance in force" meant a strictly local attack with a limited objective solely for the purpose of clearing up an uncertain situation. "In this case," Truscott proposed, "the 'uncertain situation' shall be Agrigento. What do you say?"

"I say nothing, Lucian. Not a Goddamn thing."

This was exactly what Patton wanted. Truscott's plan would keep his hands clean while getting for him the western breakout.

In the next two days the British assault petered out in both east and west. The task of breaking through the Etna Line proved too much for Montgomery. His troops, besides being battle-worn, were beginning to come down with malaria. Pending the arrival of reserves from North Africa, the Eighth Army would have to go on the defensive.

This was exactly what Patton expected when he received Alexander's directive. The swift collapse of the British strike was beginning to cast an entirely new light on the role Patton might be allowed to play—not in the east in support of Monty, but in the west on his own. Imperceptibly, the strategic plan Monty had imposed upon the campaign was losing its direction. It was reverting to the original design, with Palermo, of which Montgomery had hoped to deprive the Seventh Army, as one of its objectives.

On the afternoon of July 16th Alexander issued a new directive for Patton. Agrigento could be attacked if it "did not entail heavy fighting." And Porto Empedocle, a fishing village formerly on the prohibited list, was to be taken if possible. The directive was anticlimactic. When Truscott received it, the Rangers had already captured Porto Empedocle. As for Agrigento, his "reconnaissance in force" took it the next day after a brief fight.

With Montgomery stalled on the Simeto River and Truscott firmly settled in both Porto Empedocle and Agrigento, Patton decided to call on Alexander on July 17th to change the entire course of this campaign. If it had irked him to play wet nurse to Montgomery, he was no longer troubled. Now the opportunity of stealing a march on Monty was drawing him like an irresistible magnet. He told Alexander point-blank:

"General, I am here to ask you to take the wraps off me and change your orders to read, 'The Seventh Army will drive rapidly to the northwest and north, capture Palermo, and split the enemy's force.' "

By then Alexander knew—though he was never to concede it—that he had made a mistake when he let Montgomery rewrite the plan. He was annoyed by the Eighth Army's failure to break out toward Messina and the stagnation of the campaign in the east. Alexander agreed to Patton's request because it promised to return the initiative to the Allies, even if only on Patton's part of the front.

Patton himself clearly recognized Alexander's predicament. "I think," he wrote in the diary, "that the British have the bear by the tail in the Messina Peninsula and we may have to go in and help. Had they let us use Road 117 and take Caltagirone and Enna ourselves, instead of waiting for them, we would have saved two days and been on the north coast now.

"Alexander has no idea of either the power or speed of American armies. They [the British] attacked Catania with a whole division yesterday and only made 400 yards."

With Alexander's new directive in his pocket, Patton wasted no time. On the morning of July 18th he signaled Truscott: *"I want you to be in Palermo in five days."* It was a tall order. The city was 100 miles distant and Truscott's men would have to walk all the way.

Patton quickly drafted his plan. He organized Truscott's 3rd Division, Ridgway's 82nd Airborne (or what was left of it), and Gaffey's 2nd Armored Division into a Provisional Corps under General Keyes, to start operations against Palermo on July 19th. Bradley, with II Corps, would move straight through the island's center and attack Palermo from the east, if necessary, or turn east against Messina, if possible.

With that, Patton moved his headquarters to Agrigento, and waited for Keyes to take Palermo by July 24th. It fell on the 22nd.

On the 24th Patton returned briefly to his CP at Agrigento and held an off-the-record press conference in the hall of the huge concrete mansion where Seventh Army had its headquarters. He stalked into the room with a broad smile on his face, his blue eyes bright in the morning sunlight. He was wearing a custom-tailored whipcord shirt over his breeches. Meeks had given a special shine to his hand-made cavalry boots. He had one of his pearl-handled pistols on a hip.

"Gentlemen," he said, "we had about 200 miles to go over crooked roads to get to Palermo. Our drive was faster and over rougher ground than anything the Germans ever did. We didn't give them a chance to dig in."

Then he gave the correspondents the statistics of the blitz campaign—about 44,000 enemy captured, 6,000 killed or wounded, 190 enemy aircraft shot down, 67 guns captured.

"I feel," Patton wrote in the diary "that future students of the Command and General Staff School will study the campaign of Palermo as a classic example of the use of tanks. I held them back far enough so that the enemy could not tell where they were to be used; then when the infantry had found the hole, the tanks went through and in large numbers and fast. Such methods assure victory and reduce losses, but it takes fine leadership to insure the execution. General Keyes," he added as the first of several gestures disclaiming credit for the success of the drive, "provided perfect leadership and great drive. The praises should be his."

Yet Patton, established in the public mind and in the imagination of his own troops in Sicily as a publicity-hugging braggart, was charged with holding up the occupation of Palermo by insisting upon entering the fallen city first. This was the impression created by General Truscott's description of the climactic last few hours of the conquest, and by Donald G. Taggart in his history of the 3rd Infantry Division. According to Truscott, his men had reached the outskirts of the city at 2 P.M. on July 22nd, and requested permission to enter the capital. Patton signaled back at 2:45 P.M. that nobody was to cross into the city until he himself arrived to strut into the humiliated capital as the conquering hero.

Romantic though this sounds and appears to be, characteristic of Patton, it was not what actually happened.

Palermo was captured in an end run by several of the forces racing toward it. It was entered formally and first by General Keyes on Patton's explicit orders and according to his plan. He had reserved this honor for the self-effacing man who so brilliantly commanded the Provisional Corps.

This, then, was how Patton, in close association with

Keyes, developed the plan that led to the quick and virtually bloodless conquest of the Sicilian capital.

While the Provisional Corps was rolling northward, sweeping all resistance from its path, Patton held back the 2nd Armored Division for the *coup de grâce*. On July 20th he ordered the formation of a special unit—called Task Force X—to capture Castelvetrano, partly to protect the left and rear of the Provisional Corps, but mainly to make space for the 2nd Armored, which he was now bringing up for the climax. Headed by Colonel Darby, the Task Force was composed of two Ranger battalions, elements of the 9th Division, and supporting units. On July 21st it seized Castelvetrano and enabled General Gaffey to move the 2nd Armored to an area northwest of the city to exploit the breakthrough.

On July 22nd—the day of the showdown—Darby's task force thrust west along the coast and the 2nd Armored was committed to action. It drove rapidly northeast to the outskirts of Palermo while Truscott's 3rd Division, coming up on foot from Corleone at the incredible rate of 3 miles per hour, reached positions southeast of the city.

The lightning-like descent of the Provisional Corps on Palermo threw its defenders into panic. The local Axis commanders did not recognize the danger until the Americans were almost at the city's gates. Most German troops managed to escape in the last moment, but the Italians stayed behind waiting to be mopped up. So swift was the approach that only two of the many ships in the harbor could lift their anchors in time and sail away to safety.

Since all resistance appeared to have collapsed, General Keyes canceled a planned assault on the city, ordered the 2nd Armored Division to enter it, and instructed General Truscott to send in units of the 3rd Infantry Division to guard installations and prevent the demolition of vital facilities. This was done on Keyes' own initiative, in but a slight deviation from a plan he had suggested for Palermo's final hours. The night before, Keyes had seen Patton at Agrigento to discuss arrangements for the imminent fall of the city and to invite him to enter it first at the head of his troops. But Patton dismissed the invitation:

"You took it, Geoffrey," he said. "You enter first and I will enter it after you."

As for Patton, he had spent the whole of July 21st at

his Headquarters in Agrigento playing host to Lieutenant General Sir Oliver Leese, who commanded one of the corps of the Eighth Army.

Next morning he left Agrigento to follow his troops into Palermo on their last leg. He reached the 2nd Armored CP after dark and was received by Colonel Redding F. Perry, Chief of Staff of the division.

"Hello, Speed," Patton greeted him, "where the hell is General Gaffey?"

"I believe he's in Palermo, sir," Perry said with a grin.

"Has the city fallen?" Patton asked.

"Yes, sir. A short while ago. General Gaffey went in with General Keyes."

"Goddamnit, Speed," Patton jumped. "What are we waiting for?"

Even as Keyes, at 10 P.M., was accepting the city's surrender from two bewildered Italian generals, Patton was making his way to Palermo. Guided by Colonel Perry, he went by a tortuous route through the hills high above the cathedral town of Monreale. The night was lit up by huge fires left from the war, surrounding the city like a flaming wreath.

He began his descent into the capital through a long road running along the side of a cliff. It was lined with people shouting "Down with Mussolini" and "Long live the Americans." It somehow disgusted rather than elated him.

It was past midnight when he reached the Quattro Canti in the heart of the city, and found Keyes and Gaffey waiting for him. Then they made their way to the Piazza della Vittoria, commemorating the victories of bygone conquerors. "We took over the so-called Royal Palace for Headquarters," he concluded the day's reminiscences, "and had it cleaned by prisoners for the first time since the Greek Occupation."

That was a long time before. The Greeks had left town in 254 B.C.

To his mind steeped in history, his was a classic achievement. George Patton had conquered the most conquered city in the world. He came in the wake of Phoenicians, Carthaginians, Romans, Ostrogoths, Byzantines, Arabs, Normans, Spaniards and Neapolitans. He walked in the footsteps of all sorts of oligarchs and liberators, from the tribal chiefs of prehistoric Siculi to the Anjous, Aragons,

Hohenstaufen, Bourbons and Garibaldi, and such local despots as the Chiaramonti.

He entered the Palazzo Reale through the western gate and ascended, through the Renaissance arcades of the court-yard, passing the Palatine Chapel and the Royal Observatory, to the sumptuous Joharia apartments on the third floor with their high-ceilinged, marble-paneled rooms which were to be his quarters for the next six months.

He found the old palace—built around 1600 on foundations laid by the Saracens and the Norman Kings—only partly restored, in a bad state of neglect, and uncomfortable for modern living. "I get quite a kick out of using a toilet," he said, "made malodorous by constipated royalty." When Captain Stiller, his down-to-earth aide, surveyed the place, he told Patton:

"General, you don't really mean to live here. If you let me look, I can find a nice modern house much better than this old dump."

But he decided for the "Old Dump." It was more becoming a conqueror.

The morning after, he stepped out on the ornate balcony of his new office and saw what he had conquered in a breathtaking panorama. The broad cobblestoned Piazza was at his feet with the Cathedral and the Archbishop's Palace at his left, the Church of San Salvatore at his right, the harbor beyond them dominated by Monte Pellegrino, the crescent of hills as far as his eyes could see, to the cypress grove of the old Campo Santo.

Just then a message was handed him. It was from General Alexander.

"This is a great triumph," it read. "Well done. Heartiest congratulations to you and all your splendid soldiers."

It was a generous gesture, and Patton undoubtedly deserved it. But it went far to show how little the Commanding General of the 15th Army Group recognized the situation in Sicily in its true light.

"Sicily was to have been Montgomery's cup of tea," Martin Blumenson wrote. "It became instead Patton's dish of milk."

Actually, it was neither. The day Patton took Palermo

without a fight, Montgomery was struggling desperately to wrest Leonforte 25 miles west of the southwestern slopes of Mount Etna and some 50 to 60 tough miles from Messina. And Patton had just put 150 miles between himself and the strategic goal of the campaign at its easternmost terminus.

Did Patton's dash to Palermo prove anything? Was it as valuable a strategic feat as it seemed to be a tactical *coup?*

Si finis bonus est, totum bonum erit, said the Roman sage, and now Patton's *tour de force* made all seem well in Sicily. But the end was not in sight. If anything, his detour to Palermo tended to complicate matters. All of a sudden, the pretty strategic design of the campaign disintegrated. Instead of bottling up the egress at Messina and trapping the Axis forces before they could make good their escape across the Strait, this port of exit was left open for them to come and go more or less as they pleased.

That the Allies would gain Sicily was a foregone conclusion. But, in the end, they gained it on Hitler's terms. Even while Montgomery and Patton were plotting their selfish plans, the Führer was drafting his design along far more realistic and practical lines.

On the morning of July 12th, on D plus 2, Marshal Kesselring flew to Enna to get an insight into the situation in a conference with old General Guzzoni. Though the future course of the Allied campaign was far from clear, Kesselring quickly concluded that, in the face of the collapse of Italian resistance, it would be impossible to defend the island. That same night, back in Rome, he so advised Mussolini, but the bloated Duce refused to accept the inevitable. Kesselring then radioed Hitler, whereupon the Führer issued a directive that was to govern German operations to the bitter end.

"After the bulk of the Italian forces are eliminated," it read, "our forces alone will be insufficient to push the enemy into the sea. It will, therefore, be our objective to delay the enemy advance, and bring it to a halt west of Mount Etna."

He then ordered General Hans Hube, a one-armed Panzer veteran, saved for this campaign when he was flown out of Stalingrad just before it fell, to take charge in Sicily. Hube was given substantial reinforcements for the delaying action. One after the other, German units poured into Sicily —the 1st Paratroop Division, the 29th Panzer Grenadiers and the rest of Hube's Panzer Corps, until, as Hitler remarked, the Germans had more tanks and heavy guns in Sicily than Rommel ever had at any one time in North Africa.

On July 17th, just when Patton was coaxing permission from Alexander for his drive to Palermo, a German colonel named Bogislaw von Bonin called on Hube with specific orders for the subsequent conduct of the campaign.

"It is not to be contemplated that we can continue to hold the island," they read. "It is, however, important to fight a delaying action to gain further time for stabilizing the situation on the mainland. The vital factor, however, is under no circumstances to suffer the loss of our three German divisions. At the very minimum, our valuable human material must be saved."

Montgomery had foreseen this only three months before in Cairo when he proposed to ball the Allied fist in Sicily for a quick drive on Messina, but he became incapable on the spot to act energetically and effectively on his own anticipation. And Patton, in the heat of the battle and his rivalry with Monty, shut his eyes to this German aim. By slowing the Eighth Army to a virtual standstill south of Mount Etna, Montgomery permitted the build-up of the German forces and made things extremely difficult for himself.

Patton recognized the overwhelming importance of speed and made the most of it, but he sped off in the wrong direction. He himself had boasted on July 18th that—had he not been diverted from his original path—he could have reached the north coast of the island in about two days. He could have then turned east and raced for Messina before the Germans had time to throw up a steel barrier for the city's protection.

Life always becomes so much harder the closer you get to the summit—the cold increases, responsibility increases. In this particular case, responsibility for the disintegration of the strategic plan rested not with Patton or Montgomery but with General Alexander, whose job so clearly was to remain firm in the face of his two prima donnas and make them stick to their respective missions. When he allowed Montgomery to trespass on the American "Yellow Line" at Vizzini-Caltagirone and permitted Patton to turn west instead of continuing north and then east, Alexander abandoned the preconceived plan and let the campaign continue haphazardly, actually without a firm and purposeful design.

The hunt-and-peck method of advance which replaced the plan, Alexander's regrettable weakness and confusion, as well as Montgomery's and Patton's spirited but contradictory ambitions—all these had consequences far beyond the spectacular conquest of Palermo. A port was gained, to be sure, and one of the enemy forces was split. But by authorizing Patton's western drive, Alexander allowed his own forces to be split, giving Hube ample time to put the finishing touches to the Etna Line.

Was Alexander really any better off now than he had been when Patton first showed up at Army Group Headquarters on July 17th?

There was in Sicily only one Allied general who clearly saw the fateful deficiencies of the situation and was disgusted by Alexander's evident impotence in the face of Montgomery's and Patton's self-seeking maneuvers. He was Omar Bradley, in command of the well-nigh forgotten II Corps. He had his orders to move northward, possibly to aid Patton's conquest of Palermo by joining the assault on the city from the west, or probably to get set in the north for the drive on Messina by turning east. The day Patton moved into Palermo, flank elements of II Corps did make contact with Truscott's 3rd Division in the outskirts of Palermo, while its main force pushed on toward the north coast, the 1st Division, on the right flank of the corps, taking Bompietro. It was a woefully uncoordinated drive, and it missed the bus by failing to catch the Germans retreating from Palermo along the coastal highway. But it reached the coast and established II Corps on a line from Nicosia to San Stefano from which the final drive on Messina could jump off.

Eisenhower recognized the difference between the two drives—Patton dashing for ephemeral glory in Palermo while Bradley was hacking his way through forbidding heights toward so much more valuable objectives. In his later account he did praise Patton's speed and give him credit for shaking "the whole Italian Government so forcibly that Mussolini toppled from his position of power" in the wake of Palermo's fall. But he concluded in his own mind that Bradley, with his faithful adherence to the less spectacular, but more practical, design in the face of overwhelming odds (including his eviction from Montgomery's alternate route), was the real hero of the campaign. As a matter of fact, he was so impressed with Bradley that later in August, getting ready for "Overlord," he recommended him, rather than Patton, to General Marshall as commander of United States troops in Great Britain.

While Patton had gained a highly personal victory in Sicily and established himself as the fastest general in the United States Army, he unwittingly forfeited his greatest potential chance in World War II—command of the invasion army and of the Army Group that was to take France a year later.

There was a touch of the nebulous in the rivalry of Montgomery and Patton to the distinct detriment of realism and logic in the campaign. Both men were military virtuosos in their own different ways, but had all the whimsy and vanity of matinee idols. They played things by ear and regarded plans made for them as restrictions to be violated. Later in Sicily, Patton visited Montgomery at his Command Post and complained in his offhand, wisecracking manner of Alexander's directive that had evicted his II Corps from the crucial Vizzini-Caltagirone road on which, the chances are, the fate of the Axis forces in Sicily actually hinged.

"But Patton," Montgomery shot back in apparent amusement, "why didn't you just ignore the order? That's what I do."

Here again was a basic difference between the American and British ways of waging war. In the United States Army an order is an order. It calls for instant compliance. But in the British Army it is merely "a basis for discussion between commanders" and subject to amendments. "Had I known of this British characteristic," Bradley remarked, "I most certainly would have appealed to Patton to protest the Army Group decision on the road."

Sicily was history's vastest amphibious operation and it served as a proving ground for the decisive invasion of Europe across the English Channel. It produced a number of invaluable lessons in omissions as well as commissions, in trials and errors, in the victory as well as the setbacks which preceded it. To Eisenhower, it yielded an especially significant lesson.

"One of the valuable outcomes of the campaign," he wrote, "was the continued growth and development of the spirit of comradeship between British and American troops in action." He was right, on the level of the troops. The seasoned British gained a healthy respect for the fresh Americans, and the men of the Seventh Army learned to admire the veterans of Dunkirk and El Alamein.

Yet this same spirit of comradeship was not so whole-some at the top. If anything, Sicily had sharpened the cutting edge of the Montgomery-Patton rivalry. It became acute when Patton's contribution to the conquest of Sicily was obscured by a deliberate design to minimize his achievement lest the publicity cast a reflection on Montgomery's part in the campaign and dent his prestige.

Shortly after the termination of the campaign, Patton was visited in his palazzo in Palermo by John P. Marquand, the celebrated novelist from his adopted hometown of Boston. Patton seized the opportunity to ask him:

"You've just come from Washington. What is the reaction in the States to what American troops have done in Sicily?"

Marquand hesitated because he feared Patton would not like what he had to say, and Patton quickly spotted his embarrassment.

"No, no," he said, "don't dress it up. Go ahead and tell me."

Marquand then told him that from reading the news-papers the general impression was that "the American forces had knifed through token Italian resistance while the British had faced the brunt of the fighting around Catania."

The violence of Patton's reaction startled the author.

"By God," he said, "don't they know we took on the Hermann Goering Division? Don't they know about Troina? By God, we got moving instead of sitting down, and we had to keep moving every minute to keep them off balance, or we'd be fighting yet—and what were they doing in front of Catania? They don't even know how to run around end. All they can do is to make a frontal attack under the same barrage they used at Ypres."

Marquand, a professional judge of character, properly sensed in Patton's outburst his civilized and constructive concept of the rivalry, mixed as it was of his own self-esteem and sporting spirit, strong streak of Americanism, consummate knowledge of history and military science, pride in his troops, and his growing dislike of Montgomery's vanity and mannerisms.

"Obviously," Marquand remarked, "the General had embarked on one of those impulsive speeches for which he was already growing famous. Yet even in the midst of it—and the words in print appear more bitter than his spoken words—you were aware of an element of generosity. He was not actually evincing anti-British sentiments, nor was he speaking in jealousy or pique. He was speaking solely for his troops, aroused because their exploits had not been given proper recognition."

But Patton himself was quick to realize that he had gone a little beyond the boundaries Eisenhower had established for the Anglo-American partnership in this war. The morning before Marquand left Palermo, he asked to see Patton privately in his sumptuous office in the Royal Palace. The General received the author, sitting behind an antique rosewood desk, signing a large pile of typewritten letters.

"These letters," he said, "convey my personal thanks to individuals in the Seventh Army who have distinguished themselves in Sicily. I am glad to sign them and perhaps you know why—because usually in the Army you can expect loyalty from the bottom up more than you can from the top down, and I ought to know."

He paused and looked at Marquand before he said, "I've been in a lot of trouble lately. Only yesterday somebody from the Inspector General's office flew over to inspect the Italian prisoner camps and he now complains that the prisoners haven't got enough latrines, and they never knew what a Goddamn latrine was until I showed them."

Patton paused again. "Well," he said, "there is only one thing I want to say, and that is, the other night I remember I was somewhat critical about my distinguished opposite number in the British Army. I think I said he didn't know how to run around end and other things. Now, I seem to be in a lot of hot water lately, and suppose we just forget the episode."

CHAPTER SIXTEEN
THE SLAPPING INCIDENTS

On the evening of August 4th, General Patton called Sergeant Rosevich to his tent at his advance headquarters near Cerami to dictate the accumulated items of the previous 48 hours for his diary. He had left his fancy palazzo in

Palermo the day before and was now camping in tents and
bedding rolls on the road to Messina, close to his troops
hacking a breach through the stiff resistance of the 15th
Panzer Grenadiers.

Patton had toured the front the whole day, but his
thoughts now wandered beyond the hard-pressed sector he
had inspected. His attention was divided between the
Germans in the north fighting desperately for every square
inch of ground and Montgomery in the east accelerating
his advance toward Catania.

II Corps was to operate according to a timetable Patton
had drawn up for the race to Messina, along the coast and
the mountainous northern region of Sicily. But it was falling
behind schedule. Even on this August 4th, the 15th Infantry
Regiment of General Truscott's 3rd Division had been
unable to force a crossing of the Furiano River, while the
1st Division of General Allen could not break through
German positions in an all-out effort to take Troina. But
Monty was pursuing the Hermann Goering Division northward across the Salso River.

Though Patton seemed composed, Rosevich sensed a
mounting pressure in him, for the General was like a high-
tension wire that quivers and hums when it is overloaded.
The sergeant was well tuned to Patton. He could gauge his
temper from a fleeting frown on his face or a slight gesture
of his hands. During their long association, he had become
conditioned to the oscillations of his mood; and he was so
habituated to the incandescent diary entries Patton had
been dictating for a year and a half that nothing any more,
it seemed, could jolt him out of his equanimity.

Rosevich was somewhat taken aback nevertheless when
he realized what Patton was dictating. The General began
with his visit to the front before Troina on August 3rd,
reading from notes he had jotted down. "On the way," he
continued at his usual fast clip, "I stopped at an evacuation
hospital and talked to 350 newly wounded. One poor fellow
who had lost his right arm cried; another had lost a leg.
All were brave and cheerful. The first sergeant of C Company, 39th Infantry, was in for his second wound. He
laughed and said that after he got his third wound he was
going to ask to go home. I had told General Marshall
some months ago that an enlisted man hit three times
should be sent home.

"In the hospital, there also was a man trying to look

as if he had been wounded. I asked him what was the matter, and he said he just couldn't take it. I gave him the devil, slapped his face with my gloves and kicked him out of the hospital. Companies should deal with such men, and if they shirk their duty they should be tried for cowardice and shot. I will issue an order on this subject tomorrow."

When next morning Rosevich returned with the transcript, Patton added to it in his own hand: *"One sometimes slaps a baby to bring it to."*

As Rosevich recalls it, Patton had dictated the entry quite casually and showed no sign of regret or apprehension when he read the passage the morning after. He merely said, "This is fine, give it to Colonel Codman," his aide who was both editor and custodian of the diary. Then he leaned back in his chair to dictate a memorandum the incident had inspired.

"To: Corps, Division, and separate unit commanders," he began. The whole memo then read as follows:

"It has come to my attention that a very small number of soldiers are going to the hospital on the pretext that they are nervously incapable of combat. Such men are cowards and bring discredit on the army and disgrace to their commanders, whom they heartlessly leave to endure the dangers of battle while they, themselves, use the hospitals as a means of escape. You will take measures to see that such cases are not sent to the hospital but are dealt with in their units. Those who are not willing to fight will be tried by court-martial for cowardice in the face of the enemy."

These were the first recorded notes of the most tragic period in Patton's life. The slapping of that anonymous soldier in an unidentified hospital was but the first outburst of a violent impulse he became incapable of controlling during those days. It was followed exactly a week later by another such eruption in another evacuation hospital when the unbearable emotional tension instilled in him by the unexpected difficulties of the campaign reached its climax.

The trouble began on August 1st, when the 1st Division pushed boldly into a barren depression between Cerami and Troina. It was the gambit of the terminal offensive in Sicily with which Patton hoped to reach Messina. The day before

he had issued his directive for the major attack. II Corps
under General Bradley, with the 1st, 3rd and 9th Divisions
and supporting units, was to make the main effort along
Highways 113 and 120 from the line San Stefano-Mistretta-
Nicosia.

On the south flank, the 1st Division quickly captured
Cerami and advanced to within five miles of Troina, which
was the pivot of German resistance. On August 1st, the 3rd
Division drove eastward on the coastal highway, and the
1st Division pressed on toward Troina, its forward elements
reaching the outskirts of the town. But then it ran into
strong German defenses.

At sunset, when Patton called Bradley to inquire how the
attack was going, he received the first piece of bad news
to cock him for trouble. "Terry was hit by a powerful
counter-punch," the corps commander told him, "and was
thrown back to his line of departure."

"Goddamnit," Patton swore. "It's just like Allen."

"No, General," Bradley defended the CG of the 1st Division, who was making himself increasingly obnoxious to
Patton by his own rugged individualism. "Allen can't be
blamed for the setback. Troina was going to be tougher than
we thought. The Kraut is touchy as hell there."

The Kraut at this point was the 15th Panzer Grenadiers,
one of the élite divisions the Germans had kept in Sicily
with orders from Hitler himself to prevent Patton from
making the end run to Messina. They were fighting smartly,
making excellent use of whatever advantages the terrain
was affording them, and counterattacking with apparently
unspent élan.

This was not the only bad news Patton had to absorb.
General Middleton's 45th Division was stalled before San
Stefano on the Tyrrhenian Sea. The air support his ground
troops were getting from Major General Edwin J. House's
fliers was spotty, and only too often the American planes
were bombing their own troops. Worst of all, virtually every
one of his divisions was painfully reduced in strength.
Sergeants were commanding platoons for the lack of officer
replacements. Every killed or wounded soldier was sorely
missed, yet while casualties continued to mount, no replacements were in sight.

The day before, General Eisenhower had visited Patton
in his magnificent palazzo at Palermo and talked to the correspondents, who reminded him that on July 12th he had

told them that "a decision might be reached within two weeks." Eisenhower answered with a sidewise smile:

"I'm a born optimist, and I can't change that. But obviously it will take a little longer than we thought."

For the first time in this war things were going against Patton, and in the pinch he was beginning to lose his equilibrium. Although he was spending sleepless nights weighing his difficulties, he seemed unable to come up with any satisfactory solutions.

On August 1st, too, the Germans and Italians decided to strike back at Palermo and staged an ambitious air raid on the harbor, which already had 10 of our ships in, including a fleet of transports. It was 4:30 A.M., and the fire the enemy aircraft left behind lit up the city, which was shaken by tremendous explosions as an ammunition ship blew up in noisy installments.

The streets were deserted, except for a couple of correspondents—John Hersey of *Time* magazine and Richard Tregaskis of INS—trying to cover the burning waterfront. Suddenly a command car appeared from nowhere and Hersey recognized Patton. He hailed it and Patton ordered Mims to stop. To the reporters he seemed to be almost elated in this macabre environment—he was immaculately groomed despite the early hour and was smiling broadly in the "atmosphere of yammering ack-ack guns and exploding bombs."

Hersey asked about the damage to the harbor, and Patton said, "I couldn't get very close—too hot. There appear to be at least two ships burning. And they hit the freight yards." He added with a broad grin, "But fortunately they missed the transports altogether."

On August 2nd the news continued bad. Truscott reported that mines and demolitions were slowing the advance of the 3rd Division; and Bradley relayed intelligence from Allen that all efforts to envelop and reduce Troina had failed on the German's tenacious defenses.

Whenever Patton felt the need to bolster his own morale, he would visit the nearest hospital, because he gained solace and inspiration from the sight of men whose badge of courage was their wounds.

As much as he needed these visits to reassure himself, he thought the men needed him even more to lighten their sufferings. Patton regarded these visits as the high points of his command and his noblest task. He was always gratified to see that he was a tonic for the maimed men.

Now in Palermo, to take his mind off the bad news, he called Colonel Daniel Franklin, the Seventh Army's Surgeon, and—with a load of 40 Purple Hearts—went to call on the patients at the Base Hospital. He walked from bed to bed and talked with easy familiarity with the men.

"Where did you get it, boy?" he asked a soldier whose bandage was concealed under the cover.

"In the chest, sir."

"Well," Patton said, raising his voice, for he wanted the whole ward to hear his pep talk, "it may interest you to know that the last German I saw had no chest and no head either. To date you have captured or killed over 80,000 s.o.b.'s—that's the official figure, but as I travel around, my nose tells me that the figures are much bigger and before the end they will be double that. Get well quickly, boy— you want to be in on that final kill." He made a different speech at each ward, another to the nurses, still another to the doctors.

Just before leaving, he walked up to a bed in which a soldier was breathing heavily under an oxygen mask. When Patton realized that the man was unconscious, he took off his helmet, knelt down, pinned a Purple Heart on the pillow, whispered something into the ear of the dying man, then stood up at attention. If it was a corny performance, it did not seem so to the nurses on the ward. "I swear there wasn't a dry eye in the house," wrote Colonel Codman, who witnessed the impromptu drama.

Patton was so overcome by the experience that he went straight to the chapel of the palace to pray before he returned to his quarters, where his boss, General Alexander, was waiting to have lunch with him.

When the situation did not show any improvement on August 3rd, Patton could no longer bear the suspense at his palazzo at Palermo. He left the city and established his advance headquarters just behind Cerami, where General Allen had his 1st Division Command Post in an abandoned schoolhouse.

He spent his first day at the front encouraging and exhorting the men—doing the job he reserved for himself and which he thought he was best qualified to perform. This was what he meant when he wrote in his diary on the eve of the landing in Morocco, "I feel that my claim to greatness hangs on an ability to lead and inspire." Now, in the pressure-cooker of Sicily, he put it more plainly. "I am the best damn butt-kicker in the whole United States Army," he told General Bradley, who, under the circumstances, was not so enthusiastic about this aspect of Patton's technique of command.

"In that unhappy part of his career," Bradley later wrote, "George's theatrics brought him much contempt, and his impetuousness outraged his commanders . . . In Sicily, Patton, the man, bore little resemblance to Patton, the legend."

In front of Troina, as he mingled with General Allen's men, even his most inspired butt-kicking did not seem to work. He was appalled by what he found in the 1st Division. Having borne the brunt of two campaigns, the division had become temperamental, and even insubordinate. Discipline was lax, rules were disregarded, superiors were disobeyed. And Allen, "too much of an individualist to submerge himself without friction in the group undertakings of war," appeared to be either unable or disinclined to do anything about it. Discouraged by the hard going and left to brood about their fate in Allen's *laisser-aller* regime, his men developed too much pride in their past achievements and too much self-pity in their present plight.

Casualties had left gaping holes in the line, and Patton saw a tangible connection between them and his difficulties. Moreover, he was told that an increasing number of the men had gone to the hospital with nothing but combat fatigue, a form of neurosis for which he had neither understanding nor sympathy. The departure of these men from the tough battle for Troina was felt seriously by the hard-pressed regiments, which were becoming substantially reduced anyway by *bona fide* casualties. Since no replacements could be obtained, every man was indispensable.

It was with the fresh memories of his visit to the 1st Division boiling in him, on this August 3rd, that Patton spied signs on the road to Mistretta showing directions to the 15th Evacuation Hospital. He told Sergeant George Mims, his driver, "Take me to that Evac," not so much to seek solace this time but to see for himself how crowded it was with those combat-neurosis cases.

The 15th Evac, a typical forward hospital under canvas, was attached to the 51st Medical Battalion of II Corps during the campaign in Tunisia, and followed the corps in the Sicilian campaign. Its medical staff, headed by Lieutenant

Colonel Frank Y. Leaver, a Californian, respected Patton's obviously sincere concern for the wounded, and appreciated his profound interest in the medical facilities of his Army. But they viewed him with somewhat jaundiced eyes, nevertheless, because of lingering memories of his strict disciplinarian regime in Tunisia.

No sooner had Patton taken over II Corps from General Fredendall than an order of his appeared on the bulletin board of the hospital threatening fines up to $25 for not wearing a steel helmet at all times, or going without leggings. "Since it was impossible for a doctor to get a stethoscope in his ears while wearing a helmet," wrote Major Max S. Allen with tongue in cheek, "and still worse to attempt to operate while wearing a helmet, the order had to be ignored inside the tents, but everyone wore his helmet on going from one tent to another."

Though Patton's visit was unexpected, the 15th Evac was up to Patton's strictest standards when Mims drove him through its improvised gate to the tent where Colonel Leaver had his office. The Colonel escorted the General to the receiving tent, where they were greeted by Lieutenant Colonel Charles N. Wasden, the Receiving Officer.

The grand round inside the tent cheered Patton, because the men appeared to be legitimate casualties so far as he could judge from the abundance of bandages evident. He talked effusively with the patients, and was particularly pleased to meet the first sergeant of the 39th Infantry Regiment because its commander, Colonel Harry Albert "Paddy" Flint, was one of his best friends. Flint was an eccentric soldier in Patton's own mold. With helmet, a black silk scarf, and rifle in hand, he led his men on Troina stripped to the waist "so that he might be more easily identified." Patton spent some time at the bedside of the sergeant, talking about "Paddy," and telling the noncom how proud he ought to be to serve under such a valiant leader.

He was about to leave the tent when his eyes fell on a boy in his mid-twenties who was squatting on a box near the dressing station with no bandage on him to indicate that he had been wounded. He was Private Charles Herman Kuhl, ASN 35536908, of Mishawaka, Indiana, a bright-faced, good-looking young soldier eyeing the General with what Patton thought was a truculent look.

"I just get sick inside myself," Patton later told his friend, Henry J. Taylor, a millionaire businessman who doubled as a war correspondent in Sicily, "when I see a fellow torn apart, and some of the wounded were in terrible, ghastly shape. Then I came to this man and asked him what was the matter.

"The soldier replied: 'I guess I can't take it.'

"Looking at the others in the tent, so many of them badly beaten up, I simply flew off the handle."

What happened next was described the day after by Kuhl himself in a letter to his father. "General Patton slapped my face yesterday," he wrote, "and kicked me in the pants and cussed me. This probably won't get through, but I don't know. Just forget about it in your letter."

The letter passed the censor, but the Kuhls in Mishawaka —his parents and his wife Loretta—did exactly as Charley advised—they "forgot" about "it," probably because they were inclined to give the General the benefit of the doubt.

A carpet layer in civilian life, Kuhl had been in the Army eight months, with the 1st Division about 30 days, serving in L Company of the 26th Infantry Regiment. He had been admitted to the aid station of the 3rd Battalion at 2:10 P.M. on August 2nd, with a diagnosis of "exhaustion" made by Lieutenant H. L. Sanger of the Medical Corps. He was then evacuated to the 1st Medical Battalion, well to the rear, where a note was made on his emergency medical tag that he "had been admitted to this place three times during the Sicilian campaign."

Kuhl then was sent on to the clearing company by Captain J. D. Broom, was put in "quarters" there and given sodium amytal on a prescription signed by Captain Ralph S. Nedell.

On August 3rd he was examined by Captain T. P. Covington, who wrote on Kuhl's medical tag: "Psychoneurosis anxiety state, moderately severe. Soldier has been twice before in hospital within 20 days. He can't take it at front evidently. He is repeatedly returned."

It was by this route that Charley Kuhl eventually arrived in the receiving tent of the 15th Evac, where, through this perverse twist of war, it became his misfortune to bump into General Patton. Now he was in real trouble.

As Taylor reconstructed the incident on the basis of his first-hand information, "Patton squared off in front of the soldier. He called the man every kind of a loathsome coward and then slapped him across the face with his gloves. The soldier fell back. Patton grabbed him by the scruff of the neck and kicked him out of the tent."

When Patton was through, he turned to Colonel Wasden.

"Don't admit this sonuvabitch," he yelled. "I don't want yellow-bellied bastards like him hiding their lousy coward-ice around here, stinking up this place of honor." Then turning to Colonel Leaver and still shouting at the top of his high-pitched voice, he ordered:

"Check up on this man, Colonel. And I don't give a damn whether he can take it or not! You send him back to his unit at once—you hear me, you gutless bastard," he was now shrieking at Kuhl again, "you're going back to the front, *at once!*"

Kuhl was picked up by a group of corpsmen attracted to the scene by the noise. They took him to a ward, where he was found to have a temperature of 102.2°. It also devel-oped that he had been suffering from chronic diarrhea ever since he joined the 1st Division at the front. A blood test then showed that he had malaria.

Neither the medical staff, nor Kuhl nor his folks at Mishawaka followed up the incident, and that seemed to close the case. Patton himself dismissed it from his mind.

There was still nothing on the front to lift Patton from his depression.

On August 4th, 72 fighters of General House, each loaded with 500-pound bombs, plastered Troina, leaving it wreathed in gray dust. Next day, General Allen's units stormed a number of high positions overlooking the city, established themselves in several of them, and made things so hot for the Germans that they decided to do something about it. When day broke on August 6th, scouts of the 1st Division found the city deserted. The Krauts had sneaked out under the cover of darkness.

But when Allen pushed east from Troina, he could advance only about a mile when he was halted again by the determined *Landser* firmly established in their new posi-tions. And the 3rd Division was making little or no headway with its attack on San Fratello Ridge.

Patton continued to tour the front, looking for "tricks" to speed the advance. "We are trying to win the horse race to the last big town," he wrote to his wife, meaning Messina. "I hope we do . . . "

On August 6th he moved his camp to a new command post up the coast, in an olive grove "where Hannibal may have wandered if he ever came this way." Now he was very close to the front, within range of enemy artillery. No sooner had he settled down at the CP than the Germans began to shell it—gropingly at first, getting only "overs," then coming in with "shorts." When the shells exploded on the ridge their fragments passed directly over the CP. Patton was disgusted, but not because he was under fire. He had timed his pulse with his watch and found to his dismay that it had gone up.

Patton's chief reason for moving to the coast was to get as close as he could to an operation he had thought up to speed Truscott's advance along the seashore. They organized Lieutenant Colonel Lyle W. Bernard's 2nd Battalion of the 30th Infantry Regiment into a small amphibious force to make a landing on the coast about two miles east of Sant' Agata. The battalion—reinforced with two batteries of the 58th Field Artillery, a platoon of tanks and a platoon of engineers—jumped off the night of Aug. 7-8th and caught the Germans asleep in the orchard. By 4 A.M. the 2nd Battalion was firmly established 12 miles nearer to Messina. Most of the Germans fell back to reform their line, but Bernard picked up 1,600 prisoners nevertheless, and threw a monkey wrench into the enemy's leisurely withdrawal.

Patton was overjoyed with the success of the operation. He called Bradley to his olive grove to arrange for another amphibious envelopment, this one at Brolo to outflank the next coastal roadblock the Germans had put up at the Zapulla River. Patton was in a hurry. He scheduled the landing for August 11th, by which time he expected Truscott to be close enough to link up with the battalion at Brolo, 12 miles behind the Germans.

Bradley checked with General Truscott, but Truscott objected vigorously. He was encountering difficulties with his advance. The 7th Infantry Regiment had run into increasing German resistance. It was under heavy artillery fire, some of it coming from the long-range guns the Germans had on Capo d'Orlando. Enemy observation posts were spread too wide to enable Truscott to screen with smoke, and he was running low on smoke shells anyway. His 15th Infantry needed a mule train through these "forbidding hills and dales" to gain the ridge south of Naso.

Patton himself was astounded by the terrain. On August 7th, for example, he went to an observation post about 300 yards from a place his men had under attack. He could see the 60-mm. mortars and hear the machine guns and rifles— but it took seven hours for the troops to march from where he stood to the battle he was watching. "It is the God-damnedest country I have ever seen," he complained. "Compared with this, Indio looks like foothills."

Yet he refused to listen to Truscott's objections and insisted that the landing be staged on August 11th as he had originally scheduled it. Now Bradley interfered and asked Patton to give Truscott another day. "The amphibious attack means nothing," he argued, "unless we tie in with Truscott's forces by land." Patton remained adamant. When Bradley left the olive grove he had in his pocket Patton's final directive.

On August 8th things looked up a bit in both areas on which Patton's eager attention was riveted. Truscott took Sant' Agata. The 47th Infantry of the 9th Division reached Cesaro on the road to Randazzo. The 60th Infantry captured Monte Camolato, six miles northwest of Cesaro. But in the east, Monty was not doing too well. The Germans were delaying his advance on Messina by the direct route through Randazzo. He had to waste time on regrouping his forces for what he called "a greater effort" along the east coast.

August 9th was sheer hell again. Patton spent the entire day fretting and fussing in his olive grove, writing letters, trying hard to keep from bursting at the seams.

On August 10th, Truscott's 3rd Division moved closer to Brolo, where it was to rendezvous with Colonel Bernard's seaborne force. But the advance was not fast enough, and Bradley called Patton again, pleading with him to postpone the landing a day. Patton remained hard.

"No," he shouted. "And I don't want any more arguments."

"I was more exasperated than I have ever been," Bradley wrote.

And so was Patton.

Bradley's call left him fuming. He was not immune from once in a while suspecting his commanders of sabotaging his decisions which they disliked, and now he feared that Bradley and Truscott might pull something to delay the landing after all. He dropped everything, sent for Mims and drove to II Corps command post for a showdown with Bradley.

Patton was highly agitated on the drive and eager to get to Bradley as quickly as possible. But when he saw signs of the 93rd Evacuation Hospital in the valley near Sant' Agata di Militello, he ordered Sergeant Mims to take him there. He walked unannounced to the admission tent, where Colonel Donald E. Currier, commanding officer of the hospital, hastily advised of the General's arrival, caught up with him. Patton greeted Currier amicably. The surgeon was from Boston and was a friend of his family. The visit thus started out auspiciously.

Waiting at the entrance to the admission tent was Major Charles Barton Etter, the Receiving Officer. Then the familiar grand round began. Accompanied by Currier and Etter, General Patton moved down the aisle, going from litter to litter. He had the usual small talk with the soldiers and congratulated them on the performance of their divisions. But those who had seen him on previous such inspection trips now noticed that he was quite tense and was not acting with his customary jocular ease and friendliness. He turned almost grim when he stopped at the litter of a soldier without splints or dressing, the obvious indication of the malingerer in his eyes.

"What brought you here, boy?" he asked.

"I'm running a fever, sir," the soldier answered, and the doctor chimed in: "Yes, sir, a little over 102 degrees."

Patton raised his eyebrow, obviously not convinced that the man's temperature was high enough to justify hospitalization. He seemed to be getting ready to say it when he noticed a young soldier squatting near the exit holding a cigarette in trembling fingers.

"And what's the matter with you?" Patton snapped at the boy, his unspent irritation over the fever case turning into anger.

What followed was described most graphically by Major Etter in the report he prepared for "Surgeon, II Corps, A.P.O. 302, U.S. Army (Att'n: Colonel Richard T. Arnest)." It read in full:

1. On Monday afternoon August 10, 1943, at approximately 1330, General Patton entered the Receiving Ward

of the 93rd Evacuation Hospital and started interviewing and visiting the patients who were there. There were some 10 or 15 casualties in the tent at the time. The first five or six that he talked to were battle casualties. He asked each what his trouble was, commended them for their excellent fighting; told them they were doing a good job, and wished them a speedy recovery.

He came to one patient who, upon inquiry, stated that he was sick with high fever. The general dismissed him without comment. The next patient was sitting huddled up and shivering. When asked what his trouble was, the man replied, "It's my nerves," and began to sob. The General then screamed at him, "What did you say?" He replied, "It's my nerves. I can't stand the shelling any more." He was still sobbing.

The General then yelled at him. "Your nerves Hell, you are just a Goddamn coward, you yellow son of a bitch." He then slapped the man and said, "Shut up that Goddamned crying. I won't have these brave men here who have been shot seeing a yellow bastard sitting here crying." He then struck at the man again, knocking his helmet liner off and into the next tent. He then turned to the Receiving Officer and yelled, "Don't you admit this yellow bastard, there's nothing the matter with him. I won't have the hospitals cluttered up with these sons of bitches who haven't the guts to fight."

He turned to the man again, who was managing to "sit at attention" though shaking all over, and said, "You're going back to the front lines and you may get shot and killed, but you're going to fight. If you don't, I'll stand you up against a wall and have a firing squad kill you on purpose. In fact," he said, reaching for his pistol, "I ought to shoot you myself, you Goddamned whimpering coward." As he went out of the ward he was still yelling back at the Receiving Officer to send that yellow son of a bitch to the front lines.

2. All this was in such a loud voice that nurses and patients in adjoining wards had come outside to see what the disturbance was.

Elaborating on his original report, dated August 10, 1943, Dr. Etter later wrote to me:

"There have been many reports to the effect that I took the General's gun away from him, that I ordered him from the tent, that the General was merely waving his hands and accidentally struck the soldier. I have not seen the report [referred to by General Eisenhower] about Colonel Currier and me having to restrain the nurses. This report and the ones concerning my participation were erroneous.

"The only thing that I did, which does not show in the report, was [to] disobey the General's orders about returning the patient to the front lines. I merely hid him out in an ambulance until General Patton left the hospital and then admitted him.

"The nurses, First Lieutenants Dale Cronerweth and Lillian Held, attracted by the loud conversations and profanity, came into the tent as General Patton was leaving. They were included in the General's 'so-called apology' [see Page 337] to the personnel involved, but they were actually only bystanders."

Colonel Currier was beside himself. He rushed back to his office and put a call to Colonel Arnest, Surgeon of II Corps.

"Dick," he told Arnest, "this is Currier, 93rd Evac. You better come over here as fast as you can make it."

Patton's day of fury was not over yet.

He had made up his mind to fire General Allen, and this now seemed to be a good day to let the ax fall. He never particularly liked Allen, but he respected his courage and skill, and—after having seen the brilliant work that gallant and ingenious soldier did with the 1st Division in the Tunisian campaign—had persuaded Eisenhower to give him Allen for Sicily. Although Allen repaid the confidence with victories from Gela to Troina, he also kept irritating Patton with his individualism, leisurely methods of command, and propensity for talking back.

There was still another trouble simmering at the top of the 1st Division. Its assistant commander, General Roosevelt, was another highly individualistic soldier whose informal ways and deft human touch made him the idol of the men. A rivalry developed between Allen and Roosevelt, and it aggravated the disorder that was, Patton feared, becoming rampant in the division. He could not very well fire Allen and let Roosevelt stay. As General Bradley put it, "Roosevelt had to go with Allen, for he, too, had sinned by loving the division too much."

Bradley agreed wholeheartedly with Patton's misgivings about the two generals, and was actually relieved when Patton now authorized him to fire them. He did it in the morning of this fateful August 10th, at his command post in Nicosia, while Patton was "busy" at the 93rd Evac.

The day was to produce still another "slapping incident" before it was out, only this one involved no physical violence.

For the time being, Patton seemed to have regained his self-control, so that when he reached Bradley's command post he was almost jovial. He showed no realization of any wrong-doing when he casually mentioned the incident to Bradley. "Sorry to be late, Bradley," he said, "I stopped at a hospital on the way up. There were a couple of malingerers there. I slapped one of them to make him mad and put some fight back in him." It seemed that his hospital outburst had been a sort of catharsis for him. His nerves were calmed by his letting off steam.

Patton discussed the landing with Bradley and told him again in words that tolerated no contradiction that it had to be mounted on schedule. Bradley gave in. "As a subordinate commander of Patton's," he later said, "I had no alternative but to comply with his orders."

Patton then returned to his advance headquarters and had just finished his supper when, at 7:45 P.M., he was called to the telephone. General Keyes, the Deputy Army Commander, was on the wire.

"General," Keyes said. "I am with Lucian Truscott. He wants you to call off the landing at Brolo tomorrow morning."

"Why?" Patton snapped.

"The 3rd Division hasn't gotten on far enough," Keyes said, "to support it."

"The landing will go on," Patton said firmly.

There was a momentary silence at the other end of the wire, then Keyes said, "Hold on, General, Truscott wants to speak to you."

Truscott came on and, in Patton's description of the conversation, "strongly protested against going on with the landing."

"It will go on," Patton said again, and Truscott answered:

"All right, if you want it." Then they hung up.

The call threw Patton back into his rage. He alerted General Gay, sent for his car, picked up Major General John P. Lucas, one of Eisenhower's assistants who was visiting him at the olive grove, and drove as fast as Mims could to Caronia, where Colonel Bernard's battalion was assembled for the embarkation. He left Gay at the port with strict orders to see that the ships got off, then drove on to Truscott's command post in an olive-oil factory at Terranova, arriving at 8:45 P.M.

Patton made his presence duly felt by driving up to the CP with his foghorn blowing and raising hell with the MP's at the entrance. The first person he met inside was Captain Ransom K. Davis of the Navy, Chief of Staff of Rear Admiral Lyal A. Davidson, the senior naval officer in north Sicilian waters. David promptly seized the opportunity to add his plea to the others.

"We started an hour late, General," he argued, "and won't be able to reach the beach before 0400."

"I don't give a damn even if you won't reach it until 0600," Patton yelled. "The landing will still go on."

He found Truscott in his office walking up and down like a caged lion, with a map under his arm.

"General Truscott," he pounced on him, "if your conscience will not let you conduct this operation, I will relieve you and let someone else do it." He had General Lucas in tow, not for this specific purpose by any means, but his presence served to give emphasis to Patton's threat.

"General," Truscott said, "it's your privilege to relieve me whenever you want to."

Patton mellowed somewhat. Truscott was one of his oldest and best friends. A cavalryman like himself, he used to ride and play polo with him. He admired the dashing and handsome officer as "one of the best Goddamn trainers of ponies that ever lived."

"What's the matter with you, Lucian?" he asked softly. "Are you afraid to fight?"

But he only made Truscott angry.

"General," he shot back, "you know that's ridiculous and insulting. If you don't think I can carry out orders, you can give the division to anyone you please. But I will tell you one thing. You'll not find anyone who can carry out orders which they do not approve as well as I can."

Patton's anger was rapidly evaporating.

"Damnit, Lucian, I know that. I don't want to relieve you. I recommended you for your DSM and your major generalcy, both of which you won by your own ability. You are too old an athlete to believe that it is possible to postpone a match. This must go through. The ships have already started."

"You are an old enough athlete yourself to know that matches are sometimes postponed," Truscott replied.

"This will not be postponed," Patton said.

Truscott argued that this was a war of defiles and there was a bottleneck that was delaying him in getting his guns up to support the infantry. As a result, the infantry would be too far west to support the landing.

"If there is a bottleneck," Patton answered, "it is your place to be there and not at your division headquarters. I wish you would remember what Frederick the Great said."

"What did he say?" Truscott asked with just a touch of irony in his voice.

Patton struck a martial pose that was quite comic under the circumstances, and said:

" 'L'audace, l'audace, toujours l'audace,' that's what he said, you son-of-a-gun." His face broke into a grin. "Come on, Lucian," he added, "let's have a drink—of your liquor."

This second seaborne venture went off on schedule, with 650 men making for the beach at Brolo, which was not too good. The exits inland were difficult, running through an olive grove and up a steep bank to the coastal highway. The objective was Monte Cipolla, a spur not too far behind the German lines at Capo d'Orlando.

When Bernard and his men hit the beach, Truscott's infantry was still more than 10 miles away.

The log of signals from Bernard's SCR-193 transmitter shows how touch and go the operation was for awhile.

The men hit the beach at 4 A.M., as Captain Davis had predicted, and at 7 A.M. Bernard reported: "Blue all in."

At 9:30 A.M.—"Where's Doc and Harry?"

"Doc" was Colonel Johnson of the 15th Infantry; "Harry" was Colonel Sherman of the 7th Infantry, the two regiments on the way to relieve Bernard, but still awfully far away.

At 1:40 P.M.—"Enemy counterattacking fiercely. Do something!"

At 6:30 P.M., after a long oppressive silence, Bernard's radio was back on the air. It opened up by saying, "Give

Navy priority and let them . . ." then went off abruptly.

It remained silent until 10 P.M. When it returned to the air, the signal was:

"Doc and Harry are here . . . thank God!"

The operation was tough and costly. The Bernard force lost 167 men out of its original contingent of 650. But was it worth it? Or was Patton too impetuous in ordering it and too stubborn in sticking to it?

Patton himself claimed it was one of those things he did in the Army which made him earn his pay. After a few drinks at Truscott's command post, he headed for home because he thought that "if [he] stayed around [he] would fail to show confidence."

He spent a restless night, worrying about the operation, and also because his CP was under heavy shellfire. But shortly after reveille, Colonel Harkins, his Assistant Chief of Staff who was the duty officer, phoned him "to say," as Patton put it, "that the attack had been a *complete success.*"

However, Bradley continued to be skeptical, and questioned the sense and value of the operation. Even 8 years later he deprecated the maneuver as "this misadventure" that cost heavy casualties and gained nothing in return. However, the historians gave Patton the decision. The official history of the Department of the Army praised the operation as a "highly successful landing on the coast" with which Patton had succeeded in outflanking the enemy in the Capo d'Orlando region. By establishing positions astride the main highway, the 3rd Division was put on the road in the literal sense of the word, and the Germans were dislodged from yet another—and probably their last—defensive position they desperately needed to prevent the fall of Messina.

Patton's British friends were far more impressed with his two amphibious *coups* than most of his American colleagues. Winston Churchill spoke of them admiringly in his account of the Anzio operation. "I had of course always been a partisan of the 'end run,' as the Americans call it," he wrote, "or 'cat-claw,' which was my term. I had never succeeded in getting this maneuver open to sea power included in any of our desert advances. In Sicily, however, General Patton had twice used the command of the sea flank as he advanced along the northern coast of the island with great effect."

The highest praise came from the best qualified source —Admiral Cunningham. It was given but indirectly, to be sure, not by lauding Patton in so many words but by criticizing Montgomery and Alexander, Cunningham going as far as a British sailor could under the circumstances.

"No use was made by the Eighth Army of amphibious opportunities," he wrote in his dispatch in the London *Gazette* on April 25, 1950, adding: "There were doubtless sound military reasons for making no use of this, what to me appeared, priceless asset of sea power and flexibility of maneuver; but it is worth consideration for future occasions whether much time and costly fighting could not be saved by even minor flank attacks, which must necessarily be unsettling to the enemy. It must be always for the general to decide. The Navy can only provide the means and advise on the practicability from the naval angle of the projected operation."

But, then, Churchill and Cunningham always thought that Patton had surpassed himself in his conquest of the island while Bradley on his part never ceased to "question George's conduct of the Sicilian campaign."

Patton was far too busy with this last phase of the Sicilian campaign—and far too preoccupied with his obsession to reach Messina before Montgomery—to remember the two slapping incidents. In the rush of events, there was nobody yet to remind him of them.

The 93rd Evac was, of course, in an uproar and abuzz with mushrooming versions of the incident there. But so tightly is a corps commander compartmentalized in a theater of operations, that General Bradley received word only on August 12th, two days after it happened, and then only of the incident at the 93rd Evac near Sant' Agata.

He was working in his trailer when his Chief of Staff, Major General William Benjamin Kean Jr., brought in Colonel Arnest, his Corps Surgeon. Arnest had been to the 93rd Evac, reviewing the case with Colonel Currier and Major Etter, and talked to a number of eyewitnesses.

Bradley read the report but it did not appear to upset him. He was revolted at Patton's action, but there was little more his Army Commander could do in Sicily to rile him further. He was infuriated by Patton's boisterous tactical schemes and snap decisions, and especially by what he regarded as Patton's incomplete knowledge of an army's needs in war.

A man of humble origin, unostentatious conduct and simple habits, Bradley was irritated and shocked by Patton's manner of command. "Canny a showman though George was," he wrote, "he failed to grasp the psychology of the combat soldier." According to him, Patton provoked his men by flaunting the pageantry of his command. "He traveled in an entourage of command cars followed by a string of nattily uniformed staff officers," Bradley wrote. "His own vehicle was gaily decked with oversize stars and the insignia of his command. These exhibitions did not awe the troops as perhaps Patton believed. Instead, they offended them as they trudged through the clouds of dust left in the wake of that procession."

Having come to loathe Patton's mannerisms, Bradley was conditioned to expect the most uncouth and violent things from his overbearing and vulgar superior. So he was not surprised by this brutal assault of an enlisted man.

Holding the report, he turned to Colonel Arnest:

"Has anyone else seen this?" he asked.

"No, sir," Arnest said.

Bradley handed the report to Kean. "Seal it in an envelope, Bill," he instructed, "and mark it to be opened only by you or by me. Then lock it up in my safe."

The report had taken two days through channels to reach Bradley, and now it seemed it would be pigeonholed. Probably it would have been Bradley's duty to send it on to General Alexander, the Army Group Commander, or directly to Eisenhower, skipping the next link in the chain, his immediate superior who, of course, was Patton himself. But Bradley didn't think so. He was serving under Patton, he was loyal to Patton, and he decided not to squeal on Patton.

A report did reach General Alexander, but he, too, washed his hands of the untidy affair. Though he was Patton's superior and, therefore, duty-bound to investigate the case, take Patton to task for it and, if he decided that the slapping of an infirm soldier of his Army Group in a hospital tent was a vicious infraction of the rules, punish him for it. But Alexander felt keenly the delicacy of his own position as a Briton and refused to inject himself into what he regarded as an American matter. "George," he told Patton when the case intruded upon one of their meetings, "this is a family affair." And he left it to another American, General Eisenhower, to handle it.

Then the incident was overshadowed by the much brighter event of the capture of Messina. General Truscott made it official at 8:25 A.M. on August 17th, when he reached the center of the city and took formal possession at the Town Hall. A few minutes later a breathless British lieutenant colonel rolled up in a dust-covered tank. He was a herald from the British Eighth Army coming posthaste to stake Montgomery's claim.

General Patton entered the city in triumph at 10:30 A.M. He had on his chest his second Distinguished Service Cross, which he had received from General Eisenhower the day before—proof positive, if he needed any, that the slappings had not redounded to his disadvantage.

Dazzling in his smart gabardines, he rolled up in a command car bearing three silver stars and went straight to the token British force, six Shermans of the 4th Armored Brigade, commanded by a tall, lean brigadier named Currie. Patton shook his hands warmly and Currie told him in a cavalier fashion, "I congratulate you, sir. It was a jolly good race."

Patton was elated, of course, but that night he wrote wearily in his diary:

"Well, I feel let down. The reaction from intense mental and physical activity to a status of inertia is very difficult . . . I feel that the Lord has been most generous. If I had to fight the campaign over I would make no change in anything I did. Few generals in history have ever been able to say as much."

The diary entry in the moment of his first historic victory in World War II was a typically Pattonesque elaboration of Wellington's remark in 1815 that nothing except a battle lost can be half so melancholy as a battle won.

CHAPTER SEVENTEEN
CONQUEROR IN THE DOGHOUSE

Had General Patton been able to control his nervous temper after the first incident in the admission tent of the 15th Evacuation Hospital, his slapping of an apparently sick soldier would probably never have become public knowledge. The slapping created no hysterics in the tent. It was discussed only in passing at the hospital and the story never got beyond it. It was not reported to higher echelons by the medical staff.

Private Kuhl, a somewhat mercurial fellow with a stoic bent of mind, mentioned the incident in a letter to his family but advised them to "forget it." His parents and wife kept mum or, as the older Kuhl put it, "I am willing to let the case rest as is and drop the whole thing, and get on with the war. I have no personal feelings against General Patton. If he is a good man, let's keep him. We need good men!"

It was different with the second incident at the other hospital. The boy Patton slapped was no Sunday soldier. Pvt. Paul G. Bennett, ASN 70000001, a simple 21-year-old farm boy from South Carolina, had enlisted in the regular Army before Pearl Harbor, and served with impersonal distinction with the 105th Field Artillery Battalion in North Africa and Sicily. When his wife gave birth to their first baby he became restless, and when she sent him a picture of herself with the infant he began to show symptoms of acute nervous tension. A front-line psychiatrist diagnosed his condition as a case of anxiety neurosis—"a passing disturbance of his mind regarding some uncertain event"—probably caused by "fear that he would not be able to see his newborn baby before he died."

Bennett's condition became aggravated on August 6th when his best buddy in C Battery was wounded in action at his side. He could not sleep that night because, as he put it, the shells going over had "bothered" him. "I keep thinking they're going to land on me," he kept saying. On August 7th he became increasingly tense and showed morbid concern for his wounded friend. An aid man then sent him to the rear echelon, where he was given some sedative. But it did not seem to do him any good. He remained badly disturbed.

On the morning of this fateful August 10th, a medical officer ordered him to the 93rd Evac, even though "Bennett begged not to be evacuated because he did not want to leave his unit." It was a tragic coincidence, then, that General Patton happened to pay an impromptu visit to the hospital, virtually minutes after Bennett's own arrival in the admission tent.

At the height of the brief but violent encounter, Patton

appeared to have been shaken by his own conduct. He began to sob, wheeled around, and told Colonel Currier, "I can't help it. It makes me break down to see brave boys and to think of a yellow bastard being babied."

But whatever he himself thought of the incident, he did not think it necessary to make a report of it either to General Alexander, his immediate superior, or General Eisenhower, the Commander in Chief.

"I felt ashamed of myself," he later told Henry J. Taylor, "and I hoped the whole thing would die out."

But the incident could not be filed and forgotten with his departure. It had attracted far too much attention. It thoroughly shocked the doctors and the nurses, and became the topic of all conversations in the Seventh Army.

Then a detailed report of the incident reached General Eisenhower's headquarters in Algiers. It was Colonel Arnest's memorandum, forwarded by Colonel Franklin, the Seventh Army's Surgeon.

When Arnest realized that General Bradley would not forward his report, he opened another channel and sent it to Brigadier General Frederick Arthur Blessé, Eisenhower's Surgeon General. Blessé took the report to Brigadier General Thomas Jefferson Davis, the Adjutant General, who escorted Blessé to Eisenhower with Arnest's report.

It was 10:30 A.M. on August 17th, the very moment when General Patton was entering Messina as a conquering hero. At first blush, Eisenhower was not unduly alarmed. He told Blessé, "I guess I'll have to give General Patton a jacking up." He kept the Surgeon General in his office for some small talk. Ike praised Patton for the "swell job" he had done in Sicily but disputed his contention that there were any laggards in the Seventh Army or in any part of the United States Army, for that matter. General Blessé was inclined to agree with the Supreme Commander. His medics reported, he told Eisenhower, that, on the contrary, many American soldiers had marched over rough terrain until they had literally worn the skin off their feet. When the meeting broke up, Ike instructed Blessé to go to Sicily, investigate the incident on the spot, then report his findings directly to him.

Thus he started the ball rolling—to clear up the case in all its details, punish Patton if need be, but keep the matter strictly in the family. He clamped a tight lid on the incident because, as he said to General Blessé, "If this thing ever gets out, they'll be howling for Patton's scalp, and that will be the end of Georgie's service in this war. I simply cannot let that happen. Patton is *indispensable* to the war effort—one of the guarantors of our victory."

After Blessé left, Eisenhower called in Dr. Perrin Hamilton Long, a prominent and distinguished surgeon from Massachusetts, who was serving as his Theater Medical Consultant with the rank of lieutenant colonel. He instructed Colonel Long to make a separate investigation—"for my eyes only," as he put it—without fear or favor, brutally to the facts.

Then he sat down and wrote in his own hand a personal letter to Patton. It was a blistering epistle into which Eisenhower expressed all his disgust with the incident. He characterized Patton's conduct as "despicable." And he ordered him—in a historic and unprecedented move—to apologize to the soldier he had slapped, to all the doctors and nurses who were present in the tent at the time, to every patient in the tent who could be reached, and last, but not least, to the Seventh Army as a whole through individual units, one at a time. It was a savage punishment for so proud and cocky a general as Patton, and Eisenhower realized that he was running a serious risk. Patton might resign his commission rather than go through with it. But he took the risk, sealed his letter and gave it to General Blessé, who was leaving that afternoon, for delivery into Patton's hands.

Colonel Long's initial report left no doubt about the seriousness of the incident. After describing the event on the basis of Major Etter's report, he wrote:

"The deleterious effects of such incidents upon the well-being of patients, upon the professional morale of hospital staffs and upon the relationship of patient to physician are incalculable. It is imperative that immediate steps be taken to prevent a recurrence of such incidents."

General Eisenhower now sent for General Lucas, who was both his and George Patton's friend, and ordered him to Sicily to undertake yet another investigation, this one strictly from the soldiers' point of view.

He hoped that he would be able to close the case with that. But then the situation changed abruptly, and the incident began to cause the deepest concern to Eisenhower because he now feared that he would not be able to "keep it in the family" after all. The correspondents accredited to the Seventh Army had gotten hold of the story, and they took a very dim view of an American general's slapping a sick American boy in a hospital at the front. The Supreme Commander turned from his optimism and grimly told General Walter Bedell Smith, his friend and Chief of Staff, "I might have to send Georgie Patton home in disgrace after all."

It had taken less than 24 hours for the story to reach the press camp. It was broken by a young captain in Public Relations who happened to be in love with a nurse at the 93rd Evac. On the night of the incident he visited her while she was on duty in a tent adjoining the receiving tent where the helmet Patton had knocked off Private Bennett's head had landed. When told of the incident, the captain felt, as did everybody else at the hospital, that the incident should be reported. However, he realized that this could not be accomplished through "channels," as it seemed certain that his report would be pigeonholed at Bradley's headquarters. So he decided to tell some of the reporters whose stories he was censoring daily. The first three correspondents the anonymous captain reached in his righteous indignation were Al Newman, then with *Newsweek* magazine, Merrill "Red" Mueller of the National Broadcasting Company, and Demaree Bess of the *Saturday Evening Post*.

The day after the incident, Major Etter was interviewed, with Colonel Currier's permission, by Newman and Mueller and Bess; and again the next day by Newman and Mueller, who were now joined by John Charles Daly of the Columbia Broadcasting System. "The idea of the interviews, as we understood it," Etter recalled, "was that they could take the story directly to General Eisenhower for action without it having to go through 'channels.' "

Other reporters poured into the hospital in their wake. The press camp was ablaze with the story and its implications. They viewed Patton with jaundiced eyes anyway, violently opposed to his undemocratic methods and the childish bluster, as they saw it, in his character. They now recalled how he had ordered the mules of a poor Sicilian farmer shot because they obstructed his passage over a bridge. They remembered, too, that he had fined a soldier $25 for not wearing his leggings and never gave the boy a chance to explain that his legs were swollen with a mysterious ailment.

The correspondents discussed the case, then decided to take it up directly with General Eisenhower before break-

ing the story. Bess, Mueller and Quentin Reynolds of
Collier's left for Algiers. On August 19th they handed Smith
a complaint against Patton, with an accurate description of
the incident at the 93rd Evac. "If I am correctly informed,"
Bess wrote, "General Patton has subjected himself to general court-martial by striking an enlisted man under his
command." Bess told Smith that he and his colleagues, who
had looked into the case in Sicily, had refrained from filing
stories about it. He ventured the opinion that it would be
difficult, if not impossible, to keep such "a colorful scene,"
as he called the incident, out of the press for any length of
time.

Reynolds asserted that there were "at least 50,000
American soldiers [in Sicily] who would shoot Patton if they
had a chance." Daly mentioned as an extenuating circumstance that "probably Patton had gone temporarily crazy."
But he was most outspoken in his demand that Patton be
punished, even suggesting that he be removed from command because "he was obviously unfit to lead troops."

"All the press," Butcher noted in his diary on August
21st, "while not printing the story, are incensed."

Under this hammering, Eisenhower began to take a grim
view of the incident. He called Bess, Mueller, Reynolds
and Daly into his office and told them that he was trying to
do everything at his command to keep Patton in his job.

"His emotional tenseness and his impulsiveness are the
very qualities that make him, in open situations, such a
remarkable leader of an Army," he explained. "In pursuit
and exploitation there is need for a commander who sees
nothing but the necessity of getting ahead. The more he
drives his men the more he will save their lives. He must
be indifferent to fatigue and ruthless in demanding the last
atom of physical energy. Patton is such a commander. I
feel, therefore, that Patton should be saved for the great
battles facing us in Europe."

He pleaded with the correspondents to keep the story in
the family. A similar plea was made to the correspondents
accredited to Eisenhower's headquarters in Algiers by General Smith. The newspapermen and radio reporters—
impressed with Ike's sincerity, his handling of the case, and
his obvious need of Patton—agreed to "forget" the incident. They entered into a gentleman's agreement with the
Supreme Commander to refrain from breaking the story
either in their papers or on the radio.

By then Patton also realized that his impetuous conduct was having repercussions. Eisenhower's letters and General Blessé's arrival had brought home to him the seriousness of the situation—and yet he continued to have a split attitude toward what he had done. In one turn, he was sincerely penitent and castigated himself for his thoughtless conduct. In the next, he consoled himself that he had been right and had acted properly, even though "with little tact."

Thus on August 20th, he wrote in his diary: "After lunch General Blessé, Chief Surgeon AFHQ, brought me a very nasty letter from Ike with reference to two soldiers I cussed out for what I considered cowardice. Evidently I acted precipitantly and on insufficient knowledge. My motive was correct, because one cannot permit skulking to exist. It is just like any communicable disease. I admit freely that my method was wrong and I shall make what amends I can. I regret the incident as I hate to make Ike mad when it is my earnest desire to please him. General Lucas came at 1800 to further explain Ike's attitude. I feel very low."

No matter how peeved Patton was by Ike's "very nasty letter," he answered it on August 29th, offering his abject apologies in his most humble language.

"My dear General Eisenhower," he wrote formally on the official stationery of Headquarters Seventh Army:

"Replying to your letter of August 17, 1943, I want to commence by thanking you for this additional illustration of your fairness and generous consideration in making the communication personal.

"I am at a loss to find words with which to express my chagrin and grief at having given you, a man to whom I owe everything and for whom I would gladly lay down my life, cause for displeasure with me.

"I assure you that I had no intention of being either harsh or cruel in my treatment of the two soldiers in question. My sole purpose was to try and restore in them a just appreciation of their obligation as men and soldiers.

"In World War I, I had a dear friend and former schoolmate who lost his nerve in an exactly analogous manner, and who, after years of mental anguish, committed suicide.

"Both my friend and the medical men with whom I discussed his case assured me that had he been roundly checked at the time of his first misbehavior, he would have been restored to a normal state.

"Naturally, this memory actuated me when I inaptly tried to apply the remedies suggested. After each incident I stated to officers with me that I felt I had probably saved an immortal soul. . . ."

He closed the letter with "Very respectfully," and signed it, "G. S. Patton Jr., Lieut. General U. S. Army."

Even so, the case was drawing rapidly to its close and it seemed that it would be filed with the pathetic gesture Patton was compelled to make. In his letter, General Eisenhower explicitly directed him to apologize *en masse* to the soldier he had insulted and also to the medical staff who happened to be present. Orders were issued to the II Corps Surgeon to round up this audience and send them to the Royal Palace in Palermo for a ceremony to take place at 11 A.M. on August 22nd.

It was a Sunday. At 10 A.M., dressed magnificently for the occasion, and wearing his most formidable frown, Patton retired to the Cappella Palatina, the royal chapel of the palace, a magnificent edifice with incomparable mosaic decorations and frescoes built in A.D. 1132. Kneeling in the nave in front of the huge Byzantine marble candle holder, and caressed by the rays of the morning sun which stabbed through the eight windows of the dome, Patton prayed for almost an hour. Then he moved, ceremoniously into the magnificent Spanzadi Ruggero on the second floor, where his audience was waiting for him.

Of the various eyewitness accounts of the humiliating event, Major Etter's description is the most dramatic.

"The 'apology' went like this," Dr. Etter told me. "We were ordered to the General's office in the palace of the former King of Italy one Sunday morning. We were not informed why we were there, so we were quite startled when we were ushered before General Patton's desk in a very large room. His aide, then Brigadier General Gay, took us [groups from both hospitals] up before General Patton.

"We stood at attention while he told us that a good friend of his, in a fit of depression, had committed suicide during World War I. He felt that if someone had been 'rough with him' and 'slapped some sense into him,' his life might have been saved. He explained he considered his action for the soldiers' own good. He felt that we should understand his,

the General's, motives, that we must realize our responsibilities as officers, and watch over personnel who were in
trouble.

"With that as an explanation for his conduct, we were
advised to forget the incident and were dismissed."

Dr. Etter (now a prominent pediatrician in Memphis,
Tennessee) concluded this recollection of what he called
"an old and unpleasant subject," by saying, "This is the
whole story as best I can remember it. All of our personnel
admired General Patton and thought him a great General.
We felt that the incident was unfortunate, unnecessary
and, certainly, regrettable. My own hapless part in the
incident was that I happened to be in the right place, to be
sure, but at the wrong time."

The memories of the odious incident were receding. For
a few weeks following the ceremonial apologies, Patton
kept to his palatial residence in Palermo, resting on his
laurels behind the marvelous Norman gates of his palazzo
in a pose he thought was most appropriate for a conqueror
and discreet for a penitent.

Early in September, Patton received a visit from Norman
H. Davis, chairman of the American Red Cross. To give the
soldiers an opportunity to express their gratitude for the
services of the Red Cross, Patton assembled a large contingent of them at a theater. He escorted Mr. Davis to the
stage. This was his first public appearance since the scandal
and, of course, he was somewhat self-conscious, what with
the comments he was told were circulating about him
among the GI's.

When Davis finished his speech, he introduced Patton.
The General stepped to the front of the platform, pulled
himself up to his full height, then said with a grim face, "I
thought I'd stand up here and let you fellows see if I am
as big a son-of-a-bitch as you think I am."

The GI's went wild. They practically raised the roof of
the theater with their cheers.

Then something else occurred which suggested to General Patton that the case had been filed and forgotten. He
received word from Algiers that he was soon slated to get
his new command. The Allies had landed on the Italian
mainland at Salerno. But on September 14th a signal from
Admiral Hewitt, who commanded the Navy in the landings,
informed Eisenhower that General Clark, commander of
the Fifth Army on the Salerno beachhead, was in trouble.

Ike moved heaven and earth to aid his friend, with whom he grew into his present high command and who had rendered invaluable service to him in North Africa. But it was becoming obvious that Clark was not quite able to cope with the situation. It was doubtful whether he could hold the beachhead pending the arrival of Montgomery's Eighth Army, coming up from the toe of the Italian boot.

General Alexander suggested to Eisenhower that Patton be given command of the Fifth Army. It now seemed definite that he would be given this command, certainly before the Fifth Army began its march on Rome, scheduled for later in the year, probably around November.

And back in Washington—on October 1st, barely seven weeks after the slapping incident—Patton was nominated for the *permanent* rank of major general. Though he had been made a *temporary* lieutenant general the previous March, the promotion was long overdue, for he was still only a Colonel of Cavalry on the regular Army's permanent list.

Then, on November 21, 1943, the scandal burst into the open despite Eisenhower's best efforts to keep it quiet. Drew Pearson—who was not bound by the gentleman's agreement—"exposed" one of the incidents on his regular Sunday radio program on the American Broadcasting Company network. It was not a scoop by any means, for the story was fully known to hundreds of newspapermen who had agreed to withhold it in the national interest; and Pearson could give only a garbled, third-hand account, adding his own interpretation in his ponderous, sonorous and ominous delivery. But his airing of the stale story hit the nation with the force of a blockbuster, especially because of Eisenhower's apparent attempt to hush up the incident.

Congressmen immediately began to receive the usual mail, written mostly by irate correspondents like Mrs. Nattie Hodge of Pacolet Mills, South Carolina, for example. "I request," she wrote, "that an investigation be made in the conduct of General George S. Patton in his actions toward the shell-shocked soldier of the Seventh Army."

Mr. B. B. Waters of Greer, South Carolina, wrote: "Patton . . . should be thrown out of the Army. An officer that can't control himself any better than that is not fit to command a company, much less an Army."

One of the largest American Legion posts in Iowa wired Representative Charles B. Hoeven: "Respectfully request that you demand a full investigation of the General Patton incident with A.E.F. These are American soldiers and not Germans. If our boys are to be mistreated, let's import Hitler and do it up right." Congressman Hoeven added words of his own indignation: "Perhaps we have too much 'blood and guts' now."

Another Congressman, Joseph R. Bryson, in whose South Carolina district Bennett, the slapped soldier lived, invoked the Bible against the General: "He that is slow to anger is better than the mighty; and he that ruleth his spirit, then he then taketh a city." Other legislators chimed in, one of them demanding that Patton be moved from command of the Seventh Army to that of the Japanese Evacuation Centers on the West Coast. He could apparently think of no lower assignment than this for the disgraced general, and did not seem to care how Patton would slap the faces of "those Japs."

The situation was made worse by a statement issued to the correspondents in Algiers at a press conference called by the public relations apparatus of AFHQ. It confirmed the incident but asserted that Drew Pearson had been wrong in saying that Patton had been reprimanded by General Eisenhower. In fact, it was categorically stated that he had *not* been reprimanded.

The statement, which sounded like a whitewash presumably ordered by the Commander in Chief, disgusted the correspondents and threw the press corps into an uproar. Whereupon a second press conference was quickly called at which General Smith introduced "Red" Mueller and asked him to make the report from his notes. It was probably the only occasion in the Army's history that a civilian outsider was allowed to present such an important case on behalf of the Army, permitting the chips to fall where they may. It was also a tribute to Mueller's responsibility and reliability as a war correspondent.

During this second press conference of the day it developed that General Eisenhower was not a party to what, in the light of the earlier briefing, seemed to be the beginning of a cover-up campaign. On the contrary, Ike had done exactly what Pearson had said—he had sternly reprimanded Patton. However, it was a *personal* rebuke, the kind that does not formally go into the "201 File," an officer's personal record that contains all official citations, efficiency reports and related data, both the good and the bad.

By then the case was out of Eisenhower's hands. It became a burning national controversy handled by Secretary Stimson himself in the War Department and causing concern even inside the White House. Pressed by Senator Robert R. Reynolds, chairman of the Military Affairs Committee, the Secretary asked General Marshall to order a complete report directly from Eisenhower.

On November 24th, General Eisenhower sent a telegraphic report to Washington "in regard to the conduct of Lieutenant General George S. Patton Jr., U.S.A., Commanding General Seventh Army." It was the summary of the case extracted from the files of the incident, which had become quite voluminous, and it also contained an explanation of the seeming inadequacy of General Eisenhower's first statement to General Marshall for transmission to Secretary Stimson. In view of its historic significance, the document deserves to be reprinted in full, here for the first time:

During the Sicilian campaign General Patton was the mainspring of the effort during the sustained drive of the Seventh Army from Gela all the way to Messina. He absolutely refused to accept procrastination or any excuses for delay, with a resulting rapid advance of that Army which had much to do with the early collapse of resistance in Sicily. He drove himself as hard as he did the members of his Army throughout the campaign and consequently became almost ruthless in his demands upon individual men.

While visiting wounded in hospitals in two instances he encountered unwounded patients who had been evacuated for what is commonly known as "battle anxiety," specifically nerve difficulty. Also, one man had a temperature. He momentarily lost his temper in these two instances and in an unseemly and indefensible manner upbraided the individuals, and in one of the cases cuffed the individual involved so that the man's helmet rolled off his head.

These incidents were first reported officially to me by a medical officer, this report being followed by reports from three reputable newspapermen. Prior to receiving the report from the pressmen I took the following action:

First, to General Patton I wrote a letter advising him of the allegations, expressing my extreme displeasure, and informing him that any repetition would result in his instant relief. Further, I told him that he would necessarily make, on his own initiative to the individuals involved, amends, and, if necessary, take the necessary steps to make proper amends before his whole Army. I also told him that I would reserve decision affecting his relief from command of the Army until I could determine the effect of his own corrective action.

Second, the problem before me was whether the incidents as reported were sufficiently damaging to Patton and to his standing in his Army to compel me to relieve him, thus losing to the United Nations his unquestioned value as commander of an assault force, or whether less drastic measures would be appropriate. I sent General Lucas to make a complete investigation of the affair. I also sent another general officer to Sicily and made a short visit there myself for the purpose of determining whether or not any resentment existed in the Seventh Army against General Patton.

The following action was taken by Patton: He personally sought out the individuals involved and the persons who were present at the time the incidents took place. To these he made full apologies which it was reported to me were accepted. In addition, he visited each and every division in the Seventh Army and called together all officers, to whom he registered his regret that he should have been guilty of any conduct which could be considered unfair and un-American. The officers of these divisions in turn relayed this message to the enlisted men.

The measures taken by Patton were discussed by me with the three newspapermen who have reported the incident, and apparently they were convinced that the measures taken were adequate in the circumstances. On the top of all this I sent the Theater Inspector General to make a thorough investigation of the Seventh Army with the particular mission of determining whether or not there existed in that force any general resentment against Patton. The Inspector General reported to me that, while there was more or less general knowledge that incidents of the character described had taken place, the men themselves felt that General Patton had done a splendid over-all job and no great harm had been done.

In this connection it must be remembered that, while the conduct of Patton in these specific cases was indefensible and resented by every officer who knew of it, Patton has in thousands of cases personally supported, encouraged and sustained individuals. The net result was that throughout the Sicilian campaign the Seventh Army had a high morale. I personally supervised this investigation throughout and took those steps that seemed applicable in the circumstances because I believe that General Patton had a great field of usefulness in any assault where Loyalty, Drive and Gallantry on the part of the Army commander will be essential.

General Smith had a press conference yesterday with all of the representatives of the press and explained the essentials of the entire story as given above. This was done because of reports of the publication in the United States of exaggerated versions of the story. In this connection I commend the great body of American newspapermen in this theater because all of them knew something of the facts involved and some of them knew all, including the corrective action taken and the circumstances that tended to ameliorate the obvious injustice of Patton's acts. These men chose to regard the matter as one in which the High Command acted for the best interests of the war effort and let the matter rest there. To them I am grateful.

Summing the matter up: It is true that General Patton was guilty of reprehensible conduct with respect to two enlisted men. They were both suffering from a nervous disorder and one man in the case had a temperature. Following an exhaustive investigation including a personal visit to Sicily, I decided that the corrective action as described above was suitable in the circumstances and adequate. I still believe that this decision was sound. Finally it has been reported many times to me that in every recent public appearance of Patton before any crowd composed of his own soldiers he is greeted by thunderous applause.

On December 3rd, Secretary Stimson sent Chairman Reynolds a report dealing with both slapping incidents and explaining Eisenhower's misleading statement of November 22nd. "The situation," he wrote, "was simply to correct, for important military reasons, the untrue and damaging inferences from that incident which Drew Pearson had made in his original broadcast."

Stimson then hinted that serious military considerations were behind the handling of the case and stated bluntly that Patton's retention in high command was of the utmost interest of the war effort. "The military reasons referred to above are still important to Allied operations in the Mediterranean theater," the Secretary wrote to the Senator, "and consequently must remain secret for the present, but I assure you that they will eventually be disclosed. At that time it will be made evident why a general discussion of the details of this affair at any time prior to the completion of certain strategic plans was directly contrary to the military interests of the United States and of our allies. General Eisenhower was obliged to consider this matter from a military viewpoint rather than that of what is termed 'public relations.'

"General Eisenhower in his last report has again reported that these instances [of violence] have not affected General Patton's standing as a tactical leader, one who successfully concluded, in record time, a complicated and important military campaign, and one whom his officers and men would again be willing to follow into battle. He reports that the serious aspect of this case is the danger that the Army will lose the services of a battle-tested Army commander, and also afford aid and comfort to the enemy."

By this the irate Secretary meant to slap down Pearson for his intemperate and inopportune exposé of the slapping incidents. The high military considerations of which the Secretary spoke involved Patton's transfer to the Fifth Army, which General Alexander was urging with increasing vigor. Ambitious plans were in the making for an acceleration of the campaign and a move northward in Italy, and they needed a bold and dashing leader like Patton. Now it became abundantly evident to Secretary Stimson and General Marshall in Washington, as well as General Eisenhower in Algiers, that Patton would not be available for this assignment. Although his competence fully qualified him for the job, his new reputation in the public eye had sorely disqualified him. It was a major tragedy, for Patton personally, and for the nation and the war effort. There are ample reasons to believe that with Patton commanding in Italy, it would not have taken until June 4, 1944, to reach Rome.

Stimson was deeply disturbed by the case. Patton was one of his oldest friends. When a mere lieutenant, Patton had given the much older man "comradeship and guidance in World War I." When Stimson entered the war as a lieutenant colonel and attended a school at Langres, in France, where General Staff Corps officers were being produced for the AEF, he renewed his friendship with Major Patton, who was then running the tank training center there. Later when Patton was commanding the 3rd Cavalry and was post commander in Fort Myer near Washington, they regularly dined at each other's houses.

In September, 1943, Stimson had an opportunity to go to the aid of his friend. Patton's name was on a list of promotions of a number of officers to permanent major general about to be sent to Capitol Hill for Senate confirmation. General Marshall had recommended his promotion and then insisted on it even when a few timid souls in the War Department warned that it might create a stir should the slapping incidents become public knowledge. Then Marshall was advised in so many words to take Patton's name off the list because he was "doubtfully viewed in the White House."

Marshall went to Stimson for help, and the Secretary took up the matter with the President "to reinforce Marshall's recommendation." Mr. Roosevelt was naturally angered by Patton's "reprehensible conduct," but he remained the General's staunch admirer, and agreed with Marshall and Stimson that he was essential for victory. He left Patton's name on the list, but told Stimson, "I am going to catch hell for this when the damned thing comes out."

And now "the damned thing" was out. Stimson had to go to bat for the man who was not only one of his closest friends but also one of the country's ablest combat leaders. "The incident was not a pretty one," his memoirs stated, "but I fully agreed with Eisenhower's view that Patton's services must not be lost."

He sent Patton—whom he regarded as a "problem child" —a stern but fatherly letter. He expressed his disappointment that "so brilliant an officer should so far have offended against his own traditions."

It was Stimson's letter more than anything else that brought home to Patton the true seriousness of the situation. Until its receipt (despite Eisenhower's characterization of his conduct as "despicable" and the unprecedented humiliation he had to endure by apologizing to his troops), he was inclined to dismiss the incident with a shrug: "Oh well," he would say, "I acted hastily but I had good reasons for my action."

But the Stimson letter proved a hard blow. For the first time during the "hullabaloo," as he called the uproar, he became remorseful and conscience-smitten and, indeed, plainly worried that he had probably exceeded the limits of his exuberance and lost his best friends—Stimson, Marshall and Eisenhower. While he sounded contrite in his answer to Eisenhower's reprimand, but was in fact piqued by Ike's "nasty note" and far from convinced that he had rated it, Patton was genuinely touched and penitent when answering Stimson's letter. He apologized profusely, explaining in eloquent words the severe tension of the days that had produced his outburst. He assured the Secretary that he would never give him cause to regret his decision to stand by him at this critical juncture of his career.

Mr. Stimson later wrote: "Perhaps no decision of the war was more triumphantly vindicated by events than this one. In the summer of 1944, Patton became almost overnight the idol of many of the same newspapers and politicians who had most loudly demanded his removal in 1943."

Many years later, when collecting data for this tragic but significant episode in General Patton's career, I sought out a distinguished medical officer who also happened to be a highly qualified "practicing" historian—in fact, director of the Army Medical Services Historical Unit. I hoped to obtain from him an expert opinion of Patton's relationship with the Medical Corps and, in particular, of his attitude toward the casualty problem. He was Colonel John Boyd Coates Jr., who served with General Patton in World War II, first as his Deputy Surgeon and later as Third Army Surgeon.

"It was quite an education," Colonel Coates said, "and one that I would never have missed, knowing what I know today. Many of us of Headquarters Third U.S. Army, when we reached the United Kingdom in March, 1944, and learned authentically for the first time that General Patton was to be the new Commanding General of that Army, were not exactly enthralled, for we had heard many stories of this man which may or may not have been true.

"As a medical man I was, of course, concerned with providing the finest medical care possible to the fighting men in the Third U.S. Army. From reports (or rumors) that I had heard casually, I was far from certain just what the status of the medical service might be in combat in the Third Army under the over-all command of General Patton. This disturbed many of us while we were still in England, preparing for the invasion.

"To sum it up briefly, our fears were completely unfounded. Never have I served under a commanding general who gave more support and less unintelligent interference to the medical service anywhere. He demanded the best of every man and officer, and those who could not make the grade he either disregarded or got rid of, preferably the latter. He was interested in only one major item and that was performance. We were blessed with a superb medical service in the Third U.S. Army and General Patton supported us to the limit. Under his over-all command he permitted the responsible medical officers to run the medical service for his Army—and this is the way it should be."

Concerning the "slapping incidents," Colonel Coates said:

"I did not serve in North Africa or Sicily, but I well remember that when the story of the so-called 'slapping incident' broke in the United States, I became just as interested and inquisitive as the next individual for the complete story, especially for General Patton's own account of the affair. His personal description of this incident did not reach me until a year or so later at Nancy, France, on the evening of December 16, 1944. I was sitting in the Grand Hotel with several friends, including Colonel [now General] Paul D. Harkins, who at that time was General Patton's Assistant Chief of Staff.

"It was on that fateful December 16th that the Battle of the Bulge started. Several of us had been discussing various radiograms which we had received from the First U.S. Army, the VIII Corps of which seemed to be taking the brunt of the German attack. In some manner our conversation turned to the 'slapping incidents' and Harkins pulled out of his pocket one short typewritten sheet of paper and asked me to read General Patton's own explanation of the affair. Over a year before, Harkins, badgered by newspaper people, had asked the General to write this out in his own words.

"According to that paper, on the day of the second 'slapping incident,' General Patton had been at the front. Knowing human nature and considerable about the psychological reactions of individuals in war, I have the definite opinion that General Patton did what, at that time, he considered the correct and necessary thing to do in the interest of his command. He himself may well have been angry, tense, tired and exasperated. But in all likelihood, in his own mind, he believed he was dealing with a coward who had sought protection in a medical facility. Under the circumstances, this situation would have been totally irreconcilable to any responsible commander, much less to a commander of General Patton's character. It was unfortunate that this incident took place in a hospital—albeit the hospital was under General Patton's over-all command."

On the second anniversary of Pearl Harbor, in 1943, while returning from the Cairo Conference with Prime Minister Churchill, President Roosevelt stopped in Algiers to look in on General Eisenhower and review with him the broad and fateful future. As soon as he had landed and was seated in the General's Cadillac, he turned to him and said, "Well, Ike, you are going to command 'Overlord.' "

With this direct sentence the President cleared up the opaque confusion that had settled on Eisenhower's command in the Mediterranean. Fighting in Italy was tedious and inconclusive, and so was Eisenhower's future. After 13 spectacular months of World War II, his career had come to a halt. He was looking forward to returning to Washington to conduct the war from a desk while General Marshall replaced him in command of the crusade for Europe.

The great decision to mount "Overlord," as the invasion of the Continent was called, had been reached on May 25, 1943, at the "Trident" conference in Washington, and was confirmed in Quebec on August 24th at the "Quadrant" meeting. But it was not until the "Sextant" conference in

Cairo that Eisenhower was chosen to be its Supreme Commander instead of Marshall, whom the President regarded as absolutely indispensable in Washington.

Amid preparations for Christmas, Eisenhower went to work to organize his staff and choose his field commanders. On December 22nd he received two turkeys from Sicily as a gentle reminder from Patton that he was still around. It proved an extremely timely hint. At that very moment Ike was drawing up the list of the officers he hoped to get as field commanders for "Overlord," and the next day he sent it to General Marshall in Washington.

"My preference for American Group Commander," he wrote, "when more than one American Army is operating in 'Overlord,' is General Bradley. One of his Army commanders should probably be Patton; the other, a man that may be developed in 'Overlord' operations or, alternatively, somebody like Hodges or Simpson, provided such officer could come over to the United Kingdom at an early date and accompany Bradley through the early stages of the operation."

This was a daring list, drawn with great prophetic power. It was daring because it placed a younger and more inexperienced man, Bradley, at the top, relegating Patton to the command of an army under him. And it was prophetic because Eisenhower (who once coached football at West Point) succeeded in picking a winning team with his very first selection.

Eisenhower foresaw "some possibility of friction" with Patton over Bradley's elevation to the top field command. But he expected that Marshall would understand his motive and concur. Back in 1940, Marshall—appalled by a preponderance of deadwood among the general officers—looked over his colonels and lieutenant colonels, and picked a handful of the more promising for eventual high command. Eisenhower was one, Bradley another as was Courtney H. Hodges, then a 53-year-old colonel at the head of the Infantry School in Fort Benning. As a matter of fact, Hodges was heading for retirement and Bradley for West Point to become Commandant of Cadets when Marshall "unexpectedly" rerouted both toward their phenomenal wartime careers.

In August, 1943, four months before Eisenhower drew up his list, Marshall had indicated to him that Bradley was his candidate for the big job when he radioed Ike to send

Bradley to London immediately as the "American Army
Commander . . . to parallel activities of British army commanders." And he hinted that he had Hodges in mind for
an army command in "Overlord" when he sent him to San
Antonio, Texas, to take over the Third Army from Lieutenant General Walter Krueger, who was sent to the Pacific
at General MacArthur's request.

As far as Patton was concerned, Eisenhower was not
overly disturbed, because he knew that Patton would, in his
thoroughly chastised state, accept gleefully just about any
spot in "Overlord"; and especially because he knew that
Marshall himself had Patton earmarked for the command of
one of the American armies in the invasion.

Marshall recognized Patton's qualities probably better
than anybody else in the Army. Although he regarded him
as the "greatest tactical leader and ground-gainer this
country has produced," he was also aware of Patton's shortcomings, which, in his opinion, disqualified him for the top
job with its innumerable operational and organizational details, for the handling of which Patton was temperamentally
unsuited.

Despite his certainty that Marshall would concur in his
choice of commanders, Eisenhower thought it politic to delay the showdown over Patton as long as possible. When he
sent his list to Marshall, he also informed Bradley in London
that he had recommended him for the Army Group Command, but said nothing about giving Patton an army under
him. It was probably the smart thing to do, as Bradley himself later confirmed. "Had Eisenhower asked for my
opinion, I would have counseled against the selection,"
Bradley wrote. "For not only did I question George's conduct of the Sicilian campaign, but I seriously doubted the
wisdom of his forcing Patton to stomach this reversal of roles
in command."

Eisenhower visited Washington early in January, 1944, to
review with Marshall all the pending problems of "Overlord"; then went straight to London. He arrived there on
January 16th, with the command set-up in his pocket, fully
approved by the Chief of Staff. He had no time to see
Bradley and tell him the good news. He revealed it in a press
conference the next day, and Bradley read it in the *Daily
Express* at breakfast in the dining room of the Dorchester Hotel on the morning of January 18th. It was still
not clear from the garbled version of Eisenhower's state-

ment whether Bradley would command the First Army in the assault or the American Army Group in Normandy. So Bradley went to see Eisenhower to clear up the matter, and the Supreme Commander told him, "It's the Army Group, Brad, just like Monty."

"How about the armies?" Bradley asked.

"Hodges is going to get the First Army, Brad," Ike said, then drew a deep breath, "and Patton the Third."

Bradley's face fell.

"Don't worry, Brad," Eisenhower said, "Georgie won't object."

It was a shot in the dark. Ike had made the arrangements behind Patton's back. He never consulted Patton and could not know how he would react to what was tantamount to a demotion. But he thought he knew Patton well. And he suspected that Patton had been sufficiently softened up by then to be putty in his hands.

Now that, in the wake of the furor Drew Pearson had stirred up, Patton's transfer to command the Fifth Army in Italy had to be ruled out, his role in Sicily became painfully ambiguous. There were still important "military reasons," as Eisenhower and Stimson called them, to retain him in harness, but they seemed to be minor and, to Patton himself, rather nebulous. Left stewing and brooding in his gilded cage at Palermo, he was being used to mislead the Germans. By then he inspired respect and fear in the enemy, who came to regard him as their most dangerous adversary in the field, the Allies' counterpart of Rommel in his halcyon days. Assuming that Patton would provoke the Germans to some feverish preparations wherever he showed up, Washington decided to send him on a grand tour of the Mediterranean, hinting broadly at new assignments for him.

For a while the Germans watched the comings and goings of Patton like rubbernecked spectators following a tennis ball at Wimbledon in the finals of the Davis Cup matches. Patton was instructed to take a staff of 10 on these trips, to give the impression that he was moving in to take over; and his journeys were so arranged that the Germans could always find out about them. He was first sent to Cor-

sica, then on to Malta, and finally to Italy, with rumors deliberately launched each time that he was slated for command, now here, then there, wherever he happened to be.

Patton enjoyed the trips. The places he was visiting were
soaked in history, and his strange assignment gave him the
first and only opportunity in his life to see them. Yet he undertook the trips in a restive mood because he, unlike the
Germans, knew only too well that he was not to be given
command at any of those fronts.

By the time he reached Italy early in January, 1944, he
was deeply depressed. He was condemned to watching his
colleagues Mark Clark and Alfred Gruenther up to their
necks in war while he had to play the part of the visiting
fireman.

Even while he was touring the Mediterranean in the role
of a glorified decoy, the battle around him raged. On
November 25th Senator J. W. Bailey of South Carolina demanded that Patton be court-martialed; three days later the
Senate committee before which Patton's promotion was
pending decided to investigate his conduct before confirming it; then action on it was delayed, and the Senate Majority
Leader, Alben W. Barkley, had to work hard behind the
scenes to prevent his irate colleagues from tabling it altogether.

Patton did not succeed in making his peace with Congress
for a long time. Even in May, 1944, a Senate committee
was expressing doubts about his fitness to lead American
soldiers in the war although it had none about his professional qualifications.

Patton's reaction to the slapping scandal was uncharacteristic of the man, if only because he did not seem to react to
it at all, but let the censures and abuses resound without
offering rebuttals. Only once during those days, in a humble
letter to a Mrs. S. E. Massengale, did he *publicly* refer to the
incident. The lady had written to him directly in compas-
sionate tones, and Patton was so moved that he decided to
answer her letter, expressing his regrets over the incidents.

The General's silence was the product of a kind of panic-
conference he held on November 23rd, with members of
his staff closest to him, in the immediate wake of the Pearson broadcast. General Gay and Colonel Harkins his devoted
Chiefs of Staff; Major Stiller and Lieutenant Colonel Codman, his aides, and Dr. Odom, a prominent surgeon from
New Orleans who was his personal physician, attended it.

Patton had prepared a one-page brief for them in which he spelled out his version of the incidents and his thoughts about them. To his staff, knowing as they did of the pressures under which he had labored during those days, his outbursts were understandable and excusable. After all, they thought, Patton had never before resorted to such extreme measures, yet he repeated them twice within a single week. These men were satisfied in their own minds and souls that his violence was the product of the unbearable tension and not of any innate brutal streak in his character.

During the meeting, Colonel Codman, a debonair, sensitive, and intuitively wise Bostonian, advised Patton to do what he realized would be the most difficult for him—maintain complete silence no matter how unfair and abusive the attacks. Patton thought it over and resolved to heed Codman's advice.

It proved his most effective defense, and he was grateful to Codman for his wise counsel. During the deepest depression of those days, Patton took Codman to midnight mass on Christmas Eve in Palermo, then invited him to his quarters for a melancholy nocturnal chat. He revived the dying embers in the fireplace, produced a bottle of wine, and spent an hour and a half just chatting with his aide about things of the past and things to come. Their conversation touched upon the recent incidents, for Patton was still living in their shadow, and he told Codman in a soft voice, "You have been sound and I have taken your advice—as a friend."

"It touched me very much," Codman wrote next morning in a note to his wife.

The devoted Codman performed yet another major service for Patton to restore his faith in his usefulness and to reassure him on the correctness of his judgment. He conducted a kind of poll by sampling the mail and whatever expressions of opinions he could pick up in the circles in which he moved.

On January 15th Codman tabulated his findings, and found that the "fan mail" General Patton was receiving was "running better than the Gallup poll on the same subject—about 89 per cent pro and 11 per cent con"—and he considered only letters from strangers, eliminating all communications from friends and acquaintances. The letters that poured in during the hullabaloo in the wake of Pearson's broadcast were easy to categorize. They were either for or against the General, all written in no uncertain terms.

As Codman put it, "The letters of protest, in many cases both obscene and anonymous, confined themselves to ringing the changes on 'you are a cowardly so-and-so for striking a defenseless enlisted man.' The pro-letters, mostly from relatives of servicemen, also bore a close resemblance to one another. 'I want you to know we are proud our son is serving in your Army,' a typical letter ran. 'From the newspaper account we are not clear as to exactly what you did and why, but we want you to know we are for you. Keep going and God bless you.' "

Although Codman's findings cheered Patton, they could not altogether eliminate his despondency, especially since he feared, in the absence of any word or even a hint, either from Washington or Algiers, there were no plans to use him in future operations. This was designed to be part of his punishment. He was deliberately led to believe that his usefulness as a combat leader and, worse still, his whole career were in serious jeopardy. The General's concern for his own future was deepened by his worry for the members of his staff. He regarded them as a father would his children, and was apprehensive that if they were scattered and had to work under other commanding officers they would not fare so well as under him.

Patton sought reassurance from Wellington's experience, for the Iron Duke, one of his heroes, also had "more than his share of frustrations—of being kept in ignorance, pushed around, passed over, and generally stymied." He was reading John Fortescue's biography of Wellington during those days and lectured on his life virtually every evening to his faithful staff.

He saw the year end in total darkness, without a single ray to illuminate his future. On New Year's Day, "a very untactful telegram was received," as General Gay put it, relieving Patton of command of the Seventh Army. The message advised him "without warning" that he would be succeeded by General Clark at the head of the great army he had baptized in fire. "This was a bitter blow," Gay wrote, "to the Headquarters of the Seventh Army . . . particularly bitter in view of the fact that it was felt the Seventh Army had just completed a brilliant campaign."

"A hell of a Happy New Year," was Patton's own comment on the news. But he was still hoping that he would, somehow and somewhere, do bigger and better things in 1944.

A fortnight later there was still nothing to dispel Patton's gloom. On the contrary, on January 14th another one of his frail hopes appeared to be shattered. He had been looking forward to commanding "Anvil," the operation in the Mediterranean against southern France which was in the planning stage at the Ecole Normale near Algiers. But a letter from Colonel Harkins, who was there working on the plans, now hinted broadly that "the 'Anvil' show is off."

To ease his mind, Patton began a tour of Sicily, visiting the remnants of its past. He revisited Troina, the recent memories of which were not exactly calculated to cheer him, and looked in on Cerami, where he had had his CP during those agonizing days. Now his mind turned from the recent battle to the ancient castle which in the 10th century was the seat of Roger I, the Norman conqueror of Sicily.

The antiquities of Sicily began to absorb his interest completely and provided at least some compensation for his professional grief. He went looking for the city of Himera, which the Carthaginians had destroyed in 405 B.C., and found it with the help of Signora Marconi, the erudite curator of the museum in Palermo. All that was left of the city was a Greek temple, but it inspired Patton to a flight of historic fantasy. "It is my belief," he wrote after his visit, "that this temple marks the spot where Hasdrubal committed suicide in 397 B.C. and that the Greeks built a temple to celebrate the fact, but when the Carthaginians came back they destroyed it. On second thought, I am not sure it was this Hasdrubal or the older Hannibal. Anyhow, when he saw the battle was lost, he jumped on the funeral pile."

He was grasping ever more desperately at these straws of the past, since the present held nothing but the most bitter disillusionment for him. On the morning of January 18th Sergeant Meeks gave Patton a piece of especially disturbing news he had heard on the radio the night before. "It said, sir, General Bradley is going to command all the ground troops in England," his orderly told him.

Patton was stunned.

He turned back to the past and continued his exploration of Sicily. On January 22nd he called Captain Otis Gunn, "a silent hillbilly type" from the South who was his pilot, and went for an aerial sightseeing tour to Moyta and to Erice's Norman castle near Traponi.

When he returned to Palermo, Sergeant Rosevich awaited him with an action message that had come in during his absence. Addressed to, "C.G. 7th Army for Patton, 22 January 1944, George S. Patton, Jr., Lieutenant-General, 02605 U.S. Army" it read:

"Orders issued relieving you from assignment this theatre and assigning to duty in U.K. Request you proceed to NATOUSA, Algiers, for orders."

BOOK TWO ☆ THE TRIUMPH

CHAPTER EIGHTEEN
UNDERDOG OF OVERLORD

Nineteen-hundred-forty-four!

Will this be the Allies' rich, immortal year marked by the triumph that Churchill hoped would open wide the doors to the future?

Adolf Hitler did not think so.

He was convinced that 1944 would rudely end the Allies' dream of challenging him in the heart of the contested Continent.

On January 28th he assembled a glittering parade of his field marshals and generals at his headquarters in the Wolfschanze to review the war with them, for the first time in the New Year.

There was not much in the big picture to fill him with joy. The Red Army was pressing westward all along the immense eastern front; and in Italy the American Fifth Army had just reached the Rapido River.

But the Feührer was not interested in the big picture. He saw in scattered little things the sure promise of victory.

He was trying to hold the line, for just a little longer, until the *Wunderwaffen*—his miracle weapons like the rockets and air-breathing U-boats—would be ready to stem and turn the tide. Despite the pressures from all sides, this was a genial and confident conference.

General Günther Korten, Chief of Staff of the *Luftwaffe,* reported that the RAF had admitted the loss of 34 bombers in a raid on Berlin the night before. "But we," he added, "claimed only 23."

"Donnerwetter!" Hitler exclaimed, banging the table. "See to it, Korten, that we claim the difference tomorrow."

General Jodl reported on the fighting in Italy.

The Allies had landed in Anzio and Nettuno on January

22nd, but the promising venture appeared to be bogging down.

"They are no longer jubilant, my Führer," Jodl said. "Apparently they did not anticipate how quickly we would be able to throw our forces against them."

"Ah," Hitler smiled smugly. "I managed to pour a bit of water into their bubbling champagne." He plunged into one of his familiar lectures: "They always undertake something big, something ambitious—but when it comes to making good on it, they invariably fold. They come up against the tenacity of German resistance and get cold feet.

"You see, *meine Herren,* how important it is to have elbow room in a landing? In a small bridgehead one is completely dependent . . . There is now only one subject of dispute: Where are they going to land? I wonder where the clairvoyants are."

"In Portugal, *mein Führer,*" Field Marshall Walther Model chimed in with a quip. He referred to the crowd of "kibitzers" in that neutral country who knew better than the Lord himself what the future held.

"Yes, yes," Hitler agreed with a smile. "Everything now hinges on Roosevelt's election. The closer they get to the presidential campaign the more worried and restless they will become. But if we succeed in thwarting this thing in the south, they'll never dare to try another landing anywhere."

As if this were his cue, Jodl presented a report he had just received from Director Karl Weis, the chief engineer in charge of the expanding Atlantic Wall.

"The construction of fortifications is on the upswing again all along the French coast, *mein Führer,*" Jodl said. "According to Director Weis, the program badly lagged earlier in 1943—as a matter of fact, he says that constructions had dropped to 173,000 cubic meters in April. But in November we were up to 500,000 cubic meters again."

"You see, *meine Herren,*" Hitler said with his nose in the air, "they'll think twice before they dare to make a frontal attack on this continent."

But in London the men whose job would be to mount that frontal attack began to arrive one by one. General Sir

Bernard Montgomery flew in on January 2nd with a plane-load of oranges.

General Eisenhower arrived a fortnight later.

And Patton came on January 26th, a cold and foggy Wednesday morning.

He had needed only a day in Palermo to wind up his affairs, bid his farewells, and pack his things. His orders specified that he must take only one aide with him, so he picked Lieutenant Colonel Charles Codman, who had become very close to him during those dark days.

Codman was a very proper Bostonian with a gay and sophisticated Bohemian side and a vast circle of friends among celebrities, and a cosmopolitan air and savvy that proved as useful to Patton as his calm and sagacious counsel was at the height of the slapping scandal. He was more than just an aide—he was also Patton's majordomo, master of ceremonies, wine steward, cicerone, his shepherd through the social maze, curator of his intellectual excursions, and a kind of sob-sister in moments of stress. Codman became his absolute confidant. Now it was the suave Colonel's job to pack Patton's gear with the help of Sergeant Meeks, and especially to select his personal papers that would be lugged along to England. They were growing fast. They already weighed 150 pounds and filled three huge black foot lockers marked, "Lt. Gen. G. S. Patton, Jr.," giving his address as, "Codman & Codman, Inc., 811 Congress Street, Boston, Mass."

There was a stopover in Algiers to enable Patton to pay his respects to General Jake Devers at NATOUSA. Then he flew on to Marrakesh to change planes. Back at his old haunts, he spent a few hours at the Villa Taylor and reminisced of his days as a Moroccan proconsul when he was playing host there to President Roosevelt and Prime Minister Churchill during the Casablanca Conference.

At midnight on January 25th, Patton left Africa in a commercial C-54—I year, 2 months, 17 days and 10½ hours after he had set foot in the war on this same soil.

On this trip to England he was "cloaked in censorship"—and not for solely *military* reasons. As a matter of fact, the enemy was the last from whom his presence in the United Kingdom was to be concealed. Patton was still very much under a cloud at home, and Eisenhower felt that the publication of his new assignment at this time would get "critical reaction from the press, not only in the United States, but in the United Kingdom as well." Considerable pressure was put on the Supreme Commander by his press relations aide and psychological warfare "expert," an eager-beaver named Brigadier General Robert A. McClure. A former military attaché at the American Embassy in London, McClure professed to know his way around and gauge public opinion. He strongly advised Ike not to give Patton command of an army. "The British have keenly resented Patton's action in Sicily," he said, "and some American correspondents even felt that it would ruin you."

It was a powerful argument pinpointed at Ike's personal sensitivities, but the Supreme Commander was not prepared to accept McClure's jeremiad at face value. He knew what Patton's tactical genius meant to the pending crusade and how important it was for him personally to have him in his camp. He was, however, deeply disturbed and voiced his apprehension to Major General Albert C. Wedemeyer—who was, like himself, one of General Marshall's "fair-haired boys"—when Wedemeyer visited him in London on his way to Washington from his command in the China-Burma-India Theater. But Wedemeyer told him quietly, "Get on to yourself, Ike. Georgie doesn't need you as much as you need him."

Eisenhower instructed Major General Everett Hughes, who was close to him and was a friend of Patton, to listen around and find out whether McClure's fears had any solid foundation. "However, to be quite frank, Everett," he told Hughes, "I really don't give a damn. I'm determined to give the Third Army to George, and won't keep him under the blanket for more than a few days or maybe a week."

But the campaign against Patton continued unabated in the United States. It was only in March that Secretary Stimson announced that the War Department considered the case of the slapping incidents closed.

☆

As far as the weather was concerned, January 26, 1944, was a good day for the arrival of a man who was cloaked in secrecy. The sky was overcast and Patton's C-47 had to fly blind on instruments through a thick pea-soup from Prestwick in Scotland (where he had landed at dawn) to

Cheddington Airfield, about 35 miles northwest of London. The country was shrouded in a heavy fog.

When Patton alighted from the plane and peeped through the mist at Cheddington, he was pleased to see that a reception committee, headed by Major General John Clifford Hodges Lee, Eisenhower's deputy, was waiting for him. But Patton was not quite sure whether to be pleased or irritated, and wondered why Ike had chosen Lee to meet him. It was no secret that he could not stand Lee, but Ike probably did not know it and had picked his deputy to demonstrate how highly he regarded Patton.

The Deputy Supreme Commander was two years Patton's junior, but they had graduated together from West Point in 1909, Lee standing 12th in a class of 103, Patton ending far below him in 46th place. After that their careers had only one experience in common—they both served as aides to the colorful General Leonard Wood, Patton before and Lee during World War I. Patton went on to the glamour of the Cavalry, while Lee held down a number of engineering assignments.

A smooth-skinned, sharp-eyed balding blond man with a face Hollywood usually type-casts in the role of the glad-handing suburban clergyman, Lee was a "soldier of the old school" with a reputation for being pompous and a martinet.

Lee's presence at the airport was not considered an auspicious beginning for his new assignment. But waiting with him was Commander Butcher, Eisenhower's gregarious Naval aide. Patton was fond of him and appreciated Ike's thoughtfulness in sending him to the airfield. Butcher, however, was there on a dual mission. He had greetings from Ike for Patton, to be sure, but he had met the plane to welcome another passenger—little Caacia, one of Eisenhower's pet dogs. She flew in from North Africa, and Butcher was to take her to Hackbridge Kennels where she was to begin a six-month sojourn under strict British quarantine regulations.

Lee drove Patton through dense London fog to his own apartment; and then Patton went straight to Eisenhower to report.

"I presume, Georgie, you know what you are getting," Ike teased him a bit.

"I honestly don't know it, Ike," Patton said.

"It's my own old outfit, Georgie, the Third Army," Eisenhower said with a serious mien. "There is no better group of men anywhere, George. Hodges is about to be relieved of its command and will go to Washington awaiting his new assignment. The plans are still in the making, and you'll receive your outline in due course. Incidentally, I understand an advance party of the Third Army is on its way to England on the *Queen Mary*. It's due to arrive tomorrow or the day after, Colonel Lee will let you know. The main body will follow later, in February or early in March."

Eisenhower, who was Patton's junior in both age and permanent rank and was keenly conscious of it, looked at his friend with sympathetic but stern eyes. "I think, George," he said, "we ought to have a little talk." Patton shifted to the edge of his chair as he said:

"Go ahead, Ike, but be gentle, boy. My scars are still red."

"I have your letter here, George," Eisenhower went on, "the one you sent me from Sicily. I want you to know that I cherish it, especially where you said, 'I am at a loss to find words with which to express my chagrin and grief at having given you, a man to whom I owe everything and for whom I would gladly lay down my life, cause to be displeased with me.'"

"I meant every Goddamn word of it, Ike."

"I am sure, Georgie. But you frequently think everybody is against you, George, yet you have only one enemy in the whole world—yourself. I don't mean to sound like a Dutch uncle, but I told you innumerable times to count 10 before you take any abrupt action. You persistently disregarded my advice, but it is not just advice any longer. Well, from now on it is an order. Think before you leap, George, or you will have no one to blame but yourself for the consequences of your rashness. And I hope you value our friendship and will consider also me in the matter."

Patton was genuinely moved. He was fond of Eisenhower and had no qualms about the younger man's being put out over him. Now he responded to the bawling out with words Ike was disposed to dismiss as fulsome flattery, although Patton meant them with all sincerity.

He promised that he would watch his step, and said, "I think it's nothing short of breath-taking what's happening to us, Ike. I sincerely believe that you're on the threshold of becoming the greatest general of all times, including Napoleon."

Eisenhower blushed and squirmed a little uneasily in his chair, but Patton was quick to ease his embarrassment by sneaking a twinkle into his eyes and telling the Supreme Commander, "And as far as I am concerned, Ike, I'm just a silly old fool, Goddamnit, always putting my foot in my mouth. But don't worry, Ike. I'll be more careful in the future where I am going to have my tantrums, and they certainly won't be in a hospital."

Ike burst into one of his broad, forgiving laughs, then turned to Patton and asked, as if to indicate that the unpleasant part of the interview was over:

"Incidentally, Georgie. Are you free for dinner tonight?"

Patton faded promptly into the tremendous enterprise rapidly developing in London over which General Eisenhower was presiding like the chairman of a board.

It was a fantastic venture, and not only because of the unprecedented difficulties of the strictly military tasks ahead. The return to the Continent was designed as a joint undertaking, and coalition wars never appealed to professional military men. The United States had but one experience of this kind of war, in Europe in 1917-18, and it was neither an entirely happy nor satisfactory one.

Fortunately, in the 1930's the United States Army was not afflicted with the tradition-bound chauvinism that characterized some of the jingoistic General Staffs abroad. Planning in the United States moved slowly but intelligently and objectively, from parochialism to cooperation, anticipating the possibility of an American involvement in a coalition war. While the so-called "color" plans of the 1920's were designed for operations against one or another single power with the United States going it alone (like "Orange," for example, the plan for war with Japan), the new set of plans—called "Rainbow"—contained distinct elements of designs for coalition warfare. In May, 1939, the Joint Planning Committee of the Army and Navy stated the need for a broad strategic plan by boldly assuming that "the United

States, England, and France [would be] opposed to Germany, Italy, and Japan, with the United States providing maximum participation, in particular as regards armies in Europe."

This basic assumption, incorporated in "Rainbow 4," and especially in "Rainbow 5," became the military superstructure General Marshall began to erect in 1939 on foundations President Roosevelt had laid for cooperation with the Allies after the outbreak of the war in Europe. However, the Nazis' startling victories in Poland, Norway, the Low Countries and France created an emotional crisis in the American General Staff. Hypnotized by the German power, it regarded France's collapse and the siege of Britain as an unmitigated and irreparable disaster. These events convinced the planners that the situation of the United Kingdom was hopeless and that, therefore, the United States would have to make its own arrangements, relying entirely upon its own resources.

President Roosevelt rejected such defeatism. Even during the dark days of June, 1940, he made plain his desire that the nation and the armed forces should not plan simply on preparing for the worst. He himself meant to act instead on the hypothesis that the British Government and the British Isles would probably hold and that the military situation would remain very much as it was in the west.

Both Marshall and Patton grew up in the shadow of Pershing, but they drew different conclusions from the lessons he had taught them on this particular score. Marshall gradually came to the conclusion that his great teacher's rigid parochialism, though probably justified in World War I, could not work in a future war and that Pershing's "separate command" principle (which also involved the separate drafting of plans) would have to be replaced by the principle of merger at the top in order to assure unity of purpose through unity of command.

His attitude toward such intimate cooperation at the level of the high command became crystallized in the fall of 1940, when he realized that the British, "though so weak as to have to depend in the long run on American support, were still strong enough to make good use of it."

Patton, on the other hand, derived from Pershing only emphatic affirmation of his own innate chauvinism, which he had inherited from his Know-Nothing great-grandfather and was stimulated by his Confederate ancestors whose jingoistic influence on his outlook remained considerable. To him America was the ultimate and absolute good. While he was by no means xenophobic—for he admired the British and loved the French—he held to the principle enunciated by John Mercer Patton almost a 100 years before, opposing "the slightest control over Americans by any foreign power, religious or temporal."

In a real sense, Patton had probably the least reason to feel self-conscious about being an American in this predominantly British world, if only because his British colleagues went out of their way to demonstrate their regard and affection. At that time it was quite the *bon ton* among the British brass to think and speak patronizingly of these American newcomers to the war who had made themselves so comfortable in the driver's seat. Field Marshal Brooke in particular was most outspoken in his condescension. Even after his first meeting with Eisenhower as Supreme Commander, in London on January 24th, he noted in his diary a bit too bluntly: "Eisenhower has got absolutely no strategical outlook." And he even stooped to question Marshall's single-mindedness and honesty, as on December 3, 1943, in Cairo, when he accused the American Chief of Staff of "the worst sharp practice that I have seen for some time."

Yet Brooke led the British chorus singing Patton's praise, showing in the most demonstrative ways, of which that congenitally undemonstrative introvert was capable, the high regard in which his British colleagues held him. A few weeks after Patton's arrival in England, Brooke went to Widewing, General Eisenhower's invasion headquarters, to decorate Patton with the K.C.B., the Most Honorable Order of the Bath (which entitled him to call himself *Sir* George Patton henceforth). The staid Field Marshal, not normally given to complimenting an American general or flattering anybody, told him, "I would like to say that you have earned this more than any other general." The rather stiff Chief of the Imperial General Staff was perfectly at ease with Patton, and now even joked with him, a sign of exceptional goodwill:

"Don't wince, Patton," he told him, "I shan't kiss you."

"That's a pity, sir," Patton shot back, "because I've shaved very closely this morning in preparation for getting smacked by you."

Patton felt better off in England than in his doghouse in
Palermo, of course, but he was far from pleased with what
Eisenhower had prepared for him. The Third Army, which
he was to command, was still 5,000 miles away. It was
idling at Fort Sam Houston near San Antonio in Texas,
managed by a strange staff under a general who was on his
way out and a chief of staff in whom, from what he knew
of him, Patton had no confidence. Scattered units of the
Army were in the United Kingdom, but they were assigned
to the ETO and trained on their own. Patton became what
Bradley called "a ward of Ike," the commander of an army
without troops. Headquarters were assigned to him off the
beaten path in the Midlands. It was far from the hubbub of
the invasion build-up in southern England and 180 miles
from London where "Overlord" was taking shape.

There were also other flies in the ointment to make Patton
feel that he was, after all, the underdog of "Overlord." The
first thing on Thursday morning, January 27th, the day after
his arrival in London, he went to see General Lee to orient
himself *à-propos* the command setup. Lee told him in a
gossipy manner that Ike was definitely at the top. He had
his office in Norfolk House, the nerve center of all planning, with Walter Bedell Smith (who had just been made a
lieutenant general and had his vicious ulcer firmly under
control) as his Chief of Staff. Smith's deputy was a British
lieutenant general named Frederick Morgan, a debonair,
graying, most cooperative officer who had been the chief
planner of "Overlord" from its inception, and was now setting the final pattern on the basis of changes Eisenhower
and Montgomery had suggested in Morgan's draft.

Air Chief Marshal Tedder, whom Patton knew from
North Africa, was Ike's Deputy, and Monty was the over-all
commander of all ground elements in England, and would
be for the invasion until the establishment of an American
Army Group on the Continent. In the meantime, Bradley
was wearing two hats—as commanding general of the First
U.S. Army slated to mount the invasion and as commander
presumptive of the Army Group—and managing two
headquarters at the same time.

Patton went to see General Smith and found him very

friendly—but noncommittal. While he was in Smith's office,
Bradley happened to drop in, and now the confrontation,
to which both men were looking forward with mixed emotions, was on hand. It went off magnificently.

"Brad!" Patton exclaimed with his broadest grin, jumping
from his seat obviously delighted to see his superior.

"Good to see you, George," Bradley responded warmly
—and that was that. If there was any thought of friction
in the mind of either man it didn't spring to the surface
at their first meeting in London.

"What are your plans?" Bradley inquired.

"I'm at large," Patton said, "to do as I please—Goddamnit. I don't like it, Brad. Don't you have something for
me to do?"

"I've an appointment for lunch," Bradley said, "but why
don't you come and see me after lunch, Georgie? We can
go over things."

It occurred to Patton only when he was going down the
corridor by himself that Bradley had called him "Georgie"
for the first time.

He lunched with Air Chief Marshal Tedder, who was, as
Patton was happy to note, "genuinely" glad to see him (in
contrast to others in the British camp—Monty for example
—who, he thought, were not as pleased to have him
around). Then he went over to Bradley's office to get a peep
at "the Plan," all he could have at this time. Lee had a
private train of his own, and he was placing it at Patton's
disposal for a trip to Scotland, where the *Queen Mary* was
expected the next day with the advance party of the Third
Army. The train was scheduled to leave Euston Station at
4 P.M., so Patton had little time for the plan in Bradley's
office. He studied it earnestly, however, and did not seem
to be unduly elated, which Bradley was quick to notice.

"Well," he asked, "what do you think of it, George?"

"I don't know, Brad," Patton said. "I really don't know.
It seems to be all right as far as it goes—but I don't think
it goes far enough."

Though Bradley was eager to draw him out, Patton had
no time to probe any deeper for the apparent faults of the
plan. But the offhand remark continued to haunt both men.
Bradley was pondering it when he went to bed in his suite
in the Dorchester Hotel. And it kept Patton awake half the
night as his special train was racing through the blackout to
Scotland.

☆

He had to wait until late on January 28th to meet all that he had of the Third Army—a group of 13 officers and 26 enlisted men commanded by Colonel Edward T. Williams, an artillery expert, who was bringing them across the ocean. As far as this handpicked sample of the Third Army was concerned, this was to be the first they would hear that Hodges was out and Patton was in as their commander.

It is often strange how fates begin to roll from widely separated points of departure and converge upon a common destination. Even on January 12th, when this advance party was leaving San Antonio, Patton was still in Palermo at what was probably the deepest abyss of his depression and the most lethargic period of his enforced leisure. He had just returned from Italy hoping to find something that would end his idleness. But there was no news waiting for him, not a word to indicate that anything was afoot.

Yet on those seemingly vacuous days the wheels were already turning and his destiny was getting its latest boost. The Third Army had already been alerted for "overseas movement to the European Theater of Operations." Its first contingent was already en route to Fort Hamilton in New York to embark for Scotland. And General Hodges already knew that this was not the army he would take across the Channel to Normandy. Only Patton was in the dark about his future, and the Third Army about Patton.

He arrived in Greenock at 7 A.M. in rough weather that was whipping the gray-clad ships in the harbor, and had delayed the arrival of the *Queen Mary*. He killed the day by inspecting several depots and a hospital, and entertaining a coterie of British generals and admirals at high tea on Lee's train.

After dinner he was ready to board the *Queen Mary*, crowded with American troops arriving by the thousands for "Overlord." He was tense and curious, but was obviously overjoyed when "Molly" Williams reported to him with his contingent.

Patton shook hands with his men, then addressed them in an impromptu little speech.

"It's my pleasure to welcome you to the U.K.," he said, seasoning his remarks with a minimum of his familiar expletives, just enough to startle the men who thought the taciturn and formal General Hodges was still their boss. "I'm your new commander. There's a lot of work to be done and little time to do it. A special train is waiting on the dock to take you to our CP. We'll leave in an hour."

Despite the great joviality of the welcome and the super-abundance of brass in their reception committee (with two British generals, an air commodore and an admiral Patton had in tow), the Third Army's advance party felt in no mood to celebrate the occasion with any special exuberance. Back at Fort Sam Houston they were apprehensive that they would be left behind and forgotten in the shuffle, for little in their training under Hodges indicated that the Third Army was being prepared for the invasion of the Continent. Yet even though they had yearned for action and a more dynamic leadership, they were not quite prepared for what they were getting.

When Patton now showed up on the *Mary* to welcome them, Sergeant Bill Pajewski punched Corporal Sam McCarthy in the ribs.

"Man," he whispered in obvious consternation, "do you see what I see? It's Old Blood and Guts!"

McCarthy responded by crossing himself.

Patton had been in Britain only four days and did not even know yet what was expected of him, but he had covered an enormous territory. He had established himself in new headquarters at Peover Hall, a baronial estate in Knutsford between Manchester and Liverpool; he inspected the field headquarters of the Services of Supply and a prisoner-of-war enclosure; and looked in on the Ordnance Department, just showing the flag. He had time to spare to hobnob with British nobility and lunch with Major Alexander Metcalf, equerry to the Duke of Windsor when he was King Edward VIII.

On January 31st he was back in London to take possession of an apartment assigned to him for his visits to the capital, and to meet General Alexander M. Patch for a private conference behind its discreet doors.

"Sandy" Patch, one of Patton's oldest friends, was in transit from the Pacific to North Africa, where he was to take command of the Seventh Army. Patton was eager to talk to him about the staff he had left behind and Patch was now supposed to inherit, actually to persuade his successor to let him have his own people and get himself another staff.

Patton was fond of parodying a stanza of *I'm Growing Old*, a nostalgic poem by John Godfrey Saxe, where it said, "As I am growing dimmer in my eyes and deeper in my sighs; as I am growing wiser and older; I am growing fonder of my staff." He did not mean, of course, what the old Vermonter had in mind, a walking stick, but that small body of officers who assisted him in his command. In his highly personal regime, the staff played a peculiarly intimate role —the extension of himself. He once told General Eisenhower, "I don't need a brilliant staff, I want a loyal one." That was exactly what he had, a loyal staff that carried out his orders and ideas with unobtrusive but unfailing efficiency, and was completely subordinated and adjusted to him, his discipline, his routines, his idiosyncrasies.

While Patton was demanding absolute allegiance from his staff, like a feudal Japanese liege lord from his retainers, he was giving it his own loyalty and paternal protection abundantly in return. It did not really matter whether a man had actually proved himself or not, as long as he proved loyal.

General Eisenhower was deeply impressed by Patton's unswerving loyalty to his staff—which he regarded as conclusive proof of Patton's innate softness beneath his crusty and lusty exterior. He recorded a characteristic incident in his own memoirs:

"He once vehemently demanded that I discharge 80 of his officers because, as he said, of inefficiency and timidity bordering on cowardice. He was so exercised and so persistent that I agreed, contingent upon his sending me a report in writing. Apparently astonished by my acquiescence, he began postponing from week to week, on one excuse or another, the submission of his list. Finally he confessed rather sheepishly that he had reconsidered and wanted to discharge no one."

Patton's staff was uneven if assessed one by one on individual merits. Some members were able officers destined for meteoric careers of their own after World War II, in Korea, Germany and elsewhere. Such a man was Colonel Paul D. Harkins, son of a Boston drama critic, who was his Deputy Chief of Staff throughout the war, then moved up to become a full general, and eventually distinguished himself as the American commander in Vietnam in 1962-64.

Others were but little better than mediocrities. Yet as a whole, they constituted a precision instrument which Patton handled with the skill of a Swiss watchmaker. Like the prompter in a theater who knows the part of every player, Patton could perform in emergencies the functions of any of his assistant chiefs of staff—he nevertheless felt bare and helpless without them.

Now he hoped to persuade General Patch to release to him Gay and Harkins, Maddox, Cummings, Muller and Koch, and other members of his staff who had worked for and fought with him in Africa and Sicily. He arranged this meeting to do the persuading in the privacy of his new flat, which he had never seen before.

CHAPTER NINETEEN
IN THE LONDON FOG

It was already dark on this wintry February afternoon when Sergeant Mims drove General Patton to 22 Mount Street in the back of the huge American Embassy on Grosvenor Square, now becoming known as "Eisenhower Platz." The big Packard came to a stop in front of a low brownstone whose undersized front door opened into a small and dark hall.

Patton jumped out and looked at the shabby little house with quizzical eyes, then said to Colonel Codman, who was taking him to his new flat, "Whoever picked this Goddamn place has a genius for cloak and dagger. It seems to be the ideal hideout for a fellow like me they're trying to keep under wraps."

His flat was on the second floor. Patton and Codman groped their way up the steps on the dark staircase and Codman rang the bell, which sounded soft and sweet like the giggle of a bunch of naughty angels. The door was opened promptly by a United States Army corporal obviously detailed to take care of the establishment.

When he saw the new tenant, he came stiffly to attention and stood there saluting as Patton, motionless and mute on the threshold, surveyed the apartment he would henceforth call his own. In the dim indirect lighting he saw a paneled foyer opening into a dainty sitting room with period furniture, thick carpet, exotic prints.

Expecting even worse, Patton roared at the corporal: "Goddamnit, show me my bedroom!"

It was a chintzy boudoir, the walls and curtains all pink, enormous mirrors everywhere—even on the ceiling. It had a cushy white bear rug on the parquet. The room was dominated by a huge bed lying low and lascivious, as Codman described it, under its embroidered silk covers.

"Gee-zuss," Patton said confounded. "An Anglican bordello!"

Then catching his breath, he turned on Codman: "Who the hell picked this Goddamn brothel for me?"

"General Lee, sir," Codman said.

"He did it to spite me, the son of a bitch," he roared.

It was the most feminine setup anyone could find for the Army's most masculine general, and it was even more than just ordinarily feminine. It had been the abode of one of London's most popular and prosperous courtesans who, until her recent eviction, had practiced her trade on these pretty premises, more specifically on the giant bed under the glistening mirror on the ceiling.

Patton was suffocating. As soon as Patch arrived, he told him, "Sandy, let's get the hell out of this Goddamn crib. I'd rather be shot in the streets than spend an evening sitting around this sink of iniquity."

They went to see Robert E. Sherwood's hit play *There Shall Be No Night* with Alfred Lunt and Lynn Fontaine, at the Haymarket Theater in the West End. After the show, they went backstage to compliment the Lunts, and then on to the Savoy with them for an impromptu party. By the time Mims took him home Patton was so exhausted he no longer cared who had been the last occupant of the bed he was now sleeping in.

The growing community of "Overlord" and its bustle started a kind of social season all its own in London, and

Patton was rapidly drawn into it. He was a celebrity in his own right—both famous and infamous for what he had done in Sicily—and now, under Codman's guidance, he was spending part of his time mingling with London's own resident celebrities, including Lady Cavendish, the former Adele Astaire.

It was still mostly trivia. But then things began to quicken with a call from London on February 6th.

"Major John Poston here, sir," Patton heard a youthful-sounding voice on the telephone. "ADC to General Sir Bernard Montgomery. My general sends his compliments, sir, and requests that you report at his headquarters at 1000 on February 11."

Monty at last!

He was looking forward to the meeting with the keenest anticipation and went to London a day ahead of his appointment. This gave him an opportunity to greet a number of old friends who had arrived earlier that day. He had succeeded in bamboozling Patch into letting him have most of his staff, and now they were coming in one after another—Gay, Cummings, Odom, Koch, Hammond, Maddox and Muller. It was getting like old times. Knutsford would soon be like home.

On the morning of the 11th, Patton picked up Bradley at his office on Bryanston Square in the West End and drove him to St. Paul's School in West Kensington, which Montgomery had chosen for his headquarters. On the way, Bradley brought him up to date.

Montgomery, a slight, wiry, erect figure, unpressed as usual, received them in the dark, high-ceilinged, musty room from which he had evicted his former High Master. He was flanked by General Miles Christopher Dempsey, who was to command one of his armies in the invasion, and "Freddy" de Guingand, his Chief of Staff.

"You've seen the Plan, Patton?" he said.

"I've seen it but did not have much of a chance to study it yet," Patton answered.

"Did you like what you saw of it?" Monty asked.

"No," Patton said with a grin. "It doesn't give me anything to do."

"It was not good at all when the P.M. first showed it to me a few weeks ago at Marrakesh," Montgomery said without going into Patton's deeply felt, but jocularly voiced, objection. "I told the P.M. that the initial landing was on too narrow a front and was confined to too small an area. The *initial* landing must be made on the widest possible front, and British and American areas of landing must be kept entirely separate. I also insisted that the air battle must be won before the operation is launched."

"Ike had come to the same conclusions independently," Bradley interpolated in a rush of loyalty, "as soon as he saw the plan. General Morgan is now working on the revision."

"Yes," Monty said with a smile behind which Bradley sensed a broader meaning.

It was becoming known around Norfolk House that "Brookie" and Monty," who smarted somewhat because they had to work under an American Supreme Commander, did not think much of Eisenhower's savvy as a strategist. The crucial deficiency of the original plan was spotted by Montgomery when he spent the night before New Year's studying it in transit in Marrakesh, and by Eisenhower on January 16th, when he had his first chance to see it. By then Montgomery's objections were widely known and some Britons close to Brooke were inclined to accuse Eisenhower of plagiarizing Monty's recommendations rather than accept this as the accidental meeting of great minds.

As Brooke wrote in his diary on January 24th in one of his petulant moods: "Had a long C.O.S. meeting at which Eisenhower turned up to discuss his paper proposing increase of cross-Channel operations at expense of South France operations. I entirely agreed with the proposal, but it is certainly not his idea and is one of Monty's. Eisenhower has got absolutely no strategical outlook."

Montgomery now went further into details of the plan. Lecturing with his usual broad and sweeping pontification, he told Patton, "We must aim at success in the land battle by the speed and violence of our operations."

Patton liked the robust spirit of these words, but felt that while they might have reflected Monty's mood of the moment, they certainly contrasted strongly with his methods of waging war. He was, however, much impressed with several of Montgomery's practical suggestions. He especially liked his changes in the assault, which the planners had made far too complicated with all sorts of gadgets they thought would be needed on D-Day to break through the fortifications of the Atlantic Wall and the obstacles

Rommel was creating in the water to protect the beaches.

Montgomery described them as unnecessary, likely to encumber the troops who would storm the beaches without aiding them appreciably. He had stopped the work of the gadgeteers in an experimental armor division set up for this special purpose the year before even though it was commanded by his own brother-in-law, Major General Phillips Hobart.

On the whole, it was a spirited and very friendly first encounter. Patton proved an excellent listener on this occasion. He was keenly interested in Monty's expositions and, on his own part, didn't know enough of the plan as yet to put in his own tuppence.

Just before the meeting broke up, Montgomery changed the subject and began to speak of the larger issues of the war. Then quite abruptly he told Patton, "I am afraid the beachhead at Anzio is apt to be lost."

He revealed "in great confidence" the unlikely intelligence that "4,000 vehicles had already been evacuated on February 9th, in preparation for a possible abandonment of the beachhead."

Suddenly, for a fleeting moment, Anzio loomed in General Patton's life in one of the more mysterious and frustrating episodes in his wartime career. At 1:30 A.M. on February 16th, he was awakened at Peover Hall by Colonel Codman with an urgent message.

"I am sorry to disturb you, General," he told him, "but Commander Butcher has just called from London. General Eisenhower wants you to report to him right away."

"What do you mean right away?" Patton asked.

"Butcher said it is extremely urgent, sir."

Patton started at 6 o'clock in the pitch dark of the foggy winter morning, arriving at Grosvenor Square at 10:45 A.M. Taken to see Eisenhower immediately, he found Ike in a grim mood. He said to Patton in a most serious voice:

"I'm afraid, George, you'll have to eat crow again for a little while."

Patton was seized by one of those uneasy feelings that always went to the pit of his stomach.

"What the hell have I done now?" he asked sheepishly.

"Things are going awfully bad at Anzio," Eisenhower said, "and it seems Lucas cannot cope with the situation. We hate to give up the beachhead—it would be a tremdous feather in the cap of the Nazis and would be a greater psychological blow to us, just now when we need all the confidence we can muster for 'Overlord.' "

He paused for effect, then said solemnly:

"You will have to take command of the beachhead in Italy, George, and straighten things out down there."

"For Pete's sake, Ike," Patton exclaimed, "that's not eating crow! It's a great compliment, sir. You know, God-damnit, that I'd be willing to command anything from a platoon up in order to fight!"

Patton could not know, and died without knowing, that the idea of the Anzio strike—"the cat-claw," as Churchill called it—was suggested to the Prime Minister by the success of his two amphibious reports in Sicily during the advance on Messina. The impression they made on the Prime Minister was lasting and served to imbed Patton in his mind as an exceptional combat leader, the best of the Americans.

When the fighting in Italy became deadlocked in January, 1944, by stiff German resistance on the 50-mile front between Cassino and the sea, Churchill recalled Patton's bold strikes. He thought that the situation could be changed for the better and Rome reached faster by "pulling a Patton" in Italy with an amphibious flanking attack.

"I had never succeeded in getting this maneuver open to sea power included in any of our desert advances," Churchill wrote, recalling rather ruefully how Brooke and Montgomery had persistently refused to accept his recommendations during the campaign against Rommel. "In Sicily, however, General Patton had twice used the command of the sea flank as he advanced along the northern coast of the island with great effect."

In December, 1943, Churchill, bedded down with a siege of flu in Marrakesh, used his proximity to the scene of the battle to peddle his idea to Eisenhower and Alexander. Eisenhower was on his way to "Overlord" and washed his hands of the venture, but agreed with the Prime Minister in principle that it was a promising idea. Alexander accepted the suggestion avidly. He recognized immediately the opportunity to employ a two-handed punch to catch the Germans in a pincer movement and capture Rome. On December 18th General Brooke dropped in to see Churchill on the way back from Italy, where he had gained "nothing but depressing impressions." When Churchill broached the idea of the seaborne development, Brooke was, therefore, in a receptive frame of mind. Back in London, he plunged into "a whirlwind campaign to gather resources for the landing on the Roman coast . . . to break the deadlock."

The operation, code-named "Shingle," then took shape. Orders to mount it were issued on January 2nd. Since it was to take place in the Fifth Army's area, it became General Clark's over-all responsibility and General John Lucas' assignment to command it. On January 22nd the Fifth Army's VI Corps, supported by strong British contingents, began three simultaneous landings in the Anzio area. The British 1st Division landed at the same time, and the 3rd Division of General Truscott went ashore at beaches east of Nettuno. The Germans were caught by surprise. The assault forces reached their preliminary objectives by noon on D-Day and continued toward their initial bridgehead line about seven miles inland.

The landing threw Hitler into a rage. He resolved to defend Rome with the same tenacity he showed at Stalingrad. It took him a few days to regain his composure and organize his forces, but on January 28th he teletyped Field Marshal Kesselring, his Commander in Chief in Italy: "The next days will see the unleashing of the battle of Rome. It will decide the defense of central Italy and the fate of our Tenth Army. However, the significance of this historic battle is much greater, because the landing at Nettuno marks the beginning of the invasion of Europe, which the Allies are planning for 1944."

A German counterthrust was expected, but when it came, its power and fury found the Allies off balance. The Germans attacked with four divisions supported by 450 guns, and drove a deep and dangerous wedge into the Anglo-American line, almost forcing it back to the original beachhead. "All hung in the balance," Churchill wrote. "No retreat was possible . . . I had no illusions about the issue. It was life or death."

Though the operation was limited in scale, this was one of the great emergencies of the war. The date was February

16, 1944—less than four months before the D-Day of what Hitler called the *Grossinvasion*.

In this moment of crisis the thoughts of the Allied leaders converged on General Patton. General Alexander in particular was yearning for him to correct a situation he regarded primarily as the result of the tactical command's tragic failure on the spot. From the beginning of the operation, Alexander had viewed Lucas with considerably less than confidence, repeatedly trying to persuade General Clark to "relinquish the services of General Lucas," as he politely expressed it. But Clark refused.

When disaster now confronted him, Alexander asked, "What did go wrong with the Anzio operation?" The answer was clear, he thought—Lucas! That hapless American general had missed his opportunities by being too slow and cautious. "He failed to realize the great advantage the surprise had given him," Alexander wrote. "He allowed time to beat him."

In the great crisis Alexander went to Clark and forced the issue in language which he thought Clark would not misunderstand or ignore. "You know, the position is serious," Alexander told him. "We may be pushed back into the sea. That would be very bad for both of us—and you would certainly be relieved of your command."

This gentle injunction, as Alexander called it, brought the desired results. With Clark's agreement, Alexander sent a telegram to Brooke letting him know at last that "he was not satisfied with Lucas as commander of the corps south of Rome" and asking the Chief of the Imperial General Staff to "consult Eisenhower." Alexander complained specifically that there was no drive in VI Corps and that the British had sustained most of the losses (which was not exactly true).

He did not ask for Patton in so many words but hinted broadly that he would like to get him. "If you cannot send me a thruster like George Patton," Alexander wrote, "I recommend putting a British officer in command. I have already sent a British major general to the headquarters of the VI Corps to stir them on a little."

Field Marshal Brooke called the Prime Minister and relayed Alexander's telegram to Eisenhower. It was at this stage that Ike put in the call for Patton.

Churchill spent the night pondering the problem, and the next morning, February 16th, sent for Brooke. He had settled the command problem at Anzio in his mind in the meantime. "Send Alexander to command the troops in the bridgehead," he suggested.

"I am afraid I rather lost my temper with him over this," Brooke wrote in his diary, "and asked him if he could not for once trust his commanders to organize the command for themselves without interfering and upsetting all the chain and sequence of command."

Thereupon Churchill changed his tune and, taking a cue from Alexander's message, now proposed what he had in mind originally but did not quite dare to propose right off the bat.

"How about sending General Patton?" he asked.

Brooke agreed. He had the highest regard for Patton. He was fascinated by Patton's dash in Sicily and his capture of Palermo and race to Messina. Churchill had no difficulty in convincing Brooke that the situation at Anzio-Nettuno could be remedied virtually overnight by sending Patton to replace Lucas. And his victory in the bridgehead, combined with his impetuosity and drive, would take the Allies to Rome.

Brooke communicated the suggestion to Eisenhower, and Patton was summoned to London. Now Ike showed him a copy of Alexander's telegram and said:

"This is a very delicate matter in all respects. What it amounts to is this. Alexander is trying to get rid of Lucas and is really trying to give the job to one of his own men. I'll never consent to letting a Britisher have the command. However, we will cross that bridge when we get to it. In the meantime I'll loan you for a month. So get ready, George. You'll have to leave immediately."

Eisenhower composed a telegram to Alexander, offering to let Patton take command at Anzio on a temporary basis, called the Prime Minister and cleared it with him, then sent it off with copies to Generals Wilson, Devers and Clark at their various outposts in the Mediterranean.

The wheels began to turn. Two planes—a C-54 and B-25 —were ordered to stand by warmed up, ready to take Patton to Italy. Patton phoned Peover Hall, ordered Captain Stiller, "his fighting aide," to join him in London for the trip, then talked to Sergeant Meeks and instructed him to come along and bring his "fighting equipment."

He spent the rest of the day organizing a special staff for Anzio. General Gaffey was to go with him as Chief of Staff while Gay would stay in Knutsford to "keep the Third Army in shape." Colonel "Mollie" Williams was going as his artillery officer.

With Clark not too favorably disposed to him and a preponderance of British kibitzers at the beachhead, he worried that he would have too many monkey wrenches thrown in to prevent him from making a success of his assignment. Eisenhower promised that he would back him to the hilt. General Marshall was then told of the arrangements by special messenger.

Patton was up at daybreak next morning, making his last minute arrangements. He was planning to fly out in the afternoon. He ordered his staff to join him at 12:45 P.M. at the Mount Street flat, then drove to Middlesex Hospital, where he had an appointment with Professor Wydham to have a spot on his lip treated with X-ray. It was causing him some concern, but the doctor—a prominent cancer specialist—assured him that he had no reason to worry.

While Patton was being treated at the hospital, he was called to the telephone to take an urgent message from Ike's office. The caller was Lieutenant Colonel "Tex" Lee, one of the Supreme Commander's aides. "We are looking for you, General, all over the town," he said breathlessly.

"Well, Goddamn it," Patton said. "Here I am. What do you want?"

"General Eisenhower instructed me to tell you, sir, that you may return to Knutsford at your convenience."

That was all. The trip to Anzio was off. Apparently it was one of those trips in this war that was *not* necessary.

On February 17th, General Lucas was relieved by General Truscott, described by Churchill as "a young American divisional commander whom everyone speaks of most highly." Drawn into the crisis, then peremptorily excluded from it, Patton felt like the bride who was stood up at the altar.

Although Patton considered the strange affair a closed chapter, he nevertheless tried to find out just what had caused the abrupt cancellation of his eagerly sought mission. But all he would hear in London was, "The situation had changed in the meantime and you were no longer needed."

He found out only in the spring of 1945 that General Clark had been instrumental in foiling his trip. The mission was canceled because Clark had objected to Patton's assignment in no uncertain terms, reputedly exclaiming when the copy of Eisenhower's telegram of February 16th reached him at Caserta, "This won't do. I don't want Patton in my theater." He got in touch with London via Alexander and suggested what became a way out of the impasse—that Truscott be named instead of Patton.

Patton's final reaction to the abortion of his mission was a shrug of his shoulder. He always regarded his opportunities as unlimited and his chance to attain greatness in this war assured by fate. He did not cry over the loss of a gratuitous break that seemed to be a fluke anyway. He returned to his job in "Overlord" with greater alacrity and dismissed the Anzio interlude—this point of no departure—from his mind forever.

CHAPTER TWENTY
MASTER OF PEOVER HALL

General Patton continued to have some trouble with his lip, and returned to Middlesex Hospital from time to time for X-ray treatments. Professor Wydham reassured him that the ominous white spot was only a harmless sore caused by too much sun in Tunisia and Sicily, but Patton had made his own diagnosis.

"After all the ass kissing I have to do here," he said, "no wonder I have a sore lip."

Patton was now established in the fertile flatlands of Cheshire in west-central England near Knutsford, an urban district of some 6,500 people between Manchester and Liverpool. Knutsford's name commemorated the crossing of the Mersey River by King Canute in the 11th century. It also had a more recent claim to literary fame. The place was immortalized by Elizabeth Claghorn Caskell, the biographer of Charlotte Brontë, in her romantic tales of 19th-century British village life, *Ruth* and *Cranford*.

Headquarters was split between Peover Camp and Toft Camp, two former British military installations. Patton had his offices and living quarters in Peover Hall, an ivy-

covered, black-and-white-timbered manor house that had
been the home of the Manwaring family for 800 years and
had passed to the Peels of Knutsford when the Manwarings
died out. At the time Patton lived there, Peover Hall was
owned by a Manchester merchant.

His favorite place at the Hall was the chapel. He occupied
the Master of the Hall's pew, sitting next to the effigy of a
knight and his lady, under a pasteboard plaque that read:
"To the Glory of God and the Honor of the Manwaring
Family." The chapel now has an American flag placed
beneath a bronze plaque whose inscription reads: "This flag
is placed here to commemorate the fact that the Commanding General and his staff and members of the American
Third Army worshipped here during the Second World War,
1944."

Patton lived in style as always, hobnobbing with the
landed aristocracy of the neighborhood and dining them at
the Hall at parties that invariably ended with the showing
of American motion pictures. Yet he was, as all commanding generals by necessity are, the loneliest man at Peover
Hall. He regarded his staff affectionately, but he had no
friends in his entourage. His closest companions were Sergeant Meeks and Willie, the English bull terrier "orphaned"
when his master, an RAF pilot, was killed on a bombing
mission over Germany. Patton had found Willie in a kennel
in London and bought him, chiefly because the dog's
ferocious appearance appealed to him. He was mortified,
however, when he found on closer acquaintance that Willie
was amiable. He immediately started to train him to
acquire aggressiveness, but abandoned the effort when, on
March 10th, Willie ran into a command and reconnaissance
car and came off second best.

He lavished his affection on the dog and even had Willie,
sitting up on a chair, dine with him at his table. The dog
reciprocated, and it was quite moving to watch Patton
scuffling with his forbidding-looking but meek pet in his
moments of raucous bliss.

Patton now had virtually every member of his experi-
enced staff with him at Peover Hall—Colonel Frederick S.
Matthews as G-1, Colonel Halley G. Maddox as G-3,
Colonel Walter J. "Maud" Muller for G-4, Colonel Elton F.
Hammond as his Signal Officer, an oldtimer, Colonel
Nicholas W. Campanole, for G-5; his chaplain, Colonel
James H. O'Neill; his Adjutant General, Colonel Robert E.

Cummings; his Chief of Ordnance, Colonel Thomas H. Nixon, and many more. Colonel Oscar W. Koch, his G-2 at Fort Benning, was again working for him in that capacity. The only important newcomer was Colonel "Molly" Williams, whom he was glad to inherit from the original Third Army.

Immediately upon his arrival late in February, Koch set up the War Room in the Hall, and Patton began a daily ritual of which he was master—staff conferences at which he briefed himself and also imparted his own wisdom to the staff.

By March 1st his staff organization was complete, and he started it off on rigorous individual and collective efforts of planning. It was a gigantic effort, this preparation of a whole army for the showdown battle of the European phase of World War II. The command group and the staff had to be reorganized and adjusted to Patton's personnel and policy requirements. The impending operation had to be studied in the most minute detail, both tactically and logistically. The incoming troops had to be received, lodged, trained, and briefed. Operations plans and supply matters had to be coordinated with higher headquarters, and within the Third Army's own headquarters organization.

At Peover Hall there never was any doubt who the boss was, because everything stemmed and flowed from Patton, and vibrated with his nervous energy. But in London it was different. There he was playing it low and safe, getting that sore lip, as he put it, from licking boots. Although he was out of the doghouse, he was not quite out of the woods. Everybody else seemed to be closer to the planning of "Overlord"; closer to Ike; closer to the rapidly developing events.

Patton was to command one of the American armies in France. That, at least, seemed to be settled for good and, he ardently hoped, nothing he would do in the meantime— or would be done to him—would take the Third Army away from him. But it was not slated for "Neptune," the assault phase of the operation, in which Bradley would have only the First U.S. Army under Montgomery's over-all command. Patton still had merely a bare outline of what his

Third Army was to do after "Neptune." For the time being, he figured prominently only in a negative kind of operation —an elaborate maneuver of deception designed to mislead the enemy.

To screen "Overlord" from the Germans, General Morgan had developed a plan, called "Bodyguard," to misrepresent the Allied strategy in Europe and to induce the German High Command to make faulty dispositions for the *Grossinvasion*, as they called "Overlord." A "cover plan" called "Fortitude" was drawn up and put into effect to give the impression that Normandy would not be the main point of attack but, on the contrary, the Pas-de-Calais area across the narrower waters of the English Channel.

"Fortitude" was based on the fiction that the campaign would begin with an attack on southern Norway launched from Scottish ports in mid-July, about 45 days later than the initially designated real D-Day. Arrangements to simulate preparations for the attack on Norway included the formation of a nonexistent British force called the "Fourth Army," apparently commanded by Lieutenant General Sir Andrew Thorne. At the same time, an imaginary American force consisting of 12 divisions was conjured up with dummy troops, contrived radio traffic (conducted with purposeful indiscretion), and make-believe exercises, for the operation directed against the Pas-de-Calais.

Patton was a major fixture in "Fortitude." The Germans had already learned to respect and, indeed, fear him. He was, in fact, the only American general to impress them at all and whose name meant anything to them at this stage. They assumed that the American forces in the main invasion effort would be led by him and, therefore, the main effort would be where he would appear. (Later, when he was conspicuous by his absence in Normandy in June and July, the Germans did retain substantial forces—their entire Fifteenth Army in the Pas-de-Calais area in the expectation that Patton would land there with *Armeegruppe Patton,* as he appeared in German intelligence and situation reports.)

Patton appreciated the importance of the hoax but did not enjoy his role in it. He was especially chagrined that his clearly secondary—as a matter of fact, fictitious—part in "Overlord" removed him from the planning of the campaign in which Bradley was now leading the American contingent. A man of profound curiosity with a naturally quizzical mind, he had his antennae out in all directions, determined to pick up whatever he could, either hard intelligence or soft gossip.

But he was getting everything second-hand, While General Wedemeyer was in London, he would see Patton at Mount Street and bring him the latest news, to which the visiting fireman had easier access than the new commander of the Third Army. It was Wedemeyer who had first told him, on the afternoon of February 17th, that Truscott had been given the beachhead at Anzio which Eisenhower had assigned to Patton only the day before. Then General Hull showed up in London, on his way to Italy as General Marshall's seeing eye "to find out why Rome was not taken," and kept him posted on the Washington scene. Hull also assured Patton that he was still as strong as ever with General Marshall, and that the Chief of Staff was expecting great things from him even though Bradley was to command the assault.

That assault!

"Overlord" was now rapidly taking shape, but Patton was becoming uneasy about the direction in which it was developing. When he was briefly shown the plan by General Bradley on the day of his arrival in London he felt that something was acutely wrong with it, but could not put his finger on just what it was.

As the plan evolved after Eisenhower's and Montgomery's objection to General Morgan's original design, it committed "Overlord" to a broad but basically limited objective. The invasion was to "seize and secure a lodgment area in continental France from which further operations could be developed." It was to be executed in two "phases"—a term that was to gain significance in later months.

Phase One, given its own code name of "Neptune," was the assault and capture of an initial beachhead, including "the development of airfield sites in the Caen area, and the capture of Cherbourg."

Phase Two, or "Overlord" proper, was to be the enlargement of the area captured in Phase One, to include the Brittany Peninsula, all ports south to the Loire River, and the area between the Loire and Seine Rivers.

The entire operation was designed for 90 days. It was assumed that all objectives would be attained by D plus 90 —and there the plan came to an abrupt end. It contained no provisions for anything after that—after the lodgment area would be secured, that is.

The plan was further subdivided into two operational designs—one for the British troops, the other for the Americans. The initial assault was to be made across selected beaches between Cherbourg and Le Havre by the American and the British forces—the First U.S. Army on the right (in the west) and the Second British Army on the left (east)—both under the command of the 21st Army Group, headed by General Montgomery.

Patton's Third Army was to land through the Cotentin Peninsula between D plus 15 and D plus 60. Its mission was to be executed in two phases: Phase One called for the capture of the Brittany Peninsula and the opening of the Brittany ports (unless this had already been accomplished by the First U.S. Army); in Phase Two, after clearing the Brittany Peninsula, the Third Army was to concentrate on the right of the First U.S. Army and "be prepared to operate to the east either in close conjunction with the First Army or by swinging south of the Loire if a wider envelopment appeared to be feasible."

Patton was still vaguely apprehensive of any real deficiencies in the plan when he heard it explained by Montgomery during their meeting at St. Paul's School on February 11th. But that meeting had a catalyzing effect, because shortly afterward he suddenly recognized what he considered the plan's basic shortcomings.

It was always like this with him. Whenever a difficult problem confronted him, he would cock his brain as he would cock his pistol. He would then dedicate himself body and soul to its solution, excluding everything else from his mind, seeking in undivided concentration the answers to the questions that puzzled him. One could almost see his brain working full blast, like a delicate precision instrument under glass. He would live with the problem day and night, take it to bed with him. Sometimes it seemed he had continued the process even in his sleep, because frequently he would wake up fresh and jubilant, with the perfect solution pat-in his mind.

Some of this effort was fully rational, but part of it often seemed esoteric. Patton's vision protruded like a bent beam beyond the horizon. He could see the future projected clearly on a screen. Now his mind plunged ahead to D-Day, and he saw the course of the invasion with its turns and twists; the huge armies locked in battle; the outcome of the battle and the vistas it opened up.

It was uncanny, to be sure. In moments when he could find no rational explanation for his many accurate prophesies, or for actions he carried out on impulse or instinct, Patton was inclined to attribute to himself some occult faculties. But he was mundane enough to harness this esoteric quality and make the best practical use of it.

In reality, it would be doing injustice to him to ascribe his early recognition of what later came to be demonstrated as the limitations and deficiencies of the "Overlord" plan solely to some mystic divination over which he had no rational control. If it had a psychic source at all, his monitoring of the future had far more tangible resources. His ability to see clearly in February what would happen in July and August had a strong intellectual basis. It was triggered and aided by his consummate knowledge of the historical factors and by his exceptional talent for gauging the basic national character structure of the belligerents in its influence over their actions.

Now "Overlord" became a simple equation for him in which most quantities were available as clues for the deduction of the principal unknown quantity. Patton developed his critique of the plan on a characterological premise, by calculating how the British would react to certain challenges in given situations; how the Americans would respond; and what the Germans would do in answer to the overpowering stimulus of the invasion. He then reduced the answer from the collective to the individual level, and thus anticipated, for example, how Montgomery would act in a set situation confronting him within the framework of the "Overlord" plan.

He reread the opening sentence of the plan: "The object of 'Overlord' is to secure lodgment on the Continent from which further offensive operations can develop." Right there Patton saw a major deficiency—the plan was "timid" —it did not go far enough.

As Patton saw it at this stage—six full months before his premonitions became reality—"Overlord" might burst its seams and erupt beyond its farthest phase line. He recognized the need for another plan beyond "Overlord" to anticipate such an eventuality. Instead of devising the means merely for the establishment of the lodgment area, Patton oppressively felt the need for the broadest strategic plan— indeed, for a plan that envisaged the decisive defeat of Germany in the wake of and as the direct sequel to "Overlord."

Moreover, he thought it was "highly probable" that the British would get "boxed in" in their area and would drag the entire operation into a standstill at best, or defeat at worst. The plan assigned the conquest of the rich Calvados region astride the Orne River to General Montgomery's own Second British Army. D-Day itself was designated as the deadline for the capture of Caen, approximately 25 miles inland from the beaches, recognized from the outset as the pivot of the British effort.

Patton concluded—and firmly at that, without any quali- fications—that this would be too tough a nut for Mont- gomery to crack. Although what Monty had told him a few days before was still ringing in his mind—that "speed and violence" were his primary aims to assure "success in the land battle"—Patton doubted that he would be able to produce either the speed or the violence needed to deliver the goods.

However, he went considerably beyond mere prognosti- cation. He designed a plan of his own—which he came to call "the Third Plan"—to forestall the consequences of Monty's failure to make good on his assignment and to provide for a substitute plan that would propel the invasion with its own impetus irrespective of what happened to the Second British Army.

In barest outline, Patton's idea was to hold the Third Army in a strategic reserve ready for immediate employ- ment. Should either the First Army or the Second British Army "get boxed in," it could then be thrown across the Channel and land in the Calais region to bring the invasion forward and retain its momentum.

He could hardly wait until the next morning to share both his misgivings and his remedial plan with General Bradley. At 9 o'clock, he was in Bradley's office, outlining his grand design.

"Brad, I am worried about 'Overlord,' " Patton began.

"So am I, George," Bradley replied somewhat uncer- tainly, "but what do you have in mind specifically?"

"Remember when you first showed it to me," Patton

said, "I told you I didn't quite like it. Though I knew that
something was wrong with it I didn't know just what it was.
I have thought about it ever since. I have read and reread
that Goddamned plan, Brad, and now I think I know what
makes it bad."

Patton then told Bradley about his basic misgiving. "By
halting at the phase line on D plus 90," he said, "it could
prevent the Allies from making good on their possible
opportunity of winning the war in 1944." Then he spoke
of his apprehension along tactical lines.

"I still don't think the British have their heart in 'Overlord,' " he said, "and the plan, which is *their* handiwork,
shows it. However, that is neither here nor there. What
really bothers me is this. The plan as it now stands was
made for Monty. It was redesigned along his suggestions,
and his suggestions moved along the lines which are the
best for him and all others be damned. Monty told us, you
and me, that he wants to operate swiftly and boldly in the
beachhead, but I think he is incapable of that, congenitally
incapable. He is a good general, Brad, don't get me wrong.
I think he's the best general the Limies have. But he is not
a man for fast and bold action. He is a master of the set
battle, more concerned with not losing the battle than with
winning one."

Then he came to the crux of the matter—the crucial
problem as he saw it.

"Monty is supposed to take Caen on D-Day," Patton
said, "and it is essential that he takes it because our air
force must have those airfield sites. Well, Brad, he won't
take it. He'll need some time to get established in his beachhead and then to prepare the next move slowly and carefully. He'll take his time and in the meantime the Germans
will get ready for the counterattack."

"What do you propose, George?" Bradley asked.

"We should be prepared to land whatever troops are left
in England in the vicinity of Calais, following an air
bombardment of the nature used at Pantelleria. I have
talked to Spaatz about it and he agrees with me."

There was not much Bradley could do except listen. He
had nothing to do with this kind of planning in the rarefied
atmosphere of strategy.

Patton then reduced the "Third Plan" to paper and gave
copies of it to Beetle Smith and Tooey Spaatz, hoping it
would reach General Eisenhower through them and in the

end get to General Morgan via Ike. Spaatz responded enthusiastically. General Smith also expressed interest. But if it ever reached Eisenhower, Patton never saw any indication that it had ever been considered seriously by him or his planners.

The "Third Plan" wound up in one of the gilded pigeon-holes of Norfolk House.

In his anxiety and his enthusiasm Patton overlooked the fact that he was stepping on sensitive toes. Planning was by then completely dominated by General Montgomery, who, as one of his British colleagues put it, "had the right of it all along."

Patton was by no means alone in his anxiety. General Morgan, who headed the top planning staff, also had misgivings along those same lines. But when Montgomery, with Brooke's forceful help, succeeded in carrying his point and got the planners to change the original design by giving him what he wanted—a free hand in his assigned area—any modification of the original plan became impossible. Montgomery certainly did not want Patton or anybody else breathing down his neck, and especially taking the glory of victory away from him—a victory he did score eventually, but far behind schedule.

Patton, in his ambiguous and precarious situation, was not the ideal person to intervene in the strategic plans of the invasion, and he knew it. He, therefore, filed his "Third Plan" and tried hard to forget it, concentrating on planning for his own Third Army, whose elements had started to arrive in March.

But just when he was at last becoming a general with an actual army to command, certain incidents occurred that threatened to end his usefulness and to remove him from the theater altogether. For a brief but hectic period it seemed that Patton had again forfeited his last chance to make his eternal mark in a world war.

☆

CHAPTER TWENTY-ONE
DISMAL DAYS

During the second half of March, 1944, the Germans, after intensive efforts to track down General Patton, finally located him. "It has now been clarified," an entry in the *Wehrmacht* High Command's *Kriegstagebuch* (War Diary) read on March 20, "that . . . General Patton, who was formerly employed in North Africa and is highly regarded for his proficiency, is now in England."

This was a high compliment to Patton—he was the only American general aside from Eisenhower to rate specific mention in the War Diary up to this time. He had been quick to attract the attention of the Germans in North Africa, then impressed and intrigued them in Sicily. His personality, whereabouts and activities keenly interested the Nazi intelligence services, for through them the enemy hoped to find clues to the plans and intentions of the Allies.

The Germans had found out about "Overlord" in November, 1943, from top secret documents the valet of the British Ambassador to Turkey had stolen from his employer's old-fashioned safe in Ankara. When Eisenhower's appointment as Supreme Commander was announced on Christmas Eve, they concluded that the *Grossinvasion* had been finally decided upon. On January 6, 1944, the three section chiefs of *Abwehr*, the *Wehrmacht* High Command's central intelligence service, and the head of *Abtelung Fremade Heere-West*, the Western Branch of the German Army's Intelligence Division, were summoned to the Führer's headquarters and instructed by General Jodl to broaden their surveillance of the Allied build-up. Special attention was to be paid to Allied activities in southern Italy because Jodl assumed they would provide "invaluable clues, not merely for the intentions of the enemy in the Mediterranean, but also for the over-all intentions of the Anglo-Americans."

By February 8th enough information was on hand to enable the head of the Western Branch of German Army Intelligence to prepare a definitive estimate of the situation:

"For 1944 an operation is planned outside the *Mediterranean* that will seek to force a decision and, therefore, will be carried out with all available forces. This operation is probably being prepared under the code name of 'Overlord.' The intention of committing large forces becomes clear from the fact that the operation is expected to produce the final military decision within a comparatively short period of time . . . The distribution of enemy forces and troop movements clearly point to England as a point of departure."

At the same time, German intelligence services were ordered to follow the movements of General Patton. They located him in Italy early in January and tracked him back to his palatial doghouse in Palermo. An intelligence estimate dated January 21st deduced from "General Patton's return to Sicily" that "the Seventh U.S. Army [was] being maintained in combat readiness for future operations," presumably the *Grossinvasion*. By then it was definitely assumed that Patton would lead major American forces in the invasion. On February 4th he was the subject of a remarkable biographical sketch as one of the *Invasionsgenerale,* Allied generals the Germans expected to participate in "Overlord."

But after the January 21st report, Patton vanished from German surveillance. Several attempts were made to trace him either in Sicily or in England, but no hard intelligence could be produced about his whereabouts and mission. "Clarification" when it came represented no feather in the cap of German Intelligence. His presence in England was simply deduced from an announcement SHAEF issued on March 20th that "General Patton [had] relinquished command of the Seventh Army for another army command," which, however, was not identified.

It was then assumed by German Intelligence that he had been given command of what Axis agents in England variously called *Armeegruppe Patton* and "Ninth Army." At no time, it seems, did they succeed in identifying the Third Army by its name and organization. The War Diary continued to refer to it as "AOK 9" (Ninth Army) even after it had become operational in Normandy under its own flag and famous name.

This German preoccupation with Patton was ingeniously exploited by SHAEF to deceive the enemy. But this was not the sole reason for keeping him under wraps. The Allied high command thought it prudent to conceal Patton, not only from the enemy in Germany, but also from his own enemies in the United States.

Although he was busy organizing and training the Third Army, Patton was still on probation. On March 23rd, with fingers crossed, Secretary of War Stimson issued a hopeful statement that "the soldier slapping incident [was] closed," but Patton's employment in "Overlord" was not taken for granted by any means. It depended on his continued good behavior.

Yet even then Patton was in trouble again up to his neck. He figured in a strange case that threatened to snowball into another "slapping incident," but with more ominous overtones because it involved "murder"—the "massacre" of two groups of German prisoners of war.

The incident harked back to the Sicilian campaign. On June 23, 1943, while putting the finishing touches to "Husky," Patton embarked on a four-day tour to welcome some of his troops coming directly from the United States, and to witness a series of landing exercises at Arzeu, near Oran. With the invasion of Sicily less than three weeks away, Patton feared that his men were not quite ready for the test, either in training or spirit.

What he then found seemed to confirm his apprehensions. At Oran, he inspected the whole convoy that had brought the 45th Infantry Division from the States.

He went on to watch the landing practice of the seasoned 1st Division, anxious to have everything go smoothly because he had the top brass along to watch the exercises. General Marshall was present, accompanied by Generals Eisenhower, Bradley and Lucas, but the Navy let him down. It was 50 minutes late in putting a combat team of the division ashore and missed the beach by as much as four miles. Although the troops were not rattled by the mishap and performed in a "superior manner," Patton became filled with dark forebodings. What would happen, he pondered, if the Navy missed the beaches by such a margin in Sicily?

Pent up and exasperated, he responded with acts and words over which he *seemed* to have lost control. He took out his anger on the division and chewed out Terry Allen, its commanding general. Then he stormed the beach just as the first GI's came stumbling out of the water.

Patton confronted the startled riflemen by shouting, "And just where in hell are your Goddamn bayonets?" He went on to "blister them with his oaths" while Marshall and Eisenhower, standing within earshot, watched the scene in what General Bradley later described as "embarrassed silence."

According to Bradley, "Major General Harold R. Bull, an officer on Eisenhower's staff, nodded toward General Marshall and whispered to me, 'Well, there goes Georgie's chance for a crack at higher command. That temper of his is going to finish him yet.' "

Patton was impervious to such a possibility. Grinning, he rejoined the group and said, "Chew them out and they'll remember it." He knew he did not have to worry about the 1st Division. He was principally concerned about the 45th Division. Although it was commanded by Major General Troy H. Middleton, one of the Army's soundest infantry leaders, who had had a spectacular career in World War I, it still showed plenty of rough edges. The greenest unit in "Husky," it had the tough assignment of holding a 15-mile open beach and capturing Biscari airfield, a key objective, by D plus 2. These landing exercises at Arzeu, in the immediate wake of a long sea journey from the United States, would be all the practice the troops would get prior to the "real thing."

The exercises took place on June 25th in two installments, with the Navy compounding its previous errors. The 180th Regiment was three hours late due to naval error, and the 179th was put ashore several miles northeast of its target. And yet Middleton's expert hand was evident in their apparent readiness for combat.

Although General Patton was reassured by the showing of the 45th Division, he felt that being total strangers to war, its personnel needed one of his combustible pep talks to give them an awareness of combat. He decided to address the men on June 27th, not with just one of his routine speeches, but with a special talk that would bring home all the perils and hardships of war on this eve of their baptism of fire.

Patton spent some time working on the speech, and when he had it down in notes from which he would deliver it, he was satisfied that it was a "helluva good talk, one of my best." He delivered it in two shifts because the division was split. But he was speaking from the same notes and, therefore, both talks were virtually identical.

"Clearly all of you must know that combat is imminent," he said. "However, it is probably not so near as many of you imagine. You men of the 45th Division must face the fact that you are competing with veterans, but don't let that worry you. All of them, too, fought their first battle, and all of them won their first battle just as you will win yours.

"Battle is far less frightening than those who have never been in it are apt to think. All this bull about thinking of your mother, and your sweetheart, and your wives (who should also be your sweethearts) is emphasized by writers who describe battles not as they are but as writers who have never heard a hostile shot or missed a meal think they are.

"Battle is the most magnificent competition in which a human being can indulge. It brings out all that is best; it removes all that is base. All men are afraid in battle. The coward is the one who lets his fear overcome his sense of duty. Duty is the essence of manhood. Americans pride themselves on being he-men and they *are* he-men.

"Remember that the enemy is just as frightened as you are, probably more so. They are not supermen. We have licked the best of them, and those whom we shall face in the next fight are not the cream of the crop. Further, remember that in fist fights or in battle the attacker wins. You cannot win by parrying. Yet the enemy, being uncertain of our intentions, must parry."

Patton went on to share with these raw young soldiers the *basic doctrine of combat* as he saw it, now spelled out with amazing brevity and lucidity. He quoted General Charles L. Scott, a diminutive man who was fond of saying, "By God, I could lick Joe Louis if he wasn't permitted to attack me!" He recognized the tremendous wisdom in his quip by his old friend and mentor. "The way to prevent the enemy from attacking you is to attack him," Patton said, "and keep right on attacking him. This prevents him from getting set . . . Death in battle is a function of time and effective hostile fire. You reduce the hostile fire by your fire. You reduce the time by rapid movement.

"We Americans are a competitive race," he said in conclusion. "We bet on anything. We love to win. In this next fight, you are entering the greatest sporting competition of all times. You are competing with Americans and with Allies for the greatest prize of all—victory; and the one who wins the prize is the one who first attains victory—captures his objective. Never forget that. And remember also that the Deity, in whatever form you think of Him, is with us."

Also on June 27th, Patton drafted a message to his new army for delivery to the troops at sea. It was a message of enduring quality, for it revealed several facets of Patton— including some his critics and detractors refused to recognize and appreciate. "Many of you have in your veins German and Italian blood," he said, "but remember that these ancestors of yours so loved freedom that they gave up home and country to cross the ocean in search of liberty. The ancestors of the people we shall kill lacked the courage to make such a sacrifice and remained slaves."

Patton's mention of "freedom" and "liberty" in direct context with his blunt reference to "the people we shall kill" was characteristic. He recognized the strange paradox in the two contrasting motivations that had to propel his citizen-soldiers—the subtle ideological impulses dormant within them and an unflinching toughness with which these sheltered American boys had to be imbued. If the two could be fused into a dynamic combination, Patton believed, it would make them invincible. He would tell his troops in one breath, "The fact that we are operating in enemy country does not permit us to forget our American tradition of respect for private property, noncombatants, and women," and admonish them in the next to attack "rapidly, ruthlessly, viciously and without rest," and to "kill" even civilians who "have the stupidity to fight us."

How far Patton's pep talk to the 45th Division succeeded in turning his men from carefree habitués of drugstore counters in their hometowns into vicious killers in alien lands is, of course, impossible to gauge. However, echoes of that speech returned months later to cause him another period of acute discomfort.

The 45th Division assaulted its landing area on each side of Scoglitti, a small fishing village, at 6:30 A.M. on July 10th in what General Patton considered to be "the most important of the three American landings, because it lay nearest the Comiso and Biscari airfields." Trouble developed at once. The 180th Regimental Combat Team, whose plight in the Arzeu landing exercises Patton had viewed with mixed feelings, had an especially bad time of it. It took a plastering on the beachhead but broke through the German ring and started off toward its objectives, the two airfields. On Highway 115 (which the GI's renamed "Adolf's Alley" because "that was about where the Italians began crumbling and additional Germans were thrown in to stiffen the line") the regiment ran into elements of the Hermann Goering Division and was hurt.

The fighting was as tough and rough as Patton had predicted. The inexperienced soldiers were appalled by the ruthless determination of the Krauts. Stories of crude atrocities began to spread through the regiment. Rumors floated about that the Germans were shooting Italian soldiers to prevent them from surrendering.

"German atrocities were rampant," First Lieutenant George C. Appell recalled, "and so were ours in retaliation. My driver was captured, was tied to a tree and shot by the Goerings. Then we encountered another German trick. They would rise without weapons, waving their hands in the air and shouting 'Kamerad!' Then, when we went to round them up, they would fall flat and other Germans, concealed behind them, would open up on us. We lost many men due to this. Casualties were severe, and the procedure of taking prisoners was abandoned by both sides."

On July 14th, a detachment of A Company of the 180th, led by a young captain named Compton, was ambushed by some Germans firing from well-concealed positions. It needed all the courage and skill of these green soldiers to smoke them out of their nests. After brisk fighting that lasted for three hours, the snipers were silenced, 43 of them emerging from their holes with hands over their heads. Five were in civilian clothes or in makeshift uniforms.

Captain Compton was overwrought by the difficult action

that had cost him several of his men. When he saw that some of the Germans were in mufti, he lined them up against a barn and had them machine-gunned.

At about the same time and in the same general location, a Sergeant West of C Company was taking 36 Germans to a prisoner-of-war cage in the rear. When they were well out of the combat zone, he made them halt and shot them on the side of a road.

The tragic incidents were promptly reported to General Patton, and he issued orders for the court-martial of Compton and West.

By ordering the men to be tried, he considered the case closed, at least insofar as he was concerned.

Patton finished the Sicilian campaign, sat out his "punishment" in his gilded cage in Palermo, then went on to England to prepare the Third Army for "overlord." On March 29th he left for Northern Ireland to inspect some of his troops training there under Major General Wade Hampton Haislip, who was to command XV Corps. Patton was cheered by what he saw. He was favorably impressed with the 5th Infantry Division under Major General Stafford Leroy Irwin, one of his protégés from Tunisia, where Irwin was artillery officer of the 9th Division.

He then went on to watch the exercise of a reinforced battalion of the 8th Division, commanded by Major General William C. MacMahon, and was moved to write, "It was the best thing of the sort I have seen." During the exercise with live ammunition, two soldiers were hit, one through the calf of the leg, the other in the fat part of his arm. But they refused to drop out, the man hit in the arm going on for a mile, tossing hand grenades.

It was, therefore, in a buoyed spirit that Patton returned to Peover Hall only to be received by General Gaffey, his new Chief of Staff, with some grim news. It had something to do with the killing of those German prisoners in Sicily because, as Gaffey told him, a War Department inspector had come from Washington to investigate the case.

In the meantime, and unknown to Patton, he had become personally implicated in the tragedy. At the trial of Compton and West, defense counsel had raised the issue exactly as Patton's friends (who had advised him against the court-martial) expected. They argued that the defendants were *not* guilty because they had acted upon what was tantamount to orders from Patton himself, issued in the speech delivered to the 45th Division prior to its embarkation for Sicily.

According to the defense, Patton had told the men that "if the enemy resisted until we got to within 200 yards, he had forfeited his rights to live." And as far as the snipers were concerned, he was supposed to have told his men: "When you are sniped at, especially from the rear, the snipers must be destroyed."

Patton recognized the seriousness of the charge and the fact that it could adversely affect his continued command of the Third Army. He went to considerable lengths to prepare his "defense" before discussing the case with Lieutenant Colonel Williams, the officer sent from Washington to conduct the investigation.

☆

On April 5th, accompanied by Colonels Codman and Odom, Patton went to London to face the music. He saw to it that he had legal aid because Colonel Williams had admonished him that whatever he would say could be used against him.

"Naturally," he said, "in none of my remarks did I contemplate the murdering of men who had already surrendered." Apart from any other considerations, he said, the fact that Colonel John K. Waters, his own son-in-law, was a prisoner-of-war in German hands, had made him very careful not to be guilty of doing anything for which there could be retaliation.

The investigation satisfied the Inspector General that the defense of Compton and West had brought Patton into the case merely to confuse the issue, and was "using quite unethical methods" by trying to "manufacture evidence out of whole cloth." Even so, the matter was brought to General Eisenhower's attention, and the Supreme Commander instructed General Hughes to look quietly into the case and see if Patton was in trouble. At the same time, an account of the incident was sent to Major General Alexander D. Surles, Chief of Army Public Relations in Washington, "so that if any unscrupulous correspondent got wind of it, Surles could immediately state the facts."

Ominous though the case seemed at first, it blew out in a friendly meeting at which Eisenhower told Patton, "George, you talk too much."

The case was closed.

Patton's meeting with Eisenhower took place on April 7th. But 18 days later it seemed that Patton had reneged on the assurance he had given the Supreme Commander. This new incident erupted with screaming headlines in every newspaper in England and the United States. Patton was back in a controversy that, in the catalogue of his troubles, became known as the "Knutsford incident."

Toward the end of April, he began a series of what he called "long briefings" to explain details of the "Overlord" plan to his corps and division commanders and their staffs. On April 25th he took time out to attend the opening of a Welcome Club the people of Knutsford had organized to entertain the growing number of American servicemen at Peover and Toft camps. Mrs. Constantine Smith, head of the civic organization behind the club, had asked Patton to be the principal speaker at the opening, but he declined because, as he told Mrs. Smith, he did not want to be "too prominent." However, he agreed to attend the inaugural ceremony in a purely unofficial role.

At 6 P.M. on the 25th, accompanied by Colonel Campanole, his Civil Affairs officer, and Major Stiller, Patton motored to Knutsford. He purposely arrived 15 minutes late, hoping to sneak into the audience unnoticed. But this precaution was in vain, for the ceremony was held up pending his appearance. Dismayed at finding photographers in the courtyard taking pictures of his arrival, Patton remonstrated with Mrs. Smith. She talked to the cameramen, who promised that they would release no picture in which Patton appeared. Mrs. Smith also assured the General that no reporters were present at the ceremonies.

With about 60 persons, mostly women, in attendance, Mrs. Smith opened the proceedings by introducing Miss Foster Jeffery, regional administrator of the Women Volunteer Services, who made a speech pronouncing the club opened. Patton was then asked to say a few words. He replied that it would be proper for him to express his thanks, for, after all, this club had been organized for his men, but he cautioned Mrs. Smith that his presence must not be given any publicity. In her introduction, she then said, "General Patton is not here in his official capacity. He will be speaking to you in a purely friendly way and nothing he will say must be quoted."

Patton ad-libbed a little speech on the importance of Anglo-American unity. "Until today," he said, "my only experience in welcoming has been to welcome Germans and Italians to the 'infernal regions.' In this I have been quite successful, as the troops whom I have had the honor to command have killed or captured some 170,000 of our enemies.

"I feel that such clubs as this are of very real value, because I believe with Mr. Bernard Shaw, I think it was he, that the British and Americans are two people separated by a common language, and since it is the evident destiny of the British and Americans to rule the world, the better we know each other the better job we will do.

"A club like this is an ideal place for making such acquaintances and for promoting mutual understanding. Also, as soon as our soldiers meet and know the English ladies and write home and tell our women how truly lovely you are, the sooner the American ladies will get jealous and force this war to a quick termination, and I will get a chance to go and kill Japanese."

After the little speech, which was as innocuous as Patton could make it, a Mr. Johnson, chairman of the Knutsford Urban District Council, proposed a vote of thanks. It was duly seconded by a British colonel named Thomas Blatherwick in a lengthy address. After some more speeches by the American Consul Armstrong and a man from the Ministry of Information, a certain Mr. Mould, they played *God Save the King* and the *Star Spangled Banner* to close the proceedings.

When the informal affair was over, Patton was asked to remain for dinner, but he excused himself because he felt he "did not wish that much publicity."

The first sign that he was in trouble again came before lunch on April 26th, in a call from Brigadier General Thomas J. Davis, head of SHAEF Public Relations Division, to General Gay, Patton's Deputy Chief of Staff. Davis told

Gay that the morning papers were featuring Patton's speech at Knutsford and asked him to find out what the General had said. The trouble appeared to stem from the fact that some papers said Patton had failed to include the Russians in his remarks—an omission that, strange as it may seem today, was regarded as a serious *faux pas* in 1944.

General Davis' breathless probe was triggered by an angry message General Eisenhower had received earlier in the morning from General Marshall, advising him that Patton's alleged affront to the Soviet Union and his politically loaded remarks were provoking angry outcries in the American press and Congress. The favorite whipping boy of certain legislators and the victim of ill-informed public opinion, Patton was pounced upon for his little talk, the tenor of which was badly misinterpreted. He was attacked by both conservatives and liberals. Republicans charged that he was intruding into politics on the side of the Roosevelt Administration. Representative Karl E. Mundt of South Dakota angrily criticized him on the floor of the House as "an ally of the State Department." At the same time, left-wingers seized upon his alleged omission of the Soviet Union to describe him as a reactionary Red-baiter who had insulted our Russian allies.

The furor caught Marshall completely by surprise, and upset him for a peculiar combination of reasons. As Forrest C. Pogue, the Army's historian of the Supreme Command, described the origins of the "scandal" at the Washington end, "General Marshall, who was trying to win Congressional approval for an Army permanent promotion list including General Patton's name, was dismayed by the incident, which brought into question the Third Army commander's fitness for command and threatened to kill all Army promotions."

When Marshall's first angry inquiry arrived at SHAEF headquarters in Widewing, Eisenhower was not there to handle it with his customary diplomatic tact. He was at Slapton Sands, near Plymouth, witnessing an amphibious landing exercise of the 4th Division. In his absence, the message was handed to General Bedell Smith, his Chief of Staff, whose own name happened to be on the endangered promotion list, and Smith panicked. He answered promptly, without consulting Ike, asking Marshall if "retention of General Patton would diminish the confidence of the public and the government in the War Department." He indicated that if such were the case, "stern disciplinary action would be required." He immediately called Patton at Peover Hall and ordered him, in Eisenhower's name, "to make no more public statements."

Smith's peremptory action while he was still ignorant of the facts, his excitement and tendency to exaggerate the incident out of all proportions became mainly responsible for developing the Knutsford affair into a major crisis in Patton's professional life.

Patton's relations with Ike's chief of staff seemed to be normal enough and even friendly on the surface, with Smith sometimes going out of his way to assure Patton of his good will. But there was a simmering hostility in their real sentiments. It created an undercurrent of tension that characterized the attitude of many of the professionals to the Army's highest-ranking stormy petrel in the European Theater.

Smith's violent reaction to the "incident" was obviously produced by this insipient animosity, aggravated by memories of the Sicilian affair; and maybe by his anxious concern that Patton might be a constant source of trouble to Ike whose welfare the Chief of Staff felt duty-bound to protect. Otherwise it would be difficult to explain why Smith acted with such vehemence, recommending in effect that the American armies' best combat general, so woefully needed for the great campaigns ahead, be fired on the eve of D-Day.

Eisenhower returned to Widewing on April 29th and found the pot boiling over. Reflecting on Patton's apparent inability to hold his tongue, rather than on the merits of the case, he seemed prepared to take drastic action. He informed General Marshall that "on all the evidence now available I will relieve [Patton] from command and send him home," but left a door open by adding, "unless some new and unforeseen information should be developed in the case." He told Marshall frankly that he was reluctant to take this action because, as he put it, "there was always the possibility that the war might yet develop a situation where Patton, despite lack of balance, should be rushed into the breach."

Considering the trivial nature of Patton's *faux pas* (if a *faux pas*, indeed, it was) and what was at stake, this lumping together of his "fitness for command" and Congressional confirmation of a promotion list may seem incongruous, if not preposterous. But promotions mean a lot to professional military men, a fact that, as Commander Butcher put it, "only a regular officer could fully appreciate."

Even before Patton could be fully aware that his future in the war was in jeopardy, Marshall and Eisenhower were burning up the wires debating his fate. Between April 27th and May 3rd, six rather frantic communications were exchanged by the Chief of Staff in Washington and the Supreme Commander in London over this trivia that threatened to deprive the Allies of their most promising combat leader.

The message of April 29th went far to show that Patton was needed but not wanted, and that the high command, with the possible exception of Ike, would have been relieved to get rid of him, even on so minor a pretext as the Knutsford incident. It also showed that Eisenhower fully recognized Patton's immeasurable value to the war effort and was determined to save him, no matter how grave the provocation and pressure.

Patton, on his part, had conditioned himself to take his treatment with philosophical equanimity. He was amused rather than annoyed at being considered an *enfant terrible*. And he was actually pleased that he was tolerated as an erratic genius solely because he was considered indispensable. "I expect I take chances," he remarked, "because I do not have to earn my living in the Army, because of judicious selection of parents and besides I am a soldier— a simple soldier."

But now he was hurt by the uproar, which he regarded as contrived and unfair.

"You probably are damn fed up with me," he wrote to General Hughes who had again been deputized by Eisenhower to investigate another Patton mishap, "but certainly my last alleged escapade smells strongly of having been a frame-up in view of the fact that I was told that nothing would be said, and that the thing was under the auspices of the Ministry of Information [whose representative] was present."

Trying to be philosophical about the uproar, and regarding the incident from a long-range point of view, Patton went on to say: "I have no military ambitions after the war. Therefore, except from the question of a pension, my promotion to a permanent major general is not of paramount importance to me; and I hereby authorize you, if in

your judgment you consider it wise, to state to the Commander-in-Chief that I am perfectly willing to have my
name removed from the list of permanent generals in order
to no longer defer the promotion of other officers.

"Of course, you know what my ambition is—and that is
to kill Germans and Japanese in the command of an army.
I cannot believe that anything I have done has in any way
reduced my efficiency in this particular line of action."

However, the incident at Knutsford was gaining momentum.

He recognized its grave implications on April 30th, when
he received a "blistering letter" from Eisenhower asking
Patton "for a complete explanation and warning him of the
'serious potentialities' of the speech." It was a Sunday.
While Patton was at church, a call came from General
Smith ordering him to report to General Eisenhower
"either at 1100 or 1500" the next day.

In the meantime, General Marshall decided to let Eisenhower handle the case as he saw fit. Assuring him that
public confidence in the War Department had to be
measured against the success of the "Overlord" operation,
the Chief of Staff wrote: "If you feel that the operation
can be carried on with the same assurance of success with
Lieutenant General Courtney H. Hodges in command, for
example, instead of Patton, all well and good. If you doubt
it, then between us we can bear the burden of the already
unfortunate reaction. I fear," he added, "the harm has
already been fatal to the confirmation of the permanent
list."

Just before Patton arrived for the confrontation, Eisenhower received another message in which Marshall reiterated that the War Department's position should not be the
crucial factor in the decision he would have to reach but
"only 'Overlord' and your own heavy responsibility for its
success."

Patton reported to the Supreme Commander at 11 A.M.
and found him "very cordial and, under the circumstances,
considerate." But the issue was far from decided. Eisenhower bluntly told Patton that he might have to send him
home this time, no matter how much he himself would
regret and deplore such an order. The meeting plunged
Patton into despair. It somehow convinced him that he
had reached the end of the road. "I feel like death, but I
am not out yet," he wrote. "If they will let me fight, I will;

but if not, I will resign so as to be able to talk, and then I will tell the truth, and possibly do my country more good."

On the five-hour drive back to Peover Hall, he silently contemplated his fate, and kept reciting poetry to himself.

Arriving at Peover Hall, he sent for Sergeant Meeks and told him to pack his things, adding wryly, "We are going to have to go to the United States this time."

The correspondence between Eisenhower and Marshall continued, but the trend began to favor Patton. Two factors, in particular, aided Eisenhower in making up his mind. He concluded that the incident was far too trivial to warrant the punishment Patton's enemies were demanding. And, as so often in the past, Secretary of War Stimson entered the breach to intervene wisely and gently in his old friend's behalf.

Patton appeared to be reconciled to the worst, and his staff was shrouded in gloom when, on May 3rd, Eisenhower decided to close the case. He informed General Marshall that, aware as he was that "the relief of Patton would lose to us his experience as commander of an Army in battle and his demonstrated ability of getting the utmost out of soldiers in offensive operations," he decided to retain him in command of the Third Army. He wrote to Patton, telling him of the favorable decision "despite damaging repercussions resulting from [his] personal indiscretions," adding sternly, "I do this solely because of my faith in you as a battle leader and for no other motives."

But even before his formal letter could reach Peover Hall, Eisenhower had sent a personal telegram to his friend George with the good news. When Patton had read the message, he called out to General Gay, "The war is over," and suggested that they go and have a drink. Captain George F. Murnane Jr., one of Patton's young aides, happened to be within earshot and assumed that the war was over for his boss. He was amazed at the evident happiness with which the General, Gay and others now celebrated the occasion. "It was some time," Murnane later said with a chuckle, "before I found out my mistake."

The incident dissolved rapidly in gestures calculated to cement the Eisenhower-Patton friendship. Patton wrote a

sentimental letter to Ike, explaining his behavior with con-
summated eloquence and assuring the Supreme Commander of his unflinching loyalty and eternal gratitude.
Before the letter could arrive, Eisenhower called Patton
in person and "was extremely nice."

And yet, the incident left an indelible mark on Patton,
filling him with a deep-seated bitterness that was never to
leave him. It made something snap in his soul, and question
the invincibility of his destiny.

"My final thought on the matter is," he wrote in the
diary, "that I am destined to achieve some great things—
what I don't know, but this last incident was so trivial in its
nature, but so terrible in its effect, that it is not the result
of an accident but the work of God.

"His will be done."

CHAPTER TWENTY-TWO
RETURN TO NORMANDY

July 1, 1944, was one of those days when everything went
wrong. In the morning, General Patton dropped a heavy
blackout curtain on his foot and hurt his toe so badly that
he was in danger of losing a nail. Then he was told that the
daughter-in-law of his new landlord at Braemore House
had been killed in a collision with one of his Services of
Supply trucks. And finally Colonel Harkins reported from
London that according to the scuttlebutt the Third Army
would not become operational until the end of the month
or maybe until August.

The injury to his foot continued to plague Patton for
days (eventually the nail had to be pulled off). He got
around by wearing a spare pair of Sergeant Meeks' shoes,
which were—"fortunately," as he put it—several sizes
larger than his.

The information from Harkins was a heavy blow. The
dispositions of the final "Overlord" plan called for the

employment of the Third Army on the Cotentin Peninsula
between D plus 15 (June 21st) and D plus 60 (August 5th),
but Patton persistently hoped that it would be closer to 15
than 60. But now June was over, and though he felt there
was pressing need for him in France, there was still no
hint as to when and where his Army would join the issue.

The Germans had left substantial forces in the Pas-de-
Calais, expecting him to land there in a second major wave
of the invasion. Patton appreciated this German concern.
He was convinced that Calais would be preferable to the
Cherbourg Peninsula as the point of departure of a campaign ultimately aimed at the heart of Germany and the
destruction of the Reich. "In amphibious operations," he
wrote, "we should land as near the objective as possible.
Calais was nearer this objective than was Cherbourg."

But the ruse was wearing thin. It was becoming increasingly evident even to the Germans that the Allies had committed themselves to the developing Battle of Normandy.

Patton's restlessness was compounded of subjective and
objective elements. The fightingest general in the United
States Army, he was kept behind to bide his time while his
colleagues were in the thick of it. The strain of waiting
was becoming unbearable. "I have a horrible feeling," he
remarked on D-Day, "that the fighting will be over before
I get in." He began to sleep in his trailer and to wear his
shoulder holster to get himself, as he put it, into the proper
frame of mind.

"Time drags very badly for me," he complained. And
Codman, who watched him solicitously during these difficult
days, remarked, "Since D-Day the possibility that the war
might end suddenly had preyed on the General's mind. He
had been edgy, restive. Now he was silent, almost despondent."

But Patton's innate restiveness was never motivated by
only personal factors. It always had at least some collateral
tangible reasons he assumed had a bearing on his destiny.
Now he knew exactly what those reasons were. He thought
Montgomery was making a mess of things in Normandy.

For several days he had been following the operations
closely on his favorite map—an ordinary Michelin touring
map of France, scale 1:1,000,000—and he believed he was
seeing distinct signs that the campaign was moving inexorably toward an impasse. Not everything was bad, of

course. He had checked off Cherbourg, for example, which
had fallen to Major General J. Lawton Collins' VII U.S.
Corps on June 27th; and he expected that Bradley would
now reorient the western elements of his First Army for a
general drive southward. But he did not like what he saw
in the Omaha sector and points east, especially in the
British area around Caen.

The final "Overlord" plan with its defined phase lines had
established firm objectives for D-Day. It contemplated a
steady rate of progress that was to take the United States
forces to the Avranches-Mortain line, and the British
forces to the Flers-Argentan line by D plus 20, or June
26th. Yet now, on D plus 24, the Americans were still
about 35 miles from their second phase line; and the British
had failed to take even Caen, their major D-Day objective.

This was exactly what Patton had told Bradley would
happen. As early as February 18th and several times afterward he had warned that Montgomery, in spite of his
recognition of the importance of speed, would move slowly
and bog down *before* Caen; and that he would then improvise a campaign plan, probably at the expense of the
American forces, very much as he did in Sicily, and even in
Tunisia after Enfidaville.

Now Patton's fear that his prognosis was coming true
developed gradually as he tried to sort the facts from the
chaff of the communiqués over which, he realized, Montgomery had tight control. Monty was obscuring his difficulties with optimistic double-talk, presenting his setbacks as
the desired results of his allegedly preconceived plans. He
was misleading even his superiors with his contrived
euphemisms. Thus on June 13th, when he was a week behind
his schedule at Caen, he wrote to the Chief of the Imperial
General Staff: "Am very satisfied with progress of operations." On the 15th, he wrote to Brooke: "We are in a very
reasonable position in Second British Army," adding, however, that "the American situation is not so good."

When in the light of Montgomery's inability to reach his
objectives General Eisenhower failed to appreciate such
optimism, both Brooke and Monty dismissed him brusquely
with the rudest condescension, insisting that "Ike knows
nothing about strategy" and "Ike has the very vaguest conception of war." Even Churchill's doubts were resented.
Once he dared to question Montgomery's claims, but

Brooke slapped him down. "I flared up," he wrote on July 6th, "and asked him if he could not trust his generals for five minutes instead of belittling them."

But Montgomery could neither intimidate nor fool Patton.

On the basis of his experience in Sicily, Patton considered Montgomery an opportunist to whom phase lines and objectives meant something only when and if he actually succeeded in reaching or taking them. When he found, however, that he could not make them, he would draw up plans of his own, expediently adapted to the changed situations, then claim afterward that what he had so brilliantly done in the end was exactly what he had in mind from the very beginning. This is not necessarily bad generalship—but it is awfully slow.

With his keen sense of empathy Patton now tried to envision blow by blow the next moves Montgomery was likely to make. What he then saw in his mind's eye literally frightened him. He suspected that Montgomery would send the four corps of the First U.S. Army southward to the second phase line while he would merely maneuver his British forces at Caen hoping to draw the Germans from the Americans.

Patton had an opportunity to test his prophetic vision on June 26th, when he met Generals Eisenhower and Bradley near Exeter in England. Bradley told him that even then Monty's staff was busy drawing up a directive for the First Army along the exact lines Patton had traced by his telepathic powers. He was shocked to find that Bradley was all for it and even claimed priority as the original author of the plan, which would take the First Army in what, with considerable poetic license, Bradley called "a swift push from the grassy pasture lands of Normandy to the sleepy banks of the Seine."

"Swift push" . . . "grassy pasture lands," indeed!

As Bradley saw it, the First Army, confined as it was in a relatively small and congested lodgment area, needed elbow room and better ground farther south to use its growing forces to best advantage and fight a war of movement. It became essential to gain terrain more favorable for an offensive—but how and where? Montgomery would "pivot" at Caen while the entire First Army would advance in a single phalanx straight down the Cotentin road from La

Haye-du-Puits into Coutances in the west and from Caren-
tan to St. Lô in the east.

Bradley seemed gratified that the 21st Army Group was
in favor of the plan, and refused to agree with Patton's
reservations about Montgomery. In fact, he had only praise
for Monty's "wisdom, forbearance and restraint," assuring
Patton that the Army Group Commander was granting him
"the latitude to operate as freely and independently as
[Bradley] chose."

Eisenhower agreed with Bradley and approved the plan.
Patton returned to his headquarters with the gravest misgivings. On June 30th, then, Montgomery issued the directive ordering the First U.S. Army to make the breakout
attack while the British Second Army would continue efforts to take Caen and contain the enemy between there
and Villers-Bocage.

Afterward, when the heartbreaking difficulties of this
costly offensive were all but forgotten, Montgomery
claimed full credit for the plan in no uncertain terms, mentioning nothing of Bradley's part in its evolution. In his wrap-
up dispatch after the war, he wrote that he had had it in
his mind all the time as the proper move to make "once
we had secured a good footing in Normandy." As he explained it, "My plan was to *threaten* to break out on the
eastern flank, that is the Caen sector. By pursuing this threat
relentlessly I intended to draw the main enemy reserves,
particularly his armored divisions, into that sector and to
keep them there." It was a peculiar explanation even from a
purely semantic point of view. What was really meant by
the relentless pursuit of a threat?

At the meeting on June 26th, Bradley conceded that the
terrain into which he proposed to push swiftly was not exactly grassy pasture land but was, as he later described it,
"drowned in the rivers and marshlands of the Cotentin
neck" and boxed in everywhere by hedgerows, while the
British faced "undulating plains." He expected that the difficulties of the terrain would be offset by the weakness of
German defenses facing the First Army—in fact, he assured Eisenhower that this was the "soft spot" in Normandy, ideal for the breakout of the lodgment.

The country through which the First Army was to move
was intimately known to Patton. He had reconnoitered virtually every square foot of it from Cherbourg to Saumur in

1913, when his wife thought they were on their second honeymoon; and again in 1917 when he was training his tank corps at Langres. It was the *bocage* country through which war had moved laboriously down the centuries, and through which the Normans passed to England after the battle of Tinchebray in 1066.

It was covered by a maze of streams, marshes, canals, drainage ditches, barely passable watershed roads—and hedgerows everywhere. Patton remembered the country well—so quiet and lovely in peace, but forbidding in war. To send troops through its formidable natural obstacles was sheer madness, he thought. He decided then and there to do something before it would be too late to expedite things toward a breakout without the tortuous passage through the *Bocage*.

Patton was unusually busy during the next few days, his last at Peover Hall. He was about to move his headquarters to Breamore House in Hampshire. Before he left, he inspected XX Corps staging at Salisbury and the 2nd French Armored Division at Hull. He made a round of farewell calls on friends he had made during his five months at Knutsford—the Leicester-Warrens (who claimed descent from King Maelmorda of Leinster) and the Stockdales at Alderley Edge.

A few weeks before, in his mounting restlessness, he had begun to pack seriously and sort out the things he would not need in France. Now he took his extra clothes and a few trunks to Fern Hill for safekeeping with the Stockdales, leaving duplicate keys with them.

On June 30th he took off in a B-26 for Breamore House, in the Third Army's embarkation area, 19 miles west of Southampton. It was the ancestral home of the Hulse family, whose baronetcy dated to 1739, the year George II embarked on his 10-year war with Spain, which Patton recalled as the "War of Jenkin's Ear." Though he was to spend only a week at Breamore, he explored his palatial new residence with the keen interest of the historian who revels in the architectural glories of bygone ages.

It was truly amazing that he had found time and spared interest for such exploration in spite of his pressing duties and, especially, amid his apprehensive preoccupation with the plan fermenting in his mind. He spent the whole night of June 30-July 1st drafting it, still using only his Michelin map to guide him.

Unknown and unsung, this first in a series of bold and brilliant plans Patton devised during 1944 stands out as one of the great designs of World War II. It was, of course, never officially recognized or adopted; and it could not stave off the diastrous Battle of the Hedgerows. But it became the inspiration for the so-called "Cobra," the plan of Bradley's phenomenal breakout operation from which the historic success of "Overlord" flowed and in which Patton himself was to play a dominant part. And it presented Patton in a role in which, even today, he is still not recognized. It showed that this complex general who was regarded merely as a tactical genius was equally talented as a planner with a fascinating strategic flair and vision.

What, then, was what might be called his "Opus No. 1"?

Patton began by calling attention to an apparently striking similarity between the situation in Normandy and conditions on which the German General Alfred Count von Schlieffen had based his famous plan in 1907. "All one has to do," he explained, "is to change the pivot from Alsace to Caen." He then proposed two substitutes for the Montgomery-Bradley design.

In the first (which was the more ambitious of the two) he suggested that a provisional corps consisting of two infantry divisions and an armored division (like the one he had put together in Sicily) be landed at Moralix, an ancient fishing port on an inlet in Brittany about 100 miles west of the Cherbourg Peninsula. Deploying on an excellent road net running east via St. Brieuc and Dinan to St. Hilaire at the base of the peninsula, the corps was to attack the Germans facing the First Army, then drive on to Alençon and Argentan—and, thereafter, "depending on circumstances," to Evreux and Chartres—in "a great *coup*."

Patton was confident that such a move—which he thought would take the Germans by surprise and contribute to their disorganization in Brittany as well—would yield two enormous advantages. First, it would force the Germans on the peninsula into a lethal nutcracker. Second, it would bring about a breakout of the lodgment area into open country ideal for maneuver without passing through the *Bocage*.

He feared, however, that the initial amphibious phase of the operation might mitigate against the plan. Therefore, he devised a second design based on Bradley's projected move southward but along entirely different lines. Where Bradley was planning to make the offensive with predominantly infantry forces pushing *horizontally* across the peninsula, Patton proposed that armor be used *vertically*, in a narrow corridor, followed by two infantry divisions, and converging in a rapid dash to the sharp end of the breakout, which he pinpointed at Avranches.

His idea was to move straight down the road with one or two armored divisions abreast, convinced that such a power-thrust, costly though it may be in tanks, would enforce a breakthrough to Avranches in 48 hours.

Patton based his design on the road net of the peninsula. "If," he wrote, " 'the greatest study of mankind is man,' surely the greatest study of war is the road net." And he chose Avranches as the logical goal of the offensive because the two major roads of the peninsula, as well as several good secondary roads running parallel to them from north to south, all converged on that important junction on the little bay of Le Mont-St. Michel, which played a similar historic role in the Hundred Years War. These were, as Patton saw it, clear arteries through the dense and difficult country and, together with the so-called *route revêtue* (tarred or paved secondary roads), virtually the only "practicable" avenues to open terrain south of Avranches.

Patton's plan was a masterpiece of foresight, insight, initiative and daring. Looking at it today when the mosaic of World War II is complete, one feels a spine-chilling thrill, so ingenious and original it was. It reminds one of the robust sculptures of Jacob Epstein—mighty and eloquent in crudely hewn, compact lines. By producing the plan, Patton demonstrated that he was an artist and that creative imagination was the soul of his genius.

Following the possible course of his plan, and comparing its probable results with what was actually planned and done, one senses the difference between a work of art and a mere piece of craftsmanship. But Patton's design was not sheer fancy and artistry. It also had solid realistic craftsmanship. I have no doubt that had it been adopted and carried out, the course of the war in Normandy and Brittany would have been changed and accelerated, and history's course would have been altered.

Patton produced the plan in a squandering movement of his rich genius, because he knew that he would have a hard time getting it accepted. To see and understand what he had so brazenly sketched, the men for whom he had prepared it would have needed—but woefully lacked—his kind of imagination.

Rosevich distinctly recalls that Patton was unusually excited while committing the plan to paper. His elation resounded in the shrill timber of his thin voice, and his eagerness to gain acceptance for the plan showed in a ruse. He attributed his own original ideas to highly respected strategists, like Clausewitz, Scharnhorst and Schlieffen, whose wisdom he assumed, carried greater weight with Ike than his own strategic brainstorms.

"I don't care," Patton told his secretary. "If I don't get any credit for the idea as long as they allow me to carry it out."

Whether it would be on his own plan or on that of others, Patton now felt strongly that the time had come for the employment of the Third Army. He clearly saw that "overlord" had reached its critical stage. Though the Allies were firmly established in Normandy, they had to seize their opportunity or else—as he put it—"we will die of old age before we finish."

He had the contours of the campaign he would wage— and did wage within 40 days—clearly in mind. "It won't be playing safe," he told his staff, "or attacking with articulated lines. That's for the birds—or for Monty!"

On July 2nd General Hughes of Ike's staff dropped in for lunch at Breamore House and Patton used the opportunity to give him the plan for delivery to General Eisenhower. But the Supreme Commander was in Normandy, visiting Montgomery and Bradley, to review the finishing touches and then await the jump-off by General Middleton's VIII Corps.

There was already a lot of caustic talk in Normandy about Montgomery's "string of glorious failures," and correspondents with the 21st Army Group began to quip about his "pivoting on Caen" instead of taking it. But Bradley reassured the Supreme Commander that Monty was doing what was best for all of them and that the offensive through the *bocage* country would get the entire Army Group moving again under much more favorable conditions.

Although "Overlord" was falling far behind schedule, Eisenhower returned to London in a generally confident frame of mind. This was how Patton found him in the afternoon of July 4th—cheerful but a little exasperated by Monty's "lack of drive."

As far as Patton's plan was concerned, Eisenhower had not had a chance to look at it yet, and anyway it was far too late to substitute either one of his designs for the offensive. It had jumped off on July 3rd on the westernmost flank of the First Army. VIII Corps attacked in a driving rain with a minimum of air support and promptly ran into trouble. German resistance proved enormously stiffer than Bradley had anticipated, and progress was negligible in the face of the enemy's massed 88-mm. and large-caliber antiaircraft guns. The handwriting Patton had seen on the wall when he first thought of the pending operation was now becoming visible to Eisenhower as well, but the Supreme Commander had unquenchable faith in Bradley and, besides, there was nothing else he could do—at least not for the time being.

Patton, on his part, already had his eyes set on far greater objectives—on winning the whole war virtually single-handed. And he was ready to go. He had been alerted in the morning on July 2nd for the trip to France and was now in London to wind up his affairs. He was returning to Normandy exactly 32 years after his first visit to the country on his way home from the Olympic Games.

July 6, 1944, was George Patton's personal D-Day, and he flew into war with all the conveniences of a well-heeled tourist going to France. After the morning briefing at Breamore House, he drove to the airstrip with Codman and Stiller, Sergeant Meeks (busy with the General's bedrolls and personal luggage), and Willie, his pet bull terrier. They went in a C-47, with a jeep, its wheels blocked, lashed in the rear of the plane.

Patton came, erect, brisk and with a festive frown especially put on for the occasion. Like any traveler, he carried a book to read on the journey. It was a volume of Edward Augustus Freeman's monumental six-volume *History of the Norman Conquest*.

He had been reading the famous Oxonian's work on and off since his arrival in England, even though he was aware of its errors. They did not matter to him because he had a specific professional interest in studying the book. He was interested in what Freeman would reveal about the roads on which William the Conqueror had journeyed in his operations in Normandy and Brittany.

General Patton mounted the steps of his C-47 with quick strides, made himself comfortable in a forward seat, and secured the safety belt. The pilot came to report.

"We'll pick up our air cover of P-47's before hitting the Channel, sir," he said.

"That'll be fine," Patton said moodily. He didn't like being pampered when he was going to war.

"Do I have your permission to start, sir?"

"Go ahead."

The moment they were airborne Patton looked at his watch.

"It's ten twenty-five," he said, "exactly a year ago to the minute from the time we left Algiers for Sicily."

"This time I doubt if we will get our feet as wet," Stiller said.

"That's right, Al," Patton said. "This is a helluva way to make an amphibious landing."

The C-47, now escorted by four P-47 fighters, flew over scattered clouds straight toward the French coast.

Now the great moment to which he was looking forward so eagerly was on hand. The plane was making for a narrow airstrip just behind Omaha Beach. A few minutes later it was taxiing toward a young officer at the end of the strip waving in the pilot. He was Lieutenant Colonel Chester Bayard Hansen, General Bradley's aide. Just before the door was opened, Patton looked at his watch again.

"Eleven twenty-five," he said. "From Norfolk to Casablanca it took us 18 days. From Algiers to Gela, five days. And now France in one hour. Well, let's go. I wonder if there is still a war going on."

They drove the few miles to Bradley's headquarters in a wooded field south of Isigny. But they could make only slow progress on the crowded road, and it took them as long to get there as they needed to cross over to France.

"We drove along the beach for some miles," Patton wrote. "It is a terrible sight, with hundreds of wrecked ships. Most of the wrecks are not due to enemy action but to the storm which followed the landing for several days.

"Some of the pillboxes which the Germans had erected are remarkably strong but were all captured, which proves that good American troops can capture anything, and that no beach can be defended if seriously attacked."

Bradley received him with open arms and genuine hospitality, but Patton was quick to sense that he was but a fifth wheel in Normandy.

The businesslike atmosphere of Bradley's CP impressed and warmed him, but also filled him with envy. He had to kibitz the whole afternoon while Bradley was conferring with Generals Hodges and Collins, whose VII Corps had taken Cherbourg. They were discussing plans of upcoming operations with which Patton had nothing to do.

So close to the war yet still remote from it, Patton had to look over the shoulders of his fellow generals like a man on the subway reading somebody else's newspaper. This was not his idea of war, certainly not of his own part in it. With his nervous energy going to waste like helium in natural gas, his mood pendulated from despair to resolution. "I was obsessed with the belief," he described that "unpleasant" period, "that the war would end before I got into it. I was also certain that, by pushing harder, we could advance faster."

Bradley put him up for the night at First Army CP but did not let him sleep. He had ordered a tremendous amount of artillery fire for the night, the significance and value of which escaped Patton.

"To me all this Goddamn blasting seems futile and wasteful," he said to Al Stiller before turning in. "Have you ever heard so much firing even in World War I?"

"No, sir," Stiller said. "But at least it reminds you, General, that you need not worry about missing your war."

Next day Patton did what protocol required—made his formal call on the Commanding General of the 21st Army Group, west of Bayeux. Montgomery had his working headquarters and staff in one place and his personal, monastic command post in splendid isolation at another. This morning he was at neither. Just as Patton was coming to see him, Monty left to visit the First Army, so Patton followed him back.

The original arrangement under "Overlord" called for Montgomery to command the Army Group until the Third Army became operational when and as needed. Then General Hodges would take over the First Army and Bradley the new all-American 12th Army Group, composed of the First and Third Armies. Montgomery would continue in over-all command throughout August, after which General Eisenhower expected to take charge in the field as well.

Now, in his impatience, Patton was convinced that not only Montgomery, but Bradley, too, favored the delay. Even the day before he was informed that Third Army would become operational at last at high noon on August 1st, but he persisted in his suspicion. On June 27th General Bull, one of Ike's assistants, assured him that far from trying to keep him out, everybody was most eager, indeed, to get Third Army into an operational state.

As far as Third Army was concerned, it was in the process of being assembled. Many of its elements were still in the United Kingdom awaiting transportation. VIII Corps, which it was to take over, was still very much needed by the First Army. The future of Patton's army was being shaped by the sum total of conditions in Normandy, and not by what Patton suspected—the whim of Montgomery or the apprehension of Bradley.

But what was happening to Bradley's offensive while Patton was compelled to cool his heels in Normandy?

For 15 tortuous days it was making slow and painful progress. VIII Corps, which had inaugurated the offensive with three divisions in the west, could only inch forward, covering 6,000 yards in three days. It advanced only 8 miles in 12 days of the most bitter fighting. Exhausted and badly mauled, it was halted on July 15th, still about 12 miles from its objective, the high ground at Coutances.

Its hard experience was typical of the fighting along the entire front. St. Lô fell on July 18th, but its capture by the 29th Infantry Division marked the end of the offensive. "The fall of St. Lô," wrote Army historian Ronald G. Ruppenthal, "concluded a period of the most difficult fighting the American forces had seen thus far. Favored by endless lines of natural fortifications in the characteristic Normandy hedgerows, and aided by almost daily rains which nullified Allied tactical air support and reduced observation, an enemy inferior in numbers and deficient in supplies and equipment was able to contest virtually every yard of ground. For the American forces the period proved costly in the expenditure of ammunition and in casualties among their infantry."

Patton followed developments from close quarters in utter frustration. The costly failure of the offensive grieved him for more reasons than one. For one thing, he knew in advance that it would not—because it could not—achieve what Bradley had expected. For another, he mourned for his own plan, which he was now more than ever convinced would have attained the goal Bradley had proved incapable of reaching.

"I get quite discouraged over the slow progress being made," he wrote on July 14th. "I am sure that if I were in command I could break through in two days. All that is necessary is to take chances by leading with armored divisions and covering their advance with air bursts. Such an attack would have to be made on a narrow sector, whereas at present we are trying to attack all along the line."

On that same day he had a chance to see General Bradley at the funeral of General Theodore Roosevelt Jr., "a very brave man and a great leader," who had died in his sleep of a heart attack two nights before. He found Bradley somewhat upset by the failure of the offensive on which he had pinned such great hopes but confident nevertheless that another push, which he was already busy preparing, would compensate abundantly for the setback.

Patton was in no mood to share this optimism. His frustration had been badly aggravated by an order he received directly from Montgomery on July 13th stating in so many words that the Third Army would not become operational until after Avranches had been reached. Bradley protested that he had never seen the order, and tried to reassure Patton.

"Please don't worry, George," he said. "I will get the Third Army in as soon as I can."

Patton was checking his impatience by recalling a remark of Joe Eklund, the Swedish navigator with him on the *Arcturus,* the yacht he sailed to Hawaii in 1928. "These calms is awful, but when the wind blows you forget all about them," Joe had said.

By then he had reason to suspect that he would become operational after all, and probably within the next two weeks. Bradley was completing his own grand design, which was to do more than make up for all the hardships and heartbreaks of the inconclusive offensive, and open vistas that nobody in the First Army dared even dream of.

CHAPTER TWENTY-THREE
THE SHADOW OF BRADLEY

On July 12th, when he realized that his offensive was running into dead ends around the midriff of the Cotentin Peninsula, Bradley decided to write it off and replace it with a bolder, firmer and more elaborate design—a breakthrough at last to Avranches. Devised as a major effort with its own code name, "Cobra," the operation was to penetrate the German defenses in the Cotentin by the combination of concentrated power on the ground and overwhelming bombardment from the air. The perspective within which Bradley had conceived "Cobra" was basically the same as had motivated his July offensive; and the objectives remained unchanged—Brittany was the eventual goal, the Coutances-Caumont line the first step toward it.

Martin Blumenson, who has made the most exhaustive study of "Cobra," called attention to the difference between what "Cobra" was originally planned to be and what it became in the end—essentially the difference between a *breakthrough* and a *breakout*. The former, according to Blumenson, "signified a penetration through the depth of the enemy defensive position"; while the latter, employed *post facto* to describe the results (rather than the intentions) of the operation, meant "leaving the hedgerow country, shaking loose from the Cotentin, acquiring room for mobile warfare—goodbye Normandy, hello Brest."

In his effort to place "Cobra" in its proper historical slot, Blumenson wrote: "Reporters writing *after* the event and impressed with the *results* stressed the breakout that developed rather than the breakthrough that was planned." As it was, "Cobra" was remarkable in its conception, and superb in its execution. It became "the key maneuver," as Blumenson concluded, "from which a large part of the subsequent campaign in Europe developed."

Chastened by his recent experience, Bradley had set his expectations reasonably low but his hopes sky high. "If this thing goes as it should," he told General Collins a week before the jump-off, "we ought to be in Avranches in a week." And he told Major General Lewis H. Brereton of the Army Air Forces on July 11th, two days before the First Army published the "Cobra" plan, that "the attack was designed to break out of the Cotentin and complete the liberation of France."

Patton, on his part, was as skeptical of "Cobra" *before* the attack as Blumenson became many years afterward. But he changed his mind when he gradually discovered that "Cobra" was indeed a modified version of his own *Opus No. I.* He had no doubt that somehow he had inspired it and Bradley—deliberately or unwittingly—had copied his ideas. For "Cobra" had all the major elements of Patton's original design—the vertical attack on the road net with increased emphasis on armor, the narrow corridor concept with Avranches at its terminus. Yes, this was his plan, he thought, somewhat deboldened and bowdlerized, for Bradley would never dare go as far out as Patton was raring to go.

Of course, he had an enormous stake in its success. If "Cobra" delivered what Bradley fondly hoped it would, and punched a hole in the German defenses, the Third Army would be made operational to exploit the breakthrough and develop it into a breakout. But two flies in the ointment dampened Patton's enthusiasm even now when he was within sight of the Promised Land. First, he was given what he regarded as only a limited assignment, Brittany, and ingress to it was contingent on the First Army's ability to reach the base of the Cotentin Peninsula. And second, he was not given too much "dope" about this whole "Cobra" affair because it seemed Bradley was having some doubts about his discretion.

This was the offshoot of a "leak" that upset Bradley because he feared that his carefully nurtured and guarded plan could become known to the Germans. He told Patton all about "Cobra" on July 12th. "This thing," he said, "must be bold."

Patton agreed wholeheartedly, especially because he quickly detected in Bradley's new plans his very own ideas he had related to him on June 26th and submitted in writing on July 2nd—the vertical race down the Cotentin road net to Avranches, the whole works, now even with his original emphasis on armor. The more he learned about "Cobra" the more convinced he became that Bradley had—probably only subconsciously—developed it from the very seeds he, Patton, had planted in his mind. When Bradley gave Patton additional details of the operation as he was evolving it, Patton became positive that it was his "baby." "They are getting more and more ambitious," he noted a bit smugly, "but are exactly the ones which I proposed, so I am very happy."

Probably because of his proprietary interest in "Cobra," but also because it had, after all, a crucial bearing on his own future, Patton decided on July 16th to brief a chosen few of his higher staff about the operation.

When the regular staff conference was concluded on this ominously calm Sunday, he kept his section chiefs in the tent and asked Colonel Maddox, his G-3, to acquaint them with the details of "Cobra." General Gay made it clear that everything said during the impromptu briefing was top secret. Patton sat out the lecture without saying a word, then closed the session by admonishing the select audience to keep absolutely mum about the imminent operation.

With the loyalty of his staff what it was, those who were thus made privy to this momentous secret saw it mostly in the light of Bradley's plagiarization of their boss's ideas. In this spirit, Colonel Charles C. Blakeney, Patton's Public Relations Officer, went over to the neighboring apple orchard where the correspondents had their camp, and told them about "Cobra" with a not too oblique emphasis on Patton's actual authorship of the plan. This happened before Bradley dared reveal anything about "Cobra" to the correspondents accredited to his own First Army, except for three men he decided to take into his confidence. The others found out about it nevertheless—from Patton's correspondents who began to flaunt their knowledge and drop enough broad hints for the competition in the Bradley camp to get a good idea of what was brewing. They rushed to Bradley, complaining that Patton's boys knew exactly what they, on their part, were not permitted to know although it involved their beat; and Bradley turned on Patton with his fire hose.

As a result, poor Colonel Blakeney became the very first casualty of "Cobra." Patton was properly remorseful because he realized that it was he who had ignited the fuse. He called Bradley that night and explained the whole mix-up, trying in between to exonerate his PRO, while cussing and protesting, "I'll can him, Brad, you can bet your life I'll can him—just as soon as we find another."

Bradley knew what this meant. It usually took Patton a long time to find replacements for members of his staff who sinned, to be sure, but only from "misplaced loyalty" to him. Bradley dropped the case. "George was too contrite for me to argue further," he later wrote. But he decided to be more careful henceforth with what he would tell Patton about "Cobra."

And as for Blakeney, Patton did relieve him—but only much later and for other reasons. He would never punish a man who was loyal to him no matter how badly he would "misplace" that loyalty.

As soon as he was told about "Cobra," Patton tried valiantly to "sell" Bradley two of his pet ideas. One was to make the Third Army operational at once, and assign to it the offensive in the west of the Cotentin with *unlimited* objectives rather than the limited one Bradley had, with Coutances for its terminus. The other was to lead the attack with armor instead of infantry. Bradley rejected both suggestions, the first on his own, the second on General Collins' recommendation.

Major General Joseph Lawton Collins had come to Normandy from the South Pacific and was now commanding VII Corps with exceptional skill and spectacular success. He was, of course, an infantry general and was firmly opposed to an early commitment of armor in the offensive in which his corps was to play the lead. When the breakthrough was considered on July 12th as a possible offshoot of "Cobra," and Bradley voiced the opinion that armor would be most likely to assure it, Collins objected. "We should not count too much on fast movement of armored divisions through this country," he said. "If we make a breakthrough it is OK, but until then . . . [the armored division] cannot move any faster than the infantry."

Bradley and Collins were close friends, while relations between Bradley and Patton were still strained. Somewhat embarrassed by Patton's seniority, Bradley felt perfectly at ease with Collins, who was four years his junior in age and had graduated from West Point two years after him. He also had unbounded admiration for Collins' quiet professional competence and ability to integrate himself into the team.

Probably this was the toughest period of procrastination in Patton's life because now he had everything and yet nothing. The very location of his so-called Third Army Headquarters, in the idyllic apple orchard at Néhou, near the little Douve River, was symbolic of his paradoxical situation. High up in the Cotentin, it had been captured weeks before, on June 16th, by the 60th Infantry Regiment of Major General Manton S. Eddy's 9th Division. They were men of his own Third Army, attached to General Collins' VII Corps for the drive on Cherbourg. The war had left Néhou behind. Now only stray German mines and the junk-heap of the bygone battle's steel litter, neatly bulldozed off the roads, reminded him that he was in the combat zone after all.

At Néhou Patton had all the trimmings and paraphernalia of a major headquarters organization, not only his own, but also those of three of the four corps he would command when he became operational. Though the place hustled and bustled with the energy that always flowed from him, it was in reality a paper organization.

Patton was no Fabian. Waiting was always excruciatingly painful for him. He was becoming like Kipling's Old Man, finding it increasingly difficult to outlive his impatient years.

Now he was again seized by his morbid apprehension that he would miss his opportunity to fight in this war—obviously his last chance. He was almost 59 years old, one of the oldest generals in a war that had brought to the fore a galaxy of much younger generals. Only Courtney Hodges was his own contemporary in the highest echelons in Normandy.

His anxiety almost burst him on July 20th when word came that an attempt had been made by officers of the *Wehrmacht* to assassinate Adolf Hitler, and it seemed that the war would come to an abrupt end in the resulting chaos. Patton was visiting VIII Corps Headquarters, watching General Middleton and his division commanders getting ready for "Cobra," when the news arrived. He dropped everything and went helter-skelter to Colombières to the First Army CP, determined to put his foot down this time and insist that Bradley make him operational at once.

But Bradley was away in England, discussing problems of the saturation bombing Air had scheduled as a prelude to "Cobra." Patton had his first chance to see him three days later when he had literally nothing to do while Bradley was overwhelmed by preparations for the big push. He pleaded, "For God's sake, Brad, you've got to get me into this fight before the war is over. I'm in the doghouse now and I'm apt to die there unless I pull something spectacular to get me out."

"I've often wondered," Bradley later remarked, "how much this nothing-to-lose attitude prodded Patton in his spectacular race across the face of France. For certainly no other commander could have matched him in reckless haste and boldness." However, if Patton was driven by his pent-up emotions and the desire to vindicate himself, he went about it in a highly professional manner.

By July 21st the plot was thick enough for Patton to look forward to action any moment. He was thinking of nothing but "Cobra" and was turning up at Bradley's CP every day with ideas and suggestions, all of them calculated to broaden the scope and scale of the Third Army's part. Since they tended to go far beyond the scope Bradley had set for the operation, Patton was not getting anywhere with his recommendations and requests.

Yet it was completely clear in his own mind precisely what he would do and how he would burst the seams of "Cobra" once the Third Army was in action. It was the pattern he had devised four weeks before, the scheme he thought would work even in somebody else's care, and was now dead certain that it would perform a miracle in his own hands.

Then on July 23rd, invigorated by the bright gleam of "Cobra" in Bradley's eyes, Patton went to work in earnest. He embarked on a series of conferences to plot the course of the campaign and tried desperately to pin down his superior. But Bradley assured Patton that he would make him operational in the immediate wake of "Cobra." So now he became strictly business and tried desperately to pin down his superior. But Bradley sounded surprisingly vague on this eve of "Cobra," in the face of what Patton recognized as his glittering opportunities.

As Bradley then visualized the best possible aftermath of "Cobra," the First Army had a twofold task—to destroy the Germans remaining north of Coutances and to pursue those retreating to the south, but only as far as the base of the Cotentin. The broad and decisive breakout Patton foresaw as a strong possibility did not seem to receive proper recognition in Bradley's calculations.

Patton suggested that the Third Army be assigned responsibility for the "pursuit," by which he meant the "breakout." He pleaded with Bradley that it be made operational, and also that its area be extended to the beach for logistic reasons.

Bradley turned him down. "We'll cross that bridge," he said in effect, "when we get to it." Patton left the meeting empty-handed.

"Cobra" was supposed to begin on July 24th, but it had to be postponed a day because unfavorable weather prevented Air from preparing the ground assault. That day, Patton held his second conference "to discuss plans for the use of Third Army" after "Cobra," assuming that it would reach its objectives and Third Army would be made operational at last. Present at the meeting at his headquarters were Major General Leven Cooper Allen, General Bradley's Chief of Staff; General Middleton, commanding VIII Corps; and General Haislip, commanding XV Corps.

Patton proposed "to go in" with VIII Corps on the right and XV Corps on the left, using two armored divisions— the 6th and the 4th—from the outset. VIII Corps to take St. Malo and Brest, the XV Corps Quiberon Bay. XX corps was to follow with two armored and three infantry divisions, and halt initially at Rennes.

On *July 25th* Normandy was on fire. Bradley had unleashed his "Cobra" in the zone of General Collins' VII Corps, after saturation bombing with more than 4,000 tons of high explosives by Eighth and Ninth Air Forces had stunned and dislocated the enemy. (It was in this bombing that General Lesley J. McNair was killed by one of our own "shorts.") By nightfall, the Germans were pushed back two miles to a line running from La Butte to Hebecrevon.

But General Patton's thoughts were elsewhere. At 4 P.M. Colonel Odom, his Medical Officer, brought word that "Paddy" Flint had died of a wound received the day before while moving ahead of one of his battalions.

Flint's death was a savage blow to Patton. He was one of his closest friends, godfather of his only son. "He died," Patton wrote in a special tribute to the Vermonter, "as he would have wished to die, in battle. Probably his death was fortunate because he had been fired at too much and it had gotten to the point where he was timid, not particularly for himself but for his men. I hope when it is my time to go, I go as gallantly and as painlessly. God rest his soul."

July 26th was a spectacular day. Collins' VII Corps had broken through in the Marigny-St. Gilles region, and was exploiting its success. Middleton's VIII Corps had joined the issue and was attacking on the west flank with three infantry divisions—the 8th, 90th, and 83rd. It was cutting the Lessay-Périers road and establishing a bridgehead across the Sèvre. But Patton was busy with funerals, first Paddy's at Ste. Mère Eglise, then that of General Lesley J. McNair.

July 27th continued the rapidly mounting drama. "Cobra" was now moving inexorably toward its objectives. While even two days before Bradley was filled with apprehension that "Cobra," too, might fail, now he began to grasp that it was striking "a more deadly blow than any of us dared imagine."

"To say . . . that [we are] riding high tonight is putting it mildly," he wrote to General Eisenhower. "Things on our front really look good."

With the capture of Coutances, "Cobra" had largely accomplished its basic purpose. "By evening of 27th July," Blumenson wrote, "the situation had so evolved that General Bradley could conclude that a successful penetration of the enemy defenses had been achieved."

But it was just another tedious and empty day for Patton. After the hopeful and promising planning of the pre-"Cobra" days, his continued idleness was making him despondent. Nothing was in the air to indicate he would be called soon. Bradley was getting everything he wanted without him. Doubts began to creep up on Patton again that the war might be over before he had a chance to get into it.

When he returned to Néhou on July 23, he told Gay, "I am afraid Monty doesn't want *me* because he's afraid I'll steal his show. And Bradley doesn't want *the Third Army* because he's afraid of Army Group command."

He was both right and wrong.

Montgomery was delaying the call to Third Army in order to prolong his mastery in Normandy. With the second United States army operational, the Americans were slated to get their own Army Group, the 12th. Eisenhower would then take to the field to assume command of the two Army Groups, the British under Montgomery and the American under Bradley.

However, Montgomery was not the one who opposed Patton's *personal* participation in the campaign. It was Bradley who was really behind the delay. But he was not "afraid" of Group command as Patton suspected. He was afraid of Patton.

"My own feelings on George were mixed," Bradley wrote. "He had not been my choice for Army commander and I was still wary of the grace with which he would accept our reversal in roles."

He rationalized his personal animus on professional grounds. "Despite Patton's eagerness to aid us on the 'Cobra' attack," Bradley conceded, "for ease of control I was anxious to restrict it to First Army." Even when Eisenhower urged him to make the Third Army operational and use Patton's skill and dash to the hilt to assure the success of "Cobra," Bradley still balked. "I assured Ike," he wrote, "we could more easily unscramble a jam alone from the First Army CP than we could in conference between two Armies at an Army Group CP."

The situation was strange, indeed. The Third Army was an army in name only, but it was already fighting in fact. Its major elements—including its entire VIII Corps—carried the burden of the attack in the west. But while his troops would engage in the great adventure of "Cobra," Patton himself was to be excluded from it. Undoubtedly pressing problems of command did have a bearing on Bradley's decision to use most of the Third Army without making it operational. But emotional and personal factors were playing the decisive influence. "I was apprehensive in having George join my command," he admitted, "for I feared that too much time would probably be spent in curbing his impetuous habits."

However, Bradley was now confronted with the question of what to do next. When he drew up the original plan he was still under the influence of the dismal battle in the hedgerows and did not dare to forecast how "Cobra" might end. He would rather decide upon his next course of action from the actual results of "Cobra." Now the need to make that decision was upon him, and he realized that he would need Patton at last to exploit the breakthrough. But he was still struggling with his own grave dilemma—whether to have Patton in his command or try to get along without him. He could not decide which was the lesser of two evils. Then the situation determined the issue for him. The stunning, stupendous success of his "Cobra" was leaving him no alternative. The time had come when he could no longer do without Patton. And so, on July 28th he put in the call to Néhou.

That same morning, George Patton was busy with such routine chores as inspecting the 101st Evacuation Hospital, a bath unit, a salvage plant, a base bakery, and a gasoline dump, all of them in his own back yard near Néhou, far behind the blazing lines.

At 3:30 P.M. Captain Elliott R. Taylor, General Gay's aide, burst in upon him at the gas dump. He was so excited that he could hardly speak.

"General, sir," he gasped, "you're wanted on the scrambler at headquarters. It's General Bradley! We've been looking for you all over the place, sir."

Patton raced back to his idyllic apple orchard. Arriving at 4:45 P.M., he put in a call to Bradley as fast as he could.

"George," Bradley said, using the time-honored cliché, "this is it."

Patton drew a deep breath. "The Third Army," was his first thought. Bradley was calling him to make it operational! But that was not quite yet what Bradley had in store for him.

"You'll supervise operations in VIII Corps zone," he said, "as Deputy Army Commander, and will put in the XV Corps as soon as possible." He also told him that he would remain the mystery man of "Overlord"—kept a dark secret even in his new assignment—"to keep the Germans guessing."

What did this mean? Why was Bradley still keeping him under wraps? And what about the Third Army?

Bradley explained the arrangement with administrative expediency. When the Third Army was originally organized, it was given 4 corps (the VIII, XII, XV and XX) and 13 divisions (the 5th, 8th, 28th, 35th, 79th, 80th, 83rd, 90th Infantry, and the 4th, 5th, 6th, 7th U.S. Armored and 2nd French Armored). In the meantime, while some of its units were in the process of being shipped across, others already in Normandy had been loaned to the First Army. General Middleton's VIII Corps had been trained and equipped, and prepared for the invasion by the Third Army, but was now operating with the First.

Bradley instructed Patton to "supervise the VIII Corps exploitation growing out of 'Cobra,' " and baited the assignment by indicating that "the quicker Patton got the VIII Corps to the threshold of Brittany, the sooner he would be able to enter battle at the head of his army."

But the assignment had a short string attached to it. As Bradley envisaged it, Patton—who was to take charge of VIII Corps only after the commitment of the Third Army—was merely to "trail Middleton's columns and aid in unscrambling them should they become entangled." In Bradley's scheme, Patton was not supposed to assume command of the corps or actively influence the course of the operation.

Patton was too excited to quibble. He accepted the ambiguity and secrecy of his assignment without questioning the motives. But his staff was hopping mad because they were convinced that "topside" was playing politics with their boss. And to be sure, even with the highfalutin' title of Deputy Army Commander, Patton was in an anomalous and somewhat humiliating position.

It had long been evident to his staff that the "high command" was playing a kind of game with Patton. They felt that Eisenhower and Bradley—whom they regarded as a couple of young *parvenus* in war who never before had heard a shot fired in anger—were exploiting Patton's naïveté and eagerness to fight, and were trying to get the most out of him while keeping him down. Now they considered his assignment as Deputy Army Commander something like a gimmick Bradley was using, presumably with Ike's connivance, to insure the success of the exploitation through Patton's personal participation in it, while at the same time covering and protecting himself and seeing to it that Patton would not steal the show.

But Bradley was woefully wrong as far as Patton's "impetuous habits" were concerned. While he was still tormented by his "fears," Patton had already made the perfect adjustment to the changed command situation, and cheerfully, at that. Under the circumstances it may be proper to ask how far and how adversely had Bradley's petty apprehension influenced events in Normandy? Would "Overlord" have gotten off to a much faster start if Bradley had permitted Patton to join his command as soon as the first phase was over? Would the breakout have occurred early in July, without the cruel losses of the Battle of the *Bocages,* instead of weeks later? Would Patton have propelled the offensive as far ahead in July as he did in August and September, bringing the war with Germany so much closer to a decision, had he been allowed to participate in these operations from the outset?

Who knows? But we do know from Bradley himself that his apprehension was unwarranted. As he confessed, "George soon caused me to repent these uncharitable reservations, for he not only bore me no ill-will but he trooped for the 12th Army Group with unbounded loyalty and eagerness."

He attributed this to certain changes within Patton that had made him over into what Bradley called "the *new* Patton." There was, of course, nothing really "new" about Patton. It was rather Bradley who had undergone changes, gotten a firmer grip on his prejudice and greater confidence in himself. It was a turbulent emotional struggle within that seemingly impassive and mathematical-minded but gentle and unsophisticated man. He resolved it at last and sent for Patton—but only in the last moment when he needed him desperately and urgently to make the most of "Cobra" and do what apparently only Patton could accomplish—develop the breakthrough into the breakout.

The transition in the wake of Bradley's long-awaited call was prompt and smooth for Patton. He was in harness within an hour. This was one of the most exciting moments of his life, but for once he had his emotions firmly under control.

CHAPTER TWENTY-FOUR
THE BREAKOUT

Lieutenant General George S. Patton Jr. was now wearing four caps. One was that of the commanding general of an army, the Third, which was not operational; the second was that of deputy commander of another army, the First, over which he had no control and within which he wielded no influence. Wearing his third cap, he "supervised" VIII Corps, whose actual commander was another general.

The fourth was a dunce cap. For the time being, General Bradley told him, Patton would continue to work deep under cover. No references to his personal participation in the operations would be permitted. No stories about him and his deeds would be passed by the censors. No publicity meant no recognition. Yet by a strange twist of his manifest destiny, these were fated to be great and noble days. It was during this total eclipse that he scored one of the most phenomenal victories of his career—the breakout at Avranches.

"Though Patton remained in the background of command to the best of his ability," Martin Blumenson wrote in the official account of the breakout, "his presence was unmistakable, and his imprint on the operations that developed was as visible as his shadow on the wall of the operations tent."

As soon as General Bradley made him at least personally "operational," George Patton sent for General Haislip, a roundfaced, smooth and smiling but tough West Pointer, whose XV Corps was scheduled to enter the line between VII and VIII Corps when Third Army joined the issue under its own flag. He then collected General Gaffey, Colonel Maddox, his cool-headed, wiry G-3 out of West Point, and Colonel "Demon" Hammond, another West Pointer, who served as his Signal Officer, and drove with them and Haislip to VIII Corps Headquarters—not to supervise but to take charge.

It was a rough trip. The ground was littered with the dead rubbish of the recent battle and innumerable live mines. By the time Patton reached VIII Corps CP it was dark, but the lights were burning brightly inside the blacked-out Operations Tent where General Middleton and his staff were waiting for Patton to give him the situation report.

On July 27th VIII Corps had advanced slowly, its progress hampered more by delaying obstacles than enemy opposition. The 79th Division had overrun Lessay, and the 8th had pushed southward between there and Périers. The 90th had occupied Périers and crossed the Taute. The 83rd had patrolled aggressively across the Taute on the left flank of the corps.

Though the German units in the Cotentin appeared to be, as Major General Raymond O. Barton of the 4th Division put it, "terribly low in morale, terribly confused," they were not completely destroyed. A relatively large force had succeeded in escaping in the chaos created in part by the First Army's own confusion in the face of "Cobra's" unexpectedly great success.

General Middleton had orders from Bradley to continue southward. But his instructions were vague—Bradley merely told him to give the enemy "no time to regroup and reorganize his forces," and to "maintain unrelenting pressure on the Germans."

In every plot and plan, in every estimate, the name of a single city now recurred, either as the possible place where the Germans might make a stand, or as the inevitable, inexorable objective of the southward move. It was

Avranches. To Patton, this was a quiet moment of great satisfaction. Late in June he had already picked the place, and on July 1st put it down on paper as the most likely location of the possible breakout. He had marked it with a bold red circle on his Michelin touring map and, henceforth, had never averted his eyes from it.

Now everybody was talking of Avranches! It was "the symbol of egress from the Cotentin," as Blumenson put it, "a prize beyond compare."

On this balmy summer evening in France, Avranches was a many-splendored thing. Its capture would, as Bradley saw it, knock the gate wide open to the west. And since the "Overlord" plan had assigned the conquest of Brittany to Patton, it would make possible the immediate commitment of the Third Army.

Patton knew the place and remembered it well. A little more than 30 years before, he had toured this country with his wife in their roadster, and now the memories of that trip came tumbling back to him. Driving across the peninsula from St. Lô (where they had stopped to buy a chair and a chest), they went south to Pontorson and spent the night at an inn. Early the next morning they turned north again and, crossing the Sélune River on the low Pontaubault Bridge, almost level with the water, drove into Avranches for the day.

Patton now recalled how he and Beatrice had stood on the bluff 200 feet above the town and looked across the bay to the famous rock of Mont St. Michel, eight miles away yet clearly visible. And he remembered the ancient scars of the city. War was no new experience for Avranches. It had seen the Norsemen come and go in 889. Geoffrey Plantaganet camped there in 1141 during his conquest of Normandy, as did Edward III a hundred years later. It was the scene of some spirited fighting in the 16th century by the Huguenots. In between it still managed to flourish as an intellectual center where Lanfranc, the Italian churchman who became Archbishop of Canterbury under William I, spread the teachings of St. Anselm.

Now it was but a marker on the map, its picturesque countryside only of tactical interest to Patton. Lying between the Sée and Sélune Rivers, Avranches was the hub of a road net converging from north and east. Then south of the city the roads merged again, running in a straight line across the Sélune to a fork whose prongs led east, west and south. By looking at the map Patton realized that Avranches was far more than just the gateway to Brittany.

Supervising a single corps—"without becoming officially connected with the operations"—was a far cry from commanding an army, but Patton was quite satisfied. For he recognized in VIII Corps the ideal instrument for the overture whose notes were now forming in his mind.

Originally set up as a "direct pressure force" in the west of the Cotentin to aid VII Corps' envelopment by tying down Germans, Middleton's VIII Corps was now in business on its own. For the time being it consisted of four infantry divisions (the 8th, 79th, 83rd and 90th, two of which it was about to give up to Haislip's incoming XV Corps). Recently it had been enriched by the addition of two armored divisions, the 4th and the 6th.

Patton listened intently to the briefing as Colonel Rickey, VIII Corps G-3, showed on the map the position of the infantry divisions—the 79th at Lessay, the 8th at Périers, the 83rd across the Taute, the 90th in a bridgehead at the Sévre River.

"Where is your armor?" Patton asked, as if he did not know.

So far armor had played little part in the corps' advance. The 4th Armored started out at the western portion of the Carentan-Périers Isthmus and was pinched out there on July 15th, then held as a corps reserve. The 6th Armored had been attached to the corps only on July 25th and was still assembling at Le Mesnil-St. Martin.

The plan was to continue the advance with the infantry, which seemed to be the logical thing to do. The enemy was in general withdrawal, to be sure, and, on orders from General Bradley to "disregard the 'Cobra' limit of advance north of Coutances," infantrymen of the corps were advancing southward as quickly as engineers could clear paths for them. But a *rapid* advance appeared to be impossible in the face of the fantastic congestion of men and mines, through a profusion of wrecked and burning vehicles left by the retreating Germans along every road.

On this evening the Germans were still holding on to a patchwork front whose erratic line resembled an ever-changing amoeba. And even at its most forward points, the infantry was still about 40 miles from Avranches. Farther north, VIII Corps' progress was impeded more by obstacles than by the Germans, and the confusion and congestion threatened to become worse. How fast and how far could the infantry go under these circumstances?

Again objective and subjective motives combined in Patton to produce the solution. He was in a tremendous hurry to get to Avranches, where he would become operational, and dreaded the delay caused by the slower progress of the infantry. And he always wanted armor to lead the advance. He was now ready to give his first order in Normandy and he did not care whether he had the authority as a mere "supervisor" to give it.

"I want Wood and Grow to lead the advance," he said.

Wood was Major General John S. Wood, a rough-riding cavalryman turned tanker who had much of Patton's impetuosity and innate dash. Grow was Major General Robert W. Grow, an earthy Iowan who went into the Army from the University of Minnesota and the Minnesota National Guard in 1916, saw service in World War I both in Field Artillery and Cavalry. Patton, who had the 4th Armored from the beginning of his Third Army command and was given Grow's division on March 8th, had trained them for exactly the type of war the contours of which were beginning to emerge rapidly in General Middleton's Operations Tent.

Although Patton tried never to play favorites, his background as a tanker naturally drew him to armor, and to the 4th Armored Division in particular, probably because he had that affinity of spirit with its daredevil commanding general. It was the first of his units he visited in England, on February 1st, six days after his arrival. The division was training near Badminton in Gloucestershire, on the estate of the Duke of Beaufort where, Patton noted, "the game was invented and all the hunting took place." (The visit inspired him to put up a badminton court at Peover Hall and play daily matches with members of his staff, and especially with Colonel Williams, his artilleryman, whose skill at the game was giving him the hardest time.)

Patton was very much impressed with what he found at Wood's place—"The division is superior," was the way he expressed his pleasure at its showing. His opinion of "P." (for "Professor") Wood was spelled out in characteristic terms a few weeks later. "General Wood," he wrote after another visit, "was in a bad state as a result of having been ridden over by a jeep, which would probably have killed any other man."

Patton also picked the 4th Armored to test a paper he had prepared in mid-April on the tactical use of tanks in attack with infantry. Though still suffering from his recent injury, Wood personally conducted the test, with Patton riding along in a half-track with a radio, directing the two platoons in the exercise with a steady stream of expressive expletives he described as "just correcting errors."

It was a very important rehearsal, as Patton called it. It was the small-scale test of his greater design, the tanks jumping off to lead the attack, and infantry following in their wake.

Ever since he began to think of this campaign in the Cotentin, Patton's concept differed from the accepted scheme of attack chiefly in that he wanted the tanks to lead and the infantry to follow, while Bradley and Collins preferred the reverse. He was neither impressed nor swayed by Collins' objection that in this *bocage* country armor could not move any faster than infantry. He was convinced even before arriving on the peninsula that it could.

General Middleton was not exactly startled or stunned by Patton's peremptory substitution of armor for infantry. He was familiar with Patton's ideas on this score and, as a matter of fact, was co-author of at least part of his basic design. He happened to visit Peover Hall on April 13th, while Patton was working on his paper, "Use of Armored Divisions," and talked at length on the use of the separate tank battalion with infantry.

The concept that was about to explode in action went beyond the basic procedure of tanks leading the infantry. It involved the use of scattered tank units in paving the way for infantry advance in the face of opposition. At the slightest enemy resistance, tanks and armored cars would race around to attack on the flanks, and press on. Such constant and erratic action would keep the enemy jumping and prevent him from organizing his lines. It was to work miracles soon.

Now Middleton picked up his cue and started his tanks rolling at once. His plan of action was for twin thrusts by his two armored divisions moving abreast through two infantry divisions in a maneuver that brought from Patton the grinning remark:

"You know, Troy, such an operation would certainly get us unsatisfactory marks at Leavenworth. But this is war!"

At daybreak next morning, the two armored divisions moved out to spearhead the pursuit. Combat Command A of the 6th Armored, led by Brigadier General James Taylor, rolled southward in the west, squeezing through 79th Division to positions south of Coutances. Combat Command B of the 4th Armored, led by Brigadier General Holmes E. Dager, pushed through the 90th Division down the Périers-Coutances road, and took Coutances.

This was a signal victory by itself—and an ironic one for Patton—because the fall of Coutances marked the official termination of "Cobra."

"Thus ended Operation 'Cobra' on the Cotentin west coast in a final action not unlike the last twitch of a lifeless snake," Blumenson wrote. "Even as 'Cobra' was expiring, the battle was passing beyond the limits contemplated for the action. With the Germans reduced to impotence, the offensive was becoming quite different from the original conception."

Patton's switch from infantry to armor not only accelerated VIII Corps' advance but also placed a different complexion on the whole battle, adding to the confusion and disorganization of the enemy. Within 24 hours, the 6th Armored Division reached the Sienne River near Pont de la Rocque on the west flank of the corps, while the 4th Armored drove to Cerences. The distance between Patton and Avranches was diminishing by the minute. And now he had only two more days to kill.

Bradley had sent word that Third Army could expect to become operational at high noon on August 1st.

Patton had in his make-up much of the Elizabethan man, especially his inconsistency. He would thus preach that no superior officer should be reprimanded in front of his subalterns, yet he was doing it all the time, bawling out officers in front of their men for even minor infractions. He was caustic about Bradley's preoccupation with infantry tactics

which, he said sweepingly, no officer above the rank of
lieutenant colonel needed to concern himself with.

Yet he himself was forever interfering, more often in
minute tactical matters than in major operations. Sometimes he did it on the pretext of checking up on the execution of his orders; at other times in his firm belief that his
ideas and concepts were superior to those of others; at still
other times because he just could not repress his exuberance
and nervous energy.

But in the big maneuver developing at breakneck speed
on VIII Corps' front Patton was leaving Middleton more
or less alone. Having remade the plan in his own image and
revolutionized the procedure with the immediate commitment of the armored divisions (as well as the motorization of part of the infantry in 400 borrowed Quartermaster
trucks), he abandoned the conduct of the battle to Middleton's firm hands.

Patton simply loved to work with that general. Fifty-five-
year-old Troy Houston Middleton had joined the Army as a
private in 1910 and worked up to his colonelcy in 1939,
when he retired to become dean of administration and
comptroller of Lousiana State University. Recalled to active
service in 1941, he was given command of the 45th Infantry Division, which he took from the United States directly
into the battle of Sicily. His handling of that green and
rambunctious division impressed Patton, who recognized in
Middleton that combination of brain and brawn he valued
highest in a commanding general.

When Eisenhower pressed Patton to get another Chief of
Staff, he toyed with the idea of inviting Middleton, but decided on Gaffey in the end, on the ground that "Middleton is a brilliant man but I knew Gaffey better." However, he insisted that Middleton be given a corps in the
Third Army, and became close to him during their months
in England.

Now Patton had every reason to have full confidence in
the commanding general of VIII Corps, even though Middleton, a daring soldier but careful planner, had some reservations about Patton's free-wheeling command style and
unorthodox operational ideas. However, he did what he was
told, and that made him the perfect corps commander in
Patton's book.

Even though he let Middleton conduct the march on

Avranches, Patton was bursting with ideas, both big and small, about what he would do when Third Army became operational a few days hence. And as usual on the eve of his major involvements, he was worrying, especially about a couple of dams in the mouth of the Sélune River near Avranches. He remembered those dams and figured that if they could be broken now, the flood they produced would abate within a week, by which time he was *certain* to be *south* of Avranches.

Patton always had his eyes strained as far as they could see, focused on seemingly remote details. This was exactly how he had worried about that "Goddamn bridge" at Xivray 26 years ago on the eve of St. Mihiel. A few days before, on July 26th, he had asked General Elwood R. Quesada, who commanded the Air in "Cobra," to knock out those "Goddamn dams," but Quesada was noncommittal. Now, in the midst of everything else, and the whole war ahead of him, he called Bradley late at night because he just had a brainstorm about those dams.

"Say, Brad," he suggested, "how about using paratroops on the dams at the Sélune? I think they would be ideal for blowing them up."

Bradley had other things to worry about.

"He was not very congenial about this idea," was the way Patton paraphrased Bradley's reaction.

Now Patton was "operational" and had VIII Corps, but he still had two days to kill before he would have it all to himself with the Third Army. He was killing them by cramming into those few days an amount of work that would have required the efforts of five other generals.

He began the day on July 29th by briefing "his" correspondents. "No notes, no quotes," he barked. "I'll tell you what happened but not what's going to happen."

Then Patton drove to Coutances, dropping in at VIII Corps Headquarters on his way to the 79th Division CP to see General Ira T. Wyche, who had been wounded in the leg by a ricochet bullet. On he went, looking for the 6th Armored Division. He found it stalled on what he called "the wrong side" of the Sienne River. General Grow, the division commander, was sitting on the side of a road, while General Taylor, his assistant, was studying a big map with a group of officers, "secreted behind an old church."

"What the hell are you doing, Grow, sitting at the road?" Patton asked.

"Taylor is in charge of the advanced guard, General," Grow said.

"I don't give a damn who's in charge. Have you been down the river?"

"No, sir," Grow said. "Taylor is trying to find a place to ford it."

"Well, unless you do something, Grow, you'll be out of a job."

Then without waiting for him, Patton went down to the river and waded in to test its depth. He looked across the river to a windmill some distance away under which he could see a bunch of Germans. They looked back but did not fire at him.

"Okay, Grow," he said, back on the bank of the river, "take them across. This Goddamn sewer isn't more than two feet deep."

Later, the official history of the Army recorded this particular incident as follows: "Combat Command A, 6th Armored Division, secured crossing of the Sienne River near Pont de la Rocque on the west flank of the VIII Corps." History often has a difficult time catching up to the events it records.

There was nothing personal in Patton's intervention. He was actually fond of Grow and impressed with his division. On March 9th, the day after it had been attached to his Third Army, Patton inspected it at Martin-on-March in Wales, where it was training, and found it "in superior shape." He visited it again on April 22nd and participated in extensive firing exercises, telling Grow and his officers that they were "doing very well," a high praise from Patton.

General Grow in particular endeared himself to Patton with his no-nonsense approach to his job and his earthy personality in which intellectual tinsel was conspicuous by its absence.

Both Grow and the 6th Armored were quick to justify Patton's confidence in them. In recalling the incident later, Patton remarked, "They learned the lesson, and from then on were a very great division."

July 30th was a Sunday.

As far as the war was concerned, things were going extremely well and rushing toward the climax. Attacking through the bridgehead secured by General Taylor's Combat Command A, Combat Command B of the 6th Armored drove some three miles beyond Bréhal along the road to Granville. More important, Combat Command B of the 4th Armored pushed into Avranches, capturing two bridges over the Sée.

For the time being, its hold on the town was tenuous. Two hours before midnight the Germans began to pour into Avranches, one of their columns in vehicles marked with red crosses. What looked like a real German effort to defend the town convinced the American commander of the tank company in Avranches that caution was the better part of valor even in a hot situation like this. He ordered withdrawal.

Yet this was only a temporary setback in the seesaw battle. For Avranches was really a plum ready to be picked, and General Middleton sensed it. He ordered Grow to "put on the heat" and make for the town as fast as he could roll. Then he told Wood that taking Avranches was no longer enough. He ordered the 4th Armored to hack a path *south* of the town, secure the river crossings and, in fact, smash open the gate to Brittany.

In a very real sense, Patton's decision to have the tanks lead the advance turned the battle into a free-for-all. The fantastic speed of the attack and its constantly changing directions threw the Germans completely off base. But it also deprived the Americans of any planned and truly purposeful maneuver, although their goal was firmly implanted in their minds.

What no infantry advance could have accomplished through this congested area infested with a wildly shifting enemy, the tank advance was now rapidly achieving. The Germans were being knocked for a loop. So abrupt and unexpected was the descent of armor upon them that the major command posts of the Seventh German Army were *behind* enemy lines even before their occupants knew what was going on and that the climactic attack was on.

About three miles north of Avranches, a column of the 4th Armored Division's Combat Command B, under General Dager, passed within a couple of hundred yards of the Seventh Army's advance command post when it held the big brass of that rapidly disintegrating army, General Paul Hausser and Brigadier General Rudolf-Christoph Freiherr von Gersdorff, with their whole staffs. They ran for their lives and, unknown to Dager, managed to make their way to safety through the regular intervals of the Combat Command B column serials. First on foot, and then in vehicles they commandeered posthaste, they fled eastward to Mortain.

In the chaotic battle, Middleton could not know exactly what was happening and how close he was to the breakout. And while Patton was counting the hours, he now waited with unaccustomed patience for his moment of truth.

He even slowed down somewhat and played genial host to General Bradley, who had come over from Colombiéres to Néhou, virtually jumping with joy, to discuss the breakout with Patton. Suddenly all his misgivings had vanished. He now seemed eager to have Patton, and the two men embarked on a relationship that was to continue smooth and splendid throughout the war, to their mutual benefit and to the enormous advantage of the entire Allied war effort.

Monday broke with a rush of events difficult to follow and fathom.

Grow's 6th Armored Division overran Granville and moved quickly southeast to the Avranches area. Elements of the 4th Armored were probing southward from Avranches. And General Patton was making his last-minute arrangements to get into "this damn war" in earnest at last.

This was his last day at Néhou, and he was ready to hold his last staff conference in the War Tent before Third Army became operational. In his usual brisk manner, he marched in, his face frozen in what his staff called the No. 3 frown, yet there was a subtle solemnity in his manner. He sat down in the front row, and with his eyes firmly fixed on Koch's map on the wall, he listened to presentations by his G-2 and G-3, puffing thoughtfully on his big cigar. When the briefing was over, Patton rose, walked slowly to the front, and squared his jaw.

"Gentlemen," he began, "we're scheduled to become operational officially at 1200 on 1 August. I want to thank you all for your long endurance and faithful service while we were waiting for this great opportunity. I am convinced that you'll be equally good now that we start moving."

He paused, puffed on the cigar, squinted his eyes, and said:

"Now, gentlemen, doubtless from time to time there will be some complaints that we are pushing people too hard. I don't give a good Goddamn about such complaints. I believe in the old and sound rule that an ounce of sweat is worth a gallon of blood. The harder we push, the more Germans we'll kill, and gentlemen, the more Germans we kill, the fewer of our men will be killed. Pushing means fewer casualties. I want you to remember that.

"There's another thing I want you to remember. Forget this Goddamn business of worrying about our flanks. We must guard our flanks, but not to the extent that we don't do anything else. Some Goddamned fool once said that flanks must be secured, and since then sons of bitches all over the world have been going crazy guarding their flanks. We don't want any of that in the Third Army. Flanks are something for the enemy to worry about, not us.

"Also, I don't want to get any messages saying, 'I'm holding my position.' We're not holding anything! Let the Hun do that. We are advancing constantly and are not interested in holding anything, except the enemy. We're going to hold onto him and kick the hell out of him all the time.

"Our basic plan of operation is to advance and to keep on advancing regardless of whether we have to go over, under, or through the enemy. We have one motto, *'L'audace, l'audace, toujours l'audace!'* Remember that, gentlemen. From here on out, until we win or die in the attempt, we will always be audacious."

He broke into his broadest smile.

"Gentlemen," he said, "you've done outstanding work. And I want to thank you for it. I am very proud of you. But, after all, what you really have done has been to perform very well doing nothing. From now on, I want you to perform equally as well—doing something."

At 11:30 A.M., "Lucky" (Third Army's code name)

moved to "Lucky Forward" near St. Sauveur-Lendelin on
the Taute River. Patton waited until Colonel Hammond, his
Signals Officer, had all the lines open, then started touring
the front again.

He was planning to spend the night at Bréhal, which
Grow's 6th Armored had captured the day before and was
now CP of VIII Corps. Middleton's headquarters was
jumping with excitement. Combat Command B of General
Wood's 4th Armored had pushed into Avranches, capturing the bridges over the Sée River. And the 6th Armored
was racing southward.

By the afternoon of July 31st it was evident that the Germans would not—because they could not—make a stand at
Avranches. Bits of evidence streaming into VIII Corps
Headquarters indicated that they were abandoning the
precious area as fast as they could. Air reconnaissance saw
Frenchmen all the way from Granville to Villedieu-les-
Poéles waving the tricolor, indicating that the enemy had
retreated south of that line. Members of the French resistance reported that the withdrawing Germans were asking directions to Mayenne—a good 25 miles to the south.

General Dager was in Avranches for good with his Com-
bat Command B of the 4th Armored, directing Combat
Command A to get the bridge at Pontaubault. And the 6th
Armored was getting closer by the minutes.

Patton was smoking one cigar after another in VIII
Corps War Tent, feeling futile, as he put it, because information from the front was scant.

"Goddamnit," he said, "did Dager say anything about
those dams?"

They now became of *prime* importance. If the Germans
destroyed the water gates in these last moments and flooded
the Sélune, any immediate advance would be impossible.

Then and there at Bréhal Patton at last received two items
of news that made it difficult for him to get any sleep that
night.

At 10 P.M. word came from Grow: "Am relieving 4th
Armored in Avranches."

At about the same time, General Dager signaled: "Have
just captured two dams on Sélune River."

Patton had nothing more to worry about—not for the rest
of *this* night.

CHAPTER TWENTY-FIVE
A NIGHT IN AUGUST AND THE MORNING AFTER

On the hot, dry night of July 31st - August 1st one could almost hear the heavy breathing of history. If by some utopian magic an observer could have been perched on a celestial platform over embattled Europe, he would have seen exceptional activities in both enemy camps, from Hitler's sheltered headquarters at Rastenburg in East Prussia to 10 Downing Street in London where Prime Minister Churchill was in a huddle with General Eisenhower.

Seven minutes before midnight, seven men led by General Jodl, chief of the Führer's staff, and his deputy, General Walter Warlimont, trooped into the Map Room at the Wolfschanze to listen to an hour-long lecture by Adolf Hitler. Only 11 days before, a mine planted in this same room by dissident officers of the *Wehrmacht* had battered the indomitable Führer. By some occult protection that he enjoyed, Hitler could not be killed. But he had suffered injuries worse than death, for the bomb had shattered and shriveled him.

It was perhaps the proximity of his warped eternity and the shock of this crass assault on his sacred person that turned him from the pontiff of this strange war into a detached observer. On this night he ceased to be the visionary war lord conducting his campaign with the holy terror of his delirious intuition. For once he managed to comprehend the war in its true dimensions. He was now explaining it to his fawning, spellbound audience of smartly uniformed lackeys in rational and almost realistic terms.

The whole meaning of the events in France was still not clear, while the significance of Patton's appearance at Avranches could not yet be fathomed. Now Hitler recognized with amazing clarity the apocalyptic nature of the contest at the base of the Cotentin and heard the death toll of his dreams in the clatter of the tanks of VIII Corps.

He saw the moment as *ein gewisser Höhepunkt der Krise* —an undoubted climax of the crisis. For the first time he perceived in the west rather than the east the *Schwergewicht* —the center of gravity—of his whole war.

"Jodl," Hitler began with melancholy solemnity, "if we lose France as a theater of war we forfeit the starting point of the U-boat war. In addition, we are getting from France many things which are vital for our war effort, including the last wolfram we can hope to get.

"It is evident, and we must place this at the head of all our considerations, that it is totally impossible under the circumstances to wage a pitched battle *(offener Feldschlacht)* in France. We cannot do that. We can still manage to regroup our forces, but even then only to a limited extent. As a matter of fact, we should evacuate the coast without further ado and withdraw our mobile forces to a firm line which we should defend inflexibly. But it is already evident . . . that our forces are hardly adequate to defend even a narrow front.

"We must be clear in our mind that a change for the better in France would be possible only if we could gain superiority in the air—even if only for a brief period of time. And yet I am of the opinion that we must, no matter how bitter this may be, preserve our new *Luftwaffe* units intact inside the Reich, to employ them as a very last resort —when and where the last dice will be cast I cannot say.

"We must therefore, imbue everybody in Army Group West with the absolute necessity of conducting this struggle with the utmost fanaticism and of standing firm everywhere, because mobility—a war of movement—is impossible for us."

It was almost 1 A.M. on August 1st when Hitler finally ended his lecture. "Ah," he said with a sigh, "how much I would like to go to the West! But I simply cannot, even with the best of intentions! Flying is impossible because of my injured ears. I can stand up for a little while and can speak a little, but I have to sit down again quickly and stop talking."

This was the man who, in the summer of 1944, still had the power to direct the German forces in one of the decisive battles of history. He was a mere shadow of his former self, a human wreck overcome by pity for himself. Yet from him the decisions and the orders still flowed. And though he sensed that his problems had progressed beyond solution, he continued to pursue the shadows.

That same night found Field Marshal Günther von Kluge, *OB West,* the Oberbefehlshaber or Commander in Chief of the German forces in the West, in an improvised command post at the front south of St. Lô. He was among the first in the German High Command, and for a while virtually the only one, who recognized that the situation was passing from serious to catastrophic.

Apprehension was building up in him with growing momentum. As early as July 21st, after conferences with General Hans Eberbach of the Fifth Panzer Army and Obergruppenführer Sepp Dietrich of I SS Panzer Corps at Falaise, he had written a letter to Hitler that Wilmont aptly called both a warning and a confession of defeat.

"My discussion yesterday with the commanders in the Caen sector," von Kluge wrote, "afforded regrettable evidence that, in face of the enemy's complete command of the air, there is no possibility of our finding a strategy which will counterbalance its truly annihilating effect, unless we give up the field of battle." He concluded by saying bluntly:

"In spite of intense efforts, the moment has drawn near when this front, already so heavily strained, will break. And once the enemy is in open country, an orderly command will hardly be practicable in view of the insufficient mobility of our troops. I consider it my duty to bring these conclusions to your notice, *mein Führer,* in good time."

Von Kluge had come to the Western Front from nine months of convalescence after an automobile accident to replace Field Marshal Gerd von Rundstedt, an animated version of the wooden Hindenburg. It had been von Rundstedt's bad luck to be *OB West* at the time of "Overlord," while another famed field marshal, Erwin Rommel, the tired hero of bygone campaigns, commanded Army Group B in the direct path of the invasion.

Having failed to thwart the Allied landings at the water's edge, von Rundstedt and Rommel rushed to Hitler to propose remedies. On June 29th Rommel recommended that the Seventh German Army "should fight a rear-guard action back to the Seine, and that the armies in Southern

France should be withdrawn to help create a new line along the Seine and across to Switzerland."

Von Rundstedt went far beyond Rommel with his own recommendation. When Field Marshal Wilhelm Keitel, Hitler's Chief of Staff and toady, asked him, "What shall we do? What shall we do?" von Rundstedt replied:

"Make peace, you fools! What else can you do?"

Hitler's answer, when Keitel told him of von Rundstedt's remark, was prompt and harsh. He dismissed von Rundstedt and appointed von Kluge in his place. At face value, the new Field Marshal seemed an excellent choice. In 1940 he had commanded an army in France in the breakthrough to the English Channel; and in 1941 he led another army in the drive on Moscow. As Commander in Chief of the Army Group Center in Russia, he was given credit for "victorious defense" and won Hitler's gratitude for "accepting outrageous orders when others demurred." When he arrived at St. Germain, his headquarters in the west, on July 4, 1944, General Günther Blumentritt, his Chief of Staff, found him "cheerful and confident, indeed, almost gay about the prospects."

Then Rommel was also removed, but not by Hitler. On the afternoon of July 17th he was inspecting his defenses in the Caen sector when his car was attacked by British fighters. The vehicle crashed into a tree and Rommel was hurled to the road with grave injuries. To prevent an SS general from taking over the Army Group, von Kluge himself assumed its command in addition to his higher responsibilities. Although some of his ardor had been spent, he still seemed to be equal to the task, his mounting misgivings notwithstanding.

During this week of crisis he was initially uprooted at 1:25 A.M. on July 28th by a garbled message from the commanding general of the Panzer Lehr Division. "After 49 days of incessant fighting," the general reported, "my division is now destroyed. The enemy is advancing unchecked southward from St. Gilles."

Von Kluge immediately decided to visit the front, where he arrived in the early morning. By 9:15 A.M. he was able to phone back to St. Germain, telling Blumentritt that the situation around St. Lô had grown still worse and warned of a possible breakout.

At 5:35 P.M. on July 29th he surveyed the situation and saw his hopes clobbered by the irresistible march of the

Americans. "All told," read an entry in his war diary, *"OB West* considers the situation extremely serious."

Von Kluge spent the whole of July 30th with his left flank. Helplessly he watched the Americans moving boldly down the west strip of the Cotentin, battering his badly bruised, worn-out 91st Division. He followed avidly the American advance, now spearheaded by two armored divisions against his ruptured, chaotic front, virtually undefended at the left where the brunt of the Allied attack had been unexpected. Now he tried desperately to stem the tide with so-called *Alarmeinheiten* (emergency units) and other *ad hoc* forces. But it was too late. Avranches fell.

During this fateful night of reckoning, even before August 1st had dawned, von Kluge clearly recognized the threat in Patton's change from infantry to armor, and the greater implications of that threat. "As a result of the breakthrough of the enemy's armored spearhead," he radioed Hitler, "the *whole Western Front* has been ripped open. The left flank has collapsed."

On the evening of July 31st General Eisenhower dined with Winston Churchill. The Prime Minister was in a quandary. He needed ammunition for a speech he was to deliver to Commons on August 2nd and was properly anxious to "emphasize the British participation to his people." But Montgomery was still not delivering the goods expected of him according to the ambitious plans of "Overlord." All the spectacular events in Normandy were being produced by the Americans.

In his predicament, and for want of a better theme, Churchill proposed to reveal the existence of Lieutenant General Frederick E. Morgan behind "Overlord" and claim credit, where it was properly due, for the significant part Britons had played in the planning of this fantastic operation. Eisenhower assented readily to the lifting of the veil from the anonymous British officer whose genius had prepared this triumph. But otherwise he appeared hard put to make sense of what had happened and was now happening.

He had spent nearly the whole day dictating a report for General Marshall about his current and future operations. It was not easy at this distance to make sense of events in

France and draw any clear-cut conclusions for the future. "Hardly had he authorized the final draft of his report to General Marshall," Butcher wrote in the diary, "when he returned from the War Room with the exciting information that we had broken through not only into the Brittany Peninsula but to the east from Avranches, to slice the disorganized German forces."

Knowing little of the details at this stage, and nothing about General Patton's paramount contribution to these startling developments, Ike was inclined to give full and sole credit for the victory to General Bradley. Even today it is generally believed that Patton was merely the beneficiary of the break-out at Avranches. Actually, he was its major architect. But Eisenhower closed his cable to Marshall with the recommendation that Bradley be rewarded with a permanent major generalship. He said nothing about Patton's part in the triumph.

Even on August 4th, when Patton's rampaging forces had already thrust toward Rouen, captured Rennes, reached Fougères, and drove unchecked on Vannes, Eisenhower seemed to be singularly unimpressed with his performance and opportunities. "Ike has been impatient," Butcher wrote, "repeat impatient, and I mean impatient. He isn't excited about Patton's armored thrust into Brittany Peninsula because he figures all that will fall like a ripe apple. The thing he is interested in is bold and continuous attacks against the Germans in the central sector around Vire to destroy them so they can't retreat and fight us again, particularly in the Siegfried Line."

Butcher's entry with its reference to Ike's preoccupation with "the central sector around Vire" pointed up the confusion that the sudden fragmentation of and the omissions in the "Overlord" plan had created in the Supreme Commander's mind. He was "not excited," as Butcher put it, about Patton's armored thrust into Brittany, and by Patton's intervention in the campaign, because—under the existing plans and Bradley's prearranged supervision—Patton had been assigned only the limited task of capturing the peninsula, a mission whose accomplishment now appeared easily assured. Since Ike could not visualize either the opportunities that began to open to Patton or Patton's ability to make the most of them, he naturally concentrated his thoughts on areas covered by the sea plan and on Montgomery's and Bradley's prudent prosecution of that plan.

With Caen being, as Chester Wilmot called it, the crucible in this campaign, and with both Montgomery and Bradley working their respective passages southwest from this strategic prize, Vire was looming enormously in Eisenhower's contemplations. The most important traffic center west of the Orne River, Vire seemed to be the hub of the German defenses, the solar plexus, a blow at which promised to collapse them completely. But such calculations and contemplations were based on the assumption that the Germans were still capable of sustaining organized defenses. The Allied commanders also assumed that the enemy could still maintain a hub anywhere along its crumbling lines. The truth was that the Germans had left a gap some six miles wide between their two armies, and Vire had lost its strategic significance.

This was but one of the chances missed by the Allied high command as a result of its inability to *improvise* operations in the face of new-found opportunities. It was but one of the opportunities the Germans were afforded to save their forces for a later stand instead of losing them in this vicious nutcracker of the British and American forces.

However, General Eisenhower's communications of these crucial days demonstrated the Supreme Commander's instinctive grasp of strategy. They showed that he recognized the vistas the breakout had opened up for decisive exploitation. They further indicated that he regarded the destruction of German forces in the area as the primary task of all operations. And they showed that Eisenhower considered the decisive defeat of Germany in the west, this side of the Siegfried Line, a distinct possibility.

On August 2nd he sent General Montgomery a reminder "of the need for bold action by Allied armored and mobile columns against the enemy flanks." Ike's enthusiasm and optimism were not dampened by possible logistic difficulties. He told Montgomery that "supplies could be dropped by aircraft to such units in case of an emergency," and added, "I know that you will keep hammering as long as you have a single shot in the locker."

In his report to Marshall, Eisenhower clearly foresaw a chance for the Allies to win a decisive tactical victory. Boldly and wisely he proposed to send only a small part of his forces into Brittany while "using the bulk of the Allied units to destroy the enemy west of the Rhine, and exploit as far to the east as possible." The Supreme Commander did not regard the enemy capable of interfering with his plans. He predicted in so many words that if the Allies could have a period of 10 days to two weeks of really good weather they could achieve "a most significant success."

These were the thoughts and plans whirling around in Eisenhower's mind on August 1st. They coincided in every detail, in every expectation, with Patton's. Patton had come to these conclusions on the spot, from watching closely the haphazard battle and perceiving the opportunities the near-panic and the disintegration of the enemy began to hand to the Allies on a silver platter. Eisenhower reached the identical conclusions in his ivory tower back in England, where distance and calm enabled him to view the situation in its most intricate tactical and broadest strategic implications.

It is, therefore, regrettable that after this initial and incidental oneness of Eisenhower's and Patton's outlooks, the Supreme Commander gradually departed from those views and plans. Instead of pursuing them boldly and vigorously in cooperation with Patton, he abandoned them in favor of more cautious estimates and actions. On August 7th, two months after D-Day, he moved to France, setting up quarters near Tournières and Maisons, with his office in a huge tent surrounded by tall hedgerows. The next day, he conferred with General Bradley, still imbued with his pristine concepts of the campaign, and urged the Commanding General of the 12th Army Group to "destroy the enemy now."

"Ike was pressing for switch of Patton's forces to the northeast," Butcher recorded the gist of Eisenhower's views given to Bradley after a tour of the rear battle area northeast of Coutances, "the better to squeeze the enemy into a great pocket against the Seine River. Ike keeps continually after both Montgomery and Bradley," Butcher added, "to destroy the enemy now rather than to be content with mere gains of territory. He has instructed that the Brittany Peninsula should be taken with a minimum of forces, none to be wasted, which would be helpful in pulling the noose around the neck of Hitler's still struggling soldiers."

But Ike's proximity to Bradley soon began to dilute his own concepts and weaken his determination. Within a week he was to succumb to Bradley's influence and stand idly by as the bold campaign Patton was improvising along Eisenhower's own lines was halted and diverted, leading to difficulties even in Brittany and resulting in the enemy's escape from the noose to delay victory in the Battle of France.

General Patton was spending this momentous night of July 31st at his own headquarters, to which he had returned from Middleton's CP at Bréhal. On this eve of his Third Army's becoming operational, he felt history breathing down his neck. He was thinking of Lady Macbeth's words to Ross, "Stand not upon the order of your going, but go at once." But he still had 12 hours to kill, and now he was trying to fend off the mounting suspense of those dragging hours.

In his effort to calm the tension within him, he brought out the belongings of his dead friend, Colonel Flint, and began to sort them out for shipment to Paddy's widow in Vermont.

Despite his inner turmoil Patton was relatively composed. He had his orders and had made his arrangements. There was not always perfect harmony between the two, for Patton usually thought his own arrangements represented a vast improvement over his orders. Now, too, in his nocturnal solitude, he knew exactly what he would do, and how he would do it. He was determined to do it so fast, with such finality, that those "timid souls" hovering over him would not be able to stop him or alter the accomplished fact.

Patton even had "the sign" which he, in his innate mysticism, always needed to reassure himself that he was on the right track. When he had burst into VIII Corps Headquarters, General Middleton received him with what seemed to be a sigh of relief.

"I am glad to see you, George," Middleton said, "because here we are with lots of loose ends, and I don't know what to do. I've been trying to get hold of Bradley, but I can't find him. His orders to me were to secure the line of the Sélune River, and now we have secured it. But what am I supposed to do next?"

"Are you across, Troy?" Patton asked.

"No," Middleton said. "Brad didn't tell me to cross the river."

"Throughout history," Patton said, "it always proved fateful to stop on the wrong side of a river. I'll tell you what to do next, Troy—go across at once."

"I can't do it without Bradley's okay," Middleton said.

"I won't be taking over officially until tomorrow noon," Patton said, "but I've actually taken over on the 28th. So I am telling you on that authority—go across right away."

"But the bridge at Avranches is out," Middleton said, still objecting.

Just then, as if Patton had arranged it, two messages came in over the telephone. One reported that the bridge at Pontaubault had been damaged but was still usable. The other said that the 4th Armored Division had captured the two dams to the east of Avranches and that it was possible for troops to move across them.

"I considered this an omen of the future success of the Third Army," Patton later wrote, as usual mixing fatalism and pragmatism. "I directed that the VIII Corps start across that night, which it did. . . . Had we failed to secure a bridgehead that night, our whole operation would have been jeopardized."

What Patton meant by "whole operation" was the broad design he already had pat in his mind for the vast campaign he was prepared to wage in his own fashion. The original directive in "Overlord" had assigned only Brittany to the Third Army. But Patton regarded it as hopelessly out of date. He was brazenly going beyond its dispositions even if it meant exceeding his orders. Patton told Middleton to head for Brest with the 6th Armored and 79th Infantry Divisions. Then he sent the 4th Armored with the 8th Infantry Division to Rennes, capital of Brittany—on the way to Angers and points beyond.

Whatever the high command had in mind for the immediate future, Patton had his own ideas and started with a bang to carry them out. Although he was stretching his orders, it was none too soon. The breakthrough that he had regarded as essential for the breakout had come unexpectedly and caught the high command in the field unprepared for its consequences.

"From the beginning," General Eisenhower wrote in his memoirs, "it was the conception of Field Marshal Montgomery, Bradley and myself that eventually the great movement out of the beachhead would be by an enormous left wheel, bringing our front onto the line of the Seine, with the whole area lying between that river and the Loire and as far eastward as Paris in our firm possession."

This phase of the operation was to be accomplished by D plus 90. The success of this concept in practice hinged on the line from which the high command hoped to execute this wheel. The plan for its execution was presented formally by General Montgomery in his wrap-up conference on May 15th at St. Paul's School in London, when he said, "Once we can get control of the main enemy lateral Granville-Vire-Argentan-Falaise-Caen, and the area enclosed in it is firmly in our possession, then we will have the lodgment area we want and can begin to expand."

Patton was present, listening somewhat glumly to Monty's plan, in which he had but a vague and iffy part. His only satisfaction was an indirect tribute Monty had paid to him, an indication of the place Patton apparently occupied in Montgomery's mind. While the frisky British general referred to the various units to come under his command in France by their numerical designations, he referred to the Third Army by the name of its commanding general. In fact, Patton was the only Allied general Montgomery had mentioned specifically by name at that meeting.

Patton did not dislike Montgomery's presentation, but he felt it was a strange mixture of optimism and pessimism. He thought Montgomery was unduly optimistic in assessing the ability of his British forces to accomplish their mission in Normandy. He also doubted whether they would be capable of reaching the allocated phase lines on schedule. On the other hand, Patton thought that the plan's limiting the operation to the line of the Seine was too pessimistic. He expected something like the breakout that was to occur and felt it would open up fantastic opportunities, making it imperative to prepare provisions for its exploitation.

In the wake of the conference, Patton made a record of his expectations. He marked on his map the places where he thought the Third Army would have to fight. He had done the same thing before going to Sicily and was correct.

The historic map is extant, an enduring document of Patton's prophetic streak. Events confirmed his expectations, as well as his misgivings. As Eisenhower put it, "This part of our tactical prognostications did not work out and required adjustment." This was merely a euphemism for con-

ceding that "Overlord" had failed to produce what was
initially expected of it. The line Montgomery had sketched
on May 15th, running from Granville in the west to Caen in
the east, was supposed to be occupied by June 23rd, or D
plus 17. On April 7th, at another conference at St. Paul's
School, Montgomery assumed that the line Granville-Caen
would be firmly held on schedule, and stated unequivocally
that the second great phase of the operation could begin
shortly after D plus 20, with the left of the British forces
pivoting on Falaise and swinging with their right in the direction of Argentan-Alençon.

"This meant," Eisenhower wrote, "that Falaise would be
in our possession before the great wheel began. The line we
actually held when the breakout began on D plus 50 was
approximately that planned for D plus 5."

It goes without saying that the fantastic triumph of Patton and his Third Army during the weeks that followed
was made possible by the tedious and heroic work of the
First Army in the Cotentin, the breakthrough at St. Lô, and
Montgomery's shrewd disposition to draw the bulk of the
German units to his British forces pivoting, not on Falaise
as originally planned, but on Caen. It must be remembered
also that Patton's campaign in August was more or less the
exploitation of exceptionally favorable conditions actually
created by the forces that preceded the Third Army to this
immense battlefield.

However, the fact remains that when the Third Army
entered combat the campaign was 45 days behind schedule.
Then in 30 days—between D plus 49 and D plus 79—an area
had been secured that "Overlord" had expected to gain in
75 days (by D plus 90). The original directive then
stipulated a pause of at least a month at the Seine. It never
foresaw a continuing drive into Germany. "Operation
'Overlord,'" wrote Ruppenthal, "has been planned as a preparatory stage, its objective being the capture of a lodgment from which further operations could be carried out."

But the inescapable realities of the campaign had over-
ridden all the original plans and dispositions. By September
12th (D plus 98) the Third Army stood on a line the forecasts had expected it to reach on approximately D plus
350. As Ruppenthal put it, "Between 25 August and 12
September they [Third Army] had advanced from the D plus
90 to the D plus 350 phase line, thus covering 260 phase-
line days in 19 days."

Coming from far behind, it was the privilege of General Patton and his Third Army to drive the whole campaign swiftly forward and bring the war to the brink of total victory in less than three weeks of ingenious fighting.

CHAPTER TWENTY-SIX
BRITTANY

This was high noon, August 1st, 1944!

The Third Army was fully operational and Patton was on his own!

From all over this jampacked theater men and machines converged on the badly congested area just south of Avranches, to become committed body and soul to the indomitable will of an eager visionary.

At that moment the tanks of the 4th Armored Division were driving southward on Rennes; the 6th Armored was rolling in two columns toward Pontorson and Antrain. XV Corps was concentrating its three divisions—5th Armored, 83rd and 90th Infantry—between the Sée and Sélune Rivers, to block the Germans should they decide, or by some miracle become able, to move toward Avranches.

If the men in the tanks and the foot soldiers behind them had any inkling of what seemed to be merely an administrative switch—if they knew that they had passed from General Bradley's command in First Army to General Patton's in the Third—nothing in their conduct or stance betrayed that knowledge. Most of them were blissfully unaware of the change. The Third Army was in, to be sure, but it remained under wraps. No new shoulder patches were issued to the troops, nothing was done to stimulate *espirit de corps* or that special pride that later seized all Third Army men like a fever. Besides, Patton's presence at the front in command of his own army was strictly hush-hush.

For George Patton, the clock seemed to have stopped. At his new command post north of the Granville-St. Sauveur-

Lendelin road, attended only by Colonel Harkins, he was like a subdued reveler on New Year's Eve. All morning he looked at his watch, anxious not to miss the witching hour. His ferocious-looking but placid pet Willie chose this historic moment to consummate a fickle but passionate love affair with a local lady dog, then followed the amorous escapade with a macabre adventure, digging up the body of a recently buried German soldier, "to the shame and disgrace," as Patton put it, "of the military service."

At exactly noon, Harkins produced a bottle Colonel Campanole had left with him to celebrate the birth of the Third Army. It was what Patton later described as a bottle of alleged brandy. "We tried to drink it," he said, "but gagged."

By his own account, he was nervous. This was his normal response to momentous events from which he expected an acceleration toward his destiny. It usually overcame him whenever he was left behind to sweat out things in the oppressive solitude of the commanding general. His restiveness now was not caused by any legitimate professional apprehension. At his deserted headquarters he could not get any hard news of what was going on in the field. But he was not worried on that score. The offensive was rolling exactly as he had designed it.

The movement Patton had improvised for his troops to sustain the momentum of the breakout was highly unorthodox and potentially dangerous. The boundaries within which the Third Army had to operate were crammed. He had to push his infantry through a narrow and incredibly congested corridor between Avranches and St. Hilaire, in a maneuver that could become fatal if a traffic jam developed and the Germans pounced upon the tightly packed troops in their giant sardine can. Patton had all his generals and staff officers, except Harkins, out in the field at key points to supervise the passage of his infantry, actually to direct the movement like so many traffic cops.

The day before, he had directed Middleton to make for Brest at the top of the Brittany Peninsula with General Grow's 6th Armored and General Wyche's 79th Infantry Divisions; and for Rennes with General Wood's 4th Armored and Major General Donald A. Stroh's 8th Infantry Divisions. This was the basic mission of the Third Army under the "Overlord" plan, and it remained firm despite the radically changed situation. Patton's latest directive—to secure Brittany—had been issued to him by General Montgomery on July 27th. It was repeated verbally on August 1st, the written confirmation of the verbal order, now coming from Bradley, the new Army Group Commander, reaching Patton four days later.

At 3 P.M. on this August 1st Bradley arrived at Patton's CP for the début of the Third Army, and it seemed that Patton would be further limited in his operations. By then two of his corps commanders, General Haislip and Major General Walton H. Walker, a little martinet who patterned his life after Patton's, had drifted in to attend a meeting at which General Bradley was to show them the army boundaries.

Bradley was worried. He had information from a top secret A-1 source—probably from inside the enemy camp —that Hitler had ordered a major counterattack on Mortain. The Führer's idea seemed to be to let as many Americans as possible slide through the gap, then cut them off and annihilate them, thus dealing a potentially mortal blow to the whole invasion. Since Bradley's apprehension threatened to affect his plans adversely, Patton made light of it. As a precaution, to cover his exposed flank, he put Major General Eugene M. Landrum's 90th Division on trucks and started it forward at once.

Bradley's cautious presence on Patton's boisterous first day in action, with vistas apparently unlimited, dampened his enthusiasm somewhat. But it left him undaunted. *"General Bradley simply wants a bridgehead over the Sélune River,"* Patton told General Gaffey, his Chief of Staff. *"What I want and intend to get is Brest—and Angers."*

Brest, of course, was the precious jewel of Patton's impending Brittany campaign. By then, however, the peninsula "Overlord" had assigned to his care had ceased to intrigue and preoccupy him. The mention of Angers, historic capital of the Anjou, indicated the direction of his roving eye. The city was almost 100 miles *south* of Avranches in the Maine-et-Loire department, a logical point in the huge enveloping movement around Paris in a daring drive to the German frontier that Patton began to see in his future.

We have seen that General Eisenhower's thoughts also

groped in that same direction. But Patton was among the
first, if not the very first, in the high command on the spot
to recognize that whatever need still existed for the conquest of "his" peninsula, Brittany had lost its strategic significance. It had slipped to a position of secondary importance, the course of the battle having shifted emphasis to the
broad area south, southwest and southeast of the Cotentin.
He was already firmly convinced that the phenomenal
breakout in the wake of "Cobra" had opened up vast opportunities far ahead of the set plan, with possibilities of exploitation the mere contemplation of which staggered even
his imagination.

What was the military situation in Normandy on the
day Third Army became operational?

The front—if the haphazard battleline could be properly
called that—resembled a giant twitching snake. It extended
in convulsive bends and arcs from the water's edge just
below Avranches to the English Channel northeast of Caen.
The Allies now had about a million men in Normandy,
organized in 10 corps, with 3 more waiting to become
operational on a moment's notice. The Germans had three
corps of their Seventh Army and four of Panzer Group
West deployed from Bracey on the Sée River, about eight
miles east of Avranches, eastward along the whole line—
dense in the east, thin in the west, with virtually nothing
left for the westernmost sector of the front.

It was almost incomprehensible the change a week's
fighting had wrought. The enemy had been routed by devastating blows on the ground and from the air. There was
an everwidening breach in his positions. By July 31st his
left flank was unhinged. The gate to Brittany was knocked
open.

Though reeling badly, the Germans still managed to present an apparently cohesive defense in the sector facing the
First U.S. Army. They even succeeded in putting up stubborn resistance around Vire. But that was all. South of the
Sélune their defenses had been shattered. Most of their
units there were in pell-mell flight. What resistance continued in scattered pockets was sporadic and haphazard,
the results of the individual initiative of diehard German
commanders.

Confused and confusing though the situation was, to the
Germans as well as the Allies, there was clear indication
that a major change had occurred in the battle. It called for

a radical alteration of the set tactical plan. Yet when Third Army was made operational it was left with its basic and original mission. All Patton was supposed to gain was Brittany.

His orders on August 1st were explicit and unmistakable. He was to advance south from the vicinity of Avranches as far as Rennes, then turn west and take Brittany, mainly to open the ports of the peninsula. By then, however, the Brittany ports were no longer as crucial to the campaign as "Overlord" had expected them to be. And in the meantime the Germans had withdrawn from the peninsula all of their mobile forces, virtually abandoning Brittany to the French Forces of the Interior. Believed to be 50,000 strong (they turned out to be only about 30,000), and now centrally commanded by Colonel Albert M. Eon of the FFI (who was parachuted into Brittany with his staff to cooperate with Patton) they appeared all over the peninsula to harass the enemy and pin him down.

Thus on August 1st German strength in Brittany consisted of 10 understrength battalions of infantry, 4 motley *Ost* battalions of anti-Bolshevik Russians and former soldiers of the Red Army, and about 50,000 naval, air and service troops, mostly in and around the fortified ports. So bad, in fact, was the disposition of these units that Allied reconnaissance found miles of the supposed front entirely unmanned.

If the enemy's order of battle in Brittany was known to the 12th Army Group, nothing in General Bradley's dispositions at this time indicated an appreciation of the facts. Even Colonel Koch, Patton's G-2, appeared reluctant to discount altogether the capability of the Germans to make trouble. On August 1st he received word of the apparently westward movement of German armor from 15 miles southwest of Rennes. He alerted Patton to the possibility of a major counterattack, designed presumably "to drive a wedge to the Channel between the northern and southern columns of the Third Army," to make the southern column logistically inoperative.

Patton dismissed the warning. He conceded that such an attack might cut off his units temporarily, but he assured Koch that he could easily correct the situation. However, with his customary caution even when accepting risks, he called in Brigadier General Otto P. Weyland, who commanded the XIX Tactical Air Command in support of the

Third Army, and told him to send fighter bombers to stop the German column. When Weyland's airmen found the armor that so perturbed Colonel Koch, they undermined Patton's confidence in the spot reports of his G-2. The tanks turned out to be a column of the 4th Armored Division moving in from the *northeast,* and not from the *southwest* as Koch's information had located them.

Either by some psychic process or uncanny intelligence work on the spot, Patton was aware of the denuded stage of German defenses in Brittany, and was fully convinced that the campaign assigned to him would not tax his resources by any means. Rather, he thought, he could take care of Brittany with part of his forces and send the rest to greener pastures—toward Angers, for example. During a conference attended by Bradley, he explained the situation to his staff, but warned it with an impish grin not to let the correspondents in on the secret of the enemy's woeful weakness in Brittany.

When Bradley left, Patton went into action. Accompanied by Haislip, Gaffey and Harkins, he motored to VIII Corps Headquarters to give General Middleton a hand in coordinating the movement of the 90th Infantry Division through the incredibly congested rear area of the corps.

Patton was keenly aware of and smugly pleased with his unorthodox ways of handling such problems. Whenever he did something that was contrary to the rules of the book, he felt like spiting the staid instructors at the General Staff's school. He would tell his staff: "I'd hate to go to Leavenworth after the war. One would certainly get a 'U' for our successful operations. The Leavenworth instructors will be in a tough spot, their tactical principles will be subject to too many exceptions, historically."

He was highly flattered when a French general praised him during these days for his bold off-beat maneuvers. He was General Koechlin-Schwartz, one of his tank instructors at Langres during World War I, who now told him at an unexpected reunion in Brittany, "Had I taught 25 years ago what you are doing, I should have been put in a madhouse. But when I heard that an armored division was heading for Brest, I knew it was you."

The particular operation Patton had gone to VIII Corps to coordinate became a classic in unorthodoxy. He was cutting the 90th Division through the same town, on the same street used by the 4th and 6th Armored and two other infantry divisions. "There is no other way of doing it at this time," he told Middleton—so they did it his way.

Although the tricky operation was proceeding without any serious mishap, Patton was not quite happy with what he found at the command post. Though he had instructed Middleton to send the 8th Infantry Division with the 4th Armored to Rennes, he now discovered that the VIII Corps Commander had revised his order, sent no infantry with the 4th Armored, but sent it west instead, along the north coast into Brittany. He promptly corrected these arrangements, but was objective enough to appreciate Middleton's reason for doing what he did. Although he barked at Middleton, "What's the matter with you, Troy? I cannot make out why you're so dumb!", he remarked under his breath, "Of course it is a little nerve-racking to send troops straight into the middle of the enemy with front, flanks and rear open. I had to keep repeating to myself, 'Do not take counsel of your fears.'"

Patton was now fully in his element. He was touring the front, as was his custom, with rapid thrusts from one unit to another, showing up unexpectedly with a speed that made him appear capable of being in several places at the same time. "The Old Man has been like one possessed," Colonel Codman, his aide and traveling companion, wrote to his wife, "rushing back and forth up and down the incredible bottle-neck, where for days and nights the spearheading armored divisions, followed by motorized infantry, have been moving bumper to bumper . . . . Pushing, pulling, exhorting, cajoling, raising merry hell, he is having the time of his life.

"I am quite ready to believe that there may be other E.T.O. commanders who equal our own in mere technical proficiency. I have seen or heard of none, however, who can even remotely compare with General Patton in respect to his uncanny gift for sweeping men into doing things which they do not believe they are capable of doing, which they do not really want to do, which, in fact, they would not do, unless directly exposed to the personality, the genius—call it what you will—of this unique soldier who not only knows his extraordinary job, but loves it."

It was Sicily all over again. "An entire army," Codman wrote, "from corps commander to rifleman, is galvanized into action by the dynamism of one man. Even his military superiors find themselves irresistibly, if reluctantly, drawn into his magnetic field, and what was originally planned in the rarefied atmosphere of higher headquarters as the securing of a modest bridgehead bids fair to develop into a race across the Continent."

Patton did his touring in a jeep driven by Sergeant Mims, followed by an armored car. From time to time, at the most unexpected places, he would roar at Mims, "Halt!" and jump out to intervene in some situation he either liked or disliked. In Avranches, as the armor and infantry were moving laboriously along the overcrowded main street, he mounted an umbrella-covered police box in the middle of the square, and directed the traffic for an hour and a half.

Driving east of Avranches through the cluttered countryside, over which hung the unmistakable odor of iodoform because an ambulance column had been attacked there a short while before, he caught up with the 90th Infantry Division, led personally but somewhat sluggishly by General Landrum, between the Sée and the Sélune Rivers. Patton did not like what he saw. He thought the division was not up to par. The men were filthy. Their discipline seemed to be poor.

Patton jumped from his jeep and walked in the column for a couple of miles, darting to and fro, up and down, talking to one man after another. He concluded that the division was not as bad as it seemed. "These boys are normal," he told his aide, "but they're in bad physical shape and are badly led." Later that day the 90th had a new commanding general, Major General Raymond S. McLain, a National Guardsman whose career skyrocketed under Patton's tutelage. Under McLain, the 90th Infantry blossomed into one of the Army's best and proudest divisions.

From time to time Patton came upon his favorite people in France, the resistance soldiers of the French Forces of the Interior. They were having the time of their own lives dealing with German units left dazed and mauled in the wake of our armored advance. Each time he bumped into a group of these irregulars, most of them in their civilian clothes marked as combatants only by the tricolor arm-bands on their jacket sleeves, Patton stopped for a hearty talk in his rusty but vigorous French. "Full of goodwill and Calvados," as Codman put it, "the delighted Frenchmen un-loaded on Patton hair-raising stories about their usually brief but conclusive encounters with the Boches. Oh God, how Patton relished their tales!"

Patton was bombed, strafed, shelled—but he thrived on it. At the summit of a badly littered road over a hill he stopped to survey the scarred and scorched landscape of war—rubbish that used to be farms, fields in which the grass was burning, hundreds of stiff-legged, dead cattle. He threw out his arms as if trying to embrace the scene, and shouted to the sky, "Could anything be more magnificent?!" That split second an invisible battery opened up with a salvo, Patton had to raise his voice to a still higher pitch, as he exclaimed, "Compared to war, all other forms of human endeavor shrink to insignificance. God, how I love it!"

The immediate business on hand, however, remained Brittany.

On the afternoon of July 31st, when General Grow's 6th Armored had been ordered by General Middleton to relieve the 4th Armored in the bridgehead at Pontaubault, Grow asked Middleton:

"What do you want me to do, Troy? Should I stay in the bridgehead or move on into Brittany at once?"

"Stay at the bridgehead, Bob," Middleton told him.

But shortly before dawn on August 1st Grow was awak-ened with an order from VIII Corps "to proceed at once through Pontaubault and move westward into Brittany through Pontorson and Dol-de-Bretagne to Dinan." This was the direct result of Patton's intervention. Middleton figured that several days would pass before the exploitation would commence, but Patton intervened promptly and energetically. He had ordered Middleton to continue the exploitation without letup and gave him his dispositions for the two armored and two infantry divisions.

Grow spent the morning drawing up his plans for the advance. Hoping to get his whole division through the Avranches corridor without mishap, he planned to wait until he had his three combat commands together and only then to begin the march. Middleton went to Grow's CP in the morning, inspected the plans and approved them.

In the afternoon, Grow was directing traffic at a crossroads when a jeep suddenly stopped near him. Out jumped Patton, who immediately buttonholed Grow and told him in a low voice edged with excitement, "Listen, Bob. I've bet Monty five pounds that we would be in Brest by Saturday night."

This was Tuesday! Brest was more than 200 miles west of Avranches, at the far end of a Brittany that had to be secured every mile of the way. Aside from whatever forces the Germans had on the peninsula to contest Grow's advance, the exit of an entire armored division seemed to be hopelessly blocked. The rubble and wreckage-covered area around Avranches appeared as an insurmountable obstacle even to the deployment of the division.

Now Patton put his hand on Grow's shoulder, looked into his eyes and said, "Take Brest, Bob."

"What are my intermediate objectives, sir?" Grow asked with some solemnity, without questioning his orders.

Patton told him merely of his interest in the Brest-Rennes railroad and added, "I want you to bypass resistance."

"That's all I want to know," Grow said, and was off promptly to make his arrangements. Patton had overruled Middleton. Instead of going only to Dinan, just around the corner from the base of the Cotentin, only a few miles into Brittany, the 6th Armored was to proceed all the way to Brest.

General Grow was almost literally jumping with joy. He told his staff that they had "received a cavalry mission from a real cavalryman." This was exactly what he expected from Patton, whose G-3 he once was and for whom he had repeatedly planned similar operations to be tested in peacetime maneuvers. "It was," Grow later said, "what we had spent years studying and training for."

Reviewing the fantastic order in the historical perspective, Martin Blumenson wrote in the Army's official record of the pursuit: "To some, it might have seemed like madness to think of reaching Brest . . . in five days." But it was the rational thing for Patton to do. "Giving armored forces seemingly impossible goals to keep commanders looking beyond the ends of their noses was not unusual for Patton," Blumenson wrote. "His dramatic words 'Take Brest,' and his ignoring of intermediate geographical objectives, clearly defined his intent to exploit through—the entire length of the Brittany Peninsula. The faster the exploiting force went, the greater would be its effect. If the exploitation culminated in capture of Brest, the operation would be perfect. The ultimate objective became the immediate goal. Even though it was perhaps hardly feasible to expect a solitary division to drive 200 miles into enemy territory and single-handedly capture a fortress of unknown strength, it was exactly what General Grow set out to do."

But battle, as General Eisenhower once remarked, is never a one-sided affair. "It is a case of action and reciprocal action repeated over and over again," he said, "as contestants seek to gain position and other advantage by which they may inflict the greatest possible damage upon their respective opponents."

In his drive on Brest, General Grow was quick to experience the validity of this truism. Moving west along the Brittany Peninsula, the 6th Armored bypassed Dinan to the south on August 2nd but ran into strong opposition the Germans had managed to develop there after all, Other trouble developed, too, back at VIII Corps Headquarters, as a direct result of Patton's conduct of the operation and his arbitrary orders rather than as the consequence of any German intervention.

The 12th Army Group was not in favor of improvising the difficult campaign. The higher staffs worked feverishly on safeguarding it instead of exploiting its mounting opportunities even if they involved only calculated risks. Bradley had ordered Patton to head for the Brittany ports, but told him in no uncertain terms to "post a strong force on guard in the center of the Brittany neck." He regarded this as imperative to stave off any enemy threat from the east, especially since the contours of a massive German attack in the direction of Mortain were now becoming increasingly discernible.

On August 2nd Bradley dropped in on Middleton's CP. He found the exacting VIII Corps Commander hopping mad at Patton. He had made his arrangements in accordance with Bradley's instructions, but Patton had countermanded him. Now he was worried about his exposed left flank and rear. "I am left with nothing, Brad," Middleton complained, "between my extended columns and the main force of the German Seventh Army to my rear."

He brought out the map and showed Bradley what he meant.

"I hate to race on toward Rennes and Brest with so much of the enemy at my rear," Middleton said. "If the Germans were to break through here at Avranches to the coast, I'd be cut off way out in Brittany, with maybe as many as 80,000 of my men marooned."

Bradley exploded.

"Damnit," he said, "George seems more interested in making headlines with the capture of Brest than in using his head on tactics." He was furious. Patton seemed to be justifying his worst fears. Instead of playing on the team and following orders, he was grabbing the ball and running with it, even at the risk of endangering the whole venture, for which, after all, Bradley carried the ultimate responsibility.

"I don't care," Bradley fumed on, "if we get Brest tomorrow—or 10 days later. Once we isolate the Brittany Peninsula we'll get it anyhow. But we can't take a chance on an open flank. That's why I ordered George to block the peninsula neck."

According to General Bradley's version of the incident, he immediately called Patton at his Third Army CP but was told that he was out. He then turned to Middleton and told him, "Order the 79th down to Fougères and we'll build up there as George was told to do. We can't afford to waste any more time. If the Germans were to hit us with a couple of divisions on the open flank, we'd all look kinda silly."

That "open flank" bugaboo again! There was a running controversy around Patton over the time-honored issue of the flanks. From time to time the higher staffs turned green around the gills, as Codman put it, when prongs of seemingly unprotected Patton spearheads launched deep into enemy territory showed up on situation maps. "Three times in the last few days," Codman wrote on August 8th, "in as many tents and wooded fields, the same dialogue with minor variations:

"Division commander: 'But my flanks, General?'

"The General: 'You have nothing to worry about. If anything develops—and it won't—our tactical Air will know before you do, and will clobber it. That will give me plenty of time to pull something out of the hat.' A pat on the shoulder. 'Get going now. Let the enemy worry about his flanks. I'll see you up there in a couple of days.' "

This was one of Patton's pet phrases, *"Let the enemy worry about his flanks."* He discussed the issue innumerable times with his staff, recorded his radical views on it in his diary and reflective notes, spelled out his thesis in letters of instructions—and exasperated his superiors with his ideas. A river flowing fortuitously in the right place, a couple of planes from Weyland's XIX Tac, anything handy was often good enough for him to protect his open flanks. Sometimes he did it with mirrors, merely by simulating such protection where none actually existed; and frequently he just did not give a damn. "Let the enemy worry about his flanks!"

To General Bradley's exact professional mind this was sheer heresy. It took General Middleton some time to get used to it. But others working for Patton accepted the "cockeyed doctrine" readily and gleefully. In the Third Army people grew accustomed to a bit of Couéism when thinking of flanks and stopped worrying about them lest they draw the Old Man's wrath upon themselves.

"What the hell," he would exclaim, "are you becoming a sissy?" This was his usual rejoinder to anyone bringing up the question. Most of the time the subject of flanks was promptly changed.

Still according to General Bradley's recollection, he drove to Patton's CP in the afternoon to take him to task. Patton was just returning from one of his excursions and seemed surprised to find Bradley waiting for him. "He was stiff," Bradley wrote, "and covered with dust after a day on the front. 'For God's sake, George,' I began, 'what are you going to do about this open flank of Troy Middleton's? I just ordered the 79th down there. But I hate to bypass an Army commander on orders to a corps.'

"George smiled sheepishly," Bradley went on, "and put his arm around my shoulder. 'Fine, fine, Brad,' he said, 'that's just what I would have done. But enough of that—here, let me show you how we're getting on.' "

This was the first intervention in Patton's impromptu campaign for Brittany, and while it had some adverse effect on the operations, it did not materially alter their course. However, twice afterward in rapid succession major alterations were made in Patton's dispositions, with more serious consequences.

On August 4th Grow was halfway to Brest, while Wood's 4th Armored Division was taking Rennes, after which it was supposed to move across the peninsula to reach the coast at Vannes and seal off Brittany. Much of what was now happening in the race for Brittany was contrary to General Bradley's concept of the operation. According to Blumenson, who based his reconstruction of the events on letters of instructions and orders issued between July 29th and August 3rd by 12th Army Group, Bradley wanted Patton "to drive south from Pontaubault to seize Rennes and Fougères, then turn westward to secure St. Malo, the Quiberon Bay area, Brest, and the remainder of Brittany, in that sequence."

Patton, on the other hand, "visualized his primary mission as clearing the peninsula, his incidental mission as securing Quiberon Bay and Brest and the other ports later, his eventual mission as driving eastward toward Paris and the Seine." Unlike Bradley, Patton saw his immediate objectives far in advance of the front. In the face of the changed situation, for which the "Overlord" plan had no provisions, he was absolutely determined to slash forward and exploit not only the mobility and striking power of his armored divisions but also the German disorganization. "There seemed little point," Blumenson wrote, "in slowly reducing Brittany by carefully planned and thoroughly supervised operations unraveled in successive phases"—the kind of campaign Bradley had in mind and preferred.

Patton had two great assets aiding his kind of campaign, while Bradley's methodical operation was suffering from as many liabilities. One of Patton's assets was amazingly accurate and up-to-the-minute knowledge of what was going on even in the farthest recesses of a badly splintered front, while Bradley at Army Group was frequently groping in the dark. The other was the absolute loyalty and eager cooperation of like-minded commanders attuned to his own thinking and raring to execute his plans. Bradley worked with equally loyal men whose minds, however, moved along more conventional lines and, like their boss, tried to conduct the campaign according to the book.

Eager to take advantage of every break—indeed, building the whole campaign on this concept of opportunistic warfare—General Patton realized that he needed something special by way of an intelligence organization to ferret out the breaks. He had to have at his fingertips prompt and constant information about every change at the front. To procure this data, Patton picked Colonel Edward M. Fickett's 6th Cavalry Group, one of the cavalry units he had coaxed from Bradley a few days before, with this purpose already in mind. He renamed Fickett's unit the Army Information Service and turned it into a communications unit.

Fickett organized his fast-moving snoopers into reconnaissance platoons—each with 2 officers and 28 men, moving in 6 armored cars and 6 jeeps—and instructed them to report all activities in the areas they covered. Their reports were condensed into teletype messages and sent to Third Army's advance CP.

Fickett's rapidly roving AIS was promptly nicknamed "Patton's Household Cavalry" and attained a reputation for gathering information that left intelligence officers all the way up to Army Group Headquarters green with envy. Bypassing normal communications channels and reporting directly to Army CP (which at times was 100 miles behind the far-flung forces of the front engaged in diverse operations), the AIS enabled Patton and his staff to be better informed as a whole, better even than the corps that was directing the operations, and certainly better than Bradley's G-2 at Army Group. Most of the time his Household Cavalry was behind Patton's uncanny knowledge of the situation. And his uncanny knowledge of the situation was behind what appeared to be impetuous orders and risky maneuvers, at least to those not as well initiated. The latter included Bradley's staff, whose intelligence was woefully inadequate at this stage.

Patton's second asset consisted of the two generals who commanded the armored divisions spearheading the drive into Brittany. John Wood and Robert Grow belonged to the Patton school of warfare. As Blumenson put it in his fascinating review of the plans, personalities and problems of the pursuit, "Generals Wood and Grow in particular felt toward General Patton, who like them, was a tank officer, an affinity they could not feel toward General Middleton, bred in the infantry." Having been placed by Patton in the van of the breakout, and having assured its success with

great élan, they and their units carried out their missions
with Patton's infectious self-confidence and enthusiasm.
Their concept of warfare in the breakout and pursuit was
ideally suited to the occasion. But it exasperated and
scandalized those whose job it was to maintain an over-
whelmingly important element in war, what is technically
called *control*.

Back on August 2nd General Middleton had complained
that corps control over the two armored divisions was
"practically nil." This was only partly due to the independent
actions of Wood and Grow and the rambunctious management of armor by Patton. To a large extent it was caused
by a breakdown in signal communications, reminiscent of
the similar failure in Morocco. "The expensive signal equipment at the disposal of the Corps," Middleton wrote in his
after-action report, "was never designed apparently for a
penetration and pursuit of the magnitude of the Brittany
operation."

The bad situation was made automatically worse by the
independence of Middleton's commanders, doing more or
less as they pleased, secure as they felt under Patton's protection. "A naturally headstrong crew," Blumenson noted
wryly (but with thinly veiled admiration), "became rambunctious in Brittany." The methodical and meticulous
Middleton, an infantryman by training and temperament,
was thus caught in "a whirlwind that threatened to upset
his ideas of orderly and controlled progress." While Grow
and Wood had Patton behind them in their free-wheeling
operations, the corps commander enjoyed Bradley's anxious
support in his efforts to restore a semblance of order to the
campaign after Patton had taken charge.

Out of this clash of personalities and from the problems
created by the abrupt change from "the positional hedgerow warfare in the Cotentin to wide-open exploitation in
Brittany" emerged dispositions that tended to thwart the
impressionistic maneuvers Patton was conducting on the
operational level—somewhere between tactics and strategy
—in favor of orderly advances to specific objectives by units
forming a compact front—a situation Bradley and Middleton hoped to achieve and strived to save from the Patton
hurricane. Headaches ensued all along, and situations developed that taxed Bradley's patience and tested Patton's
ingenuity to work beyond his orders and get away with it.

After the capture of Rennes on August 4th Wood was

tempted to move south to Châteaubriant, but his orders specified a westward move to Quiberon Bay as his next
objective.

Wood was counting on Middleton. Hoping to get his
orders changed to suit him, in a situation that was in a state
of flux anyway, he pretended à la Patton that he had received
no mission for his next move. Determined to straighten out
his eager-beaver tank commander, Middleton drove to 4th
Armored Headquarters, where he was given a most exuber-
ant welcome, Wood throwing his arms around the Corps
Commander.

"What's the matter," Middleton asked, "have you lost
your division?"

"No," Wood said. "But Goddamnit, they [Eisenhower
and Bradley] are winning the war the wrong way."

Wood nearly succeeded in coaxing from Middleton his
consent for the eastward drive. In the end he was ordered
to stick to a slightly compromised version of his basic
orders—to block the roads south of Rennes, to dispatch part
of one combat command southwest to secure the bridges on
the Vilaine River near Redon, and to make maximum use of
his reconnaissance units to secure the Vilaine River line.

The arrangement was confirmed in a list of missions
issued by Middleton to his commanders upon his return to
his CP.

Gaffey had come upon Middleton's routine list of missions shortly after midnight. He immediately went to Patton
because he realized that both the letter and the spirit of the
order issued to Wood were contrary to Patton's concept of
the 4th Armored Division's role in the campaign. He told
Gaffey to send an inoffensive memo to Middleton, reiterat-
ing Patton's "assumption," as it was politely phrased, that
"in addition to blocking the roads [south of Rennes]"—the
defensive role the Corps Commander had assigned to the
4th Armored—"you are pushing the bulk of the division to
the west and southwest to the Quiberon area, including the
towns of Vannes and Lorient," exactly what Middleton did
not intend to do but which was, as Gaffey emphasized, "in
accordance with the Army plan."

Without waiting for Middleton to act on the "assumption," Patton sent for Colonel Fickett and dispatched a unit
of his Household Cavalry directly to Wood with a message.
He ordered him unequivocally to move to the west, to Vannes and Lorient, to cut the Brittany Peninsula at its base.

All VIII Corps Headquarters could do after that was note the action and record the mission—without comment.

Grow's original orders, issued by Middleton in the wee hours of August 1st, sent him into Brittany, but instructed him to go only as far as Dinan, not too far, at that. Patton then blew the order wide open and told the 6th Armored to go all the way to Brest. He specifically ordered Grow to move as fast as possible, *bypassing all resistance*.

But at 1:45 P.M. on August 3rd, when Grow was already beyond Dinan, Middleton again revised his orders by radioing him: "Do *not* bypass Dinan and St. Malo. Message follows by courier." The message consisted of a piece of scratch paper on which Middleton had penciled, "Protect your front and concentrate so that we can move in on St. Malo tomorrow."

Grow was handed the message while observing an attack on Mauron by General Taylor's Combat Command A. The engagement was an unexpected intermezzo caused by an accident. Driving to the west after having bypassed Dinan (where patrols found a sizable German concentration in prepared positions), Combat Command A made the wrong turn at a fork and ran smack into the organized German resistance it was supposed to evade. Grow read Middleton's note and was stunned. It was already Wednesday! How in hell could he be in Brest by Saturday if he had to remain where he was and wait until Major General Herbert L. Earnest's task force and portions of Major General Robert C. Macon's 83rd Division took St. Malo?

Caught between Patton and Middleton, Grow decided to protest the order. He radioed VIII Corps requesting reconsideration, but received no answer. He then sent an officer courier with a message to the same effect. By 5 P.M. he had no choice and told his Chief of Staff, "Corps has changed our mission."

He began to make the necessary tactical changes, leaving Combat Command A near Mauron, telling Combat Command R (Reserve) to be ready to move on Dinan, and planning to send Combat Command B north to outflank the city. There was only one hitch, and Grow was inclined to see in it an act of God. He could not establish radio contact with Combat Command B. Here was, he thought, his opportunity to obey Middleton's orders while heeding Patton's instructions as well.

Grow began to toy with the idea of letting Combat Command B continue westward alone, but gave it up because he concluded that such a subterfuge would violate Middleton's order. He went looking for Combat Command B, and when he found it near Loudéac he instructed Colonel George W. Read Jr., its commander, to stay where he was for the time being—on the road to Brest, to be sure, but headed toward Dinan.

He still hoped that Middleton would let him continue on to Brest, but the officer he had sent to VIII Corps with his plea returned late that night, reporting that "The answer was no."

Then around 11 A.M. on August 4th Patton turned up unexpectedly at Grow's CP in a wheat field near Merdrignac. It was immediately evident that the Army Commander was furious, controlling his rage only with difficulty. He opened up by yelling at Grow, who had just emerged from his tent with a broad smile:

"What in hell are you doing sitting here? I thought I told you to go to Brest."

"My advance was halted, sir." Grow paled as he said it.

"On what authority, Goddamnit?" Patton roared.

"Corps orders, sir," Grow answered. His Chief of Staff then handed over Middleton's penciled message. When Patton was through reading it he put the note into his pocket, murmuring under his breath, "And he was a *good* doughboy, too," meaning Middleton, of course. Then he turned back to Grow.

"I'll see Middleton about this," he said quietly. "Don't take any notice of this order, or any other order telling you to halt, unless it comes from me. Get going and keep going till you get to Brest."

With that he climbed back into his jeep and drove off.

Even before Patton could take the matter up with Middleton—in fact, but a few minutes after he had left—a message was handed to Grow from VIII Corps. Middleton had undergone a change of heart. He now granted permission for Grow to continue toward Brest after all. At 11:25 A.M. Grow flashed the news to all of his commands: "Division proceeds at once on original mission to Brest. Dinan will not (repeat not) be attacked."

Grow then signaled Middleton that he would be ready to resume the advance shortly. But it took the division the entire afternoon to get ready. The thrust on Brest was delayed a day, its sharp edge blunted.

"Although Grow thereupon advanced day and night," Wilmot wrote of the aftermath of this aborted diversion, "evading enemy rear guards with the help of French guides [who had assured Grow that Brest was ripe to fall], he could not make good the 24 hours that had been lost." While he was covering the last 100 miles, the Germans withdrew their coastal garrisons from Western Brittany into the port.

Grow arrived at Brest on August 7th and attacked immediately. But the defenders foiled his initial assault, whose spontaneity was not exactly conducive to success. Even then the Germans were surprised to find the 6th Armored north of the city.

A scant day earlier the port had been but weakly defended, and the chances are that it would have fallen to Grow's spontaneous attack. As a result of the delay it did not capitulate until September 18th, and then it needed a 10-day assault by three infantry divisions, at the price of almost 10,000 American dead and wounded.

"This costly siege of Brest," General Bradley wrote in his *post mortem*, "has since been described by some as a wasteful and unnecessary campaign, executed primarily because of blind obedience to an outdated 'Overlord' plan that called for its capture." He went on to concede that "Overlord's" premise on the need for the Brittany ports had been invalidated, but asked, "Why then did we spend three divisions on Brest?"

His answer failed to take into account the delay Middleton's peremptory order had caused in Grow's promising drive. "The decision to take Brest," Bradley wrote with reference to its eventual siege and capture, "was not dictated by any outdated 'Overlord' plan of maneuver. I went ahead with the costly siege at Brest, with Eisenhower's approval, not because we wanted that port, but because [Major General Hermann] Ramcke [the garrison commander, an aggressive and fanatical Nazi] left us no other solution."

But Bradley continued to gloss over the fact that if Grow had reached Brest on August 6th instead of a day later, the plum could have been picked with ease, for the garrison was not yet strong enough to withstand the armored assault. It was only later that Brest's defenses became "spiked with troops from the crack 2nd Parachute Division" and Ramcke, rushing in to make a stand, decided to fight to the bitter end.

What is the historian's verdict on the aborted coup?

"By the time General Grow was able to launch his preliminary attacks . . . on 11 and 12 August, the Brest garrison numbered about 35,000 Army, Navy, and Air Force troops," Blumenson wrote. "But before then, even without such overwhelming strength, the Germans had made evident their decision to defend with determination. The extent of their fortifications, the size of the fortress complex, and Hitler's orders to resist to the last man were more than sufficient to keep a lone armored division from taking the largest port in Brittany."

He concluded: "Yet it was a spectacular achievement, an exhilarating accomplishment that went virtually unnoticed because of action elsewhere on a much larger scale."

What Patton had recognized instinctively in February, 1944, and with crystal-like clarity late in June now began to dawn on Bradley and others in the high command. "Overlord" had failed to provide for the situation that was confronting the Americans in Normandy. In every respect the sacrosanct plan was now hopelessly outdated.

Even on August 2nd General Bradley still clung to the original plan, with Patton's entry into Brittany representing the main American effort. As Bradley saw it, the entire Third Army was to be committed in Brittany, the whole of Brittany, and nothing but Brittany. This included XV Corps of General Haislip, waiting in the wings to join the issue. Under the plan, XV Corps was to advance along the north shore of Brittany, and it was only on August 1st that Haislip was told that the operation had been canceled. At any rate, this stubborn adherence to the outdated "Overlord" was badly cramping Patton's style at a time when "Cobra's" explosive outcome clamored for an entirely new orientation and a rapid acceleration of the whole campaign.

The break came on August 3rd. That day General Bradley (in a move for which General Montgomery was quick to claim credit) altered the course of the campaign by telling Patton to secure Brittany, not with his entire army, but with "a minimum of forces." In a telegram to Field Marshal Brooke, with whom he was keeping in closer touch than with Eisenhower and Bradley, his working colleagues, Montgomery wrote: "I have turned only one American corps westward into Brittany as I feel that will be enough."

More important were the implications contained in a Letter of Instructions Bradley issued on August 3rd in which he stated unequivocally that the primary mission of the American units under his command were to "go to the forces in Normandy who were to drive eastward and expand the continental lodgment area."

Simultaneously Eisenhower was developing identical concepts. He had come to the conclusion on August 2nd that "within the next two or three days," Bradley would "so manhandle the western flank of the enemy's forces" that the Allies would create "virtually an open [enemy] flank." By gaining the initiative, he could select the next move as he pleased. He considered it "unnecessary to detach any large forces for the conquest of Brittany," but would rather "devote the greater bulk of the forces to the task of completing the destruction of the German Army."

This was exactly what Patton had in mind, but he did not need weeks (and the overwhelming evidence in Normandy) to reach *his* conclusions. Yet even after the crucial decisions of August 3rd, the mission Bradley assigned to the Third Army was both offensive and defensive. Aside from Brittany, it was to secure a 60-mile stretch of the Mayenne River between Mayenne and Château-Gontier, and seize bridgeheads across the river. At the same time it was to protect the right flank along the Loire River west of Angers.

This was the cue for XV Corps to enter the stage and for General Walker's XX Corps to start working. Although his orders had the usual limitations, Patton was again thinking and planning far beyond them. He put Walker down on the Mayenne to take care of whatever protection was needed. Then he started Haislip off in various directions. XV Corps was to drive southeast to the river, but Patton told Haislip on August 5th, "Don't be surprised if you get orders to move to the northeast or even to the north." This implied an eventual Third Army advance some 50 miles beyond Laval to Le Mans.

Unlike Bradley, whose caution was still getting the upper hand and who was still mainly preoccupied, naturally enough, with safeguarding the enormous victory resulting from his success with "Cobra," Patton was thinking exactly as Eisenhower did.

He had, as Blumenson put it, sniffed the opportunity to encircle the Germans west of the Seine, and he liked what he smelled. But it needed yet another major crisis in the command situation, with a final blow to Bradley's cautious approach to the campaign, before he could go all-out after the scent.

CHAPTER TWENTY-SEVEN
THE CHAINS OF COMMAND

On July 27, 1944—the eve of the breakout when General Patton still had no inkling concerning his part in the war— Colonel Kent A. Hunter of his Public Relations staff picked up a choice bit of incidental intelligence in the correspondents' camp near Néhou. One of the reporters confided to him that General Marshall, in a candid review of the command situation in Normandy, had said:

"Bradley will lead the invasion. But he is just a limited-objective general. When we get moving, Patton is the man with the drive and imagination to do the dangerous things fast."

Hunter hastened with his prize gossip to Patton, whose gloom of the moment nothing could dispel. "This is very fine if true," he merely said. He then turned back to the frustrating chores of an army commander who had no army to command and who was not permitted to contribute anything constructive to this historic phase of a phenomenal campaign.

True or apocryphal, for we have only the anonymous correspondent's word for it, the statement attributed to General Marshall touched upon a crucial issue of "Overlord." In the final analysis it was the problem of command —probably more than any other single problem— that was to dominate the evolution of the campaign in August.

Command in war is a mystic quantity. It is infused with intangible elements flowing from the subliminal quotient of the human equation. For a long time victory in war was regarded as a miracle conjured up by that strange hero-figure, the military genius, standing in solitary splendor on his *Feldherrnhügel*, the vantage point of the supreme war lord, looking down on the battle below. Caesar was such a hero-figure. His art, as Theodor Mommsen defined it, consisted of "making possible through the suddenness of his resolutions what at first sight appears impossible." Napoleon regarded himself as such a master spirit of war. Ranke confirmed the validity of the Caesarian-Napoleonic claim when he said that great captains are, indeed, the souls of the army.

General Eisenhower, on the other hand, was inclined to credit luck with an inordinate share in the molding of the victorious commander. But von Moltke was probably closer to the truth when he warned that "luck in the long run is given only to the efficient," as Patton's case tended to show.

The romantic aura surrounding the great commander like a halo was carried over into the 20th century by the totalitarian countries. In Germany, Hitler's alleged military genius was considered the decisive factor in the war, supposedly doubling by its mythological prowess the physical power of his divisions. In the Soviet Union, Stalin himself was deeply imbued with the Napoleonic delusion. Once he personally amended his official biography by adding, "Comrade Stalin's genius enabled him to see through the enemy's plan and defeat him." The Duce of Italy basked in the reflected glamour of Fascist militarism, firmly believing that his amateurish dabblings in military matters were far superior to the thinking and transactions of the trained professionals.

Actually this was an archaic concept, as outdated in World War II as the blunderbuss. "Today," Montgomery wrote, "kings and emperors [or, for that matter, even dictators] do not take command in the field, and we find that the relationship between a general and his army in the past has little resemblance to the present times. The great military geniuses of those days forged their own instruments, and then cut their way to victory unhampered by political control. It is very different today."

War had undergone not only its industrial revolution, but

also a managerial revolution. As Hanson W. Baldwin put it, modern war is the product of many minds. "Napoleon," he wrote, "with his hands thrust in his coat, could no longer survey the modern battlefield and choose the opportune moment to order a cavalry charge. War today is a management process." And Alfred Vagts wrote that "the development of warfare, apart from the demand for an ultimate pyramidal point of decision and political authority, [holds] no role for the solitary military genius; he had been replaced by managerial staffs of experts, a change not all generals liked to admit." Gerhard Ritter, a German historian writing in 1944 under the handicaps prevailing under the Nazis, aptly expressed it as a subtle warning to Hitler: "The acquisition of strategical mastership outside a strict military education is no longer possible today."

Where did Patton fit into this new order?

He somehow proved that there are exceptions even to the most universal and rational rules of command, and that psychological factors in a gifted individual continue to have at least some influence in even the most modern organization, including, of course, the military. I, for one, believe that his combination of dash and daring on the one side and enormous professional skill and savvy on the other qualified him even for the Supreme Command, which was eventually denied to him through the failure of his superiors to recognize and appreciate the intrinsic and overwhelming value of such a combination.

However, his superiors must not be blamed exclusively or even too strongly for not having given Patton the place in World War II his genius deserved and which he, if given the job, would have probably justified. When he arrived in England in January, 1944, to take part in "Overlord," he already had a number of strikes against him. In the circles where the ultimate decisions were made he was regarded as a monumental bore and troublemaker who, it was reluctantly admitted, was indispensable.

Even so, it was not genuine disapproval of and mortification at his boisterous and thoughtless extracurricular deeds that were instrumental in turning his superiors against him. Even Patton's slapping of the two soldiers in hospitals in Sicily was initially regarded as an inevitable offshoot of his bizarre method of command, and was attributed to his highly emotional dedication to his job. It came to be considered intolerable only when it produced a scandal. His impromptu remarks at Knutsford were far too insignificant to warrant the righteous indignation and stern retaliation they provoked when they became distorted in publication.

Eisenhower was his staunchest supporter throughout the war. Even Patton conceded that without Ike's energetic intervention to secure his participation in "Torch" he would have been left behind in a humdrum Stateside job to stew in his own juice. Yet even Eisenhower was willing to discard him at one point during the Knutsford crisis when it became evident that Patton was creating trouble for him and represented an intolerable ballast weighing on his own personal responsibilities, as well as his future.

While in the end practical considerations outweighed whatever apprehensions existed, and Patton was retained in the Army so it could benefit from his drive and skill, he was kept down as far as possible and deliberately obscured. He was given assignments in which his superiors believed he could not create any serious trouble for them. Even General Semmes, who was persistently most cautious and discreet in his description of Patton's personal conflicts, conceded this much. "It is generally believed," he wrote, "that the high command, while believing in Patton's great tactical ability, genuinely feared his 'rashness.' Hence one of Bradley's prime missions was to keep a restraining hand on him, sometimes by order, and sometimes by diversion of supplies, or troops, to other armies."

While he was thus kept in line and held with firm rein (as far as it was possible), Patton performed brilliantly, frequently against overwhelming odds. Often showing off in incidents in which his conduct had the earmarks of the dilettante, the superb professional that he was always came through when the occasion demanded.

Within 24 hours of his Third Army's becoming operational in Normandy he was performing with all the skill of which he was capable. His conduct of the campaign in August—when even his very presence in Normandy was unpublicized and Bradley's supervision tended to be stifling—was nothing short of astounding. It was a kind of gargantuan *coup de main*, which he improvised from one moment to another and sustained with constant on-the-spot decisions.

It drew the highest praise from his victims, the Germans, who by their tradition and experience were well qualified to recognize exceptional proficiency in war. In his comment on the breakout and its aftermath, Percy Ernst Schramm, the distinguished historian who was one of the keepers of the German High Command's war diary, stated: "The breakout paved the way for a new situation. The struggle that hitherto resembled 1918, with two more or less static fronts, now developed into a war of movement whose speed surpassed, if possible, that of the [German] campaign of 1940." Professor Schramm elaborated upon his wartime remark in a communication to me, giving Patton first and foremost credit for this development.

General Siegfried Westphal, who was von Rundstedt's Chief of Staff in the west and opposed Patton with brain and brawn to the best of his ability, wrote to me: "As far as General Patton was concerned, I was of the opinion even then that he was by far the outstanding commander in the [enemy] camp. Above all else, Patton was remarkable for his determined and bold actions. This was quite in contrast to Field Marshal Montgomery, who was known to me from North Africa. Montgomery was always extremely cautious, unwilling to take any risks."

General Blumentritt, Westphal's predecessor at von Rundstedt's side, wrote: "We regarded General Patton extremely highly as the most aggressive *Panzer-General* of the Allies, a man of incredible initiative and lightning-like action. He resembled our own *Panzer-General* Guderian. His operations impressed us enormously, probably because he came closest to our concept of the classical military commander. He even improved on Napoleon's basic tenet —*activitée, vitesse—vitesse.*"

General Hermann Balck, a shrewd but taciturn soldier who commanded Army Group G, which later opposed the Third Army at the Siegfried Line, summed it up bluntly: "General Patton was the outstanding tactical genius of World War II. I still consider it a privilege and an unforgettable experience to have had the honor of opposing him."

And the great von Rundstedt himself told Liddell Hart: "Montgomery and Patton were the two best that I met. Field Marshal Montgomery was very systematic . . . That is all right if you have sufficient forces and sufficient time."

In an interview with Patrick Mitchell, correspondent of *Stars and Stripes* in Germany, he said unequivocally: "Patton was the best!"

Montgomery failed, somewhat conspicuously, to include even a single American general among his examples of outstanding commanders. But when he sketched the essential traits and qualifications of the great military leader in war, he described Patton after all, even if only by unwitting inference. According to him, "The man who aspires to rise to high command has got to make an intense study of the military art, and equip his mind professionally with all he needs—so that he will be ready when the moment arises, when the opportunity comes his way."

He must be, Montgomery continued, a man of decision and action. He must be calm in crisis and decisive in action. He must be a good judge of men, a good picker of subordinates. He must be tough, and ruthless in dealing with inefficiency in battle. He must know his soldiers and be recognized by them. "And he must be prepared," Monty concluded, "to take a chance when the situation favors boldness." Unintended though it most probably was, this catalogue of virtues described Patton astoundingly well.

Patton was also fascinated by the problems of command, both in general terms and insofar as they concerned himself. He once devoted an entire article in the *Cavalry Journal* to his ideas of leadership.

As far as the commander was concerned, he had no illusions about his psychological fabric, and was even somewhat caustic in his views. "In my experience," he later wrote, "all very successful commanders are prima donnas, and must be so treated. Some officers require urging, others require suggestion, very few have to be restrained."

Patton was, of course, not the sole architect of these stunning victories in the summer of 1944. They were produced by a remarkable combination of skills and personalities, in a difficult coalition war in which national idiosyncrasies and strong personalities continuously threatened to clash. The Anglo-American coalition of World War II was the most efficient and, therefore, the most successful such alignment in all the history of warfare because, to quote Vagts'

felicitous assessment, the common liberalism of England and the United States proved a better lubricant of war than the totalitariansim of the Axis.

The close and harmonious cooperation was the product of concessions and compromises. The coalition brought to the fore commanders with transcendent human qualities who were able to control their prejudices and were willing to make the necessary adjustments.

The very evolution of the top command structure in "Overlord" demonstrated the crucial influence of enlightened compromise. The basic concept of the cross-Channel invasion as the potentially most lucrative route to German defeat had the Americans—led vigorously by General Marshall—for its staunchest advocates. The British, under the influence of Field Marshal Brooke, could never work up more than lukewarm enthusiasm for it. When it fell to Brooke to issue the orders for drawing up preliminary plans for the invasion, he said pithily to the officer chosen to do the planning, "Well, there it is. It won't work, but you must bloody well make it!" Despite their misgivings, the British came to support "Overlord" royally, gallantly and selflessly, and assumed the major responsibility for preparing it in a long and tedious—and, as it turned out, brilliant—intellectual process.

In the immediate wake of the Casablanca Conference, a special organization called COSSAC (Chief of Staff to the Supreme Allied Commander) was established in London, and General Morgan of the British Army was named to head it on the assumption that "members of his staff would serve as a nucleus for the future Supreme Headquarters." General Morgan developed COSSAC along the lines of the traditional and tested British staff system (for which, incidentally, General Marshall had unbounded admiration).

Recognizing the British superiority in planning and Britain's substantially longer experience in the war, President Roosevelt and Prime Minister Churchill agreed initially that a British officer be named Supreme Commander of "Overlord." Until April, 1943, Brooke had been slated to get the job. But then it was decided that in view of the eventual preponderance of American forces in "Overlord," the Supreme Command should go to an American—General Marshall in particular.

Even though Brooke showed magnanimity in going along with the decision, he would not have been human if he had not resented the appointment of an American. He was told of the decision on August 15, 1943, in Quebec, and he described that particular Sunday as a black day for him, his mood upon hearing the news as "swamped by a dark cloud of despair."

Although Marshall was the logical candidate for the Supreme Command, Eisenhower was given the job in the end because the Chief of Staff was considered indispensable and irreplaceable in Washington. Patton was never considered for the top job, not even by himself or those closest to him who had unbounded admiration for his talents. He was, even after Morocco and Tunisia, if not exactly an unknown quantity, still an unfulfilled promise. His impressive accomplishments were somewhat clouded by glaring errors and occasional halfbaked arrangements and were overshadowed by his arbitrary and seemingly impetuous acts. His record in 1942 and 1943 was spotty, and Eisenhower showed genius in judging his man, as well as courage, when he continued to husband Patton for the showdown and eventually gave him his historic chance.

During this crucial period of the war in July-August, 1944, the fate of the grand Allied campaign was in the hands of five men. Four of them happened to be Americans—Eisenhower, Bradley, Hodges and Patton. Only one, Montgomery, was British. Like the ingredients of a chocolate malted, the character traits of these exceptionally gifted commanders now whirled about in an invisible mixer to produce the battle. This handful of men, forming the high command in one of history's vastest campaigns, presented a fascinating combination of those skills and talents, personal assets and liabilities that together shape the course and outcome of wars.

General Eisenhower was clearly the strategic genius in the group, perfectly suited for the Supreme Command. By the same token Patton was the outstanding tactical genius, best qualified to translate the Supreme Command's ideas and plans into bold and decisive action in the field.

Bradley was shrewdly placed between the two, and in due course he became the perfect bridge between Eisenhower and Patton. But at this stage he had not yet found himself comfortably at home in this war, either as the custodian of Eisenhower's strategic concepts or as the comptroller of Patton's broad and ingenious but unorthodox tactical designs. For all his know-how and organizational ability, for all the sweep of his scientific military prowess, for all his comprehension of war and mastery of plans, Omar Bradley was still somewhat uncomfortable at the top. He was unsure and a bit vacillating, not by any means in the handling of his million men, but in his relations with and attitude toward this single man—George Patton.

It was somewhat difficult for him to accustom himself—psychologically, that is—to his enormous new responsibilities and to develop the flexibility this unprecedented war demanded. For a while he was shaken and uneasy when he found himself suddenly confronted with two inescapable realities the fighting in Normandy had produced. The war he was directing was not going by the book. And his most important commander in the field—the unpredictable and ruggedly individualistic George Patton—turned out to be the general he least wanted on his team.

The erratic relationship between Bradley and Patton at this stage was an appreciable impediment to the most efficient prosecution of the campaign. It was aggravated by the fact that Eisenhower gradually came to lean toward Bradley in the conflict and tended increasingly to accept Bradley's counsel and ideas even when his own concepts coincided with Patton's ideas and his strategic instinct told him that Patton, rather than Bradley, was right.

The unsatisfactory Bradley-Patton relationship of the first fortnight in August was not the only personality problem of command to affect the campaign and result in lost opportunities. Another was presented by General Montgomery and the British command in Normandy.

On August 1st the command structure of "Overlord" in France underwent a radical change. With the establishment of the 12th (American) Army Group, Bradley came into his own as Army Group Commander, working through Hodges and Patton, who commanded the First and Third U.S. Armies. The British now had their own household in the 21st Army Group, which had Montgomery for its commander, operating through Lieutenant General Miles C. Dempsey, who commanded the Second British Army, and Lieutenant General H. D. G. Crerar, commanding the First Canadian Army.

Montgomery was still left with another hat to wear. He remained the over-all chief of ground operations pending General Eisenhower's assumption of that command in France, the date of which, the scuttlebutt had it, Montgomery tried to postpone as best he could. So nominally Bradley (and Patton as well) remained under Montgomery, who had the last word in the conduct of the operations.

Patton expected that once he got going Montgomery would be the difficult one among his superiors to deal with, on what he attributed to selfish grounds. In his contemplation of hierarchical rivalry, Patton never considered Bradley an antagonist. He regarded Montgomery as the only general in the Allied camp with whom he would have to compete and who was worth competing with. Monty was, he readily conceded, a good and ingenious commander, somewhat like himself except for his caution; and, as he repeatedly remarked, he suspected the Briton of ulterior motives, on account of the man's king-size vanity, in order to steal the show.

But Montgomery proved the perfect boss in Normandy. He was, of course, preoccupied with his own troubles. The Germans shared the prevailing opinion that the seasoned British veterans were far more formidable and dangerous as foes than the green and presumably uncouth Americans. They, theyfore, concentrated their forces opposite the two British armies, enabling Monty to claim afterward that he himself had planned it that way all the time—to draw the enemy to himself by "pivoting on Caen" and give the Americans all the great opportunities in the campaign in the face of much lighter German resistance.

Montgomery was watching Patton's free-wheeling operations with unconcealed admiration and, indeed, he regarded them as the perfect implementation of his own grand design. He was exercising his superior command with exquisite discretion and tact, never interfering with Bradley's tactical arrangements and tacitly supporting his prudent directives. But at the same time he did nothing to restrain Patton and, in fact, gave him a free hand even when and where Bradley sought to stop him or slow him down.

In his remarks to General de Guingand, his Chief of Staff and closest confidant in the field, and in his communications to Field Marshal Brooke, with whom he kept up an almost daily correspondence, Monty was lavish with praise of Patton, approving both implicitly and explicitly what he was doing. His personal admiration manifested itself in little things that were characteristic of his sentiments. In his letters to General Bradley, for instance, he rarely omitted to send his regards to George Patton, again singling him out as the only American general he deemed worthy of personal recognition.

It was an exasperating factor in the campaign, with its adverse influence on the entire "Overlord" design, that Montgomery was not doing as well as expected in his own sector. He was doing even worse, Eisenhower was inclined to think, than the stubborn German resistance warranted. The tedious development of the offensive in the British sector came as a grave disappointment not only to the Supreme Commander, but even to Churchill who, unlike Field Marshal Brooke, was not disposed to accept Montgomery's eloquent explanations at face value. In the final analysis, the slow escalation of the campaign south of Caen was Montgomery's fault, but only insofar as he had accepted responsibilities under what General Morgan called the "Overlord Master Plan," exactly as Patton had anticipated, for a far greater and faster mission than he was inherently, organizationally and materially capable of accomplishing. Far from actually failing in their basic task, the British performed as well as could be (and should have been generally) expected.

In assigning the missions in "Overlord," the planners overlooked some of the intangible factors that frequently play an inordinately and surprisingly great part in shaping war. They casually skirted the issue of national characteristics in their influence on man's actions, and neglected to consider the creeping fatigue of the British soldier, underfed and overwrought, his endurance sorely taxed, his vim and vigor somewhat blunted in what for him was the fifth year of a terrible war.

On the assumption that the British supplied the more experienced contingents for the Allied Expeditionary Force, the planners loaded them down with the more difficult and trickier tasks. In fact, the American soldiers were looked upon with some misgivings. Their performance in battle was candidly expected to be inferior to that of British soldiers. The planners hoped for the best, of course, but did not take any American ability for granted and made their arrangements accordingly.

This proved a mistake—understandable and perhaps even inevitable, but a mistake nevertheless, and one that could have or should have been avoided. Even Field Marshal Rommel, it seems, knew better. "In Tunisia," he wrote, "the Americans had to pay a stiff price for their experience, but it brought rich dividends. Even at that time, the American generals showed themselves to be very advanced in the tactical handling of their forces, although we had to wait until the Patton Army in France to see the most astonishing achievements in mobile warfare."

Rommel concluded with an observation that now seems especially pertinent: "The Americans, it is fair to say, profited far more than the British from their experience in Africa, thus confirming the axiom that education is easier than re-education."

Anxious to work in complete harmony, the preponderantly British planners tended to underplay the national differences lest they fell victim to a strange sort of nepotism. The result was a master plan in which the British unwittingly were given the benefit of most of the doubts, to their eventual detriment and to the detriment of the over-all crusade for Europe.

The underestimation of the ordinary American male's military prowess was bad enough. Probably even worse was the planners' miscalculation of American generalship. By D-Day in June, 1944, only two American commanders— Bradley and Patton—had emerged to impress them as outstanding performers with a promising war potential in the big league. All the others rated only question marks. Some were considered quite good, others indifferent. Some were expected to be pretty bad in action, an assessment that was inevitably influenced by memories of the Kasserine Pass and Anzio. As it turned out, American generalship proved almost uniformly excellent, and in a number of cases superior.

The British attitude was also due to the familiar condescension of the so-called city slicker toward the country cousins. This was by no means a one-way street. The Americans were also inclined to regard their British associates with suspicion and some of that same condescension. Once, during a trans-Atlantic telephone conference listened to at both ends by a number of people, the voice speaking from the Pentagon concluded a long dissertation with the exclamation, "But for Christ's sake, don't tell the British!" When the speaker indignantly inquired why his injunction had been greeted with laughter at the London end, he was told that his remark had been monitored by two British generals and a British admiral.

These then were some of the omissions and commissions in the creation of "Overlord." Their effect became unmistakable as soon as the plan was put into operation, influencing the command structure and making for grave problems in the field.

It may be tempting to contemplate what would have happened if "Overlord" had been given a different command—General Alexander, for example, as over-all ground commander, Montgomery in command of the British, Patton commanding the American army group, and Bradley in charge of the Third Army working *under* Patton. But it is preposterous and pernicious to ponder such iffy questions of the past—and useless, anyway. History would not be what it is, the record of man's crimes and follies, if logic and decency governed its events and great decisions.

CHAPTER TWENTY-EIGHT
THE FALAISE MYSTERY

It was close to midnight on August 6, 1944, at "Lucky Forward," Third Army Headquarters, in another apple orchard near St. Sauveur-Le Vicomte. The Third Army had been operational less than a week, but when General Patton now looked at Colonel Koch's big map in the G-2 tent before turning in, this was what he saw.

● General Grows' 6th Armored Division was within striking distance of Brest. On its right flank, Combat Command B of Colonel Read was just south of Morlaix and Lesneven.

● The 83rd Infantry Division of General Macon was at the gates of the St. Malo fortress.

● General Earnest's Task Force A was a bit beyond St. Brieuc on its westward drive along the north coast of Brittany.

● An infantry team of General Stroh's 8th Infantry was in Dinan, the rest of the division near Dinard.

● The 4th Armored of General Wood was in Vannes, advancing on Lorient.

This much for Brittany, whose capture was, even three days before, supposed to be the sole mission of the Third Army. Patton was looking *back* on his Breton campaign and *forward* to juicier plums elsewhere as Koch's markers showed the following situation:

● Major elements of General Haislip's XV Corps were across the Mayenne River, driving rapidly on Le Mans.

● General Wyche's 79th Division was almost in Laval.

● The 35th Division of Major General Paul W. Baade was on the way to join General Walker's XX Corps. The eager corps of the balloon-shaped little general was protecting the southern flank with a single division, Major General Stafford LeRoy Irwin's 5th Infantry.

And this was only the Third Army. To the west, other markers showed General Hodges' First Army at Ambrières-le-Grand, at St. Pois, and, yes, *inside* Vire. The city had been cleared at last by Major General Charles H. Gerhardt's 29th Division of Major General Charles H. Corlett's XIX Corps, rendering V Corps of Major General Leonard T. Gerow temporarily unemployed.

The situation was still changing, virtually from minute to minute, despite the late hour. A buzzer broke the silence and Corporal Charley Andreen, on duty at the map with Corporal Dave Landow, put up another marker—a spearhead of Major General Lunsford E. Oliver's fresh 5th Armored Division had reached the outskirts of Château-Gontier. Then the buzzer sounded again and another marker went into the map to show that a reconnaissance troop of the 8th Infantry was at Châteaubriant, where four days before General Wood had longed to go when seized by a sudden wanderlust.

Master Sergeant Julius S. Kerekes' eloquent map told the complete story of these fabulous operations. This was no longer a crammed battle within its clearly demarcated field. This was a major campaign by itself, within the generous boundaries of the Third Army—running from Précy to Le Mans via St. Hilaire-du-Harcourt and Mayenne. Patton had coaxed plenty of elbow room from Generals Bradley and Hodges the day before, and for once he got what he wanted.

Gaffey grinned back because he knew what Patton meant. By being on the "outside" the Third Army could operate freely and drive on virtually every point of the compass.

"An accident of geographical position," noted the after action report in the cocky language of the Third Army, "enabled the Army on 5 August to advance in every direction—east toward Le Mans, south and southwest through Laval and toward Lorient, west toward Brest and north toward St. Malo—but the dash and drive with which the Army carried the fight to the enemy wherever he could be found was no accident. That was the way Third U.S. Army fought."

Yet Patton was still not satisfied.

Why the hell isn't Wyche *inside* Laval? How come McLain couldn't put enough snap into that green 90th Division to cross that Goddamn Mayenne River faster? What is keeping Macon from taking St. Malo?

He had gone to the VIII Corps CP to find out what was delaying the capture of that Breton port, and was not satisfied with what he had found. "Apparently it is simply the fact," he fumed, "that the people are too damn slow, mentally and physically, and lack self-confidence."

Patton caught himself in one of his unreasonably irascible moods and concluded that it was time for him to retire and recharge his batteries. He dreaded fatigue. "There are more tired division commanders than there are tired divisions," he used to say. "Tired officers are always pessimists."

He went to bed.

The next morning he was fresh and pleasant, and then something happened that galvanized him into feverish activity. At 8:30 A.M. Gaffey and Koch brought to his trailer a bedraggled American air officer accompanied by a lieutenant and an officer of the FFI. The air officer was Lieutenant Colonel Howard G. Coffey, fresh from a harrowing adventure. He had been shot down near Angers three weeks before, was picked up by the FFI and hidden near the city. When the battle exploded, the FFI guide drove Coffey from Angers to Châteaubriant, picking up the lieutenant on the way. It took three days to cover the 100 miles.

Colonel Coffey had electrifying information for Patton.

"We drove by back roads, sir, with our eyes open, but didn't see any large formed bodies of Germans," he said. "All we saw were German signal detachments taking up wire and moving east."

"How about the bridge at Angers?" Patton asked eagerly.

"It's intact, sir," Coffey said. The Frenchman nodded his agreement.

This was a splendid bit of news. Somehow Angers drew Patton's thoughts like a magnet. It was the farthest he had hoped to go when Bradley told him to secure only the bridgehead at the Sélune River and stop there. A lot had happened since. But Angers was still an attractive goal.

"Hammond," Patton barked at his Signal Officer after only a moment's contemplation, "is your phone working?"

"Sorry, sir," Hammond said, "it isn't. Our lines have been blown out."

Patton hesitated only briefly, then turned to his Chief of Staff.

"All right, Gaffey," he said, "you take Colonel Carter [Lieutenant Colonel Bernard S. (Bunny) Carter, Codman's best friend and Colonel Koch's French-speaking assistant] and go to Vitré. Pick up a combat team, the tank battalion and recce troop of the 5th Division, and take Angers. The gentleman here"—he pointed at the FFI officer taking in everything with incredulous eyes—"will show you the way. And yes, tell Irwin to send a battalion to Nantes to keep the Boches from interferring. Hammond!"

"Yes, sir," the signal chief snapped.

"Get word to Wood to send elements of the 4th Armored southward on Nantes, to help Irwin."

If all this sounds simple enough, as the logical exploitation of an open opportunity in the face of apparently no resistance, well, in truth it definitely was not. Patton went for Angers—which was 100 miles from where he had come in at Avranches on August 1st—at the very moment the Germans were pushing in with a vicious blow that was rapidly assuming the proportions of a full-scale counteroffensive. This was the trump Hitler had up his sleeve, the existence of which Bradley had hinted to Patton a week before.

The operation, which became known as the Mortain counterattack, had been thought up by Hitler at his headquarters in East Prussia, a thousand miles from the hard-pressed West Front, as his strategic remedy for his plight in Normandy. He developed the plan by looking at Jodl's big map of the front, the apparently overextended advance of the Third Army attracting him like a moth to the flame On the map, and at the safe distance of Rastenburg, the idea seemed nothing short of brilliant. The Seventh German Army was to advance through the United States line between Mortain and Avranches to the sea and annihilate the American forces cut off to the south and in Brittany.

By the time Hitler had the plan down on paper he was infatuated with it. He described it as "a unique, never recurring opportunity for a complete reversal of the situation." He convinced himself that all danger from the rapidly developing invasion of the Allies would be over by August 10th, and sat back to await what he told Jodl would be the greatest triumph of his life and the crowning achievement of his career as a war lord.

The Führer's high opinion of the pending operation was not shared by the man assigned to execute it. When Field Marshal von Kluge received his directive on August 3rd, he threw up his hands in despair. He considered the plan far too grandiose and impossible to carry out—"the apex of conduct by a [supreme] command," as Major General Rudolf-Christoph Freiherr von Gersdorff put it, "ignorant of front-line conditions, taking upon itself the right to judge the situation from East Prussia." At 8:35 A.M. on August 3rd, von Kluge phoned General Jodl to tell him about his misgivings. But by 11 o'clock he was no longer questioning the infinite wisdom of the Führer. He was doing as he was told, without any further remonstrations.

Von Kluge was an able soldier, but he was a weak and corrupt man. He had sold his soul to Hitler for lavish cash grants from the Führer's privy purse and was completely committed to him for better or for worse. But he was also somewhat bolstered in his new resolution to go ahead with Hitler's plan and orders—"to run all risks and use every means to thwart the breakout even at this late stage," as he eventually told Jodl—because in the meantime his forces had scored some unexpected local successes, even if only defensively. A ghastly gap in the Seventh Army front could be closed. A new front could be established in the south. The one in the west seemed to be on the verge of being consolidated.

Only Patton continued to cause him trouble. It was on this day of doubts and hopes in von Kluge's doomed life (he was to commit suicide two weeks later) that the Third Army broke into Brittany, took Rennes and reached Vitré, Châteaubriant and Redon. By then, however, von Kluge had hypnotized himself into even welcoming this American drive, rationalizing that it would deliver to him still more Americans to cut off and destroy.

Patton followed developments with mixed feelings. He countered Bradley's repeated warnings (based on exceptional intelligence, the origin of which was never disclosed) with glib platitudes. "I don't think you have anything to worry about, Brad," he said. "The Kraut is only bluffing to cover his withdrawal!" But it was mostly auto-suggestion to reassure himself in the face of the developments that could, he feared in his secret heart, throw his whole vast maneuver out of kilter. He continued most of his operations on his scattered fronts, even arranged new ones like the charge at Angers, but stopped the 80th, the 2nd French Armored and the 35th Divisions in the vicinity of St. Hilaire, "just in case something might happen."

It happened on August 7th. Shortly after dawn von Kluge unleased the counterattack with massed armor in the direction of Avranches. It penetrated the line at the junction of Corlett's XIX and Collins' VII Corps, overran Mortain and rolled on to Juvigny and Le Mesnil-Tove before it could be stemmed with the help of aircraft. The First Army, as usual, bore the brunt of the counterblow, its 30th Division of Major General Leland S. Hobbs being hit the hardest and several other elements becoming isolated in the Mortain area.

Despite the initial success of the ambitious attack, skepticism continued to prevail in the German High Command, as indicated by several caustic marginal notes in the war diary. To an entry that read, "The hope persists that the breakout can be halted," someone at the Führer's headquarters added the irreverent question, *"Where?"* The record of a phoned directive that had ordered General Hans Eberbach to lead the counterattack carried the penciled remark, *"Ordered by whom?"* A notation of Hitler's "intention to pursue the enemy after the success of the counterattack" had the subtly sardonic comment, *"The Führer's intention!"* with a poignant exclamation mark.

Bradley managed quickly, calmly and brilliantly to stabilize the situation by committing General Barton's 4th Infantry Division and the 2nd Armored of Major General

Edward H. Brooks, transferring the 35th Division to First Army and making a number of other arrangements. When, on August 8th, the enemy continued his efforts to deepen the penetration, the First Army held fast on all lines while elements of the 2nd Armored began to push back the Germans at Mortain. The situation was most succinctly summed up on August 9th by a laconic entry in the German war diary: "The attack of Panzer Group West (reorganized for the enterprise as *OB Panzer 5*) in the direction of Avranches has failed to produce the hoped-for success."

Instead of throwing the First Army back into the sea and chopping up the Third Army in Brittany, Hitler's ill-fated panacea further aggravated the German situation. But the Führer was not through yet. Even while von Kluge was trying desperately to convince him of the utter hopelessness of the situation, Hitler was pushing *OB West* to regroup his forces and reopen the attack, convinced as he was that the first onslaught had failed only because it was launched "too early, in insufficient force, and in unfavorable weather."

The assault was renewed on August 11th, but by the next day the First Army succeeded in completely defeating the German effort to break through to Avranches. General Collins' VII Corps recovered the ground lost to the enemy, and Hodges' army, the incomparable workhorse of the American expeditionary force, resumed its march toward Sourdeval and St. Sauveur-de-Chalieau.

Patton now conceded that the German threat had been no bluff, but that was the only concession he was willing to make. At no time during the counterattack did he slow or stop his own drives. On August 7th, when the German blow exploded the First Army front, he pressed Haislip on to Le Mans. On the 8th he sent the 79th Division into the city. When, he ran into Bradley that day and was told that "the danger from the counterattack had passed," he rushed back to his CP and wrote out in his own hand the remarkable order for what, as we shall see momentarily, became one of the historic operations of the war—the attack of XV Corps on the line Alencon-Sées. And he ordered the 2nd French Armored Division of Major General Jacques Leclerc, which had arrived in France a week before, to get moving and secure the Sées-Carrouges line in preparation for much greater things, the shape of which he had seen in the smoke of the Mortain attack.

The other objective was his pet project of the moment,

whose development he was following most avidly. It was the
coup to capture Angers. On August 8th the 5th Division
invested both Angers and Nantes; on the 9th it closed in on
Angers, and on the 10th it captured the city. General
Walker's restive XX Corps had scored its first victory, in an
operation Patton had designed on the spur of a moment.

It was just one of those things. When he had decided upon
it in the wake of Colonel Coffey's sudden appearance with
cheerful intelligence about the apparent absence of German forces in the Angers area, Patton must have had some
doubts of his own about the venture, because he remarked
in an aside, "I am doing this without consulting General
Bradley, as I am sure he would think the operation too
risky." Then he added, "It is slightly risky—but so is war."

This was a very big war—by now more than two million
men were battling in Normandy, Brittany and points south
—but during this first fortnight in August it seemed that it
was not big enough to accommodate both Bradley and Patton. The sudden appearance of Patton in the campaign resembled the thrilling moment at a rodeo show when the
gates of a pen are thrown open and the prize bronco of the
ensemble thrusts into the arena. If one is permitted the
metaphor, Patton was the bucking bronco of the show and
Bradley the rider trying frantically to stay in the saddle.

During these days Patton was gaining ground and apparently clinching the campaign with a largely improvised
maneuver of unprecedented power and velocity, bursting
"Overlord" at its seams. At the same time Bradley was working almost desperately to restore a semblance of order to
the campaign and conduct it in a set and prudent manner
on schedule, according to some reasonable design. He himself was drifting away from the outdated master plan and
was becoming bolder, without being carried away, by the
sweep of his victories. But he was trying to substitute a
design of his own, adapted to the changed situation as it was
seen by his G-2, and as far as it could be gauged in the flux.

Unlike Montgomery, who secluded himself in his personal caravan isolated even from his headquarters staff, Bradley was a gregarious commander. Whenever he could spare
the time, he toured the fronts. Now he was en route most of

the time, trying to follow Patton and draw him, with smooth words if possible and with orders and other means if necessary, into the orbit of his own plans.

By nature Bradley was a paragon of prudence, always anxious to fulfill the responsibilities expected of him. This had been instrumental in General Marshall's decision to give the American command in the invasion to him, and in endearing Bradley to General Eisenhower. Ike, too, bore the ultimate responsibility for the success of the invasion. He knew that success always had many parents but failure was an orphan, and he did not cherish the prospect of becoming orphaned by some major mishap in France caused by reckless or sanguine actions, either his own or any of his commanders'. Although Bradley's enormous professional competence made him a superb hunter, he preferred a bird in hand to a bigger and more picturesque bird in the bush.

In his cautious approach to the campaign Bradley was now motivated mainly by strictly professional considerations. For one thing, his G-2 could not keep up with the events and rendered conclusions and interpretations that were frequently erroneous. As a result, Bradley was, despite his position at the apex, not as well informed about the actual plight of the Germans as his commanders in the field, at the broad base of the pyramid where things were popping. He was, therefore, prone to overestimate the enemy's strength and his ability to make trouble. He appeared to be justified in his appraisals, and was fortified in his views, by the Mortain counterattack, which seemed to show that the Germans had the will and the power to strike back, and probably even to place the vast Allied enterprise in jeopardy.

Equally important—and probably foremost in Bradley's mind—was the logistic aspect of the immense venture. It was what he liked to call the tyranny of supplies that forced him to cling to the master plan longer than seemed warranted. No matter to what extent the plan had become outdated by the course of the fighting, its basic logistic provisions remained in effect, and supplies continued to be regulated by its original arrangements.

Bradley could not very well commit himself to a plan—however promising it was and appropriate it might be to the different circumstances—if he could not expect power and adequate logistical backing. With the supply situation being what it was, he had no choice. He had to fall back on the master plan and that, in the light of the breath-taking speed of events, made him seem even more cautious than he was by temperament.

Patton sensed that he was making Bradley uneasy and nervous, but he was not wasting any sleepless nights over it. He tried his best, with humility that he could turn on or off as the occasion required, to placate and accommodate his superior. Despite his self-confidence and the glittering triumphs, he realized that he was still on probation and that in any showdown his conflict with Bradley might bring about, Eisenhower would opt for Bradley and let him go home.

Patton went out of his way during these days to be "nice" to Bradley. He let him feel at every turn that he recognized him as the boss. He rarely, if ever, voiced any firm objections to the group commander's orders, no matter how they threatened to cramp his style; he tried to make himself as inconspicuous as possible at times and extremely hard to find whenever he was off on one or another of his independent ventures, like the race for Brest or the *coup* to take Angers.

On August 31, Patton flew with Bradley to Morlaix, then went to VIII Corps Headquarters with him to see Middleton about Brest, whose defenders were still putting up tenacious resistance. Bradley was not, as he put it, sanguine about the capture of the Breton port, and Patton seized the opportunity to remark that he was getting tired of fighting on four fronts indefinitely. The remark was a sly plant. He hoped it would persuade Bradley to give him a freer hand where the pickings were better by releasing him from his tedious responsibilities in Brittany. The trick worked. "Bradley, as usual, had been thinking the same thing," Patton later wrote.

The Third Army staff never doubted that Bradley was making good in France by expropriating their boss's ideas, actually plagiarizing them either deliberately or unwittingly. Thus Codman wrote to his wife: "As of August 1st . . . General Bradley has adopted practically all of General Patton's plans."

If these things worked hardship on Patton, he was either too busy to show it or careful to conceal it. Any man less devoted to his job and less eager to serve his country would have felt strongly and resented bitterly the humiliating treatment to which he was subjected by much younger and less experienced men, actually his juniors even in perma-

nent rank. Communiqués issued by SHAEF were blooming
with names of places he had captured and headlines blazed
with victories he had scored, but his name appeared nowhere. His presence in France in action and the fact that
the Third Army had become operational continued to be
cloaked in secrecy. But it was becoming the worst-kept
secret of the war. It was certainly no secret to the Germans.

According to their war diary they had concluded as
early as July 17th that Patton had no longer been held back
in England for the supposedly main effort of the invasion
in the Pasde-Calais area: "A steady flow of units belonging
to *Armeegruppe Patton* to the bridgehead in Normandy indicates that there will be no major enemy landing in the area
of the Fifteenth Army." By the end of the month the Germans were so certain of this that orders were issued for the
transfer of major elements of the First and Fifteenth
Armies to the combat zone.

The activation of the Third Army on August 1st became
known almost immediately to the enemy, for, after all, wars
cannot be conducted behind closed doors, and secrets have
a way of crossing their barriers. Actually, German patrols
had captured several up-to-the-minute documents clearly
marked "Headquarters Third Army—APO 403" and at
least one field order so headed and signed "G.S. Patton, Jr.,
Lieutenant General, U.S. Army, Commanding."

Patton began to loom large not only in the minds of the
German generals who had the misfortune of dealing with
him at close quarters, but even in the reports of the German
combat correspondents. Only a week after his arrival at the
front his presence was revealed in so many words by the
German Transocean News Agency, whose material was
beamed by short-wave radio to the United States in English.

Patton was annoyed, not so much by his personal treatment at the hands of SHAEF as by the effect he feared
such management of the news with its blatant discrimination against the Third Army was likely to have on his men.
He considered high morale an absolute *sine qua non* for
the efficiency of his army and promoted it energetically and
ingeniously by all sorts of means. He was determined to
make every man serving under him imbued with a special
esprit and the soldiers of the Third Army the "cockiest
bastards" in the whole expeditionary force.

But while his own attitude toward the discrimination was
functional (worked off in special expletives), that of his

staff was highly emotional, so much so that the animus toward SHAEF at Third Army Headquarters threatened to interfere with the efficient prosecution of the war. General Marshall took notice of this brewing palace revolution and sent one of his aides to determine the extent of these animosities and how justified the suspicions really were. The observer spent some time on his clandestine investigation, and by the time his report reached Washington it was December. Virtually the morning after it was placed before Marshall, the battle erupted in the Ardennes, providing, as we shall see, some graphic illustrations for the observer's conclusions.

By then, however, everything was sweetness and light between Bradley and Patton, partly because they had found in Montgomery a common denominator of their discontent. More important though, Bradley had been drawn close to Patton, and not just on the principle of joining the man he could not lick. The bond of friendship the war gradually forged between these two great commanders made for exceptionally smooth and effective cooperation and became, I believe, one of the cornerstones of the victory.

But by then it was too late to make up for the past. The chance of destroying the German army in France before it could retreat behind the Siegfried Line and the probability of ending the European war in 1944 had gone. The shock effect of Patton's impact on the campaign was dissipated. Too many good opportunities had been missed, including one of the greatest of the war—the opportunity of catching the German forces in a *Kessel* (pocket), the likes of which Hitler's generals never managed to conjure up on the Eastern Front.

☆

The bold idea of encircling the Germans in France in the immediate wake of the landing began to kindle Patton's imagination as soon as he was shown the master plan of "Overlord." He would speak glibly and a bit flippantly of the "timidity" of a plan that carried the campaign to a D plus 90 phase line merely to secure a lodgment area bordering on the Seine in the east and made no provisions either for the collapse of German defenses inside the lodgment area or for the follow-up after it had been secured on the original schedule. Patton's criticism was based on sheer guess-work, for he could not know how the Germans would re-spond to the invasion. Nor was he by any means better informed about their condition, capabilities and morale in France than were any of his colleagues.

He was on much firmer ground after the invasion, and especially after the breakthrough at St. Lô when he could see with his own eyes—and maybe clearer than some of his colleagues—that German strength in France was disin-tegrating. And he became firmly convinced that a mortal blow could be dealt the Germans in Western Europe when he found that he could maneuver virtually at will at places the planners of "Overlord" expected to reach only 100 and maybe 200 days after the invasion.

Even Patton's intention, voiced on August 1st, to go all the way to Angers with the first wave of the flood, 100 miles from the point of entry of his army, rather than to the Sélune River, his actual objective only 10 miles away, was more bravado than serious design. But his ideas began to harden, now along strictly scientific lines, only three days after the Third Army had become operational, when he realized that he would not need XV Corps for the Brittany operation. He also had two additional corps, XII under Major General Gilbert R. Cook, one of his best friends, and XX, for maneuvers not fully or explicitly covered by "Over-lord."

The first record of Patton's plan to encircle and destroy the German army in France dates to August 4th, when he met General Haislip near Fougéres and told him to drive to the water line between Mayenne and Château-Gontier, about 30 miles to the southeast. Then he alerted General Walker and ordered him to take his XX Corps (which con-sisted of a single infantry division) south to the Loire. Fi-nally, he told Haislip to hold himself ready for bigger things.

He was expecting great things from Wade Hampton Haislip. The 55-year-old bulldog-faced, firmly packed Vir-ginian had had to work his passage into Patton's confidence, but by now he was firmly in, closer to the Army Command-er than even Middleton. He was one of the Army's best edu-cated officers—West Point 1912, Infantry School 1924, Command and General Staff School 1925, Ecole Supéri-eure de Guerre 1927, Army War College 1932. He spent 19 years in various service schools, either studying or teaching. Though Haislip was at St. Mihiel and in the Meuse-Argonne, and had commanded the 85th Infantry Division since April, 1942, Patton was somewhat wary of him when he was given XV Corps. He considered him "musclebound in the fanny" from too much sitting around in swivel chairs in the War Department. His last desk job "before joining the Army," as Patton mockingly put it, was that of G-1, Assistant Chief of Staff for Personnel, War Department General Staff. But he proved as competent in the field as he had in the office.

The drive Patton now entrusted to Haislip was a stab in the dark. There was little, if any, accurate information about the German forces in the area into which Patton was sending his two corps. Air reconnaissance was no help. "Each day we would get a thick book from the air force and we would have to try to figure out what if anything in it applied to our little spot on the map," General Haislip recalled later. "By the time we could figure it out, we were far away from there." Patton's Household Cavalry was not functioning yet. No contact had been established with about 2,500 organized members of the French Resistance groups presumably operating around Mayenne.

"Nobody knows anything about the enemy," Corps G-2 cautioned General Haislip, "because nothing can be found out about him."

The orders of August 4th were verbal and fragmentary. By the time he received their written confirmation the next day, Haislip had taken Mayenne. Patton told him, as he had told Grow, "Bypass all resistance." He did not have to bypass any. There was no resistance. Nobody knew *anything* about the enemy simply because there were hardly any Germans left in Haislip's path.

Now Patton flashed the word: "Don't stop!"

He told Walker to hurry up to the Loire to protect Haislip's south flank.

The eyes of XV Corps were now focused on Laval, about 17 miles to the southwest, and on Le Mans, *almost 50 miles to the southeast.* Before it could start rolling, however, the corps had to cross the Mayenne, a steep-banked stream about 100 feet wide and 5 feet deep. All the bridges except the one at Mayenne had been blown. There were other problems to surmount besides the river. The corps had both flanks open. And its objectives beyond the stream were bigger cities, like Le Mans with a population of 75,000.

But Haislip had been seized by Patton's fever. At 10:45 A.M. on August 6th he issued an order to the officers of the corps: "Push all personnel to the limit of human endurance." He told them, even as Patton would have said in a similar situation, that their "action during the next few days might be decisive for the entire campaign in Western Europe."

That same day major elements of the corps crossed the Mayenne; the 79th Division took Laval; then, on August 8th, it entered Le Mans. XX Corps was on the Loire. The entire situation in France had changed. The crisis of the German army was almost at hand. The war in Europe was approaching a climax.

At 4:40 P.M. on August 5th Patton had phoned Haislip at Mayenne, changing the axis of the corps' advance from the southeast to the east. Now it was about to be changed again, this time to the north. One of the steel arms of the Allies had suddenly stretched out to crush the German army in France in a lethal embrace.

It was not General Patton's job to plot the campaign. But he was making it easier for the planners to do their job. He was, of course, not the only one to recognize the great opportunity. Its outlines were becoming increasingly evident to anyone who could read a map or had even a perfunctory knowledge of the order of battle in France.

On August 1st the Germans had their badly bruised Seventh Army of three corps in a south-north bending line between St. Hilaire-du-Harcourt and Tessy-sur-Vire, the latter the most advanced point of the enemy front. Their Panzer Group West, consisting of four corps, held an S-shaped line between the Vire River and the Channel.

By August 6th the German front had been pushed back everywhere except in the eastern extremity of the long line. It was now running almost straight from southwest to northwest, from St. Pois to the Channel. The German forces had been regrouped for the Mortain counterattack and were reinforced by six divisions. In the specific area of the prospective pocket they now had massed 19 divisions, including two Panzer divisions.

In the Allied camp, on this August 6th, the most important development, aside from the drive of XV U.S. Corps, was the Canadian First Army of General Crerar south of Caen. It was getting ready for a southward drive to Falaise, a tannery and textile town of some 4,000 people in the Calvados, in whose Norman castle William the Conqueror was born. The advance, ordered by General Montgomery on August 4th in answer to repeated proddings of General Eisenhower "to press the attack," was scheduled to jump off at 11:30 P.M. on August 7th.

Even though the Supreme Commander was discreetly behind the drive, its direction from Caen toward Falaise represented the thinking of General Montogomery. Eisenhower had suggested on July 31st that a determined attack by General Dempsey's Second British Army coupled with an attack of Bradley's forces, mainly those of the First U.S. Army, would "clean up the area west of the Orne once and for all." But Montgomery was looking beyond the Orne.

On August 4th, in a paper called "General Operational Situation and Directive," he spelled out his intentions. He hoped to pin the Germans against the Seine, as the "Overlord" master plan had stipulated, and was about ready to issue the order for a general drive to that river. But he felt there was a more immediate opportunity "to cut off the enemy," as he put it, "and render their withdrawing east difficult—if not impossible." In another paper, issued on August 6th, he announced his intention to "destroy the enemy forces within the boundaries of the 'Overlord' lodgment area."

This was a strategic design of the first magnitude. The destruction of the Germans west of the Seine would be "such a damaging blow," Montgomery said, that it might "hasten the end of the war." To accomplish this, he ordered three Allied armies to swing into the German forces and the fourth to catapult forward to outrun them.

At this point General Bradley was not yet convinced of Monty's logic. He had agreed to Patton's drive on Le Mans as a preliminary for a move toward the Paris-Orléans gap. And he had ordered Hodges to secure the Domfront-Ambriéres-le-Grand area as a preliminary for a drive toward Alençon. But he was still worried that the Germans might "turn and leap."

In his Letter of Instructions No. 3, dated August 6th, Bradley judged the enemy capable of "assembling strong armored forces in the vicinity of Domfront," and expected him to mount an attack from there westward to Avranches. He was right, too. The German attack he had expected came within 24 hours, on Mortain. But after that, Bradley ceased to be a prophet of gloom. He not only accepted Montgomery's concept but actually improved upon it. When he was satisfied that he had pulled the sting from the German attack, he looked at the map and concluded: "By mounting their attack, the Germans incurred the risk of encirclement from the south and north."

It was shortly after lunch on August 8th at 12th Army Group Headquarters at Bradley's swank château near Coutances. General Eisenhower happened to be there when Bradley reached his conclusion. If he needed a push to act, Eisenhower was only too glad to give it. During those days he had written to General Marshall about the possibility of destroying the Germans, and now the opportunity presented itself, as shown by the pins in Bradley's map. He kept urging both Montgomery and Bradley to "pull a Clausewitz"—to destroy the Germans rather than be satisfied with mere gains of territory.

With Eisenhower breathing down his neck, Bradley called Montgomery on the phone to secure his approval "for a bold course of action designed to encircle the German forces west of Argentan and Falaise." Thinking along identical lines, Montgomery readily agreed. But to make sure that he would play his part in the "bold course of action," General Eisenhower decided to talk these things over with him in person. After dinner, he motored to Montgomery's headquarters "to make certain," as Butcher described it, "that Monty would continue to press on the British-Canadian front" toward Falaise. By then, Crerar's Canadians were on their way. It was a historic event in itself, for this was the first time in a war that Canada had a fighting force in action large enough to rate the name army.

All this represented a radical change in the arrangement of Bradley's 12th Army Group. His previous dispositions envisioned a drive toward the Seine. But the new plan called for a north ward turn of both the First and Third Armies, driving on Flers and Argentan instead. Stopping on the boundary line from Mortain to Domfront and Carrouges to

Sées, the Americans would form the southern jaw of the
vise. Coming from the north, British forces would act as the
other jaw between Tinchebray and Falaise.

General Bradley's order to Patton, as the first step toward
the formation of the southern jaw, read: "Advance on the
axis Alençon-Sées to the line Sées-Carrouges prepared for
further action against the enemy flank and rear in the direction of Argentan." Argentan was designated the outside
limit of Patton's advance.

Bradley's order reached Patton on August 9th. He was glad
to get it, but he read it with mixed feelings. It was another
of his own ideas reaching him in the form of an order from
Bradley.

On the previous morning Patton had moved his command post to St. James near Laval (Lucky's third move
forward in a week) and was visited there at 9 A.M. by General Bradley. He had come to tell Patton that the danger
from the Mortain counterattack had passed and to discuss
with him the next move in the light of this gratifying development.

Patton grabbed the opportunity to tell Bradley about the
plan he was working on—turning XV Corps north from Le
Mans instead of pushing it on to the Seine or Orléans—to
encircle the Germans and destroy them in a pocket developing through the Canadian advance.

Bradley told him that he was thinking along those same
lines, so Patton pulled out all stops and outlined his plan
with all its bold details. He suggested that they attack with
the axis either on Chartres or on Dreux about 75 miles to
the northeast, but Bradley turned him down.

Patton still argued. "This is a helluva big envelopment,
Brad," he said in effect. "And there are likely to be plenty
of Germans in that Goddamn pocket. We need elbow
room."

Bradley was adamant. He told Patton that the attack
would have to move on Le Mans-Alençon-Sées axis, in a
straight line up north. Alençon was only 25 miles from Le
Mans, Sées but 12 miles from Alençon; then came Argentan, another 12 miles slightly to the east, and finally Falaise,
about 15 miles still farther to the west. The line running

from Le Mans to Falaise marked out the contours of the encirclement. But it was closing in a small area containing tens of thousands of German troops in various stages of disorganization, threatening to become the kind of congested battlefield Patton dreaded.

"If we move on the Alençon-Sées axis," he persisted, "we won't have space for the kind of maneuver this operation requires. On the other hand, if we went for Chartres or Dreux . . ."

No, Bradley said. It would have to be Alençon and Sées.

It was better than nothing. Bradley left to meet Eisenhower near Coutances; and Patton, accompanied by General Hughes, went hunting for an elusive phallic symbol in Dolde-Bretagne. The talk with Bradley had left him both elated and depressed. His elation was not helped, and his depression was not alleviated by what he saw later that day when he looked in on the 83rd Division stalled outside of St. Malo.

On the drive back to St. James, Patton was quieter than usual. He was no longer thinking of the doughboys near St. Malo. He was preoccupied with Haislip's drive to the north. When he got back, he called for a folio-size pad of lined yellow sheets and, in his neat handwriting but with his abominable spelling, wrote out the order for the attack of XV Corps on the line Alençon-Sées, almost a full day before Bradley's directive reached him.

It was a historic order. It was not Patton's fault if it did not make history.

"The purpose of the ensuing operation along the axis of Le Mans-Alençon-Sées is to drive the German Army heretofore confronting the First American and Second British and Canadian Armies along the Channel coast, against the Seine between Paris and Rouen." This was the set plan under "Overlord," and Patton was complying with it. But then he began to deviate.

"In consonance with this plan you will advance along the axis Le Mans-Alençon-Sées, with the purpose of initially securing the line Sées-Carrouges, both inclusive, prepared for further advance utilizing the 5th Armored Division, the 79th and 90th Infantry Divisions and the Second French Armored Division, which is hereby attached to your corps."

He concluded by telling Haislip: "This letter is for the purpose of giving you the plans as now envisioned. Irrespective of anything in this letter, your mission is and will continue to be to destroy Germans in your front."

The order had two major points of departure from the set plan. Both were written in the special Aesopian language Patton had developed for communications with his commanders when he was giving them instructions exceeding his own orders. They came to understand it.

In this case Haislip knew what Patton had in mind when he wrote almost parenthetically, *"prepared for further advance."* It meant, Haislip knew at once, that he was not to stop upon reaching the Alençon-Sées area but was to push on to Argentan, then on to Falaise to meet the Canadians coming from the north. And the mission "to destroy Germans in your front" was Pattonese for the encirclement.

The big new mousetrap was being set. And the Germans were beating a hasty path to it.

On August 8th the Canadians seized Fontenay-le-Marmion, Requancourt and Garcelles-Secqueville. Five minutes before 2 o'clock in the afternoon their 4th Armored and the 1st Polish Armored Division attached to Crerar's army passed through the infantry to start their exploitation toward Falaise. The drive was expected to be a cinch. The night before and on this day the Eighth U.S. Air Force and the RAF Bomber Command had dropped more than 5,200 tons of bombs, in the second heaviest air support in Normandy, exceeded only by that given the British on July 18th. Yet the drive of the two armored divisions was almost stopped cold by unexpectedly strong enemy opposition.

The next day the 4th Armored overran Bretteville-le-Rabet while the Poles seized Cauvicourt and St. Sylvain. The fighting was heavy and costly. Falaise was about 12 miles away. Little progress was made on August 10th and 11th. On the 12th the Canadians were still held up astride the Falaise road.

But that day Haislip reached Alençon and Sées, and began to implement Patton's coded instructions. He started *immediately* toward Argentan.

By then, for this segment of the Third Army, the sky became the limit. Patton himself was riding with the advance.

When he left his CP in the morning of August 11th he told his Chief of Staff:

"Well, Gaffey, to coin a phase—this is it!"

He was firmly convinced that it was. As he saw it, the total destruction of the Seventh German Army was only a matter of time.

During the morning he visited XV Corps Headquarters northeast of Le Mans, then began the grand round, dropping in on the 79th Division, the 5th Armored and the 90th Division. After lunch he went looking for General Leclerc who, like himself, was running around the front. Although Patton followed him farther, as he afterward put it, than caution should have permitted, he could not find Leclerc.

He got a kick out of the Frenchman's eager courage. Patton loved France. It was his second country. Anything French warmed his heart. A whole French armored division had set it on fire.

Using "Leclerc" as his *nom de guerre* while serving de Gaulle after the fall of France, Philippe François Marie de Hautecloque was a soldier's soldier. Smart, intense, dashing and competent, he had fought in Africa, first with a handful of adventurers crossing the Sahara, eventually with this armored division. In the spring of 1944 the division was transferred to England to represent the reborn French army in "Overlord."

Re-equipped with American matériel and retained in the Third Army, the 2nd Armored Division sneaked into France on July 30th, humping up over the dunes from the beach, then making for the first village in its native land. It was a small place, with only a handful of people—mostly women and elderly folk—in the square, indifferent to the spectacle. They had seen too much in recent weeks. The column did not strike them as unusual. But then, through the hatch of the lead Sherman, popped the head of a tanker, shouting to a *citoyenne* on the sidewalk in the unmistakable *argôt* of Paris:

"Dis, donc, ma mignonne, on t'emmène à Paname, hein?"

"The lady's jaw dropped almost to her ample bosom," wrote Codman, who had witnessed the scene, "and the eyes of the other villagers bulged as they caught sight of the small tricolor flag painted on the tank's side." By the time they came to, the first French fighting unit to land upon the soil of occupied France was well out of town. But even before they reached the next town, the grapevine had filled

THE TRIUMPH

the *place* with a throng—men, women and children loaded down with flowers, fruit, bottles, jugs of cider, loaves of bread.

Leclerc's *2me Blindée* had arrived. Patton assigned it to XV Corps and within 24 hours Haislip reported that it was killing Germans "with gusto and efficiency." Now leaving for the front, Patton remembered to remember the French tankers.

"Codman," he told his aide, "be sure we take along a bagful of Bronze Stars for Leclerc's sons of bitches."

But Leclerc was giving him trouble.

Ordered by General Haislip to skirt the Forêt d'Ecouves on the West on his march to his Carrouges-Argentan objective, Leclerc disobeyed. He passed the forest on both sides and drove straight through it in three columns. The procedure did speed up his own advance, but it blocked the road reserved for the 5th U.S. Armored Division, causing the latter to delay its attack toward Argentan by six hours. It was enough time for the Germans to rush a unit into the breach. Had the attack been launched as scheduled, General Oliver's armor would have captured Argentan. Now it was making little progress.

But Patton could never work up a real rage where Frenchmen were involved. When Haislip blasted Leclerc, Patton calmed him.

"My gosh, don't get so upset, Wade," he said. "He's just a baby."

The gap between Patton's units moving north and the Canadians moving south was now about 20 miles wide. Patton was making his final dispositions.

Leclerc had thrust to Carrouges. The 5th Armored had taken Sées. But the Canadians were still stalled. Dismayed by their slow progress, Montgomery phoned General Crerar on August 11th and ordered him to intensify his efforts to capture Falaise, adding that it was "vital that it should be done quickly." He was now fully committed to the encirclement. "Obviously," he said, "if we can close the gap completely, we shall have put the enemy in the most awkward predicament."

He instructed Crerar to continue south from Falaise and rendezvous with the Americans, who were to stop at Argentan. That was the boundary between the British and American army groups. Probably expecting that the Canadians would make it after all, Montgomery saw no reason why he

should relax the traffic across the boundary line and let
the Americans enter his territory.

In the meantime the Germans began to see the shape of
things to come. First to recognize the gathering threat was
Sepp Dietrich, an uncouth Bavarian who was once Hitler's
bodyguard, later transferred to the *Waffen SS* and rose
rapidly in both rank and influence. He was now a *General-
Oberst*—the equivalent of lieutenant general—in command
of the Fifth Panzer Army, whose LXXIV Corps was likely
to be caught in the *Kessel*. At 10:35 A.M. on August 13th
Dietrich teletyped this warning to Lieutenant General Hans
Speidel, Chief of Staff of his Army Group: "If the front held
by the Panzer Army and the Seventh Army is not withdrawn
immediately and if every effort is not made to move the
forces toward the east and out of the threatened encirclement, the army group will have to write off both armies.
Within a very short time resupplying the troops with ammunition and fuel will no longer be possible. Therefore, immediate measures are necessary to move to the east before
such movement is definitely too late. It will soon be possible for the enemy to fire into the pocket with artillery from
all sides."

Now it was the 11th hour! It was too late to do even what
Dietrich had proposed. All the top German commanders,
from Field Marshal von Kluge at *OB West* headquarters at
St. Germain to General Eberbach, who had taken over
command on the spot from the badly wounded Colonel
General Paul Hausser (and whom Patton later described
as "the ugliest man in uniform" he had ever seen), expected the doom to descend upon the pocket momentarily.
It was apparent to them that their weak forces could not
maintain for long, if at all, the slender defensive line opposite the XV Corps.

Yet the line held.

It held, as Blumenson put it, not because of German
strength but because of an abrupt cessation of the American
attack.

What happened?

As early as August 8th, when he first discussed the idea of
the operation with Bradley at St. James, Patton had voiced

his doubts about "Monty's ability to close the gap at Argentan." Bradley was not sure if he agreed with hs skepticism. A few days before at 21st Army Group Headquarters when Montgomery outlined the plan, General Dempsey had offered to bet Bradley that the British would beat the Americans to Argentan. They seemed to be extremely keen about the operation.

But now on August 11th Patton saw his doubts confirmed.

The opportunity seemed far too great to let it slip by the wayside. There may be as many as 100,000 Germans in that pocket, maybe more. Here was a unique chance to destroy them, as Eisenhower preached, instead of just gaining ground. If they are annihilated here, they won't be able to fight elsewhere. Patton no longer felt bound by the protocol of war. Montgomery or no Montgomery, boundaries or no boundaries, Canadians or no Canadians, he became determined to act on his own.

During his visit to XV Corps CP he told General Haislip, "Pay no attention to Monty's Goddamn boundaries. Be prepared to push even beyond Falaise if necessary. I'll give you the word."

Haislip said he did not think he had enough troops for what Patton had in mind, especially to secure the east-west roads north of Alençon. Patton left immediately to round up additional forces. He directed Walker to assemble XX Corps on the Mayenne-Le Mans line, then drive northeast to the line Sées-Carrouges, make contact with XV Corps, and await orders. He left a regimental combat team of the 80th Division to maintain the bridgehead at Le Mans. He alerted Major General Lindsay McD. Silvester's 7th Armored Division to move from its assembly area to the rear of its line of departure. He called General Wood and told him to be prepared for a possible eastward move of the 4th Armored Division. He phoned Bradley and asked for the return of the 35th Infantry Division, attached temporarily to First Army to help with stemming the Mortain counterattack.

At 11:30 P.M. on August 12th Haislip signaled Patton at his CP near Laval that the 5th Armored was about to secure Argentan and mentioned rather pointedly that he had no mission beyond that. Should, however, Patton authorize him to proceed "northward," Haislip said he would be ready to move the 5th Armored through the French division for a drive to a rendezvous with the Canadians.

Patton put in a call to Bradley.

"We've got elements in Argentan," he said. "Let me go on to Falaise and ' we'll drive the British back into the sea for another Dunkirk."

"Nothing doing," Bradley replied. "You're not to go beyond Argentan. Just stop where you are and build up on that shoulder. Sibert tells me the German is beginning to pull out. You'd better button up and get ready for him."

"Sibert" was Brigadier General Edwin Luther Sibert, Bradley's G-2. What he had told Bradley about the Germans pulling out later stood out as one of the grave intelligence blunders of the war. "Incorrectly believing," Blumenson wrote in his *post mortem*, "that elements of 19 German divisions were already stampeding eastward through the gap, [Bradley] thought it conceivable that they would trample the thin line of American troops."

But Haislip had his answer within 70 minutes of his own call. At 12:40 A.M. on August 13th, Gaffey signaled the word from Patton "to push on slowly in the direction of Falaise, allowing your rear elements to close. Road: Argentan-Falaise your boundary inclusive. Upon arrival Falaise continue to push on slowly until you contact our Allies."

In the morning, leaving a containing force behind at Argentan, the 5th Armored began the slow drive toward Falaise. XX Corps was attacking toward Chartres for the rendezvous with XV Corps. Patton signaled Haislip that he was trying to scrape up additional forces for the final push.

In the north the Canadians were five miles from Falaise. The gap was now only 15 miles wide. Americans, Canadians and Poles were inching forward in the face of stiff German opposition.

A reconnaissance party of the 5th Armored pushed to within a few miles of Falaise.

Now it was 11:30 A.M., August 13, 1944.

The telephone rang in Patton's operations tent at St. James. Major General Leven Cooper Allen, General Bradley's Chief of Staff, was calling. General Gaffey took the call.

Lev Allen told Gaffey that by order of General Bradley the Anglo-American boundary in the Falaise-Argentan area was not to be crossed under any circumstances and that the advance of XV Corps was to halt forthwith on the Argentan-Sées line.

Gaffey found Patton in his trailer and told him about Bradley's halt order.

"You're kidding," Patton said. His face was flushed, his lips paler than usual. His jaw had dropped. He seemed worried.

"No, sir," Gaffey said. "Lev Allen spoke for General Bradley."

Patton put through a call to 12th Army Group Headquarters at Coutances, asked for Bradley. Allen answered.

"General Bradley is at Shellburst," he said. It was the code name of SHAEF Advance Headquarters near Tournières. Patton tried to reach his boss there but Bradley was out. He called Allen back.

"Listen, Lev," he pleaded with the Chief of Staff, "try to find Brad for me and ask him to reconsider his order. And get in touch with Monty about the boundary. He may agree to let us go through."

General Allen located Bradley at Shellburst and conveyed Patton's request to him. Bradley was with Eisenhower, so he raised the burning issue with the Supreme Commander. Eisenhower was looking forward to the closing of the gap and the destruction of the German forces in the pocket. On August 9th he had written to General Marshall: "Under my urgent direction all possible strength is turned to the destruction of the forces facing us . . . Patton has the marching wing which will turn in rather sharply to the northeast from the general vincinity of Le Mans and just to the west thereof, marching toward Alençon and Falaise." But now he hesitated. When Bradley strongly advised him against XV Corps' drive, the Supreme Commander endorsed the halt order. Bradley then told Allen to tell Patton that the answer to his request was negative.

In the meantime, Brigadier General A. Franklin Kibler, 12th Army Group G-3, phoned Montgomery's headquarters trying to get permission for Patton to go beyond Argentan. He spoke with General de Guingand, Montgomery's Chief of Staff, who told him bluntly: "I am sorry, Kibler. We cannot grant the permission."

It was now 12:15 P.M. Patton called Allen again.

"Lev, listen," he said, the high pitch of his voice betraying his nervous excitement, "Haislip is on the Argentan-Sées line as directed. He has reconnaissance beyond it. It's perfectly feasible for XV Corps to continue the operation. Did you speak to Brad?"

"Yes, George," Allen said. "The answer is still no."

Then he repeated the order. Haislip's corps was to halt on the Argentan-Sées line and consolidate.

They hung up.

Patton turned to Gaffey. "The question why XV Corps halted on the east-west line through Argentan is certain to become of historical importance," he said. "I want a stenographic record of this conversation with General Allen included in the History of the Third Army."

It was Sunday afternoon.

At 2:15 P.M. General Haislip received Patton's order transmitted by General Gaffey. The order directed him to stop further movement to the north; not to go beyond Argentan; and to recall at once any elements that might be "in the vicinity of Falaise or to the north of Argentan."

Instead of pressing the attack toward the Canadians and closing the gap, XV Corps was instructed to "assemble and prepare for further operations in another direction."

The action General Haislip thought would be "decisive for the entire campaign in Western Europe" was cut short with a check-string. The opportunity to defeat the Germans in 1944 suffered its *first* setback.

At Shellburst, General Bradley was, according to Butcher, "playing bridge as calmly and peacefully as if he had just come off the golf course."

Patton later wrote: "This was a great mistake, as I was certain that we could have entered Falaise and I was not certain that the British would." In conversations with his staff and others, he was even more explicit.

United States Army historians seemed to agree with Patton that "halting the XV Corps at Argentan" was "a tactical error, a failure to take full advantage of German vulnerability." On the basis of the most careful review of the events, Blumenson concluded that Bradley had made the decision to halt XV Corps probably on five interrelated grounds:

(1) General Montgomery, the over-all ground force

commander, apparently refused to move the boundary and thus appeared to be opposed to further American advance.

(2) He (Bradley) was not convinced that American troops could move through or around Argentan in the face of increasing enemy resistance.

(3) The closing of the gap would have exposed XV Corps, which had none of its flanks protected.

(4) Bradley was misled by estimates of his G-2 which "inclined to the incorrect view that the bulk of the German forces had already escaped the pocket."

(5) The Canadians were about to launch their second attack to Falaise.

As far as the Canadians were concerned, "the evidence suggests," according to Wilmot, "that the thrust from the north was not pressed with sufficient speed and strength."

While Bradley was made the butt of the controversy, Blumenson suggested that Eisenhower must, in the end, bear the responsibility for the failure to close the gap. "If Patton, in a subordinate role, could only rage," Blumenson wrote, "and if Bradley thought he might offend a sensitive Montogomery, Eisenhower, who was in France and following combat developments, might have resolved the situation had he thought it necessary to do so. Yet General Eisenhower did not intervene. Interfering with a tactical decision made by a commander who was in closer contact with the situation was not Eisenhower's method of exercising command. Long after the event, General Eisenhower implied that the gap might have been closed, which, he thought, 'might have won us a complete battle of annihilation.'"

CHAPTER TWENTY-NINE
VICTORIES AND WOES

On August 12, 1944, General Eisenhower was at General Bradley's headquarters when the news of Alençon's capture by XV Corps arrived. The place reminded Bradley of something he had promised General Haislip. Since the lid was still on Third Army, its XV Corps was, of course, also hush-hush. No reference was made to it in the joyous communiqués announcing its triumphs.

The secrecy was rather contrived. The enemy knew exactly, not only what, but also who, was hitting him. Bradley's innate objectivity and exquisite sense of fair play suggested to him that it was being carried somewhat too far. And now, the capture of Alençon made him anxious to ask the Supreme Commander to lift the veil from Haislip and XV Corps. Eisenhower readily agreed.

Bradley then felt that this also was a good opportunity to get Patton back into the limelight, and recommended that they pull out the censorship stop as far as the whole Third Army was concerned. This was simple common sense. Censorship concealed Patton and his army, not from the enemy, but from the American people. Yet it was so airtight that not even Mrs. Patton at home could know that her husband was in action. But nobody could fool her. From July 28th on, she marked the map where she thought her husband's influence was unmistakable and, as Semmes put it, "mentally inserted" Patton's name in the communiqués.

Patton himself appeared to shrug off the issue as far as he personally was concerned but mentioned several times to Bradley, "How in hell can Third Army have a high morale with all this Goddamn secrecy cloaking its victories?" He was never remarkable for a passion for anonymity, and Bradley knew that he was suffering intensely from his nameless part in the amazing triumphs of these days.

But Eisenhower balked. Probably he thought Patton needed a little more time and a few more victories to redeem himself in the eyes of his Stateside critics. But what he told Bradley showed that he was also thinking of himself.

"Not yet," he answered to Bradley's recommendation that they restore Patton to the headlines. "After all the troubles I've had with George, I have only a few gray hairs left on this poor old head of mine. Let George work a while longer for his headlines."

By then, back in the United States, Patton's champions came to feel strongly that it was certainly grossly unfair to benefit from his skill while denying him the joys of publicity. On the morning of August 13th the Washington *Evening*

Star exploded the issue. Citing a *German* news agency which had repeatedly exposed Patton's presence in France, the paper suggested in an editorial that it was high time to give the controversial general his public due. The editorial was promptly reported to General Eisenhower, and the Supreme Commander relented. On the evening of August 15th Patton was listening to the British Broadcasting Corporation news when he was jolted out of his seat.

"I've just learned from the radio," he told Sergeant Rosevich, who was coming to his office for some dication, "that I'm commanding the Third Army in France."

However, efforts continued to play down the Third Army's part in the campaign and especially to mute the crescendo of Patton's galloping fame. "SHAEF's Public Relations Division," wrote Forrest C. Pogue in his official history of the Supreme Command in the ETO, "had the task not only of censoring stories to prevent breaches of security and the disturbance of good relations between Allies, but also of publicizing the exploits of various units to aid morale."

With Patton in France this presented a problem. As Pogue put it, "This became difficult when commanders like General Patton, by their personal color and their slashing advances, overshadowed the hard work of other commanders and armies."

Trusted correspondents—like Ernie Pyle—were told to put more oomph into their dispatches about the First Army and go a bit slower in their coverage of Patton and his Third. When the "difficulty" of which Pogue spoke continued, General Eisenhower decided to meet it head on. By his orders on September 6th, General Bedell Smith, his Chief of Staff, issued a paper called "Policy re Release of Information to the Press," in which SHAEF dealt with the problem bluntly. Telling the Public Relations Division in no uncertain terms that its briefing officers should call especial attention to General Hodges and his First Army, Smith wrote: "In other words, try to attract a little more attention to Hodges and Bradley as against Patton's colorful appeal to the press."

Even this intervention did not succeed in gaining for the First Army the recognition it so abundantly deserved. Actually, the "policy" backfired. When it leaked to Third Army it became responsible for stimulating suspicion of SHAEF and even of Bradley among Patton's people.

At the conclusion of the daily staff conference on August 14th Patton made a little speech to commemorate the two weeks of the Third Army in action. The map in front of which he stood spoke eloquently of its achievements. At the end of the first fortnight, elements of the army were inching their way to Orléans, 50 miles due south of Paris and 155 miles east of Avranches, where they had come in on August 1st.

The third phase of the first campaign was about to begin. The Third Army was racing toward the Seine and yet another big envelopment, with Mantes-Gassicourt and Elbeuf for its key points. Its advance to the east, both north and south of Paris, remained relentless in accordance with Patton's design to overrun the enemy's planned strong points before its defenders could make them really strong.

Now he told his little audience in the tent: "As of today, the Third Army has advanced farther and faster than any army in history."

On that day, while the Canadians were still struggling on the Caen-Falaise road, VIII Corps of Patton's army was fighting in Brittany for those elusive ports; XV Corps was mopping up in the Alençon-Sées-Argentan area, preparing to drive east on Dreux; XX Corps was beginning its drive toward Chartres; and XII Corps, fresh in the fracas, was going to Orléans, the teeming capital city of Loiret in north-central France.

Yet the victories also cast thin shadows of woes and produced occasional disappointments which, if viewed in the historical perspective, as they must be, take some of the sheen off their glitter. Obscured by the din and speed of the advance was the fact that not everything in Patton's first campaign was as favorable to the Allied cause as he thought when he stressed rapidity and distance in his review.

Generalship on the German side was astonishingly and incredibly bad, and not merely because of Hitler's remote-control interference. Now that they had come up against a well-trained, well-equipped, well-supported and well-led foe, these German generals turned out to be very much less than supermen. By contrast, American generalship was

astoundingly good, from Eisenhower down to the leaders
of combat commands and task forces. It amazed the world
and surprised even the worried men who had put together
the "Overlord" master plan. But at the top where the big
decisions were made and the major campaigns were conducted it was not as top-notch as it could have been.

As a result, for all its spectacular nature and for all its
promises, the situation was ambiguous. It was made equiv-
ocal by the very triumph the Third Army had scored and
the stupendous territorial gains it had made. There was
much in this situation that justified General Bradley's misgivings and left him uneasy even in the light of his great
successes in August.

In Brittany, Patton had lost his £5 bet to General Montgomery. Brest did not fall at the end of a five-day operation. The big Breton ports resisted repeated onslaughts
upon them with a tenacity which indicated that man-to-man
the German soldier, despite the blunders of his generals
and the setbacks in Normandy, remained a formidable foe.

Now it became profoundly clear that the basic mission of
the wise general was what General Eisenhower preached
(but, unfortunately, did not always practice)—to destroy the enemy rather than to gain ground. What good was
it to gobble up territory if the enemy, evicted from it, was
left to fight another battle? The Supreme Commander's
classic principle, based on his study of Clausewitz, did not
penetrate to Bradley and Patton. For all his vast historical
scope and the scientific turn of his military mind, Patton
was not a fan of Clausewitz, probably because the German's tactical principles tended to clash with his own. And
Bradley was confronted with the accomplished facts of the
campaign, accomplished by a commander over whose actions he did not always have complete control.

The idea of merely containing the Breton ports until they
become ripe to fall—"I don't care if we get Brest tomorrow
or 10 days later," as Bradley put it to Middleton on August
2nd—had left a substantial German force more or less intact on the peninsula. More important, it tied down VIII
Corps when it was needed and could have been used to better advantage elsewhere.

Gradually Bradley came around to recognizing the deficiency of his original concept and to regretting that he had
prevented Patton from rolling up the Germans in Brittany
with a fast and furious campaign. On September 9th, when

VIII Corps was licking its wounds and regrouping after another costly but futile effort to take Brest (including the bloody battle for the crest of Hill 103), he supposedly told Patton: "I would not say this to anyone but you, and have given different excuses to my staff and higher echelons, but we must take Brest in order to maintain the illusion of the fact that the U.S. Army cannot be beaten."

St. Malo fell on September 3rd, Brest on September 20th. But the other ports had to be contained to the bitter end of the war.

The failure to close the Falaise-Argentan gap and annihilate the Germans inside the pocket released thousands of enemy troops for subsequent battles. Even today nobody can account for all the Germans who managed to escape. On August 23rd Hitler ordered *OB West* to send him a report on the divisions that had succeeded in escaping from the pocket, but the report, if it was ever submitted, has never been found. On August 20th, in its daily report, Army Group B claimed that "approximately 40 to 50 per cent of the encircled units succeeded in breaking out and joining hands with the II SS Panzer Corps." Later estimates ranged from 20,000 to 80,000 men, the first figure presumably too low, the latter almost certainly too high. The Allies did not take too many prisoners out of the pocket, probably fewer than 50,000, and only 10,000 German dead were counted on the battlefield when the pocket was closed at last on August 19th.

The Germans were quick to recognize the significance of this and regarded our failure to close the gap as a tremendous victory for themselves. The Falaise operation continues to be listed prominently in German accounts among the triumphs of the *Wehrmacht*. Professor Schramm thus wrote in his commentary to the war diaries: "Although the enemy employed his air force on an unprecedented scale [a total of 8,000 tons of bombs were dropped in but two major air support operations], we succeeded in withdrawing our forces eastward from the *Kessel* . . . . A substantial portion of heavy equipment was destroyed by the encircled troops; more of it was lost in the breakout; but more than half of it could be rescued nevertheless. Consequently, the breakout at Falaise, in which the 3rd Parachute Division especially distinguished itself, remains one of the great passages of arms of this campaign. The second opportunity the enemy had during this retreat-operation to cut off and destroy a whole army was thus thwarted."

Much later—during the tough fighting on the Moselle and in the Bulge—German Hermann Balck's tenacious forces included many a *Landser* who would have been dead or in some Allied prisoner-of-war camp had the battle of the Falaise-Argentan pocket been carried to its logical conclusion by the Allies.

The Third Army's drive in August was historic, deserving the high praise lavished on it by the Germans. While 500 miles apart, and protecting the 485-mile flank on the Loire River, it advanced 400 miles in 26 days, liberated 47,829 square miles of French soil. But there was a significant figure in the statistics that counsels caution in the assessment of this triumph. As of August 26th, German casualties inflicted by the Third Army totaled 16,000 killed, 55,000 wounded, and 65,000 captured. In its whole wartime career of eight major campaigns, the Third Army killed 47,500 Germans and wounded 115,000. While its final bag of prisoners totaled a staggering 1,300,000, those captured during this first campaign between August 1st and September 24th, which carried the army from Avranches to the Moselle, amounted to fewer than 100,000—94,199 to be exact—or about 7 per cent of the eventual total.

In August and September the Third Army was capturing Germans at the rate of 1,713 a day (a figure that slumped to a daily average of only 193 in the fighting to force the Moselle line). It may be proper to compare this figure with an average daily bag of 9,749 prisoners-of-war after March 13, 1945, when the German army began to disintegrate in earnest and the victory of the Allies became truly assured.

In France many circumstances and factors combined during this auspicious August to aid Patton in his remarkable campaign and to encourage him to think highly of the apparently decisive contribution the Third Army was making to a possibly early termination of the war. One of them was the fact that most of the time he was fighting in a vacuum. To be sure, this was exactly how he had planned and wanted it. The orders to Grow and Haislip—"bypass resistance"—showed his intentions. He was forever looking for "breaks," usually found them (frequently thanks to the superb intelligence he received from Colonel Fickett's Household Cavalry), then made the most of them. But this method glossed over strong enemy concentrations. It did not have for its basic mission the annihilation of the enemy's forces, no matter how Patton exhorted his commanders to "destroy the German army" and egged on his men to "kill Germans."

By "breaks" Patton meant gaps in the front, the finding of light held or vacant stretches in the enemy lines through which he could advance quickly and penetrate to his rear. To make the most of these "breaks," Patton devised a special maneuver on a very low operational level, apparently an implementation of his favorite tactical principle, "Hold them by the nose while you kick them in the pants." For this campaign, in the wake of "Cobra's" unexpectedly great success and the devastating effect of the Avranches breakout, Patton prepared no specific plan because he thought that no formal plan could be effective in the virtually total absence of organized German resistance.

For the chaotic German retreat, frequently in small batches or groups, and for dealing with the hastily formed *Kampfgruppen*—emergency units put together from remnants of the shattered divisions offering sporadic resistance on the initiative of their mostly *ad hoc commanders*—Patton applied a special treatment. He was leading his staccato assaults with armor, and he used it like cavalry. Instead of utilizing his armored divisions *in toto,* or even in intact combat commands, he split them up into small combat teams. Their mission was to break through the gaps, pounce upon the retreating Germans unit by unit, in hit-and-run raids, so to speak, smashing whatever links they had to their rear and carrying the war to the hinterland in what was a large-scale but haphazard guerrilla type of warfare.

He was applying to a real-life enemy in earnest what he had tried out in the maneuvers in 1941, when his tactics resulting "in a lot of small fights throughout the entire battle area" provoked General McNair's remark: "This is no way to fight a war." While Patton's tactics now compounded the Germans' confusion, they also contributed to some chaos in our lines. And while he did penetrate to the enemy's rear in these lightning raids, he usually confined his piecemeal operations to skirmishes with stragglers, instead of interfering strategically with the enemy's communications zone. While he did succeed in places and in parts in preventing the enemy from forming a front, he did not destroy enough of his units to make more than a dent in his strength.

Patton's search for "breaks" was not entirely due to his eagerness to plunge forward as far and as fast as possible. To a considerable degree it was caused by his realization that the American infantryman fighting under him at this stage was not yet quite as proficient in war as this do-or-die confrontation with the Germans required.

General Omar N. Bradley, the infantrymen's infantryman with whom he frequently raised the issue, was in complete agreement with Patton on this score. Pending substantial improvement in the prowess of the American infantryman he expected to come with experience, Patton preferred not to risk major tests in any pitched engagements.

This may seem unfair to the memory of the 12,825 Third Army men killed, wounded or missing in the fighting of these days, and sound a bit harsh to the surviving veterans of this campaign, yet the fact remains that many of Patton's spectacular forward plunges occurred in the face of very light or no resistance. While Crerar's Canadians had to hack their harrowing path down the Falaise road through crack units of the German Panzer Army, XV U.S. Corps raced to Alençon encumbered by only the feeble opposition of German units the corps history described as "badly hurt" and as "remnants of divisions in the process of wholesale reconstitution."

General Haislip himself said that "there were no units worth mentioning" on his right flank. He characterized those worth mentioning as being of "negligible combat strength." Sées was defended by the bakery company of the "badly hurt" 9th Panzer Division. Whatever concentration of enemy units was suspected to be in the corps' northward path, Haislip bypassed in accordance with Patton's instructions.

On the drive to the Seine, Third Army found "scarcely any Germans between Vitré and the Loire River." The roads to Dreux and Orléans were devoid of enemy forces. Resistance encountered around Chartres was strictly local. On August 19th "no effective obstacle save the river itself barred a crossing of the Seine."

On the other hand, whenever resistance developed and could not be bypassed, the Third Army drive slowed. Thus on August 19th at the Seine, XV Corps found only the badly disorganized remnants of inferior German units. In the pinch, a lowly *Hauptsturmführer* (captain) of the *Waffen SS,* a young man named Wahl, took it upon himself to organize a defense for the crossing sites. He managed to assemble a handful of tanks, then attracted to his *ad hoc* force combat remnants of the 17th Panzer Grenadiers and contingents of the 1st SS Panzer Division. It was not much of a force but, aided by the terrain and the weather, it proved enough to hold up General Oliver's 5th Armored Division for five days on its drive to Louviers.

During these days Patton's famed personal intervention was sorely needed. His well-known proficiency as "the best Goddamn butt-kicker in the U.S. Army" was very useful. Wherever he could, he bolstered the fighting spirit of his men and pushed them through the occasional sticky spots. Following his example, and prodded by him, general officers intervened personally and continuously with individual acts of great valor to impress and invigorate their green troops.

On August 23rd, on the Seine near Ponthierry, a corps commander—General Walker (a roly-poly tanker of whom Patton once said "he'll do well unless he blows up")— took personal charge of minor local operation which benefited only a group of French criminals whose prison the attack had "liberated."

Walker happened to pass the CP of Combat Command R of General Silvester's 7th Armored Division and found it stalled on what Patton liked to call the wrong side of the river. Preparatory to crossing the stream, the unit had been ordered to pave the way of an infantry company to a prison-island in the middle of the Seine, linked to the left bank by a partially destroyed bridge. But the order was not being carried out. In true Pattonesque manner, Walker took charge, and pushed the men on to the island. They quickly secured it under heavy fire from the east bank of the river. Patton awarded Walker the DSC and gave another to his aide, First Lieutenant David W. Allard, who had swum across the Seine under fire to collect information for the Corps Commander.

Whatever the shortcomings of the campaign, nothing indicated either in Patton's notes or conversations that he was unduly worried about them. His rapid advance, the beauty of his mission, his beloved France all around him in the vicinity of Saumur, where he had spent his happy sojourn exactly 30 years before, combined to fill him with euphoria.

If possible, his euphoria was now mounting with every passing day. What he was looking forward to as the crowning gratification of his Francophilia was drawing closer. Patton was approaching Paris rapidly and irresistibly. The liberation of the great City of Light, so ignominiously soiled by its Nazi squatters, was a highly sentimental issue with him, a matter of personal honor. This was partly behind the haste with which he was driving on Orléans and Dreux, south and north of Paris. He had discussed the matter with General Montgomery and extracted the promise that he would be entrusted with the coveted mission that undoubtedly would be the high point of the crusade for France. Montgomery was apparently determined to keep his promise. In an order issued on August 20th he instructed Bradley to "assemble [his] right wing west and southwest of Paris and capture that city when the Commanding General considers the suitable moment has arrived—and not before." After the war, Montgomery thought it important enough to clarify the statement by declaring unequivocally that by "Commanding General" he meant General Patton and that the statement was intended to read, as he himself put it, "Paris should be captured when General Patton considered that a suitable time had arrived."

However, there was considerable hesitation on General Eisenhower's part whether to liberate Paris at this time. From a purely military point of view, the termination of the city's bondage presented no problem. Any one of Patton's three corps in the general area could have taken the city on short order and without much difficulty—Haislip's XV Corps at Dreux, Walker's XX Corps at Chartres, or Major General Manton S. Eddy's XII Corps at Orléans. At this moment the three corps formed a semicircle around the city, their closest point of advance only about 35 miles from its outskirts.

Even so, Eisenhower sought to defer the grand liberation as long as possible on logistical and political grounds. He feared that supplying the liberated metropolis with food, fuel and other essentials would overtax the facilities of General Lee's Communications Zone, already badly strained by the vastly extended American lines. And politically, Eisenhower expected complications with General Charles de Gaulle, whose cooperation with the Allies usually left much to be desired.

However, events inside the city forced Ike's hand. The Parisian resistance forces refused to wait for him to make up his mind. On August 7th they came out of their hideouts, unpacked their cached weapons, seized key points, and forced the German commandant, General Dietrich von Choltitz, to make arrangements for the soonest possible liquidation of his rule.

At 8 o'clock in the morning on August 23rd, white-gloved, immaculately groomed MPs herded five dust-covered, bedraggled, worn-out civilians into General Gaffey's office in a tent southwest of Chartres, involving Patton's headquarters in one of the less seemly melodramas of the war. Led by a Swede named Rolf Nordling, who claimed to be the brother of the Swedish Consul General in Paris, the strange delegation consisted of Alexandre de Saint-Phalle representing the Parisian branch of the Committee of National Liberation; Jean Laurent, a former secretary of General de Gaulle's cabinet; an agent of MI. 16, the British Secret Intelligence Service, who called himself "Monsieur Armoux," and a German officer in mufti, Major Hermann Bender, representing von Choltitz. They had come all the way from Paris in a minuscule Citroen, their way through the Allied lines paved by the mysterious Monsieur Armoux's open-sesame credentials.

Nordling told Gaffey that they had come to arrange the orderly transfer of the French capital from the Germans to the Allies. The Chief of Staff hurried to Patton, who was immediately seized by a sense of history. Assuming that the group had come to surrender the city, he sent for Sergeant Rosevich to take down the conversation, and asked Colonel Hammond to send over a couple of Signal Corps cameramen to take pictures for posterity.

But Nordling was not bearing any such gifts. As Patton understood his mission, he had come merely to "get a suspension of hostilities in order to save Paris and probably save Germans." Patton could not care less. He sent the delegation on to General Bradley at Army Group.

By then Patton was no longer personally interested in the liberation of Paris. He had been dealt a cruel blow a few days before, apparently by Eisenhower, who took away from him the one mission he had craved with all his heart.

On August 13th, Eisenhower met with Bradley informally for bridge, but Bradley used the opportunity to bring up the question of Paris. He had urgent information about the *fait accompli* the Resistance had created in the city, and was concerned that the Germans might institute reprisals against the insurgents unless the city was taken out of German hands. General Sibert, his G-2, was especially insistent that the city be liberated with great dispatch, and Bradley urged Eisenhower to give the order. Reluctantly the Supreme Commander agreed.

Although there is no record of the conference and, therefore, it is not known in what way Patton was discussed, from what developed in the wake of the meeting it is reasonable to assume that Ike turned thumbs down on giving him any part in the liberation.

It was left to Bradley to break the bad news to Patton. He did it on August 15th, as tactfully as he could, explaining the decision with a subterfuge. He spoke of some intelligence warning of an attack on Argentan by five Panzer divisions. Citing this threat, Bradley instructed Patton to halt his move to the east on the line of XX Corps at Chartres, the XV Corps at Dreux, and the XII Corps at Châteaudun. Patton knew immediately what this implied. He was not to go to Paris. Still he remained hopeful.

But he failed, and now he was beginning to see the light clearly. While Bradley himself decided to move his own advance headquarters, Eagle Tac, from near Laval 115 miles east to the vicinity of Chartres, only a stone's throw from Paris, he reiterated Patton's orders to stay put and freeze his front. Then, on August 19th, he informed Patton that Eisenhower had resolved to let "only the French division" go into Paris, and hinted that Ike had given First Army the mission.

Patton was bitterly disappointed. His staff was stunned. It regarded the decision as the last straw in Eisenhower's increasingly apparent measures to exclude Patton from the glory road, at least as far as he could.

By all means Patton should have been given the job. He was France's best friend and greatest admirer in the whole army. It was the phenomenal advance of his Third Army that made the city ripe for the taking. His own forces were nearest to the city. The *2me Blindée,* Leclerc's armored division, which was brought to France especially for this glorious purpose (for it had long been resolved in high Allied councils that a French unit at division strength must be the first Allied force to enter the city) was attached to his XV Corps.

But General Eisenhower picked General "Gee" Gerow for the job. His V Corps was idling near Chambois, 100 miles from Paris, after it had helped to close the Falaise-Argentan gap at last at 7:30 P.M. on August 19th. It needed some doing and shifting to prepare V Corps for its unexpected task. And it caused some headaches.

On August 17th the French division was taken from Patton and transferred to Gerow. It was explained that General Leclerc simply had to be shifted to firmer hands because he was cutting up under Patton who, in his love of anything French, was inclined to pamper him too much and let him get away with insubordination that was detrimental to tactical interests.

It was true that Leclerc was becoming unruly and restless. Gallant, skilled and recklessly brave, he was a whole man, a compleat soldier, and a thoroughbred tanker after Patton's heart. He had paid with blood and sweat for his impending honor. The Germans had captured him in 1940. He escaped, changed his name to protect his family in occupied France, made his way to de Gaulle, and led a desert striking force across the Sahara from Fort Lamy to Tripoli to join Montgomery's Eighth Army. This was his fifth year at war, four of them hard and humiliating. Now the sweet scent of France, the native soil under his feet, the heady summer of the Calvados, the proximity of Paris, and the excitement of his historic mission had made him drunk with impatience.

On August 14th he asked General Haislip to query Patton when the *2me Blindée* would be sent eastward from Argentan to liberate Paris. Without waiting for an answer, he put the show on the road, starting the march on Paris on his own initiative and authority. Gaffey was quickly summoned. He ordered Leclerc to stay where he was.

The next day Leclerc wrote Patton an unsigned letter threatening to resign and kick up an embarrassing political fuss unless he was permitted to go to Paris at once. That evening he called on Patton, who gave him a cordial reception and assured him that he would have the honor of liberating Paris.

That seemed to pacify Leclerc. "Strangely," Patton remarked, "we parted friends." But he told General Wood, who happened to be present at the heated meeting, watching the highly agitated Leclerc make his point with the

Gallic eloquence of his hands, "You see, John, he's a bigger pain in the butt than you are."

Leclerc became despondent with First Army. His relations with Hodges and Gerow were strained. The American generals, who did not have Patton's compassion for things Gallic, were exasperated by the Frenchman's rampant insubordination, and treated him harshly if not contemptuously. Leclerc, in turn, accused the generals of being Francophobes. He refused to accept his transfer and continued to consider himself—in name, that is—a member of the Third Army family.

On August 22nd V Corps was made ready for the big event. Leclerc's division was alerted for the mission. To back him up, General Barton's 4th Infantry Division was shifted from VII to V Corps and sent rolling as fast as it could toward the city from the south, leaving one reserve combat team behind at the Seine for its original task of securing a crossing.

Patton followed events with jaundiced eyes, to say the least. But when the great moment arrived with General von Choltitz's surrender of the city to Leclerc at 3:15 P.M on August 25th, in a stiff ceremony at Gare Montparnasse, he consoled himself with what he called poetic justice in three incidents. They pleased him no end.

First, he received a special call from General Pierre-Joseph Koenig, Supreme Commander of the French Forces of the Interior, whom General de Gaulle had designated as the Military Commandant of the liberated city. Koenig was en route to Paris but he detoured to Patton's CP to pay his respects and thank the American general. The fine gesture moved him to tears.

The other two incidents moved him to smiles.

General Gerow had established himself in von Choltitz's orphaned shoes, somewhat in the role of conqueror, with headquarters in the Hôtel des Invalides, in the shadow of Napoleon's tomb. There he waited three days before he notified de Gaulle that he was ready to turn over command of the city to French hands. He was told promptly and bluntly that he need not bother. General Koenig had already assumed that command on August 25th. And Koenig let Gerow know that the administration of the city had been handled "exclusively by French authorities since the moment of liberation."

"Good for old Koenig," Patton said when he was told of the incident.

Then he was told, too, that the British Broadcasting Corporation had credited the Third Army with the liberation of the city. As he recorded his reaction to the BBC's gratifying announcément, "This seemed to me poetic justice, as I could have taken it had I not been told not to. Later, I found that when the French 2nd Armored entered Paris, they told everyone they belonged to the Third Army and not to the First."

Three members of the Third Army did make their way into the liberated city, but only as transients on one-day passes. They were Colonel Codman, who was the wine-buyer of the S.S. Pierce Company of Boston in civilian life; Colonel "Bunny" Carter, who used to manage the Paris branch of the J. P. Morgan bank on Place Vendôme, and their driver, a corporal named Shoulder.

They bumped into Colonel David Bruce, on an oh-so-secret mission heading the O.S.S. contingent in Paris, who said, when he spotted the debonair Codman in the Ritz, "Ah, there you are, Charley. Now I *know* everything is normal."

But somehow Ernest Hemingway, ensconced in the Claridge's Bar and brooding over a glass of Perrier Jouet '29, summed up best the feelings of the Third Army.

"This is nothing," he said. "Just a bunch of crap."

CHAPTER THIRTY
"THE SURE THING"

The drive from the rain-soaked airstrip to Eagle Tac, General Bradley's advance CP near Laval, was only a 20-minute ride. But those few minutes loom in the history of World War II like the moment of truth in a bullfighter's career.

Riding in a commandeered Red Cross jeep, Lieutenant
General Patton was bobbing up and down in his seat, not so
much from the bumps in the road as from the inner bounce
of his nervous tension. He had reason to be bouncy and
tense. The night before he had had a brainstorm, hitting
upon a *strategic* idea so big and bold that it scared even
him. He had concluded that it would be possible to drive
into Germany through the West Wall within 10 days and
maybe even win the war in Europe right then and there,
in this summer of 1944, before the autumn rains turned
the battlefields into impassable quagmires. He had the operations plan worked out in his mind, ready for his staff to
put down on paper.

He had told General Gay, his Deputy Chief of Staff
and closest confidant in his entourage, "Now is the moment, Hap! They are ours for the taking. If we delay, the
price will be written in blood."

As an apprehensive afterthought, Patton added: "It is such
a sure thing that I fear someone will stop it."

On this murky, wet August 22nd, he was taking the plan
to General Bradley, hoping to win over the Army Group
Commander and enlist his aid for getting the green light
from General Eisenhower.

As was his wont, Patton burrowed himself completely into
the plan and identified himself with it body and soul. As
General Gay put it, all his hopes, his aspirations, his
dreams were tied up in it.

His pet plans always became highly personal matters with
him. Those who were for them were his friends, those
against them his enemies. As Patton now saw it, this would
be the acid test not only of Ike's leadership, but also of their
friendship. A few days before, he had been plunged into
deepest gloom over his failure to get Ike's permission to
lead the force that was to liberate Paris. But now his depression was gone. It gave way to buoyant energy and unbridled enthusiasm as he nursed "the Sure Thing" on its
passage to Bradley.

He was abruptly returned to reality when he found out
that Bradley was away from Eagle Tac attending a conference with Eisenhower and Montgomery. August was drawing to a close, and with its end would come radical changes
in the high command. General Eisenhower was slated
to assume personal command of Allied armies in France.
Patton was counting the days to that shift, like so many

shopping days to Christmas. More and more he had come
to blame Monty for his difficulties, and especially for the
abortion of the big maneuver in the Argentan-Falaise gap.
"The day Monty ceases to command U.S. troops," he told
his intimate staff, "we'll give thanks to God."

In Bradley's absence he buttonholed General Lev Allen,
Chief of Staff of the 12th Army Group, and confided the
plan to him. Allen seemed to like it. As a matter of fact, he
said, General Bradley was thinking along identical lines, except that he wanted to use two armies with six or maybe
seven corps instead of three corps Patton thought would be
sufficient for the operation.

There was nothing more Patton could accomplish at Eagle
Tac, so he drove to Sens on the Yonne River, 70 miles east
of Orléans, the farthest point of the Third Army's advance.
The capture of the old ecclesiastical city, where the massacre of the local Huguenots in 1562 rekindled the War of
Religions, fascinated him and filled him with unbounded
pride in his army.

On August 20th General Eddy (who had taken over XII
Corps from General Cook when the latter became disabled
with a serious circulatory ailment) had ordered General
Wood to make a 70-mile dash for Sens with his 4th
Armored Division. Followed by the 137th Infantry Regiment of the 35th Division, Wood bypassed Montargis,
which Hitler had ordered strongly defended, raced to
Souppes-sur-Loing on the Loire, crossed the river and continued to Sens, where he arrived on the afternoon of August
21st.

The enemy refused to believe their eyes when Wood's
spearheads drove into the city. It was crowded with German officers in their Sunday best who had come to visit
the famous 12th-century cathedral of St. Etienne, one of
the oldest Gothic monuments in France.

When Patton was told at Eagle Tac that Wood was already
on the east bank of the Yonne, he became eager "to
have a look and be seen by the troops." In Sens he handed
out a batch of Bronze Stars, then went sightseeing to the
cathedral built by the same William of Sens who also
worked on the edifice at Canterbury. Nothing could
demonstrate more dramatically the breath-taking speed of
Patton's campaign than this change of the guard in Sens. A
scant 20 hours before, the great cathedral had been
crowded with German sightseers; now Patton stood in the

same spot, admiring the magnificent windows painted by
the great Jean Cousin, whose *Last Judgment* is one of the
treasures of the Louvre.

What with the excitement over Paris, he realized that the
next few days were not propitious to promote his plan. So
Patton, for once the forgotten man in the joyous hullabaloo,
settled down to perfect it. An opportunity to test his design
offered itself the next day at Droué, 10 miles west of
Châteaudun, whence Lucky Forward had moved the day
before. General Alphonse-Pierre Juin, Chief of Staff of the
reborn French army, had come to visit.

He immediately ingratiated himself with Patton, telling
him, "Your daring, *mon général*, was Napoleonic." Patton
showed him the plan. Juin thought it *was* Napoleonic. He
agreed that the weakest spot in the Siegfried Line was east
of Nancy in the direction of the Saar—a spot Patton had
picked simply by studying his Michelin touring map. He
told Juin:

"I am not particularly worried about that Line because
I believe American troops can break through *any* Goddamn fortifications."

Early on August 23rd Patton received word that Bradley
was back at Eagle Tac and was ready to see him. Now their
meeting became a must, and not merely to chase the rainbow of his "Sure Thing." Other, more immediate, problems
began to burden him. He was about to be weakened badly
by the transfer of XV Corps to First Army, due to take
place this very day. What with that corps gone and VIII
Corps tied up in Brittany, he was left with only four divisions, one of which he had to freeze in the vicinity of
Orléans.

What was the use of plotting an all-out drive with three
corps and thinking of attacking to the Rhine when he had
available only as many divisions as corps he would need for
the big drive? "I cannot possibly go east with such a
skeleton force," he told Colonel Maddox, his G-3, with
whom he was reviewing the "Sure Thing" in long discussions. "I'll try to persuade Bradley to let me steal or borrow
all or part of VII Corps."

Then there was the growing problem of supplies. It was
beginning to cause Colonel Muller, his G-4, sleepless nights,
sending him to Patton with increasing frequency to warn
that something had to be done before it would be too late.
Patton was, as Bradley knew only too well, not particularly

interested in logistics. "I've my G-4 to worry about such details," he would say lightly. But now he could no longer evade the issue. His supplies were getting perceptibly short. The fantastic advance of the campaign and the logistic burdens of his three-front war began to interfere with his current operations and to threaten future ones.

Before leaving for Laval in the morning, Patton sent for "Maud" Muller and took him along for a man-to-man discussion with Brigadier General Raymond G. Moses, Bradley's Assistant Chief of Staff for Supply.

He found the Army Group Commander waiting at the airstrip, with only a few moments to spare for their conference. Bradley was on his way to Shellburst, where, he told Patton, he expected to have a noisy meeting with Eisenhower and Montgomery. "I've never seen him as mad as this before," Patton told Colonel Muller on their return to the CP.

For Bradley, the situation presented a fantastic paradox. He had scored greater victories in a shorter span of time than probably any field commander in history. He was riding the crest of the wave. It seemed that final victory over Hitler's vaunted *Wehrmacht* was a foregone conclusion. In frivolous moments of justifiable optimism it was even expected to occur before the end of this year.

Bradley was suffering from an embarrassment of riches. He had become too good a general for his own good. His immense successes now came back to plague him. He had taken on the Germans in a head-on clash in "Cobra" and won. Then he accepted their foolish challenge at Mortain and won again. While originally he expected to wage the decisive battle in this duel for France east of the Seine, he had so disorganized the enemy and had so knocked him off base that virtually the whole of France east of the river lay wide open.

And yet this triumphant general—this modest, self-effacing man who had become a conquering hero—had ample reasons to be uneasy and upset. The unbelievable extension of his front was beginning to overtax his supply arrangements. But logistics, even with Bradley's keen awareness of their importance, now appeared to be only a secondary issue compared with what was rapidly becoming his Number One problem—Montgomery.

A few days before, they had locked horns over the burning question of what to do next. Their meeting ended incon-

clusively, pending a decision at the top. But their dispute
continued to simmer. Now Bradley was flying to Shellburst
for what he expected would be a showdown fight for his
concepts and plans as opposed to Montgomery's ideas for
the future.

The big question was—what next?

This was the same question that confronted General
Eisenhower on August 17th when he sat down to dictate a
letter to General Marshall about his own prospects and
plans. His forces had reached the Seine River as planned, 15
days ahead of schedule. The basic mission of "Overlord"
had been accomplished. The lodgment area was more than
secure.

The master plan prescribed a pause there to give the
troops some rest, replace their losses, bring in reinforcements (including fresh divisions from the United States because the British were scraping the bottom of their manpower barrel), replenish the equipment of the combat units,
build up the Communications Zone for the next push, con-
struct pipelines for fuel, improve the roads, restore the rail
net—in other words, to make up for the ravages of the bygone campaign and prepare for the task ahead.

Eisenhower wrote to Marshall about his "feeling" that the
beating the Allies had administered to the Germans would
not make such a pause necessary after all. But he was still
struggling with the crucial question of what to do next—
whether to stop on the Seine or to go beyond it. Two days
later he reached the decision. The Allies would, he wrote
to Marshall, "dash across the Seine." The river had lost its
lure. His eyes were set on the Rhine, 250 miles to the east
—in Germany.

It was a momentous decision, second only in importance
to Ike's famous resolution to go through with the invasion
on June 6th despite the prospect of inclement weather. On
August 19th Eisenhower told Montgomery and Bradley of
his decision, and he could not have made them happier.
They both agreed with the Supreme Commander that the
drive should be continued relentlessly while the enemy was
still staggering. But there the two commanders parted company. Montgomery proposed a single thrust north of the
Ardennes toward the Ruhr by three Allied armies—two
British and one American—under his command. A fourth
army, presumably Patton's Third, would be virtually

pinched out and held in position on the Meuse. Whatever Monty had in mind, the inference seemed to be clear. He did not want Patton to be in on the end run.

Bradley, on the other hand, recommended a double thrust. Under his plan Montgomery would be given but a single American corps from the First Army, instead of the entire army as Montgomery proposed, to support his main effort to the Ruhr. The Third U.S. Army would simultaneously unleash a second drive across the Rhine, to Mannheim, Karlsruhe and Wiesbaden, assisted by the remainder of the First Army.

The fight for the competing plans started at once.

Montgomery was not pulling his punches. He was lining up allies to support his design, drumming up an acute crisis in the mind of his mentor, Field Marshal Brooke (who was always willing to be critical of Eisenhower's strategic planning), and even involving Prime Minister Churchill in the dispute.

Now Bradley was flying to Shellburst to force Eisenhower, as he told Patton, to choose between the two plans. In truth it involved more than just that. It had to be a choice between two nations. As Bradley pointed out, "One involved a predominantly American effort; the other was basically British."

Patton was keenly interested in what Bradley was relating to him. He had assumed that the big brass would abide by the "Overlord" phase line and order a halt at the Seine. This assumption had been mainly responsible for triggering his plan to drive on. And it stiffened his back to put up an all-out fight for it. He had assumed that Bradley also favored the halt and would be difficult to win over, but was gratified to learn from General Allen the day before that the Army Group Commander was raring to go.

Bradley was now complaining, "To tell the truth, George, I am quite worried. I feel in my bones that Ike will not go against Monty and the American armies will have to turn north in whole or in part. As a matter of fact, Air Marshal Leigh-Mallory was with me all day trying to sell me on the idea."

There was no time to discuss the "Sure Thing." Bradley's plane was ready to take him to Shellburst. As Patton, worried and deep in his thoughts, stood at the airstrip in the drizzle, he could not know that the conference for which

Bradley had just left would lose him a cherished plan but
win him an indomitable and invaluable friend and ally for
the rest of the war.

General Marshall was giving Eisenhower a completely free
hand in making the decision. Bradley's arguments on this
particular issue carried but limited weight with the Supreme Commander, while Patton had no influence whatsoever on him. He had not seen or heard from Eisenhower for
weeks, had not received even a brief "well done" from
him for his drive. Then there was also the sacrosanct chain
of command. Patton had to work through Bradley. He
would sometimes do certain things on his own initiative
without first consulting Bradley, but he would never go directly to Ike or Marshall over his superior's head and behind
his back.

But the pressure from London was enormous. Eisenhower needed his best grin to bear it. The suspicion with which
some Britons viewed the problem was plainly documented
by Field Marshal Brooke in his diary entry of August 28:

"Difficult C.O.S. meeting where we considered Eisenhower's new plan to take command himself in Northern
France on September 1st. This plan is likely to add another
three to six months on to the war. He straight away wants
to split his force, sending an American contingent towards
Nancy whilst the British Army Group moves along the
coast. If the Germans were not as beat as they are this
would be a fatal move; as it is, it may not do too much
harm. In any case I am off to France tomorrow to see Monty
and to discuss the situation with him"—behind Eisenhower's back, he could have added.

This was how Brooke and Monty always did these things.
While Bradley would never have thought of taking his beefs
directly to General Marshall, Montgomery was in constant
communication with "my dear Brookie," as he addressed
the Chief of the Imperial General Staff in his private letters
in which he poured out his heavy heart. Brooke, on his part,
kept Monty steadily posted on what was going on in the
highest Allied councils and frequently alerted him to anything that even remotely threatened to become detrimental
to their cause. Such a relationship was highly irregular. It

violated the chain of command and, more specifically, an agreement Eisenhower had made with Brooke to give him sole authority over his British commanders. It was grossly unfair to General Eisenhower personally, especially since references to him in this explosive Brooke-Montgomery correspondence were highly abusive at times.

The Supreme Commander knew about it, was exasperated by it, but could not do anything about it. He wrote: "This habit may have been based upon sound reasons of which I know nothing, but it was always a shock to me, raised in the tradition of the American services, to find that the British Chiefs regularly queried their commanders in the field concerning tactical plans."

Eisenhower was genuinely fond of Montgomery, admired him very much, and regarded his strange mannerisms as simply incidental liabilities over his enormous assets. But he could never work up a real liking for Brooke, who, he thought, was "adroit rather than deep, and shrewd rather than wise" and who "lacked that ability so characteristic of General Marshall to weigh calmly the conflicting factors and so reach a rocklike decision." He attributed Brooke's constant mingling in his affairs with Montgomery as the offshoot of the peculiar British command relationship and part of the pageantry of intrigue that traditionally split the War Office and the British Army into cliques.

By the time Brooke reached Monty's headquarters at 2 P.M. on August 29th a solution of the problem appeared to be in the making. "Apparently," Brooke wrote, "[Montgomery and Eisenhower] succeeded in arriving at a suitable compromise." But he added the reservation, "It remains to be seen what political pressure is put on Eisenhower to move Americans on separate axis from the British."

Montgomery and Patton were poles apart in their planning, but there was an affinity in their characters and thinking. Essentially each wanted the same—the single thrust. But Montgomery claimed it for himself while Patton now worked as hard as he could from his position of distinct disadvantage to secure the drive for the Third Army with an assist by a single corps he hoped to get from the First.

While Bradley was flying west to Eisenhower to hear the verdict, Patton was driving the short distance to Eagle Tac for the supply conference. Muller thought his mercurial boss was unusually subdued, but Patton was merely off on one of his thinking sprees. He was like Josiah Holland's sun-crowned, tall man who lived above the fog in public duty and did his thinking in private. Whenever Patton became engrossed in working out an enigma, he retired into his own hard shell, became oblivious to the world around him, and thought methodically, his agile brain conjuring up all the paraphernalia he needed for his thoughts—maps, references, figures, orders of battle, historical precedents, and even arguments pro and con.

His meeting with Bradley had disturbed him and pulled a cloud over his sunny plan. It became obvious that he could not expect to get any part of VII Corps to augment his meager forces for the drive east. And it now appeared likely that the big drive through the West Wall to the Rhine might founder on Eisenhower's decision. Patton expected the Supreme Commander to succumb to Montgomery, let him mount the thrust, and give him the American forces he was asking for.

It struck him like a dismal prospect—but then suddenly Patton brightened. His hard thinking had produced results. Like a man who had just emerged from a trance, he turned to Colonel Muller.

"Maud," he said in one of his rare moments of such intimacy with his G-4, "mark this August 23rd. I've just thought up the best strategical idea I've ever had. This may yet be a momentous day."

Now he could hardly wait to get to 12th Army Group Headquarters. So he won't get the VII Corps! So he might have to go north first to aid Monty! It no longer mattered. He had an alternative plan and he thought it was grand.

At the CP he dashed into the Chief of Staff's tent and pinned down Allen.

"Look here, Lev," he said, "if Ike orders us to go north to help Monty the XX Corps could do it faster from Melun and Montereau, and the XII Corps from Sens, than any-one else. By heading to Beauvais we could pick up the 4th Division, which will be south of Paris tomorrow, and then get the 79th and possibly the 5th Armored by having them cross at Mantes. After reaching Beauvais we can parallel the river and open the Seine to the British and Canadians. What's more, by having our supplies come across at Mantes, we could reduce our present haul by 50 per cent."

General Allen took it down, checked on his map the points Patton had mentioned, and said, "It seems fine to me, General." Coming from the lean and friendly Mormon who was always informal but cautious when expressing his opinions, this sounded like enthusiasm to Patton.

"Tell it to Brad when he comes back," Patton urged. "I'm going back to my CP to have my staff put both plans in writing—the one I told you yesterday about going straight east, and this one going north. If Bradley approves the attack to the north he has only to wire me 'Plan A' by 1000 tomorrow. If I don't hear from you fellows by that time, I'll then move east as per my 'Plan B'."

Back at his command post, Patton summoned his planning staff and told them: "We are to do what Monty hasn't done yet—keep the Hun from escaping. I'm not going to sit on my butt and allow the Hun to organize in front of me. We'll attack his line and go north at the same time."

But he was jumping at conclusions.

The signal he received from Eagle Tac next morning instructed him to stay where he was. Then early on August 25th, while preparing to move his CP—now for the eighth time—to a place 10 miles south of Pithiviers, he received a call from General Bradley asking him to be at Chartres, where Eagle Tac had moved in the meantime, at 11 A.M.

Patton found General Hodges there when he drove up, and Bradley quickly brought him up to date. Eisenhower had decided to move beyond the Seine at once. To Patton this sounded anticlimactic. He had anticipated the decision. When, on August 19th, XV Corps had reached the lower Seine northwest of Paris (in a zone actually assigned to the British), he had told General Haislip to push on. At 9:35 o'clock that night, Haislip sent word to General Wyche to take his 79th Division across the river. Shortly afterward, men of the 313th Infantry Regiment single-filed on a narrow dam in torrential rain and utter darkness and secured the first Allied bridgehead east of the Seine. They were followed at daybreak by the 314th Infantry. By nightfall on August 20th the division was on the east bank with tanks, artillery and tank destroyers.

What followed was best described by the war diary of the Germans' Army Group B, which gave a dramatic account of the industry with which the 79th Division exploited its historic bridgehead. It not only extended and improved its foothold, repelled counterattacks, interdicted highways, ferry routes and barge traffic lanes, but also captured the command post of the Army Group at La Roche-Guyon and sent the German headquarters troops scurrying eastward to Soissons, 75 miles away.

Moreover, General Dempsey's Second Army had also jumped off toward the river. On August 24th, in face of "almost negligible resistance," his 15th Division reached Le Neubourg and began preparations to cross the Seine at Louviers, 12 miles away.

Patton hoped to switch his own drive into high gear, but the orders Bradley doled out dampened his enthusiasm. Eisenhower was still considering the two competing plans. In the meantime, Bradley ordered Hodges to cross the Seine at Melun and Mantes (both of which, as Patton wryly remarked, had been captured by the Third Army) on bridges (which had been erected by Patton's engineers). Lille, in the north of France on the Belgian border, toward which Montgomery was planning to attack with his thrust, was designated as the general direction of the First Army's drive.

As for Patton, he got back XV Corps as well as Leclerc's *2me Blindée*, increasing his force to seven divisions—three armored and four infantry. Using XV, XX and XII Corps, he was ordered to advance in the direction of the line Metz-Strasbourg. It was a far cry from the "Sure Thing," but Patton was not entirely displeased with his assignment.

"The direction is part of my plan," he told General Gay.

The next three days were busy ones as Patton toured his lively fronts.

On August 26th, trailed by a flock of Signal Corps cameramen on assignment to take pictures for a story to be called "A Day with General Patton," Patton drove to the 5th Division CP near Montereau, just outside Paris, to compliment General Irwin on a great job at the Seine and to hand out DSC's to Lieutenant Colonel Kelley B. Lemmon Jr., Captain Jack S. Gerrie and Technical Sergeant Dupe A. Willingham. They had distinguished themselves in a spirited fight with the Germans on August 23rd.

He then drove on to Melun, straddling the Seine at the apex of a long, V-shaped bend where the river was almost

300 feet wide, to visit the 7th Armored Division. General Silvester's tankers and artillerymen had crossed the river there on a treadway bridge to reinforce the precarious east-bank bridgehead secured by armored infantrymen the previous day.

By August 25th the Third Army had four bridgeheads across the upper Seine south of Paris between Melun and Troyes. Patton visited them all.

He regarded some of the transactions of these days as mere shadow-boxing. He undertook them on orders from above, but did not think that any real gain could be made from these attacks to the south. Although the Third Army was moving forward with great strides, Patton felt a letdown. These operations hardly held out any real excitement. His men took Château-Thierry of World War I fame, then jumped forward in the direction of Vitry-le-Francois, Châlons-sur-Marne and Reims. On August 28th the Third Army was 250 miles east of Avranches, fewer than 150 miles from the German frontier at Sulzbach.

Up to this point, Patton's army had suffered only 1,930 killed out of a total of 18,239 casualties. But 5,414 of his total were of nonbattle origin. Although Patton would cry for every wounded and mourn every dead, it was not too high a price for such gains.

It would be too much to say that these jumps east of the Seine required any undue exertion on the part of the Third Army. German opposition was sporadic and confused. In most of the places where resistance was encountered the Germans were usually easy to dislocate and force into withdrawal.

During these days the toughest job was to get Leclerc's 2me Blindée back into the war from Paris. Its soldiers had dissolved in the delirious city, which feted and pampered them with impassioned joy. The men vanished into private homes to be dined and wined, and sleep off the hardships and humiliations of the war in downy beds, in the arms of ad hoc mistresses. A whole detachment, for want of a proper billet, established itself at Madame Hélène's, enjoying the delectable attention of Madame's mundane sorority with everything on the house that was not a home until it was told by irate FFI men that Madame's établissement was to be closed down because her poules had shown too much of the same delectable attention to les Boches. Patton needed Leclerc's division badly to relieve the 35th Division, which was overdue at XII Corps but had to be kept back to guard the right flank. The Frenchmen were supposed to revert to him on August 29th. It required Bradley's energetic intervention to assure their return a week later.

With so much to choose from, General Patton was in a strange quandary. The drive on Metz was an integral part of his grand design. He was approaching the Saar with giant steps and could race to the West Wall. But now he was torn between the "Sure Thing" and the "best strategical idea" he had ever had. With Beauvais as its pivot, he saw in the latter "a glowing opportunity" to pull another envelopment on the Argentan pattern. By turning north, as he had suggested to Army Group on August 23rd, and wheeling toward Beauvais, he could "stick armored spearheads into the flanks of those German forces that had escaped across the Seine."

The idea may have been splendid, but not everybody, even at Patton's own headquarters, regarded it as foolproof. To some it appeared to resemble the old Schlieffen plan in reverse, with all its disadvantages. And such a wheeling to the north would have delayed the drive toward the German border, an objective that never ceased to relax its hold on Patton's imagination.

His problem was solved for him on the morning of August 28th, when General Bradley arrived to discuss the drive of the Third Army and, in a sense, straighten out its commanding general. There was no equivocation in Bradley's orders—Patton was to forget about the envelopment and the wheel turning to Beauvais. He was to go east toward the upper Rhine, in due course, that is, for that objective was still 250 miles away.

"How about a line on the Meuse?" Patton bargained, for he was a past master of the *quid pro quo*. The question provoked pangs of memory, for that was where, at St. Mihiel, he had had his baptism of fire with his toy-tanks in World War I. The line also contained one of history's immortal objectives, Verdun.

"I don't think you ought to extend your line that far to the east," Bradley said. "You'd be better off on the Marne."

But Patton continued to argue, and Bradley approved the drive to the line Verdun-Commercy on the Meuse. In the light of what was to happen in a day or two, it is questionable whether Bradley really meant to give Patton what he wanted, or agreed merely to cut him short.

Patton was taking no chances. Fearful that Bradley might reconsider, he went into action at once to start his army moving to the Meuse. He sent General Gay to General Walker with orders for XX Corps to move on Verdun. Then he went to General Eddy to start XII Corps off to Commercy.

While he was with Eddy, a message was handed to him. It was from Muller, urgent. It reported that for reasons unknown, Third Army's ration of gasoline—140,000 gallons —had failed to arrive.

"Goddamnit," Patton blew up on the impact of the shock. Just then General Wood came into the room and Patton said to him, "I don't know what this Goddamn thing means, John. Maybe it's a backhanded move to stop me." He paused for a moment, then added in a lower tone, "I doubt it."

His first impulse was to call Bradley, but he dropped the idea. The CP had only radio link with 12th Army Group Headquarters, and Patton assumed the Germans were monitoring it.

"I don't want the Boche to know," he told Wood and Eddy, "that we're getting low on gasoline."

On August 28th Colonel Oscar W. Koch, Patton's meticulous intelligence chief, handed his chief "Estimate No. 9," a study of the situation as it presented itself to the G-2 of a victorious army. For his study Koch deserved the Medal of Honor, for it represented a courageous deed far, far beyond what other men in his position would have regarded as their call of duty.

The air was heavy with optimism. From everywhere cheerful estimates floated to Patton's desk, including one from Major General Kenneth Strong, Eisenhower's own G-2, that said without any strings attached: "The August battles have done it and the enemy has had it. Two and a half months of bitter fighting, culminating for the Germans in a blood-bath big enough even for their extravagant tastes, have brought the end of the war in Europe within sight, almost within reach." Another SHAEF G-2 estimate spoke of the German army in the west as no longer being "a cohesive force but a number of fugitive battle groups, disorganized and even demoralized, short of equipment and arms."

General Eisenhower was not misled by his G-2's cheerful prognostication. He refused to concede that the Germans had been decisively defeated. As a matter of fact, he expected considerable travail ahead for his armies because, as he put it, the German forces had "succeeded, in spite of defeat and disorder, in withdrawing significant numbers of their troops across the Seine."

The same caution now stared Patton in the face from his own G-2's sober estimate. "Despite the crippling factors of shattered communications, disorganization and tremendous losses in personnel and equipment," Colonel Koch wrote, "the enemy nevertheless has been able to maintain a sufficiently cohesive front to exercise an over-all control of his tactical situation. His withdrawal, though continuing, has not been a rout or mass collapse.

"Numerous new identifications in contact in recent days have demonstrated clearly that, despite the enormous difficulties under which he is operating the enemy is still capable of bringing new elements into the battle area and transferring some from other fronts. . . . Barring internal upheaval in the homeland [which, incidentally a First Army intelligence estimate of about that same date expected to occur within 30 to 60 days] and the remoter possibility of insurrection within the *Wehrmacht,* it can be expected that the German armies will continue to fight until destroyed or captured."

Patton was inclined to dismiss Koch's estimate. When he had read it, he told Koch, "After a careful study of the situation it appears to me that there is no real threat against us from anywhere so long as we do not let imaginary dangers worry us."

Koch got the message. But he continued to be skeptical and cautious. Strangely enough, he survived at Patton's side throughout the war. Patton kept him and admired him for those very traits he would have blasted as "Goddamn defeatism" in anybody else. In his own boundless optimism and enthusiasm he needed a G-2 like Koch, and he knew it. But he never warmed to the colonel sufficiently to call him by his first name.

Now the crisis over the two plans—Montgomery's and Bradley's—was coming to a head. And Patton, with a new bitterness that was beginning to rend his soul, saw the "Sure

Thing" recede into limbo. He had come to recognize his own brainstorm in Bradley's broad design and gained encouragement from the recognition because he hoped that Bradley's influence on Eisenhower would help it. It was a straightforward plan, nothing essentially fancy about it. In Bradley's own description, it called for emphasis on a thrust to the Reich straight through the middle of France to the Saar and beyond the Saar to the Rhine in the vicinity of Frankfurt. Bradley figured he would need both of his armies for this effort. He hoped it would be accompanied by what he called "a secondary thrust" of the British and Canadian armies up the Channel coast to Antwerp.

But Montgomery insisted that all the Allied strength be concentrated on a drive north through Amiens and Brussels to the Ruhr. Its path would cover almost twice the distance of the drive Bradley was proposing. And Montgomery was pressuring Eisenhower to approve the northern thrust even if it meant, as Bradley put it, the total abandonment of the American advance to the Saar.

This was the crux of the matter.

Knowing the manner in which Montgomery was waging his war, his careful preparations and hoarding of supplies, Bradley and Patton feared that the northern thrust would not leave enough supplies for the Americans ever to get to the Saar. Patton believed he saw shades of Sicily. All Monty wanted the Americans to do (aside from those units he hoped to get for this thrust) was to sit on their backsides and cover his flanks, while he would be grabbing the ball and running with it for a touchdown, exactly as he had planned it in Sicily when he put the Seventh U.S. Army down on the open beaches.

Montgomery saw it differently, of course. The Americans had had their day in this campaign and now it was his turn. He had sat on *his* backside long enough in June, July and August, drawing the bulk of the German forces in Normandy, while the Americans—and Patton in particular —could rampage with virtually no serious opposition. Besides, he did not plan his thrust as an all-British venture. He had asked for the Hodges army to go along on the ride. He wanted only one American army to stay in position on the Meuse. As far as Patton was concerned, the Montgomery plan was unacceptable to him because the American army Monty wanted to leave behind happened to be his Third Army.

No matter how much Patton was coming to distrust Eisenhower, the fact was that on this particular issue the Supreme Commander was on his side. When, on August 23rd, Montgomery presented his bold plan assigning the Third Army to the "defensive role of flank protection during the advance of the Second British and First American Armies to the Ruhr," Eisenhower told him:

"The American public would never stand for stopping Patton in full cry, and public opinion wins war."

"Nonsense," Montgomery shot back angrily. "Victories win war. Give people victory and they won't care who won it."

But Eisenhower continued to believe that the halting of Patton would be "politically impossible"—and on this thin thread now hung the future of the Third Army in the caldron of this coalition war.

The decision could not be delayed much longer. On August 30th it began to cast its shadows ahead.

The pressure on General Eisenhower became almost unbearable. Insisting that if the Supreme Commander would support his 21st Army Group "with all supply facilities available," Montgomery said he could rush right on into Berlin and end the war. "At the moment," Eisenhower later wrote, "his enthusiasm was fired by the rapid advances of the preceding week and, since he was convinced that the enemy was completely demoralized, he vehemently declared that all he needed was adequate supply in order to go directly into Berlin."

When Eisenhower wrote "vehemently" he really meant "vehemently." During those days Montgomery showed little restraint in his treatment of the Supreme Commander or any respect for his position. At one of their meetings on this hotly contested issue, when Eisenhower was weakened by an injured knee and could hardly move about, Montgomery subjected him to a series of indignities. At the beginning of their conference Monty demanded that the Supreme Commander's Chief Administrative Officer—who, incidentally, was a British Army lieutenant general—be excluded from the discussion while his own aide be allowed to participate. Eisenhower agreed. Montgomery then proceeded to blast the Supreme Commander and his plans "in language which was far from parliamentary." It was a British historian who wrote of the meeting: "A man of less generous nature might have reacted violently to his outburst but, as the tirade gathered fury, Eisenhower sat silent." He did not stay silent for too long. When Monty once stopped to catch his breath, Ike placed a hand on Montgomery's knee and told him in a low but firm tone:

"Steady, Monty! You can't speak to me like that. I'm your boss."

Patton had a sneaking suspicion that the decision was going against him but he refused to throw in the sponge. On August 30th he flew to Chartres because he had heard that Major General Harold R. Bull, Eisenhower's G-3, would be there, and he was anxious to win him for his cause. As they assembled in Bradley's new mahogany-paneled, 26-foot trailer, he asked to be allowed to present his case for an immediate advance to the east and, as he put it, rupture of the Siegfried Line before the Germans could regarrison and re-equip it. He pointed to the known facts of hard intelligence—"The enemy is weak and disorganized in the zone of Third Army's advance." And he called attention to the Germans' considerable strength and powerful positions in the north.

As far as the West Wall was concerned, Patton argued that he could penetrate it in a few days with light losses. "But if we permit the Hun to man those massive emplacements," he said, "it'll take weeks and thousands of casualties."

There was a lot to his argument, especially with regard to the West Wall (which our side insisted on calling "Siegfried Line" after the *Siegfriedstellung* of World War I memory).

It was clear that the break into Germany would be difficult and costly if carried across the vast fortifications Hitler had built on the western border of the Reich to contain the Anglo-French forces in 1939 while he was dealing with the Poles. In the meantime, however, the Wall had become an empty shell. It was stripped of equipment needed elsewhere. Its garrison was removed from its sinecure to the lively fronts. Its grass was allowed to grow into pastures and cattle were permitted to feast among its measured defenses. The casemates were padlocked and the keys thrown away. Even in August, Hitler hoped to make a stand somewhere in France, maybe on the Somme-Marne line. He indulged in the belief that the West Wall had outlived its uselessness, so to speak, until it was almost too late—*almost* too late.

Thanks to intensive prisoner-of-war interrogations, a

careful study of captured documents and especially information gained from intercepted radio messages by Signal Intelligence, Patton had a good idea of the state of the abandoned Wall. "It was definitely known," wrote Colonel Robert S. Allen, a G-2 officer on his staff, "that not only were these positions unprepared for defense, but the field commanders did not even know their exact locations. They were frantically clamoring for liaison officers to show them where to dispose units."

In a communication to me, General Westphal, then Chief of Staff of *OB West,* presented this picture of the German situation in the area toward which Patton was casting eager glances:

"When I arrived at *OB West* to take over as Chief of Staff from General Blumentritt, the German situation in the West was nothing short of disastrous. The defeated Army of the West was in disorderly flight. It appeared hopeless to expect that the flood could be stemmed, even at the Rhine crossings.

"As for the West Wall, it had been dismantled two years before, in favor of the Atlantic Wall. The fortifications were stripped of all weapons, ammunition depots were empty. In most cases, not even the keys could be found to unlock the gates to the various subterranean gun emplacements. The tactical value of the concrete bunkers was virtually nil. For one thing, they had been erected in breathless haste, with evident emphasis on showmanship and quantity, neglecting quality and proper tactical considerations. I happen to know this first-hand because I was serving in Trier, the central sector of the line, when the Wall was being erected in 1938-39.

"The much-vaunted and so-called West Wall thus possessed merely a symbolic value. It offered not even the slightest obstacle, yet evidently impelled the Allies nevertheless to approach it with a carefully prepared drive instead of penetrating it in a lightning assault with relatively light forces. This actually astonished us at headquarters. We then experienced a similar surprise in February-March, 1945, when our enemies persisted in regarding the Rhine as a serious obstacle to their advance, something it never was in reality.

"When I accompanied Field Marshal von Rundstedt, the Commander in Chief, on an inspection trip to the West Wall during those days, I heard him conclude that it would be absolutely incapable of offering any serious resistance, an estimate in which I concurred wholeheartedly.

"I would like to state unequivocally that we would have been totally incapable of putting up any serious resistance and foiling a drive across the western boundaries of the Reich had General Eisenhower decided upon a truly determined, concentrated and ruthless advance at this point. At that time, headquarters of *OB West* was located in the vicinity of Koblenz. Whenever after sunset we could hear the rattling of chains in the street where the Field Marshal had his quarters, he would ask, 'Can this be Patton?' The question was posed in jest, of course, but it did not lack the most serious undertone.

"Had the Allies assigned all available ground and air tonnage for the transport of fuel, and had they used airborne units to establish bridgeheads east of the Rhine, it would have been possible for them to penetrate deeply into the Reich, push the West Front up against the East Front, and win the war before the end of the year 1944.

"This is no hindsight," General Westphal wrote in conclusion. "I have always regarded it as a miracle that we succeeded in halting the eastward flight of our defeated West Army and, after many worrysome weeks, managed to build another, even if only on a very thin front."

This was exactly what Patton told General Bull on August 30, 1944, from this side of the barrier he was so eager to cross. "Their resistance is merely a thin crust," he said. "It has no depth. The Hun has no effective reserves behind it."

He realized that his "Sure Thing" would be really sure only if he exploited this abysmal weakness of the enemy at once and reached the West Wall while the formidable vacuous caverns were still in their abandoned state, stripped of all weapons and ammunition reserves. And what with the advance of the Third Army, he did not expect the Germans to leave the Wall abandoned for too long, or to permit the area toward which he was driving to remain so woefully undefended.

Patton was right on both scores. On August 17th Field Marshal von Kluge, broken in body and soul, and harassed by the Gestapo for his alleged involvement in the July 20th plot against Hitler, committed suicide while he was en route to the Führer's headquarters to account for his failure and

supposed disloyalty. He was replaced by Field Marshal Walther Model, a stiff-necked tactician Hitler regarded as highly for his skilled campaigns in the east as for the absence
of any blue blood in his veins.

Even as Patton was pleading with Bull to let him jump to
the West Wall, Model was reorganizing the remnants of the
divisions he had managed to extricate from the debacle on
the Seine, and was sending them to the Châlons-Reims-Sois-
sons area with the purpose of opposing the Third Army.
"This meant," as Wilmot put it, "that just as the British
were about to break out from the Vernon bridgehead, Patton was drawing to the east the only mobile forces capable
of checking their advance." And Hitler was even then drafting an order for Model to "concentrate the most powerful
armored force he could on the upper Moselle with the object of counterattacking Patton's army and striking into the
American flank."

At the same time, orders were being flashed to stationary
garrisons all over the Reich and to idle fortress battalions,
to training regiments, officer candidate schools, even to a
squad of deep-sea divers in the *Kriegsmarine* and to the
Arbeitsdienst, the labor organization, to assemble contingents for an immediate march into the West Wall. Before
long, Hitler had 135,000 men thus stamped out of the
ground to repopulate the casemates, bunkers and galleries.
They were not uniformly good. If anything, they were almost uniformly bad. One battalion consisted solely of men
suffering from duodenal ulcers. Another had only men with
defective hearing. They were kept together in special units
by some perverted stretching of the German obsession with
organization and *Ordnung*. Whatever their shortcomings,
the prospect developed that this crucial gap at the German
frontier would soon be filled with men and equipment to
bar Patton's passage.

But on this August 30th, when Patton was pleading with
General Bull, Field Marshall Model's forces were still
straggling toward the line Châlons-Soissons. The West
Wall was still but a gigantic vacant lot, populated by
squatters—refugees from heavily bombed German cities in
the area. At the conference in Bradley's swank trailer
(which, Patton said, looked like a "Goddamn chapel," probably because it had an altar rail for its partition and was
darkened by blackout curtains) Bradley seemed to go along

with his plea. But Bull sounded discouraging. Patton left the meeting completely dispirited. He saw his worst apprehensions coming true. "It is such a sure thing that I fear someone will stop it," he had said on August 21st. It was about to happen.

CHAPTER THIRTY-ONE
BONE DRY

While General Patton was at Chartres on August 30th for the meeting with General Bull, General Bradley took him aside and told him with some embarrassment that he would get very little gasoline from then on, and possibly none at all for the next few weeks. Bradley gave several reasons for putting Third Army on "A" ration when Patton's projected moves required more than the unlimited "C."

Vast quantities of gas were needed to supply liberated Paris, and not only to keep the wheels of the big city turning. Most of the diverted gasoline was consumed by the endless columns of trucks that carried an enormous variety of relief supplies into the city—from food and drugs to freshly printed Free French franc bills and contraceptives. Even wine had to be poured into the city—mostly the popular Prémontaines variety—for Parisians set in their culinary ways. They would probably have revolted if deprived of this staple indispensable to even the most modest French table.

Serious though this unexpected added strain was on the American supply organization, it was not the decisive factor in throttling Patton. The real trouble originated at SHAEF.

The day before, in a stunning decision, General Eisenhower finally gave Montgomery what he wanted, even though for some time he had allowed Bradley to hope that his plan had the inside track. According to the Supreme Commander's directive of August 29th, however, Third

Army would be allowed to move to the Meuse as best it could, but the main effort was to be made by the British in the north.

Monty had already jumped off and was heading toward the Somme at Amiens with a powerful drive. He was aided by XIX and V Corps of the First U.S. Army, which had turned northeast from the Seine and were advancing rapidly toward Belgium. They needed all the gas they could get, everything the Services of Supply could scrape up, straining all transportation facilities to the breaking point.

Bradley was almost apologetic when he told Patton this, especially when he spoke about the shortage of supply trucks. He appeared to be irked not only with Montgomery, but also with General John C. H. Lee, head man of SOS. It seemed that in the midst of this oppressive strain on gasoline stocks Lee had decided to move his own palatial and vast headquarters from Cherbourg to Paris. He consumed 25,000 gallons of precious gas on the transfer and took hundreds of trucks out of circulation.

Bradley was also outspokenly critical of General Eisenhower for having given in to Montgomery's persistent demands for far more tonnage than Bradley thought the 21st Army Group reasonably needed. Montgomery had first presented a shopping list for all kinds of goods he required but could not get from his own supply administration. Then he claimed he could not support his thrust unless he was given a fleet of American trucks to carry these goods.

When SHAEF instructed the 12th Army Group to give Monty the trucks he requested, Bradley diverted them from the First Army. But then that army was ordered to roll northward with Monty and needed those very vehicles. Bradley took the trucks from Third Army, describing this juggling of American vehicles as "hijacking poor Patton's trucks."

Behind Monty's desperate need of the American trucks was one of the war's great scandals. Just before the northern thrust, the alarming discovery was made at the 21st Army Group that the engines of 1,400 British-built three-tonners—as well as all the replacement engines for this model—had faulty pistons, rendering them useless. The capacity of these trucks was 800 tons per day, enough to supply two divisions. The lost tonnage Montgomery had to compensate for with the vehicles taken from Patton amounted to about 40 per cent of the total the Third Army was to receive after the radical cutback of supplies to a daily 2,000 tons.

Bradley and Patton were shocked by Montgomery's insistence on supplies well beyond his apparent needs. Bradley was firmly convinced that he could have delivered his thrust with less of everything. "Had Monty pared down his ammunition requirements," he wrote, "and concentrated instead on gasoline, Patton might have advanced farther . . . . I argued strenuously with Eisenhower on Monty's extravagance in tonnage, but without success, for I was unable to budge him. Meanwhile Patton worried, then moaned and stormed as the growing shortage of QM trucks caused his gasoline supplies to dwindle."

In his state of shock at seeing his "Sure Thing" dry up with the rapidly evaporating gasoline stock, Patton did not know what to make of Bradley's commiseration and protestations. He was mystified by the Army Group Commander's attitude, as was, even years later, Chester Wilmot, the Australian journalist-historian who wrote *The Struggle for Europe*. Were Bradley and Patton fellow victims of Montgomery's shenanigans, Eisenhower's equivocations, and favoritism? Or was Bradley himself a silent party to them? In his account of these momentous days when the real struggle for Europe was being waged in the secrecy-cloaked offices of the Allied high commanders, Wilmot recalled how Bradley, on his own initiative, had tried to slow Patton and how he had hoped to stop him at the Marne instead of letting him advance to the Meuse.

Wilmot called attention to Bradley's ready acquiescence in cutting Patton's gasoline allotment virtually to nil, and wrote, "If Bradley thought that this would restrain Patton, he was wrong." The inference was quite clear.

At this critical moment in his career Patton was not yet seeking scapegoats for the heartbreaking crisis his army was facing. He did not stop to assign blame to Eisenhower or Bradley, or even to Montgomery. Rather, he dashed out of Bradley's command post and rushed back to his own headquarters to act upon this alarming knowledge with the greatest of dispatch and energy.

At La Chaume he found the confusion of Chartres vastly compounded. Colonel Muller received him with the news that of the 400,000 gallons of gasoline he had requested in his daily telegram for this August 30th, only 32,000 gallons had arrived. Then Gaffey came in with word from General

Eddy, whose XII Corps was supposed to race to Commercy. Eddy had called the army CP advising Gaffey that if he pushed on to Commercy he would arrive there with all his gasoline gone. Gaffey, in Patton's absence, gave Eddy permission to halt halfway, at St. Dizier.

Eddy was at St. Dizier, sitting tight and waiting for gas, when he received a call from a totally outraged Patton, who upbraided him for his failure to go to Commercy and countermanded Gaffey's permission. "You get off your fanny as fast as you can," Patton roared, "and move on until your engines run dry, and then move forward on foot, Goddamn-it! We must and will get the crossings on the Meuse! In the last war I drained three-fourths of the gasoline from my tanks to keep the other fourth going. You can do the same thing!"

The whole CP was vibrating with Patton's own excitement. The gloom and despair vanished momentarily with the return of the Army Commander to his CP. He plunged into action with every ounce of his energy to push on his cherished drive. He admonished his staff, "We have no time to lose!" He told his officers in the bluntest language that they were up against *two* enemies—the Germans and their own high command! He did not doubt for a moment that he could take care of the Germans. But he was not so sure that he could win his bout with his superiors.

The peculiar command situation was partly responsible for his plight. General Marshall had placed Bradley between Eisenhower and Patton to restrain the latter's alleged impetuosity and put a brake on his supposedly reckless drive. Their relationship had improved vastly since the disappointing events of Argentan, and Bradley was becoming increasingly inclined to side with Patton in his clashes and controversies. Yet his position was awkward and ambiguous. He could not very well join Patton's permanent palace revolution against SHAEF. But at the same time he was no longer so determined to keep Patton down. As we shall soon see, it was to take only another week for Bradley—now thoroughly irritated by Eisenhower's long forward pass to Montgomery—to loosen the reins and give Patton the freedom of action they both craved.

Patton's position was anomalous. At this crucial juncture of the campaign, when the stakes seemed to be a decisive victory over the *Wehrmacht,* he could expect only qualified support from his own Army Group Commander. He could not appeal directly to his old friend Ike. For one thing, this would have been a gross violation of the Army's strict etiquette. For another, Patton had no link with him.

At this stage the Supreme Commander was completely isolated, not only from Patton, but virtually from the realities of the war. His move to France did not turn out to be such a good idea. By establishing his command post at Camp Shellburst near Granville, Eisenhower removed himself from his working staff in London without bringing himself appreciably closer to his commanders in the field.

While he was in England he could make flying trips to the front to see his two Army Group Commanders. But now he had to stick to his headquarters on the west coast of the Cherbourg Peninsula, 400 miles from Monty's front near Belgium, 150 miles from Bradley at Chartres, and 225 miles from Patton at Sens. His G-2 was far behind the events, partly because it was extremely difficult even for corps G-2's to keep up with the rapid advances and partly because Ike's communications system at Granville was a mess. In the haste of his move there had not been time for the Signal Corps to set up the vast and intricate network the Supreme Commander needed for his communications. For some time Shellburst had no outgoing telephone lines, not even a wireless telephone link between Eisenhower and the headquarters of his Army Groups. While Hitler was linked to his commanders in the field by a teleprinter net, Eisenhower was dependent solely on the radio, which was both slow—what with the time spent on coding and decoding—and undependable. Urgent communications to him requiring immediate action needed 24 hours to clear. Then it usually took another 24 hours to get Eisenhower's answer out into the field. A "Most Immediate" signal once sent to Montgomery in the north was 36 hours in transit. It arrived with several paragraphs missing, and it took another 48 hours to complete.

The situation became badly aggravated on September 1st, when Eisenhower replaced Montgomery as over-all ground commander, while Monty was made a field marshal to compensate him for his loss. At a time when the battle was developing at breath-taking swiftness at points 250 to 450 miles apart, the Supreme Commander, now wearing two hats, was either completely out of touch or only in a most tenuous contact with it.

It was under circumstances like this that he had to make

the crucial decision. He made it nevertheless, groping and hoping in the dark. Although it did not change the ultimate outcome, it delayed it by weeks, if not months.

And nobody in the ETO was more convinced of this than General Patton.

The problem of supplying the rampaging armies became a burning issue. On its successful solution now depended not only the continuity of Eisenhower's crusade but, indeed, the victory of the Allies.

"A tank without gasoline or a vital part might better be a pillbox," General Orlando Ward, one of Patton's armor leaders in Tunisia, liked to say. To get the tank is the job of Ordnance. To operate it is the job of the troops. To get the gasoline for it so that it can be operational is the job of the Services of Supply. And the job of SOS is "logistics." Derived from "proportion" or "calculation," the word applies to that branch of military science which embraces the moving and supplying of armies. As any hard-pressed supply officer will tell you, it has little, if anything, to do with logic.

The crucial interdependence of operations and logistics was most pungently expressed by the legendary Confederate cavalry general, Nathan Bedford Forrest. He summed up the whole vast military science in the famous words, "I git thar fustest with the mostest men." The "fustest" may not always work. It is certain *not* to work if it is not supported by the "mostest," supplies as well as men.

To military men, logistics means the "mostest." Whether or not there is some secret course at the higher service schools that teaches avarice in supplies I do not venture to guess. But it is an incontrovertible fact that commanders are invariably imbued with the mercenary spirit of the *Ballyshannon's* treasure hunters. They are never satisfied with what is alloted to them and are always clamoring for more in men and matériel.

The instruments of their greed are their Assistant Chiefs of Staff for Supplies, G-4's in Army shorthand. The good G-4 has the hoarding instinct of the squirrel and the rapacity of a Barbary pirate. Even Bradley, whose innate modesty and fairness somewhat tempered his predatory sense, esteemed

his longtime G-4, Colonel Wilson, with the smug pride
Fagin regarded his flock of little pickpockets. Maintaining
that all was fair in love and war, Bradley praised Wilson for
developing chicanery into a high art in the business of supplies. "He fully merited his reputation for piracy," Bradley
gleefully said.

Montgomery's well-known gluttony made him dependent
on Brigadier Miles Graham and Colonel "Rym" Lyner, his
sturdy aides in charge of Administration and Supplies. They
were go-getters of the first order, completely devoted to
their covetous chief, absolutely immodest in assessing their
needs, and totally ruthless in acquiring them.

Patton was different. He took logistics for granted. He was
not avaricious and was not hugging his supplies. But he
expected that everything required for the execution of his
plans would be there when needed. He thus abandoned to
his G-4 the responsibility for assessing his requirements and
procuring the necessary supplies in proper abundance. It was
not the easiest job in the world to serve Patton as Assistant
Chief of Staff for Supplies. The fact that he had the same
G-4 from 1941 at Fort Benning to the end of World War
II showed that he had succeeded in finding a supply officer
who met his exacting standards. He was Walter J. Muller, a
stocky but agile, firm-jawed, broad-faced, fast-talking, fast-
moving professional who had spent all his life in the Army
since the day he was born at old Fort D.A. Russell in Wyom-
ing in 1895.

Muller (whose remarkable career in the Army ranged
from army brat to major general) graduated from West
Point in 1918, too late for active service in World War I.
But he spent four years in various infantry assignments in
postwar Germany and France. After graduation from the
Command and General Staff School he served increasingly
in the field of supplies with General Chaffey's new Armored
Force at Fort Knox, then as G-4 with Patton's Armored
Corps at Fort Benning.

Muller went with Patton to the Desert Training Center at
Camp Young in California, was his G-4 in North Africa and
Sicily, and now slaved and stewed in that same assignment
with Third Army. " 'Maud' Muller was the getttingest G-4 in
the ETO," Colonel Allen wrote of him. "If it was to be got,
he got it—and often when it wasn't . . . [He] operated on
the fixed policy of keeping several steps ahead of Patton on
supplies. It was a very sound rule," especially in an Army

whose commanding general was not interested in the details of logistics. They were far too mathematical for his unarithmetical mind and, besides, they had the tendency of interfering with his bold plans and his free style.

In the Third Army, Mueller's successful "scavenger hunts" were followed with amazed admiration and made him a legend, no mean achievement in a job as lacking in glamour as logistics. "At times," Allen wrote, "there were irate outcries from other quarters, but no one in Third Army paid any attention to them. They were viewed as merely the disgruntled wails of envious malcontents."

It was the peculiar feature of the war at this juncture that its *de facto* conduct had shifted to the supply specialists and transport technicians—to General Lee in SOS, to Brigadier General Raymond G. Moses, a genial 53-year-old New Yorker with an engineering background, at 12th Army Group; to Brigadier Graham at 21st Army Group, to Colonel Wilson at First Army. In the Third Army, Patton remained the grand seigneur as ever. His nervous tension was making the CP quiver and jump. But for these two or three historic weeks, even at his highly centralized headquarters, the balance of power shifted to Colonel Muller.

At the outset of the campaign Muller had no real reasons to complain. The supply situation was reasonably good throughout the ETO, and probably best at this Johnny-come-lately Third Army. Even though some of his demands (for blankets and overshoes, for examples) had not been met, and his supplies were low in a few categories, rations and ammunition were plentiful. To be sure, his Class III supplies began to give him headaches the moment he came in. It was the all-important POL—petrol, lubricants, oil. Even on August 6th his stock of POL was sufficient for only 1.3 days.

But the Communications Zone then got behind the Third Army with substantial deliveries, enabling Muller to build up a reasonable POL reserve. Between August 7th and 16th Com Z made regular daily deliveries of only about 6,000 tons to First Army, but well over 13,000 to the Third, and more than half of the latter consisted of gasoline, grease and oil. The average of Muller's needs in August was about 6,000 tons each day, of which about 1,500 tons were POL and 2,500 were ammunition.

But just when Third Army reached the Seine and its needs had grown by leaps and bounds to meet Patton's new plans and aspirations, deliveries fell off. Com Z was finding it increasingly difficult to move even daily maintenance supplies forward. On August 27th Bradley authorized army levels of Class I and III supplies (rations and POL) at five days and Class V (ammunition) at but three units of fire, as against seven days and seven units respectively when Third Army had become operational. But even the reduced authorizations proved a meaningless gesture in view of the difficulties Com Z was experiencing with moving anything forward. By the end of August up to 95 per cent of all supplies lay in depots at the beaches. There were virtually no stocks between Normandy and the army dumps 300 miles away, and there developed a shortage in trucks to keep up the flow over that distance.

Now Muller was stymied and Patton was frustrated. And nothing the harassed and exasperated G-4 of Third Army could do, by fair means or foul, could get Patton what he most desperately needed—gasoline. Even as the army was on its way to the Reims-Vitry line, toward an objective beckoning with the best spirits of France in the cavernous, dark wine and champagne cellars of the region, Muller was feeling the pinch.

In the meantime, personal items and medical supplies became so short that Patton, concerned for the welfare of his troops, ordered Muller to give blankets and drugs the highest priority. Then the Air Transport Command came to their rescue. Its C-47's were pressed into service to fly in supplies. On a single day, August 25th, 207 aircraft landed at Orléans with 507 tons of supplies, mostly rations. The next day they airlifted 80 tons of medical supplies to Third Army. "The ATC literally was keeping the columns rolling," wrote Colonel Allen. "The C-47's were as vital to the spearheads as were their tanks and guns."

Lady Luck also aided Muller in replenishing his stocks. The Third Army captured 10 tons of medical equipment at Orléans, 15 tons at Dreux, and 20 at Fontainebleau; and it found 300 miles of German telephone wire in a cave near Chartres. Probably even more important, the capture of Sens yielded 37 carloads (over 100,000 gallons) of German gasoline and oil. This well-timed fortune of war enabled Patton to *start* his operations east of the Seine. It goes without saying that Colonel Muller forgot to report this fortuitous discovery to SOS.

But his splitting headache remained POL. The XII

Corps alone was consuming between 200,000 and 300,000 gallons of gasoline to move 50 miles. But on August 24th, when Patton assigned to it objectives that lay 150 miles ahead, and even more, it had only 31,000 gallons of gasoline on hand.

The corps sped on nevertheless and reached Châlons-sur-Marne, where Gaffey permitted General Eddy to halt and whence Patton then ordered him forward, on foot if necessary. It did not become necessary. Just when his prospects seemed darkest, Eddy came upon more than 100,000 gallons of German gasoline at Châlons. By carefully restricting its movements, XII Corps could continue to the Meuse.

But it was a drop in the bucket. The gasoline situation was becoming acutely critical. None of the quantities specified in Muller's daily telegrams would arrive. One day only 197,000 tons were received out of 250,000 he had requested. The next day receipts were 135,000 tons short of the 450,000 requisitioned. And then the C-47's also stopped to keep the columns rolling. Like the trucks, they had been diverted to another mission by SHAEF.

In the letter sanctioning Montgomery's thrust, Eisenhower directed that airborne forces be used to clear a path for him. According to the plan, the drop was to be made on Belgian soil, 13 miles east of Lille. As Eisenhower saw it, this airborne force would bag the German Fifteenth Army on its hasty withdrawal from the Pas-de-Calais. Patton did not know anything about the operation, but Bradley hurried to Eisenhower, pleading with him to cancel it and to leave him the aircraft. "The drop had been scheduled for September 3rd," Bradley recalled. " 'We'll be there before you can pull in,' I warned, but Eisenhower stuck by his guns."

Now the emergency had Lucky Forward completely in its grip. Influenced by Patton's suspicions, his staff, in its attitude toward the situation, was highly emotional, as flammable as the overdue gas. There was no shortage of gasoline on the Continent, it claimed. PLUTO, an elaborate system of pipe lines across the Channel, was pouring fuel into the dumps in Normandy at the rate of 260,000 gallons a day. Getting it to the line units would have posed no problem had not Eisenhower diverted the C-47's to the airdrop. (Incidentally, it never came off. The night before it was to begin, the First Army's tanks reached the area where it was to take place, exactly as Bradley had predicted.)

During these days Patton encouraged the Third Army to go to ludicrous lengths to requisition gasoline. Trucks rolling into Paris were hijacked with their precious cargo. Raiding parties siphoned off fuel from strange dumps. "There was rumor," he later wrote with tongue in cheek, "which, officially, I hoped was not true, that some of our Ordnance people passed themselves off as members of the First Army and secured quite a bit of gasoline from one of the dumps of that unit. To reverse the statement made about the Light Brigade, this is not war but is magnificent."

To dramatize the plight of his army, Patton would drive to Bradley's Eagle Tac at Chartres with the last drop of gasoline in the tank of his jeep and ask permission to have it filled up at one of the gasoline pumps of the Army Group. But this was no joking matter. SHAEF was using POL as a lever. Although Third Army had been given tacit permission to continue its drive while Monty was thrusting northward, this permission was made illusory by apparent orders to withhold the necessary supplies from it.

Patton and his staff were now absolutely convinced that the spigot was being deliberately turned off to stop Third Army's forward move. On August 31st Patton returned to Bradley once more with his most urgent and frenzied plea. "Damnit, Brad," he said, "just give me 400,000 gallons of gasoline and I'll put you inside Germany in two days." But he left emptyhanded.

Patton was now determined to defy Eisenhower and continue the advance in spite of Bradley. If it was insubordination, he had sound reasons for it. He was not trying to grab all the glory for the Third Army. He was not just stubborn, crazed with the obsession of carrying out his own plans. Indeed, he was never more cold and calculating, never on more solid ground. Field Marshal Model was rapidly completing the concentration of his troops in the Third Army's path. Colonel Koch had already identified seven German divisions in the area. The empty West Wall was rapidly filling up. It was becoming desperately obvious that Patton had to make the break into Germany before it would be too late.

Unbeknown to him, the situation was becoming even more serious than he thought by a development in the enemy camp. Hitler had come to recognize in Patton the gravest and most immediate threat to him. He had teletyped orders to Model to forget everything else and stop the Third Army. Then he sent for General Balck, an intrepid tank commander who had made a name for himself on the Eastern Front, to get ready for the biggest assignment of his life.

Frantically seeking a solution for his oppressive problems and still indulging in the dream that he could stem and turn the tide, the Führer was developing the idea of a powerful counterthrust in Belgium via the Ardennes to push the Allies back to the sea, and maybe to Paris. The only threat to this bold maneuver, as he saw it, was George Patton. So the mission he had prepared for Balck was to hold Patton while he, Hitler, was mobilizing his forces for the counterthrust—his last adventure, which became the tragic Battle of the Bulge.

So the cry was "Hold Patton!" on both sides of the fence. It was undoubtedly the strangest and most paradoxical situation of the entire war. Eisenhower had given orders to hold Patton exactly when Hitler had issued identical orders!

But Patton still refused to be held. He had reached the Meuse and had pushed through Verdun. He was only 35 miles from Metz, barely 70 miles from the Saar, with nothing, as Bradley conceded, to bar his way except the still empty fortifications of the West Wall. He was in a position to attack toward the Moselle. From there the Rhine was only 100 miles away.

On August 30th Patton issued an operational directive, confirming his orders of the previous day, *to push on beyond the Marne and the Meuse, and make straight for the Rhine*. "All I need are those lousy 400,000 gallons of gasoline to win this Goddamn war," he cried. He needed more than that. His supplies, Muller told him, had dwindled to the breaking point. His soldiers in the van of his advance needed shoes, heavy underwear and socks. His tanks needed spare parts. But most of all, and worst of all, the Third Army needed gasoline.

On August 31st the 7th Armored, followed closely by the 5th Division, established a bridgehead across the Meuse at Verdun. The revitalized 90th Division was at Reims and the 4th Armored had crossed the Meuse at Commercy and Pont-sur-Meuse.

On that same day, Muller reported to Patton that he had not received a single drop of gasoline.

The Third Army was bone dry!

CHAPTER THIRTY-TWO
THE SHADOW OF EISENHOWER

Now it was September. The place, a delightful woodland dell near Châlons-sur-Marne to which Lucky Forward had moved. It was Patton's 10th command post in less than two months. For those with time on their hands this was the perfect neighborhood. Nestled in the heart of the Champagne region, the place somehow rippled with the same natural carbonation that made its famous product bubble.

The Third Army was the butt of jokes and envy of the ETO. From here on, its spirited showing was widely and snidely attributed to each man's internal combustion produced by the delectable fuel the army had found in the warehouses of Reims and in the seemingly endless labyrinthine caves of the hills around Epernay.

Even Colonel Cole, the Third Army historian, permitted himself an irreverent reference to this fact in his serious study of the Lorraine campaign when speaking of the army's extraordinary "spirit of optimism and a contagious feeling that the final victory [of World War II] was very close at hand." Recording deadpan the capture of those caves and warehouses, Cole quipped, "It is unnecessary to dwell on the importance of this event" beyond noting that it had "acted to heighten still further the spirits of General Patton's command and gloss over the first sobering effects of the oncoming gasoline shortage."

The captured stocks were enormous—the choicest cognacs and liquors, wines and champagnes, the last some of the finest like Moët, Bollinger, Perrier Jouet and Mumm, and including the outstanding vintage 1937. The thrill of it all was heightened by the fact that most of the bottles bore the stamp, *Reserviert für Angehörige der Deutschen Wehrmacht* (Reserved for members of the *Wehrmacht*).

The loot was put to excellent tactical use. The crews of the C-47's flying in supplies were given copious gifts, a practice that resulted in an uncontrollable urge in the Air Transport Command to volunteer for missions to the Third Army.

General Patton did not preach or practice temperance. But he did not cherish the idea of being the commanding general of an inebriated army. After allowing a brief binge in August, he ordered guards posted at the captured depots to forestall *impromptu* "liberations," and organized regulated distribution throughout the army. The caches found at Reims were reserved for Thanksgiving Day, with seven bottles of wine or cognac set aside for every officer and soldier.

But if the troops were cheered by this boozy bonanza (for they knew little of the difficulties their army had run into on its irrepressible drive), it could not lift the gloom from headquarters. Patton in particular was fidgety and bitter as he tried to sweat out the gasoline famine without going to pieces.

Early on September 3rd, accompanied by Colonel Nick Campanole, his G-5, and Major Stiller, his rugged aide, he decided to fly to XII Corps Headquarters. The day began well. At Ligny-en-Barrois, General Eddy greeted him with the splendid news that he had captured another 100,000 gallons of gasoline and could move on to his next objective at the word go.

But the word was stay. The front was quiet. The Third Army, practically immobilized for lack of fuel, could afford only sporadic stabs over short distances in the hope that such feints would conceal its plight. The 2nd Cavalry Group had patrols on the Moselle. The 319th Infantry Regiment of the 80th Division moved from the west to the east bank of the Meuse. The only halfway ambitious operation was mounted by the 7th Armored Division, which set out north from Verdun. It had covered some 30 miles toward Sedan when it ran out of fuel. General Eddy then recalled it, but the division could not comply with the order—it had no gasoline for the return journey. So it just sat there, in front of Sedan, while XII Corps was frantically trying to scrape up enough gasoline to get the division back.

With virtually nothing to do, Patton went sightseeing. He drove to Commercy on the Meuse, then on the new CP of the 319th Infantry at Gironville, to give Colonel O. L.

Davidson the regimental commander, a pat on the back for having crossed the river the day before.

It was a sentimental journey. This time Patton did not need any psychic *déjà vu* to conjure up memories of the region. He had been there, everywhere, just nine days short of exactly 26 years before.

There in the distance was Toul where Pershing's IV Corps had its headquarters in 1918. Next to it in the hilly country was Essey-lès-Nancy where he had met General MacArthur on the morning of September 12, 1918, walking about under shellfire, looking for a gap through which he could push his brigade. There was Pannes, too, which he had captured with a single tank and where he had started his lonely journey into the Hindenburg Line. And there was Montsec, the scene of much hard and wasteful fighting during the closing days of World War I. On top of it, Patton recalled, was a huge monument commemorating the American dead of St. Mihiel. "I wonder if the Hun has left it there," Patton remarked nostalgically to Major General Horace L. McBride, commander of the 80th Division.

Though the view was mellowed by his memories, this hallowed land between the Meuse and the Saar was now staring at him ominously. It was not as empty as it had been only a few days before. The Germans had moved into the vacuum in force, including recent arrivals from Italy.

Even as Patton was looking out to this promised land, Hitler was thinking of him. The Führer had just given orders to Field Marshal Model to attack from the Nancy-Langres area toward Reims, roll up the right flank of Third Army, and cut American lines of communication. And he was drafting a follow-up order to his Seventh Army to "continue to fight a delaying action forward of the West Wall," especially, as he put it, at the "mighty obstacle" of the Meuse.

Friendship is an unstable anchorage even under less trying conditions. Frequently a single misunderstanding proves sufficient to turn lifelong amities into bitter enmities. The events of these hectic days—in which the course of the war was shaped by the strong convictions of headstrong, high-spirited men puffed up with ambition and vanity—now threatened to ruin a relationship that had stood as one of the cornerstones of American successes in this conflict.

It was not that Eisenhower had come to dislike or distrust Patton more. His feelings toward "Georgie" and his high opinion of him as a tactical wizard remained unchanged. But Patton had come to trust Ike less. It is never wise, as Samuel Johnson warned us, to let friendship die by silence and negligence. Rightly or wrongly, Patton now felt that this was exactly what was happening to his relationship with Ike. The Supreme Commander was, he sincerely believed, neglecting him deliberately and giving him the silent treatment.

Patton had been restive ever since he saw his own great plan flounder in the apparent vacillations at SHAEF. He was deeply hurt when Montgomery was given the green light to deliver what promised to become the knock-out blow to the Germans. He was thoroughly shocked when his own secondary drive, authorized under the same decision, was apparently sabotaged by what he considered a reckless manipulation of supplies.

But he blamed SHAEF, that mysterious mass of chairborne warriors, "the men around Ike," rather than Eisenhower himself, for his woes. He had some valid reason to suspect that the SHAEF planning staff was behind the Supreme Commander's decision because he knew that it regarded the northern route to the Ruhr as the most likely to lead to the collapse of Germany. On May 3rd, 1944, it had produced a draft called "Post-Neptune Courses of Action After the Capture of the Lodgment Area," outlining the main objectives and the axis of the advance. It was a vague plan but quite firm in its advocacy of the angle of the attack from the Seine. The draft proposed that the main advance be slow in the direction of the Ruhr after a careful build-up at the Seine, with a secondary attack south of the Ardennes.

Never taken seriously, the plan was now completely outdated. For instance, its timetable assumed that the Allies would reach the German frontier on D plus 330, or on May 2, 1945, and at a point north of Aachen, at that. Knowing, however, how people cling to their original ideas, Patton thought that the authors of the old plan had succeeded in influencing Eisenhower to give Montgomery the go ahead simply because it was his 21st Army Group that was poised to move against the Ruhr. Thus blaming the faceless planners, he was prepared to absolve Eisenhower.

Even on September 1st, when the Supreme Commander assumed tactical command of his forces on the Continent (now totaling 2,100,000 men) in addition to his strategic responsibilities, Patton still felt that this could be a turn for the better.

His attitude stiffened due to a radio broadcast he heard. That morning, Patton woke up at Chartres as Bradley's guest, on his way back to his own command post after a quick trip to Brittany. They had flown to Morlaix for a meeting with General Middleton and Lieutenant General William H. Simpson, commander of the Ninth U.S. Army which had landed in Southern France on August 15th, to arrange the transfer of VIII Corps to Simpson's army. By the time Bradley's C-47 arrived back at Chartres, it was too late for Patton's cub to take him to Châlons, so he accepted Bradley's invitation and spent the night at 12th Army Group.

When he was ready to leave for home, he heard the familiar words, "London calling!" on the radio, and stayed to listen to the BBC's 8 o'clock news. What he then heard spoiled the rest of the day for him. "General Eisenhower said that Montgomery was the greatest living solider," was the way Patton repeated it to his staff, "and was now a field marshal."

In the supersensitive state of his mind, he was inclined to read more into a statement of Eisenhower that the BBC had paraphrased than the Supreme Commander intended to convey. On August 31st, on the eve of his assumption of the tactical command, Eisenhower flew to London especially to smooth the waters, as Commander Butcher expressed it, badly roiled by the impending event. At a press conference held at the Ministry of Information, he outlined the command setup in order to correct certain British misapprehensions.

"He praised Monty," Butcher recorded, "and said that anyone who misinterpreted the transition of command as a demotion for General Montgomery simply did not look facts in the face. He said Montgomery is one of the great soldiers of this or any other war and he would now have the job of handling the battles on his side of the front. It would be most unfortunate if this plan of campaign, which had de-

veloped as it was conceived from the start, should be interpreted as a demotion or as a slap at anybody."

Actually, Montgomery was hurt. He had tried to persuade
Eisenhower to leave him in over-all tactical command even
after he had started the drive to the north because, after all,
he would continue to command substantial American
forces. But Eisenhower was under some pressure from General Marshall to take over from Montgomery, and he himself now felt that the time was ripe to end Monty's supervision over Bradley.

Alerted by Montgomery, Field Marshal Brooke tried
what he could to delay or frustrate the change-over. On the
evening of August 30th he went to see Prime Minister
Churchill, in bed with a minor attack of pneumonia, to explain to him "the difficulties that had been arising with
Eisenhower taking control from Monty and wanting to direct the American forces on Nancy and Frankfurt, leaving
the British forces to deal with the German forces in Northern France."

The Prime Minister did not volunteer to intervene. But
he told Brooke that he would make Monty a field marshal,
"the appointment to coincide [September 1st] with the date
of Eisenhower assuming command of Land Forces." Churchill felt that such "a move would mark the approval of
the British people for Montgomery's leadership," and hoped
that it would assuage his hurt pride.

Patton figured nowhere in these maneuvers but he felt
strongly about them. For the first time since August 1st he
felt tired and bored. He spent the day of the change-over
quietly at his headquarters, working on humdrum administrative matters, even as bits of action reports floated into his
CP about valiant efforts of his men to break the lull. A combat command of the 7th Armored went to Etain, halfway
between Verdun and Metz, on gasoline of rather mysterious origin. And using captured gasoline, the 3rd Cavalry
Group patrolled eastward, almost to the Moselle. But nothing could dispel Patton's gloom. It was one of his darkest
days.

The next morning, on September 2nd, he was preparing
to visit his immobilized front in the area of XV Corps when
a phone call from Chartres directed him to go immediately
to Bradley's headquarters, where he was expected by 11
AM. The weather was too bad to fly. He had to drive the
130 miles to Chartres, arriving at 12:45 o'clock. He found

Hodges with Bradley, and also Major General Hoyt S. Vandenberg of the Army Air Forces. Then he almost fell out of his boots when he spotted General Eisenhower in this little crowd of top brass.

It was their first meeting in more than two months. It was also, Patton felt, a good opportunity for Ike to congratulate him on the breakout and for his drive to the Meuse. But probably peeved by Patton's tardiness, the Supreme Commander was strictly business. With a formality that antagonized Patton, he settled down to explain his plans.

If Eisenhower's decision of August 30th created confusion in the minds of some of his commanders, this meeting served merely to compound it. Eisenhower was at Bradley's CP primarily on a conciliatory mission, as a sequel to his London trip. In London he had used his consummate diplomatic skill to smooth those troubled British waters. Here in Chartres he hoped to soothe the feelings of his American commanders and to reassure them that he had not sold them down the river. The meeting did not produce a firm line of action or a fixed plan for the future. It did not reach out for the strategic solution. Rather it harked back to that pre-D-Day draft with its slow-motion prospects east of the Seine. On August 29th Ike had given the green light to Monty for his thrust to the north. Now in Chartres, it seemed, he was giving it to Bradley, too, for his thrust in the center. That, at least, was Bradley's interpretation of what Eisenhower said at the conference.

The meeting began with Eisenhower offering an explanation for his support of Montgomery's plan. From what he heard, Patton gained the impression that Ike was no longer convinced the war against Germany could be won either quickly or easily. Eisenhower did not seem to share either Montgomery's or Bradley's optimism. He said he had never really expected the British to go all the way to the Ruhr—or even to Berlin in one fell swoop, as Montgomery insisted he could—but rather he hoped they would secure the Belgian ports on the North Sea, which he badly needed, and cut off, and destroy if possible, whatever remained of the German Fifteenth Army in the Pas-de-Calais.

Patton listened with growing impatience. Eager to impress the Supreme Commander and gain support for his own eastward drive, he seized upon the adventurous forays of his troops east of the Meuse the day before, and presented them with a flourish to demonstrate the Third Army's power and élan even in adversity.

"We have patrols on the Moselle near Nancy," he said with a full throat, and even stretched the truth a bit by adding, "Patrols of the 3rd Cavalry had actually entered Metz. If you let me retain my regular allotment of tonnage, Ike, we could push on to the German frontier and rupture that Goddamn Siegfried Line. I'm willing to stake my reputation on that."

"Careful, George," Eisenhower said somewhat wearily, "that reputation of yours hasn't been worth very much."

He said it with his disarming smile, but Patton was hurt by the quip. Then he remembered that a day or so before he had received from the United States the first shipment of newspaper clippings of articles printed about him and the Third Army since the release of their participation in the campaign. He was pleased to conclude from them that apparently all was forgiven back home and he was riding the crest of a new popularity. So he suppressed his irritation, hitched up his belt, and smiled back at Ike.

"That reputation is pretty good now," he said quietly.

When the meeting boiled down to the brass tacks of future plans, Eisenhower agreed to a renewal of the drive to the east by Bradley's Army Group—by Third Army, that is, aided by General Gerow's V Corps from Hodges' First Army. They were to attack toward Mannheim, Frankfurt and Koblenz, exactly as Bradley had planned, with one exception. It would have to be done with but one corps of the First Army instead of getting the entire army for the drive. The two other corps would have to remain with Monty, at least for the time being.

Then Eisenhower qualified his approval still further. Bradley's drive would have to be contingent on the success of Monty's thrust, he said, because the British had prior claims on supplies.

"We have advanced so rapidly," he said with his newly acquired realism, "that further movement in large parts of the front even against very weak opposition is almost impossible. The closer we get to the Siegfried Line the more we will be stretched administratively and eventually a period of inaction will be imposed upon us. The potential danger is that while we are temporarily stalled the enemy will be able to pick up bits and pieces of forces everywhere and reorganize them swiftly for defending the Siegfried

Line or the Rhine. It is obvious from an over-all viewpoint we must now as never before keep the enemy stretched everywhere."

Patton still tried, with Bradley's eloquent support, to persuade Eisenhower to give the Americans at least equality with Monty's 21st Army Group. "We have an excellent plan, Ike," he argued, "for a drive through the Nancy-Epinal gap. The Siegfried Line isn't manned yet, and the Huns have little if anything in the area to stop us. If you let me go and give me what we need, we can be in Germany at the Rhine in 10 days."

But Eisenhower remained adamant. He would let Patton proceed and attack the Siegfried Line—"as soon as the Calais area was stabilized." Until then, he held out the promise of only limited supplies.

He was now convinced more than ever, he said, that no amount of juggling his supplies would enable either Montgomery to get to Berlin or Bradley and Patton to Frankfurt. Those separate *all-out* thrusts were out. As he saw it, the logical move was to take advantage of all existing lines of communications in the advance toward Germany, and push both army groups forward—with emphasis now here, then there—on what he called a broad front.

He conceded that Montgomery had refused categorically to agree with his logic. Far from justifying the Supreme Commander's broad-front concept, Monty had argued that the scarcity of supplies actually mitigated against it. According to Montgomery, inadequate supplies made it simply mandatory to concentrate on a single major thrust with everything we had—on his thrust if possible, on Bradley's thrust if need be, but on a single thrust. A compromise solution which Eisenhower favored would fatefully weaken Allied power and prolong the war. "We have now," Eisenhower quoted Montgomery, "reached a stage where one really powerful and full-blooded thrust toward Berlin is likely to get there and thus end the German war."

While Eisenhower made it quite clear that he disagreed with Monty, Patton now found himself in the uncomfortable position of agreeing with the Briton's seemingly devastating logic. But he thought he was far better qualified than Monty to make the drive to the heart of Germany. Much in the recent history of the campaign appeared to support his argument. "Patton had proved himself to be a master of exploitation," Wilmot wrote in his review of the great argument, "and his troops were already across the Seine. Montgomery had no such reputation and his troops had not yet reached the Seine. Neither the British nor the Canadians had yet shown a capacity for advancing with the dash and drive the Americans had demonstrated so brilliantly since the breakout."

But no matter how Patton argued, coaxed and cajoled, he could not divert the Supreme Commander from the broad-front strategy to his drive. The "Sure Thing" that had filled him with such excitement and optimism only a few days before had vanished in the blue cigar smoke of this strange meeting. But at least he was not going home entirely empty-handed. Eisenhower promised that the Third Army would get its new gasoline allotment right away, and Patton told his planning staff upon his return to Châlons:

"As soon as we get sufficient gasoline, I have permission to secure crossings over the Moselle and prepare to attack the Siegfried Line."

But he was not kidding himself. He realized that his one big opportunity in this war had been missed.

☆

The more he thought of the meeting at Chartres the more discouraged Patton became. The Supreme Commander now appeared in his mind as the major, if not the sole, obstacle in his path to win the war with the Third Army by exploiting the disorganization and weakness of the enemy, to which his own campaign had made the major contribution.

The duel for France so far had wrought havoc with Hitler's highly touted *Wehrmacht*. For this fleeting moment it actually seemed that it had been damaged beyond repair. In the three months since the invasion the Germans had lost 1,200,000 troops in killed, wounded and missing, about 500,000 of them in the west (with 200,000 of this number bottled up in the coastal fortresses in Brittany and elsewhere). Their matériel losses were impossible to estimate. The historian of the 30th U.S. Infantry Division expressed the consensus when he wrote: "There was a quality of madness about the whole debacle of Germany's forces in the West . . . . It looked very much as though Adolf Hitler . . . might be forced into surrender long before American and British units reached the Rhine. That was the avowed opinion of Allied soldiers on the Western Front, and German prisoners were of the same mind, often stating that it couldn't last for another week."

This was exactly how Patton viewed the situation. And he was both dismayed and furious when he found out that Eisenhower did not see it the same way.

By now his relations with Eisenhower presented a study in ambivalance. This, of course, is the alternating current of love and hate of which Freud wrote extensively. It is not for me to probe the psychological springs of General Eisenhower's sentiments toward Patton or to attribute to him feelings and motives by methods of contrived psychoanalysis. He himself covered the subject fully in his memoirs, leaving the impression that his devotion to Patton never diminished, even though his patience had been sorely tested several times, and his determination to preserve Patton in his command had wavered once or twice.

Patton's relations with Eisenhower showed a curve that shot up all the way in the summer of 1942, when Ike had sent for him to take command of the Western Task Force in "Torch." It then declined, slowly at first, then more rapidly, until his friendship gave way to hostility, bitter at times.

What the personal sources of this antagonism were, I do not presume to know and do not care to guess. I am inclined to think that none was purely personal. At any rate, after the series of embarrassments Patton had caused General Eisenhower, from the slapping incidents to the Knutsford affair, and after Eisenhower had become Supreme Commander, their personal relationship ceased almost entirely, and it became strictly professional.

This was a relationship that had spanned a quarter of a century, and while they were never on truly intimate terms, they had remained aware of each other long before a world war was to bring them more closely together.

Although only five years separated them in age, a whole world set them apart in the strict caste system of the Army. Patton was the scion of a wealthy patrician family. Eisenhower, who was born in Texas and grew up in Kansas, had the log-cabin type of background. He was a member of a devout family and was never to shed completely the influence of his uncompromisingly pacifist mother, not even when he was the Supreme Commander of a fighting multi-million-man army.

Patton graduated from West Point in 1909, two years before Ike had even become a plebe. He had had a spectacular and sometimes rip-roaring career in the Army, even in peacetime, but Eisenhower had been given the dreariest assignments. While Patton was with Pershing in Mexico, Ike was an assistant mustering officer at Fort Sam Houston or Camp Wilson in Texas. When Patton sailed with the AEF to Europe, Eisenhower worked with the Illinois National Guard, then became an instructor at the Officer's Training Camp at Fort Oglethorpe in Georgia. And when Patton took the first American tanks into combat at St. Mihiel, Eisenhower was in Pennsylvania, at the Tank Corps Training Center at Camp Colt.

It was then that the two men first heard of each other. Eisenhower was, in a sense, training men for Patton. At Camp Colt he had 600 officers and 9,000 soldiers under him, and was shipping them to Patton overseas as quickly as he could prepare them. They talked about the young major who had trained them, and Patton was impressed with their training. He was looking forward to meeting Eisenhower.

When Patton returned from the war and went to Fort Meade on his aborted assignment with the short-lived Tank Corps, he found Major Eisenhower there, studying at the Infantry Tank School, and serving as an assistant to General Rockenbach. Together they took part in a truck-convoy maneuver over 10,000 miles of American roads, to study mobility, the problems of supply to mechanized columns, and some general logistics. For a brief period they had limited social contacts at Fort Meade, confined to a few dinners at each other's quarters. Patton and Eisenhower discussed armored tactics and shared utopian dreams about the future of the tank, while Beatrice Patton and Mamie Eisenhower engaged in the usual small talk of army wives. Mamie liked the Pattons and especially admired Bea for her ability to keep her obstreperous husband in line.

At this time, too, Patton did a minor favor for Eisenhower. He introduced him to General Fox Conner, who was looking for an executive officer in Panama. Ike got the job, and after that their paths separated. Patton went on to his swashbuckling cavalry while Ike forked off to some more dreary assignments at Camp Dix, Fort Benning and Fort Logan. He served as recreation officer in Baltimore and recruiting officer in Colorado. His first real break came when he was detailed to France with the Battle Monuments Commission for eight months to write a guidebook to the World War I battlefields and supervise the erection of the monument at Montsec near St. Mihiel.

No two men could have been more different. Patton was every inch the romantic, old-fashioned cavalry officer who carried his aristocratic equestrian dash into everything he did. Eisenhower was the prototype of the staff officer—self-effacing, superbly tactful, diplomatic. He had a remarkable career as chief of staff to other officers, including Douglas MacArthur, under whom, as he himself once put it, he had studied dramatics for several years in the Philippine Army. MacArthur once characterized Ike as "small-minded," but only because his young aide had advised him against taking on the rank of field marshal in the Philippines.

Then suddenly the two officers' paths crossed again. Eisenhower made it from Chief of Staff of Third Army at Fort Houston to Assistant Chief of Staff to General Marshall, in charge of operations and war plans. He sent for Patton, whom he remembered well from their frustrating tank days at Meade, to take charge of the only all-American task force in "Torch."

Relations between these contrasting personalities remained excellent for a while. The older man, senior in rank, willingly subordinated himself, never letting either his seniority or his oversized ego become a barrier between them. Patton actually rejoiced in Eisenhower's meteoric rise. He realized that without it he would probably have been filed and forgotten in some desert hole in the United States, doing what Eisenhower had done in World War I—training tankers for somebody else to command.

He had still another reason. Patton had a strong streak of chauvinism in his make-up and was glad to see an American officer getting the top job in the coalition. He expected Ike to carry the ball for the United States and put the British in their proper place. It was on this note that his first resentment seeped in to cloud his attitude toward Eisenhower. He disliked the way Ike was leaning over backward to create what he called a "feeling of partnership" between Britons and Americans.

Patton's latent resentment flared up on July 13, 1943, during the difficult initial stage of the Sicilian campaign. When Ike visited him at his CP, which was still on the

Monrovia, he gave Patton a spirited dressing down in front of others for his failure to send periodic reports to Malta about the progress of the operation.

"How the hell do you expect me to do my planning," Eisenhower demanded, "if you don't let me know what's going on?"

This first outburst of Ike's celebrated temper sent the blood rushing to Patton's ruddy face. He was annoyed and showed it. He regarded this as an artificial issue that Ike had raised merely to show who was boss. When Ike left the *Monrovia,* the incident banished from his mind, Patton still seemed to be smarting. He saw the Commander in Chief off, standing stiffly at the top of a rope ladder, "looking," as John Gunther put it, "like a Roman emperior carved in softish stone." Patton retaliated by refusing permission to the correspondents who accompanied Eisenhower to land on the beaches.

Yet these were minor slurs and insignificant incidents. They did not really loosen the bond the war had developed between them. It began to come apart, however, with the slapping incidents, which also started the strange ambivalence in Patton's attitude to Eisenhower.

☆

The subsequent deterioration of Patton's sentiments as far as Ike was concerned was not apparent to those who observed the two in their personal contacts. Patton always refrained from showing his resentment, either to Ike or in the presence of strangers. But when he was alone with his personal staff, and especially with his diary, he stopped being contrite and flattering. He left behind a document that showed his true feelings and the real quality of his strangely ambiguous relationship.

He was willing to give Eisenhower credit for his masterly management of the Anglo-American coalition, but was not equally generous in his assessment of the Supreme Commander's military knowledge. In effect, Patton charged that the war had proved too much for Eisenhower's professional talents and that, by trying to make up with diplomacy for what he evidently lacked in strategic and especially tactical know-how, Ike had surrendered to the British.

He also accused Eisenhower of running the war with an

eye on his own future in politics and that his cordial relations with the GI's had been motivated by Ike's ultimate ambition to become President of the United States.

The idea that Eisenhower had such sweeping political ambitions first struck Patton on June 26, 1944, when he accompanied Ike to Cornwall to inspect units of the 35th Division. Patton noted that the Supreme Commander was treating the GI's like a politician kissing babies.

He was convinced from then on that Eisenhower had been bitten by the presidential bug. He did not object to it. As a matter of fact, he expressed the opinion that Ike would make what he called "a better President than he is a general."

It was Eisenhower's apparent aloofness in France and the distance he was putting between himself and Patton that started the relationship downhill. The first real break came at this conference at Chartres on September 2nd. By then whatever opportunity existed to develop their professional association into a really warm personal friendship was gone. This was where the ambivalence came in. For whatever else he may have been, Patton was no ingrate. He never forgot a favor. And even in his most bitter moments of resentment he always remembered Eisenhower's crucial role in this glorious finale of his long career. But from here on this became an "I-owe-Ike-everything—but . . ." kind of relationship.

The next three weeks in this September put it to its most severe test. When they were over, Patton was seriously thinking of putting in for transfer to China or maybe to Admiral Chester W. Nimitz's command in the Pacific.

Now Patton was like Porgy. He had plenty of virtually nothing. To make the most of what little he had, he introduced the rock-soup method, after the shrewd gimmick of an itinerant begger. "A tramp," he explained to his staff," once went to a house and asked for some boiling water to make a rock soup. The lady was interested and gave him the water, in which he placed two polished white stones. He then asked if he might have some potatoes and carrots to flavor it a little, and finally ended up with some meat.

"In other words," he spelled out the practical meaning

of the parable in his situation, "in order to attack, we'll
have to pretend to reconnoiter, then reinforce the reconnaissance, and finally put on the attack—all depending on
what gasoline and ammunition we can secure."

Colonel Muller played his game of supplies like a virtuoso.
Frequently when the going was easy with little or no resistance, he would cut back his ammunition request and get
gasoline for the released tonnage to speed the advance. But
even when the fuel shortage was most acute, Patton insisted that personal items like blankets, for instance, and
Class I rations be given absolute priority.

On September 4th at Patton's new CP near Châlons,
where, he noted, Aetius defeated Attila the Hun in A.D.
451, the only hostile action of the day occurred right there
at his headquarters. He was visited by Mrs. Anna Rosenberg, a tiny career woman who was the able head of President Roosevelt's War Mobilization and Reconversion Office. The indomitable Mrs. Rosenberg was dressed for her
tour of the front line in a very tight pair of khaki slacks,
which aroused the animosity of Willie. The pseudo-fero-
cious pet that would not normally hurt a fly went after the
lady with unaccustomed vengeance, and gently, but firmly, sank his teeth into her leg.

And then, the lull ended abruptly.

At 11 A.M. General Bradley arrived with orders for the
Third Army. Patton immediately sent for his three Corps
Commanders, Generals Walker, Haislip and Eddy. Bradley then explained the plan. The situation in the north having been stabilized, Third Army would start getting half of
all available supplies and could move again, to cross the
Moselle.

It was a minor miracle, reflecting Patton's energy and
drive, that the Third Army was where it was on this eve
of its next big push. Initially, when the Seine was crossed,
Bradley wanted Patton to stop on the Marne, but succumbed
to his plea and permitted him to go on to the Meuse. By
the time the Third Army reached the river, it had two
strikes against it. It was not supposed to go any farther by
order of the 12th Army Group. And even if it wanted to,
it was not believed it could because of lack of gasoline.

But nothing could stop Patton. He funneled his driblet of
(mostly stolen) gasoline into a handful of tanks and rolled
stubbornly ahead. Within the army he deadlined thousands
of vehicles and clamped ironclad conservation measures on

the others. Now on the eve of the new offensive, he stood beyond the Meuse, virtually at the gates of Metz and Nancy, both of which appeared to be at his mercy.

Bradley no longer had any reservations about Patton. He was now his Number One fan and chief booster, an ideal boss. And he was full of admiration for him at Châlons. "A less aggressive commander than Patton," he wrote, "would probably have hoarded the pittance that came his way and halted his line for winter safekeeping behind the Meuse River line. But George plunged boldly on beyond the Meuse 30 miles farther to the Moselle, where he promptly grabbed a bridgehead south of the fortress city of Metz."

The gloom of the past week was gone. Patton was back in his element like an actor after an intermission.

Elaborating on Bradley's orders and boldly rewriting them, he directed XII Corps, which was to lead the "plunge," to cross the Moselle, secure Nancy and be prepared to continue to Mannheim and the Rhine.

Then he embarked on what Bradley hopefully called the headiest and most optimistic advance of the European war. The enthusiasm was contagious and a feeling of victory gripped the Third Army. The men expected the war to end momentarily. The scuttlebutt among the troops as they were trucking forward was that they would soon be redeployed to the China-Burma-India Theater. "This optimism," Bradley recorded, "pervaded even the headquarters commands, where staffs held their breath, tallied the tonnage, and talked of getting home by Christmas."

Patton gave the signal, and the dormant front suddenly burst alive.

The 317th Infantry Regiment of the 80th Division was the first to jump off shortly after daybreak on September 5th, expecting to cross the Moselle at Pagny and in the Blénod-Pont-à-Mousson area. But something happened. The enemy was suddenly there to deny them passage.

The 317th tried again, and after fighting for a day and a night, it managed to get a battalion across at Pont-à-Mousson. This was a new experience for the men of the 80th Division. They no longer had things their own way.

The 318th Infantry was encountering its own difficulties at Hill 326 overlooking Marbache. And the 319th was trying desperately to expand the Toul bridgehead to include Fort-de-Gondreville but proved unable to reduce Fort de Villey-le-Sec on the way to its objective.

The next day the offensive was broadened as the 7th Armored opened the attack of XX Corps to force the Moselle. Four combat reconnaissance columns started toward the river at 3 A.M. to search for crossing sites. The main body attacked at 2 P.M., with two combat commands leading and the reserve following. They did not get too far. On the north, Combat Command A was brought to a halt at Ste. Marie-aux-Chénes; then Combat Command B was held up near Rezonville and Gorze.

Even worse, the 317th Infantry had to abandon efforts to cross the Moselle when the enemy, now swarming everywhere, succeeded in overrunning the 3rd Battalion's hard-won bridgehead. The day's only success was the capture of Hill 326, but the attacks of the 319th Infantry on Fort de Villey-le-Sec remained futile.

Patton was stunned.

"All this comes from the fatal decision of the Supreme Commander," he told his aide, Major Stiller, "to halt the Third Army until the Pas-de-Calais area was cleared up."

It was his first bloody nose in the war. And it hurt nobody because he was convinced that it could have been avoided.

☆

On September 8th it seemed that things would get still worse.

The Germans now went over to the attack.

At daybreak in Aumetz, the 106th Panzer Brigade, an SS unit fresh from the Reich, suddenly moved forward between the 359th and 358th Regiments of the 90th Division. A detachment penetrated to division headquarters, awakened General McLain by firing at his quarters at 20-yard range, broke into the division's classified files and captured a quantity of papers, raised general hell and then withdrew to join the main force of the attacking brigade. The young Nazis were on the verge of scoring the first appreciable German victory of the campaign when the Third Army finally found itself. A spirited counterattack virtually destroyed the German contingent. It lost 30 tanks, 60 half-tracks and some 900 men.

While all this was going on, the 2nd Infantry battered the outer fortifications of Metz, a formidable objective because of its strongly prepared positions, some of which

dated to the Franco-Prussian war of 1870-71. Although the
enemy at Briey surrendered, things were not going as well
as Patton expected. The 5th Division managed to gain only a
precarious foothold on the east bank of the Moselle at Dornot. Four companies of the 11th Infantry Division and
elements of the 23rd Armored Infantry Battalion of the 7th
Armored were pinned down in their shallow bridgehead by
heavy enemy fire. All efforts of the 11th Infantry to push on
to Fort Blaise proved futile and costly. To complicate
things further, the enemy began counterattacks against the
80th Division and succeeded in retaking Marbache.

It was not too good a day for the Third Army.

The seesaw battle continued on September 9th, but the
outlook was not entirely dark. General Bradley looked hopefully to the Third Army's ability to wear down the resistance of the relatively meager German forces, or draw them
to its area, thus opening the way for V Corps to launch a
frontal assault on the West Wall.

On September 11th Bradley issued orders to the First
Army to break through the West Wall and secure crossings
over the Rhine in the vicinity of Koblenz, where Field Marshall von Rundstedt, who had returned to the west, had his
headquarters. Under the same order Third Army was to
secure crossings at Mannheim. The great offensive was
scheduled for the 14th.

The situation was fraught with a strange ambiguity. It
filled the Allied commanders in the field with sanguine hope.
But it burdened General Eisenhower with problems that
seemingly defied solution.

Patton, whose actions always had a highly personal historic
continuity, was deeply moved by his memories of 1918.
They both blessed and burned him. What he could not
accomplish with his toy tanks 26 years before—win a major
break at a decisive point of the front—he was now determined to achieve at the head of his army.

Standing between him and the attainment of his goal was
the West Wall. It held him with that vibrant fascination
which had animated him when he faced the Hindenburg
Line in World War I. Although he would talk contemptuously of Hitler's fortified line, it actually intrigued him. He

was like Hagen in the Nibelungen saga, seeking the vulnerable spot in Siegfried. Patton was impatient to break through
the line. For one thing, he was eager to have the worrisome
barrier behind him. For another, he craved the distinction
of becoming the first Allied commander to breach it.

The West Wall meandered along the German border like
a giant worm, from Clève to the Swiss border just north of
Basel. It was tantalizingly within Patton's reach in XX
Corps sector; exasperatingly remote in the area of XII
Corps, and seemingly beyond the grasp of his XV Corps
holding the southern flank on the line Assy-Chaumont-
Neufchâteau below the Marne-Rhine Canal.

This was September 11, 1944, a day of some historic
significance. It was unseasonably cold and wet. The fighting
in the mud was tough and inconclusive all along the Third
Army's front. Armor's efforts to get behind the enemy line,
in accordance with Patton's favorite tactics, became frustrated. The 4th Armored was at the Moselle, General Wood
maintaining his CP within the actual fighting line. But it
lacked equipment for a bridge to cross the river. The 35th
Division had managed to get across at Crevechamps but
was promptly pinned down in its precarious foothold. Resistance was encountered everywhere—at Bainville-aux-
Miroirs, at Bayon, on the hills overlooking Brémancourt,
near Neufchâteau. At Pont St. Vincent the Germans even
succeeded in pushing two companies back to the west bank
of the Moselle.

What rankled Patton most was not the enemy's desperate
effort to contest the foregone conclusion. As he later put it,
"I was convinced then, and have since discovered I was
right, that there were no Germans ahead of us except those
we were actually fighting. In other words, they had no
depth." He had made up his mind to drive for the Rhine
across the West Wall.

But he was upset because the high command was apparently playing a game with the Third Army. According to
the latest scuttlebutt, plans would be changed again to give
the *First* Army a bigger role at the West Wall. "I wish,"
Patton said to his planning staff when the rumors reached
him, "people would stop changing their mind, especially
when they always do so at our expense."

The West Wall was a magnetic objective for the First
Army as well. Its V Corps under General Gerow had advance elements of the 5th Armored Division near the Our

River right at the German border. Patrols of the division had a good close-up of the Wall, a strange mixture of old pill-boxes and more recent chicken coops.

This had become a race, but Patton felt sorely handi-capped. He was fighting on borrowed time. He had been told that emphasis would be shifted again to the north where Montgomery was racing through Belgium toward the German border. The British would get their batteries recharged, again at the expense of the Third Army, which was expected to stay put, holding a defensive position on the west bank of the Moselle. When advised of these prospects by Bradley, General Patton pleaded, "Don't stop us now, Brad, but I'll make a deal with you. If I don't secure a couple of good bridgeheads east of the Moselle by the night of the 14th, I'll shut up and assume the mournful role of the defender."

Bradley gave him the extension, and Patton more than made good. On September 12th, the 2nd Infantry Regiment of the 5th Division improved its position in the bridgehead at Arnaville in the face of coordinated counterattacks. By noon the engineers finished bridging the Moselle, and tanks and tank destroyers of the 7th Armored crossed into the bridgehead. In XII Corps area the 317th Infantry Regiment of the 80th Division stormed across the river at Dieulouard, was followed promptly by the 318th, and then weapons and vehicles started across. By nightfall the bridgehead was expanded to include Ste. Geneviève, Loisy, Bezaumont and La Côte Pelée. The 4th Armored expanded the Lorey bridgehead south of Nancy; and farther south, the 314th Infantry of the 79th Division cleared Charmes and sent a battalion over the river to gain still another foothold. If all this was still a bit precarious, for the Germans continued to oppose the advance bitterly, Patton was not unduly wor-ried. He told General Eddy, who was, as usual, somewhat concerned about his flank, not to worry but to take a stiff drink and prepare to storm the West Wall.

But then these frenzied preparations suddenly became anticlimactic. The Third Army lost the race. At 5:55 P.M. on September 11th, the First Army reached the West Wall and penetrated it. It was a spectacular event despite the minuscule scale on which it occurred.

Earlier in the afternoon the second platoon of Troop B of the 5th Armored's 85th Calvary Reconnaissance Squad-ron reached the western end of a bridge on the Our River.

The span had been demolished, but Staff Sergeant Werner W. Holzinger, who led the platoon, waded into the water and found it was shallow enough for his men—Corporal Ralph F. Diven, T/5 Coy T. Locke, Pfc. George F. McNeal and a French guide named DeLille—to cross. On the west bank they climbed a hill to what seemed like a cluster of farmhouses. On closer inspection they turned out to be camouflaged concrete pillboxes, some 19 or 20 of them. The pillboxes were surrounded by installations which convinced Holzinger and his men that they were inside a *Kampfstellung* (combat sector) of the West Wall.

Holzinger's platoon gave V Corps something to crow about. Its G-3 Journal recorded that at 6:05 P.M. on September 11, 1944, one of its patrols had been the first Allied unit to make it into Germany, near the village of Stalzenburg, a few miles northeast of Vianden, Luxembourg. It was a few hours short of exactly 26 years after Patton's solo excursion into the Hindenburg Line. As if a spell had been broken, other patrols of First Army followed immediately.

Now it seemed that these penetrations into Germany would usher in a new phase in the campaign whose basic directive had instructed General Eisenhower to "undertake operations aimed at the heart of Germany and the destruction of her armed forces." The distance to the heart of Germany still seemed to be rather long. But the destruction of the enemy forces in the west appeared to be at hand.

Up to this point, from the end of "Cobra" and the breakout at Avranches, the campaign had the character of a pursuit. The Germans were on the run. "Except for the Third Army," wrote Charles D. MacDonald in his official history of the Siegfried Line campaign, "which had been handicapped for five days while bearing the brunt of a general transportation shortage and gasoline drought, the Allied drive had reached its zenith during the period 1-11 September."

During these 11 days the British had rolled from the Seine to the Belgian-Dutch border; the First U.S. Army had eliminated a German pocket near Mons, in Belgium, bagging 25,000 prisoners, and elements of Bradley's 12th Army Group to Patton's north had inched their way to the West Wall. On this day the Allies reached a line that pre-D-Day planners had expected would be gained at about D plus 330, on May 2, 1945. The advance was ahead of schedule

by 233 days. According to a post-"Neptune" planning forecast, which expected German surrender on D plus 360, the
Allies were but 30 days from final victory.

Patton alone seemed to be awkwardly placed to make the
most of the situation. He was experiencing some trouble at
the Moselle, and even at the most forward point of his advance he was still 25 miles from the West Wall. He could
barely endure the disappointment. His plight was the fateful
consequence of the enforced halt.

Now, too, he was held down by inadequate supplies.
Pointed references were made to the difficulties he was experiencing with the enemy in front of him. He tried desperately to convince SHAEF that he was up against a thin
crust of Germans with little if anything behind it, that he
would pick up the ball and run as soon as he had adequate
supplies to break through the crust.

The German resistance was exactly as Patton saw it. It
did not stem from any real physical power, certainly not
in depth. General Eisenhower now had 49 divisions for a
knockout blow, opposed by 48 German divisions. But when
Field Marshal von Rundstedt returned to the front a few
days before, he was dismayed to find that the divisions with
which he was supposed to keep the Allies out of Germany
existed mostly on paper. On Hitler's explicit orders, 5 of his
48 divisions were bottled up on the Channel Islands and in
the coastal fortresses. The others were woefully underman-
ned. Von Rundstedt estimated that the actual forces under
his command were equivalent to only 25 divisions.

In equipment, Allied superiority was stifling. In guns it
was 2½ to 1, in tanks 20 to 1. The Allies had some 14,000
planes, against which the Germans could pit only 573
serviceable aircraft. The entire *Luftwaffe* was down to
4,507 planes, and none of those in Germany and the
Eastern Front could be spared for the west.

During these days when the Germans were, as Patton
sensed, at their lowest point of strength and power in the
west, and when a concerted action, as he envisioned it,
could so harm them that recovery would be impossible, they
suddenly gained a new lease on life. It was the Argentan-
Falaise situation repeating itself on a vastly greater scale.
Again it was the Allied failure to exploit the great opportunity that enabled the enemy to fight on for another eight
months.

Earlier, when the order came from Eisenhower to continue beyond the Seine, Patton had responded to it with his two great plans—the one oriented to the north to pocket the Germans fleeing from the Seine, the other to drive straight ahead to the heart of Germany. He was allowed to execute neither, and when he tried to take things into his own hands, he was stopped by the arrangements at SHAEF that diverted his supplies to Montgomery's drive.

"If the German High Command had anything to be thankful for," Blumenson wrote, "as *OB West* staff members later recalled, it was that the Allies failed to conduct an immediate and ruthless exploitation of the Seine River crossing at Mantes-Gassicourt [by Patton's Third Army] by an enveloping movement along the east bank of the Seine to Le Havre."

That kind of maneuver would have crashed open the gate to Germany, exactly as Patton had predicted. The plan he had evolved for this eventuality was, as he put it, the best he ever had. Yet it never gained the distinction even of mere consideration by General Eisenhower if, indeed, it had ever reached his level.

And Patton's "Sure Thing," the forward thrust through the West Wall, was thwarted at a time when General Eddy, the most cautious and conservative among Patton's commanders, wrote in his diary:

"It seems strange to me that we should be sitting here . . . I am convinced that if we could obtain the necessary fuel this war might be over in a matter of a few weeks."

CHAPTER THIRTY-THREE
PERIOD OF CONFUSION

Patton called it "the Unforgiving Minute." Bradley referred to it as "the Big Bust." To Monty it was "something of a wreck."

They all had the same thing in mind—the situation in France in September, 1944—the period of confusion when, it seemed, the war had been won, then lost again for seven more months.

While "the momentous error" did not become a scandal— for things that end well tend to erase past errors and diminish recriminations—it did develop into a controversy that continues to haunt the history of Eisenhower's crusade. It simmers across boundaries, irritates national and personal sensitivities, jeopardizes friendships forged in the heat of war, and, somehow, summons Patton's ghost.

The issue revolves around the questions:

Could the war have been carried to a victorious conclusion in the Indian summer of 1944?

Was it necessary to let it drag on till May, 1945?

And whose fault was it that it did drag on?

History abounds in such loaded questions in the wake of every war. There always comes a time in their course— often but a fleeting moment—when it seems that the last showdown is at hand and the final victory of one side or the other is just around the corner. Frequently an eager commander in the field mistakes his triumph in a big battle for the decisive victory in the war. And when the gods and his superiors, who are supposed to know better, dispute his contention, he usually persists in the conviction that he is right and the others are all wrong. Victories in battles are deceptive triumphs. They place the burden of proof not on the men who won them, but on those who are in charge of the war and must be guided by the assumption that no matter how many battles may be won, the war itself can still be lost. Nobody knew this better than Pyrrhus of Epirus. And nobody should have realized this sooner than Adolf Hitler of the Thousand-Year Reich.

Patton himself—at first in the privacy of his headquarters and then posthumously in *War As I Knew It*—was bitter and vindictive in his discussion of the issue. Had he been permitted, he claimed in so many words in his *post mortem*, to go all out, the war would have ended sooner and more lives would have been saved. "Particularly I think," he wrote, "this statement applies to the time when, in the early days of September, we were halted, owing to the desire, or necessity, on the part of General Eisenhower in backing Montgomery's move to the north."

What was the price the Third Army paid for the delay?

According to Patton's meticulously kept "score sheet," his casualties on September 17, 1944, amounted to 3,841 killed,

18,241 wounded, and 4,120 missing—a total of 26,202 in all categories (excluding noncombat casualties). His final score sheet of May 8, 1945, showed a grand total of 136,865 casualties, including 21,441 killed in action. The two score sheets lend poignancy to his claim that in September "there was no question of doubt but that we could have gone through and on across the Rhine within 10 days" and to his conclusion that "this would have saved a great many thousand men."

It is easy to understand why Patton felt so strongly on this score. The war had come to its turning point, presenting a fantastic opportunity that was not likely to recur. His own career had reached its climax in this sizzling September, his destiny its highest fulfillment. Though he continued to flourish and gained additional honors and glamour, he never again experienced the tension and suspense of those days in France when the historic triumph within his grasp turned into pitiable, humiliating inaction.

Was he right, as he himself so categorically asserted? Was this, indeed, the unforgiving minute demanding bold and concerted action?

Who is qualified to answer these questions? Yet they are being answered from time to time, either with unabashed partisanship or with doctored evidence in official histories. Even though no answer can be conclusive and completely free of bias, it is possible, nevertheless, to examine the issues in the hope that some answers at least might suggest themselves.

If this was a period of confusion, there were abundant reasons to be confused. The great "Overlord" plan had just expired at the Seine. The follow-up "plan," hastily drafted on May 3, 1944, was vague, unimaginative, and pessimistic. When the Seine was reached, a snap decision made the pursuit proceed posthaste without regard for the crucial problem, the total destruction of all German forces in France. No exact plans regulated the pursuit. In the crisis, General Eisenhower, now in over-all command in the greater combat zone, proved incapable of exercising either the strategic or the tactical leadership the changed situation demanded.

As a result, each dynamic army commander in the field could plot his own designs. And the more dynamic he happened to be, the bolder and weirder his plans turned out to be. Thus this promising pursuit toward the ultimate goal was planned at different headquarters, always from the narrower angle of each competing commander. Although it should not be assumed that selfish interests had dominated these men and that they had lost sight of the common good in devising their schemes, it cannot be denied that parochial considerations, egotistical motives, conceit and vanities had at least some influence on their plots.

From the Seine on, and to the Rhine, the war came to be conducted under three different and essentially contradictory plans, with a different emphasis on each.

One was the Supreme Commander's strategic design, which fell back on the vague SHAEF draft of May 3rd. While the planners chose the Ruhr, as the potentially most lucrative strategic goal of "post-Neptune operations," they cautioned that it would be "dangerous to attack by a single route and thus canalize the advance and open it to a concentrated enemy attack." Eisenhower adopted his planners' outdated scheme and decided in favor of "a broad front both north and south of the Ardennes," to give the Allies the advantages of maneuver and the ability to shift the main weight of attack.

The other was Field Marshal Montgomery's kinetic plan to place all available resources on his thrust to the Ruhr, pursuing it with such force and power that it would lead to the inevitable collapse of all German resistance.

The third was the Bradley-Patton plan of the thrust in the south with a gigantic enveloping maneuver, reaching Berlin with one of its prongs, racing all the way to Vienna with the other. It was a slightly modified version of Patton's "Sure Thing."

With each of the three plans in execution, the war became pulled and pushed in several directions but with inadequate power in any of the thrusts. It became quickly and abundantly evident that each plan suffered from some inner deficiencies and from the consequences of the confusion.

What Patton called the "Sure Thing" was almost too simple and too good to be true. It was based on two major assumptions: First, that the easiest way to breach the West Wall was in his sector through what he called the "Nancy Gap;" and, second, that no substantial German forces stood in his path to contest the breach and his subsequent rapid advance.

His plan called for a drive with two corps abreast and a third echeloned to the right rear, with armor leading, from Nancy through Château-Salins to Sarreguemines. The Wall was to be breached on a 40-mile line between Saarbrücken and Wissembourg. Aided by a corps attached from First Army, Patton would then drive in the direction of Kaiserslautern between the Haardt Mountains and the Blies River valley, on either Mainz or Worms, then continue northeast through the flatlands to Frankfurt—and points beyond.

He had picked the Nancy Gap by studying ordinary road maps.

Later he checked his choice against a study of the West Wall prepared by his G-2 and Colonel John Conklin's Engineers, and found it fully confirmed. "The two places already picked," he wrote, "for a probable breakthrough by a study of the road map exactly accorded with what a meticulous study of contoured maps had developed."

His shop talks of those days indicated that Patton was not awed by the West Wall. He agreed avidly with General Wood's cocky guess that it was only a big bluff, and figured that he would need only 3 of the 10 days he had scheduled for the drive to Worms to get through the fortifications. After that, he told Wood, there would remain only the task of mopping up scattered, demoralized enemy units inside Germany.

His own low opinion of the West Wall gained support from a report prepared by the 5th Armored after several of its units had penetrated the defenses to a depth of eight miles, as far into Germany as Prüm. "The Siegfried Line," the report stated, "although a strong natural position, is not what it was ballyhooed to be by the Germans . . . It will not be too difficult to break."

Despite its apparent excellence and Patton's unbounded enthusiasm for it, his plan never had a chance to be accepted, or even to be taken seriously anywhere beyond General Bradley's command post. Patton did his plotting either in ignorance or in defiance of Eisenhower's decision to support Montgomery's thrust to the north. This by itself mitigated against the plan. But there were other factors, too, that made it appear considerably less "sure" a thing than Patton thought it was.

There were absolutely no means at the disposal of the Allies to support a drive of 400 to 600 miles into Germany, even if Eisenhower had agreed to place all his eggs in Patton's basket. And it was highly doubtful whether Patton could have enjoyed the kind of air support that proved so instrumental in his race across France. Colonel Herbert W. Ehrgott, Chief of Staff of IX Engineer Command, which had the task of building and maintaining airfields in the combat zone, argued conclusively against the notion that it would have been possible to go into Germany within those 10 days.

"Had Patton continued through the Saar Valley and the Vosges," he wrote, "it must have been without close air support and with a very small contribution in the way of air supply beyond the Reims-Epernay line. We could have fixed up Conflans, Metz, and Nancy-Azelot in time to have done some good, but the next possible fields were at Haguenau and Strasbourg, with no fields except Trier between there and the Köln-Maastricht Plain.

"I would not have liked to tackle the job of supplying Patton over the Vosges and through the Pfalz during that October. I don't doubt that we could have carried about two armored and one [motorized] division up to Köln, but then where? Certainly not across the Rhine. A good task force of Panzerfaust, manned by Hitler youth, could have finished them off before they reached Kassel."

Yet air support on a substantial scale would have been indispensable to Patton's success. Although the Germans had only 500 planes in France, they had several thousand inside the Reich, and would have used them vigorously to interfere with the invaders.

In his enthusiasm and impatience, Patton also glossed over other important impediments. He refused to recognize that his troops were tired and needed a rest. He chose to disregard the certainty that the Germans' resistance would be far more effective on their home ground than on the alien soil of France. Even as he was worming his way deeper into Lorraine, the welcoming crowds thinned out, the cheers waned and hostility increased. He preferred to dismiss the fact, actually staring him in the face at the Moselle, that none of the favorable conditions of the breakout and pursuit existed in a drive into Germany. The war of movement that Bradley had ushered in with "Cobra" was already turning, even if imperceptibly as yet, into a war of position.

If the failure of the Allies to realize their hopes of victory at this time followed in part, as Pogue thought, from undue pessimism on the part of the "Overlord" planners, Patton's great plan suffered from an overdose of optimism. He had devised it without much regard for logistic considerations, hoping, as was his wont, that a bold operation would succeed by its own momentum, on its own resources.

Montgomery's plan predated Patton's by 14 days. He had discussed it in detail with Bradley as early as August 17th, at which time Bradley appeared to be enthusiastically for it. But only two days later, after a conference with Patton, his enthusiasm evaporated, probably because Patton showed him how deeply Monty's scheme would cut into Bradley's domain and how little it would leave for the 12th Army Group to do.

Bradley's animosity toward Montgomery's plan, and then to Monty himself, increased steadily during these days. Until the Cotentin campaign in July, Montgomery had held a certain spell over Bradley. He impressed his American colleague with the clarity of his mind and the strength of his personality, neither of which ever made any great impression on Patton. Back in Tripoli, in February, 1943, Patton had had his first opportunity to listen to Monty's exposition of a pending campaign, the orchestration of the British Eighth Army's advance on the Mareth Line and the American II Corps' holding operation in Tunisia.

Montgomery was especially eager to impress Patton, "that remarkable American character," and dazzled his audience with a spirited lecture on "how to make war." But on his way back to his hotel, Patton irreverently told Major General Sir Brian Horrocks, who was then commanding a corps in Monty's famed army, "I may be old, I may be slow, I may be stoopid, but it just doan mean a thing to me."

But initially Bradley was much impressed with Montgomery's gift of reducing complex situations to their simplest terms, and his way of spelling out problems and their solutions in crisp, brief, numbered paragraphs. And he liked Monty's custom of taking infinite pains to explain to his associates exactly what he wanted from them and how he expected them to deliver it.

Now, however, a conflict developed between the two generals' spheres of interest. When Monty began to insist that two corps of the First Army, fighting with him in the north, be transferred to his command, the spell broke abruptly. Bradley began to suspect Monty's motives, resent his encroachments upon the prerogatives and domains of others and even to question the true clarity of his expositions. The more he moved away from Montgomery's orbit, the closer he came to Patton, until their views merged completely and they acted in unison.

The vehemence with which Montgomery represented his own interests and the apparent avarice behind his demands became important factors in alienating his colleagues now. Promoting his personal plan with every fiber in his body, he was asking too much for himself, leaving virtually nothing for others. He also gave the impression that he was trying, after his controversial showing in the beginning, to vindicate himself and hug the whole glory of winning the war single-handedly.

No matter how plausible and promising his plan was, and how powerful his arguments sounded in its support, there were elements in Monty's record in France to plant some doubts in Eisenhower's mind. For one thing, the memories of his slow-motion campaign around Caen were still too fresh. This evidence of the recent past somewhat undermined Eisenhower's faith in Monty's ability to conduct the kind of fast power-drive of which he spoke.

The fact that Monty had his own grave problems—that he had to wage his war with full recognition of the British limitations in manpower and supplies, and that he, in the face of them, was wisely determined to win with superior generalship and a minimum of fighting—did not move Eisenhower sufficiently for him to adapt the war to Montgomery's special needs and methods.

When Monty's drive was under way at last and he moved his armor 250 miles in a week, he demonstrated that he had, as Wilmot generously put it, "a capacity for movement and exploitation of Patton himself." Yet even then several mishaps occurred which made it appear unlikely that Montgomery could push on to his distant goal even if he had everything his way.

One of Eisenhower's main reasons for giving priority to the northern thrust was his eagerness to capture the port of Antwerp. He was persisting in the belief that the Allies could not force the Seine line and operate successfully beyond it until they had ports for the reception of fresh troops and supplies directly from the United States. He had zeroed in covetously on Antwerp, especially when VIII Corps had failed to secure the Breton ports on schedule.

However, when the port area was within his grasp, Major General George Philip Bradley Roberts, whose 11th Armored Division (British) had captured the city, neglected to secure the bridges over the Albert Canal at the northern edge of Antwerp, although they could have been seized "within a few hours." As a result, the Schelde Estuary, the 60-mile water entrance to Antwerp, remained in German hands for some time and the opening of the port was delayed until late in November. Thus one of the major objectives of Montgomery's thrust was not attained.

Then later in September, Montgomery's drive suffered another setback at Arnhem, where the Germans succeeded in defeating an ambitious operation (that included the greatest mass landing of airborne troops ever attempted) designed to outflank the northern end of the Siegfried Line. The Rhine remained a barrier. The threat to the Ruhr was neither so great nor so immediate as Montgomery had hoped.

With the deficiencies of the competing plans what they were, it was imperative to have at the top a firm hand to prevent the fragmentation of the war into free-wheeling campaigns conducted by prima donnas. At this crucial juncture of the war General Eisenhower's control suddenly lapsed. Just when he needed his utmost physical integrity and mobility, he suffered a painful injury that virtually incapacitated and immobilized him.

On September 2nd, upon his return to his headquarters from his flying trip to Bradley's CP for the conference with Patton and Hodges, a broken muffler on his C-47 necessitated a change to an L-5, a small liaison plane. His pilot landed on the beach near Ike's villa (named "Montgomery") in a rising tide that threatened to engulf the little craft. While helping the pilot push the plane to higher ground, Ike twisted his knee badly in the soft sand. "He has to sit with his leg straight," Commander Butcher recorded, "and is quite uncomfortable. But worst of all, the stiff leg makes difficult his normal movement around the country to see the commanders."

Even before the accident, signs were accumulating that the problems Eisenhower had to solve began to overwhelm him. This became abundantly evident when, upon General Marshall's urging and in deference to domestic American considerations, he assumed personal command of the land battle at its most confusing and critical stage. This turned out to be unfortunate.

"In the role of Supreme Commander," Wilmot wrote in his sympathetic characterization of Eisenhower at this stage, "he had shown himself to be the military statesman rather than the generalissimo . . . Being an honest and modest man, Eisenhower was conscious of his lack of experience in the tactical handling of armies, and this gave him a sense of professional inferiority in dealing with men like Montgomery and Patton who had been through the mill of command at every level. Because he had no philosophy of battle which he himself had tested in action, Eisenhower was reluctant to impose his own ideas, unless the decision was one which he, as Supreme Commander, had to make . . . He had a remarkable capacity for distilling the counsel of many minds into a single solution, but when his commanders were scattered over France, he was open to persuasion by the last strong man to whom he talked."

Montgomery, of course, was the strongest among his peers. Moreover, he, in his exalted position as second only to the Supreme Commander himself, had the easiest access to him. On the other hand, Ike's relations with Patton had grown frail and remote.

Patton's contact with SHAEF was tenuous by necessity but his relationship with Supreme Headquarters in general was not too bad. Despite his suspicion of the motives and competence of "the men around Ike," he was jovial with them and they reciprocated in kind, though they remained rather quizzical. They respected his skill, admired his drive, but frowned upon his mannerisms and raw language. They regarded him as something of a buffoon and a bit queer, with that silent condescension with which the illegitimate sons of grand dukes were viewed at the Czar's court.

Eisenhower himself was cordial but perceptibly more reserved than he used to be in their less harassed days. Their contacts became infrequent. They had not met in the whole of August. They met four times in September, twice in the field and twice at Versailles (to whose Trianon Palace Hotel near the Petit Trianon SHAEF had moved). Their meetings were friendly but perfunctory. Eisenhower had no hidden hostility toward Patton and none of his angry re-sentiment. But he was now the Supreme Commander and had grown into his bigger shoes. Mindful of Patton's lower position in the strict military hierarchy, below Montgomery and Bradley, and dubious of the quality of his judgment, he was not prepared to take either advice or pressure from him. Most of all, he did not look with any favor on Patton's sudden emergence as a strategic planner, especially at this time when planning was his biggest headache.

As a matter of fact, Patton was virtually the only top man in his command to whom he could say no without hesitation and with whom he could be blunt. He had gotten accustomed to arguing with Patton long before, during their salad days at Fort Meade; then he acquired a no-nonsense firmness in his dealings with him during the embarrassing incidents in Sicily and England when he, as Eisenhower put it, had to save Patton from himself.

A man who liked to be liked, Eisenhower would tolerate incompetency and mistakes silently because it pained him to hurt the feelings of his friends. In March, 1943, he frankly told Patton, "I ought to relieve General Anderson [the British commander of the Allied army in Tunisia to which Patton's II Corps belonged] but I don't want to hurt his feelings." Once, when he should have issued an order he had reason to believe that Bradley disliked, he refrained because he did not want to injure his friend's feelings. But he had no such qualms in his relations with Patton. To him he could speak straight from the shoulder, and this was exactly what he did when Patton pestered him with his own plans and demands.

The very qualities which made Eisenhower a successful Supreme Commander now prevented him from becoming an effective and forceful commander in the field. "His great talent lay in holding the Allied team together," Wilmot thought, "and in reconciling the interests of different nations and services. In the situation which had now developed, however, Eisenhower's conscientious tolerance and inclination to compromise were liabilities. The occasion called for a man with a bold plan, a Commander in Chief who knew what was essential and had the will to impose his strategic ideas without regard for personalities or public opinion."

This did not mean that the famous Eisenhower temper never flared up or that he had no firm opinion of the prima donnas who were making his life so miserable at this time.

When Patton called on him at Versailles on September 21st, Eisenhower reiterated his decision that, for the time being, the main effort would be left with the British and the northern flank of the First Army. But when Patton returned to his own CP, he told his staff with unconcealed glee, "He was more fed up with Monty than I've ever seen him. In fact, he called him a sonuvabitch, which is very encouraging."

The situation did not call for compromise. Yet it was with a compromise that Eisenhower hoped to solve it. In the course of the solution, several collateral errors were committed which compounded the confusion. Thus it was a mistake on Eisenhower's part to use supplies as a lever of his influence. He was probably wrong in his assumption that he could not force the West Wall with fewer than 60 divisions. He persisted in this belief even when the Germans' effective strength was down to about 25 ill-equipped divisions while the Allies had 48 divisions at full strength and adequately supplied.

The Supreme Commander was unduly concerned with his open flanks. He regarded the "linking-up of the whole front" as "mandatory," in order to "prevent the costliness of establishing long, defensive flanks along which our troops could have nothing but negative, static missions." He continued to worry about his flanks even after Patton had demonstrated that they could be held by air power or secured through a prudent and ingenious use of terrain.

Even so, Ike's strategic plan might have been appropriate had not the outcome of the Normandy battle rendered it outdated. Hitler had committed every possible mistake the Allies needed to secure the lodgment area. He had decided to fight for every bit of *bocage* and whittled down his forces in the tedious process. Then he counterattacked at Mortain, and sacrificed the only divisions he had to hold the front together. By staying too long at Falaise, he had made an organized withdrawal to the Seine line impossible.

Thanks to Hitler in a great part, there was no actual strategic need for a broad front, except to compromise the differences between Montgomery on the one side and Bradley and Patton on the other without giving either what he actually wanted. Eisenhower's predilection for "action everywhere" was no mere whim or conciliatory gesture. It was part of his education, a strategic concept ingrained in him with the lessons he had learned at West Point. "Like

nearly all senior American military commanders at the
time, except the genius MacArthur," wrote Sir Arthur Bryant in his commentary on Field Marshal Brooke's (Lord
Alanbrooke's) diaries, "he was a believer in the classic Civil
War doctrine of frontal assault, of 'Everybody attacks all
the time.' "

The resulting situation demonstrated the cumulative consequences of these errors. Patton in particular was to suffer
from them almost fatally. The long front they created
extended his responsibilities much too far to the south, into
an area completely devoid of strategic importance. And the
decision rendered the tactical situation of the Third Army
both heart-breaking and untenable by giving it only enough
gasoline to join the battle but not enough to win it. At the
same time Montgomery was also frustrated and exasperated
by the compromise. When Patton was granted permission
(and given the gasoline) to drive beyond the Marne, the
First Army had to drive forward on its right to cover the
Third Army, when it was needed in the north to support
Montgomery's drive for the Ruhr.

Broad as the front now extended, it soon became quiet
all along its enormous length. Montgomery came to a halt
in the Low Countries. Hodges was stopped at Aachen. Patton was halted in front of the Saar River. And the Germans
gained what they did not dare to hope for in their fondest
dreams—time to recover from the near-lethal blows in
France.

If, on September 15th, Patton had any misgivings about
his future, he did not show them. Supplies were flowing
again, not as much as he wanted, but enough to sustain
him. He was full of pep. Having gained a new lease on life
and allowed to dream again, he worked with Generals Eddy
and Wood on what was left of the "Sure Thing," for he
had picked XII Corps to mount the attack through the
West Wall toward Worms.

The Third Army was active along its entire front, but
its gains were not in the old mold, barely enough to justify
Patton's sanguine plan. The major venture of the day was
the 90th Division's attack on the fortifications of Metz,
some old, others new, all now held firmly by fresh troops

rushed into the breach. The day was marked by increasing German counterattacks, both sides suffering heavy casualties.

Then Patton flew to Bradley's command post for another conference with General Bull from SHAEF. It was a gossipy meeting, most of the small talk revolving around Monty and the pressure he was putting on Eisenhower. They also discussed a pending shuffle of their forces, but it was of such a long-range prospect that Patton told Bull, "By the time I get these divisions, the war will be over." He was all set to give it a big push.

Patton spent the next day with Eddy and Wood, getting them ready for the storming of the West Wall he had scheduled for September 18th, barely two days away. He was in one of his buoyant moods, fully confident that he would still be able to bring off the "Sure Thing." He suggested (rather than directed) that they attack in a column of three divisions, with the 4th Armored leading the assault. The primary objective was to secure a gap in the Wall. Then Eddy had to be prepared to rush some armor, backed by one combat team, straight to the Rhine in the vicinity of Worms, to grab the bridge before the Germans had time to blow it up. A second unit was to hold the gap open, while the third division would mop up whatever Germans were left between the Moselle and the West Wall.

On September 17th Patton's attention was diverted from the front. The smoldering controversy with Montgomery had flared up again. Bradley called in some excitement to tell him that Monty wanted them to stop where they were because he was ready for the second phase of *his* big push. Bradley was totally exasperated by now and told Patton with an acidity that was rare for him, "He says he'll make a *dagger*-thrust at the heart of Germany but I think it's more likely to be a *butter-knife* thrust."

Patton told Bradley not to worry. "In view of Monty's ambitions," he said, "I'll get so involved that they won't be able to stop me. Eddy will start tomorrow morning for the West Wall, and then we'll be off running. So play it dumb, Brad! Don't call me until after dark of the 19th. After that we won't have any reason to worry about Monty's dagger-thrust."

Bradley agreed to this daring plot, but then a hitch developed after all, and Montgomery had nothing to do with it. While preparations continued for the eastward push, the

Germans began to infiltrate into Lunéville in the projected path of XII Corps' rush to the West Wall. The old ducal city of Lorraine remained in possession of the Americans, but their hold became tenuous.

Then on the 18th, just when Eddy was to jump off for the West Wall and Worms, the enemy launched a full-scale counteroffensive and Lunéville erupted. The 2nd Cavalry Group in the city was hit by the first blow and fell back. But led personally by General Wood, the 4th Armored (which on this day was to lead the attack on the West Wall) stemmed the onslaught and forced the enemy southward. By nightfall the Germans withdrew to Parroy, apparently having spent their sting, but the offensive forced Patton to rearrange his forces and delay the big push. Even so, he signaled General Eddy: "The attack on the West Wall is still on as suggested."

The morning after, when the 4th Armored was mopping up the Germans left over from their Lunéville debacle, Patton reviewed his plan for the eastward drive. He found it as good as ever. He now decided to push forward with all he had in XII Corps, using the Moselle-Rhine Canal to protect his right flank. But he was experiencing some trouble at his front, and had certain premonitions that made him fidgety.

Metz was still the biggest fly in the ointment. Walker could not take it, and arrangements were not ready yet to contain it. For the first time during these days of revived hope, and despite his great expectations from Eddy's push, Patton seemed to be nervous. Then the sky fell in on him.

On the morning of September 23rd, Patton was about to visit the front in XX Corps area when a call from Bradley made him hop into his jeep and drive as fast as he could to Verdun. Bradley received him with stunning news.

"Monty won again," he said with a fallen face. "I have orders to send an armored division north to aid him and to assume the defensive. What's more, our supplies have been cut back again."

The 7th Armored Division was just getting ready to cross the Seille River near Metz when it received the order to drop everything and join XIX Corps of the First Army in the north. To Patton it now seemed that the whole Third Army was breaking up. Aside from Silvester's armor, he was about to lose XV Corps again—Eisenhower had given it to General Devers. He also had a pointed hint that he would have to give up one or two infantry divisions to cover the Luxembourg Gap for Hodges.

Patton had had it. Whatever hopes he had left were blasted beyond repair. His dream of breaking through the West Wall and being in Germany "within 10 days" was shattered. This particular war was over for him.

When he got back to his headquarters, Patton summed up his disappointment in a pungent question by asking General Gay, "Well, Hap, how would you like to go to China and serve under Admiral Nimitz?"

CHAPTER THIRTY-FOUR
A MATTER OF OPPORTUNITY

General Patton's reaction to the shift from the offensive to the defensive in his sector was characteristic of the man. It was both formal for the record and highly informal within the safe confines of his headquarters. In his case this meant that he was strict and businesslike in obeying his orders but violent in criticizing them. As soon as he had Bradley's directive, he penned a "Letter of Instructions"— Number 4—to his commanders, acquainting them with the new scheme of things. Marked "Top Secret," it was not to be circulated below the grade of general officer. The Letter was concise, lucid, and remarkable for its restraint. It was also interesting, for it showed Patton's broad interpretation of his orders, leaving as much of the offensive as possible even in his defensive arrangements.

"The acute supply situation confronting us," he wrote on September 25, 1944, "has caused the Supreme Commander to direct that, until further orders, the Third Army, with its supporting troops, and those of the Ninth Army placed in the line, will assume the defensive.

"It is evident that the successful accomplishment of this mission will require particular concentration upon two points:

"First, this change in attitude on our part must be completely concealed from the enemy, who, should he learn of it, would certainly move troops from our front to oppose other Allied Armies.

"Second, we must be in possession of a suitable line of departure so that we can move rapidly when the Supreme Commander directs us to resume the offensive.

"We will not dig in, wire, or mine, but will utilize a thin outpost zone backed at suitable places by powerful mobile reserves."

He ordered all batteries to register all possible avenues of tank attacks. He urged that counterattacks be planned and executed by mobile reserves. And he mapped out a "line of departure" to be secured and maintained "for the future offensive," ending the Letter on this note of confidence and hope:

"We only await the signal to resume our career of conquest."

While Patton expected some lively action from these arrangements and hoped that they would be an antidote to any slackening of his men's offensive spirit, he did not indulge in illusions. He realized fully that his was the predicament of the Red Queen—it took all the running one could do to keep in the same place.

In his own inner circle he vented his disenchantment with little control over his true feelings. At a press conference he called to explain the situation off the record, he was as caustic as he could be, pointing an accusing finger at *Field Marshal* Montgomery (whose brand-new rank became a sardonic handle in his hands). Monty was his favorite whipping boy in such adversities, if only because he knew that criticism of the British commander evoked sympathetic response in the correspondents, including the Britons assigned to his headquarters.

"Yesterday," he told the correspondents gathered in the PRO tent, "the Field Marshal ordered SHAEF to have Third Army go on the defensive, stand in place, and prepare to guard his right flank. The Field Marshal then announced that he will, after regrouping, make what he describes as a lightning dagger-thrust at the heart of Germany. 'They will be off their guard,' the Field Marshal predicts, 'and I shall pop out at them like an angry rabbit.' "

Larry Newman, correspondent of International News Service, expressed the consensus in the press tent. "That guy in there," he enthused, "all by himself, without benefit of high-priced writers, music or scenery, that guy is eight-eighty entertainment."

The correspondents received Patton's jabs and jokes with guffaws. And the more they laughed the more Patton clowned it up. This, however, was no laughing matter. Facing this sophisticated crowd and encouraged by its hilarity, he put on one of his flamboyant shows. But deep down in his heart he was sad and deeply shocked.

In his intimate circle Patton was displaying his outrage without theatricals, placing the blame squarely on the "Supreme Commander" and the "timid souls" around him, especially General Lee of Com Z.

At dinner with his aides, nervously crumbling a slice of toast, he exclaimed over a glass of awful-tasting chlorinated water, "How long, O Lord, how long? We roll across France in less time than it takes Monty to say 'Regroup' and here we are stuck in the mud of Lorraine. Why? Because somewhere up the line some sonuvabitch who never heard a shot fired in anger or missed a meal believes in higher priorities for pianos and ping-pong sets than for ammunition and gas."

He was cut short by the ringing of the field telephone in the next room. General Bradley was calling him. He took the call, his mood of the moment coloring his words as he said:

"Hello, Brad, this is George. What the hell does SHAEF want *now*?"

Patton was never madder with SHAEF and never prouder of his men than during these hapless, haphazard September days in 1944. He had molded his army in his own image. As the Germans were catching their breath and returning to the attack, it stood its ground, each man fighting with Patton's skill and spirit. It was a remarkable show of go-to-itiveness and stick-to-itiveness, changing back and forth from one to the other virtually at a snap of Patton's fingers. The passion of the great pursuit had spent its intoxicating force. It was replaced in his soldiers by a boisterous pride in their army's past achievements and by unbounded confidence in ultimate victory which, to most of his men, still seemed to be just around the corner.

Patton himself was still running like a sprinter beyond the finish line. But gradually even he had to realize that the spurt was at an end. The angry surge of this pursuit of triumph had turned into a chase of phantom hopes. The enemy had arrived to contest every inch in his path. The wild vicissitudes of war were upon him.

As usual, there was a baffling contrast between Patton's boisterous outward behavior and the sober rationale of his inner thoughts. He behaved as he did because he thought it would be a sign of weakness and surrender if he conceded defeat or showed his despondency. The uncured ham in Patton misled even the learned historian of his own army. Long after the war Hugh M. Cole charged that Patton had been reckless and unrealistic in planning his drive to the Rhine because he "showed no anticipation of any stubborn enemy resistance at the Moselle."

This is not borne out by anything on the record. His two stillborn plans—the northward turn in the direction of Beauvais and the thrust to the Rhine—were made with a firm and knowing eye on the German order of battle. He hoped to be permitted to turn north to envelop the disorganized enemy fleeing from the debacle at the Seine, and by destroying the Germans in a *Kessel* to prevent them from moving east and southeast into the path of his main drive. He was keenly conscious of the historic significance of his two plans and of the consequences of their abortion. "If the doings of the Third Army and its general," he wrote later, "are subject to inquiry by future historians, the two points just mentioned should be a warning." And he reiterated the basic premise on which he had based his plans: "It was evident at this time that there was no real thrust against us as long as we did not allow ourselves to be stopped by imaginary enemies."

Today we know, of course, that Patton was right, even if only for a few days. But events were tumbling so fast in the latter part of August that even a few days could have made all the difference. Few commanders have the special gift of recognizing their sudden opportunities and possess the courage to seize them at a moment's notice. Most of them are, while certainly not slow-witted, bound by carefully drawn plans and their firm orders.

What were the German dispositions in the Moselle sector during those August days when Patton hit upon his "Sure Thing"?

There was, to begin with, a grave personal crisis at the top of the German High Command with a hiatus in *OB West*. Hitler had filled only one of the late Field Marshal von Kluge's two jobs, that of his tactical command of Army Group B, by appointing Field Marshal Model to it.

Model's boundary in the south extended to the line Neufchâteau-Bayon-Strasbourg, some 45 miles below Nancy, running up to the Marne-Rhine Canal, with the West Wall between Trier and Strasbourg for its eastern terminus. South of that line was Army Group G, pushed up from Southern France by Lieutenant General Alexander S. Patch's Seventh U.S. Army. It was commanded by Colonel General Johannes Blaskowitz, with headquarters at Gérardmer. A square-faced, competent old pro from East Prussia, Blaskowitz was firmly established in Hitler's black book, for he not only was no Nazi like Model, but also was a mildly vocal opponent of the regime. He was in the West by tolerance, his days in command numbered, and he knew it, which was by no means conducive to any great enthusiasm on his part for holding fast to what he regarded as a lost cause.

During these last days in August, Model's First Army, committed on an 80-mile front from Sedan to Bayon (where it opposed Patton) looked impressive on paper. But it was an empty shell. Its commander, General Kurt von der Chevallerie, had managed to salvage in his retreat across the Meuse only 9 battalions of infantry, 2 batteries of field guns, 10 tanks (the entire Army Group B had only 100 tanks), 3 antiaircraft batteries and 10 75-mm. antitank guns.

Below Bayon at Charmes, Blaskowitz had elements of the 21st Panzer Division with virtually no tanks it could call its own, and the battered remnants of General Walther Lucht's LXVI Reserve Corps. Farther south was his Nineteenth Army, commanded by General Friedrich Wiese, a veteran of World War I who had sat out the lean years of the Weimar Republic as a police officer.

Patton's proposed advance was thus contested by two German armies, as far as the formal order of battle went. But these armies existed mainly in the bureaucratic catalogue of intelligence officers. As of August 21st, when Patton had devised his plan for the breakthrough into Germany "within 10 days," the Germans were exactly as he believed them to be—conspicuous by their absence.

By then, however, the Patton name began to mean something at Rastenburg, where Hitler was plotting the revival of his front in the west. The Führer had recognized in him a major threat to his welfare and was now in the midst of scraping together whatever forces he could find, to pit against Patton and halt his advance which, as Hitler foresaw, could very well breach the abandoned West Wall.

From his distant headquarters in the Wolfsschanze, Hitler was issuing one *Führerbefehl* after another to re-establish a coherent front in the west. In a strangely ironical sequence, the mounting crescendo of his arrangements coincided with Patton's growing internal difficulties.

On September 7th he sent Field Marshal von Rundstedt back to the west, into von Kluge's empty shoes as *OB West*. Apparently forgiving the old man's outburst—"End the war, you fools!"—he now endowed him with sweeping powers, placing into his orbit every unit in the west, including naval and *Luftwaffe* forces, and all *ad hoc* troops, the so-called *Volksverbände* or people's units in the process of being formed by plumbing the depths of his manpower reservoir.

On September 26th, the Führer began to issue a series of orders "for the interior defense of the Reich," designating the whole of Western Germany as a combat zone. On October 8th he issued a special directive for the strengthening of the southern sector of the West Front. He concluded, for the time being, this effusion of orders with a directive significantly called *"Halten des Westwalls unter allen Umständen,"* ordering the holding of the West Wall under all circumstances.

The broader purpose of these vast arrangements, miraculous in their scope and characteristic of Hitler's revived faith in the future, was hinted at in a 17-word passage in the directive of September 3rd. *"Spätere Hauptaufgabe ist,"* the text read in the German original, *"ein Angriff mit zusammengafassten Kräften gegen die tiefe Ostflanke und den Rücken der Amerikaner."* It was his first written reference to what became the Ardennes offensive.

Let us now trace Patton's course from the buoyant birth of the "Sure Thing" and his dash beyond the Meuse to the humiliating denouement of the Third Army's first reverses, all within six weeks.

On August 21st, when the pat plan of the race for Worms first popped into his brain, the Third Army stood on the Seine. Haislip's XV Corps was completing the historic operation its exultant commander had called "a Lulu", firming up and expanding the bridgehead across the river in the Mantes-Gassicourt area. Walker's XX Corps was driving to Arpajon and Rambouillet. The XII Corps, under its new commander, General Eddy, had just captured Sens and was pushing through Pithiviers.

The Seine had been reached and crossed. But it was not yet certain whether General Eisenhower would sanction a drive beyond "Overlord's" final phase line and let this fantastic pursuit proceed to its farthest point of exploitation.

Then on August 23rd, in the heady atmosphere of the liberation of Paris, Eisenhower's green light was flashed to his armies, and the dash beyond the Seine was on. The Marne was reached on August 29th, at Châlons and Vitry-le-Francois. Walker took Reims. The next day Eddy overran St. Dizier, halfway to the Meuse, then reached the river at Commercy and Pont-sur-Meuse.

Behind Patton was most of France. Now he was continuing toward the Moselle, where he would put his drive into still higher gear for the break through the West Wall and the thrust into Germany.

Imperceptibly at first, then with increasing evidence, the atmosphere of the campaign was changing, the environment seemed to be growing less congenial. This was still France, to be sure, but it was Lorraine—what the Germans called Lothringen and claimed as their own—a gently rolling plateau of pastures and fields, framed by the Vosges and the ridges at the Moselle with their precious vineyards. It was a piece of Europe with which kings used to play chess. In the dynastic jumble of the past, it had Frenchmen, Germans, Austrians and even a Pole for its rulers. Its hapless people had been shifted to and fro between France and Germany four times in the less than 75 years between 1870 and 1944. Trampled upon by opposing armies as they came and went, these people looked with jaundiced eyes upon conquerors.

Many of them, moreover, did not seem too happy or eager to be liberated. Among them were thousands of die-hard Nazis planted here after 1940, when 35,000 French-speaking citizens of the region were either expelled or deported. For the first time, the Third Army was encountering sullen hostility among the supposedly French populace. Espionage and sabotage increased. Most of the 337 flagrant cases of such shenanigans the Third Army encountered in its campaigns occurred here, and the majority of the 42 enemy spies apprehended by its intelligence troops were caught in Lorraine.

But the drive had its compensations. From the moment he plunged beyond the Marne, Patton was racing toward one of the world's classical battlegrounds. The objectives of his drive had famous historic names—Nancy . . . Verdun . . . Etain Douaumont . . . St. Mihiel . . . Metz. Where millions fought and hundreds of thousands of them fell in past contests, now no hostile forces seemed to be waiting to impede his progress. Sure enough, Verdun was taken without a fight. Commercy was picked up "like a ripe plum."

For Patton personally all this had the sentimental impact of a class reunion a quarter-century after graduation. While his men were overrunning one familiar place after another, he ceased to be the triumphant general of a conquering army. He became a humble pilgrim, visiting the spots tagged in his memory—a roundhouse at Conflans that withstood the bombings of two World Wars; a manure pile in Langres with, believe it or not, the same man squatting on it now as 26 years before; his old billet in Madame de Vaux's chateau in Bourg; the *salle-à-manager* of the Hôtel de France in Chaumont, and Pershing's old headquarters in the city, with the tiny office by the gate of the barracks which was the "seat of my first considerable command"—that of the Headquarters troops—in 1917.

In the meantime, the campaign was rolling on, so smoothly that it hardly needed Patton's supervision and exhortation. His spearheads were at the Moselle. Nancy was within his grasp, as was Pont-à-Mousson. And Walker's XX Corps was on the Etain road, encountering virtually no resistance as it moved toward Metz.

Even though Nancy was the key to his projected thrust beyond the Moselle, Metz intrigued him more. A very old and beautiful city whose 65,000 frightened inhabitants now tried to adjust again to yet another big battle in their back yards, it had the kind of bloody history and military reputation that fascinated Patton.

Of pre-Roman origin, Metz came into its own in the 12th century as an autonomous imperial city and powerful episcopal see. It saw various armies come and go until, thanks indirectly to Napoleon I, it became a *focus* of war. In 1814, apprehensive that they might have to deal again with the deposed Emperor, the Allies earmarked it as their point of entry into France from the Saar. And in 1870 it became the pivot on which Achille François Bazaine, the nefarious Marshal of France "whose incompetence was rivaled only by that of Napoleon III," based his defenses in the war with Prussia. Some 300,000 troops clashed here in a bizarre battle that ended with the capitulation of Metz and the surrender of its 180,000 defenders after a two-month siege.

Nancy has never been fortified in modern times, but Metz was turned into what military men call an "impregnable" fortress. A network of two dozen forts was built, 22 of them in two tiers around Metz and in a line between the city and Thionville—the so-called Metz-Thionville *Stellung*—with two more farther north at Illange and Königsmacker. They ranged from strong-points to major installations, formidable *groupes fortifiés* like the Jeanne d'Arc and the Driant works on the outskirts of Metz.

Originally intended for the defense of France, they fell into German hands in 1870 and were retained until 1918, when they reverted to France and became a peripheral part of the Maginot Line. In 1940 the Germans regained the forts and kept them, until this summer of 1944, in a state of more or less adequate repair.

Haphazard and incomplete as Allied planning had been for the campaign beyond the Seine, the Metz system did not figure prominently in the calculations of SHAEF. In the light of the ease with which France was being cleared, it was not expected to represent any real threat. Then just when it seemed that Metz, like Verdun, would fall without a fight, things took an unexpected turn. During the next two and a half months the city came to epitomize the difficulties and hardships the Third Army had to endure as its big parade turned into a desperate slugging match.

Strangely enough, General Patton had anticipated some complications here long before he knew that the conquest of Metz would be assigned to him. On March 9, 1944, on his grand tour of the units of his budding Third Army in England, he visited Chisledon to inspect elements of General Walker's XX Corps.

Forty-five year old Walton Harris Walker was known to Patton most favorably from St. Mihiel, where the squat little West Pointer, Class of 1912, commanded a machine-gun battalion with exceptional gallantry. In 1941 he joined the Armored Force, in which he gained a reputation as a hard-driving, tough trainer of men.

Probably to compensate for the nonmilitary bulk of his frame, Walker was a hell-raising daredevil, a martinet who strutted about always immaculately groomed, with a perennial frown on his amply upholstered face, his broad chest thrust out over a formidable midriff, never shirking a scrap. Patton regarded him with a mixture of admiration and amusement. Everything Walker did was an imitation of Patton's ways. He was huffing and puffing constantly to keep up with his mercurial idol.

Patton spent the evening of March 9th talking shop at Chisledon. Sitting around the dinner table with Walker, General Oliver of the 5th Armored Division and Colonel Eugene Regnier, who had one of its combat commands, he turned the conversation to the West Wall and the task of breaching it. A scheme of attack was evolved then and there for a drive to the Rhine via Metz. They knew very little of the nature of its fortifications but assumed that they would need some special attention. It struck them as potentially dangerous to bypass such a strong-point while thrusting some 150 miles ahead in an impetuous and chancy drive.

Metz became a hot topic again on August 26th. On that day Patton flew to see Walker at his CP near Fontainebleau and told him that he had permission from Bradley to "go it alone" in the direction of the line Metz-Strasbourg, even to break into Germany through the West Wall. He explained his plan for two corps to drive abreast, the XII making for Nancy and the "Gap," while Walker's XX would be going via Metz.

At this stage Metz was still 170 miles away, a forbidding distance under normal circumstances, but nothing was "normal" in this campaign. So Patton told Walker to start thinking of Metz and how he would deal with it. All this sounded brash and premature, especially since Walker was experiencing some difficulty with his advance. The 2nd

Infantry Regiment of his 5th Division had come up against unexpectedly strong resistance at Melun on the Seine, necessitating Walker's personal intervention to secure a bridgehead. But after that the corps started to roll. By the 27th, the day after Patton's visit, it took Nogent-sur-Seine and turned north for the big push to the east on the Reims-Verdun-Metz-Saarbrücken road.

On August 28th Walker closed in on Reims and took the city the next day. He sped on to Verdun and established a bridgehead across the Meuse on the 31st, completing a 175-mile power-drive in just five days, against scattered resistance. Even as the corps was advancing, it was feeling the pinch of a growing gasoline shortage. Then on the 31st it ran dry—when it was only 35 miles from the Moselle at Metz, and but 50 miles from the West Wall.

For the next five days XX Corps was immobilized! It was a heartbreaking, ignoble anticlimax to its career in this campaign. On its north flank, the 90th Infantry Division was squatting at Reims "with hardly enough gasoline left to keep the field ranges on the kitchen trucks burning." The 7th Armored and 5th Infantry Divisions could make the last few miles to the Meuse only by siphoning fuel from supply and transport vehicles. The crossing at Verdun was the last step in the rapid 400-mile advance XX Corps had made since August 6th. Of the 17 tanks in the task force sent to Verdun, only 3 made it. The others ran out of gasoline on the way. While waiting for fuel, Walker rationed the few hundred gallons of gasoline he had, and sent his cavalry on sporadic scouting missions to the north and east.

The reconnaissance forays of a few cavalry platoons in a handful of armored cars and jeeps broke Patton's heart because they clearly indicated what he could have accomplished had not the "iron grip of logistics" (the official euphemism for the stifling gasoline shortage) stopped the Third Army dead in its tracks. On September 1st, for example, a platoon of the 3rd Cavalry Group, consisting of three armored cars and six jeeps, took possession of Thionville, the great northern anchor of the fortified *Stellung*, and held it for several hours, shooting up the place at will. It was a futile and frustrating enterprise, for no major forces of XX Corps could follow to make the conquest stick. The city fell two months later, after heavy and costly fighting.

On September 2nd a platoon from the 43rd Cavalry

Reconnaissance Squadron made it to Haute Kontz, north of Thionville, established an observation post on a 430-foot hill over the Moselle and radioed back to Walker's CP: "No enemy visible on either side of the river. Many good places for bridges, all undefended." But by the next morning the whole squadron became idle because it did not have a drop of gasoline left to operate either its vehicles or its motor-driven radios. However, even those sporadic raids served a useful purpose. They misled the enemy into believing that XX Corps was regrouping for a drive to the northeast. It was simply inconceivable to the German High Command that an American force would halt for lack of gasoline.

During these days of enforced inactivity, while Patton fumed helplessly, General Walker busied himself with drawing up plans for the drive to the Rhine, with Metz as his next objective. It was imperative to take the fortress as soon as incoming supplies enabled the corps to move. It had to be captured before the Germans could garrison it because everything in and around Metz favored the defenders and would enable even a substantially inferior force to compel a siege. However, Walker now found out that we were blissfully ignorant of the system of fortifications. Neither Colonel Koch nor his own G-2 had any hard intelligence about the type or strength of the various forts, and little reliable information even about their exact locations. Excellently camouflaged and hidden behind and beneath natural growth of sod and bushes, the works remained concealed from aerial reconnaissance. And Walker did not have enough gasoline to send in patrols to reconnoiter them on the ground.

During those days, as Colonel Cole eloquently described it, there was little XX Corps could do but "commit ambitious future plans to paper, wait, make a sterile record of the optimistic and pleading messages radioed in by the cavalry, put out daily periodic reports with the dour phrase, 'no change,' engage in gunnery practice when German planes came over at night in fruitless attempts to destroy the Verdun bridges, and hope that gasoline would soon arrive." Even the infantry became immobilized, for no artillery, bridging equipment, rations, or ammunition could be moved to support them.

Five fateful days! It is possible that they added hundreds of days to the war in Europe!

On September 3rd some gasoline started to trickle in,

and a modest flow opened up the next day. Enough fuel became available for the cavalry groups to broaden their reconnaissance before the main forces could start moving. But it became immediately apparent that things had changed in the meantime. When, on August 31st, the corps came to a standstill, FFI informants reported that there were no substantial German forces anywhere in the path of the advance, and the few units remaining in scattered small pockets in the area consisted of the pitiful remnants of burned-out regiments. They also told the Corps G-2 that several bridges south of Metz were still standing.

But when on September 4th a cavalry reconnaissance patrol reached the bridge at Pont-à-Mousson, it found that it had been blown up. There were other such ominous signs everywhere to indicate the sudden presence of the enemy in force. Several attempts to enter Arnaville were beaten back by a phantom unit now holding a place where no enemy forces could be seen even two days before. Five cavalry task forces probing toward Metz encountered strong resistance at every turn.

At Gravelotte (a key point in the Metz defenses where Marshal Bazaine made his last stand 74 years before) the Germans made their presence felt in an especially humiliating manner. They ambushed and captured Colonel F.W. Drury, commander of the rampaging 3rd Cavalry Group, in what to the Germans must have seemed poetic justice. It was Drury's fortuitous capture of 4,000 gallons of gasoline on August 31st that made the raids possible at all.

It was now obvious that the situation had undergone a radical change while XX Corps had been idle. Just how abrupt it really was became evident by the experience of 2nd Lieutenant R.C. Downs, whose platoon had made Haute Kontz on September 2nd and reported that no Germans were in evidence. But when Downs returned to the same observation post on September 5th, he found the east bank of the river occupied by enemy troops pouring in from all directions. And the same FFI agents whose report was generally negative less than a week before, now reported that substantial German forces with heavy equipment had been observed entering Metz itself.

What happened?

On August 24th, shaken by the rapid advance of the Allies toward the German border, Hitler issued *Directive No. 772965/44 gK Chef.* over his own signature, ordering the immediate establishment of the *Weststellung* all along the Moselle, from Trier to Epinal. He thus created a continuous 180-mile front where none existed before. He designated the Metz-Thionville area (to a depth of 25 miles to St. Avold) a fortified combat zone, and directed that it be manned forthwith and held at all cost. It was the very line toward which Walker was moving.

Hitler's order was executed with superb dispatch and efficiency, showing that the enemy was still capable of defending himself. By September 3rd the area was swarming with Germans. Where Walker would have found a virtual vacuum had his advance continued unabated there now stood elements of two corps.

Directly to the south and straddling the boundary of XX U.S. Corps stood XLVII Panzer Corps, commanded by General Heinrich Freiherr von Lüttwitz, a bemonocled Junker version of Patton. A former cavalry officer and an outstanding horseman, Lüttwitz was a pioneer in the mechanization of the German Army. He was, like Patton, notorious for his mannerisms and impetuosity, and famed for his personal bravery. He was no stranger to Patton. Lüttwitz had commanded the 2nd Panzer Division in the Falaise pocket, where Patton rated it "the best Goddamn armored division the Huns have in the West." When now his G-2 located XLVII Panzer Corps in the area and identified Lüttwitz as its commander, Patton gave orders to "bring him back alive" and produce him at once in his headquarters because, he said, "I'd like to ask the bastard a few pointed questions." He rejoiced in the presence of a dashing cavalryman-tanker on the other side of the fence and regarded Lüttwitz as an *Ersatz für Rommel*, whose absence from his front Patton keenly regretted.

While it was a mere shell only a fortnight before, the reinforcements pouring in from Trier and Saarbrücken made the First Army the strongest of all German armies in the West. To complete the revitalization, Hitler fired the placid General von Chevallerie and replaced him with Otto von Knobelsdorff, a Panzer general who sported a dainty Führer mustache. On September 5th, when Walker was ready to move again, Knobelsdorff had almost five divisions on the 15-mile Metz-Thionville line, with an organized front to meet the resumption of the American advance.

Even more important, Metz had been placed in Condition Red, the city regarrisoned and the forts manned with impromptu units, the 559th Volksgrenadier (VG) Division and one going by the odd-name of Division Number 462. The "462" was a makeshift division commanded by Lieutenant General Walther Krause with the faculty of the various service schools at Metz, its rank and file consisting of outstanding student troops picked for officer and NCO training. Although it never had more than 4,000 officers and men, the division performed with exceptional gallantry and effectiveness during the battle of Metz.

The garrison of Fortress Metz also included two replacement battalions, one machine-gun company, one engineer battalion, a couple of antiaircraft battalions, one artillery battalion, four companies of the *Waffen-SS* Signal School, and a handful of *Luftwaffe* troops, all of them stamped out of the ground in but two weeks to deny the fortress to the Americans.

CHAPTER THIRTY-FIVE
METZ AND MUD

Patton was full of pep and hope. His batteries recharged, he exuded unbounded enthusiasm and optimism. "Be prepared to continue to Mannheim and the Rhine," he told General Eddy, adding, "and don't worry about your flanks!" To Walker he said, "See you in Metz."

Walker jumped off at 3 A.M. on September 6th toward the Moselle. His attacks at Metz continued fruitlessly until he told Patton on September 16th that he did not think he could take the city. This was also the day when Bradley confided to Patton that Field Marshal Montgomery was working on General Eisenhower to stop "all the American troops . . . so that he, Monty, could make a 'dagger-thrust with the 21st Army Group at the heart of Germany.' " It was no time to slow down anywhere and, by slackening his efforts, give Monty what he wanted. Quite the contrary, Bradley's call induced Patton to become so involved in operations that higher headquarters could not stop him.

Patton was as eager as Walker to dispose of Metz, but this was no mere threat to pep up Walker. Just then it seemed that XII Corps, which had taken Nancy, would achieve the breakthrough, rush the West Wall and break into Germany. Walker obviously did not cherish the prospect of twiddling his thumbs at Metz while Eddy was running for the touchdown. He immediately sat down to draft a plan that he, considering the circumstances, grandiosely named "Operation Thunderbolt." He designed it as a combined air and ground attack to the bitter end. But the weather turned bad, grounding the planes. Then another shortage developed—ammunition became woefully scarce. The combination of the two unforeseen crises forced Walker to abandon "Thunderbolt" even before it began.

The first phase of "Thunderbolt" called for the seizure of Fort Driant, the biggest of the forts around Metz, guarding the southwestern ingress to the city. The major obstacle to the capture of Fortress Metz, Driant possessed considerable appeal for Patton and his commanders in XX Corps. Especially attracted was Colonel Charles W. Yuill, commander of the 11th Regiment, which had been so badly hit in its precarious Dornot bridgehead. A romantic hero type with something of Patton's dash (although he was a mere foot soldier), Yuill was not bowed by his sobering experience at the ill-fated bridgehead. If anything, he was raring to avenge that setback. He thought that the capture of Driant by his regiment would more than repair its reputation. He hit upon the old-fashioned idea of taking the big fort by storm, in an operation reminiscent of the costly actions of World War I in this same area. He set out to develop a plan of his own, hoping to sell it to General Irwin, his division commander, to General Walker, and maybe to Patton himself.

By zeroing in on Driant, Colonel Yuill picked the hardest nut to crack. It was not only the most elaborate installation in the entire system, but also the one the Germans had kept in best repair. They built it in 1902 (it was named Driant by the French in 1918 after a famed lieutenant colonel of Chasseurs who fell at Verdun) and maintained it even after the other forts had been stripped to provide guns and steel for the Atlantic Wall.

The Driant group of forts stood on a tall hill, fading unobtrusively into the landscape, fringed by trees, enclosed by dense barbed wire, bisected by moats and ringed by concrete machine-gun emplacements and armored observation posts. It consisted of the *enceinte,* the central fort, surrounded by a water ditch, and five batteries, four inside the fort proper (with six 100-mm. and six 150-mm. guns) and one, the so-called Moselle Battery of three 100-mm. guns, just outside the enclosure. Inside the enclosure were three huge concrete blockhouses and as many big bunkers. Permanent infantry trenches zigzagged through the fort, and thousands of feet of communications tunnels ran underground, with one branch leading to the Moselle Battery and another to Ars-sur-Moselle, a few hundred yards to the east. From three observation posts along the southern end the defenders enjoyed a superb view of the Moselle valley and of the crossing sites of General Irwin's hard-pressed 5th Division.

With but perfunctory intelligence at his disposal, Yuill went ahead with his planning, and devised a scheme of attack. Preliminary saturation bombing with 1,000-pound aerial bombs and napalm would be followed by high-explosive bombs and strafing of the interior. The frontal attack was to be mounted by two infantry companies and a tank-destroyer company.

Colonel Yuill took his plan to Brigadier General A.D. Warnock, the Assistant Division Commander, with whose help he then "sold" it to General Irwin and also to General Walker, who quickly became Yuill's most ardent supporter in the enterprise. Walker gave Yuill permission to storm the fort with one battalion, as a kind of dress rehearsal to test the strength of Driant's defenses and the practicability of his plan.

The assault jumped off at 2:15 P.M. on September 27th. It lasted until 6:30 P.M., when Yuill withdrew his little force. At the price of only 18 casualties in the two infantry companies (the tank destroyers never managed to get into the scrap), the operation produced what Yuill thought were valuable lessons in fortress warfare, something for which no units in the Third Army had received any training. However, the lessons were all negative. The preliminary bombardment, bombing and strafing brought only negligible results. Hardly denting the installations, they actually raised the morale of the defenders because they received positive proof that the concrete works of Driant gave them plenty of protection. Maneuver on the ground was seriously impeded by the thick wire entanglements and by fire from pillboxes, whose location was unknown to the attackers when the operation began.

The assault never succeeded in penetrating the interior of the fort. The closest Yuill got to the *enceinte* was about 300 yards from its moat, where his men were halted by small-arms fire. But nothing could dampen his enthusiasm, which was now fully shared by General Walker.

The morning after the four-hour assault they carried the plan to Patton and petitioned him for permission to mount a full-scale attack as the opening phase of operations against Metz itself. General Irwin was a West Point graduate in the Class of 1915 who had so impressed Patton as the 9th Division's artillery commander in Tunisia that he made him commander of the 5th Division in England and had no reason to regret it. But now Irwin irritated his mentor by presenting reservations to the Walker-Yuill plan. He pointed out that the test-assault had proved only that Driant was more intricate and powerful than expected, and that the operation, brief and limited as it was, had exposed a number of difficulties. But Walker dismissed Irwin's objections. He criticized Yuill and his officers for not having shown greater aggressiveness in the assault and assured Patton that more determined leadership in a reprise would succeed in reducing the fort.

General Irwin was on the spot. He could not very well go against his Corps Commander. On the other hand, he was convinced that Walker was unduly optimistic and that the venture should be abandoned. With the exemplary courage of his convictions, he told Patton bluntly, "My men need rest, sir, and special training in this kind of operation. I think the fort ought to be taken by encirclement, but then, we have no maneuver troops for that either."

General Irwin received powerful support from two of Patton's own advisers—General Gay, his Deputy Chief of Staff, who was instrumental in developing Third Army tactics, and Colonel Maddox, his G-3. They had made an extensive personal reconnaissance of Driant on September 26th, then watched the first assault the next day. Contrary to Walker's critique, Gay and Maddox found leadership of the officers good and morale of the men high throughout the attack. But they considered Driant virtually impregnable. They told Patton in almost as many words that it was sheer madness to mount a frontal attack because, Gay said, in his and Maddox's opinion neither Driant nor Metz could be taken by storm. Their own solution coincided with General Irwin's proposal—a double envelopment of Metz with five divisions, three infantry and two armored. They warned that anything less would not be sufficient to reduce Driant.

Patton's own reference to this critical operation is confined to a single paragraph and two brief follow-up comments in *War As I Knew It*. "For about 10 days," he wrote, "we had been contemplating trying out the defensive qualities of the German forts covering Metz west of the Moselle. The 5th Division believed that Driant, one of these forts, could be taken with a battalion. On the 3rd of October, they put their plan into execution and had considerable initial success. However, after about seven days of it we decided to quit, as the operation was too costly."

What really happened was quite different. Patton himself had been bitten by the bug of Walker's all-out enthusiasm for the project. He dismissed Irwin's reservations, Gay's objections, Maddox's warnings. On September 28th, after listening to Yuill's explanation of the assault plan, he gave tentative approval for the systematic reduction of Fort Driant, with a single proviso. General Eisenhower was expected the next day at Etain, where Third Army now had its headquarters. He wanted to discuss the operation with Ike, Patton said, to find out what the Supreme Commander thought of it.

On September 29th General Eisenhower was shown the plans of the operation, presented to him as a local maneuver, and he approved them. It goes without saying that Eisenhower's approval promptly silenced whatever objections to the venture still remained.

Final orders to reduce Fort Driant were then issued, with instructions to the 5th Division to start simultaneous preparations for subsequent attacks on the other forts of Metz as well, including the "Verdun," the big fortified group east of the Moselle.

The attack jumped off on October 3rd under the most adverse conditions. Scheduled to start in the morning, it had to be postponed several times because the air support failed to show up. The weather was so bad that the preliminary aerial bombardment had to be canceled. The men went in at high noon behind a brief and feeble artillery barrage that did not do them any good but thoroughly alerted the defenders.

Company B of the 11th Regiment made it into the fort nevertheless, but the fighting remained inconclusive. Everything seemed to favor the defenders. By nightfall it was obvious that the first attack had failed. The Germans kept coming up from their tunnels, filtered into the rear of the attackers, badly shot up the platoons, and forced them to withdraw. Even worse, small groups of Germans mounted forays into the American positions all through the ensuing night. When dawn broke, those Americans who were still in the fort were badly disorganized.

If Irwin hoped to call off the operation, Walker was determined more than ever to go on with it. He told Irwin to "hang on and extend his hold on top of the fort area," and the division commander relayed the order to Yuill. Then Patton intervened with a blistering order of his own. He instructed Walker to "take Driant even if it took every man in the XX Corps." And he added ominously, "I cannot allow an attack by this army to fail!"

But fail it did. By October 9th the situation was confused beyond belief. Now convinced that he had made a mistake when he approved the operation, Patton sent General Gay to XX Corps to extricate the 5th Division from its predicament. General Warnock, whose initial enthusiasm for the Yuill idea had waned when he had to intervene and take personal command of the task force, frankly told Gay, "As far as I can see it, the jig is up." He explained:

"Further attacks within the fort would be far too costly. In my opinion, Driant must be surrounded, the enemy all driven underground and destroyed there. We need four more battalions for this."

His recommendation was rejected out of hand, and General Gay, using the authority Patton had conveyed to him, ordered that the operation be abandoned and the fort evacuated without delay.

But General Walker asked Gay to let him mount a last attack through the tunnel. Skeptical as he was, Gay went along with the Corps Commander, but it was of no use. Walker's last desperate assault failed. The American forces then withdrew from Driant during the night of October 12-13th, a few hours short of 10 days after the misbegotten operation had begun.

General Patton was badly shaken by this reverse, one of only two operations he later described as errors on his part.

He was especially disturbed by the pressing need to break off the venture because, by an unfortunate coincidence, he was suffering this setback just when General Marshall was due at the Third Army front. He had hoped to welcome the Chief of Staff with the glittering gift of the captured fort.

On the morning of October 11th General Bradley arrived at Lucky Forward to find out what was going on at Driant. Patton called in Walker to explain the situation. Walker now had his second thoughts and recommended to Bradley and Patton that they pull out of the attack "as the glory of taking the fort was not worth the sacrifice in men which it demanded." Bradley eagerly concurred, and Patton gave the order. What made this reversal especially depressing was the realization that he should never have allowed himself to be persuaded to sanction the operation.

Several factors were responsible for this and other setbacks on the Third Army's front. The American troops were not used to the intricate fighting the German newcomers in this sector imposed upon them. The Germans at this front were fresh, their morale amazingly high, jacked up by Hitler's apparent self-confidence conveyed to them by the Goebbels propaganda machine. By contrast, Patton's troops were completely exhausted at this tail end of their 400-mile advance.

Patton himself was probably the most exhausted of all. His fatigue was badly aggravated by the frustrations and annoyances, by the disappointments and reverses he had to endure. For the first time in the campaign he decided to take off a day and rest.

He now dismissed Metz from his mind. The Germans at the fortress were given a reprieve. The city, which had been within his grasp and would have fallen "like a ripe plum" had not his advance been halted, did not capitulate until November 25th, almost three months behind Patton's original schedule.

CHAPTER THIRTY-SIX
THE ROAD TO THE BULGE

Spasmodic though this war had become with its diverse and mounting complications, it was still grand history in the making, producing momentous events worthy of commemorative observances in later years. But General Patton, in his innate impatience, was not content to wait for posterity to celebrate these significant occasions on their anniversaries. On December 8, 1944, he paused momentarily to take stock —to commemorate such an "anniversary" which, however, was measured in mere weeks rather than years in the rapid flow of developments.

It was exactly one month before that he had embarked upon the so-called Saar campaign and begun the intricate maneuver that led him into Metz, the first conquest of that vaunted fortress in what he estimated was 1,301 years. During this month of relentless fighting, aggravated by unseasonably rude weather, he had liberated some 1,600 square miles of alien soil containing 873 towns; he had taken more than 30,000 prisoners and had killed and wounded about 88,000 Germans.

Whenever Patton had adequate supplies to feed and sustain his operations, his thrusts were irresistible, highly lucrative and relatively cheap. His own battle casualties during this month totaled considerably less than one-third of the enemy's—23,000 Americans killed, wounded and missing. Though his army was now under strength by some 11,000 men, due mainly to noncombat casualties caused mostly by the weather, he was ready to continue his march from the precarious bridgeheads at Dillingen and Saarlautern, still fighting from river to river, from pillbox to pillbox, even from house to house.

This December 8th dawned auspiciously. The 2nd Infantry Regiment of the 5th Division, which had fought and bled so valiantly while assaulting its coveted objective, had received the surrender of Fort Driant at last. In XII Corps area, the 35th Division was attacking across the Saar, its 134th Infantry crossing the river by bridge south of Sarreguemines, the 320th by assault boats to the east. The 134th cleared Sarreinsming and pushed on northeast under heavy German fire. Meanwhile, the 328th Infantry of the 26th Division mounted an assault on two forts of the Maginot Line within its sector, while the 104th Infantry, fighting to the right, took four mutually supporting forts in the Aachen area.

Patton was eagerly looking forward to the pending operations. He expected to make it to the Rhine this time— more than three months behind his original schedule, but better late than never.

He was confident, too, that he would get through the German-held portions of the Maginot Line without any undue difficulties, and crack the West Wall as well. His refusal to be awed by these fortifications may have impressed some of his listeners as sheer bravado. But his seeming flamboyance was fully justified on November 29th, for example, when he drove from Château-Salins to St. Avold across one of the supposedly strongest stretches of the Maginot Line. Elements of the 80th Division had just fought their way through this sector, yet they told Patton they had not even noticed that they were crossing a fortified zone.

This was not a new offensive in the strict sense. Rather it was the continuation of the campaign Patton had started on November 8th, after that wet and cold October he spent in Lorraine, stuck in the mud. Throughout that exasperating, futile month, Patton was fussing and fretting in the strait jacket into which he thought SHAEF had confined him. Looking back on his eight hectic and wonderful weeks in Eisenhower's "crusade," he could see much to fill him with enormous pride. Yet the situation his sweep had produced now impressed him as being far from satisfactory.

The "crusade" that promised to crush the Germans, and that at one point looked as if it would bring final victory within a critical fortnight, had developed into a stalemate that favored the enemy. As the Third Army after-action report put it, "When in September the shortage of gasoline forced Third U.S. Army to slow finally to halt its advance, the enemy took full advantage of the situation." Enabled to reinforce their line with hastily organized units of incompletely trained and upgraded green troops, the Germans entrenched to stabilize their front. Then they mounted one counterattack after another in a frantic effort to gain time and fortify a terrain that favored them anyway.

Even so, the enemy was unable to prevent the Third Army from forcing the line of the Moselle. The Americans pushed across the Meurthe River and established a number of bridgeheads across the Moselle, but their progress was slow and costly. Terrific battles had to be fought as the Third Army strove to breach the outer defenses of Metz, for example. But just when it seemed that Patton would regain his old momentum, his drive was halted again and he was ordered to hold his positions until a supply build-up would permit a resumption of the offensive. By this time an acute shortage of ammunition was added to that of gasoline.

A heartbreaking hiatus followed. The picture reminded one of an action movie in which all movements are suddenly frozen by stoppage of the projector. On Bradley's long front—extending from Aachen in the north to Bayon in the south, a 160-mile stretch tantalizingly close to the German border—nearly all operations had come to a halt. On October 13th the First Army was fighting house to house inside Aachen. But efforts to close the Aachen gap petered out when frontal assaults yielded only 1,000 yards in the face of sharp-edged German counterattacks, forcing the embattled veteran 1st Division to suspend the offensive. The Ninth Army was still assembling. And the Third Army had to abandon plans to take Maizières-lès-Metz, or do anything truly constructive, when the ammunition shortage compelled Patton to freeze all artillery ammunition larger than 3-inch shells.

The Third Army was not exactly idle even during this enforced halt. It improved its scattered bridgeheads over the Moselle in order to secure the best possible jumping-off positions for later operations. It patrolled aggressively, frequently on a substantial scale. It was building up supplies of gasoline, ammunition and winter clothing. And probably most important, it was drafting plans for the resumption of the offensive.

On October 17th General Gaffey presented a detailed outline of the plan in a staff conference presided over by Patton and attended by Gay, Harkins, Maddox, Muller and

Koch. It was virtually the first such formal planning session at Patton's headquarters, indicating in itself how things had changed. The happy period of inspired improvisations and quick seizure of opportunities was over. Now Patton was spending more time with Gaffey and Gay, and the rest of his special staff, planning minutely each portion of his maneuvers. Recalling those days, he wrote: "It will be noted that both the plans for the operation for the capture of Metz and the Saar campaign were worked out with much greater detail than our operations while going across France." The reason for this was evident. "Touring France," he continued, "was a catch-as-catch-can performance where we had to keep going to maintain our initial advantage. In this operation we had to start moving from an initial disadvantage."

Gaffey's plan provided for an attack by XII Corps with three infantry divisions to secure a bridgehead over the Seille. This accomplished, the 4th and 6th Armored Divisions would move through the infantry, the 6th Armored securing the high ground east of Metz while the 4th Armored would go straight through, crossing the Saar north of Sarreguemines and, with God's help, as Patton put it, roll on to the Rhine.

The ingenious plan called for the infantry action to begin two or three days before the actual D-Day of the offensive. On D-Day, XX Corps was to cross north of Thionville to join XII Corps, with the 10th Armored turning north. It was to force another crossing of the river at Saarburg, to be followed by the 90th Division. After that, the 10th Armored would join the 4th Armored on its march to the Rhine in the direction of Mainz. By this maneuver Patton expected to have two armored divisions moving rapidly toward the river, the 6th Armored rolling through the West Wall.

On October 19th Patton wrote a personal letter to General Bradley to acquaint the Army Group Commander with his plans for the earliest possible resumption of the offensive. He assured Bradley that the German forces in front of him were all the enemy had to oppose the Third Army and repeated what he had already said in August, under different circumstances—that "once these forces were destroyed or captured the Third Army stood a good chance of penetrating the West Wall and driving rapidly to the Rhine." Patton was at his cautious best when taking Bradley into his confidence. He explained that such an operation would represent no departure from "the secondary role" assigned to Third Army. Rather it would be so timed to precede or follow an offensive by any of Bradley's other armies and would be designed solely to "disjoin the German scheme of defense." However, Patton told Bradley that given what he needed and permission to proceed, he could make it to the West Wall "in not to exceed D plus 2 days."

On the 22nd, Bradley and his Chief of Staff, General Allen, visited Patton at Nancy to review the situation, and Patton asked permission to resume the offensive *at once* with Gaffey's plan. He conceded that an acute ammunition shortage was preventing the 12th Army Group from mounting an all-out attack with its three armies. But he argued that a shrewd pooling of the Army Group's ammunition resources would enable the Third Army to jump off *within 48 hours,* with excellent prospects of success.

Bradley remained conservative. "I'd rather wait," he countered, "until we all can jump off together."

He pleaded all he could. But when he had exhausted his power of persuasion, all he had managed to coax from Bradley was permission to resume the offensive "on or after November 5th," a fortnight hence at best.

Behind Bradley's caution was something Patton did not know. On October 18th, even as Patton's plans were being typed, General Eisenhower met with his "chief subordinates" to draw up a detailed directive including tentative dates for his armies to resume the attack. Everybody was given a "probable date"—the top-priority mission again going to Montgomery—except Patton. Although the others were to commence their offensives between November 1st and 10th, no date was set for the Third Army. Referring to its future in rather nebulous terms, Eisenhower's directive stipulated merely that Third Army would resume its advance "when logistics permit," and would have but a limited mission even then—driving in a northeasterly direction covering the right flank of the First Army.

Under these circumstances, Bradley's consent had to be vague and conditional. But Patton interpreted it as firm and final. He had the plans ready, and now he plunged into preparing the offensive in his customary manner, with visits to his various units. Although morale was high throughout the Third Army "despite the mud, the rain, and the tedium of enforced inactivity," Patton thought it advisable to prepare his men for combat with his specially honed pep talks. A speech he delivered to the 95th Infantry Division, newly arrived on November 4th, summed up his basic theme. "It is 132 miles to the Rhine from here," he said, "and if this army will attack with venom and desperate energy, it is more than probable that the war will end before we get to the Rhine. Therefore, when we attack, go like hell!"

The passing of time was excruciatingly slow, but inevitably November 5th came. But the awful weather now forced the postponement of the attack for 72 hours, adding to Patton's agony. Even on November 7th it rained the entire day. It was one of those "long days" in his life when the clock seemed to have stopped. He spent the day quietly, reading the Bible and praying until 7 P.M., when Generals Eddy and Grow burst into his headquarters. They had come to plead with Patton to call off the attack because of the heavy rains and the swollen rivers.

"The attack will go on," Patton told them categorically, "rain or no rain. And I'm sure it will succeed."

When Eddy and Grow insisted that the jump-off be postponed, he told them gruffly, "I think you better recommend the men you would like appointed as your successors."

Patton put on his usual tough front—the frown and stance he invariably assumed on the eve of all his offensives —but deep within him he, too, had doubts. He was not as strong as he had hoped to be. The XV Corps had been taken away from him on September 29th. And though he was given III Corps in return on October 10th, it would not become operational until December 6th, a month after the new offensive. All Patton now had on the fighting line were Walker's XX and Eddy's XII Corps. The Third Army's combat strength was down to about 220,000 troops, with some 18,000 men bedded down with the flu, trench foot and the other ailments caused by the inclement weather.

On the other hand, Patton's persistent probing attacks had enabled him to establish a fairly strong line from which to jump off. Especially to the north of Metz, he was strong enough to cross the Moselle at will and at any point.

He went to bed in full uniform and slept fitfully until 3 A.M. on November 8th, when he awoke abruptly to see if the Lord had answered his prayers. It was raining harder than ever. Patton became jittery. He brought out Rommel's book, *Infantry Attacks,* and happened to open it at a page where Rommel described the heavy rains of September, 1914, in France and how the Germans had got along despite the weather. He read for half an hour, then returned to bed somewhat reassured, and fell asleep. He was awakened at 5:15 when his artillery opened up with the preparatory barrage. The sonorous staccato banging of the 400 guns sounded like the slamming of all the doors in a big empty house. This artillery fire would be all he would get to soften up the Germans. Patton had expected some 2,000 planes to give him air support, but when he looked out into the dismal dawn, he realized that no plane could fly in this abominable weather. Well, he thought, it will have to be done without air support. "His will be done!"

He stepped outside to watch the spectacle. The rain had stopped and a few brave stars were twinkling faintly in the firmament. But under this peaceful sky, the very ground on which he stood was trembling. The whole eastern sky was aglow with the flashes of the guns. "I thought how the enemy must have felt now that the attack he had dreaded so long had come at last," he later told Major Stiller.

While Patton was watching and thinking, the attack jumped off. By dawn, the 90th Division, to which he had assigned the main effort, had completed a secret move to the Cattenom Forest and attacked across the Moselle through the strongly fortified Königsmacker area and the Maginot Line. The 10th Armored Division was moving northward in the mud just behind the infantry spearhead. An engineer detachment was clearing the east bank of the river to enable the 337th Infantry to cross over in assault boats south of Uckange.

Now it was 6 o'clock. The XII Corps also began its drive straight toward the Saar, three regiments of the 80th Division abreast on the north flank leading the attack. By then the startled Germans were noisily in the game. Firing vigorously and accurately, they prevented a company of the 337th Infantry from bridging the river. Effective enemy fire then halted the 320th Infantry just before it could reach its first objective on the Morhange plateau.

But on the whole the offensive was off to a good start and it was rolling well—*without* air support.

At 8 A.M. a call came from General Bradley.

"What are your plans, Georgie?" he asked.

"I am attacking, Brad," Patton said smugly. "Can't you hear our guns?"

"What?!" Bradley sounded incredulous. "You're attacking without air support?!"

Patton had not told Bradley that he had decided to jump off irrespective of the weather and without air support for fear that he might call off the attack. But now Bradley sounded fine. "Splendid, Georgie," he enthused. "Hang on, Georgie, Ike is here and wants to speak to you."

"Georgie," Patton heard the familiar voice, now even more silky than usual, "this is Ike—your Supreme Commander, you know. I'm thrilled, boy! I expect a hell of a lot from you, so carry the ball all the way!"

"Thanks, General," Patton said, with a grin in his voice but with the stiff formality he always used when talking to the Supreme Commander on business. "We will, sir, we sure will!"

The rain had resumed, but it was a mere drizzle when Patton, Stiller and Codman set out to tour the front. So much smoke was being used at the crossing that little of the action could be seen. But at 10 A.M. the smoke lifted, the rain stopped, the sun broke through the clouds, and—as if by some miracle—the planes came after all "streaking like shining arrows," Codman wrote to his wife, "against a sky now interlaced with crisscross vapor contrails and the smoke spirals of our planes' markers."

Patton's eyes lit up like the star on a Christmas tree. "What do you say to that?" he asked Codman with a lump in his throat. "They came after all, and in this Goddamn weather! I'm almost sorry for those Kraut bastards!"

By late afternoon, General Eddy reported that virtually all his units had reached their objectives, and General Walker was sending in reassuring signals from XX Corps. Then the rain returned.

At supper, Patton was—for the first time in weeks—his old relaxed and talkative self. He spoke of Eddy's plea to postpone the attack and of his own unyielding determination to go on with it. "It takes a lot out of you to prepare such an attack," he said, "and Eddy had cold feet because he was tired. I've always maintained that there are more tired commanders than tired troops. But I knew he'd be all right once the show got on the road."

This was the Third Army's third campaign since August 1st.

The siege of Metz was carried forward with determination and dash by XX Corps. The XII Corps did as it was ordered—established bridgeheads across the Saar. It was not an easy job, for the rains had left the terrain muddy and the river at record flood level. Its bridging demanded prodigious labor and great gallantry on the part of the engineers.

Aided chiefly by the weather, the Germans managed to prevent the major breakthrough Patton had hoped for. But they withdrew slowly into their West Wall defense, abandoning the whole of the Maginot Line. Despite the fanatical resistance of green and ill-equipped enemy troops, Metz was taken by assault on November 18th (for the first time since 415 A.D.), while the belts of forts protecting it were reduced one by one. Fort St. Quentin surrendered on December 6th, Fort Plappeville on the 7th, the redoubtable Fort Driant on the 8th. The last of the great strongholds, the formidable Fort Jeanne d'Arc, fell on the 13th.

Despite the brilliant Gaffey-Gay plan (which, of course, reflected Patton's ideas) and the hot steam that Patton had personally breathed into the attack, he did not quite get what he wanted, certainly not on his sanguine schedule. "I had hoped to win this battle by the 11th [of November]," he wrote, "as it was my birthday and my lucky day in North Africa. However, I did not win it."

But he had reached positions all along his front from which he *could* drive into the West Wall and maybe points beyond, provided SHAEF let him.

For once, however, the Germans were not overly impressed with the famous Third Army and its vaunted commanding general. A new man was in charge, one of the few top generals left in the *Wehrmacht* who believed with Hitler that the Third Reich still had a chance in this war.

He had been hand-picked by Hitler for a special mission —to do to Patton exactly what Patton liked to do unto others: to hold him by the nose while kicking him in the pants. The kicking part had an "if possible" proviso attached to it and was not the crux of the matter. The important element in this crucial mission was to *hold* Patton and pin him down while Hitler was preparing to give the Allies the surprise of their lives.

The new broom in the west was General of Panzer Troops Hermann Balck, a deceptively friendly-faced, blond and blue-eyed soldier. He looked smooth and soft like a poet but was a rough and tough martinet and a dedicated mercenary of Hitler.

When all his generals in the west had turned out to be flops, Hitler reached out to the East Front to find replacements for them. This was why he picked Balck, commanding general of the Fourth Panzer Army on the Vistula, to take over from Colonel General Johannes Blaskowitz, "an officer of the old school, with all the staunch virtues associated with his native province of East Prussia." Blaskowitz had commanded Army Group G in the south of France and succeeded in extricating his forces in a brilliant maneuver when they were pounced upon by the Seventh U.S. Army coming in through the back door from the Mediterranean to join the duel for France. But Blaskowitz was through as far as Hitler was concerned. For one thing, he dared to talk back to the Führer, first during the Polish campaign and now in Alsace-Lorraine. For another, Hitler had made him personally responsible for not having defeated Patton by flinging him back on Reims. It was an absurd complaint, but that made no difference. Blaskowitz was out and Balck was in as the new commanding general of *Armeegruppe G*.

The full story of Balck's sudden transfer to the west is extremely important because it smoothes out one of history's stubborn wrinkles and places the origin of the Battle of the Bulge in the right perspective. The record of Balck's execution of his mission is significant because it shows the high price we really paid for the decision to stop Patton in his tracks again and again and to hold him down when he was able and raring to go.

The Battle of the Bulge is sometimes characterized as Hitler's final desperate gamble, the last straw at which he grabbed. Nothing could be further from the truth. The Ardennes offensive was a major and carefully conceived maneuver, not merely to avert the defeat of the Third Reich, but also to administer a decisive blow to the Allies. It was developed long in advance and prepared with exceptional care, respectable ingenuity and considerable investment in human and material resources.

Speaking of the evolution of the Ardennes offensive in the context of the war in the west, Professor Schramm aptly wrote in his commentary to the German High Command's war diary:

"Although one had to report thus far mainly the *defensive measures* in the course of which major defeats were suffered and substantial territory was lost by the Germans, the period between the end of September and the end of December can be viewed properly only when taking into consideration that it was used for the preparation of an offensive that, thanks to farseeing planning, painstaking preparation and careful concealment, could be unleashed on December 16th with total surprise and would abruptly and fundamentally change the entire situation on the whole West Front. The initiative held so firmly and so long by the Anglo-Americans had been regained by the German High Command."

Describing the pre-history of General Balck's assignment, Major General Friedrich Wilhelm von Mellenthien, his Chief of Staff both in the east and the west, wrote:

"The front of Fourth Panzer Army on the Vistula was now [in August] firmly held, but General Balck and I were not destined to remain long in a relatively quiet sector. The Normandy campaign had ended in the frightful disasters of Mortain and Falaise, Paris fell on August 25, and the spearheads of Patton's Third Army were already probing eastward toward the frontiers of the Reich. In September, General Balck received a summons to report at Hitler's headquarters; he was to be appointed to the command of Army Group G in the west, and I was to accompany him as Chief of Staff."

Closeted with Balck and von Mellenthien, Hitler confided what he regarded as one of his two greatest secrets in the war, second only to his decision in October, 1940, to attack the Soviet Union, then his ally. The Führer began with a review of the situation in the west, where, he said, "the Anglo-American advance was bound to come to a stop on a line running from the mouth of the Scheldt along the West Wall to Metz, and from there to the Vosges. Supply difficulties would force the enemy to halt." Hitler then declared that "he would take advantage of this pause to launch a counteroffensive in Belgium."

The date of this conference was September 18, 1944. Only two days before, Hitler had startled his top advisers with the announcement that he was determined "to inflict upon the Western Allies a crushing defeat that would influence in his favor the final outcome of the war." Measures to implement the decision even predated the announcement. Orders to constitute the Sixth Panzer Army, seen as the backbone of the attacking force in the Ardennes, had already been issued on September 6, 1944.

As Hitler saw it, he had little fear that Montgomery in

the north would break into the area where he planned to assemble and deploy his forces for the offensive. On the other hand, he was apprehensive that Patton might, in spite of his supply difficulties, overrun the area centering on Trier. He told Balck, "I am looking forward to November as a likely date for this operation." He then gave him the fateful mission in what von Mellenthien described as "formal orders."

"You are to hold Alsace-Lorraine in all circumstances," the Führer said. "You have to fight for time. On no account must you allow a situation to develop in which my forces earmarked for the Ardennes offensive would have to be sidetracked to Army Group C."

Balck plunged into his task with more ardor than efficiency and luck. He arrived at Molsheim in Alsace, where Army Group G had its headquarters, on September 20th, and took over from Blaskowitz the next morning. Hardly was he settled behind his new desk when he ordered his first spoiling attack. It was the battle for Château-Salins, a place Patton would have left far behind had he been able to continue his advance in August.

Looking at the map, Balck decided peremptorily that it was imperative to halt XII U.S. Corps and eliminate the American bridgeheads across the Moselle. He alerted his First Army under General Otto von Knobelsdorff to attack on its left flank and ordered his Fifth Panzer Army, ably commanded by the ascetic General Hasso von Manteuffel, to resume its assaults on the 4th U.S. Armored Division. So unexpected was such an ambitious German move at this time that General Wood had just ordered his tired men of the 4th Armored to take a day off and rest.

The Germans jumped off on the morning of September 22nd, their tanks protected by dense fog. But they did not get too far. Wood quickly got his armor into action, halted the attack west of Juvelize and inflicted such heavy losses on the enemy that the 111th Panzer Brigade was left with but 7 tanks and 80 men at the end of the day.

This was hardly an auspicious introduction of Balck to his new command. But he persisted and the battle continued (thanks chiefly to von Manteuffel's leadership) until September 29th, when Balck was forced to call it off. Realizing at last that his forces were far too inadequate for the venture, he went personally to *OB West*, demanding that Field Marshal von Rundstedt give him at least three more divisions to sustain the attack. But von Rundstedt had nothing to give. He needed everything he had, and more, to stem the First U.S. Army's concurrent attack toward Aachen.

Though his first enterprise had not come up to expectations, Balck was satisfied nevertheless. He had assumed that Patton was both determined and able to force his way through to the Saar and even to the Rhine (and, as von Mellenthien later remarked, Patton "might well have done so if he had been given a free hand"). The venture around Château-Salins was costly, but there were signs in the American camp that led Balck to believe that it had been worth the investment. In fact, on September 30th General Eddy, under the pressure of his staff, agreed to withdraw his XII Corps behind the Seille on the theory that "further German infiltration could not be halted."

The withdrawal was canceled by Patton, who was infuriated by Eddy's decision. His intervention was recorded in the journal of the 6th Armored Division, which noted (with what Cole called some discreet expurgation), "Gen. Patton emphatically stated that he would not give up another foot of ground to the Germans."

But Balck thought he had checked the Third Army and so reported to Hitler. He continued to do his best with the meager and miserable forces at his disposal, believing that it was his skill and leadership which were holding up Patton and preventing him from breaking into the zone where Hitler was assembling his forces for the Ardennes offensive. A conceited and cocky man, Balck refused to attribute his "success" to Patton's difficulties. In his ignorance of the facts he even developed some contempt for his American adversary.

"Never have I commanded such motley and badly equipped troops," he wrote to General Jodl at Hitler's headquarters in a personal letter on October 10th. "If we succeeded nevertheless in consolidating our lines, and could even afford to give up the 3rd Panzer Grenadier Division to the north, it was due mainly to *the bad and timid leadership of the Americans* . . . and to the unprecedented fight put up by my troops, including those ill-assorted hordes."

It was left to General von Mellenthien's postwar account of Balck's regime at Army Group G to correct the impression and give "credit" where it was due. "We now know," he wrote, "that Patton was compelled to halt by Eisenhower's orders of September 22. The Supreme Allied Commander had decided to accept Montgomery's proposal to make the main effort on the northern flank, clear the approaches to Antwerp, and try to capture the Ruhr before winter. Third U.S. Army received categorical orders to stand on the defensive." He went on to say:

"The rights and wrongs of this strategy do not concern me, but it certainly simplified the problems of Army Group G. We were given a few weeks' grace to rebuild our battered forces and get ready to meet the next onslaught."

On November 25th General Patton drove into Metz, his "steamboat trombone" turned on full blast to herald his coming, for a review of the city's conquering heroes, the dog-tired officers and men of General Irwin's workhorse 5th Division. It was a joyous spectacle with the typical Pattonesque ritual—the dispensing of medals and ribald pleasantries. But then, remembering the tough fight for Metz, Patton turned serious and told the men:

"Our success was primarily due to continued offensive . . . day and night . . . relentless and unceasing . . . and to the fact that we used maneuver. We held the enemy by the nose and kicked him in the pants . . .

"It is needless to point out to men like you the pre-eminent value of disciplined valor . . . You have demonstrated your courage and have, I am sure, realized the safety which results from courageous actions . . .

"In my dealings with you, I have been guilty on too many occasions, perhaps, of criticizing and of loud talking. I am sorry for this and wish to assure you that when I criticize and censure I am wholly impersonal . . . For every man I have criticized in this Army, I have probably stopped, talked to, and complimented a thousand . . . You know that I have never asked one of you to go where I feared to tread. I have been criticized for this, but there are many General Pattons and there is only one Third Army. I can be expended, but the Third Army must and will be victorious.

"I am very proud of you. Your country is proud of you. You are magnificent fighting men. Your deeds in the battle for Metz will fill the pages of history for a thousand years."

It was the usual patchwork speech made from notes Patton had prepared in North Africa and Sicily for the various occasions that called for speeches. Though he would refer to them with what sounded like smug condescension—"I let 'em have Form Number 7," for example—he always meant every word he said and invariably so worked himself into an emotional trance over these warmed over talks that he wound up with tears in his eyes.

But the triumph at Metz did not blind Patton to certain shortcomings that were becoming more and more evident in the conduct of the war.

As far as mere *tactics* were concerned, even his own army was growing somewhat stale and sluggish, despite the experience it was gaining in increasingly difficult fighting and the hellcat spirit he was constantly breathing into his men. While patting General Irwin on the back Patton also told him that his division was not getting any better—hell, he said, it wasn't even as good as it used to be. The same applied to the 10th Armored, whose drive in Saarburg he found too slow. But it was undergoing its baptism of fire and maybe couldn't do any better yet. At least its cocky self-confidence and the generally high morale of its men compensated for its apparently arrested development.

Patton realized, however, that his own woes were largely the result of strategic decisions made on the higher echelons where the conduct of the war had reached what to him seemed the far end of a mental *cul de sac.* He was now convinced that Clemenceau had something in his famous quip—at least up to a point. War *was* too serious a matter to be entrusted to *certain* generals. Patton had come to regard this particular war as far too intricate a venture to be left entirely to the tender care of SHAEF, ensconced as it was in soft comfort in and around Paris, hundreds of miles *behind* the fighting fronts.

The distance from the combat zone at which SHAEF had to operate naturally robbed it of much of the urgency and immediacy that seized front-line fighting troops. This, in turn, imbued the men whose job it was to plan the strategy of the war with the complacency and circumspection that are typical of any deskbound bureaucracy keeping regular hours. As Commander Butcher remarked during these exciting days at the front, Paris was as beautiful as ever, but it was "certainly *not* exciting."

Other strictly functional factors also tended to reduce SHAEF's efficiency as an instrument of supreme command in what, in August and September, was the fastest war of movement in history. Though it had moved from Granville to Versailles, it was still quarantined from the fronts by an embarrassing and exasperating inadequacy of its system of communications. Frantic efforts were being made to get the signal equipment General Eisenhower needed to convey his ideas and orders to his commanders and to ascertain from them as quickly as possible exactly what was happening in their various sectors.

The situation became so bad in October, 1944, that Sosthenes Behn, president of the International Telephone and Telegraph Company (serving as a colonel in the Signal Corps), was summoned to Paris to devise remedial measures. In the meantime, SHAEF remained pretty much in the dark as far as the day-by-day problems and needs of the Allied armies were concerned. Eisenhower himself usually found out about them only when he personally toured the combat zones, a change he liked immensely but could ill afford. It was on one of these inspection trips that he discovered that his armies were being slowed by still another cramping supply scourge, a shortage of artillery ammunition.

Patton's frustration was aggravated by these haphazard communications. They hampered him considerably and made him founder because, after all, he could not wage war entirely on his own, his umbilical cord to the mother organization completely severed. The situation led to uncertainties and recrimination, creating a charged atmosphere of antagonism in which malicious rumors flourished. The situation was certainly not conducive to the most efficient prosecution of the war, especially when Patton was staking success on speed in decisions and action, insisting like Lucan the Latin poet that "Delay is always fatal to those who are prepared."

On one of those rainy days in October, Commander Butcher showed up in Nancy on a delicate mission—to check on rumors that the Third Army was bitterly critical of SHAEF, accusing it of blatant discrimination and favoritism. The previous month, when the Third Army's activities were on and off as a result of what Patton thought were SHAEF's contradictory dispositions, Wes Gallagher of The Associated Press had returned to Paris from a tour of the fronts and confided to Butcher that "officers and personnel of Patton's Third Army [were] burned up because they [felt] the British have been favored by General Ike with transport and permitted to advance while the Americans in the Third Army were stalled because of lack of gasoline." Gallagher told Butcher that officers of Patton's army were saying freely that "Eisenhower is the best general the British have."

The situation appeared to be deteriorating so badly that Butcher thought a personal visit to Third Army Headquarters might do some good. Patton was fond of the Columbia Broadcasting System executive who had become Eisenhower's confidant, and since Butcher now arrived with a generous supply of cigars, he had added reason to roll out the red carpet. He invited Butcher to attend his regular morning briefing and introduced him to the staff as "Admiral Butcher," to the acute discomfort of the mere commander in the Naval Reserve.

After the session, Patton took Butcher to his office and showed him his plans on a map. Butcher then seized the opportunity to bring up those rumors about Third Army's dissatisfaction of Ike as the best *British* general. Patton protested vigorously. He was an intrepid swordmaster, of course, even in his human relations, but he knew when to use the blunt edge of his blade lest he cut into the soft tissue of sensitivities in circles whose hostility could redound to his disadvantage. He was always careful to mask his true feelings in his contacts with "sightseers" from SHAEF who could carry his critical views back to Eisenhower.

"He replied," Butcher recorded on his return to Paris, "that although some may naturally have felt bitter because the Third Army finally had been stopped, not so much by the enemy as by lack of gasoline, this did not represent the true feeling of himself or his Army."

This, of course, was the politic thing to say. But it did not reflect Patton's real feelings. He had come to discuss his misgivings with growing vehemence not only with his confidants at his command post, but also with such visiting VIP's as Generals Patch, Spaatz and Doolittle. They were his friends. And their own views usually echoed Patton's opinions.

His staff conferences, and even his evening meals at which he was surrounded by the chosen people of his staff, became seminars. Patton would review the course of the war in brilliant dissertations and frankly criticize its conduct by the higher-ups. His own experience since August 1st had fully confirmed his old dictum that wars were rarely, if ever, won by a cautious adherence to rigid plans.

Patton persisted in his belief that he had been stopped in his tracks by "a change of plan by the High Command, implemented [as he politely phrased it], in my opinion, by General Montgomery"—just when he was "certainly very full of hopes" and visualized himself "crossing the Rhine." Yet he attributed his troubles after the resumption of what became only a half-hearted offensive—half-hearted, that is, not on his part but as a result of the necessities imposed upon all armies by SHAEF's supply difficulties—to the great "Overlord" plan. Its basic deficiency had come home to roost; its failure to provide for operations beyond the Seine had forced Eisenhower into snap decisions and compromise solutions. This led to improvisations in which neither the Supreme Commander nor his closest associates in the field, Montgomery and Bradley, excelled. On the other hand, Patton was a past master of what could be called the *commedia dell'arte* type of warfare, for which only a general plan existed, the scheme of action being adapted to given conditions and changing circumstances.

There was enormous fluidity on the German side, but this was neither anticipated nor matched by our own Supreme Command. As a result, after the Seine the Allies had to wage the war on Hitler's terms. And Patton had to conduct his campaigns by actually stealing his marches and mounting his offensives, not in accordance with existing plans but frequently in defiance of them.

This war in Europe created a strangely paradoxical situation. It was not the enemy's interference that thwarted our original design. Rather it was our own unexpectedly brilliant showing against the vaunted Germans' woeful performance in France that disorganized whatever plans Eisenhower and SHAEF had drawn up to deal with them. The resulting confusion was compounded by the fact that SHAEF had only a vague, more or less incoherent—and certainly tentative—plan for this eventuality, where a firm and fixed design was needed.

Patton felt strongly—almost with physical pain—the absence of consistent direction from the top. He was like the brilliant concertmaster of a great orchestra, a virtuoso in his own right, trying to follow a conductor who did not quite know or failed to comprehend the delicate nuances of a score.

From time to time, in the intimacy of his personal entourage, he would say bluntly, "Our whole trouble is that we don't really have a Supreme Commander." This did not mean that he totally disapproved of Eisenhower and denied him recognition of any ability in his backbreaking job. He certainly did not go along with Ike's rude British critics who dismissed him with Field Marshal Brooke's contemptuous words, "Eisenhower is no real director of thought, plans, energy or action."

Even amid his often violent criticism Patton gave Eisenhower full credit for his skill in holding the strings of his coalition firmly in his hands and dexterously manipulating his commanders on them. Patton had no illusions about the psychological difficulties that confronted Eisenhower in his dealings with his prima donnas. It was a job somehow comparable to that of an opera director who has to arrange his repertory with one eye on artistic values and another on the vanities of his divas.

His objection to Eisenhower boiled down to what he regarded as his two major deficiencies. One was his failure to endow his "crusade" with a firm strategic orientation in the light of the war's strange and, indeed, unexpected evolution. The other was his apparent inability to provide for his commanders what S. L. A. Marshall called "grand tactics."

Eisenhower's tragedy was that he permitted himself to be pushed into what turned out to be a trap. He had succumbed to General George C. Marshall's suggestion that he take over the ground command in Europe and involve himself in the tactical conduct of the war, for which he was not actually suited. He took upon himself this enormous operational responsibility in addition to his strategic job, which alone was beginning to overtax his resources. Consequently, both strategy and tactics suffered, leading inevitably to a drifting beyond the Seine and eventually to the prolongation of the conflict.

Looking at the evolution of Ike's "crusade" from a historical perch, the grave difficulties from which it came to suffer coincided with Eisenhower's assumption of the ground command on September 1, 1944. Until then the tremendous campaign was moving in high gear. After that the momentum was stopped and the clutch was shifted into reverse. In Patton's own circle, Eisenhower's inexperience and apparent ineptness as a field commander were keenly felt and bluntly discussed.

General Eisenhower would certainly disagree with, and properly resent, the charge frequently raised in the Third Army that he had conducted the war from the Seine to V-E Day without a practicable master plan. Eisenhower was the war's busiest general. He had to deal with the politicians breathing down his neck; with his distant superiors especially General Marshall) whose views he had to respect, and with his high-strung, individualistic commanders in the field. It was far too diverse and taxing a job for any one man, and the fact that Ike mastered it as well as he did assures for him an enduring niche in what Disraeli called the most limited assembly of posterity.

The fact remains, however, that Eisenhower was by necessity much closer to SHAEF wherever it was than to his field commanders, whom he visited only from time to time and with whom he could maintain only a tenuous contact. Working closely with his own planners and developing his compromise solutions in situations that allowed for no compromise, he could not, even by the most constructive and brilliant effort, do justice to both strategy and tactics. Yet he not only believed firmly in the excellence and efficiency of his solutions, but actually mistook them for a master plan. Much later, when everything had worked out satisfactorily despite all the ups and downs of the "crusade," he wrote to General Marshall:

"Naturally I am immensely pleased that the campaign west of the Rhine that Bradley and I planned last summer and insisted upon as a necessary preliminary to a deep penetration east of the Rhine has been carried out so closely in accordance with conception. . . . I hope this does not sound boastful, but I must admit to a great satisfaction that the things Bradley and I have believed in from the beginning and have carried out in the face of some opposition from within and without, have matured so splendidly."

The letter was dated March 26, 1945, when the collapse of the German army in the west was reflected in the 10,000 prisoners Patton was taking each day. It raises a few questions to which history may give different answers. The credit Eisenhower was so handsomely sharing with Bradley was probably gratuitous, for it was Bradley who had joined Patton forcefully and eloquently in *opposing* Eisenhower's plan and "the things [he] believed in from the beginning." Patton himself regarded the plan of "last summer" as one of the great mistakes of the war. But he left it to posterity to make the final assessment when he wrote, in late August, 1944, when the Eisenhower plan was originally conceived, that "hereafter many pages will be written . . . on the events which produced it."

As he saw it, and as far as he was concerned, *no* plan at all would have been preferable to the one the Supreme Commander had evolved and with which he professed such "great satisfaction."

When Patton returned to Nancy in the evening of November 25th, he was no longer buoyed by the pleasant intermezzo he had spent with the officers and men who had taken Metz. He had gone north to Thionville to be on hand when XX Corps opened its drive to the Saar, hoping to take Saarburg in this sweep and maybe getting as far as Trier, only about 10 miles farther north. What he learned at General Walker's CP was not too bad, but neither was all of it good. On the northern flank, in the zone of the 10th Armored Division, the 385th Infantry was battering at the formidable Orscholz Line, mainly to relieve elements of its 3rd Battalion, which had fought its way into Butzdorf the day before only to be cut off. Now, assisted by tanks and aircraft, the regiment succeeded in relieving its isolated unit, but was then forced to pull back.

Before the day was out, Major General James A. Van Fleet, to whose 90th Division the 358th Infantry belonged, decided to withdraw the regiment because it was "unfit to continue the attack." However, driving on with his two other regiments, the 359th on the left and the 357th on the right, he continued to attack steadily toward the Saar and reached Oberesch by nightfall, only 4 miles from the river.

The Saar campaign was in its 17th day. By now Patton knew that Saarburg, one of its main objectives, would not fall to him as quickly and easily as he had hoped when planning the offensive. He was becoming worried that it might be denied to him altogether because the Germans, now alert to Patton's shrewd design, began to assemble their forces in that very sector.

These German moves had their quota of mystery, but so has every move in war. The explanation seems to lie not in what the Germans were doing, but in what we were failing to do. The First and Ninth U.S. Armies were virtually inactive except for VII Corps of the First. So presumably the Germans felt safe to thin out their line opposing them and to concentrate in front of the Third Army, whose drive they recognized as something of a menace. As it turned out, XX Corps' operations did upset the enemy, and not only because they threatened his front on the Saar. They were becoming increasing dangerous to the big trump card Hitler was preparing to play.

What Patton found waiting for him at his headquarters was not calculated to lighten his gloom. Arrangements were in the making to alter the boundary between XII Corps and the Seventh Army of General Devers' 6th Army Group, whose 2nd French Armored Division had just taken Strasbourg in the south but was facing the difficult task of consolidating its impressive gain. Had the boundary then been changed as G-3 of Seventh Army had demanded, the Third Army would have been pinched out. Knowing how his boss would react to such a demand, Gaffey voiced vigorous dissent and prevailed. The immediate danger threatening Patton from his own 12th Army Group (which was inclined to approve the boundary change) could be averted. But the danger from the enemy was becoming more serious by the hour as the continued inactivity of the two great American armies to the north enabled the Germans to shift more units into Patton's path.

That night Patton talked over his misgivings with his staff, speaking candidly about the inactivity of the Ninth U.S. Army and the slow progress of the First. The latter was using only its VII Corps in arduous fighting around the Hürtgen Forest battling natural and man-made defenses along the German border.

"The First Army is making a terrible mistake," Patton said, "by leaving Middleton's VIII Corps static where it is. It is highly probable that the Germans are building up east of them for a terrific blow."

Patton's sixth sense—what Eisenhower had praised as Patton's uncanny ability to worm himself mentally into the enemy's thinking and anticipate his moves—was working again. Just what are the Germans doing, he asked, aside from concentrating these second-rate units in front of him? Why are they so determined to prevent him from breaking into the area around Saarburg? And while he was thinking ahead, trying to answer these questions, he also thought

back, to November 10th, in particular, to an event recorded
in unusually harsh language. "Bradley called up at 1710,"
he wrote, "and, in my opinion, crawfished quite flagrantly
in forbidding me to use the 83rd Division."

What was behind these strong words? And what was
ahead of them?

The Gaffey-Gay plan of October 17th for the Saar campaign was excellent as far as it went. It became bold and
brilliant by the time Patton finished editing it. Forever seeking the opportunity denied him in early September, he
broadened the plan to include a possible breakthrough in
XX Corps area with a powerdrive to the Rhine. Thus the
mission of XX Corps became not only the destruction of the
German forces in the general area of Metz, but also what
was called, with deliberate obscurity, "a quick shift in the
axis of advance to the northeast." This second phase envisaged the establishment of a firm bridgehead across the
Saar in the vicinity of Saarburg from which the attack
would continue along the Metz-Saarlautern axis to the
Rhine.

The concept presupposed control of the Saar-Moselle triangle and the capture of Trier, the ancient Augusta Trev-
erorum founded by the Romans, seat of the Western emperors and see of archbishops whose temporal rule once
extended far beyond their diocese. Now the city was a
major stronghold whose capture would kill two birds with
one stone—it would turn the whole West Wall in the Third
Army's sector and open up a corridor leading directly to the
Rhine, only 50 miles away.

Patton regarded XX Corps as sufficiently strong to carry
out this ambitious mission. It had been bolstered by the
arrival of the 95th Division, commanded by Major General
Harry L. Twaddle, who had activated and trained it, and
had brought it to Lorraine straight from the United States
via England; and by the 10th Armored Division of Major
General William H. Morris Jr., a West Pointer known to
Patton most favorably from St. Mihiel, where Morris had
received the DSC for his gallant handling of an infantry battalion. All told, Walker had three infantry divisions and an
armored division for the operation. But Patton would make
it even stronger by borrowing the 83rd Infantry Division
of Major General Robert C. Macon from VIII Corps of the
First Army.

In the final version of the plan, the 83rd was assigned a

crucial role, one that was to make possible the breakthrough. Patton planned to "send the 83rd Infantry Division (minus the 329th Infantry) through the 90th Division bridgehead behind the 10th Armored Division.The 83rd was then to attack northward, clear the Saar-Moselle triangle, and establish a bridgehead over the Saar at Saarburg."

It was a terrific plan, another of Patton's blessed designs in which pure creative art was blended with the plain ingredients of military science taught at Leavenworth. Since Saarburg was clearly the crux and the initial pivot of the operation, Patton organized a special task force to race for the town and take it as soon as the 90th Division had a bridgehead across the Moselle near Thionville.

With Saarburg secured, the 90th Infantry and 10th Armored would embark on the second phase, turning northeast to Trier and beyond, if possible, to the Mainz-Darmstadt-Frankfurt area on the Rhine. In the meantime, the 83rd would come down from its line in southeastern Luxembourg and mop up the triangle. When these details were worked out, Walker's orders read: "Eliminate the Metz garrison, secure grossing of the Saar in the Saarburg area, *and, upon order, continue the offensive toward northeast.*"

According to the Third Army staff, General Bradley agreed wholeheartedly to "the employment of the 83rd Division in this portion of Patton's plan." And Patton was supposed to have said to Bradley, beaming, "General, if this plan goes through, we'll make real history."

Patton took it for granted that he had the 83rd all the way and had his staff draw up plans with the division integrally in the big picture. They continued to plan along these lines even after October 30th, when General Bradley wrote to Patton, attaching a number of strings to the lend-lease of the 83rd. In the letter Bradley limited the use of the division to a minor role so that it could revert to VIII Corps as soon as possible.

Patton chose to disregard Bradley's letter. He was confident that all the limitations would be promptly rescinded once the results of his offensive tore open the path to the Rhine. As usual, he was banking on buying what he needed with the dividends his venture would yield.

The offensive began on November 8th, with the fate of the 83rd still hanging in midair. It was standing by to move through the 90th Division bridgehead behind the 10th Armored. Then at 5:10 P.M. on November 11th Bradley called Patton, apparently only to inquire how things were going. It was Patton's birthday and he was in high spirits. "Everything is just fine, Brad," he said in his most vigorous style. "I think we'll make a killing before the day is out."

He had reason to be so optimistic. The 90th Division had nearly doubled the size of its crucial bridgehead. The formidable Fort Königsmacker had surrendered to the 358th Infantry Regiment. The 95th Division had established a bridgehead across the Moselle, whose flood waters had reached their crest and began to subside. Eddy's XII Corps was also doing well, and Patton, all set to call in the 83rd Division, began to see himself on the march to the Rhine.

But then, without warning, Bradley threw a vicious curve to him.

"Incidentally, Georgie," he said casually, "I don't like the way Walker is planning to handle the 83rd Division. I made it explicitly clear that you can have operational control only to a limited extent. As a matter of fact, I don't think you should have the 83rd at all."

For once Patton was speechless. When he recovered from the blow, he told his superior, "But Brad, I need the division! I've made all my plans with them in mind!"

"Walker is disobeying my orders," Bradley replied, now sounding quite peeved, "and I won't let him have the 83rd. No use arguing, George. The decision is final. I'll phone Hodges to this effect."

That night when Patton told his staff about it, he virtually hissed the words through lips tight from his bitterness: "Gentlemen, I am quite sure that this is the first time in the history of war when one-tenth of an attacking general's command was removed after the battle had been joined. Moreover, I am sure that it is a terrible mistake, because by using the 83rd we could take Saarburg easily. Without it we won't get Saarburg, and will be bothered by the triangle between the Moselle and the Saar."

The incident may seem trivial in the huge context of the war. General Bradley on his part did not regard it as sufficiently important to rate even a passing mention in his memoirs. Dr. Cole dismissed it with a footnote in his history of the Lorraine campaign, adding: "The question of the use of Macon's division was one of the very few, in the entire European campaign, which found General Bradley and General Patton in serious disagreement."

Patton died convinced that Bradley's decision to take the division from him when he needed it most was one of the great mistakes of the war—probably the decisive factor in making possible and, indeed, inevitable, what became the Battle of the Bulge.

But at this stage of the game Bradley did not know and Patton could only suspect what Hitler had in store for them. So Patton just swallowed one more disappointment and re-adjusted his timetable for the trip to the Rhine. It was becoming nothing short of pathetic, his being stopped again and again, always on the threshold of what he thought would be a decisive triumph of his arms. First in August, when he *knew* that his "Sure Thing" would take him into Germany "within 10 days." Then twice in September. And now in the midst of his Saar campaign with its enticing vistas!

What next?

He was due at Colonel Koch's quarters, where the heads of his staff sections were holding a party to celebrate his 59th birthday. Patton showed his annoyance by having more than his usual quota of "Armored Diesels."

"They're damn good, Oscar," he said appreciatively to his host, calling Koch by his first name, a sure sign that he was mellowed after the bitter blow of the day and cherished the sympathy of those in this grim-visaged war who were closest to him.

It was a Goddamn autumn of discontent.

"At the end of November," wrote Cole about this dubious period, "the Third Army was closing up to the Saar River. As yet, General Patton's intention to secure at least one bridgehead east of the river in each of the two corps zones had not been realized. It appeared likely, however, that the bulk of the Third Army would soon be across the Saar. Beyond lay the West Wall, which, insofar as the section facing the Third Army was concerned, remained an unknown quantity.

"The optimistic prediction by higher headquarters that Patton's troops would reach the Rhine by mid-December had been quietly forgotten. The Third Army commander himself had gradually abandoned the hope of a quick break-through to the Rhine; at this stage he seems to have been

concerned simply with driving steadily forward, going as far
as his strength and supplies would permit."

SHAEF, too, was concerned about the situation but, for
once, its ideas were to Patton's liking. On November 28th
Eisenhower's planning staff came up with an idea that promised to propel the Allies forward, with Patton doing most of
the propelling. "More important than the capture of
ground," stated a SHAEF study of "Immediate Prospects of
Western Front" prepared by General Bull's G-3 section,
"would be the destruction of the Germans in the area
between the Moselle and the Rhine." It was to be done by
a joint offensive of the Third Army and General Devers'
6th Army Group. "It is probable," the SHAEF paper went
on, "that this offensive will attract considerable German
resources from the northern and central sectors, and it is
possible that this movement of reserves may resolve the
impasse at the Roer."

Though the idea had a breathtaking strategic sweep of
its own, with possible consequences that could have become
decisive, the planners were still limited in their vista by
their primary concern for Montgomery, whose priority in
all plans was enduring despite his failure to make good on
his assignments. "Although," SHAEF G-3 added significantly, "the joint Third Army-Seventh Army offensive is not
in the most important sector of the front"—a contention
Patton was only too willing to contest—"it offers the best
chance of quick returns and of getting the main offensive
under way once more."

Patton himself was thinking much bolder than Cole gave
him credit for and was planning more sweepingly than even
this indirectly favorable SHAEF paper would encourage
him. The hard fighting of November had produced substantial gains for his army. He had inflicted damage on the
enemy, reducing the combat strength of the First German
Army from eight infantry and four Panzer divisions so substantially that it now had only one battalion to each 4-mile
sector and but four and a half guns for each mile of the
front line.

But Patton was not satisfied. His offensive had failed in
the objective he had *in petto* when he planned it—it did not
effect any penetration of the West Wall and did not
materially hasten the advance on the road to the Rhine.

Now he was working again to remedy the situation. All
the plans he was hatching during these first days of Decem-

ber converged on the climactic objective of the campaign. It was the decisive breaching of the West Wall in order to return, once beyond it, to a war of movement he hoped would duplicate his rapid progress in France, but on German soil this time.

The breakthrough, as he called it, was contingent on what Patton described as "probably the most ambitious air blitz ever conceived." Planned as one of the war's heaviest bombing attacks, with some 3,000 planes participating, it was to hit the West Wall in front of Kaiserslautern and smash a wide path for his troops. Scheduled for December 19th, it had been "conceived" on December 6th when a glittering array of Air Force brass had flown into his CP at Nancy for a planning session.

The delegation was headed by Generals Spaatz and Doolittle, accompanied by Major General Hoyt S. Vandenberg, commander of the 9th U.S. Air Force. The visitors spent the night in style at the Grand Hotel, sitting up late to plot the "big show" with Patton. It was planned to last for two or three days and was expected to destroy much of whatever resistance the Germans would be capable of putting up.

Spaatz and his colleagues were more than just willing to help. They were actually eager to give Patton anything he wanted or needed. His relations with the Air Force were proper and smooth. They were also exceptionally close in the personal sense of intimate friendships on both individual and collective levels.

Here was still another apparent contradiction in Patton's make-up. This "ancient warrior," as he liked to fancy himself, was actually the most up-to-the-minute soldier. He was not like Browning's man in armor—he was not his armor's slave. For Patton was, quite contrary to the widespread impression, an amazingly broad-minded commander to whom no other branch of service was inferior, no new weapon was alien, no new doctrine repugnant. Emotionally rooted in the history of war and the anachronous chivalry of bygone centuries, he avidly adopted all the novel mechanical wonders that burst onto the battlefields straight from the pages of H.G. Wells.

The veteran and fervent cavalryman took to the tanks with love at first sight. The tanker then, with all the ardent *esprit* of his corps, had nothing but respect and admiration for the infantry. As Lieutenant Colonel Wisdom H. Stewart recalled, "one of General Patton's last laments was that he was ineligible for the Combat Infantryman's Badge" because it was restricted to officers of the grade of colonel and below. He was, of course, whole-hearted in his recognition of the airplane's influence in modern war, its overwhelming importance to his own operations, and of the value and valor of the men who flew them.

Knowing how dependent his own success was on air support, Patton shrewdly singled out the airmen for special attention and friendly treatment. He drew General Weyland, the debonair and brilliant young commander of the tactical Air assigned to his Third Army, into his personal circle. Fanning their friendship at every turn and promoting Weyland's good-will with lavish words of praise and gratitude, he gave him and the whole XIX Tac a feeling of importance and a keen sense of belonging. There was nothing Weyland and his airmen would not have done for Patton in return.

And he literally pampered the special group of air observers working for him directly and personally as his seeing eyes, producing in them a fiercely sacrificial spirit of loyalty matched only by those on his staff closest to him. They were willing to fly for him in all weather conditions to get the information they were best qualified to procure. The virtually constant air surveillance of his sector was a crucial factor contributing to Patton's astounding omniscience, which in turn assured success in most of the operations he undertook.

He also cultivated Spaatz and Doolittle, to whom he was tied by firm bonds of sincere personal friendship. He invariably rolled out the red carpet for them whenever they dropped in. A few weeks before, on November 9th, he had entertained them at Nancy with exquisite French food and the best of champagne in what was almost a formal dinner conjured up by Codman. It was the day after the Saar campaign had jumped off, more or less into the blue, without any air preparation because the impossible weather had grounded the fighter-bombers. But coming from the angry clouds like bolts of lightning, the planes appeared in force as soon as conditions enabled them to take off, giving the new offensive a tremendous lift. Thanks to their unexpected intervention, the day that began rather uncertainly became, in Patton's phrase, "the brightest and best we had for two months."

It started to rain again at 5 o'clock in the afternoon, and the weather continued dismal on November 9th. The rivers were flooded. The tanks and trucks were marooned, the planes apparently grounded. Yet while Patton was with General Irwin's 5th Division to spur with his presence (in the absence of air support) its attack south of Metz (by footbridge and assault craft across the swollen Seille River), he looked up and saw "thousands of planes" coming over. They were the fighter-bombers of Doolittle's 8th Air Force —1,476 of them to be exact—flying valiantly through the thick soup. They promptly covered the spreading battle-field, bombed the obstinate Metz forts and attacked crucial targets all along the front.

Patton was profoundly moved by Air's cooperation under the circumstances and said so in warm words when he dined Spaatz and Doolittle later that evening. In what was meant as a poignant toast, he turned to General Spaatz and said, "I am very grateful to you, Tooey, because frankly I regard the wonderful air support we are receiving under these adverse conditions as an expression of your and Jimmy Doolittle's personal friendship."

"You bet it's the expression of our friendship," the delighted airmen shot back. "You're the kind of ground commander, Georgie, we *like* to help out."

During their planning session on December 6th, they assured Patton that they would come through on December 19th, rain or shine, with everything they had to aid his breakthrough. But having been stopped twice before on what he was convinced was the eve of the decisive moment for a breakout, Patton was fated to be diverted again, deprived of the opportunity of presenting for collection the promissory note Spaatz and Doolittle had been so pleased and eager to give him.

After that momentary pause for reflection on December 8th, Patton continued the drive relentlessly toward what he called his "big date with the air boys." But the going was tough and slow. On the 9th he committed the full strength of the 90th Division to the battle of the Dillingen bridgehead in the face of repeated counterattacks that proved debilitating to both sides. His precarious bridgeheads across the Saar

remained under heavy enemy fire. Though spot checks produced reports of local successes—in XII Corps area a couple
of Class 40 bridges could be completed; a battalion of the
137th Infantry was mopping up in the western part of Sarreguemines, and the 328th Infantry had captured the two
forts in the Maginot Line—efforts to push forward continued to be almost futile as the supply problem showed
signs of worsening again. And the weather was not getting
any better.

Patton was seized by the same feverish impatience that
had overcome him 15 months before in Sicily when he was
driving on Messina. "In order to make our date with the
Air Force for the Third Army breakthrough to the Rhine,"
he wrote, "which was initially set at December 19th, we had
to get to the Siegfried Line prior to that date, so from then
on the operation on the front of the XII Corps became a
horse race against time."

On December 12th, in XII Corps area, the 35th Division
began an attack across the Blies, gaining a weak hold at
Habkirchen. Bliesbruck was cleared on the near side of the
river, and the 328th Infantry succeeded in getting forward
elements across the German border. But on the next day
the Germans counterattacked furiously at Habkirchen,
where the 35th Division became involved in a difficult and
inconclusive battle in weather so bad that Patton described
it as his *primary* enemy.

With his consummate faith in his super-powers, he now
refused to go along with the people who always talk about
the weather but never do anything about it. He summoned
Colonel James H. O'Neill, the Third Army Chaplain, to his
office in Nancy for a special conference in which he hoped
to fuse the concrete tenets of military science with the presumably inscrutable abstractions of theology.

"Chaplain," Patton told O'Neill, "I want you to pray for
dry weather. I'm sick and tired of these soldiers having to
fight mud and floods as well as Germans. See if you can't
get God to work on our side."

"Sir," the Chaplain replied, "it's going to take a pretty
thick rug for that kind of praying."

"I don't care if it takes the flying carpet," Patton said.
"I want you to get up a prayer for good weather."

"Yes, sir," Chaplain O'Neill said. "But permit me to say,
General, that it isn't the customary thing among men of

my profession to pray for clear weather to kill our fellow men."

"Chaplain," Patton began to fume, "are you teaching me theology or are you the Chaplain of the Third Army? I want a prayer."

"Yes, sir," Colonel O'Neill said. When he was outside, he asked Harkins, "What do you think the Old Man wants?"

"The General wants a prayer," Harkins said crisply, because, as he put it, this whole transaction was perfectly clear to him. "He wants it right now, and he wants it published to the Command."

"Oh, God," O'Neill said, "this is a tough one." But he produced the prayer exactly as Patton had ordered.

"Almighty and most merciful Father," it read, "we humbly beseech Thee, of Thy great goodness, to restrain these immoderate rains with which we have had to contend. Grant us fair weather for Battle. Graciously hearken to us as soldiers who call upon Thee that, armed with Thy power, we may advance from victory to victory, and crush the oppression and wickedness of our enemies, and establish Thy justice among men and nations. Amen."

The Lord was in no special hurry to answer the prayer. It was only on December 23rd that He and His inscrutable wisdom deemed it the right time to stop the rains and clear the weather. The timing was superb, because, as we shall see, Patton by then needed clear skies to correct a situation the earlier bad weather had helped to create.

Whatever it was that made the difference, somehow the war had changed, in its whole atmosphere as well as in its physical aspects, from the thrusting aggressiveness that had propelled the crusade after the breakout in August to this groping and inching through the mud of the clay-mixed topsoil. There was an element of uncertainty in the war, cramping Patton's style and clouding his martial spirit. There was nothing vague in his own mind, to be sure, about the way he intended to wage the war. But he was not running the show. He had to fit himself into the greater strategic complex. His orders from above, he wryly complained, rarely proved conducive to the execution of his own plans or to the fulfillment of his hopes. War was war, however, and Patton was doing as well as possible. But somehow this was no longer the kind of war he savored and in which he was at his best.

After those late August and early September days, his forward march never succeeded in regaining its original breathless momentum. This was now substantially due to the Germans, who quite miraculously managed to put up spirited and effective resistance each time they had been knocked to the floor and taken a count of nine. They were not expected to get up again, but they did and were saved, as Patton sometimes put it, by the bell tolling for them at SHAEF.

Some of the slow progress was caused by a miasmic nervous tension that was filling the Allied air and infecting Patton's volatile command, imperceptibly but harmfully like malevolent bacteria in a drop of seemingly clear water. The question was not *where* do we go from here. It was *when*, Goddamnit, would we get there, with all the monkey wrenches littering Third Army's path.

But now the "when" and the "where" were becoming fused as Patton was once again looking forward to his thrice-postponed journey to the Rhine. On December 13th the finishing touches were put to his plans for the huge air-ground assault on the West Wall. On the 14th preparations continued for the attack in the area of XX Corps while XII Corps was crossing the Saar on Bailey bridges.

On December 15th the 90th Division opened an all-out assault on Dillingen and the Prims River bridge on the Dillingen-Saarlautern road, and the 95th Division continued its advance in the Saarlautern bridgehead. Though the enemy was now contesting every inch of ground, Patton was making steady progress toward the "big show" on December 19th, from which he was now sure to squeeze the coveted breakthrough.

☆

CHAPTER THIRTY-SEVEN
BASTOGNE

"So they've got us surrounded,
the poor bastards!"

Anonymous GI in Bastogne;
December 22, 1944

As far as General Patton was concerned, it began with what sounded like another one of 12th Army Group's ill-timed meddlings. It was December 16th, after dinner at 10 rue Auxerre in Nancy, when the telephone rang. General "Lev" Allen, Bradley's Chief of Staff, was calling. What he then told Colonel Harkins, who took the call, threw Third Army Headquarters into one of its periodic uproars.

Army Group was ordering Patton to stop the 10th Armored Division of General Morris from whatever it was doing and transfer it to General Middleton's VIII Corps up north that same night.

"What?" Patton roared, biting a piece off the big cigar he was smoking amid the pleasantries of this after-dinner period. The division was standing by, having been alerted on the 11th to meet what looked like a German attack developing in the 90th Division area around Dillingen. But mostly it was getting ready for the big role Patton had assigned to it in the attack scheduled to erupt on December 19th with that 3,000-plane air blitz.

At first sight this seemed worse than the case of the 83rd Division the month before, because Patton then merely lost something he did not really have. But the 10th Armored was his, and he sorely needed it. So he phoned Bradley at Luxembourg, where 12th Army Group now had its headquarters.

"Listen, Brad," he pleaded, "don't spoil my show. Third Army has sweated and bled to bring this damn thing to a head. Without the 10th Armored we won't be able to exploit the breakthrough at Saarlautern." Then he stated as strongly as he could: "If you take Morris from me, you'll be playing into the hands of the Hun."

"I don't question your logic, George," Bradley said with what Patton thought was tension in his voice," but it's *necessary* to move the division to Middleton *at once.*"

Patton tried to prolong the argument but Bradley cut him short.

"I've got to hang up, Georgie," he said curtly. "I can't discuss this matter on the phone."

This was the first "official" word Patton had that the *Wacht am Rhein*—as the Germans had code-named their Ardennes offensive—was on. Early in the morning Field Marshal von Rundstedt had opened an all-out attack with three armies (two of them Panzer), hitting VIII U.S. Corps so hard that the impact threatened to pulverize its four divisions by nightfall.

Patton did not have any details of the attack, but he sensed instinctively that this time Bradley had some serious reasons for taking an armored division from him. "I guess they're having trouble up there," he remarked to Codman, adding in a low reflective tone, "I thought they would."

Patton had long been irked by the protracted inactivity of much of Bradley's forces in the north, not because he envied their sinecure or needed their help, but because he regarded their idleness as dangerous. He never underestimated the enemy. He always expected him to do what he would have done under similar circumstances. So now he expected the Germans, smart foes that they were, to seize this opportunity and mess up VIII Corps a bit.

As for himself, he was incapable of standing still, even when ordered, on two grounds—one personal, the other professional. For one thing, he was congenitally mercurial and agile. For the other, he knew that idle troops in the front line always courted disaster. When his own advance had been arrested at the Moselle on September 25th, Patton was prompt to make elaborate arrangements against total inactivity. "We will not dig in, wire or mine," he told his commanders, "but will utilize a thin outpost zone backed at suitable places by powerful mobile reserves." And he ordered them to patrol aggressively and mount "limited operations" from time to time to conceal from the enemy the bitter fact that, for all practical purposes, they were as idle as a moribund mackerel.

On November 25th he had voiced his apprehension that Middleton's inactivity might entice the Germans to attack him. Patton's fears mounted as VIII Corps, exposed though it was in the Ardennes, continued to sit still and serve as a kind of rehabilitation area for divisions hurt in the other sporadic operations of this baffling period.

In a meeting on December 12th, he told his staff in so many words that he regarded an enemy breakthrough in the First Army's zone as a distinct possibility. He actually instructed General Gay and Colonel Maddox to make "a study of what the Third Army would do if called upon to counterattack such a breakthrough."

Patton was not just playing his hunches by being so concerned. There was some solid data coming to his desk to justify his fears. Colonel Koch's section was working overtime, utilizing all its diverse and mysterious sources, to develop an estimate of the enemy's situation and fathom his intentions. Third Army G-2 was snooping all the time, and far beyond the area of its own responsibilities. It sought to provide coverage up to 150 miles to the north and south of Third Army's flanks, the limits of the army's tactical air reconnaissance. The distance also represented a day's maximum march by motor of enemy troops that could possibly show up in front of the Third Army. Moreover, any substantial enemy action against either the First Army or the Seventh Army to the south was likely to affect the Third Army as well. Such a possibility was always of immediate concern to Patton's studious Intelligence chief.

In November, G-2 had identified a number of German units in the process of leaving Westphalia. Inexplicably, too, German armor had vanished from the Third Army's front, indicating that a major force consisting mainly of Panzers was being assembled somewhere, presumably in the north. Koch began to grope for an answer to the questions these enemy movements posed. So on November 23rd he wrote in the daily periodic report: "This powerful striking force, with an estimated 500 tanks, is still an untouched strategic reserve held for future employment"—as a matter of fact, for use in what he called a "coordinated counter-offensive."

On December 7th his daily report again called attention to these "enemy reserves with large Panzer concentrations west of the Rhine in the northern portion of 12th Army Group's zone of advance." On the 9th Koch briefed Patton informally on the possibility of a German attack and the enemy's capabilities to mount it. On the 11th he stated emphatically, "Overall, the initiative still rests with the Allies. But the massive armored force the enemy has built up in reserve gives him the definite capability of launching a spoiling offensive to disrupt Allied plans."

The recounting of these excerpts from Colonel Koch's daily reports are not meant to claim clairvoyance or omniscience for Patton's industrious G-2. Those daily periodic reports contained much data, some good, some indifferent, some of it plain bad. In the mass there always was something that in retrospect appeared to be prophetic, even if it had not been designed to pinpoint the future when it was originally put down on paper, usually as one of *several* possibilities.

Colonel Koch himself told me that most of the time Patton, with his psychic seismograph, was far ahead of his G-2 in sensing hardly perceptible tremors in the enemy camp. But Koch was inspired by his chief's inner eye. Now he thought he saw in the concentration of that unemployed "powerful striking force" the clear-cut possibility, and even the probability, of an imminent enemy attack.

His section succeeded in reconstructing the contours of two German assembly areas—one in the north, between Düsseldorf and Cologne west of the Rhine, the other farther south, in the general area of Gerolstein north of Trier. Since in the northern assembly area the Germans were moving their forces by day, Koch assumed that these troops were decoys. But those in the southern spot were moving stealthily under the cover of darkness, leading him to believe that they represented the "striking force" proper being assembled for a specific purpose. He ventured the opinion that an attack developing from these movements would be north of the Third Army's zone of advance. But he warned Patton that it might be large enough to affect the Third Army as well, and interfere with Patton's own impending offensive.

On the morning of December 16th these amorphous bits of information Koch had pieced together so laboriously became full-bodied intelligence. At 6:30 A.M., during a special secret briefing session handling so-called "special intelligence," Captain John J. Helfers presented the hardest fact

yet developed about those enigmatic Germans north of
Trier.

Helfers belonged to a unit of Third Army discreetly called
the "Black Market." It was Colonel "Demon" Hammond's signal organization's most demoniacal branch.
Headed by a trigger-smart young major named Charles
Flint, the unit (called SIS for Signal Intelligence Service)
maintained constant vigil on the enemy's communications
traffic and "translated" intercepted messages by breaking
their intricate codes and ciphers.

On the night of December 15-16th Helfers was the duty
officer at SIS, monitoring the German traffic as usual and
"translating" the intercepts as far as possible. Now he told
Patton that what he had found in the intercepts had convinced him that the concentration north of Trier was breaking up, the troops moving toward a mysterious destination.
Patton was keenly interested in Helfers' report, if only because he thought it might just be possible that the Germans were heading in his direction. So he turned to his
G-2 and asked, "What do you make of it, Koch?"

The bespectacled, professorial colonel produced a sheaf
of small index cards (on which he regularly jotted down his
conclusions) and was about to read his answer from them
when a message from SIS was handed to him. It reported
that the Germans had gone on radio silence.

"Well," Patton asked, "what do you make of *that?*"

"I don't know what it means when the *Germans* go on
radio silence," Koch said. "But when *we* place one of our
units in radio silence, it means they're going to move. In
this particular case, sir, I believe the Germans are launching an attack, probably at Luxembourg."

Patton took it from there. "If they attack us," he said,
"I'm ready for them. But I'm inclined to think the party
will be up north. VIII Corps has been sitting still—a sure
invitation to trouble."

He asked Gay and Maddox how they were coming along
with the study he had ordered on December 12th, then
made his instructions more specific.

"I want you, gentlemen, to start making plans for pulling
the Third Army out of its eastward attack, change the
direction 90 degrees, moving to Luxembourg and attacking north."

Inspired and, as it turned out, invaluable though his
order was, it was the product of sheer intuition. For Patton

really did not know what the Germans were up to, and
where and how their offensive would loose its venomous
sting.

When December 17th dawned, the Ardennes offensive was
in full bloom. The momentous secret Hitler had hoarded so
long and succeeded in preserving so well was out at last.
What became known (by Churchill's phrase) as the Battle
of the Bulge was to last for the next 42 days.

The purpose and dimensions of this daring enterprise that
Hitler had confided to General Balck on September 18th
were spelled out in greater detail by General Jodl on
November 3rd in a dissertation left to us as the best account of the pre-history of the battle. In a hush-hush meeting at the headquarters of Field Marshal Model's Army
Group B (to which a galaxy of senior German generals had
been admitted only upon signing a document binding them
to ironclad secrecy), Jodl elaborated upon the "plan" the
Führer had related to Balck in its barest form a month and
a half before.

"It is the unalterable decision of the Führer," Jodl said in
a tired voice, trying without success to display enthusiasm
for the venture he was describing, "to launch a decisive
offensive in the West from Field Marshal Model's sector."
He explained that the attack would be staged there because
a breakthrough in that particular region by the forces on
hand would be what he called a "guaranteed certainty."

"In view of the thinness of the enemy forces in the
Ardennes," Jodl explained, putting his finger on the Allies'
weakest point, "the Supreme Command has decided that
the Monschau-Echternach sector is the most suitable. The
enemy has suffered heavily in his offensive battles, his reserves are in general located immediately behind the front,
and his supply situation is strained.

"The enemy line is thin, nor does he expect the Germans
to attack anywhere, least of all in this sector. Therefore, by
full exploitation of the element of surprise, in weather conditions which will keep the Allied air force grounded, we can
reckon on achieving a rapid breakthrough. This will permit
mobile operations by our Panzer forces, which will swiftly
seize the bridgeheads over the Meuse between Liège and Na-

mur, bypassing Brussels to the east, and will drive irresistibly for Antwerp."

Three complete armies were to take part in the offensive under the over-all command of old Field Marshal von Rundstedt, Hitler's battered jack-in-the-box who would jump out whenever his Führer pushed the button—the Sixth SS Panzer Army under the former SS bully, Sepp Dietrich, now a full general of Panzer troops; the Fifth Panzer Army of General Hasso von Manteuffel (who was at that moment engaged in the critical defense of the Heinsberg-Aachen area), and General Werner von Brandenberger's Seventh Army, composed mainly of foot soldiers.

Although nobody mentioned him by name, Patton hovered in spirit over this super-secret meeting of his top adversaries. General Balck was there, for example, bliss-fully ignorant that even while he was listening to Jodl's exposition, Patton was issuing his firmed-up orders for the Saar campaign. But his American opposite number was always foremost in his mind, so now he asked Jodl as an im-plied warning:

"What if the enemy"—meaning the Third Army—"suc-ceeds in getting Metz after all and breaks through the West Wall to the Rhine?"

"The Führer is determined to carry out the operation re-gardless of risks," Jodl said. "Even if the impending Allied attacks on either side of Metz and toward the Ruhr should result in great loss of territory and of fortified positions, he is nevertheless determined to go ahead with this attack."

Then von Manteuffel rose. "I don't think we need anti-cipate strong reaction coming from the north on the east bank of the Meuse," he said in his precise style. "I believe, and General Dietrich shares my assumption, that only insig-nificant reserves are located behind the enemy's divisions in the line. But I am rather worried by the possibility of strong enemy counteraction from the south."

"General von Brandenberger will have six infantry divi-sions and a Panzer division in his Seventh Army to cover the southern and southwestern flanks," said Jodl.

"Yes, I know," von Manteuffel countered coldly, with re-markable prescience, "but I have to anticipate strong enemy forces—maybe even the bulk of his forces—in action in the Bastogne area by the evening of the third day of our at-tack."

Jodl repeated that von Brandenberger would be strong

enough to deal effectively with such an intervention, adding merely, "His army will gain time for the construction of a strong defensive line along the Luxembourg border by means of demolitions."

Although the Germans had to assemble, equip, train, maintain, supply and deploy three armies of up to 25 front-line and 8 reserve divisions, the Allies managed to discover nothing whatsoever about the pending attack. SHAEF's intelligence emanations of the period do not indicate even Colonel Koch's fragmentary and incidental knowledge.

Even worse, everything the Allies did during the incubation period of Hitler's offensive played into his hands. When Bradley had made it impossible for Patton to break through to Trier and Koblenz by withholding the 83rd Division, he indirectly aided the Germans by assuring the security of one of their assembly areas. The decisions reached by Eisenhower in his October 18th conference did little, if anything, to aid the Allies. But they unwittingly helped Hitler to perfect his design. When VIII Corps was set down around Arlon in southeast Belgium, thinned out on a 75-mile front on the assumption that a single—and rather motley—corps would be sufficient to defend the Ardennes sector, SHAEF handed Hitler the direction of his attack on a silver platter.

Even the Allied slugging match in the Hürtgen Forest and the attack toward Aachen, successful though they seemed on their own merits, aided Hitler. By concentrating on the Aachen area, the Allies enabled the Germans to assemble along the Düsseldorf-Cologne line and just north of Trier, completely safe not only from any molestation by our forces, but apparently even from our ground and aerial reconnaissance.

"The fighting in the Aachen sector," von Manteuffel wrote, "served as an excellent cover both to hide the intentions of our High Command and also to conceal the massing of troops for our planned offensive."

War is like a ship, strictly compartmentalized. And the bigger the war the more divided it is. Up in Belgium, a whole American army (in many respects the best we had in the war) was being attacked by 200,000 fanatical Germans with everything they had, from specially souped-up tanks to silly tricks of so-called "psychological warfare." The enemy was running roughshod over the hapless (and, indeed, helpless) VIII Corps—isolating two of its regiments and pushing on to St. Vith; driving relentlessly to Wiltz; overrunning Osweiler and Dickweiler; and chopping the 4th Division into chunks of quarantined units. Yet even General Hodges, commander of the embattled First Army, lived with the blissful illusion that this was only a nuisance raid —a spoiling attack at most—and was telling his corps commanders, "Isolated parties have made deep penetrations, but the enemy have not penetrated our lines in force. . . . Our position is not critical."

At his headquarters in the Hotel Alpha in Luxembourg City, General Bradley hardly knew what to make of this crazy situation. He had been with General Eisenhower at Versailles on December 16th, discussing some vexing replacement problems, when the first flash of the German offensive arrived at SHAEF. Supreme Headquarters was subsisting in an air of smug confidence, conducting the war in a deliberate and rather leisurely manner along the lines of the "broad front" strategy.

A letter President Roosevelt had written to Churchill on December 10th reflected the complacency inspired by by SHAEF. "For the time being," it read in part, "even if a little behind schedule, it seems to me the prosecution and the outcome of the battles lie with our field commanders, in whom I have every confidence. We must remember that the winter season is bringing great difficulties, but our ground and air forces are day by day chewing up the enemy's dwindling manpower and resources, and our supply flow is much improved with the opening of Antwerp. *General Eisenhower estimates that on the Western front line he is inflicting losses in excess of the enemy's capability to form new units.* I still cannot see clearly just when, but soon a decisive break in our favor is bound to come."

As for Eisenhower, he had expressed his personal estimate in a letter to General Marshall in which he assured the Chief of Staff that everybody in his command was "in surprisingly good heart and condition." He derived hope from the fact that "the enemy was badly stretched in the west and was forced to shift his units constantly to protect various points threatened by the Allies." Ruling out the possibility of an enemy attack, he was willing to concede only that the Germans might be "able to maintain a strong defensive front for some time, assisted by weather, floods, and muddy ground." The letter was dated December 5, 1944.

On December 15th Field Marshal Montgomery sent Eisenhower an "appreciation" of his own, in which he stated categorically: "The enemy is at present fighting a defensive campaign on all fronts; his situation is such that he cannot stage major offensive operations."

In an atmosphere like this, and lulled into overconfidence by their Intelligence chiefs (who, as Robert E. Merriam aptly put it, were "vying with each other for the honor of devastating the German war machine with words"), it is hardly surprising that Eisenhower and Bradley could not immediately gauge the extent of the Nazi venture. Now, when the first news was in, and probably embarrassed that such a thing could happen to him, Bradley appeared stunned. He was bereft of any constructive ideas, but Eisenhower rose to the occasion and suggested that he take an armored division from Simpson's Ninth Army and one from Patton's Third and send them to each side of what he believed was the limited attack area.

Even then the Supreme Commander seemed to be more awed by Patton than Hitler. He bolstered Bradley for Patton's anticipated protest by advising him how to shut up Georgie. "Tell him," he said, "that I'm running this damned war."

Back at Nancy, Patton was also groping in the dark while sitting on his familiar pole, the horn of a dilemma. He had his own urgent business to attend to. His big offensive was developing according to his plans. The preliminaries of the hoped-for breakthrough were being properly taken care of. In the light of events on his front, he regarded his prospects as even better than before, for it was becoming evident that poor Balck was becoming weaker by the day.

There was a pathetic discrepancy between Balck's orders and his capabilities. On November 29th he was told to stay where he was and refrain from withdrawing another yard from his positions. In his plight, Balck resorted to vigorous whistling in the dark, masking his despair with strong and optimistic words. He asked von Rundstedt for the Panzer Lehr Division, fully committed in the Sarre-Union sector farther south, "for but two days," as he put it, "to wipe out the American gains made on November 27th and 28th."

When his request was turned down, he issued resounding orders to his commanders. On November 30th he instructed General von Tippelskirch, who had relieved von Knobelsdorff, to make "one attack after another," and was talking boldly of an operation he had up his sleeve "to recover Alsace and Lorraine."

But while his chief adversary was daydreaming, Patton was planning ahead with precision and zest. Now he decided to send Major General John Millikin's fresh III Corps into the expected breach behind the 35th Division to exploit the breakthrough, which he was taking for granted.

In the meantime, he tried to puzzle out, for want of specific information, what this German attack in Belgium really meant and what it might portend for his own offensive. During the morning briefing on the 17th, Koch reported that the Germans were continuing their attack on VIII Corps, but also appeared to be moving into the area fronting on Third Army's own XX Corps.

Patton thought it over for a moment, then said, "One of these is a feint, one is the real thing. The more I think of it, though, the more I become convinced that the thing in the north is the real McCoy."

Then he threw the ball to Colonel Maddox, his G-3, who responded with an impromptu *précis*. "It's a perfect set-up for us," he said. "The Germans will have to commit all their reserves to maintain this drive. That means that they can't reinforce against us or Seventh Army. If they will roll with the punch up north, we can pinwheel the enemy before he gets very far. In a week we could expose the whole German rear and trap their main forces west of the Rhine."

It was not such a bad idea at that, but for once Patton was the cautious one.

"You're right," he said, "that would be the way to do it. But that isn't the way those gentlemen up north fight. They aren't made that way. That's too daring for them. My guess is that our offensive will be called off and we will have to go up there and save their hides."

Even so, Patton was still hoping that he would be able to mount his offensives. After the briefing he instructed General Eddy at XII Corps to get the 4th Armored Division engaged at once because, as he phrased it, "I felt that if we did not, it, too, might be moved to the north by higher authority."

Recalling the useless expediency of this disposition, Patton later candidly conceded: "The fact that I did this shows how little I appreciated the seriousness of the enemy attack on that date."

But whatever doubts he still had about the nature of the threat and whatever hope he still cherished that he could go through with his third desperate attempt to get to the Rhine vanished on December 18th with another telephone call from Army Group Headquarters. This time Bradley himself was on the wire, and Patton answered the call on his private line. He usually picked up his phone when it rang, rarely waiting for some aide to answer it.

Well, Bradley now got him at once and told him, "I want you to come to Luxembourg as soon as you can, and bring along Koch, Maddox and Muller. I will have to tell you something I'm afraid you won't like, but it can't be helped."

They met in the crowded war room of 12th Army Group in the brick railroad building where Bradley had his working headquarters. General Sibert and his G-2 staff had posted on the big situation map the enemy divisions already identified—14 thus far, 7 of them Panzer units. When Bradley first looked at that map upon his return from Ike's villa at Germaine-en-Laye, he exclaimed to General Allen in language somewhat uncharacteristic of him but aptly adapted to the situation, "Pardon my French, Lev, but just where in hell has this sonuvabitch gotten all his strength."

The so-called Patton legend, which makes the man into an insufferable, selfish bore, has its own version of this confrontation. It portrays Patton in a rage, telling Bradley off and insisting that he will go through with his own offensive, the First Army be damned. Patton was deeply disappointed, to be sure, but he never for a moment placed his own designs ahead of the common need. On the contrary, he pushed into the breach with a Samaritan's eagerness to help. If the allegedly explosive conference proceeded in an atmosphere of high tension, it was due to the gravity and the uncertainties of the situation and not to Patton's cantankerousness and egotism.

"What the hell," Bradley later quoted Patton as saying when told that his Saar offensive was off, "we'll still be killing Krauts."

"What can you do to help Hodges?" Bradley asked, and Patton answered crisply, without a moment's hesitation. On the way up he had guessed what this conference would be about and made his dispositions in anticipation of Bradley's questions. He said earnestly:

"Brad, my three best divisions are the 4th Armored, the 80th and the 26th. I'll halt the 4th Armored right away and concentrate it at Longwy, beginning tonight. I'll start the 80th on Luxembourg tomorrow morning. And I'll alert the 26th to stand by and be ready to move on a day's notice."

Bradley was satisfied. Instead of getting a bitter argument, as he had expected, he got three divisions by just asking.

Patton drove home in the pitch darkness, totally blacked out. There were rumors abroad that a special goon squad of Nazi infiltrators was at large behind our lines, hunting for Allied generals. Then just when he was ready to turn in shortly after 11 P.M. he was summoned to the telephone. It was Bradley calling again.

"Georgie," he said, "Ike is coming to Eagle Main tomorrow morning for a special confab. Be there at 1100 sharp."

"Will do," was all Patton said.

When he hung up, he called in Gay. "Hap," he said, "I'm going to Verdun tomorrow morning for a conference with General Eisenhower. I want you to call a special staff session for 0800 tomorrow."

With that he went to bed and, as he later quipped, slept through the night like a *good* baby.

The staff session the next morning opened with the usual briefing, with Patton in his regular seat in the front row, listening a bit more intently than on routine days. Then he got up, turned to face his familiar audience, and made a little speech.

"Gentlemen," he said, "what has occurred up north is no occasion for excitement. As you know, alarm spreads very quickly in a military command. You must be extremely careful in a critical situation such as this not to give rise to any undue concern among the troops."

He paused for a moment, took a deep breath, then went on:

"Our plans have changed!

"We're going to fight, but in a different place!

"Also we are going to have to move very fast!

"We pride ourselves on our ability to move quickly. But

we're going to have to do it faster now than we've ever done before. I have no doubt that we will meet all demands made on us. And whatever happens, we will keep right on doing as we have always done—killing Germans wherever we find the sons of bitches."

The emotional veneer of his mood vanished abruptly as he now turned to an explanation of the changed plan he already had pat in his mind.

"Assuming that we'll have VIII Corps of First Army and our own III Corps," he said, "I intend to use them on any two or three possible axes. From the left, the axes of attack are in order of priority as follows—from the general vicinity of Diekirch, due north; from the general vicinity of Arlon, on Bastogne; and from the general vicinity of Neufchâteau, against the left nose of the Hun salient."

He looked at his watch. It was exactly 9 A.M. "Gentlemen," he said, "I'm going to Verdun to see the Supreme Commander. I want you to polish up the plan separately for each of the axes. I'm leaving a code name for each eventuality with General Gay. Be ready to jump with the one whose code name I'm going to phone back."

He drove through the grilled gates of his headquarters at Nancy (for the last time, as it turned out) at exactly 9:15 A.M.

If Patton was awed by his responsibilities, he was not, as you would think, overawed by the special genius of his generalship. "When it is considered that Harkins, Codman and I left for Verdun at 0915," he later wrote, "and that between 0800 and that hour we had had a staff meeting, planned three possible lines of attack, and made a simple code in which I could telephone General Gay which two of the three lines we were to use, it is evident that war is not so difficult as people think."

The historic Verdun conference of December 19, 1944, was, I submit, one of the high points of Dwight D. Eisenhower's generalship in the war. He was variously described as having been pale and nervous, showing not only signs of the strain but also of an intimate kind of concern, as if he worried about his personal future in the aftermath of this crisis. Actually, Ike was in top form, concise and lucid,

holding the conference with iron hands to its key issue—
the Allied counterattack. It was obvious to all that he knew
what he wanted and was the full master of the situation.
He had in full measure that special inner strength which
always filled him when he was called upon to make the
absolute decisions.

And Patton was described at this same meeting as acting
like a clown, providing ill-timed comic relief to the stark
melodrama. This could not be further from the truth. He
was as subdued as his colleagues, much quieter than usual,
and silent most of the time. He spoke only when Eisenhower addressed him directly. If his answer then smacked of
his usual bombast it was because he was talking from a
position of strength the others could not fathom or appreciate. However, he knew what he was saying because he
knew what he intended to do.

Present at the conference in the barren board room of
the French barracks in Verdun where Eagle Main was situated were, aside from Eisenhower and Patton, Air Chief
Marshal Tedder, General Devers of the 6th Army Group,
General Strong, the SHAEF G-2, and a large number of
staff officers. The session began with a brief exposé by
Strong, then Eisenhower took over. He needed only a few
succinct sentences to outline his plan, then turned straight to
Patton.

"George," he said, "I want you to go to Luxembourg and
take charge of the battle, making a strong counterattack
with at least six divisions."

"Yes, sir," Patton said, though he did not know exactly
where he would get those three additional divisions.

"When can you start?" Eisenhower asked.

"As soon as you're through with me," Patton answered.

"What do you mean?" Eisenhower asked, somewhat taken
aback by Patton's answer. The others shifted in their chairs,
obviously annoyed by the Third Army Commander's apparent flippancy.

"I left my household in Nancy in perfect order before I
came here," he said, "and can go to Luxembourg right
away, sir, straight from here."

Eisenhower looked more kindly at Patton as he now
asked, "When will you be able to attack?"

"The morning of December 22nd," Patton said and,
seizing the opportunity to dampen Eisenhower's enthusiasm
a bit, he added pointedly, "with *three* divisions."

The reaction to Patton's deadline was electric. "There was a stir," wrote Codman, who witnessed the scene, "a shuffling of feet, as those present straightened up in their chairs. In some faces, skepticism. But through the room the current of excitement leaped like a flame."

It was a seemingly impossible undertaking to which Patton was now committing himself. As Codman put it, "To disengage three divisions actually in combat and launch them over more than a hundred miles of icy roads straight into the heart of a major attack of unprecedented violence presented problems which few commanders would have undertaken to resolve in that length of time."

Now even Eisenhower lost his temper. "Don't be fatuous, George," he said sternly.

Patton answered without ruffling his voice. "This has nothing to do with being fatuous, sir," he said. "I've made my arrangements and my staff is working like beavers this very moment to shape them up." He explained his tenative designs, then added, "I'm positive I can make a strong attack on the 22nd, but only with three divisions, the 26th and 80th Infantry, and the 4th Armored. I cannot attack with more until some days later, but I'm determined to attack on the 22nd with what I've got, because if I wait I lose surprise."

The meeting broke up into scattered groups to iron out details. Eisenhower retired with Patton, Bradley and Devers to discuss the shift of fronts. They decided to assign part of the Third Army to General Patch's Seventh Army, which was to become static between Saarlautern and the point to the south where it was touching the Rhine. Patton then took stock of the forces he thought he would get for the job. He had his own three corps of course—the III of Millikin, the XII of Eddy, and the XX of Walker. He was taking over Middleton's VIII Corps from First Army and was getting the 101st Airborne Division, commanded by Major General Maxwell D. Taylor, part of the new Airborne Corps just forming under General Matthew B. Ridgway. But he was giving up the 87th Division and the infantry regiments of the 42nd to Seventh Army.

Patton moved from the conference to the nearest telephone to call Gay and give him the code word. It started the 4th Armored rolling on Arlon by way of Longwy and the 80th Division on Luxembourg via Thionville. The 26th became fully alerted pending specific orders to move.

He was ready to leave. Eisenhower accompanied him to the front door and, referring to the fact that he had just been made a full general, told him facetiously, "Funny thing, George, every time I get another star I get attacked."

Patton was back in his natural flippant frame of mind.

"And every time you get attacked, Ike," he shot back with an impish grin, "I bail you out."

The miracle of the Third Army's turnabout can be appreciated only when it is understood what all this meant in staff work. "Until the Battle of the Bulge," Bradley later wrote, "I did not share George's enthusiasm for his Third Army staff which, unlike those of both the First and Ninth Armies, lacked outstanding individual performers . . . However," he now conceded with a somewhat left-handed compliment, "five months in Europe had seasoned that staff and the greatly matured Patton succeeded in coaxing from it the brilliant effort that characterized Third Army's turnabout in the Bulge."

This, then, was what Patton's "mediocre staff" did in just five days, between December 18th and 23rd, under the mounting pressure of the Ardennes offensive:

● Colonel Maddox's G-3 changed from a three-corps front running north to south to a four-corps battle line split in two—one running east to west in the Ardennes, the other north to south in the Saar.

● Colonel "Speed" Perry, the officer who had served as Patton's guide into Palermo, moved hundreds of combat and supply units in 133,178 motor vehicles, traversing more than 1.6 million miles.

● Colonel Muller and his G-4 established an entirely new supply system, set up scores of new depots and dumps, and shifted 62,000 tons of supplies in just 120 hours, working round the clock.

● Colonel Hammond's signal men constructed a vast new communications network, using some 20,000 miles of field wire, and kept it going under extreme winter conditions in the face of vicious enemy interference.

● Colonel Koch's G-2 prepared and distributed hundreds of thousands of new maps and terrain analyses of the changed battle area, drew up estimates of the enemy situation, and kept the Order of Battle up to the minute.

● Colonel Coates, Third Army Surgeon, transferred and erected numerous evacuation hospitals.

"It was all wrought quietly and efficiently by a teamwork without parallel in the ETO," wrote Colonel Robert S. Allen, "a teamwork rooted deeply in great know-how, in great confidence in itself and its Commander, and in great fighting spirit."

So brilliant was the staff work backing him up that Patton was able to handle this enormously complex maneuver entirely by telephone, "Improvising from day to day," as Bradley put it, "to stretch the capacity of his road." He now consoled himself over the forfeiture of his own offensive with the utmost importance and crucial nature of his new assignment. He hardly had time to stop and fume over finding an unexpected fly in the ointment. During the Verdun conference General Eisenhower had said nothing about the possibility of changing the ground command. But the morning after, he virtually dethroned Bradley and shifted command in the Ardennes to Field Marshal Montgomery even though no British troops were involved in the vast enterprise.

There endures a bit of mystery about this strange shift that infuriated Patton and left a lasting sore in Bradley's memories of the war. On the afternoon of December 20th, Winston Churchill called Eisenhower at Versailles to give him some gratuitous advice. Field Marshal Brooke, the chief of the Imperial General Staff and his top-ranking military counselor, was using the American setback in Belgium to remind the Prime Minister, "Didn't I tell you so?!" While Churchill valiantly resisted Brooke's influence on his own attitude toward the Americans, now, in ignorance of what was happening, he became inclined to go along with Brooke's line of thinking.

"Montgomery and also we here in England have, as you are aware," the Prime Minister wrote to Field Marshal Jan Christiaan Smuts of South Africa on December 22nd, "pressed for several months for the emphasis of advance to the north of the Ruhr, and have on repeated occasions urged that our strength did not enable us to undertake two major offensives such as the one against Cologne and that across the Saar."

It was the old phonograph record, only it sounded more scratchy than ever, being played so shortly after Montgomery's debacle at Arnhem and during his latest period of protracted "re-grouping." But heeding Brooke's advice in this frame of mind, Churchill agreed to speak to Eisenhower and suggest that "he give to Montgomery the whole command north of the breakthrough, and Omar Bradley everything south of the breakthrough, keeping control himself of the concerted operations."

Eisenhower replied that he had already "issued orders exactly on these lines in the morning." As a result, Montgomery had, from December 20th on, 18 American divisions under his command in addition to his 21st Army Group with its 16 divisions. He was assuming entire charge of the battle area, Churchill advised Smuts, even though, as he pointed out, there was "nothing to suggest that the Germans have the power to mount a full-scale offensive against" his own main front.

The bitterness that resulted from this arrangement, and especially from the conspicuous lack of diplomacy with which Montgomery was to exercise his command, has no bearing on Patton, so we may as well gloss over it. In a sense, Monty's reappearance on the periphery of Patton's orbit had a salutary effect, if only because it introduced an element of sporting competition into the race to oust the Germans from their gains as quickly as possible. Bradley, on his part, suffered what was tantamount to demotion and disavowal, but he took it well. He remained at his headquarters in Luxembourg, Namur and Verdun throughout the battle and interfered with Patton as little as possible.

For once Patton was really on his own, to do as he pleased and make war as he liked. He spelled out the general idea that imbued him in this campaign and with which he, in turn, sought to imbue every officer and man fighting under him. "Everyone in this Army must understand," he said upon arriving at his new CP, "that we are not fighting this battle in any half-cocked manner. It's either root-hog, or die. Shoot the works. If those Hun bastards can do it that way, then so can we. If those sons of bitches want war in the raw, then that's the way we'll give it to them."

With that he turned his full attention to the first business at hand, what was to become virtually his major business in the Bulge——the problem posed by an insignificant little market town in southeastern Belgium.

Its name was Bastogne.

Patton's tortuous road to Bastogne began on December 19th. Though the distance between Verdun, his point of departure, and his eventual destination via Thionville and Luxembourg was only 90 miles, it took him seven days to cover it.

When the big meeting broke up, Patton had his mind made up. There was nothing more he could do at Nancy. The city where he had spent many weeks and from which he had directed his Saar campaign now receded into a pattern of his life that had come to its abrupt and irrevocable end. He startled Codman when he told him, "I won't be returning to Nancy. Tell Mims to get the jeep. We're leaving in five minutes *for Luxembourg.* And phone General Walker that I want to see him at Thionville on my way up."

He reached Thionville at twilight, had his talk with Walker at dinner, borrowed a pair of pajamas and a toothbrush, and spent the night at XX Corps' command post. He left early the next morning and arrived at the Hotel Alpha in Luxembourg at 9 A.M.

The quaint old capital of the little duchy, back to normal only a few days before, had undergone a quick and dismaying change. A heavy pall of anxiety lay over the city as groups of its stunned citizens gathered in the streets and the squares in silent despair, reminded by the rumble of guns only 7 miles away that the war had returned. The only American flags still displayed fluttered in the brisk winter wind over the scattered locations of U.S. installations. At the Hotel Alpha the flustered members of the Army Group staff reminded Patton of harassed tenants taking stock of their belongings on the eve of moving out of a house that had been sold over their heads by a callous landlord.

Patton was driven into the city by Mims, whose sole passenger he was. The general, who always traveled in style with an entourage, arrived at his new command post without a single aide, for Codman had returned to Nancy to arrange the moving of the "household." How different this was from his bumptious arrival in Tunisia in March, 1943, under similar circumstances, when he drove into Djebel Kouif with sirens shrieking in a cortege of armored scout cars and half-tracks!

Yet Patton did not feel bare. The most flexible of generals, as Eisenhower once described him, he could always take care of matters—both the big things and the little details—by himself. "On the 19th," he wrote to his wife from Luxembourg, "it was decided to send me up here to stop the Germans . . . The next day, the staff of the Third Army, which consisted of myself and Sergeant Mims, visited two corps and five division commanders, reshuffled two divisions, and telephoned for the engineers, tank destroyers, extra tank battalions, etc."

Driving him back to his billet at the Alpha at the end of the day and having observed his general on this hectic tour doing single-handedly the intricate work of a company of staff officers, Mims hit upon the idea of a drastic economy move. "General," he told Patton, "the government is wasting a lot of money hiring a whole general staff. You and me has run the Third Army all day and done a better job than they do."

The battle was now four days old and it was going badly. In V Corps area two divisions had to withdraw to defensive positions before the Elsenborn ridge, but even so, the Germans managed to penetrate their new line. The enemy kept up pressure everywhere in the area of VIII Corps—at St. Vith, at Marvie, at Waldbillig—driving with seemingly unspent fury on the prearranged course—the Fifth Panzer Army toward Brussels and the Sixth SS Panzer Army toward Antwerp.

The total pattern of the German drive was still not quite clear. As a result, all Allied arrangements had to be improvised. Yet it was on this December 20th that the hard-pressed Allies definitely adopted an idea that, in the end, frustrated Hitler. They focused on two spots, seemingly insignificant in the greater order of things and virtually overlooked by Hitler in the avarice of his design. One was St. Vith, a village of a thousand souls in the Malmédy district near the German border. The other was Bastogne.

The creative imagination that singled out Bastogne as the key in the Allied arrangements survives as one of the great inspirations in the history of military art. In the German plans the town figured but incidentally as a possible supply center. The original "Watch-on-the-Rhine" plan provided for two Panzer divisions to bypass the town and push on westward, leaving one of the lesser divisions, the 26th Volksgrenadier, to pick it up without a fight. However, on

December 19th, the entire Panzer corps involved in this
part of the enterprise was slowed by a combat command
of the 10th U.S. Armored Division. And the Volksgrena-
diers were halted in front of Bixory before they could get
to Bastogne.

Suddenly the little market place loomed in German eyes.
"The importance of Bastogne was considerable," von Manteuffel recalled. "In enemy hands it must influence all our
movements to the west, damage our supply system and tie
up considerable German forces. It was therefore essential
that we capture it at once."

But by then it was too late. The town virtually overlooked
in the German plans had become the fulcrum of the Allied
calculations. Patton had picked it off his road map on
December 19th, while drafting tentative plans for the eventuality of his involvement. He had designated it as an axis
of his presumptive attack from the general vicinity of Arlon.
But he had no exclusive claim by any means to the inspired
choice. Bastogne was in a real sense the meeting place of
many minds.

Probably the very first to think of it as a bastion was
Major General John Francis Martin Whiteley, a 48-year-
old British veteran of World War I who went to war again
in 1939 from his peacetime staff jobs in India and the War
Office. He wound up with SHAEF in May, 1944, as Deputy
G-3 under the American General Bull.

Early on December 17th, when most of SHAEF was still
frantically groping even for stopgap solutions to its sudden
problem, General Whiteley went straight to General Walter
Bedell Smith, SHAEF Chief of Staff, with the suggestion
that Bastogne be made a pivot in the Allied defenses. He
recommended that substantial forces be committed to its
defense immediately so that it could be held by any and all
means even if it became engulfed by the German flood.
Smith went along with Whiteley's recommendations and
issued orders to find some reserves at once to garrison the
town.

Almost simultaneously, General Middleton also chose
Bastogne for what became its historic part; and on December 19th General Bradley made elaborate dispositions for
its defense. When Patton reached Luxembourg on the following days, he was confronted with a definite decision and
was told that the substantial forces of which Whiteley had

dared merely to dream were already established in the improvised fortress.

When later that day he toured the front and met General Middleton at Arlon, he instructed the VIII Corps Commander to give ground so that the enemy would extend himself still more before he would hit him. But he concurred wholeheartedly in the decision to hang on to Bastogne.

"I don't think," he said, "the enemy dare pass it without reducing it."

Though Middleton was one of the authors of the Bastogne plan, he now cautioned Patton. He was deeply impressed with the difficulty of sustaining Bastogne in the flood. Referring to the inevitable plight of its defenders, Middleton told Patton, "They'll be surrounded unless they get help."

"They will get help!" Patton said, and returned to Luxembourg at once to arrange it.

And so Bastogne became the apple of our eyes—what Reichsmarshal Hermann Goering later called "the keystone of the entire offensive."

It was a strange and haphazard fate for the little town. In none of the many wars that had ravaged this area did Bastogne itself play a significant or conspicuous part, probably because nothing in its configuration ever recommended it to the strategists as a possible strong point. The town lay flat in the embrace of a crescent of rolling hills covered by light forests, its sole potential importance being that it was the hub of seven spokes in the southern Ardennes road net.

A modest market town of some 4,000 people, Bastogne was in the Luxembourg province of Belgium, so called because the Belgians had taken it from the Luxembourgeois in 1839 in an act of crass ingratitude. When the Belgians rebelled against the Netherlands in 1830, the Duchy of Luxembourg, created by the Congress of Vienna a few years before, sided with them. But no sooner was Belgium established as an independent country than it reached out and grabbed the province from its recent ally. Some international complications ensued. But the province remained part of Belgium and prospered along with the rest of the country, raising cattle in its rural parts and mining coal in its industrial district. Arlon, its capital, had some reflected significance, but Bastogne remained quiet and sleepy until it was awakened to its historic role with a bang.

Patton was making good on his commitment. The offensive he had promised for December 22nd began at 6 A.M. on the appointed day, with III Corps jumping off and making fair progress. In the west, General Gaffey's 4th Armored column reached Burnon and Martelange. To the right, the 26th Division had to march 16 miles before it could make contact with the enemy in the Rambrouch-Grosbous area. The 80th Division advanced 5 miles, then ran into stiff resistance at Merzig, but managed to clear the town.

Inside Bastogne it was a red-letter day. When Whiteley's recommendation was acted upon, SHAEF could not find any reserves to send to Bastogne, so it had to resort to the 101st Airborne Division of General Taylor, resting at Reims after its ill-fated 58-day involvement in Montgomery's Arnhem operation.

The division was uprooted on the evening of the 17th and shipped posthaste to Bastogne, where it joined a combat command of the 10th Armored, the 750th Tank Destroyer Battalion, elements of the 9th Armored Division, some artillery, and a Quartermaster unit composed entirely of Negro soldiers.

General Taylor happened to be in Washington, and so Brigadier General Anthony C. McAuliffe, artillery commander of the division, was acting division commander and also was in over-all charge of the bastion. By now the Germans had become alerted to the importance of the town to their venture and detached substantial forces to invest the *ad hoc* fortress.

Patton was still far too preoccupied with his imminent attack to devote undivided attention to Bastogne, which was being supplied as best as Air could in the abominable weather. Even on this December 22nd Patton referred but perfunctorily to the bastion. He was inclined to regard the Germans' sudden interest in Bastogne on this scale as their first reaction to his own attack.

At that moment Bastogne was under siege by two of Hitler's most dashing generals, Fritz Bayerlein of Afrika

Korps fame, and Patton's old adversary at Argentan, the famed cavalryman, General von Lüttwitz, who were charged with reducing this obstacle without delay. Assuming that McAuliffe's fate was sealed inside the ring, Bayerlein decided on a dramatic gesture. He sent a four-man delegation with a white flag of truce into the fortress, demanding that the defenders surrender. When their spiel was translated to McAuliffe, he answered with a single word that was to electrify the Allied armies in the whole of the Bulge.

"Nuts!" he said and had the puzzled Germans (who did not know what the idiom meant) escorted back to their line.

And more than that. In the evening McAuliffe launched a series of forays, so surprising the Germans that they hastily had to scrape up forces to repel these attacks. The forays, and what Merriam called McAuliffe's "puzzling but nonetheless vehement reply," now convinced the Germans that they could not gain Bastogne without a struggle. Although the siege continued and the future of the town's 18,000 defenders remained in the balance, the resolution to hang on to Bastogne was stemming the tide. "From the evening of December 22nd," von Manteuffel wrote, "the situation at Bastogne was reversed: henceforth the investing forces were to be on the defensive."

Although his attack was not going well, Patton's major preoccupation now shifted to the relief of Bastogne. This was December 23rd, and though it had snowed during the night, the day broke clear, promising excellent flying weather. The spell appeared to be broken. When making his estimate on the eve of the offensive, General Strong predicted that the Germans might attack "whenever [they] had a prediction of six days of bad weather." Now those six dismal days seemed to be up. For the first time in weeks the weather was actually *fine*. The clear skies were promptly filled with Allied aircraft—7 groups of fighter-bombers, 11 groups of medium bombers, a division of the 8th Air Force, and a smattering of RAF planes.

Patton was jubilant. He called Colonel Harkins to his office in Luxembourg and received his Deputy Chief of Staff wearing a smile from ear to ear. "Goddamnit, Harkins," he exclaimed, "look at the weather! That O'Neill sure did some potent praying. Get him up here. I want to pin a medal on him."

Chaplain O'Neill was still in Nancy, but now he was rushed to Luxembourg on Patton's orders. The weather was still fine the next day when he walked into the General's office. Patton jumped to his feet and approached the embarrassed Colonel with hand outstretched. "Chaplain," he greeted him, "you're the most popular man in this Headquarters. You sure stand in good with the Lord and soldiers." Then he pinned the Bronze Star Medal on his chest.

"Everyone offered congratulations and thanks," Harkins recalled, "and we got back to the business of killing Germans."

Now the relief of Bastogne shot to the top of Patton's list of priorities. He chose Combat Command B of the 4th Armored Division to break through to the besieged-bastion. He had unbounded faith in that unit, partly because it was commanded by Brigadier General Holmes E. Dager, whom he had learned to respect when the 4th Armored was training in England under General Wood and to admire when Dager spearheaded the breakout after Avranches.

But Dager ran into lively opposition south of Chaumont and was forced to give up the attempt. In the meantime, VIII Corps was maintaining the Bastogne perimeter against pressure from all sides, while in the area of III Corps, CCR sneaked to the west flank of the 4th Armored Division from Bigonville, launched a surprise attack, and secured the road from Vauxles-Rosières to Chaumont, leaving it to CCB to capture the latter.

The final chance to break into Bastogne came at 2:30 A.M. on December 26th, when General Gaffey raised Patton and requested permission to push elements of his 4th Armored through with a tank charge. Patton eagerly told him to go ahead. Led by Colonel Wendell Blanchard, an officer who had learned his *métier* at Benning in the 2nd Armored Division under Patton, forward tanks of Gaffey's Reserve Combat Command (commanded by Colonel Creighton W. Abrams) rolled into Bastogne, and made contact with the garrison. But the corridor was too narrow and precarious for vehicles to follow.

Next day, however, trucks and ambulances began to move into the city on the road Abrams had opened, and

the siege of the city was officially ended. Then reinforced
by units of the 9th Armored and the 80th Infantry Divisions, Gaffey's 4th Armored set to broadening the corridor
and opening the highway running from Arlon to Bastogne.
On December 29th, the road was secured, and the stage
was set for the last phase of the campaign—the drive on
Houffalize. For all practical purposes, the battle Hitler had
foisted upon the Allies was over.

The Ardennes offensive was, somewhat like the Battle of
Jutland, a rather untidy affair whose haphazard and dolor-
ous course exposed both the good and the bad in the high
command of both sides. It reverberated with recriminations
and nasty charges. It gave birth to spurious claims and
doctored histories. The clamorous clash of its major pro-
tagonists, pitted against one another within each of the two
camps, long survived the actual clash of arms. Sometimes
the din of the battle was drowned out by the noise of the
controversy it begot.

Patton's own 38 days in the Bulge produced more nonsense to embellish or distort the dubious Patton legend than
any other period of his wartime career. Some of his
wisecracks were given wide circulation and used to document, so to speak, the charge that he was irresponsible and
a blustering egomaniac. It is true that when apprised of the
magnitude of the German attack he had exclaimed, "Fine,
we should open up, and let the Hun get all the way to
Paris. Then we'll bite off the rear of their attack." But
nobody who knew the *real* Patton would repeat the quip
as evidence against the man. For how could any seriousness
be attributed to such a remark by a commander who
steadfastly refused to return a single conquered hamlet in
France to the *Boche*.

He was accused of having pleaded to be allowed to go
on with his attack against the West Wall despite the
emergency in Belgium, suggesting that he and the Germans
engage in a race "to see who can get the farthest." This
idiot charge, taken seriously by many despite its patently
apocryphal nature, is summarily disproved by Patton's intuitive preparations to respond to the German challenge
when it was still but a gleam in Hitler's eyes.

He was depicted as something of a buffoon at the Verdun conference for assuring Eisenhower that he could be in action in the north within 22 hours. This despite the fact that his promise was based on precise plans he had completed prior to his departure for Eagle Main, not even knowing what Eisenhower had in mind for him. Today we all know how faithfully and promptly he kept his promise.

In the welter of bitter and self-seeking argumentations around the Battle of the Bulge, Patton actually amazes the historian with his stillness and humility, with his sense of proportion, and with his strict professional approach to his enormous task. Occasionally he did refer to certain opportunities, the proper exploitation of which he thought could have forestalled the disaster. Months after the battle Patton recalled how Bradley had taken the 83rd Division from him in November, 1944, and related that episode to the Ardennes adventure. "If Bradley had not welched on his agreement," he said, "we would have taken Saarburg within 48 hours after we got Königsmacker. The Germans were on the run, and, with 83rd striking down from the north, the seizure of the town was certain. Once we had it, they couldn't have stopped us from taking Trier.

"And if we'd had Trier it would have been impossible for the Germans to have launched their Ardennes offensive. With Trier in our possession, they could not have massed their forces in the Eifel as they did. I'm firmly convinced that Bradley's refusal to allow me to use the 83rd, as he had promised, was one of the underlying causes of the Battle of the Bulge."

And he would also review the pre-history of the freak offensive with some wind of criticism, censuring Middleton, for example, for squatting on his fanny, letting the Germans get him like a sitting duck; and he mildly criticized General Gerow of V Corps for not breaking into the Germans' assembly area in the north.

But never during or after the battle did he claim for himself and his army anything more than their proper due. Dropping all his familiar bombast and bravado, he never rationalized his triumph in the Bulge as the foreordained outcome of his superior generalship. Patton never pretended to be better than he really was. During the recent Saar campaign General Van Fleet's 90th Division went for the formidable Fort Königsmacker en route to Saarburg, crossed the Moselle into a precarious bridgehead, and was

saved from harsh enemy retaliation only by a sudden
flash flood that caused the river to rise several feet within
a few hours. When the 90th secured the famous fort on
November 12th, Patton called a press conference and told
the correspondents about the exploit of the division,
characterizing it as one of the greatest in the war.

When one of the reporters asked him whether he had
known in advance that the Moselle would flood, Patton
answered with a smile, "Well, I could tell you that I was
a great strategist and knew it was going to happen. The
real truth is that both we and the Germans were caught
by surprise."

Now in the Bulge, Patton was like Emerson's man who
in moments of presumptuous pride, quickly looked to the
stars to remind himself what a tiny speck he really was
in the vast universe. On Christmas Eve a violent German
maneuver forced Dager into a withdrawal with the loss of
five tanks. Patton was quick to accept responsibility for the
mishap, attributing it to the fatigue of Dager's men caused
by his (Patton's) insistence on fighting around the clock
until Bastogne was liberated.

Throughout the battle he was humbled by the magnitude
of the task confronting him and especially by the unequaled
valor of the American soldier, which he regarded as the
decisive factor in the outcome. In his opinion the Battle of
the Bulge produced but one hero to be placed on the
pedestal of this moment—the common soldier on *both*
sides who was led into this misbegotten adventure by his
leaders, too sanguine and greedy on the German side, too
complacent and fumbling in our own camp.

In the final analysis it may be just a "myth," as Merriam
dubbed it, that the Battle of the Bulge was *won* by Patton's
Third Army. But the contention that the Third Army's
contribution was confined, as Merriam asserted, to the
liberation of Bastogne is also just a "myth." In the hands
of tabloid historians who simplify things to fit broad topics
into the narrow confines of our comprehension, Bastogne
became the romantic epitome of the vast encounter. In
reality it was far more than just a symbol, handy to reduce
this complex clash to its simplest denominator. It was, as
General von Manteuffel, a strict disciplinarian in both war
and historical presentation, demonstrated, the crucible in
which the whole battle was brewed.

By the remarkable incident of its defenders' courage,

Bastogne became the pivot on which—at first by accident and then by design—the entire enterprise turned from its beginning almost to its end.

Its magnificent tenants were not Patton's men. But Bastogne was his plum in the Bulge, and the battle to sustain it as the pivot against steadily growing German opposition was the Third Army's job. This meant far more than just the liberation of a besieged garrison. And so, by the sheer importance of its objective and the manner in which it carried it off, the Third Army has proper claim to an equal share in the triumph, leaving it to pedantic historians to argue over what in this superb exertion was but "myth" and what was blood and guts.

CHAPTER THIRTY-EIGHT
"ONE MORE GREAT CAMPAIGN"

General Patton ushered in the New Year of 1945 with a flamboyant gesture. He had issued orders to every battery in the Third Army to open up at exactly midnight and keep firing for 20 minutes. At the split-second during what the Germans call *Sylvester-Nacht* (the night before New Year's Day named for St. Sylvester), the front erupted in an inferno of sound and fury, as if Patton's guns were barking out his own festering protest—why the hell was this war still on when it could have been won and done with months before?

He hoped that this terrific collective salvo would be more than just a lot of seasonal noise and that at least some Germans would be hit. Later he was pleased to hear that when the sound of the bombardment had subsided the shivering Germans could be heard screaming in their frozen woods.

It was the meanest winter in 38 years. The weather was consistently bleak, the ground was covered with a thick blanket of coarse snow. The sharp wind blew in from the north and whipped up angry flurries, like tiny fragments of broken glass, that pierced the faces of the G.I.'s. It was 5° below zero at St. Vith, 7° below at Wiltz, a steady zero at Bastogne. Where the bulldozers had flattened the snow, the ground was a solid sheet of ice.

Out of this frigid nature protruded the contours of the pock-marked countryside with its charred ruins, for neither the snow nor the creamy fog could hide the scars and sores of the recent battles. It was a kind of 20th-century animated Valley Forge. Everything connected with the war was frozen stiff, from the numb, frostbitten limbs of the dogfaces to the strategy of the high command. The falling snow and the closed skies kept the air forces grounded. Even individual observation planes had a hard time taking off on the icy airstrips. Armor could operate only with grave difficulty by day, and hardly at all at night. The tractors that pulled the heavy and medium artillery had to be towed by special-duty trucks. Illnesses like flu and trench foot caused by the merciless weather almost equaled combat casualties—the "score sheet" of January 2nd listed 56,706 wounded in action and 55,675 felled by the climate. Virtually the entire army had to live outdoors because the below-zero temperature froze and broke the water systems, heating installations and the sewers.

Unlike the enforced intermission at the Moselle in October, 1944, this was war at its rawest. But for Patton personally it was one of the quietest periods of the conflict. For once his broad panoramic view of the future was blurred by the immediate problems confronting him in his own sector. He was humbled by the ardor and valor of the private soldier on both sides who had to wage this strange battle left very much to his own resources. And his doubts muted not only his usually sanguine expectations, but even his familiar eloquence and bombast.

The acute danger period was over, but the Third Army was not yet out of the woods. Its counterattacks were yielding only modest results, and hard won at that. While several units were making progress, others appeared to be bogged down. The 35th Division, for example, proved incapable of relieving some of its elements isolated at Villers-la-Bonne. The Germans continued to cling tenaciously to Lutrebois, and it seemed that no amount of nudging could dislodge them.

Bastogne was still the fulcrum of the Third Army's efforts. The III Corps was containing the enemy salient southeast of the town, its 4th Armored Division laboriously enlarging and frantically protecting the precarious corridor. How touch-and-go the fighting was could be seen best by following the fate of the 6th Armored from day to day. On New Year's Day it took three towns east of Bastogne, but had to give up one. The next day it drove into Oubercy and Michamps, only to be driven out of the latter.

When the day broke on the 3rd the division suddenly found itself in a defensive role, forced to fight furiously to repel a spirited enemy attack from Michamps. In the meantime, a task force organized of elements of the 101st Airborne Division and a combat command of the 10th Armored had to be thrown into a breach northeast of Bastogne to block furious German attacks toward the town.

On January 3, Patton visited the division's command post at Bastogne, and while he was there the Germans took the outpost under fire, drawing the appropriate reply from the Americans. The shelling presented a pretty spectacle in the snow, but it was not especially reassuring. "We can still lose this war," Patton wrote the night of January 4, and told his staff, "The Germans are colder, hungrier and weaker than we, to be sure. But they're still doing a great piece of fighting."

In his eagerness, Patton was backed to the hilt by his staff. If possible, the offensive spirit of his section chiefs even exceeded his own. On December 26th, in a staff memorandum signed by Harkins, Maddox and Koch, they advised him: "It is our belief that the Third Army should continue the offensive and carry the fight to the enemy, and destroy him without delay."

As usual, the enemy was not the only adversary who bothered him. Ever since he took the Third Army into the Bulge, Patton had been very much his own boss. General Bradley, brooding at his tactical headquarters and plagued by haphazard communications, did little to interfere with the Third Army's operations. Even so, his rare interventions proved enough to upset Patton. "In one case," Patton wrote, "while he did not order, he strongly suggested that instead of attacking north of Diekirch and cutting the enemy off at the waist [as Patton had planned], we should put in a new division southeast of Bastogne so as to insure the integrity of the corridor."

Patton heeded the suggestion (or, as he later put it, let

himself be "overpersuaded" by Bradley) and deployed the 90th Division as recommended, but too far west. He assumed full responsibility for the "error," yet wrote afterward: "Had I put the 90th Division in north of Diekirch, I am sure we would have bagged more Germans and just as cheaply."

At 9 A.M. on January 8th, 12th Army Group intervened with a crash plan, suggesting that he attack Houffalize that same day, using the 101st Airborne and the 4th Armored. Patton argued against the proposition, chiefly because he had planned a general attack for the next day, with General Van Fleet's 90th Division moving through the 26th, along the ridge road to the northwest, south of Wiltz.

He was now planning meticulously. He had worked out this particular plan with exceptional attention to all details in a special conference on January 6th attended by General Millikin of III Corps and General Van Fleet. Apparently nothing was overlooked to assure the success of the operation. Colonel Hammond was instructed to use a Signal Corps Deception Group at Van Fleet's CP to mask the movement of the 90th Division with fake radio traffic.

In the end, Patton went ahead with his operation, but it yielded a scant 2 miles. The attack was continuing when Army Group called again with another plan. This time Patton was *ordered* in so many words to place one of his armored divisions (presumably Gaffey's 4th) in reserve south of the city of Luxembourg. The order was induced by rumors of an imminent German counterattack at Saarbrücken.

On January 10th, Army Group got into the act again, cramping Patton's attack still further. Misinterpreting enemy troop movements, Army Group G-2 concluded that the Germans were about to resume their offensive, this time with an attack in force from across the Saar River just north of Trier. Although neither attack materialized, Army Group's intervention aborted Patton's own budding operation. "These two instances," he wrote, "for which Bradley was not personally responsible, indicate the inadvisability of commanding from too far back."

Reviewing his situation, Patton was smugly satisfied. Every unit of the Third Army was in what he regarded as its proper place, so poised as to be most effective to the detriment of the enemy, but safest for its own good. If he could not conduct successful operations from these positions, he told his staff, it would undoubtedly be due to the power and skill left in his enigmatic enemy and not to any faulty arrangements on his own part.

Then on January 11th Patton suddenly realized that all the air had gone out of Hitler's big balloon. This, in retrospect, may seem to be a belated recognition. As early as the third day of the offensive General Jodl of the *Wehrmacht Führungs-Stab* had realized that it had failed. Patton was not much behind Jodl with his estimate of the greater issue, even if his day-by-day difficulties and the hard fighting had left him apprehensive and gloomy.

His belief that the Germans had spent themselves beyond their means was supported by some of Colonel Koch's hard intelligence. On December 24th, when the Ardennes offensive was but eight days old, Koch's efficient and alert prisoner-of-war interrogation team had called attention to the dismal state of the German prisoners, who complained bitterly that they had gone without food for days. On the 24th, too, Signal Intelligence had intercepted a distress call from the 5th German Parachute Division, one of the crack enemy units in the offensive, asking for help, especially food and ammunition. Two days later another G-2 report based on prisoner interrogations re-emphasized the fact that the Germans were becoming increasingly hungry.

When Koch presented the report during the morning briefing, Patton exlaimed, "I think the Hun has shot his wad! This is the time for us to attack!"

But it was too early to act so violently upon the scattered intelligence. The Third Army had much of its toughest fighting and Patton some of his biggest problems in the Bulge still ahead of them. But by January 11th there could be no doubt that the jig was up for the Germans and especially that the end of the Bastogne operation was in sight. Patton had anticipated this and was ready to exploit the situation promptly, preparing the way to Houffalize for the rendezvous with General Collins' VII Corps coming from the north, thus closing this unpleasant chapter of the war. More than that, he was all set to resume the attack toward the West Wall which the Ardennes offensive had so rudely interrupted.

How did Patton do his "anticipatings"?

In this particular case, as soon as he became convinced that the Battle of the Bulge was drawing to its close, he had a study made of the river lines and road nets in the area of General Walker's XX Corps, which he expected to spearhead the resumed offensive.

The study showed that the Germans could cross the Saar at three points—in the vicinity of Saarburg, at Saarlautern and at Saarbrücken—where, as he put it, "I would have attacked had I been the Germans." He ruled out the first two possibilities and focused on Saarbrücken. Patton decided to resume the offensive then and there with what he had. He drove to Thionville, where XX Corps still was maintaining its CP, to discuss the plan with Walker, and "arrange the blow." But his arrangements proved premature.

For the time being, his immediate job was to get to Houffalize. The attack jumped off on January 13th, was slow at first, then gained speed. At last, on the 16th, Captain Herbert Foye's 41st Cavalry Squadron of the 11th Armored Division of the Third Army established contact in the town with Colonel S. R. Hinds' 41st Armored Infantry Regiment of the 2nd Armored Division of General Collins' magnificent VII Corps.

Patton drove to Houffalize, which he found "extremely well liberated." What turned out to be hardly more than a sightseeing trip left him with a healthy respect for the soldiers who had fought this fantastic battle and with humility at the sight of the dead. At one point he ordered Mims to stop the jeep to pick up a German machine-gunner at the roadside who seemed to be seeking help with arms outstretched. The man was dead. He had been "instantly frozen" when killed in a sitting position, his stiff, extended arms still holding a belt of cartridges. Farther on he halted again to inspect a strange row of black twigs sticking out of the snow. They turned out to be the frozen toes of dead soldiers. This was war in a refrigerator. Its quick-freezing process had turned the dead the color of claret—"a nasty sight," Patton remarked.

But now, for all practical purposes, the big battle was over and won. On January 29th it was made official, and Patton could take stock. At a press conference called that day to mark the conclusion of the impromptu campaign—his eighth in a little more than two years—he said:

"The purpose of our initial attack can be stated very briefly. We hit the sons of bitches on the flank and stopped them cold. Now that may sound like George Patton is a great genius. Actually he had damned little to do with it. All he did was to give orders."

In his own *post mortem* he wrote with some justifiable flourish:

"During this operation the Third Army moved farther and faster and engaged more divisions in less time than any other army in the history of the United States—possibly in the history of the world." But the triumph had its price, and so Patton closed the chapter of the Bulge with a special "score sheet." As of January 29, 1945, 14,879 of his men had been killed in action, 71,009 wounded, and 14,054 were missing, a grand total of 99,942 casualties. The Bulge itself had cost him 50,630 of these men.

Patton always viewed his victories in the sacrifice of his soldiers. On January 6th he was driving to Arlon, where General Millikin had his headquarters, when he passed through the rear of the 90th Division going into battle. The men had been in their trucks for some time in the sub-zero weather—actually it was 6° below zero. On the right side of the road an endless column of ambulances was bringing back the wounded. It was a grim scene of war under leaden skies, yet when the men spotted Patton in his jeep they jumped up and gave him a cheer that melted the frost.

"It was the most moving experience of my life," he wrote, "and the knowledge of what the ambulances contained made it still more poignant."

It was with that episode in mind that he concluded his *post mortem*: "The results attained were made possible only by the superlative quality of American officers, American men and American equipment. No country can stand against such an army."

The Bulge had cost the Germans some 120,000 casualties they could ill afford and a mass of invaluable material. But Hitler continued to pull rabbits from his battered hat. His new V-weapons, rolling off the assembly lines in rapidly growing numbers, began to be used tactically as well against vital military targets. His aircraft industry was making good progress in producing fighters with the new jet propulsion, which the desperate Führer expected would have "a decisive influence on the whole course of the war." Strangely enough, he was seconded in this assumption by the Allied air commanders. They warned Eisenhower that "if the enemy could succeed in putting these planes into the air in considerable numbers he would quickly begin to exact insupportable losses from our bombers operating over Germany."

In August, 1944, the consensus in the Allied camp was that the power of German resistance had been exhausted. Now the estimates of SHAEF G-2 swung in the opposite direction. Allied Intelligence, confused by the unexpected power of the Ardennes offensive, assumed that the Germans were capable of putting up strong resistance even west of the Rhine, and could, if need be, withdraw behind the river in good order and in good time. Bolstered by what was described as the formidable barrier of the Rhine, the enemy could, SHAEF mused, make life extremely difficult for the Allies and prolong the war beyond anything "practicable" for either side.

There were, however, serious miscalculations in Hitler's hopes and SHAEF's estimates. For example, Allied Intelligence could not properly gauge the influence of the Red Army's new offensive on the West Front, an influence, indeed, that proved crucial even for the outcome of the Battle of the Bulge. And Hitler could not know, or probably just refused to recognize, how quickly and completely the Allies would recover from the shock of the bizarre battle he had imposed upon them.

Patton's short-lived and rather uncharacteristic pessimism of this period was shaped by the foxhole perspective of the field commander who had just emerged from a bloody battle in which he had ample reasons to admire the enemy soldier's skill and morale. But Eisenhower was rather optimistic, even amid the gloom of a growing legion of Jobs at his headquarters. He saw clearly from his elevated perch that (1) victory of his arms was a foregone conclusion and (2) it was but a matter of time. He was not prepared to delay the decision much longer. If a plan was needed to bring it about, he had one ready. *"One more great campaign,"* he wrote, *"aggressively conducted on a broad front, would give the death blow to Germany."*

On December 20th, when the Ardennes issue was very much in doubt, he began to talk it around. It was a persuasive demonstration, if any was needed, that the Supreme Commander never regarded Hitler's big gamble as a comeback. But the plan was neither a revolutionary concept nor a new one. It was the organic continuation of his original compromise solution of August, 1944—his broad-front strategy given a new lease on life. It had produced some remarkable successes, but also a number of painful problems. It had resulted in the inconclusive offensives of the autumn of 1944, and in the stalemate that made possible the Ardennes venture of the Germans.

And like his old plan, the new also seemed to please no one.

At this stage General Patton was still far too busy with his own considerable problems to be interested in outline plans. He was also in the dark about Eisenhower's intentions. He had last seen Ike at Verdun on December 19th during the crisis conference and had never even heard from him either on the phone or by telegram after that. As a result, as we shall see, his opposition to the plan was slow in developing.

The British, however, exploded against it, and so vehemently that the coalition was thrown into its worst crisis. Brooke and Montgomery again took it upon themselves to represent what they honestly regarded as "British interests," on the tacit understanding, though, that what was good for Monty was good for the entire Allied cause. The basic issue was the problem of command. In the emergency of December, Montgomery had been given operational command of all troops north of the Ardennes. He not only strove to retain that assignment but also hoped to be named ground commander of all of Eisenhower's forces except those under General Devers in the far south. In other words, he aspired for total operational command in the field, the job Eisenhower had been holding since September 1, 1944. After that, the Supreme Command would be but an empty shell.

The tragedy of the Bulge supplied a handy peg on which to hang this new campaign. It took the form of a violent onslaught on the plan *pro forma* and on Eisenhower and his broad-front strategy *de facto*. It became *bon ton* in certain British circles to saddle the Americans with all the blame for the Ardennes offensive and present Montgomery as the one man in the Allied high command who had actually warned them of the possibility of its coming.

The American commanders, wrote Arthur Bryant, reflecting the British view of December, 1944, "had chosen to ignore the two most elementary rules of war—concentration and the possession of a reserve to counter the enemy's moves and keep the initiative. As a result, though Germany was all but broken, she had been able, like a wounded tiger, to inflict on them grave injuries."

Bryant went on to say: "The war, instead of ending in 1944, had been prolonged into another year and, unless a very different method of conducting it was now to be adopted, not only [the British] position, but that of Europe was desperate." There was only one remedy, according to Bryant, as Brooke and Montgomery saw it. It became imperative "to induce the American high command, while shaken by its reverse, to concentrate at last on a single decisive blow and to prevent Eisenhower and Bradley from again indulging in their preference for attacking everywhere at once."

Field Marshal Brooke was the first in the British camp to hear of the revival of Ike's old plan and also the first to oppose it with his consummate skill in backstage intrigue. He happened to be in a rather bad shape, both physically and emotionally. "I have now done three years of this job," he wrote in his diary on January 1st, "and am very, very weary." It is possible that his weariness reduced his tolerance and increased the intensity of his opposition, though he never needed much of a provocation to criticize Eisenhower's concepts or question his competence.

As soon as word of the plan reached him, Brooke alerted Montgomery. "We must watch," he wrote to Monty on December 21, 1944, "that things do not go wrong again, and I hope, therefore, you will continue to keep in close touch with me in these matters."

On this cue Montgomery promptly rushed to the center of the stage. He was convinced that the humiliation in the Ardennes had made the Americans a soft touch for concessions and pulled out all stops to gain them while the getting seemed good. He began to insist bluntly and unequivocally that his 21st Army Group, reinforced by at least one entire American army, be given "all available offensive power" for what Eisenhower had called the "one more great campaign," relegating the remaining American forces—and especially Patton's Third Army—to virtually total inactivity.

The stakes were high, and Monty was fighting dirty. When Bradley called on the Field Marshal at his monastic headquarters in a Dutch farmhouse on Christmas Day, Monty jumped on him and pummeled him with the bluntest of words, telling him that he had fully deserved his setback in the Ardennes. And when Eisenhower visited three days later, Monty became so crude that his bad manners began to disturb even his mentor. "It looks to me as if Monty," Brooke wrote, "with his usual lack of tact, has been rubbing into Ike the results of not having listened to Monty's advice."

Montgomery was putting the screws on Eisenhower to change the plan to suit him. "I suggest," he wrote to the Supreme Commander after their meeting, "that your directive should finish with this sentence:

" '12 and 21 Army Groups will develop operations in accordance with the above instructions. From now onwards full operational direction, control and co-ordination of these operations is vested in C.-in-C. 21 Army Group [Montgomery himself] subject to such instructions as may be issued by the Supreme Commander from time to time.' "

He then compounded the affront with bad taste by telling Ike: "I put this matter up to you again only because I am so anxious not to have another failure. I am absolutely convinced that the key to success lies in:

"(a) all available offensive power being assigned to the northern line of advance to the Ruhr.

"(b) a sound set-up for command, and this implies one man directing and controlling the whole tactical battle on the northern thrust.

"I am certain," he concluded, "that if we do not comply with these two basic conditions, then we will fail again."

This was too much for even the long-suffering Supreme Commander used to Montgomery's arrogance. Still trying valiantly to control his temper, he wrote back: "You know how greatly I've appreciated and depended upon your frank and friendly counsel, but in your latest letter you disturb me by predictions of 'failure' unless your exact opinions in the matter of giving you command over Bradley are met in detail."

Eisenhower expressed the hope that the issue could be settled on their own level without the necessity of submitting their differences to the Combined Chiefs of Staff. "The confusion and debate," he wrote, "that would follow would certainly damage the goodwill and devotion to a common cause that have made this Allied Force unique in history."

But he still seemed to be laboring to devise a solution that would give Montgomery operational control by another name. While the centrifugal force of the British threatened to jeopardize what Bradley called the integrity of U.S. command, centripetal pressure from two opposite forces firmed Eisenhower for turning down Montgomery. One was applied by Bradley and Patton, the other by General Marshall.

As soon as Bradley and Patton learned of the threat, Bradley rushed to Eisenhower to let him know where he and his army commanders stood in this explosive controversy. But when he raised the issue, Eisenhower fended it off impatiently with an evasive answer, forcing Bradley to state his position in uncompromising terms.

"You must know, Ike," he said, "that I cannot serve under Montgomery. If he is to be put in command of all ground forces, you must send me home, for if Montgomery goes in over me, I will have lost confidence in my command."

As Bradley described the scene that followed, "Ike flushed. He stiffened in his chair and eyed me hotly." Instead of reassuring Bradley that he would never acquiesce to Monty's demand, Eisenhower seemed to indicate that he was planning to go along with it. "Well," he told Bradley, "I thought you were the one person I could count on for doing anything I asked you to."

"You can, Ike," Bradley said. "I've enjoyed every bit of my service with you. But this is one thing I cannot take."

He was able to reinforce his position by telling Eisenhower that Patton also would ask to be relieved. As a matter of fact, the uncharacteristic intransigence of Bradley's stand had been largely generated by Patton. A few days before, Patton had received word from the United States that "some Englishmen" were lobbying in Washington to get high-level American support for Montgomery's aspirations. He immediately went to Bradley and related this prize piece of information to him and was pleased to hear from Bradley that he "would feel obliged to ask for relief rather than submit 12th Army Group to Montgomery's command." Patton clasped Bradley by the arm and said solemnly, "If you quit, Brad, I'll be quitting with you."

News of the revival of Montgomery's campaign in his own behalf was quick to reach General Marshall in Washington. The Chief of Staff regarded the claim as preposterous, especially since there were now 50 American divisions committed in the west compared with only 15 British divisions. On December 30th he sent Eisenhower a telegram advising him that it would be totally unaccepable to him, to

President Roosevelt, to the Joint Chiefs and, indeed, to the American people to give Monty what he was so ardently seeking.

Field Marshal Brooke, who saw nothing improper in keeping Montgomery posted on everything that was going on in the highest commands, immediately advised his protégé of General Marshall's telegram counseling him to keep quiet for the time being while he, Brooke, would continue the fight against the Eisenhower plan and for Montgomery's demands. On January 10th Brooke then did exactly what the Supreme Commander had hoped would not come to pass. He submitted the controversy to the Combined Chiefs in a formal request to review the Eisenhower plan.

"Insisting," Pogue wrote, "that there would not be sufficient strength for two main attacks, the British asked that one major thrust be selected and that only those forces not needed for this purpose be used for other operations. This approach would rather effectively *rule out any action by the Third Army.*" He then added: "In presenting their questions, they appeared to be in a position of championing Montgomery against his superior."

What began as a private controversy between Eisenhower and Montgomery now became a burning Allied issue. It led to what Robert E. Sherwood described as "the most violent disagreements and disputes of the entire war." At one point General Marshall—in his exasperation with the British—made it known that if Eisenhower's plan were not accepted by Brooke and his associates he would recommend to Eisenhower that he had no choice but to ask to be relieved of his command.

How bitter the controversy became was evident in one of Montgomery's letters to Brooke. Dated January 22nd, it read in part: "I fear that the old snags of indecision and vacillation and refusal to consider the military problem fairly and squarely are coming to the front again. . . . The real trouble is that there is no control and the three Army groups are each intent on their own affairs."

Then taking cognizance of his major rival, around whose fate, in the final analysis, the issue essentially revolved, Montgomery wrote: "Patton today issued a stirring order to Third Army saying the next stop would be Cologne. One has to preserve a sense of humor these days, otherwise one would go mad."

At their meeting on Christmas Day, Montgomery thought Bradley appeared in rather bad shape, looking thin and worn. "Poor chap," the Briton wrote later, "he's such a decent fellow and the whole thing is a bitter pill for him."

But Monty had drawn the wrong conclusions from Bradley's appearance. If the American was thin and worn, it was because he had been working a full week trying to stem the German tide in the Ardennes. If he seemed ill at ease, it was because he was hopping mad at Montgomery and was trying to conceal it. That night Bradley dined quietly with Patton. After the meal, they had a long talk.

"He told me," Patton recorded their conversation, "that Montgomery stated that the First Army could not attack for three months, and that the only attacks that could be made would be made by me, but that I was too weak. Hence, we should have to fall back to the line of the Saar-Vosges, or even to the Moselle, to gain enough divisions to permit me to continue the attack."

The proposition was repugnant to them, and not soley on military grounds. Patton later wrote that he considered this a "disgusting" proposition. It threatened to have tremendous political implications, if only because, as he phrased it, it would "probably doom to death or slavery all the French inhabitants of Alsace and Lorraine, whom such move would abandon to the Germans."

Returning to his headquarters, Patton called a staff conference and threw the problem to his section chiefs, calling for a joint memorandum embodying their opinion of Montgomery's idea. The memo was ready the next day, December 26th. It was a carefully considered and brilliantly reasoned argument against the Montgomery design, refuting his contentions in seven major points, one of them shrewdly psychological. "The American (soldier and public) psychology must be considered," the memo stated. "Although it cannot be evaluated, it would probably be seriously affected by a voluntary withdrawal. The American soldier has tried with all of his skill and heart to gain the ground now in our hands. To give it up might be catastrophic both from a psychological and military point of view. Third Army troops know and understand the attack. They do not know or understand the retreat or general withdrawal."

On December 27th Bradley left for another meeting with Eisenhower, at which Montgomery was expected to be present but as usual failed to show up. He set out properly primed by Patton, who had urged his friend to demand that the First Army command be immediately returned to him. "If Ike puts you back in the driver's seat, Brad," he said eagerly, "we'll bag the whole German army."

Bradley returned from Paris with a number of gifts. He had succeeded in getting two divisions released to Patton and brought back for him a second Oak Leaf Cluster for Distinguished Service Medal with a very nice citation. And it appeared that he had also managed to put some starch into the Supreme Commander's general attitude toward Monty. For immediately after the meeting with Bradley, Eisenhower left for a showdown with Montgomery at the latter's tactical headquarters in Holland.

"General Ike had informed Monty," Butcher reported, "that he could not agree that one Army Group commander should fight his own battle and give orders to another Army Group commander. The plan for the advance to the Ruhr envisioned the placement of one complete U.S. Army under Montgomery's command, which General Ike considered militarily necessary and believed also that it reflected his confidence in the Field Marshal. . . . Monty responded, sympathetic with the great burden of responsibility which the Supreme Commander was forced to bear, and said that whatever the decision, he can be relied upon completely."

It was upon his return from Monty's headquarters that Eisenhower found Marshall's unequivocal telegram waiting for him, the contents of which had been promptly reported to Monty. It was a blatant breach of confidence, as Montgomery implied in his memoirs, but the indiscretion served a constructive purpose. "I have always been under the impression," Montgomery wrote, "that Eisenhower did not know I had been told about Marshall's telegram." However, he added, "That telegram finished the issues of 'operational control' as far as I was concerned and I knew it would be useless to open it again."

On his part, Eisenhower resolved the issue by falling back on his original compromise solution. On December 31st he drafted an "Outline Plan" that incorporated practically all of Montgomery's demands except his hankering for "operational control."

Basic to the plan was the destruction of "enemy forces west of the Rhine, north of the Moselle, and to prepare for crossing the Rhine in force with *the main effort north of the Ruhr*." The emphasis was General Eisenhower's.

The plan anticipated the victorious conclusion of the Bulge battle with the meeting of Patton's Third Army and VII U.S. Corps under Field Marshal Montgomery's temporary command. With that, the plan stipulated, General Bradley would "resume command of the First U.S. Army."

"Thereafter," Eisenhower wrote, "First and Third Armies to drive to northeast on general line Prüm-Bonn, eventually to Rhine;" while Montgomery's 21st Army Group, "with Ninth U.S. Army under operational command," was to return to the preparations of "Veritable," Montgomery's plan for a Canadian attack between the Maas and the Rhine originally contemplated for January-February, 1945, but delayed by the Ardennes offensive.

The plan was to operate in two phases—one at the Rhine, the other in the Rhineland and beyond. Monty's *main* drive into the Reich was to progress "from the Lower Rhine north of the Ruhr and into the North German Plain." Bradley would make a complementary attack from the Mainz-Frankfurt area "to join up with the Russians." There was also to be a subsidiary effort by General Devers' Sixth Army Group in the south.

Montgomery appeared to be satisfied. "I studied the outline plan," he wrote. "It did all I wanted except in the realm of operational control, and because of Marshall's telegram that subject was closed." He concluded: "In fact, I had been given very nearly all that I had been asking for since August. Better late than never."

On January 12th, even as the Germans were accelerating their withdrawal from the Bulge, General Bradley visited Patton to survey the situation. Patton assured him that the link-up with VII Corps was a matter of but a day or two, and that Bradley was actually on the eve of getting back the First Army. Bradley, on his part, then told Patton that he hoped to attack east with the First Army toward Cologne while the Third Army would maintain pressure from the vicinity of St. Vith. "I don't really care where we attack," Patton said, "as long as we attack. Because if we don't, Brad, the Germans certainly will."

On the 23rd they met again to discuss plans at a somewhat longer range and to coordinate designs drawn up by Patton's staff with those drafted by Bradley's Army Group. They fitted perfectly like the pieces of a jigsaw puzzle. According to this joint design—the fortuitous meeting of minds—two corps of First Army were to attack the West Wall north of the VIII Corps area while Third Army would do the same to the south with one strong corps, Middleton's VIII. The III and XII Corps would hold the line, then follow the advance of VIII Corps on its right.

CHAPTER THIRTY-NINE
TO THE RHINE

In a sense, all this politicking and long-range planning was little more than academic. The over-all situation was still far too complex and wrought with many imponderabilia that made exact prognoses very difficult, if not impossible. The Germans had lost their Ardennes gamble but their power to remain in the war for even another year appeared to be still substantial. On closer scrutiny it became apparent that the real sources of that power were spiritual rather than material. But so persuasive were Hitler's evangelism and Goebbels' propaganda that even the coldly calculating and increasingly skeptical professionals of the *Wehrmacht* high command began to see rays of hope. Strange as it may seem, German estimates of the period regarded the future as rosy in spite of the resounding failure of the Ardennes venture and the daily growing menace of the powerful new Red Army drive.

On January 4th, for example, a colonel of the General

Staff, Wilhelm Meyer-Detring, who was section chief in the Operations Department of the *Wehrmacht Führungs-Stab*, presented a comprehensive appreciation of the situation in the west and spoke with unabashed optimism of German prospects, as he put it, to retain the initiative. "The basic objective remains," he told Hitler, who was in the audience at the afternoon session, "the piecemeal destruction of the enemy armies whenever and wherever an opportunity is afforded."

As for the future, Colonel Meyer-Detring spoke hopefully of "the re-establishment of a strong position in the Vosges" for the purpose of "cutting off those elements of the enemy which still remain in northern Alsace. This will give us the base for new offensive operations." The Germans had had a smattering of intelligence about the command controversy in the Allied camp and derived additional hope from an apparent clash between Montgomery and Bradley. On January 6th, 16 days after the event, the *Kriegstagebuch* recorded that Monty had assumed command of the First and Ninth U.S. Armies. Assuming that the arrangement had been designed to be permanent, German Intelligence interpreted this as the beginning of poor Bradley's end. "This means," the interpretation read, "that General Bradley has been put on ice."

But while Hitler hoped and Eisenhower planned along more or less imaginary lines, Bradley and Patton appeared to see the situation as it really was. They recognized the element of last-ditch determination in the German war effort as an acute danger; and they had a healthy respect for the sting still left in the *Wehrmacht,* even in its hastily assembled *ersatz* divisions. They were convinced, nevertheless, as were Eisenhower and Montgomery, that a powerful blow, well aimed, smartly directed and adequately supplied, would demolish what was but a house of cards in Germany. But unlike Eisenhower and Monty, they were dubious of Monty's ability to carry out the mission the Supreme Commander had assigned to him. Craving for themselves the stellar part, Bradley and Patton never ceased to hope (seemingly against hope) that emphasis of the plan might be shifted to 12th Army Group after all.

The trouble was that most of the time Patton was playing the role of Lazarus at the big feast of the Allied war effort, receiving, like the Biblical beggar, merely the crumbs of the sumptuous meal. This is an important feature of his story in World War II and a puzzling sidelight of its conduct by Eisenhower. From the beginning to the end of the "crusade in Europe" there always was a gaping discrepancy between what Patton wanted to do and what the Supreme Commander was willing to let him do.

It is no reflection on the valor and skill of the British soldier when it is said that Brooke and Montgomery, while claiming the main effort for the predominantly British 21st Army Group, were not actually capable of making the most of the opportunity afforded them. Although the British were probably right in their occasionally vehement advocacy of what Monty had called "the *one* big thrust," they did not have the physical forces to mount it and bring the war to its logical conclusion in a sweeping drive. By his military philosophy, temperament and the nature of his generalship, and as great a commander as he was, Field Marshal Montgomery did not have what it took to conduct sustained power drives (on shoestrings, if necessary) leading to the ultimate decision. On the other hand, even if Patton alone was probably not the man to do it, the combination of Bradley and Patton was.

However, this crucial factor of command was either not recognized or deliberately glossed over, presumably in the interest of "Allied unity." Under the circumstances, the eager and brilliant Patton, condemned to play second fiddle, had to scheme each time he wanted to break his chains. Fortunately, by this time, he had Bradley's wholehearted support for his permanent rebellion, and more. He could safely depend on the enormous professional competence and unwavering loyalty of his unspectacular Army Group commander to push him on or hold him back as the situation demanded.

When the Battle of the Bulge ended the war in the west had only about 100 days left. But what a One Hundred Days they became in Patton's career! During that period he mounted four full-scale campaigns and wound up, somewhat baffled by the end when it came, inside Czechoslovakia with something resembling the military version of an unfinished symphony.

This was no longer a war of staccato moves. In Patton's hands it suddenly became a machine of perpetual motion.

The Battle of the Bulge ended on January 29th. On that day, as Colonel Harkins recorded it, "the 13 divisions of the four corps of the Third Army were abreast the Moselle, Sauer and Our Rivers, ready to crack the Siegfried Line from Saarlautern, north to St. Vith."

On the very day one of his difficult battles ended, Patton started another. Exhausted but undaunted, VIII Corps opened an offensive on the 29th, one battalion of its 4th Infantry Division crossing the Our River. The 90th Division was to get over during the night. The 87th Division, still some distance from the Our, was closing in for the assault crossing.

The VIII Corps was followed by III Corps immediately to the south. The XII Corps was assembling and deploying to join the issue. And XX Corps was getting ready to start operations a little later. From Patton's point of view this was a kind of honeymoon. It seemed that, for once, he would be given the full scope he wanted and needed.

But the "honeymoon" was deceptive. He still had two wars on his hands. One was the "easy" one against the Germans. The other was more difficult, for he had to wage it against his own superiors. "Goddamnit, Brad," Patton once exclaimed, "why the hell won't SHAEF leave us alone? I'd rather fight the Hun than Ike and Monty all the time."

Just two days before the offensive resumed, President Roosevelt and Prime Minister Churchill had met at Malta, en route to the Yalta Conference with Marshal Stalin, to discuss strategy and coordinate their plans before meeting the Soviet leader. Churchill had coined the code name "Cricket" for these discussions, but to Bradley and Patton the outcome did not seem to be quite that. For Patton it spelled the end of the honeymoon that had barely begun. The Malta meeting froze the Eisenhower plan as it was, giving Montgomery too much and what Bradley and Patton regarded as far too little for them.

In the final stages of the Bulge operation, as we have just seen, Patton had fought himself clear for a major thrust. His XII Corps was regrouping and was being brought up to strength. It was now in an excellent position to move on to Bitburg in Germany, Patton's first major objective.

Eddy planned to attack on the morning of February 6th, but Patton told him, "Make it the 4th."

"Goddamnit, General," Eddy exploded, "you never give

me time to get ready. The trouble is you have no appreciation of the time and space factor in this war."

"Is that so?" Patton countered. "If I had any appreciation of it we'd still be sitting on the Seine."

So it was decided that it would be the 4th, and Patton called Army Group Headquarters to clear the attack. General Bradley was in Paris again, conferring with Eisenhower. In his absence Patton talked to General Lev Allen, the Chief of Staff, who had no objections. But Allen called back within the hour.

"No dice, George," he said in a small voice. "You are to commit nothing—pending further orders."

Patton was stunned. He ordered Eddy to suspend his preparations, then called a staff conference to review what he immediately recognized was another change in the fluid situation. "This doesn't sound good to me," he told his section chiefs. "I'm afraid we're going to be halted again in the middle of a going attack in order to start another one you know where, that has little promise of success. I have the sneaking suspicion that SHAEF is out as usual to exalt the Field Marshal."

To drown his apprehension, he went to join his men, visiting every company of Major General Harry J. Maloney's 94th Division. He was in a dark mood, and went into a rage when he found that the division had the worst ratio of noncombat to combat casualties in the Third Army. "If you can't do something to improve this situation," Patton told Maloney, "you'll be a noncombat casualty yourself, and pretty soon." But then he relented, patted Maloney on the back and said with the hint of a smile, "You're doing fine otherwise—but Goddamnit, do something about those slackers."

When he got back to his CP a call from Bradley was waiting. "Monty did it again, George," the Army Group Commander said. "You and Hodges will go on the defensive while Montgomery will resume the offensive in the north." Then, anticipating Patton's reaction, he continued, "It wasn't Ike this time. Orders from the Combined Chiefs. Brooke even got General Marshall to go along with him. I don't know what made him agree. Probably he's anxious to get those 14 British divisions sitting on their butts in Belgium back into action."

"What are they hoping to accomplish?" Patton asked.

"Montgomery wants to secure a wide stretch of the Rhine

as quickly as possible," Bradley replied, "so that we would
have a quick entry if Germany collapsed suddenly."

"Horsefeathers," Patton said. "I'm convinced that we have
a much better chance to get to the Rhine first with our
present attack. When are the British supposed to jump off?"

"Probably on the 10th," Bradley answered.

"I doubt if Monty will be ready by the 10th," Patton said.
"But what are *we* supposed to be doing in the meantime?"

"You can continue your attack until February 10th,"
Bradley said, "and maybe even after that, provided your
casualties aren't excessive and you have enough ammunition
left."

Patton then attended an Army Group conference at
Namur to listen to the official version. Upon his return he
summoned his corps commanders and planning group to a
conference of his own to acquaint them with these new
developments and give them the benefit of his vociferous
doubts. He started the meeting in a frivolous mood, regaling his audience with one of his Montgomery stories.

"The Field Marshal was outlining his plans to Eisenhower," he said with an impish smile, "and concluded as follows: "I shall dispose several divisions on my flank and lie in
wait for the Hun. Then, at the proper moment, I shall leap
on him. . . ."—Patton paused dramatically to drive home
the punchline—". . . like a savage rabbit."

But then he became deadly serious.

"Gentlemen," he said, "I participated in a Group conference with Generals Bradley, Hodges and Simpson. General Bradley informed us that General Eisenhower had been
ordered by the Combined Chiefs of Staff to make the main
effort in the north, under Field Marshal Montgomery. For
this offensive, the Field Marshal is to get nine United States
infantry and several armored divisions. . . . Third Army
will be required to transfer several divisions to Ninth Army.
We will get the bad news later. Whatever it is, we will
comply promptly and without argument. However, it is very
obvious now who is running this war over here and how it
is being run."

Patton had made up his mind to disobey his orders. "Personally I think," he said, "that it would be a foolish and
ignoble way for the Americans to end the war by sitting on
our butts. And, gentlemen, we aren't going to do anything
foolish or ignoble."

He had three avenues open to him to continue operations

within the newly imposed limitations. By then VIII Corps
had been halfway to Prüm and the heart of the West Wall
defenses in Patton's sector. So VIII Corps could continue
the attack toward Prüm or it could halt, leaving XII Corps
to mount the attack on Bitburg. Or, as a third possibility,
both corps could attack simultaneously.

"Personally," he said, "I favor the last."

That settled it. They decided to go for both Prüm and
Bitburg, but since they had to conduct the two-pronged
drive "under the counter," so to speak, Patton counseled
strictest secrecy. "Let the gentlemen up north learn what
we are doing," he said, "when they see it on their maps."

Shortly after the meeting Patton was handed a signal
from 12th Army Group summoning him to Bastogne for a
conference with General Eisenhower. This sounded ominous. "Do you think, Hap," he asked his Chief of Staff apprehensively, "that this might have some connection with
our attack?"

He was convinced that Ike had gotten word of his
"insubordination" and was calling him to Bastogne for a
dressing down. He later compared his experience to Nelson's
predicament at Calvi when he had learned the night before
the attack on Corsica that the enemy was stronger than had
been assumed, but withheld the intelligence from Jervis
because he feared he would call off the operation. As it
turned out, the Bastogne meeting was a purely social call.
When Patton realized that the Supreme Commander had no
inkling of his intentions, he decided to keep mum, just as
Nelson had done at Calvi.

What became known as the Eifel Campaign—the Third
Army's fifth—was now on in earnest. It gained momentum
on February 6 with XII Corps' advance on the Kyll River
and the clearing of the Saar-Moselle triangle by XX Corps.
It ended on March 12th, with VIII Corps completing the
mop-up west of the Rhine. Trier was taken on March 1st.

But, of course, it was not as simple as it sounds. Patton
had to hatch one of his elaborate plots to acquire the strength
he needed to take the city. Even then, he captured it in violation of orders.

Trier had begun to intrigue him in mid-October, 1944,
when he was planning the Saar Campaign. In one of those
inspired fits that produced his best ideas, Patton saw a
chance to capture the city with the help of the 83rd Division, which he hoped to borrow from VIII Corps. When the

division was denied him, Trier escaped his grasp. Then came the Ardennes offensive, and Patton had to bide his time. Now the hitch was that he did not have the force he needed or the authority to capture the city. He was determined to get both and take the city as a bonus of his Eifel Campaign.

On February 14th, chaperoned by Colonel Codman, Patton went to Paris on his first leave since October 24, 1942. He traveled in style, in the private, self-propelled, palatially appointed railroad car that had belonged to Reichsmarshal Goering, and checked into the Hotel Georges V off the Champs-Elysées. The swank hotel was, in the words of a directive issued by Com Z, "General Lee's private residence" where the "assignment of accommodations carried with it the understanding that such persons are his [Lee's] guests and the billeting of any person has his official approval."

This was supposed to be strictly a pleasure trip. Patton's schedule called for some shopping, including a set of silver-plated flatware for his private mess with the insignia of the Third Army engraved on every piece, a night at the Folies Bergère, and a shoot for driven ducks at the Royal Preserve of the former kings of France. But Patton was mixing pleasure with business. He used the occasion to excellent advantage to mend his fences at SHAEF and to do some brisk soliciting in the relaxed atmosphere of the jaunt. He was especially keen on the shoot General "Beetle" Smith had arranged in his honor because Generals Bull and Whiteley, Ike's operations chiefs, were expected to be present, and he wanted something very badly from his friend "Pinky" Bull.

What he wanted was the 10th Armored Division. Just prior to his departure he and General Walker had suddenly realized that the 94th Division was ready for a breakthrough in the Saar-Moselle triangle, provided it could be supported by an armored division. Patton had none to spare and looked around for one to borrow. The 10th Armored seemed to be the logical choice, if only because it had been part of XX Corps before the Ardennes offensive necessitated its abrupt transfer to VIII Corps. With the division back in the fold, Patton was convinced that anything would go—he could clear the triangle, take Trier, and even make a run on Koblenz.

In Paris, Patton laid the groundwork for the return of the division by telling Smith and Bull how well he could use it. But he refrained from specifically asking for it. But on the 19th, back at his headquarters, he put in the call. Now his proselytizing, as he called it, paid off. "Okay," Bull said, "you can have the 10th Armored, but only for a single operation, to clear the triangle."

The division joined XX Corps the next day, and with it Patton realized that the capture of Trier was a distinct possibility. But things in general remained frightfully complicated. He now had the strength he needed to take Trier, but still lacked the authority to go for that prize.

On February 21st, in another carefully plotted scheme, Patton coaxed tacit permission from General Bradley to include the capture of the elusive city in his Eifel Campaign. It was a fantastic day, this February 21st! Of Eisenhower's armies, the Third was the only one actually fighting. Montgomery's 21st Army Group with the Ninth U.S. Army; Bradley's First Army, and Devers' two armies were "sitting on their hunches," as the saying went at Patton's headquarters. But in his sector the front was aflame from one end to the other.

This was what Third Army did on this momentous day:

● In the area of the VIII Corps, the 90th Division seized five towns and cleared a sixth. The 11th Armored Division widened the breach in the West Wall, capturing Roscheid. The 6th Armored Division took two villages east of the Our and cleared two others.

● In the area of XII Corps, the 80th Division enveloped and destroyed the enemy in his West Wall positions between the Our and Gay Rivers, captured one town and cleared two.

● In XX Corps area, the 10th Division drove to its final objective in the Saar-Moselle triangle, clearing five localities; it then drove northeast to Saarburg, which it largely cleared, and mopped up to the Saar in the Ockfen area. The 94th Division overran a number of towns and villages between Orscholz and Saarburg, and cleared everything in its zone eastward to the Saar.

Behind the front, Bradley and Patton were locked in a conference, trying as best they could to keep a sense of proportion in the face of the resounding success of the Eifel Campaign. Bradley was, as usual, the reluctant harbinger of a SHAEF plan, an ambitious three-phase design. Under the plan, Montgomery was to establish a firm bridgehead across the Rhine north of the Ruhr and First Army was to invest Cologne. The Third Army was to drive to the Eifel and launch an offensive through the Palatinate "as the prelude to an assault up the historic Frankfurt corridor into central Germany."

Patton and his staff listened to Bradley's presentation with mixed feelings. In their opinion the whole design was "widely at variance with the actual ground situation." SHAEF had assigned the main effort to the north, where the Germans were the *strongest,* while casting Third Army to play a subsidiary role in the area where the enemy was *weakest.* But Patton recognized his opportunity, even if SHAEF had not, and asked Bradley as casually as he could, "It is my understanding that I have the authority to push the attack of the Third Army east to secure the Kyll River as extended south by the deep gorge generally 10 kilometers east of the crossings over the Saar River; and furthermore, if opportunity presents itself for a quick breakthrough by armor supported by motorized infantry to the Rhine River, then I have the authority to take advantage of that situation."

Bradley expertly caught the ball. "Of course," he shot back with a faint smile. "You would have to exploit any opportunity like that."

Now it was Patton's turn to smile, ever so faintly. "No more was said," wrote Colonel Allen, who witnessed the meeting, "and a few moments later the conference broke up. Patton had all he wanted."

Within four days the Saar-Moselle triangle was cleared, Saarburg secured, a string of firm bridgeheads established across the Saar. Trier came directly within reach and Patton ordered the 10th Armored to attack immediately toward the tottering city.

It was one of the war's strangest ventures. Patton had been given the 10th Armored solely to clear the triangle and was supposed to return it into SHAEF reserve as soon as its mission was accomplished. Nothing was said of Trier in the bargain. Now SHAEF was beginning to bombard Patton with inquiries why the 10th Armored had not reverted to its reserve. Even Bradley warned him, "Georgie," he said, "if you use the 10th Armored to take Trier you may be sorry."

Patton decided to take a chance. Late at night on the 26th he was given a breather. Bradley phoned that SHAEF would let him keep the precious armor, but for only 48 hours. "You either take Trier in two days," he said, "or you'll have to return the 10th Armored to SHAEF." Now the capture of Trier became the kind of race against time and space Patton had come to enjoy since his dash for Palermo and Messina. He made this one a two-pronged race. On the 28th, while the 5th Division of XII Corps was clearing the west bank of the Kyll River, the 76th Division of Major General William R. Schmidt drove off toward Trier. In the XX Corps area the 10th Armored intensified its drive toward the city, rolling as fast as it could across vicious minefields and in the face of bitter resistance from innumerable pillboxes.

There was no time to lose. The 48-hour respite was up. Patton either captured Trier at once or forfeited his chance, because the armor was due back at SHAEF the next day. Cutting all lines to "higher authority," he now gambled everything on taking Trier within these next 24 hours. On March 1st, reinforced by elements of the 94th Division, the 10th Armored reached the outskirts of Trier in the morning, drove into the city in the afternoon, began to clear it in the evening, and completed its capture during the night.

The next morning Patton was handed two top-priority messages that had come in at dawn. One was from SHAEF, ordering him to bypass Trier "as it would need four divisions to capture the city." The other was from General Walker, reporting that the 10th Armored and the 94th Infantry Division had just captured Trier. Patton immediately sent for Sergeant Rosevich and dictated an urgent telegram to SHAEF via 12th Army Group.

"Have taken Trier with two divisions," the message read. "What do you want me to do? Give it back?"

While Patton was thus dealing effectively with one formidable foe, another adversary suddenly loomed large in his domain, in the person of a lowly sergeant. Although it had but an incidental bearing on the war, the showdown between the general and the young sarge deserves this passing mention. It adds another pastiche to the Patton story. And it demonstrates, probably more poignantly than anything else, the basic democracy of the American army, and Patton's innate ability to adapt himself to it with ease and grace, despite his autocratic ways.

On February 16th, Captain Butcher, General Eisenhower's aide, called General Gay at Third Army CP, and told him: "Sergeant Bill Mauldin is scheduled to spend 30 days in your theater, so it may not be a bad idea if Mauldin and General Patton got together and had a little chat."

Mauldin was, of course, the famed cartoonist of *Stars and Stripes*, whose unforgettable Willie and Joe, a couple of weary, unshaven dogfaces, never ceased to irritate Patton. Bill had spent three years with the 45th Division, then kicked around in some fifteen other divisions, making innumerable friends but also a number of powerful enemies with Patton in the van.

During his first winter in Italy, Bill produced a number of brash and biting cartoons depicting the hardships the combat soldiers had to endure, and was reprimanded for them by the deputy theater commander who went so far as to forbid their distribution in his area. But then, right in the middle of the controversy, one of the corps commanders asked for the original of one of the banned drawings.

Mauldin took the drawing to him, worrying that his uniform was somewhat mixed and his hair uncut. But the corps commander put him at ease at once by asking: "How's your battle with the rear echelon progressing?"

Mauldin replied that he had nothing against the rear echelon, only some of its generals who accused him of undermining morale. "When you start drawing pictures that don't get a few complaints," the general told him, "then you'd better quit, because you won't be doing anybody any good."

After that Bill felt a lot better.

But Patton's opposition to Mauldin and his stuff was implacable. He took up the matter with Colonel Egbert White, publisher of the *Stars and Stripes,* suggesting that either Mauldin start shaving his characters or the paper stop featuring them, but White gave him no satisfaction. Patton then took his beef to Eisenhower, but the Supreme Commander dismissed the complaint with a hearty laugh and a spirited defense of Willie and Joe.

And now, Sergeant Mauldin was to infest the very Third Army where a necktie, conspicuous for its absence in his cartoons, had a distinct place in the war effort and was regarded as second in importance only to a bazooka, maybe. The soldier-artist's introduction to the Third Army was boisterous but not unexpected. He was stopped by the first MP he met, who asked him: "Where the hell is yer gawdam helmet?"

Mauldin began to say that he had just plain forgotten it, but the MP cut him off. "Don't you gimme none of yer gawdam lip, dammit—I heard that one before."

This went on until Bill got sore, blew his top, and was given a ticket. He retaliated with a cartoon, poking fun of the forbidding sign at the boundary lines of the Third Army, admonishing one and all to sartorial perfection— then went to see Patton.

The confrontation produced no fireworks. The general and the sergeant discussed the problem in quiet and civilized language, each defending his view and neither giving ground. When it was over, nothing changed, either in the appearance of Willie and Joe and their sardonic approach to war, or in Patton's opposition to them. The case was closed with a notation by General Gay on February 27th. "Undoubtedly," it read, "Sgt. Mauldin is a great cartoonist, and much to [my] surprise, he is merely a boy."

In a last effort to break the spell of Mauldin's presumably evil eye, Patton decided to blanket the Third Army with competing cartoons depicting the dogfaces the way he liked them—virile, full of vim, and clean-shaven. He found a young artist named Tom Hudson at his own command post and ordered him to draw a series of cartoons, Goddamit—wholesome and funny ones, none of that gawdam Mauldin stuff. But when Tom, after a promising start with emphasis on sex rather than combat, began to show the Mauldin touch, Patton discontinued the contest. From then on, Willie and Joe were tolerated as the only two unkempt, unshaven dogfaces in the Third Army.

While Patton was racing against what Eddy had called space and time, as well as against the restrictions the Combined Chiefs had imposed on him, he was, in the innermost recesses of his sporting soul, also competing with Field Marshal Montgomery. Their competition came to be interpreted as a running feud, although it was closer to being an affair of honor, like a duel. To a large extent Patton's hero-worshiping staff was the source of this historical misinterpretation because in its total loyalty it could not, or would not, comprehend the delicate nuances of the rivalry.

Montgomery's close subordinates were far more sophisticated. Equally dedicated to their chief, they were nevertheless (as the memoirs of de Guingand and Horrocks show) alert to his shortcomings. Unswerving as they were under his leadership in their loyal and efficient pursuit of his designs, they were not unmindful and unappreciative of the major contributions Patton was making.

On the other hand, Patton's passionately partial staff was incapable of appreciating that the Third Army was, to paraphrase Pope, but a part of the stupendous whole. Consequently, it viewed with suspicion, disapproval and scorn just about everything Montgomery did. In their partisan fervor, Patton's officers were not tempered by and failed to benefit from his own sense of proportion. He, too, had come to dislike and condemn Montgomery, and made him the scapegoat for some of his troubles. In his free-wheeling addresses to his staff and in conversations with confidants, Patton would present the Field Marshal as the villain. Yet his negative attitude toward his British colleague, and what seemed to be his implacable hostility, were hardly more than skin-deep. Often they were but part of his theatrical stance, more sound than fury.

Far from damaging the common cause, this contest between two superb practitioners of the military craft was actually good for it. Their personal bout drove both men to top performances. It invigorated much of Eisenhower's great crusade. And it impelled the various offensives briskly forward. One is almost inclined to wish that more of the Allied commanders had been imbued with their competitive spirit.

Now, too, Patton's energetic drive was, to a degree, both motivated and propelled by their rivalry. When he spoke jocularly of Montgomery's imminent "Veritable" operation and dismissed him with Monty's alleged characterization of himself as a "savage rabbit," he did it to inflame his own commanders with an unbridled spirit of this competitive enterprise. The rivalry gained added impetus from the facts of the battlefield. Patton, driving against weak German defenses, could make rapid headway. But Montgomery, facing the bulk and the cream of German opposition, had to move slower and was intermittently bogging down.

On February 8th, two days after the jump-off in the area of Patton's VII Corps, "Veritable" began "in overpowering strength after the most concentrated artillery bombardment of the war in the West." Thus was unfolded Eisenhower's Rhineland plan, with the immediate objective of driving Montgomery's troops "through the Reichswald and into the undulating sweep of the Lower Rhineland" to achieve a decisive breakout.

The drive was quick to reach Cleve, but there it came to a halt. Mistaking the arrival of the 15th (Scottish) Division of Major General C. M. Barber at the outskirts of Cleve for the breakthrough, General Horrocks, commander of XXX Corps, ordered the 43rd (Wessex) Division of Major General G. I. Thomas to exploit it, with disastrous consequences. The two divisions became hopelessly entangled. It was not until February 11th that Cleve could be cleared, and the Reichswald by the 13th. The Germans had brought up substantial reserves and succeeded in frustrating not only the hoped-for breakout, but even the preliminary breakthrough.

In the meantime, Patton was rolling on unchecked. The Germans proved totally incapable of halting his sweep across the Eifel and to the Rhine north of Koblenz. Elements of 11 enemy divisions, pocketed between the Third and First U.S. Armies, were destroyed, only a small fraction managing to escape across the Rhine. The Eifel Campaign was drawing to its end. The contours of a new campaign— the Third Army's sixth—moved within sight.

This was to become known as the Palatinate Campaign (with the capture of Koblenz), of which Wilmot wrote: "Patton's sweep through the Palatinate was the counterpart of his 'end run' south of the *bocage*." Yet he had to finagle again to accomplish this remarkable feat. This may seem a flippant and irresponsible way of putting it but, unfortunately, it was true. While in the final analysis each of his campaigns was properly authorized in general terms (for not even Patton could free-lance in a world war), the sweep and success of each was triggered by some sly trickery Patton had to employ in certain psychological moments to gain permission, first to mount campaigns instead of conducting what were supposed to be merely supporting drives, and then to broaden his invariably limited missions into triumphal marches. To gain his victories (in which the results usually justified his means and the fact that he had exceeded his orders), he had to play a lot of backstage politics and apply ingenious subterfuges. It required as great a skill in these endeavors as Bradley's and Patton's consummate prowess and know-how to produce the desired results.

The Palatinate Campaign, in particular, necessitated deception to befuddle, not the Germans, but Patton's own superiors (with a complicated signal maneuver staged by Colonel Hammond). On March 9th Patton was summoned to General Bradley's headquarters, now established at Liège, for a conference at which General Eisenhower was expected to attend, but mainly to be decorated a Grand Officer of the French Legion of Honor and receive the Croix de Guerre with Palms.

The situation in the Third Army's sector was extremely fluid and promising. Patton's VIII Corps had completed its drive to the Rhine and started mopping up. In the XX Corps area, the 10th Armored Division had closed along the Salm River, cleared a number of villages and towns, then turned north to the Dorbach area, where it put in a bridge and established a bridgehead. Potentially most significant was the regrouping of the 4th Armored Division in the area of XX Corps for an attack toward Treis to secure a bridge on the Moselle.

Prior to his departure, Patton's staff had put the finishing touches to the plan for the drive through the Palatinate. Under it, the participation of the 80th Division was imperative if the drive was to bag Koblenz and create the preconditions regarded as necessary for the campaign. However, the division, kept in SHAEF general reserve, was not available to the Third Army.

At 10 P.M. on March 9th, while Patton was still at Liège, General Eddy, commanding XII Corps, called General Gay and told him that "the 2nd Cavalry under Colonel Charles H. Reed had secured a bridge intact across the Moselle River." Eddy asked Gay what he should do. Gay took it upon himself to order Eddy to exploit this success forthwith and secure a firm bridgehead. Then he called Patton in Liège to tell him the good news. He suggested that he get authority to launch the planned Palatinate Campaign.

Patton immediately went into conference with Bradley and Eisenhower, explaining the situation. They both gave permission to exploit the capture of the bridge. He then asked for the 80th Division, and Eisenhower was glad to give it to him. Patton called Gay and ordered him to launch the Palatinate Campaign.

At about 1 A.M. on the 10th Eddy called Gay again to tell him that the report of the bridge's capture had been a mistake. Gay did not need any prodding to respond to the information in Patton's own manner. He told Eddy that the telephone was out of order and he could not hear what he was saying. But no matter what, Gay said, the Palatinate Campaign was on.

Upon returning to his headquarters, Patton was told the story of that confounded bridge. A tank battalion of the 4th Armored had moved south to Carden on the river opposite Treis and found the bridge intact, as initially reported. But when the first tank was halfway across, the bridge blew up. It no longer mattered. Patton instructed Hammond to cut the lines to "higher authorities" until further notice, then ordered Eddy to put in as many bridges as possible and go on with the action. While Third Army Headquarters played deaf and dumb, Eddy put three bridges across the Moselle, all that were needed for the drive into the Palatinate.

Another coincidence further aided General Patton in the campaign, permission for which he had procured under such slightly false pretenses. On the morning of March 16th, he received a message that General Eisenhower would arrive within a couple of hours. The Supreme Commander, accompanied by General Bedell Smith, was on his way to 12th Army Group Headquarters to visit Bradley, but could not land there. He decided to come down on Patton's airfield instead. Although the notice was extremely short, it sufficed for Patton to roll out the red carpet. When Ike and Smith arrived at 1:40 P.M. he had an honor guard lined up at the airfield, then took Ike on a sightseeing trip through the triangle to Trier. That night he entertained him at a sumptuous dinner party, with four winsome Red Cross ladies among the guests.

When he thought the moment was properly convivial, Patton asked Eisenhower whether, in the light of what he had seen of the Third Army's work, he could not give him another armored division. The Supreme Commander immediately obliged. He took the 12th Armored from General Patch's Seventh Army and released it to the Third, where Patton promptly assigned it to XX Corps. It was in action on March 18th, driving with two combat commands through the 94th Division toward the Rhine in the Worms area.

At the tail end of the Eifel Campaign, remnants of nine German divisions, cut off west of Cochem, withdrew south of the Moselle and by March 12th managed to establish a hastily formed defense line in the Hunsrück Mountains, trying to protect the north flank of General Balck's dwindling Army Group G. But Patton had developed a major threat to the enemy forces manning the West Wall—a danger the Germans could not ignore.

Their fears were fully justified. By driving to the Rhine, the Third Army had exposed the enemy's right flank and created the opportunity to resume a devastating war of movement for the first time since last August in France. Crossing the Moselle south of Koblenz, General Gaffey's 4th Armored Division ripped across the enemy's rear, followed closely by infantry units of General Eddy's XII Corps. Shortly afterward, the armor of General Walker's XX Corps plunged through the West Wall and attacked toward the Rhine, linking with units of XII Corps to trap the remnants of 10 enemy divisions in the Hunsrück Mountain region. At the same time, Patch's Seventh Army was attacking to the north through the West Wall.

Panic seized the Germans. They attempted to set up a defense line west of Mainz and Mannheim, but failed to hold the Third Army's charging armor. The 4th Armored penetrated far into the Palatinate and into the Seventh Army's zone, cutting off all but one of the enemey's Rhine River escape crossings. The 10th and 12th Armored drove the enemy eastward toward the Rhine. His withdrawal quickly becoming a rout, the enemy dashed for Speyer, the only crossing of the Rhine left him.

Chopped to pieces by Patton's armor rushing on them from three directions, attacked relentlessly by the fighter bombers of General "Opie" Weyland's XIX Tactical Air Command, and pursued closely by infantry, the Germans lost the bulk of two armies, yielding more than 80,000 prisoners. Other Third Army units gained control of Koblenz on March 18th. The Palatinate Campaign ended three days later with the Germans having been pushed across the Rhine everywhere in the Third Army's sector.

Patton was now back in the race in direct competition with Montgomery. The prize this time was what Monty had called "the greatest water obstacle in Western Europe"—the Rhine at last.

Little had been heard of the 21st Army Group since March 12th, a day Brooke commemorated in his diary with some nostalgia: "12.3.45!" he wrote. "It is sad that this date will not return for another hundred years. It looks so nice!" Operations "Veritable" and Blockbuster" were concluded on the 10th. The Ninth U.S. Army, fighting under Montgomery, took over the defense of XVI Corps' sector after an unexpectedly successful power-drive to the river. The entire left bank of the Rhine from Nijmegen to Cologne was in Allied hands. The stage was set for "Plunder," the majestic operation, as Montgomery referred to it, to trasnfer Eisenhower's vast northern army of 35 divisions to the east bank, envelop the Ruhr, and open up the plains of Northern Germany for Allied armor.

In the scope of its arrangements and in the obligato of its hullabaloo, "Plunder" appeared to be second only to "Overlord." The spectacular crossing was advertised beforehand as Montgomery's crowning achievement in the war, greater even than El Alamein. The Field Marshal was balling his fist for the venture, in which he expected to meet "the flower of what remained of Hitler's Western Army." He had assembled the Second British Army under General Dempsey, the First Canadian Army under General Crerar, and General Simpson's Ninth U.S. Army. Some 250,000 tons of stores had been accumulated, including a multitude of amphibious vehicles, assault craft and bridging material.

The magnitude of the preparations was graphically described by Churchill. His romantic imagination inflamed by the operation, he was looking forward to it somewhat in the spirit of Julius Caesar at the Rubicon. "All our resources were to be used," he wrote. "Eighty thousand men, the advance-guard of armies a million strong, were to be hurled forward. Masses of boats and pontoons lay ready. On the far side stood the Germans, entrenched and organized in all the strength of modern fire-power."

The Prime Minister journeyed to the Rhine to witness the crossing in the classic manner, "from a hill-top amid rolling downland," and saluted Marshal Stalin from the historic spot, in an emotional telegram. "I am with Field Marshal Montgomery at his HQ," he wrote. "He has just ordered the

launching of the main battle to force the Rhine on a broad
front with Wesel at the center. The operation will be supported by 2,000 guns and by the landing of an airborne
corps. It is hoped to pass the river tonight and tomorrow
and to establish bridgeheads. Once the river has been
crossed a very large reserve of armor is ready to exploit the
assault." Unmentioned in the dispatch were hundreds of
heavy bombers and 3,000 fighters under Air Vice Marshal
Coningham standing by to support "Plunder."

But the operation had several dark blotches that made it
seem somewhat less than the greatest show on earth Montgomery had intended to be. His personal zeal had already
intruded. In spite of the presence of the Ninth U.S. Army in
his fold, Montgomery had reserved the assault across the
river for the second British Army, leaving his Americans out
in the cold. "Ninth Army was flabbergasted," wrote its historian. "The instruction of the Field Marshal left General
Simpson's command with no part to play in the assault."

Simpson protested and Montgomery issued a new directive. But then two events occurred that made this monumental venture seem rather anticlimactic. Early in March
the Ninth U.S. Army embarked on an operation called
"Grenade" and drove from the Roer River to the Rhine, extending its northern flank all the way to Wesel. With his
power unspent, Simpson then suggested to Montgomery that
he be permitted to cross the river. "There is no doubt that
Simpson could have crossed with ease between Duisburg
and Düsseldorf," Wilmot wrote. But he was "restrained" by
Montgomery. "The 'master of the set-piece assault and the
tidy battle,'" Wilmot remarked, "he did not appear to
realize that American 'untidiness' and improvisation, however dangerous when the enemy was strong, could now yield
great dividends. An improvised crossing of the Rhine, even
in the 'wrong' place, might distrub his own plans, but it
promised to disrupt and confound the enemy's."

Then a windfall made "Plunder" appear almost superflu-
ous. On March 7th elements of the 9th Armored Division of
the First U.S. Army, advancing along the northern edge of
the Eifel, found the Ludendorff railway bridge at Remagen
standing and intact. General Hodges himself telephoned the
incredible news to General Bradley, who shouted into the
phone, "Hot dog, Courtney, this will bust the Kraut wide
open!" Breathing down his neck was General Bull, Eisenhower's G-3, who, only moments before was forcing Ei-

senhower's set plan on Bradley with the "larcenous proposal" to take three or four divisions from 12th Army
Group.

Bradley, who had immediately recognized the opportuni- ▸
ty presented with the capture of the bridge at Remagen, now
turned to Bull. "There goes your ball game, Pink," he said,
but Bull shot back, "You're not going anywhere down there
at Remagen. It just doesn't fit in with the plan." But Bradley
appealed the decision and was told by Eisenhower, "Get
across with whatever you need—but make certain you hold
that bridgehead." But within 24 hours SHAEF corrected the
Supreme Commander's exuberance. The next morning
Bradley was ordered "to commit no more than four divisions
at Remagen," an obvious intervention "in the interest of the
plan."

This was the situation at the Rhine when Patton also
reached the river. On March 21st his XII Corps was ma-
neuvering briskly along the Rhine, elements of the 2nd Cavalry Group standing firm between Frei Weinheim and Mainz;
the 90th Division closing in on Mainz and clearing most of
its zone west of the Rhine, and the 5th Division executing
similar operations in its area. The 4th Armored was driving
north along the west bank even as the 11th Armored was
completing its second drive to the river, with elements of the
division entering Worms.

Patton toured the front to see what was happening. By
then it was the 22nd and all the German exits over the
Rhine in the Third Army's area had been cut off. Back at
headquarters after dark, he found that a record number of
prisoners had been captured during the day—some 11,000
Germans—indicating the near-collapse and demoralization
of the enemy. He was also told that elements of the 10th
Armored had made contact with units of the Seventh Army,
completely pocketing the German troops. It was a fantastic
situation, inducing General Gerow, now commanding the
Fifteenth Army, to wire Patton: "Congratulations on surrounding three armies, one of them American."

"What are we waiting for?" Patton exclaimed.

He gave the signal to cross the Rhine as they were, without air support and artillery preparation, without airborne
troops landing behind enemy lines, without even complete
authority to do so. In the immediate wake of Patton's orders,
the 5th Division reorganized for assault across the river at
Oppenheim, then began crossing two battalions at 11 P.M.

on the 22nd with little, if any, difficulty. It got six battalions across by daylight with a total loss of 34 men killed or wounded.

The Rhine as a barrier with the flower of the German army deployed on its east bank existed mostly in Montgomery's imagination. His enormous arrangements for the crossing now revealed his failure, as Wilmot phrased it, to appreciate how near collapse the Germans were. This time even Bryant applauded Patton's coup. "While the British Commander in Chief was preparing for his crossing on March 24th," he wrote, "Patton had opened a new offensive. Having marched north at Christmas to contain the German breakthrough in the Ardennes and having gloriously avenged that battle in the early days of March by driving through the Eifel to Koblenz, the Third Army Commander now struck southeast across the Moselle in two armored drives. . . . Within a week, encircling the Siegfried Line defenders, he had rounded up many thousands more dispirited and demoralized Germans and cleared the whole remaining west bank of the Rhine.

"Then, once more—and this time rightly—jumping the gun to forestall Montgomery, the great cavalry leader obeyed Bradley's injunction to 'take the Rhine on the run' and, on the night before the British were to make the crossing in the north, slipped a division across the now almost undefended river a few miles south of Mainz and established a second American bridgehead."

Patton greeted the crossing, at first subdued like a mischievous child afraid of being punished for some trespass, and then with an exuberance that seemed excessive even for him.

On March 23rd, while Bradley was finishing his second cup of coffee at breakfast, a phone call came in from Third Army. It was Patton.

"Brad," he said, "don't tell anyone but I'm across."

"Well, I'll be damned," Bradley shot back. "You mean across the Rhine?"

"Sure am," Patton said. "I sneaked a division over last night. But there are so few Krauts around there they don't know it yet. So don't make any announcement—we'll keep it a secret until we see how it goes."

During the morning briefing, Lieutenant Colonel Richard R. Stillman, Third Army liaison officer at 12th Army Group, spelled out the coup. Smilingly alluding to Montgomery's enormous preparations, he said: "Without benefit of aerial bombing, ground smoke, artillery preparation, and airborne assistance, the Third Army at 2200 hours, Thursday evening, March 22nd, crossed the Rhine River." It was, as Bradley put it, the first assault crossing of that river bastion by a modern army.

Patton phoned Bradley again after dark. He was no longer whispering the news as in the morning. Now he was shouting it into the telephone:

"Brad, for God's sake," he said with his treble voice at its highest pitch, "tell the world we're across! We knocked down 33 Krauts today when they came after our pontoon bridges. I want the world to know Third Army made it before Monty starts across."

"In connection with this crossing," Patton later wrote, "a somewhat amusing incident is alleged to have happened. The 21st Army Group was supposed to cross the Rhine on March 24th and, in order to be ready for this earthshaking event, Mr. Churchill wrote a speech congratulating Field Marshal Montgomery on the *first* assault crossing over the Rhine in modern history. This speech was recorded and, through some error on the part of the British Broadcasting Corporation, was broadcast, in spite of the fact that the Third Army had been across for some 36 hours."

On the very day that "Plunder" jumped off, Patton accompanied by Eddy, Codman and Stiller, staged his own triumphant crossing of the Rhine. Halfway across he stopped on the pontoon bridge and "spit" into the river—in the bowdlerized version of what he had actually done to celebrate the event.

Giving the enemy no chance to recover, Patton flung two bridgeheads over the Rhine within five days, then followed with two more. Units of VIII Corps made a second assault crossing south of Koblenz. All four could be expanded rapidly. The enemy's frightful losses in the Palatinate and his concern over the First Army's bridgehead at Remagen had left him with inadequate forces to contain the Third Army within its Rhine bridgeheads.

Now storming through the Mainz-Frankfurt-Darmstadt triangle, Patton advanced to the Main and, on March 25th, seized bridgeheads over that river in the vicinity of Hanau and Aschaffenburg. Frantic German attempts to contain the Main bridgeheads failed to stave off the breakthrough. By the 28th, the 4th Armored had driven 30 miles northward to join forces with the First Army and pocket thousands of German troops in the Wiesbaden-Bingen area.

Advancing rapidly toward Kassel and Fulda, Patton again refused to give the enemy time to man defense lines. His armor drove swiftly down both sides of the Werra River to Eisenach, then across the Fulda River, and 20 miles beyond Fulda, blasting German hopes of making a stand along the Eder, Fulda or Werra. Resistance was met only at Kassel. But Patton's onrushing armor seized Mühlhausen, Gotha and Suhl, then held up its advance to enable infantry units to mop up the bypassed enemy forces. Patton was leaving it to the First and Seventh Armies to protect the Third Army's wide-open flanks by their own advances.

By April 10th, the Third Army was pushing toward the Mulde River. Its armor on the rampage again, it bypassed Erfurt, Weimar, Jena and Gera, and pulled up on the outskirts of Chemnitz, covering 80 miles in a five-day drive. The campaign ended on the 21st at Eisenhower's orders. As Patton's after action report phrased it, the Third Army had been "restrained by higher headquarters from advancing east of the line Mulde-Zwickmulde-Plauen-Hof-Bayreuth." Actually, Patton had been halted by SHAEF in order for him to assume another mission Supreme Headquarters regarded as urgent and imperative, but which, as we shall see, proved to be Patton's most futile and frustrating diversion.

It was the day after Adolf Hitler's 56th birthday—his last. The war in Europe had but 17 days to go. Cooped up in his elegant bunker under the Reichs Chancellery on the Wilhelmstrasse, Hitler was already dictating his testament to Frau Gertraude Jung, his private secretary. "More than 30 years have passed," it began, "since the day in 1914 when I first volunteered my modest services for World War I which had been foisted upon the Reich."

Patton had been conducting his uninterrupted drive from the frozen fields of Belgium to the German Mulde (on whose banks the trees had begun to leaf and the perennials to blossom) in his own special manner, personally supervising every major move and involving himself in even minor tactical matters. Even so, he was just about the only one at the top echelons of his command who showed no signs of the strain. Others around him were beginning to break.

On April 20th, just as the 11th Armored Division of General Eddy's XII Corps was driving into Grafenwohr to capture an immense cache of arms and ammunition, Eddy had to be evacuated. He had been suffering from high blood pressure for some time but concealed his condition from Patton, determined to stay in the fight even if it killed him. Then Colonel Thomas H. Nixon, Patton's Chief of Ordnance, was felled by a dangerous stomach ailment. Even one of the Corps Surgeons became seriously ill and had to be replaced just before the curtain fell.

But General Patton was in the best of health, full of his usual vim. On April 14th, invited to attend the inauguration of the Rhine Bridge at Mainz and cut the ceremonial ribbon, he scornfully refused the pair of oversize scissors Major General Ewart G. Plank, his host from Com Z, had handed him for the ritual. "What are you taking me for, a tailor?" he grunted. "Goddamnit, give me a bayonet!"

CHAPTER FORTY
YONDER ARE THE RUSSIANS

It was almost midnight, April 12, 1945, at Hersfeld, an ugly little town just north of Frankfurt, at General Patton's latest command post, in an armored force training center from which the Third Army had just evicted its *Wehrmacht* tenants. It had been a busy day for Patton. Early in the morning Generals Eisenhower and Bradley had flown in to inspect an industrial salt mine at Merkers, where the 385th Infantry Regiment of the 90th Division had stumbled upon the gold reserve of the Reichsbank and an inestimable hoard of treasure the Nazis had stolen from the occupied countries and the Jews.

The gold alone was valued at $250,000,000. Nobody yet cared or dared to put a price tag on the looted works of

art and assorted bric-a-brac. The loot included a conglomeration of things from sets of priceless Sèvres porcelain to
gold bridges removed from the mouths of victims the Nazis
had put to death in the gas chambers.

Patton was in one of his more flamboyant moods. He
felt like a medieval conqueror, what with all this gold at his
feet, and kept up a running line of quips while he guided
his guests on this sightseeing tour. The vault with the gold
was in a pitch-black shaft, accessible only by means of a
rickety old elevator. As this antique was descending on its
single cable at high speed, Patton counted the stars on the
shoulders of its passengers and remarked with a poker-face,
"If that clothesline should break, promotions in the United
States Army would be considerably stimulated."

The abandonment of this treasure chest was but one of
the unmistakable signs that Hitler's Thousand-Year Reich
was falling apart at its seams in its 13th year. The gold
hoard had been discovered on April 6th. On that day a few
men from a Quartermaster detachment captured the headquarters of a German corps, complete with its commander,
a Generalleutnant Hahn, and his staff. On the 7th the
400,000th prisoner of war was checked into one of the
Third Army's P/W cages. And the next day at Tanbach a
patrol of the 357th Infantry Regiment of the 87th Division
came upon a truck convoy loaded with the complete secret
archives of the German Navy, fleeing to a secret hiding
place.

Then something happened that, for three desperate
weeks, refilled Hitler with the delirious expectation that
somehow he could still extricate himself from his lethal
predicament. President Franklin Delano Roosevelt died
unexpectedly. The Führer regarded his passing as a divine
gift, perhaps even as the turning point of the war.

Even a few weeks before, in a staff discussion of the dismal future, Hitler had pinned his hopes on Roosevelt's
removal from the war. Although only a miracle could have
now helped him, he was still counting on some rational domestic development in America to rid him of his hated
adversary. "Remember," he told General Guderian, "that
there are many Polish voters in America who have considerable influence on the Catholic clergy. And the priests
are beginning to be fed up with Roosevelt's brand of
Christianity." But he no longer needed such help to lose
Roosevelt. The "miracle" had happened. The President was

removed from his path by a massive cerebral attack while resting in Warm Springs, Georgia.

Patton heard the tragic news quite by accident. He had stayed up late with Eisenhower and Bradley. Then, just when he was about to retire, he noticed that his watch had stopped. He turned on the radio, tuned it to the BBC to get the time, but what he heard was the bulletin announcing Roosevelt's death at Warm Springs. He immediately awakened the Supreme Commander and General Bradley, then spent the rest of the night with them, talking about Roosevelt and trying to gauge the ramifications of his death.

Though Patton belonged to a nation in which George Bernard Shaw had divined a volcanic political instinct, he himself was merely volcanic. With his background of wealth and the circles in which he moved, Patton was intuitively opposed to the New Deal and would have, if pinned down, spoken out strongly against Roosevelt's policies. Yet he was personally attached to the President, who was, first and foremost in his mind, his Commander in Chief.

Their relationship was distant but excellent. They had met during World War I, when Roosevelt, then the Assistant Secretary of the Navy, visited France and bumped into Patton during an inspection tour of Langres, where the American tankers were training. In 1942, Patton went to war with the President's personal good wishes, then played host to him during the Casablanca Conference. They remained in touch throughout the war, Patton sending occasional souvenirs to the Commander in Chief and Roosevelt acknowledging them in charming, bantering personal notes.

On July 27, 1943, Roosevelt surprised Patton with a signed photograph in appreciation of the spectacular capture of Palermo. Patton responded by presenting to the President "a very dirty map which I have been carrying in my pocket through most of these operations [in Sicily], showing what we have taken to date." The Commander in Chief receipted the gift in a "Dear George" letter dated August 4th:

"It is good to have yours of July 27th and that most interesting map which you carried is a real addition to the Library at Hyde Park. It will go next to the original field maps which General Degoutte gave to me after I had been with him for two days in 1918 on the advance from the Marne to the Vesle. You are doing a grand job in the advance. It was suggested by Pa Watson and Wilson Brown and Harry Hopkins that after the war I should make you the Marquis of Mount Etna. Don't fall into the crater!"

Patton replied on October 7th, in the same vein:

"Please accept my most sincere thanks for your generous letter of August 4th. My sure knowledge of how busy you are makes me appreciate more than ever your kindness in writing. With reference to Mount Etna, I think that I had better stay away from that place because if all the horrid things I am supposed to say, as reported in the newspapers, were true, the Devil would certainly pop out of the Mountain and catch me. But I believe there is a historical precedent for becoming a Marquis 'in absentia' because, as you remember, the Italians made Lord Nelson the Marquis of Bronte on the west slope of Etna, and it is well known that neither he nor Lady Hamilton ever visited the place—how sad."

Properly briefed by Secretary Stimson and General Marshall about Patton's qualities and his indispensability, the President stuck by him during the two great crises even when some of his White House counselors urged him to get rid of Patton, whom they considered a grave political liability. At the height of the slapping incidents Mr. Roosevelt reassured him in a confidential personal message. He sent him a very friendly letter with Archbishop Francis Spellman during the exciting August days in 1944. Patton responded in October with the gift of a ship's model Colonel James Polk of the 3rd Cavalry Group had "captured" in Brittany. He apologized for the delay in answering the President's letter with an explanation he was sure would please Roosevelt: "My excuse is that in carrying out your plans I have been quite busy fighting Germans."

General Patton repaid the President's goodwill by remaining steadfastly loyal to him in the face of several efforts to poison his mind against Mr. Roosevelt. At least one direct attempt was made to set him up as the leader of a conservative movement in post-war America that was, as its proponents put it, designed to recapture the country from the New Deal.

On March 13, 1945, Henry J. Taylor visited Patton in Luxembourg and after dinner treated the General to a long and eloquent, but embarrassing, political lecture. Taylor was in Europe covering the war for the United Press. But he also had a second identity. A successful and prosperous businessman in the pulp and paper industry, and an econo-

mist of a rather conservative hue, he was bitterly opposed
to Roosevelt and the New Deal. Now he seized the opportunity to explain how wicked the Democrats really were,
when Patton thought that only the Germans were evil, at
least for the duration. Taylor hinted broadly that Patton
would be needed after the war in a major political role.
But Patton discouraged him with the emphatic words, "I
am not a politician and certainly have no desire to become
one."

And now Roosevelt was dead.

On the day of his death, advanced armored spearheads of
General Simpson's Ninth Army drove 57 miles to the Elbe
near Magdeburg and established a bridgehead over the
river. Farther north, elements of his 5th Armored Division
reached Tangermünde, only 53 miles from Berlin. Allied
soldiers were storming the inner bastion of Hitler's tottering
Festung Europa, from Arnhem, where the Canadians had
just opened a major assault, to Jena in the heart of Germany.
There, in 1806, Napoleon had won his decisive battle with
the Prussians. But now the old Thuringian city on the Saale
River was only a whistle stop on the Third Army's eastward
dash.

The Russians, advancing with 180 divisions in the conflict's mightiest offensive, had moved from the frozen plains
of Southern Poland to the Oder River, and were now hammering at the peripheries of Berlin's defenses, where Hitler
was squatting in his bunker. To the south, however, in
Hungary, for example, their going was much slower. They
had to fight for every farmhouse turned into a miniature
fortress, for every street corner around which lurked a sui-
cide-sniper. Every inch of ground was desperately defended,
not by the natives of those lands, but by German soldiers in
whom propaganda and experience had infused a hatred and
fear of the Bolsheviks.

The war was taking a subtle turn as the final decision
neared, shifting with growing momentum from the primarily
military to the predominantly political sphere. It was becoming increasingly evident that while the war aims of the
Western Allies and the U.S.S.R. were identical—namely the
defeat of Nazi Germany—their peace aims were vastly dif-

ferent. The time had come for both sides in the anti-German camp to jockey for positions from which either could dominate Europe and manipulate its fate after the war.

These were momentous days, on whose actions and arrangements hinged the future of Europe. Yet suddenly the United States had lost interest in and influence over the political shaping of events. There had been in Washington a shrewd and equitable division of labor between President Roosevelt and General Marshall, a silent understanding that had guaranteed the most efficient prosecution of the war. Roosevelt rarely meddled in military matters, leaving them entirely to Marshall; and the Chief of Staff never presumed to encroach upon political matters, whose management he properly regarded as the prerogative of the Chief Executive.

With Roosevelt's death, this equilibrium was upset. Since President Truman was not yet *au courant* with his great new job, to which he had become a sudden heir without adequate preparation, there was nobody at the top in the United States to deal with political issues just when they began to gain dominant importance. As a result, emphasis in the entire American conduct of the war was shifted unequivocally to the military sphere, which was becoming more defunct with every passing day.

Now Churchill was alone in the west, trying desperately to create a geopolitical balance on the shattered Continent and working feverishly, when it seemed almost too late, to establish firm positions for our side from which to oppose the post-war aspirations of the Soviet Union. But even he had to subordinate his urgent political schemes to the purely military designs of the Combined Chiefs, to whom the political future of Europe seemed immaterial. All that mattered to them was the immediate course of the war, which they sought to direct from a distance of 4,000 miles.

General Marshall now emerged as the dominant figure, and his narrow military concept became basic in all efforts to wind up the fighting. His influence was not entirely without contradictory elements. On the one hand, he declared (through the Joint Chiefs while Roosevelt was still alive) that "the commander in the field is the best judge of the measures which officer the earliest prospects of destroying the German armies or their power to resist." On the other, he left no doubt in Eisenhower's mind where he stood in these matters and that he expected the Supreme Commander to act upon them. Only 16 days after Roosevelt's death Marshall cabled Eisenhower: "Personally and aside from all logistic, tactical or strategical implications, I would be loath to hazard American lives for purely political purposes."

On April 7th Eisenhower had told Marshall that he was "the first to admit that war is waged in pursuance of political aims." But now, on the 29th, he answered Marshall's cable by saying: "I shall not attempt any move I deem militarily unwise merely to gain a political prize unless I receive specific orders from the Combined Chiefs of Staff." Such orders were never given. The Combined Chiefs, sitting in Washington and dominated by Marshall, deemed it beyond their scope and jurisdiction even to consider the political aspects of the war, no matter how pressing they had become.

"Military factors," Eisenhower wrote in his post-war explanation of his failure to push his victory to its utmost geopolitical limits, "when the enemy was on the brink of defeat, were more important in my eyes than the political considerations"—as for example, those involved in Berlin, which in his opinion "no longer represented a military objective of major importance."

When left alone to develop his own strategic concepts, Eisenhower usually proved an astute disciple of Clausewitz. But now, under Marshall's unmistakable influence, he lost sight of the Prussian philosopher's dictum that war is merely a continuation of politics and that victories in military maneuvers are rated in history according to the political gains they produce.

Eisenhower clearly recognized that Germany was in her last throes. But he still refused to take anything for granted. During the closing days of the war, as we shall soon see, he went out of his way to organize elaborate measures to prevent the Germans from retreating into a stronghold in the Alps from which they could prolong the war and Germany's agony. And he divided the almost completed task of defeating Germany between his own forces and those of the Soviet Union.

In this orientation of his concluding strategy he followed ideas that dominated the thinking of the highest American military councils. It reflected an astounding feeling of inferiority that prevented not only Ike, but especially Marshall and MacArthur, from relying entirely upon their own resources and power to finish the job without further Soviet assistance. Both Marshall and MacArthur kept insisting that the Red Army be brought into the Pacific war or else, they warned Roosevelt, Japan would endure for at least another year, if only by continuing the war from Manchukuo. And Eisenhower insisted upon the Russian pressure from the east, irrespective of its political price. In this context, Berlin became nothing but a "prestige objective" in an assessment amazingly devoid of any political—or even military—vision.

"We were less concerned," General Bradley wrote after the war, "with post-war political alignments than the destruction of what remained of the German Army." And in a variation on the same theme he added: "I could see no political advantage accruing from the capture of Berlin that would offset the need for the quick destruction of the German army on our front. As soldiers we looked naïvely on this British inclination to complicate the war with political foresight and nonmilitary objectives."

Contrary to the widespread belief, Eisenhower's hands were *not* tied by any "secret deals" the statesmen had allegedly made at Yalta. The famous conference in that Crimean resort did not cut up Europe into spheres of interest. Though Roosevelt was accused after the war of surrender to Stalin by abandoning to him Berlin, Czechoslovakia, big chunks of Central Europe and the Balkans, no such arrangements had been made, no such promises ever held out. An area had been mapped out in Germany which was to be left to the Soviet Union. But it was never proposed, much less agreed upon in any binding arrangements, that the military forces of the Western Allies should not enter the Red Army's hypothetical zone of occupation *in their pursuit of the defeated enemy*. Berlin was never surrendered to the Russians to take and do with as they pleased. As Wilmot put it, "at Yalta, this question had not even been discussed, perhaps because in the military circumstances then prevailing it had seemed academic."

Moreover, in this momentous spring of 1945, the strategic situation in Europe was far different from that which existed at the time of the Yalta Conference only two months before. Germany was fighting a two-front war—two separate wars, in fact. Although in February she still had considerable power on both fronts, she now had none left in the west. On the other hand, Hitler, in his last desperate twitches, had succeeded in creating a strong defense line on the Oder and the Neisse. On a front stretching from the Baltic to the mountainous north of Czechoslovakia, the Germans were defending every bit of ground while the Red Army had to wait for the establishment of its lines of communications through Poland. In Hungary, too, the Germans were holding fast on a coherent front; and they were blocking virtually the only approach to Vienna by refusing to release their hold on the Bratislava Gap on the Danube.

If politically nothing stood in the way of Eisenhower's progress to Berlin, Prague and Vienna, militarily only his undue pessimism or caution was blocking his path in these hours of decision. The plan of his final offensive that emerged from these considerations became crystallized late in March. The Supreme Commander then resolved to neutralize the Ruhr and, after that, to concentrate the mass of his forces under Bradley's, rather than Montgomery's, command, specifically in the Kassel region, and make a power-drive due east through the midriff of Germany. His objective was to split the Reich in two and link up with the Red Army in the Leipzig-Dresden area.

On March 28th he cabled the plan to Washington and London, and also directly to Marshal Stalin in Moscow. As a matter of fact, he had taken Stalin into his confidence on his own, without consulting Churchill and Truman, or the Combined Chiefs. Churchill protested vigorously but vainly. And Eisenhower completely misunderstood the motive for his objections. According to him, the Prime Minister was "greatly disappointed and disturbed" not because, as was the case, he had opened up the heartland of Europe to the Soviet Union, but on parochial grounds "because my plan did not first throw Montgomery forward with all the strength I could give him from American forces in a desperate attempt to capture Berlin before the Russians."

The plan represented a belated victory for Bradley and Patton. It gave them at last the main thrust, a privilege and power they had sought for so long without avail. But, at this late stage, it was a hollow victory and, in fact, not to the advantage of the cause of the Western Allies. On a word from Eisenhower, the British under Montgomery or the Ninth Army of General Simpson could have descended on Berlin and easily taken the German capital even though the Red Army was standing at its very outskirts. Or he could have ordered Patton's Third Army into Prague and Vienna. But Eisenhower was not giving the word to advance. The word from him was to stop.

General Patton was in the eye of the hurricane. For once he was truly a pawn of destiny—and a destiny, at that, which was far greater and more dramatic than just his own. On his moves now depended the fate of a continent whose future was in the balance between freedom and servitude. A Russian deserter who had managed to make his way to the Third Army from a unit of General Andrei Vlasov, a former Stalinist general now fighting with the Germans in Czechoslovakia, hit upon the theme of the day when, with tearful eyes, he offered congratulations to his American interrogator.

"How fortunate you are, you lucky Americans!" he said. "You are rid of Hitler. But we, your companions in victory, still have our Stalin."

Patton's historic mission in this chaotic finale of the war was as crucial and far-reaching as it was essentially simple. He was to push forward as fast and as far as the Third Army could go until it met the Red Army and could go no farther. This promised to be a broad and bold sweep. Taking Patton deep into Czechoslovakia to Prague and maybe beyond, and into Austria as far as possible, would have given the West control of the greater part of Czechoslovakia and Austria.

The Third Army's penetration of territory the Soviet Union was craving (as indispensable for its advance to the European heartland from its Euro-Asian frontier before the war) appeared possible because the Red Army was falling behind in its timetable. Taking cognizance of the Russians' progress farther north, General Eisenhower had drawn a stop line for the forces of the First Army. An order 12th Army Group issued on April 12th restricted Hodges' advance to the Mulde, beyond which none of the units of his First Army were to move unless explicitly authorized. Hodges made his arrangements accordingly. He permitted only small patrols to cross the river and roam about, looking for the Russians. They found some on April 25th at three spots—at the Mulde, at the Elbe and beyond the

Elbe. On the 26th, in the area of First Army's V Corps, United States and Soviet forces established formal contact at Torgau when the commander of the 273rd Infantry Regiment of the 69th Division met the commanding officer of the 173rd Regiment of the Red Army's 58th Guards Division.

But in Patton's sector, at least as far as he could scan, the Red Army was nowhere in evidence. Neither, for that matter, were his actual enemies, the Germans. Advancing to the right of the First Army, Patton was moving south-westward at breakneck speed, his progress impeded only by the heavily wooded terrain of the Thüringer Wald. All organized opposition had practically ceased on April 11th, enabling the Third Army to roll 15 to 20 miles a day. The cost of the advance was infinitesimal. On the 23rd, for example, its casualties totaled 45 men—3 killed, 37 wounded, 5 missing. But more than 9,000 prisoners were taken.

On April 11th General Bradley outlined a stop line for Patton as well, restricting the advance of the Third Army to a line slightly to the west of the Czechoslovak border, thus presumably abandoning the whole of that country to the Red Army. But Bradley and Patton had a tacit agree-ment that the stop line was merely tentative and that the Third Army would be permitted to advance as far as the incoming Red Army's advance would let it. As a matter of fact, a few weeks later Bradley granted explicit orders to Third Army to cross the Czechoslovak border and advance to a line running north and south through Budweis-Pilsen-Karlsbad. More important, he told Patton to be prepared to advance farther eastward.

Nevertheless, on April 22nd, the Third Army was halted in its tracks and reoriented toward the Isar and the Inn. It was ordered instead to cross into Austria to seize Linz, the farthest authorized point of its penetration. For the Third Army the day marked the beginning of the end. "By April 22nd," Patton wrote in his account of the last round-up, "it was obvious to me that the end of the war was very close." But his view was not completely shared by SHAEF. An influential group of Operations and Intelligence special-ists at Supreme Headquarters in Paris continued to insist that German resistance was not about to cease. Fanatical Nazis were said to be preparing massive concentrations of troops and supplies in the Alps with an eye to prolonging the war.

The possibility of such a turn first occurred to General Strong early in March when certain intelligence data reaching him from Germany spoke in specific terms of a mountain fortress of enormous proportions—a "National Redoubt," as it became known—garrisoned by fanatical young Nazi soldiers sworn to resist to the bitter end. Strong included information about this in the March 11th issue of his "Weekly Intelligence Summary." "The main trend of German defense policy," the summary read in part, "does seem directed primarily to the safeguarding of the Alpine Zone. This area is, by the very nature of the terrain, practically impenetrable. The evidence indicates that considerable numbers of SS and specially chosen units are being systematically withdrawn to Austria—and that some of the most important ministries and personalities of the Nazi regime are already established in the Redoubt area."

The SHAEF G-2 went on to paint a forbidding picture of the possible implications of this development. "Here," Strong wrote, "defended both by nature and by the most efficient secret weapons yet invented, the powers that have hitherto guided Germany will survive to reorganize her resurrection; here armaments will be manufactured in bombproof factories, food and equipment will be stored in vast underground caverns and a specially selected corps of young men will be trained in guerrilla warfare, so that a whole underground army can be fitted and directed to liberate Germany from the occupying forces."

A few weeks later SHAEF G-2 prepared a special monograph about the "National Redoubt," based on the mass of seemingly high-class intelligence data pouring in from all directions. It was suggested by SHAEF G-3 that "emphasis be placed on offensives to interfere with rumored enemy plans to build a National Redoubt in the mountainous area running from western Austria as far north as the lakes below Munich and as far south as the Italian lakes."

Some of SHAEF's planners were inclined to dismiss those "rumors" as Nazi propaganda and to let the mysterious "National Redoubt" divert the Allies from their most direct course to Germany's defeat. But others, both inside SHAEF and far beyond, took the threat seriously. One of those impressed with this last-minute menace was General

Marshall in faraway Washington. On March 27th he bluntly recommended that General Eisenhower change the line of attack from Nuremberg toward Linz or from Karlsruhe toward Munich "to prevent the enemy from organizing resistance in southern Germany."

The plot then thickened on both sides. In the Allied camp, the "National Redoubt" materialized to such an extent that it began to interfere seriously not only with local operations specifically directed against it, but, indeed, with the over-all strategic conduct of the war. When the Ninth Army reached the Elbe in mid-April, General Simpson asked Bradley's permission to attack toward Berlin and capture the capital. The request was relayed to the Supreme Commander, who turned it down. He ordered Simpson to split his forces, holding the Elbe line with one unit, turning north toward Lübeck with another, and sending a third against the "National Redoubt." Explaining his order, Eisenhower told Marshall on April 15th that he regarded these objectives, and especially the "Redoubt," as vastly more important than Berlin.

A political intelligence report SHAEF issued on April 14th again presented the "Redoubt" as a distinct threat to Allied plans and listed it as one of the sources of a certain optimism SHAEF G-2 still believed it detected among the Nazis. When Nuremberg fell, Eisenhower remembered Marshall's recommendation and directed General Devers to "shift the Seventh Army into southern Bavaria and the Tyrol to make certain that the enemy did not establish a National Redoubt in that region."

Even on April 30, when Germany's complete collapse was epitomized by Adolf Hitler's melodramatic suicide, General Eisenhower still believed that a continuation of German resistance was possible. He spoke of "another offensive" in a letter to Marshall, with priority given to "the southern drive toward Linz and the Austrian Redoubt." This preoccupation with an "Alpine fortress" but eight days before Germany's unconditional surrender showed how well the Nazis had succeeded in capturing the imagination of the Supreme Commander with a phantom stronghold. For, in fact, the "National Redoubt" was nothing but smart Nazi propaganda at best and a shrewd maneuver of deception at worst. Nevertheless, it succeeded in throwing the well-laid Allies plans out of kilter and, in its ultimate consequences, in influencing the post-war balance of power in Central and Eastern Europe.

What was truth and what was fiction about the "National Redoubt"?

In a report to me, Wilhelm Höttl, a deputy chief of the German Intelligence Service under Ernst Kaltenbrunner and General Walter Schellenberg, described in detail the maneuver that could be called "Operation Bugaboo."

According to him, toward the end of 1944 a dissident group within the German Intelligence Service had concluded that peace with the Allies was no longer possible on the basis of equal partnership at the conference table. A plan was developed to persuade the Americans to refrain from abandoning Germany and Austria to the Russians by presenting evidence of Soviet double-dealings, including documents indicating that Stalin was trying to conclude a separate peace with Hitler. But this plan was quickly abandoned. It was then decided to approach the Americans along another tangent.

German Intelligence knew from several of its agents that the American and British high command was unduly apprehensive that German resistance would continue indefinitely from a so-called Alpine fortress. These agents also reported on various Allied estimates, which assumed that such a redoubt could be maintained for a protracted period of time—an assumption that would have been correct had the redoubt actually existed.

The idea of developing a redoubt in the Alps did come up, and certain preparatory steps had been made toward its establishment. But that was how far the physical development of this super-fortress had progressed. In November, 1944, Gauleiter Franz Hofer of the Tyrol drafted a memorandum for Hitler outlining the means and the potentialities of a last-ditch stand in the Alps. Hofer gave the memo to Reichsleiter Martin Borman, the Führer's deputy, for submission to Hitler. But Borman regarded the whole concept so blatantly defeatistic that he refused to bring it to Hitler's attention.

When Borman later learned that Hitler himself had been told by German Intelligence of Allied fears regarding a "National Redoubt," he showed him the memorandum and arranged for Hofer to report on the idea to him. Hitler recognized it for what it was worth—a splendid means of

deception—and instructed Hofer to begin at once the construction of a fortified ring around the area where the
Allies suspected the stronghold to be. The Gauleiter of
Kärten, Dr. Friedrich Rainer, was then drawn into the plot
to lend a hand.

Elaborate arrangements were made by Hofer and Rainer
to make the building of the "Redoubt" appear as realistic
as possible. Teams of geologists and members of the faculty
of the SS Mountaineering School were sent to the region
to survey it for fortifications. The area soon resounded with
the thunder of explosions of SS men detonated tons of
dynamite in the Alps. Plans were drafted for the transfer
of troops into the stronghold, together with a massive shifting of industries and stores needed for their support.

All this was nothing but make-believe with appropriate
sound effects. The Allies' apprehension had no actual basis.
As a matter of fact, the bulk of the Allied intelligence data
about the redoubt had been manufactured by German
Intelligence and was planted with Allied Intelligence with
the help of double-agents.

This, then, was the status of the formidable "National
Redoubt" when German dissidents managed to establish
contact with Allen W. Dulles, resident director of the Office
of Strategic Services in Switzerland. The dissidents proposed
to buy a *pax Americana* for Germany through Dulles, and
the price they proposed to pay was definitive information
about the "National Redoubt." As Herr Höttl, one of the
dissidents, put it, they assumed that information exposing
the dreaded redoubt as a hoax would certainly be worth
something to the Allies.

 · The first meeting with Dulles and his associates produced
ample evidence that the threat of this mysterious Alpine
stronghold was weighing heavily on Allied minds. Dulles
was then told in categorical terms that the so-called *réduit*,
as it was called in Switzerland, was but a phantom conjured
up by Nazi propaganda. He was also assured that all possible arrangements to concentrate troops in the Alps for a
prolonged stand in their natural fortifications had been
effectively sabotaged by winning over into dissidence every
senior officer who could, by assignment or experience, be
employed to command mountain troops or conduct operations from such a strong base.

Nevertheless, this was the objective Patton was given for
his next mission, diverting him from his race toward

Czechoslovakia. Once again there was a serious discrepancy between Eisenhower's purposeful dispositions and Patton's intuitive designs. The Supreme Commander was keeping after the Germans on his broad front wherever they were. But even on April 29th, only nine days before V-E Day, he was giving "first priority" to the northern thrust toward Kiel and the southern drive toward the "Redoubt."

"If additional means were available," wrote Pogue on the basis of Eisenhower's papers, of which he was custodian, "he planned to attack enemy forces that were still holding out in Czechoslovakia, Denmark, and Norway." But while Eisenhower thought that the Western powers should forestall the Soviets in Denmark and Norway, he "concluded that the Red Army was in perfect position to clean out Czechoslovakia and would certainly reach Prague before the U.S. forces."

Patton was not concerned about German troops sweating out the end in Denmark and Norway. He no longer cared about any priorities Montgomery was enjoying on his northern thrust. He was now completely absorbed in the problem of Czechoslovakia. Unlike the Supreme Commander, he was convinced that the Third Army was in a better position than the Russians to clean out Czechoslovakia and reach Prague before the Red Army.

When the Third Army was stopped abruptly for its new mission, it started doing something it had never done before —it regrouped on a quiet front. Patton called Bradley to apologize, dead-pan, that for the first time in a long while the Third Army was not making the front pages. But the humdrum chore was performed in a brisk and prancing manner, like the morning workout of a race horse. Bradley assured Patton that he was well pleased with his skillful regrouping at record speed.

Even on April 16th, when word of the changed direction of the attack had first reached Patton at his CP in Hersfeld, Third Army was moving fast and hitting hard against what the communiques characterized as "scattered resistance." The VIII Corps was encountering most of it on its south-southeast push but maintained its momentum. The XX Corps was closing along the Zwick Mulde River. The

XII Corps was clearing Hof and mopping up in Bayreuth, the city of Richard Wagner, the capture of which seemed poignant amid this *Götterdämmerung*. Then everything stopped and changed. Responding to the abrupt shift of the gear, Third Army reshuffled itself behind some combat activity confined mostly to patrols.

Probably because he could not bear the sight of mere regrouping, Patton flew to Paris on the 17th for a 24-hour leave. There he paid hospital visits to his son-in-law, Colonel John K. Waters, who had been captured in Africa and released when Hammelburg was liberated, and saw his old friend, General Hughes, in the Hotel Georges V, where he was again General Lee's "guest." It was there on the next morning, during a leisurely breakfast with Hughes, that he read in *Stars and Stripes* that he had received his fourth star. The item was in a box in the center of the front page but Patton, engrossed in an article about the Third Army in a column on the right, did not notice it until Hughes called it to his attention. He was only moderately elated. "It's nice," he said, "but I'd have enjoyed it more if it had come in with the first batch."

Patton employed his day in Paris to good advantage, picking up information about the war from people who were so much closer to SHAEF. In retrospect, everything may have looked pat and foreordained in this last roundup of merely putting into place the few remaining stones of the huge mosaic. But it was not at all like that to the men on the spot, not even to top-ranking generals like Patton.

In the popular image the great commanders are dazzling, romantic, oversized figures. They stand on their mounds at the perilous edge of the battle guiding its cold currents and compulsive course. They bend a million-headed army to their indomitable will, mocking at fear and not affright, as the quiver, in Job's phrase, rattleth against them, the glittering spear and the shield.

They are unique characters, to be sure, in a heroic mold, for who else among us can plot their vast schemes and move their multitudes of men. Yet in reality they are neither omnipotent nor omniscient. Indeed, they are bound by elements of war that are far beyond their reach. "You can ask me for anything you like," Napoleon said to an impatient aide, "except time." Toward the end he ruefully conceded that even he could not unbend the bow.

As for their omniscience, their knowledge of the broad

scene is forever encumbered by either too much or too little information, and by the variegated evaluations and interpretations of the available intelligence. For all his consummate training in the best service schools of the United States Army, and with all the intricate technological aids of modern generalship at his disposal, Eisenhower was not immune from these limitations. And despite his instinctive, empathic and artistic bend, Patton was not exempt from the rule. So Eisenhower did his planning, not just within his bounded responsibilities, but especially within the ingrained infirmities of his enormous job. And Patton acted upon his orders as best he could, but only within the inviolate frame of reference of a modern general.

His instinct counseled him to go for Czechoslovakia before it would be too late. But he did not resent or resist his orders to attack the enigma of a redoubt. He moved with vigor, efficiency and dispatch. Within a few days he succeeded in providing the evidence Eisenhower needed to conclude that the vaunted Alpine stronghold was but a myth.

On April 20th, its extensive regrouping virtually completed, the Third Army began to sideslip southward for the new drive. It jumped off two days later. Meeting enemy opposition only at Neumarkt and Regensburg, and along the lines of the Altmühl, Danube and Isar Rivers, its powerful three-corps attack swept the Germans into Austria.

Final victory was in the air. Now that Patton's quick sweep down the Danube had dispelled the likelihood of resistance from the Alps, Czechoslovakia loomed again in Bradley's and Patton's imagination. It still did not seem too late to forestall the Red Army. On May 2nd Berlin fell to the Russians. Continuing westward through Mecklenburg and Brandenburg, the Second White Russian Front effected a junction with British forces along the line Wismar-Wittenberge. To the left, troops of the First White Russian Front reached the Elbe southeast of Wittenberg and linked up with the Americans.

Yet in Czechoslovakia the Ukrainian armies were still held up and were fighting for every yard. The Red Army troops earmarked to take Prague were still busy at Dresden and Görlitz inside Germany.

May 2nd was remarkable in the Third Army's career of conquest, mainly for a passing incident. The 80th Division reached the Inn River and began crossing it near a place called Braunau in Austria. The town had no special significance in the campaign except that in 1889 Adolf Hitler was born there. The Führer's birthplace had become a shrine during the Nazi era. But now its defenders surrendered the town meekly to a combat command of the 13th Armored Division without even a fight.

It was only on May 4th, while his 11th Armored Division was hammering at Linz, his ultimate objective on the anti-redoubt drive, that Patton received permission to resume the Czechoslovak phase of his last campaign. He sweated it out at his command post all day until 7:30 P.M., when Bradley called him with the good word.

"Ike has just called," he said exuberantly. "You have the green light for Czechoslovakia, George. When can you move?"

"Tomorrow morning," Patton whooped back.

His dispositions were now paying the expected dividends. He had kept the 90th and 5th Divisions and Colonel Reed's 2nd Cavalry Group busy with special orders to secure crossings over the mountains into Czechoslovakia "so that," he wrote, "in case we had to attack Prague, we would at least be through the passes before anything hit us." And General Gay, on whom Patton's sixth sense had rubbed off, had alerted Brigadier General John C. Pierce's 16th Armored, a green division aching to get into the war before it was over. The V Corps, consisting of the 1st, 2nd and 97th Infantry Divisions, and the 9th Armored Division, was put under Patton, so he now had the largest army he ever commanded—about 540,000 men. From where he sat, Czechoslovakia looked like a cinch.

Even so, Bradley sounded skeptical when Patton assured him that he could turn again overnight and attack in the new direction the next morning. But he was not *overly* skeptical. "As we were pretty well used to each other," Patton later wrote, "he believed me."

Patton's eagerness kept puzzling Bradley, so now he asked, "Why does everyone in the Third Army want to liberate the Czechs?"

Patton said nothing about the Russians. "Oh, Brad," he answered, "can't you see? The Czechs are our *allies* and consequently their women aren't off limits. *On to Czechoslovakia and fraternization!*" he yelled into the telephone. "How in hell can you stop an army with a battle cry like that?"

Between 8 and 10 A.M. on May 5th XII Corps jumped off, its 5th and 90th Divisions crossing into Czechoslovakia, its 11th Armored and 26th Infantry Divisions taking Linz. Patton's new V Corps joined the issue with the 1st Division. It was now commanded by Major General Clift Andrus, who reminded Patton of his hottest day in Sicily when Andrus was artillery officer of the embattled 1st Division at Gela.

Conveying Ike's explicit instructions, Bradley directed Patton to restrict his advance to a northwest-southeast line running through Pilsen. But in a suggestive undertone he added that he "could and should reconnoiter vigorously as far as Prague." For the man who had captured Palermo in an operation labeled "reconnaissance in force," this, of course, meant that he had Bradley's subliminal permission to *take* Prague. And Patton made his arrangements accordingly.

Czechoslovakia was now under the Third Army's massive attack:

The 1st Division was driving on Karlsbad; the 97th Division of Brigadier General Milton B. Halsey was attacking toward Pilsen; in the left sector of its zone XII Corps had set the stage for the drive on Prague; the 2nd Squadron of Reed's Cavalry Group was speeding to Klatovy to accept the proffered surrender of its garrison; elements of the 42nd Cavalry Squadron took Prasily; the 90th Division opened up the road through the Regen Pass for the debouchment of Patton's armor; the 5th opened up three additional roads and crossed the Tepla River, and the 4th Armored was reconnoitering routes to Prague, which it was to attack in full force the next morning.

Also on May 5th, an OSS team headed by Captain Eugene Fodor, an eager American of Slovak origin who had begun his military career as a conscripted artilleryman in the Czechoslovak army, drove into Prague on one of the strangest journeys of the war. Taking the main road from Pilsen, the OSS unit drove east in a jeep flying a fair-size American flag. En route they passed through endless columns of German soldiers, including the bulk of an SS division, marching west looking for United States forces to whom they could surrender.

The jeep, driven by a starry-eyed young adventurer from Brooklyn named Shapiro, entered Prague without incident. The OSS team was immediately engulfed by a tide of exhilarated patriots who had liberated their city, as had the Parisians under similar circumstances. Now they were waiting frantically for the Americans to take them off the hook.

Gene Fodor was taken to the basement headquarters of the patriots on Wenzel Square in the heart of the city, where General Frantisek Kratochwil, commander of the Prague partisans, formally "surrendered" the ancient capital of Czechoslovakia to this wayward OSS team. Fodor immediately turned around and raced westward through the plodding Germans, looking for Patton to inform him of the break and, he hoped, to guide the Third Army into Prague.

He found the Commanding General of the Third Army with Major General Clarence R. Huebner at V Corps Headquarters near Pilsen, arranging for a combat team of the 9th Armored to send a spearhead to Prague. Patton was elated by Fodor's news. But it threw him into a quandary. His orders stipulated that he stop on the line through Pilsen, and Prague was 60 miles to the northeast. But Prague needed him badly. Its self-liberation had left the city hanging precariously in midair, so to speak, between German forces under Field Marshall Ferdinand Schoerner and the Red Army approaching laboriously from the northwest.

Patton called Bradley, told him that Prague was ripe for the picking, and asked, "Is this stop line through Pilsen really mandatory? Can't you let me go into Prague? For God's sake, Brad, those patriots in the city need our help! We have no time to lose!"

Bradley's sympathies were fully with Patton and the patriots, but he had his own instructions. He said he would call Eisenhower at once to get the answer, when Patton had a brainstorm. He now suggested that he would "get lost" on May 6th, and while he would be incommunicado his troops would enter Prague. He would then come out of hiding and report to Bradley—from a phone booth on Wenzel Square.

Bradley sounded as if he liked the idea but refused to commit himself all the way to that phone booth in Prague without clearing it with Ike. He put in the call to Eisenhower, for he could not afford to be just half-safe in a situation of extreme delicacy like the liberation of Prague, which he knew had important political strings attached.

The Supreme Commander was at his firmest in ordering Bradley to stop Patton. The day before, General Eisenhower had been in touch with General Alexei Antonov, the Red Army Chief of Staff. He suggested to Antonov that, after the occupation of the line through Pilsen, the Third Army be allowed to move to the Moldau and the western suburbs of Prague. Antonov dissented strongly. He urged Eisenhower "not to move the Allied forces in Czechoslovakia east of the originally intended line"—to avoid, as he put it, "a possible confusion of forces."

Antonov then added ominously that "the Soviet forces had stopped their advance to the lower Elbe east of the line Wismar, Schwerin, and Dömitz at the Supreme Commander's request, and that he hoped General Eisenhower would comply with Russian wishes relative to the advance of U.S. forces in Czechoslovakia."

As Ike saw it, he had no choice. He dropped the proposition and assured Antonov that he would halt the Third Army on the prearranged line. Now he ordered Bradley to find Patton wherever he was and tell him that under no circumstances was he to go in force beyond the Budweis-Pilsen-Karlsbad line. Moreover, the city of Prague was not to be touched.

In the morning on May 6th, when he was returning from church, Patton was called to the phone. It was Bradley, calling to convey Ike's orders.

"The halt-line through Pilsen *is* mandatory for V and XII Corps, George," he said with the utmost emphasis. "Moreover, you must not—I repeat, *not*—reconnoiter to a greater depth than 5 miles northeast of Pilsen. Ike does not want any international complications at this late date."

"For God's sake, Brad," Patton protested, "it seems to me that a great nation like America should let others worry about complications."

But Bradley was off the phone. And Prague was off the Third Army's shopping list. "By this action," Pogue wrote in the official history of the Supreme Commander, "[Eisenhower] left Prague and most of Czechoslovakia to be liberated by the Red forces. Except for minor adjustments of boundaries and the closing up to lines of demarcation, operations of the Western Allies were at an end."

On May 7th Patton was busy the whole day guiding Judge Patterson, the Under Secretary of War, on a sightseeing tour through his sector. It was 8 P.M. when he got back to his headquarters. A top secret message from SHAEF was waiting for him:

"Final German surrender fixed for 0001B May 9."

Patton was in no mood to celebrate. For the first time in the war he was feeling frightfully lonely and tired.

CHAPTER FORTY-ONE
A TIME OF WAR, AND A TIME OF PEACE*

> *To every thing there is a season, and a time to every purpose under the heaven:*
> *A time to be born, and a time to die . . .*
> *A time to kill, and a time to heal; a time to break down, and a time to build up . . .*
> *A time to get, and a time to lose; a time to keep, and a time to cast away;*
> *A time to rend, and a time to sew; a time to keep silence, and a time to speak;*
> *A time to love, and a time to hate . . .*

May 6, 1945, was the Third Army's last day of fighting.

Germany's defeat was now total and irrevocable. The disintegration of the Third Reich was complete, its power smashed, its pretenses shattered. And yet, in its final throes of agony, bands of young Germans were still in the thick of it here and there, punching like a dazed pugilist after the knockout blow. As a result, in the Third Army's sector, this was still a day of war while everywhere else in the west the imminence of Germany's surrender was casting its calm on inert fronts.

On May 7th, then, the German High Command—or what was left of it—surrendered all land, sea and air forces unconditionally to the Allies. The instrument of surrender

* Ecclesiastes, III, 1-8

was signed at General Eisenhower's tactical headquarters at Reims at 1:41 A.M. Central European double daylight saving time, to become effective at 1 A.M. on the 9th. As soon as the news was received in the field, all offensive operations were halted. The organization of defensive positions began, just in case . . .

On the 8th, at last, the Third Army also established contact with the Red Army. At Armstetten, in the area of XII Corps, it was the final mission of the 11th Armored Division. Then elements of XX Corps met the Russians, the 65th Division in the vicinity of Strengberg, the 71st at St. Peter.

In Czechoslovakia, though, the war continued for another day. Three Ukranian armies were pursuing the Germans westward and, on the 9th, troops of the First Ukranian Front entered Prague. By then there was nothing Patton could do about it. The mission of the Third Army had been concluded.

In 281 days of campaigning in Western Europe, the Third Army had liberated or captured 81,522 square miles of territory, including 47,828 square miles in France, 1,010 in Luxembourg, 156 in Belgium, 26,940 in Germany, 3,485 in Czechoslovakia, and 2,103 in Austria. During the greater part of the nine months and eight days of fighting the Army maintained a front of from 75 to 100 air miles—the longest on April 20, 1945, when it measured 200 miles. Some 12,000 cities, towns and communities had been liberated or captured, including 27 cities of more than 50,000 population.

The Third Army was at the peak of its strength when the last campaign ended on May 8th. Its effectives totaled 92,187 on August 1, 1944; 220,169 on August 31st; 437,860 the day hostilities ceased. Its casualties totaled 160,692, including 27,104 killed, 86,267 wounded, 18,957 missing in action, and 127 captured by the enemy. In marked contrast, the casualties the Army had inflicted upon the enemy totaled 1,443,888 officers and men, of whom 47,500 had been killed, 115,700 wounded, and 1,280,688 taken prisoner.

"I can say this." Patton wrote in assessing his part in the victory, "that throughout the campaign in Europe I know of no error I made except that of failing to send a Combat Command to take Hammelburg. Otherwise, my operations were, to me, strictly satisfactory. In every case, practically throughout the campaign, I was under wraps from the

Higher Command. This may have been a good thing, as perhaps I am too impetuous. However, I do not believe I was, and feel that had I been permitted to go all out, the war would have ended sooner and more lives would have been saved."

At the regular morning briefing on May 8th, Patton addressed his staff, thanking each member for what he had done. He assured them: "No one man can conduct an army. The success of any army depends on the harmonious working of its staff and the magnificent fighting ability of the combat officers and enlisted men." Choked up, he concluded the emotional speech with the words:

"Well, as the Church says, 'Here endeth the Second lesson.' "

At 11:30 A.M. he held a final briefing for his war correspondents, of whom only two—Robert Cromie of the Chicago *Tribune* and Cornelius Ryan of a London daily paper—had spent all their time in Europe with the Third Army. During the briefing, Larry Newman of International News Service asked him, "General, why didn't we take Prague?"

"I can tell you exactly why," Patton answered, enjoying for a brief moment the look of eager expectation in the eyes of his audience. "Because," he continued slowly, "we were ordered not to."

On May 10th he issued *General Orders No. 98* terminating the war.

The shooting stopped, perhaps a bit abruptly for Patton, but now the shouting began. The man who exactly two and a half years before was known to only a relative handful of professional soldiers and polo enthusiasts was now a historic figure. The letdown was tremendous, but Patton was uplifted quickly by the acclaim he was receiving. The general damned in Sicily and censured for a harmless lapse of his tongue in England, the tough old warrior who had escaped the sack only by the skin of his teeth, was now, next to Eisenhower, the most popular hero of the great crusade. The ordeal was forgotten in the triumph that had its glittering rewards—the cheering of crowds in London, Boston, Denver, and Los Angeles, official and unofficial accolades in Paris and Stockholm, the tearful gratitude of the people of Luxembourg greeting him in the role Patton savored most—that of the liberator.

His triumphal return to America evoked different reactions in different people, for Patton remained a baffling figure to the bitter end. To Dwight Macdonald, probably his most articulate critic in the United States, he was "brutal and hysterical, coarse and affected, violent and empty." Macdonald judged Patton by his floating reputation and by a brief newsreel clip that showed him addressing a crowd in Los Angeles on his visit to his boyhood environment. "Gray-haired and erect," Macdonald wrote, " 'Old Blood and Guts' had a fine presence; paternal, gruff, a bit diffident, with a warm smile every now and then as he talked."

But what he said left Macdonald appalled. "These utterances of Patton's," he wrote, "are atrocities of the mind; atrocious in being communicated not to a psychoanalyst but to great number of soldiers, civilians, and school children; and atrocious as reflections of what war-making has done to the personality of Patton himself."

In the eyes of Milton F. Perry, another of his biographers, whose interest in Patton was stimulated by their mutual love of sidearms, the General epitomized the ideal fighting man. "Here was the Patton all America knew," Perry wrote in his account of Patton's arrival in Boston on June 7, 1945, "and the nation was not disappointed. Photographs and newsreels clearly showed the 'pink' gabardine riding breeches, the tightly tailored combat jacket he had taken to wearing and four rows of ribbons adorning the latter. Discernible on the left sleeve were five overseas bars, one for every six months spent outside the United States during World War II.

"Above was the Third Army shoulder patch, and, below, four herringbone-shaped chevrons for an earlier war. Around his waist was the brown leather, brass-trimmed General Officer's belt, and the riding boots he liked so well encased his legs. In his hands, as he accepted the plaudits of the dignitaries, he nervously clutched a swagger stick.

"His was the return of the hero."

The real Patton at the end of the war was somewhere between these two clichés. This complex man was probably most faithfully presented at the Hatch Memorial Shell in his adopted home town of Boston when he was called upon to address the crowd. He strutted to the platform, an impeccably groomed warrior created by the close cooperation of his Lord and his tailor, and, in his high-pitched voice, began an address that sounded in accord with the visual image. But then Patton hushed the crowd with a moving speech that was remarkable for the man's integrity, for it retained his martial stance yet was humble and moving.

"It is foolish and wrong," he said, "to mourn the men who died. Rather we should thank God that such men lived." And after his rip-roaring address in the Memorial Coliseum that so scandalized Macdonald, he showed his humility in another speech on the steps of the Los Angeles City Hall. He pointed to the rows of ribbons on his chest and said, "Gallant men won these medals, but we only wear them." At both places tears welled up in his eyes. Overcome by the grim memories of the recent conflict, he could not go on. He sat down, presenting the incongruous spectacle of the hard-boiled soldier hunched in his chair, wiping his eyes.

But he was still running with the breathless momentum of the war. Apparently for the sake of keeping home-front morale high for the war against Japan, Patton persisted in his boisterous ways and continued to raise eyebrows with hell-raising speeches at inopportune moments in improper places. At the Church of Our Saviour in San Gabriel, which his grandfather Don Benito Wilson had founded, he led the Sunday School in the singing of hymns. But in the next breath he treated the class to one of his bloodier speeches, urging continued preparedness in terms far less temperate than George Washington's similar appeal.

He was criticized several times for frenzied words and emotional outbursts by clergymen, intellectuals, and even the *Stars and Stripes*. He had to explain as best he could what he had really meant when he tried to link peace with preparedness but unfortunately sounded like a warhawk calling for the resumption of fighting against a different enemy.

Patton was somewhat slow in realizing that V-E Day had made the home front peace-conscious again, and that henceforth he would have to think carefully before jumping into his impromptu harangues about the dangers he feared were still confronting his nation. The last thing he did in Washington in late June before returning to Germany was to visit wounded veterans at Walter Reed Hospital and to attempt to "clarify" various newspaper reports about his incendiary remarks. But he failed to calm completely the controversy that was beginning to envelop him again. His clash with Bill Mauldin was revived in the papers. His apparent addiction to war for war's sake was subjected to critical scrutiny. Before long, the image of the conquering hero was blurred again.

But he was receiving ample recompense for all the hard knocks, and Patton appeared to be enjoying to the hilt the crowds and the flowers and the parades. There was, however, a dark blotch in this sunbaked high noon of his career —the ambiguity of his relationship with Dwight D. Eisenhower.

It is difficult to define the source of the discontent, and it would be odious to explain it in terms of projected psychoanalysis. Yet, in truth, the association of these two great soldiers had suffered as the war progressed and was quite blurred at its end. The vexation of Patton's high-strung, sensitive staff with SHAEF in general had occasionally assumed proportions of rancor, and some of it was directed —now splenetically, then derisively—at Eisenhower's own person. The ill-humored quip that Ike was "the best general the British had" originated at Third Army Headquarters and became so widespread by constant repetition that inevitably it reached the Supreme Commander's ears.

It betokened the prevalent attitude of Patton's people and was not exactly calculated to endear them to the victim of their barb. Patton, on his part, went to some lengths to dissociate himself from such blatant allegories of scorn. But Ike could not help knowing that his friend George, too, had his own quota of reservations about his friend from their happier days at Fort Meade.

His innate patience and tolerance, his sunny disposition and cordial nature endowed Eisenhower with a generous capacity for forbearance. But in Patton's case his magnanimity was stretched almost to the breaking point—further even than in Monty's case. And Eisenhower, who had a streak of resentment in his make-up, plus a light touch of vindictiveness, repaid, in his own subtler ways, Patton's animosity toward him.

Patton had felt distinctly the finely honed edge of the Supreme Commander's punctilious hostility when Eisenhower passed over in icy silence his occasional trickeries to gain his ends and failed conspicuously to praise him for the resounding victories he usually scored in their wake. During their meeting at Bastogne toward the close of the Battle of the Bulge, Eisenhower was jolly and effusive, but said nothing in direct praise of Patton's feat. Later, in his joy over the capture of Trier, Patton phoned Bradley with the news and could distinctly hear that Eisenhower was with Bradley. But he was sorely disappointed when the Supreme Commander did not deem it necessary to add his own congratulations to those of Bradley.

It was only on March 17, 1945, after the Third Army had stormed through the Mainz-Frankfurt-Darmstadt triangle, that General Eisenhower offered his first congratulations to Patton on his phenomenal progress since August 1, 1944. Ike had arrived at Patton's command post that morning and asked to be taken into the briefing session. When it was over, he rose to make an impromptu speech to the startled assembly. Now he pulled out all stops.

He began by saying that members of the Third Army were such seasoned veterans that they had become blunted by their own greatness. He urged the officers and non-coms in the room to be "more cocky and boastful" because otherwise, he said, people would not realize how good the American soldier really is. He mentioned specifically General Gaffey's 4th Armored Division, which had been delayed at the Nahe River near Bad Kreuznach before it secured a crossing and continued its southward drive. Eisenhower referred to the critical accounts in the newspapers of Gaffey's struggle and added with some heat, "But Goddamnit, they didn't mention the fact that the 4th Armored had been held up on account of the unprecedented speed with which it had advanced."

Then turning to Patton, Ike said warmly that not only was he a great general and a good one, but also "a damned lucky stiff," the ideal combination—for did not Napoleon prefer luck to greatness? Patton was so astounded by this praise that he recorded the event in full, concluding the entry with a characteristic remark: "I told him this was the first time he had ever complimented me in the two and a half years we have served together."

It proved to be also the only time. Less than a fortnight after the spectacular pat on Patton's back, Eisenhower wrote a personal letter to General Marshall praising his commanders in general terms, but taking special pains to stress the stellar contributions of Bradley and Hodges. Of Bradley, he wrote: "He has never once held back in attempting any maneuver, no matter how bold in conception, and never has he paused to regroup when there was opportunity lying on his front. . . . I consider Bradley the greatest battle-line commander I have met in this war." The praise seemed somewhat extravagant, not on its own merit, but by Bradley's inferential comparison with Patton.

Of Hodges, he wrote that from the end of February "his drive, clear-headed and tactical skill have shone even more brightly than they did in his great pursuit across France, in which First Army's part was the most difficult given to any United States formation but brilliantly and speedily executed, often against much resistance." Eisenhower added that although it was not his intention to detract from the splendid performance of his other commanders, he felt it was proper to tell Marshall these things because "others had received credit for things that Bradley and Hodges were primarily responsible for."

However, Omar Bradley amply made up for Patton's strange omission from Eisenhower's dithyrambic letter to Marshall. On June 30, 1945, when the time came to prepare Patton's efficiency report for his 201 File, Bradley wrote a rating that combined poetic justice with some poetic license:

"Colorful, courageous, energetic, pleasing personality, impetuous. Possesses high degree of leadership, bold in operations, has a fine sense of both enemy and own capabilities. An outstanding combat leader. . . . Of the 10 general officers of this grade known to me, I would list him Number One as a combat commander. Renders willing and generous support to the plans of his superiors, regardless of his personal views in the matter."

On April 12th Patton wrote to his wife: "I love war and responsibility and excitement. Peace is going to be Hell on me."

When the war in Europe was over and he began to feel the pangs of the let-down, Patton started moving heaven and earth to be sent to the Far East. He used a visit of General "Hap" Arnold to his headquarters in Germany to ask the Air Force chief to intervene on his behalf with

General Marshall; then wrote directly to the Chief of Staff, pleading with him to expedite his transfer, "willing," as he put it, "to go in command of a division."

At his final briefing on V-E Day, Patton assured his staff that it would be "going to China" very soon to take on the Japanese. So confident was he that he would be permitted to "earn his pay" a little longer in that other war that in his last meeting with the correspondents he told them, "The Third Army is heading for the Pacific."

But on May 20th, less than fortnight after V-E Day, Patton's hopes faded. "The desire to fight is evaporating," he wrote to his wife, "and these soldiers will not be much good unless they get in soon." As far as he personally was concerned, he added, "I doubt if I will go to China unless something happens to Doug [General Douglas Mac-Arthur]."

Patton had more reason than most of us to hope for an abrupt termination of the war with Japan in the not too distant future. In April he had been told by John J. McCloy, the Assistant Secretary of War, that the United States was developing an atomic bomb of cataclysmic power which was expected to force Japan to her knees without an invasion. At about the same time he played host to a group of scientists combing occupied Germany for evidence that the Nazis, too, had made headway with the military application of nuclear fission. He was gratified to learn that they had found the German effort to be far behind the American-British development. But he was dismayed that a single super-bomb might terminate his usefulness as a combat commander. Patton started to argue, in his mind, against such an eventuality.

For a fleeting moment in May it seemed that he would be given a chance to get back into the war, even if only on a minor scale. On the 16th, when Patton was in London on his way to visit his old haunts around Knutsford, he was paged at Claridge's to take an urgent call. It was from General Bull, SHAEF G-3, ordering him to report to General Eisenhower at Reims.

He was back in harness by 5:30 o'clock that afternoon, closeted with Eisenhower, who was explaining a problem that had just arisen and which, it seemed, needed Patton for its solution. The veteran Croatian Bolshevik Josip Broz, who had emerged from the war as the ruler of Yugoslavia with the *nom de guerre* Marshal Tito, was casting covetous eyes on parts of Albania and Italy, especially on the Adriatic port of Trieste and the Venezia-Giulia region. Determined to keep Tito in his place, President Truman had instructed General Marshall to arrange for a show of force in northern Italy by an American army, and Marshall had ordered Eisenhower to send Patton.

The next couple of days were devoted to the demonstration, for which Patton was to be given XV Corps from the Seventh Army. The plan was to bluff on the Enns and, if Tito called it, to cross the river. But the mission was canceled as abruptly as Patton's assignment to the Anzio beachhead was in January, 1944, and apparently for the same reason. According to the scuttlebutt at Third Army Headquarters, General Mark W. Clark, the Commander in Chief of the Allied forces in Italy, again succeeded in preventing Patton from insinuating himself into what Clark regarded as his exclusive preserve.

Then, during his visit to the United States, Patton's last hope for the transfer to the Pacific was crushed. On June 13th he called on President Truman at the White House, then went to the Pentagon for a conference with Secretary Stimson and General Marshall. He was told categorically that his transfer to the Pacific was out.

The issue was quick to provoke speculation; and a touch of mystery was added when Secretary Stimson, in a press conference the next day, ruled out all questions on Patton's future assignment. There were rumors that Stimson and Marshall were for Patton's transfer, but General MacArthur strongly opposed it. MacArthur later denied that he had ever objected to the shift of Patton to his theater, but the decision to leave Patton in Europe while the war against Japan still presented considerable difficulties was never explained.

Whatever it was that persuaded Marshall to deny Patton his wish, it was not the imminent dawn of the atomic age or the belief that the end of the war with Japan was in sight. The first A-bomb was detonated at Los Alamos, New Mexico, on July 16th. Until then, nobody privy to this enormous secret could know whether it would work. And the decision to use it against Japan was reached on July 30th at Potsdam, when Japan appeared to reject an Allied ultimatum of July 26th to cease resistance.

At the time of Patton's presence in Washington, General Marshall was still firmly convinced that the war in the

Pacific would last another year or maybe longer. On the day of his conference with Patton, American armies were fighting on Luzon and Okinawa. Marshall was busily planning for "a prolonged Pacific war." Although he had plans ready for "an attack on Kyushu and Honshu in 1945," they depended on the rapidity of redeployment from Europe, which he expected would require a minimum of four to six months.

As late as June 4th the Operations Division regarded "the point in our military progress at which the Japanese will accept defeat" as "unpredictable." It was assumed that "probably it will take Russian entry into the war, coupled with a landing, or imminent threat of landing, on Japan proper by us to convince them of the hopelessness of their position." General Marshall concurred completely in the assumption.

Even on July 24th, eight days after the A-bomb had been successfully tested, Marshall's over-all strategic concept still was that "the invasion of Japan and operations directly connected therewith are the supreme operations in the war against Japan." But apparently there was no place for Patton in those supreme operations.

With the disappointing outcome of his Washington mission, the war receded into the background and the vexing problems of the conqueror descended upon Patton once more. Before he knew it, he was back in the role for which he was least suited. He was an American proconsul again, as in Morocco 30 months before. But this was Germany! In complexity and intricacy, the problems confronting him far surpassed anything he had found in Casablanca.

In the last analysis, though, they could be reduced to just two. One was the proximity of the Russians; the other was the painful legacy of Nazism facing him at every turn.

Tito's sudden stirring had brought into sharp focus the budding crisis of post-war Europe. Patton spelled out the underlying factors in the Yugoslav's move in a diary entry on May 18th: "The question at issue is not so much Tito, but as to whether or not he is the pawn of the Russians and, if so, whether he is being used as a red herring to pull us to the South so that the Russians may resume an offensive in Central Germany; or whether the Russians are actually backing Tito with the idea of getting a port, or ports, on the northern end of the Adriatic."

This was the beginning of his final anxious preoccupation with the Russians. Patton was only mildly interested in what he called "the Russian problem" and was hardly irritated by it until he met General Wladislaw Anders in Cairo in December, 1943. The commanding general of the 2nd Polish Corps in exile in World War II, Anders was, in his younger years, on the staff of a Russian division in the Tsarist army, where he had ample opportunity to observe the Russians at close quarters. An intense but enlightened patriot, he disliked the Russians in general and the Soviet Union in particular. In Cairo he told Patton that "the Russians had deliberately murdered quite a few thousand Polish officers." It was the first Patton heard of what became the hot issue of the so-called Katyn massacre.

"If I ever marched my corps of two divisions in between the Russians and the Germans," Anders told Patton, "I'd attack in both directions."

Patton's education was subsequently broadened by a number of persons who had no illusions about what he had come to regard as an unholy alliance with Stalin and which he expected would blow up in our face sooner or later. He obtained his most authoritative information from W. Averell Harriman, the Ambassador to the U.S.S.R., who visited him at Nancy on the eve of Thanksgiving Day in 1944.

Patton took Harriman to General John S. Wood's command post, so far forward that it was almost on the fighting line. The hard-bitten Wood had pitched his own tent, soaked by the heavy rains of this dismal autumn, in the quagmire of the contested countryside. "I took him to the 4th Armored Division," Patton wrote, "to show him that the Russians were not the only people who had to contend against mud."

Harriman was eminently qualified to bring Patton up to date on the explosive Soviet issue. Probably earlier than anybody that high in the Roosevelt Administration, he recognized that the conflict between Bolshevism and the democracies, suspended for the duration, would erupt with greater force than ever as soon as the shooting stopped. He told Patton that Stalin had paid the Third Army the highest compliment by saying in the presence of the Red Army Chief of Staff, "The Red Army could not have conceived and certainly could not have executed the advance made by the Third Army across France.

But he also warned Patton (who was unmellowed by the praise) that Stalin was "a strong, ruthless revolutionist, and therefore a very potential threat to future world conditions." He described the discipline in the Red Army as "the most rigid and ruthless he had ever seen" and its officer caste as "the new nobility."

"This is a strange result of Communism," Patton noted in his diary.

Later his aversion and apprehension were confirmed by a high Polish churchman and by Commandant Philippe de Forceville, the senior French liaison officer with the Third Army. Both men regaled him with first-hand information about the new Soviet rule in Poland. "It seems to be quite a hell of a mess," Patton remarked.

In his natural belligerency, he assumed that the problem could be solved only by a clash of arms. Here, he thought, was the seed of World War III. As far as could be traced, his first public expression of this view occurred on a day most prominent in the Marxist calendar—May Day in 1945.

Word had reached Patton that a German prisoner-of-war camp at a place called Moosburg was holding a precious gift for him. Among the Allied prisoners there was Major Al Stiller, his old friend and aide, who had been captured on the ill-fated Hammelburg expedition. Patton rushed to Moosburg, found Stiller and personally liberated him.

The camp contained some 30,000 Allied prisoners, including a large Red Army contingent, the pariahs among the "inmates." Wearing tattered uniforms, they looked a motley and dejected crew. While Patton was busy with Stiller and was acknowledging a spontaneous ovation by the other Allied prisoners, the Russians assembled near the gates, apparently ready to check out.

"Then," wrote Codman, who witnessed the scene, "a remarkable thing happened. The senior Russian officer blew his whistle, barked a sharp command, and through the now open gateway the Russian column marched out at a fast, rhythmic clip. Bearing, precision, staying power, discipline. Somehow the beards were no longer unkempt. They bristled with stored energy, and the faded tunics took on the lines of dress uniform."

Patton dropped everything to watch the extraordinary spectacle. He mounted a crate to get a better view of the Russians "now magically reconverted into seasoned troops," as Codman put it, "veterans of a hundred battles," as they set out on the long journey home. Patton turned to Codman and said, his eyes shining with admiration, "That's it, the Russian infantry!" He paused for a moment as his next thought seemed to banish the gleam from his eyes. "But it can be done," he said grimly, "and that is undoubtedly just what we shall have to do."

Like most of the bents of Patton's mind, his attitude toward the "Russian problem" was also shaped by two mainsprings, one highly personal, fused with all the passionate bias of his hectic soul, the other detached and strictly professional. Personally he just did not like the "new" Russian, the puzzling human automaton the cultural anthropologists of the O.W.I. called "the Soviet man." This was an irrational and arbitrary sentiment, if only because he did not know any Soviet people well enough to size them up accurately or fairly. Whenever the visit of a Soviet delegation was announced, Patton instructed Colonel Koch to prepare a set of doctored maps for them and told General Gaffey or Gay to show them as little as possible as elaborately as could be feigned. He then left his headquarters and stayed out of reach until the visitation passed.

The few Red Army officers he could not avoid did not change his preconceived opinion. They impressed him as sullen, taciturn, rather crude and rude fellows whose doubt and mistrust seemed to ooze through their pores like malodorous perspiration. From his own upper-class world (his real status which no amount of Rabelaisian language could compromise) Patton regarded the bullet-headed senior officers in the Red Army as a bunch of imperfectly housebroken, Falstaffian rubes.

He was at his childish worst during one of his first formal meetings with the Russians at a joint review in Berlin shortly after the termination of hostilities. Only the unexpected good humor of a Soviet general then averted what for a tense moment threatened to erupt in a minor but embarrassing international incident. It was evident during the parade that Patton was a celebrity to his Soviet colleagues. They kept eyeing him and were flashing awkward smiles in his direction throughout the review. Patton responded with his frown No. 5, which was reserved for s.o.b.'s at the bottom of the class. Despite this discouraging gesture, one of the Russian generals sent an interpreter to Patton, inviting him for a drink after the show.

"Tell that Russian sonuvabitch," Patton barked back, "that from the way they're acting here I regard them as enemies and I'd rather cut my throat than have a drink with one of my enemies."

The interpreter paled. "I am sorry, sir, but I cannot tell the general *that*," he stammered, in a state of shock.

But Patton *ordered* him to translate everything he said word for word, and the interpreter reluctantly complied. The Russian broke into a broad smile, said something, and the interpreter told Patton, "The general says that he feels exactly like that about you, sir. So why, he asks, couldn't you and he have a drink after all?" They did.

Once, after the visit of a Soviet general, Patton remarked that it could not be denied, the Bolsheviks had raised the level of the Russian people—from common soldiers and ordinary workers to sergeants and foremen. That was as far as he was willing to go. He could not imagine that he could ever become chummy with his opposite numbers in the Red Army, the portly marshals whose enormous chests were hung with medals like prize bulls wearing their ribbons at a 4-H show, simply because he did not think that they were his kind of gentleman.

On meeting Marshal Georgi Zhukov at an inter-Allied review on September 7th celebrating V-J Day, he wrote to his wife: "He was in full-dress uniform much like comic opera and covered with medals. He is short, rather fat, and has a prehensile chin like an ape but good blue eyes." Of Marshal Feodor I. Tolbukhin, commander of the Third Ukrainian Front, whom he met at the headquarters of the 4th Russian Guards Army during his investiture with the Order of Kutuzoff, First Degree, he wrote in his diary: "He was a very inferior man and sweated profusely at all times." That was all.

Patton added this general impression: "The officers, with few exceptions, give the appearance of recently civilized Mongolian bandits."

His low opinion of "the Soviet Man" colored his ideas about the entire Soviet system. There was nothing intellectual or philosophical at the bottom of his attitude. It is doubtful whether Patton either knew too much or really cared about the ideological and other theoretical implications of Communism. More than likely he would have probably approved it had it succeeded in producing a better and nobler human being, a nicer and more sophisticated, friendlier individual than this morose, suspicion-ridden, vodka-guzzling "Soviet Man."

Patton's hostility to the Communists was not of the common crackpot variety. Unlike Macauley's hypocritical Puritan, he hated bear-baiting—or, for that matter, Red-baiting—not only because it gave pain to the bear but also because it gave pleasure to the spectators. One would think that Patton would have given credit to the Bolsheviks for at least producing the fine soldiers of World War II. But no! He admired the toy-soldier precision of the Russian infantry and respected the Red infantryman's death-defying equanimity in the face of overwhelming odds. But he could not see much difference between Kutuzoff's docile muzhiks marching against Napoleon's grenadiers and Stalin's stolid hordes storming into the muzzles of Nazi guns.

It was in the military sphere that Patton came to grips with the "Russian problem." It continued to intrigue him for the rest of his life also in geopolitical terms. On October 13th, in the quiet of his reduced last headquarters at Bad Nauheim, he reviewed the ramifications of the Soviet Union's new position in the world and placed in his diary ideas on the topic that were, in the perspective of the years, remarkable for their foresight.

Patton spent November 17th brooding over the problem. The day produced a long dissertation, which became the final summation of the views burning in him. He wrote:

"It seems highly possible that the Russians have spheres of influence in Korea, Manchuria and Mongolia. Now, while in many of the states . . . alleged democratic forms of government exist, they are actually under the thumb of the Russians and it is quite certain that the Russians will not permit any large-scale economic relations between the Bolshevik-ruled countries and the rest of the world because if they did, too many foreigners would be able to look behind the curtain and see what actually goes on in these communist countries . . .

"One result of the Bolshevik conquest of half of Western Europe is that they have reduced the scale of living in those countries to the Russian scale, which is very low, and furthermore, have prohibited the United States and England from selling to about a third of their former markets. In view of the fact that the world financial arrangements were based on sales to and between all members of the world nations, the removal of a third of these nations is bound to upset the political economy of England and America, and therefore throw large numbers of men out of work and consequently make them readily acceptable victims of the virus of Communism."

Strangely enough, these economic views of the Soviet expansion coincided with the expectations of an influential group of Soviet economists led by Academician Eugene Varga. The latter, too, looked forward to grave economic crises in the Western democracies as one of the paradoxical consequences of their victory in World War II. Fortunately for the free world, the United States wisely anticipated the possibility of such a dangerous development and countered it with energetic and ingenious measures, like the Marshall Plan, thwarting both the expectations of the Varga group and the gloomy predictions of Patton.

Patton's pent-up misgivings, his exasperation with the apparent leniency of the official American policy toward the U.S.S.R., erupted in a strange phone conversation with General Joseph T. McNarney, his old friend who had come to Germany to serve as Eisenhower's deputy and was Acting Theater Commander in Ike's absence. At that time, a spirit of cooperation still persisted at Eisenhower's headquarters in the huge I.G. Farben building at Höchst near Frankfurt. Patton's impatience with the policy ran away with him when McNarney relayed a Soviet complaint that he was too slow in disbanding and confining several German units in his sector of military government.

"Hell," Patton exploded, "why do you care what those Goddamn Russians think? We are going to have to fight them sooner or later; within the next generation. Why not do it now while our Army is intact and the damn Russians can have their hind end kicked back into Russia in three months? We can do it ourselves easily with the help of the German troops we have, if we just arm them and take them with us; they hate the bastards."

Patton had put his foot in his mouth again. It was a serious *faux pas*, this reference to those "German troops," and it shocked McNarney.

"Shut up, Georgie, you fool!" he told Patton. "This line

may be tapped and you will be starting a war with those Russians with your talking!"

But Patton refused to shut up. "I would like to get it started some way," he said, "that is the best thing we can do now. *You* don't have to get mixed up in it at all if you are so damn soft about it and scared of your rank—just let me handle it down here. In 10 days I can have enough incidents happen to have us at war with those sons of bitches and make it look like their fault. So much so that we will be completely justified in attacking them and running them out."

Mortified, McNarney hung up. Patton turned to Colonel Harkins, who was in his office during the conversation (and later related it to General Semmes). "I really believe," he said with a smug smile at McNarney's evident discomfort, "that we are going to fight them, and if this country does not do it now, it will be taking them on years later when the Russians are ready for it and we will have an awful time whipping them. We will need these Germans," he concluded on a theme that was getting the upper hand in his entire thinking, "and I don't think we ought to mistreat people whom we will need so badly."

Patton could not know it, of course, but this conversation with its fantastic indiscretion and political naïveté was the beginning of his end. It convinced McNarney that Patton was on the wrong track and was, indeed, unfit to govern the defeated Germans in whose land Nazism was not yet defunct by any means. It was only a matter of time before Patton was to suffer the last humiliation in his life, the one whose scars he was to take to his grave.

His rather rabid views of the Russians and his belief in the inevitability of a war with them within a generation sharply contrasted with General Eisenhower's philosophy of peace and his ideas about the post-war world. Ike had developed a personal friendship and understanding with Marshal Zhukov, the man who reminded Patton of an ape. Moreover, Eisenhower was firm in his adherence to both the latter and the spirit of the various agreements reached at Potsdam, aimed not so much at the punishment of the

Germans, but at making sure that Germany as a nation would not rise again and become a menace to the world.

Eisenhower persisted in this even when members of his own staff and his high-ranking associates, irritated by increasing Soviet violations of those same covenants, urged him to refuse to withdraw American troops from the Elbe to the area the Potsdam agreement had allocated to the United States. "The argument was," Eisenhower wrote, "that if we kept troops on the Elbe the Russians would be more likely to agree to some of our proposals, particularly as to a reasonable division of Austria. To me, such an attitude seemed indefensible. I was certain, and was always supported in this attitude by the War Department, that to start off our first direct association with Russia on the basis of refusing to carry out an arrangement in which the good faith of our government was involved would wreck the whole cooperative attempt at its very beginning."

It was obvious from the outset that Eisenhower's diplomacy and his conciliatory regime would clash with Patton's intransigence and impatience. The tragic dénouement of the clash could not be far off.

With his eyes transfixed on the showdown with the Soviet Union, Patton began to irritate not only the Russians, but General Eisenhower as well. And he shocked others high in the American Military Government in Germany who were not so prepared as Patton seemed to be to forget the recent past and forgive the Germans their debasement and the Nazis their crimes. Since the Third Army had wound up the war in the south, Patton was appointed Military Governor of Bavaria, with temporary jurisdiction over certain territories beyond it, including the part of Czechoslovakia he had liberated one step ahead of the Red Army.

During those days, Robert D. Murphy, the distinguished diplomat who had headed the nebulous American conspiracy against the Vichyites in North Africa and was now Eisenhower's diplomatic adviser, had two separate talks with Patton in which they discussed the problems of the General's delicate duties. Patton candidly asked him on each occasion whether Murphy thought he had fought his last battle. "He inquired with a gleam in his eye," Murphy later wrote, "whether there was any chance of going on to Moscow, which he said he could reach in 30 days, instead of waiting for the Russians to attack the United States when we were weak and reduced to two divisions."

Perhaps it was a mistake, especially in view of the Moroccan experience, to give General Patton the job of an American proconsul again. For he possessed none of the subtlety the task required and was far too inclined to explode into ill-advised action on his own hasty and combustible ideas. He was not the right man either by experience or training, by philosophy or temperament for the delicate assignment of rehabilitating that part of Germany where the cradle of Nazism had rocked and where the stench of Hitler's regime was still polluting the air.

But nothing in his conduct of the war or in his former attitudes to the Germans indicated that such a rapid change of heart would occur in him. Throughout the war the German was the *Boche,* the *Kraut,* the *Hun* to him. He would wax so emotional that he frequently burst into tears when proclaiming all the horrid things he had in store for so vile an enemy.

This aversion, produced by the natural enmity of war, seemed to have deepened into an implacable hatred when then the Third Army overran the Ohrdruf concentration camp near Gotha and Patton witnessed this morbid evidence of the Nazis' despicable crimes. General Eisenhower was shaken to his marrow by what he found in these horror camps with their neat, tiled gas chambers. And so were the other American generals Ike had ordered to inspect them to get a first-hand impression of Nazi bestiality. But none was more profoundly shocked than Patton.

Upon his return to his command post from the first visit to the Ohrdruf camp, he called in Sergeant Rosevich to dictate a lengthy memorandum about what he had seen. Rosevich still remembers most vividly how the mere recollection of those terrible scenes held Patton in its grip.

"Colonel Codman and I," Patton dictated on April 12th, "together with a party which included General Eisenhower, General Bradley, and General Weyland, drove to Ohrdruf from the XX Corps Headquarters and visited a prison camp for slave labor who had been employed in a munitions factory in the vicinity. This was one of the most appalling sights I have ever seen.

"One of the former inmates acted as impresario and showed us first a gallows where men were hanged for attempting to escape. The hanging was done with a piece of piano wire, and the man being hanged was not dropped far enough to break his neck but simply strangled as a result of the piano wire. It is alleged that the German generals who were killed after the attempted assassination of Hitler in July [1944] were hanged in the same manner.

"The rope is so adjusted that after a drop of about two feet the man's toes can just touch the ground, so that death takes some time. Two prisoners next to be hanged are required to kick the plank from under him.

"We then saw a whipping table which stands at a height of just to a man's stomach. The person to be whipped then had his feet fastened in a sort of stocks. He was then pulled across the table by his hands and beaten with a stick, about an inch and a half in diameter, over the buttocks and back. The impresario claimed that he had received 25 strokes. He was such a well-fed looking man that I had an idea he may have been one of the executioners.

"Just beyond the whipping table was a pile of about 40 bodies more or less naked, all of whom had been shot through the head at short range. The ground was covered with dried blood. These men had become so exhausted as to be useless for labor and were disposed of in this humane (?) manner. In a shed near this place was a pile of about 40 completely naked bodies in the last stage of emaciation. These bodies were lightly sprinkled with lime, not for the purpose of destroying them, but for the purpose of removing the stench. When the shed was full—I presume its capacity to be about 200—the bodies were taken to a pit a mile from the camp, where they were buried. The inmates claimed that 3,000 men, who had been either shot in the head or who had died of starvation were so buried since the 1st of January.

"When we began to approach with our troops, the Germans thought it expedient to remove the evidence of their crime. Therefore, they had some of the slaves exhume the bodies and place them on a mammoth griddle composed of 60-centimeter railway tracks laid on brick foundations. They poured pitch on the bodies and then built a fire of pinewood and coal under them. They were not very successful in their operations, because there was a pile of human bones, skulls, charred torsos on or under the griddle, which must have accounted for many hundreds.

"Generals Walker and Middleton had very wisely decided to have as many soldiers as possible visit the scene, which I believe will teach our men to look out for the Germans."

But very soon Patton was willing to gloss over the past and evaluate all Germans—Nazis, anti-Nazis and others alike—in the light of their potential usefulness in a war against Russia. Perhaps it was his staid new job and his sedate new duties that made this volatile man so restive and reckless and irresponsible in the face of his grave responsibilities. On August 10th he had expressed his feelings about his post-war occupation, and how difficult he found it to unwind, with no place to take his bustling energy and exuberance.

"Now," he wrote in his diary, "all that is left to do is to sit around and await the arrival of the undertaker and posthumous immortality. Fortunately, I also have to occupy myself with the de-Nazification and government of Bavaria, and the recruiting of the industries of the German people so that they can be more self-supporting."

By then the German was no longer the *Hun*. Patton had begun to regard him as his future ally in a joint crusade against the Bolsheviks.

The incongruity of his actions in Germany emerged from the strange and rebellious contradictions within this man. On July 28th, for example, he toured his part of Czechoslovakia in triumph, to the vociferous acclaim of the populace. At Susice the grateful townspeople he had liberated from the Germans' yoke greeted him with gifts, and Patton, responding with one of his emotional outbursts, kissed a little girl with an enthusiasm that seemed to symbolize his collective embrace of the whole community. At the conclusion of his trip he was given Czechoslovakia's highest decoration, the Order of the White Lion and War Cross. Yet only a few days later he provoked the wrath of the Czechs by ordering the removal of some 1,500 Polish Fascists the Nazis had foisted upon them, to protect the Poles from the retribution the Prague government was preparing to mete out.

By September, Patton was in hot water. His employment of a German whose record clearly showed that he had been a member of the SS was publicly criticized. And he was censured for a statement attributed to him, questioning the wisdom of getting rid of a group of Bavarian bankers and industrialists with the stain of Nazism in their past. Many of them were employers of slave laborers, whose death camp Patton had described in such moving words only five months before.

His apprehensions about the Soviet menace began to obsess him, somewhat in the manner in which a similar obsession was to drive James V. Forrestal to suicide. He now equated everything in Germany in these terms. After a visit to Berlin, he wrote to Mrs. Patton that the sight of the devastated city had given him the blues. "We have destroyed," he wrote, "what could have been a good race and we are about to replace them with the Mongolian savages and all Europe with Communism."

The Germans were quick to sense that they had a friend in General George S. Patton. They greeted him wherever he went in Bavaria "with cheers," as Semmes recounted it, "and by throwing flowers from the windows, shouting, 'He is our savior. He has saved us from the Russian mob.' "

The situation became so bad that General Eisenhower had to caution Patton, twice in quick succession—first, on August 27th, during a special conference called to discuss the control of Germany, and again in stronger terms in a letter dated September 12th. In the latter, Eisenhower demanded that Patton carry out the de-Nazification program as he was told instead of mollycoddling the Nazis.

The inevitable then happened with the proverbial banana peel on which he made his fateful slip. On September 22nd, as soon as the ban prohibiting the quotation of general officers was lifted, Patton called a press conference at his walled and turreted headquarters in Bad Tölz. He was interviewed by a handful of correspondents including Raymond Daniell of the *New York Times*, Edward Morgan of the *Chicago Daily News*, and Carl Levin of the *New York Herald Tribune*.

The explosive issue of his treatment of the Nazis was among the first to be raised. The reporters knew that Robert Murphy was in Munich with Dr. Walter Dorn, his deputy, to investigate Patton's controversial handling of the Nazi problem. They were also looking into his relations with the U.S.-sponsored government of Fritz Schaeffer, whose "ultra-conservatism," as it was charitably put, was distasteful to Ike.

Patton responded eagerly to the questions, unmindful of the fact that he was skating on extremely thin ice. But once he got started on the problem that had come to be foremost in his mind, he kept going in deeper and deeper. He belittled the de-Nazification program of the Allies and as-

serted that the Military Government "would get better results if it employed more former members of the Nazi
party in administrative jobs and as skilled workmen."

Patton never lacked the courage to act upon his convictions. Even the most cursory investigation by the Murphy-
Dorn team into the situation in Bavaria had disclosed that
more than a score of Nazi party members in the mandatory
removal class were still occupying key positions in the
Schaeffer government. And though Eisenhower had ordered
Patton to fire Schaeffer, nothing was being done to carry out
the order.

Even so, the reporters gasped when they now heard from
Patton himself that there was a deliberate design in all this
apparent madness. One of them, sensing the opportunity of
coaxing Patton into a major story during one of his fits of indiscretion, asked casually, "After all, General, didn't most
ordinary Nazis join their party in about the same way that
Americans become Republicans or Democrats?"

Patton failed to recognize the trap. He promptly proceeded to fall headlong into it. "Yes," he said, "that's about
it."

The reporter had his headline. "American General Says
Nazis Are Just Like Republicans and Democrats" it read,
and words to that same effect appeared in every newspaper
in the United States and around the world.

Patton had done it again, and this time there were no
extenuating circumstances or considerations in his favor.
The war was over. He had outlived his essential usefulness.
He was expendable. Now Patton had no period of grace, no
time to accustom himself to his new notoriety. The reaction
was prompt and violent. In a sense, his sin was worse than
the slapping of a couple of his soldiers near Troina. He had
insulted a majestic and vindictive foe—the institution of the
American two-party system.

While the storm raged with growing fury until it reached
tornado proportions, Patton remained strangely, almost
morbidly, calm and composed. There was in his poise the
kind of attitude the French describe in the phrase *je m'en
fous*—which, in Patton's own earthly language, translated
into not giving a damn. And there was something else in his
behavior during these hectic days that was missing in Sicily
and England during his "incidents" there. Patton's outburst
was not followed by a display of humility. There was, in fact,

a defiance in his attitude, the truculence of a little boy who is convinced that the swiping of cookies is his Godgiven right.

The latest scandal embarrassed and annoyed General Eisenhower, especially since he was becoming increasingly exasperated with Patton's recurring antics. Several times in the past few months he had had to admonish Patton that his patience was being stretched to the breaking point and that the time would soon come when no amount of forebearance would enable him to take Patton off another hook. Eisenhower thought that a baffling change had come over Patton. Something was driving him into callous and arbitrary acts; he was arrogating undue privileges to himself; and he was behaving as if his assured place in history had filled him with reckless arrogance.

This latest cycle had begun on April 18th, when Patton fired a SHAEF censor (over whom he had no authority) for having passed a story about the ill-starred Hammelburg raid. "Ike had taken Patton's hide off," Butcher then wrote. "But I think Patton must have as many hides as a cat has lives, for this is at least the fourth time General Ike had skinned his champion end runner." But now it seemed that Patton was down to his last hide.

General Eisenhower realized at once that this time he could not save Patton's skin. But he was still determined to give his stormy petrel the benefit of the doubt and the due process of a fair investigation. He instructed Robert Murphy to ascertain all the facts of the case and assess the damage Patton had done by falling into a sly reporter's trap. But the pressure to punish Patton became so great that Eisenhower decided to take personal charge even before Murphy's report was in his hands.

On September 24th, he ordered General Bedell Smith, his Chief of Staff, to call Patton on the phone, trying to clear up the incident without the necessity of employing more radical measures. Ambassador Murphy had a luncheon date with Patton that noon and had arrived early at the General's villa at the Tegernsee, on the former estate of Max Assmann, deposed head of the Nazi Party's defunct publishing house. He was chatting with Patton while a gifted Polish artist named Boguslav Czedkowski was painting the General's portrait.

Patton was serene, attired in his Sunday best for the sitting, with seven rows of ribbons on his chest, a pearl-handled pistol hanging from a broad leather belt, one gloved hand holding the other glove and a riding stick. The rays of the afternoon sun played with the ruby of his West Point ring, which he wore on the middle finger of his right hand.

The long war had taken its toll. Patton looked tired. His fair hair had turned gray and become sparse. There were permanent rings under his eyes. Wrinkles danced around his lips, which seemed thinner and paler than before.

Smith's call came after the lunch while Patton was confering with Murphy in Assmann's abandoned study. As Murphy, its sole eyewitness, described the scene, "We were interrupted by Patton's efficient WAC secretary who announced an urgent telephone call from Frankfurt." General Smith was on the line.

"There was no love lost between Smith and Patton," Murphy continued, "and the latter suspected trouble. Pointing to the extension telephone, he said to me, 'Listen to what the lying s.o.b. will say.' I did not know that the decision had been taken to relieve Patton of his command until I heard Smith performing his duy as tactfully as possible. Patton vigorously pantomimed for my benefit his scornful reactions to Smith's placatory remarks."

In actual fact, Smith was not calling to relieve Patton. He was merely conveying Ike's orders that he eat crow by calling another press conference immediately for the purpose of taking back everything he had said on the 22nd. Smith also instructed Patton to read to the correspondents two paragraphs from Eisenhower's letter of September 12th, which had spelled out the official policy regarding the treatment of Nazis in no uncertain terms.

Patton faced the press again in accordance with his orders, and complied with Ike's instructions to the extent of reading the crucial passage from the letter.

"As you know," Eisenhower had written, "I have announced a firm policy of uprooting the whole Nazi organization, regardless of the fact we may sometimes suffer from local administrative inefficiency. Reduced to its fundamentals, the United States entered this war as a foe of Nazism; victory is not complete until we have eliminated from positions of responsibility and, in appropriate cases, properly punished every active adherent of the Nazi party.

"I know that certain field commanders have felt some modification to this policy should be made. That question has long since been decided. We will not compromise with

Nazism in any way. I wish you to make particularly sure that your subordinate commanders realize that the discussional stage of this question is long past and any expressed opposition to the faithful execution of the order cannot be regarded leniently by me. I expect just as loyal service in execution of this and other policy applying to German occupation as I received during the war."

But otherwise he did not retreat much from his original position. In a prepared statement, he now said:

"It is my considered opinion that I am carrying out his directives with the same vigor and loyalty as I carried out those which resulted in victories at Casablanca, El Guettar, Sicily and here. I am convinced that as the result of my efforts I shall be just as successful here as I was in those other places. However, you must remember that results cannot be obtained overnight. It took the Third Army 281 days to conquer its portion of Germany and it will certainly take us a reasonable time to denazify and reorganize our portion of Germany.

"Unquestionably, when I made a comparison of so vile a thing as Nazism with political parties, I was unfortunate in the selection of analogies. The point I was trying to bring out was that in Germany practically all, or at least a very large percentage, of the tradespeople, small business men and even professional men, such as doctors and lawyers, were beholden to the party in power for patronage which permitted them to carry on their business or profession and that, therefore, many of them gave lip service only; and I would extend this to mean that when they paid party dues, it was still a form of blackmail. These are the type of people whom, while we will eventually remove them, we must put up with until we have restored sufficient organization to Bavaria to insure ourselves that women, children and old men will not perish from hunger or cold this winter.

"I believe that I am responsible for the deaths of as many Germans as almost anyone, but I killed them in battle. I should be un-American if I did not do my uttermost to prevent unnecessary deaths after the war is over. With the exception of these people, it is my opinion, to the best of my knowledge and belief, that there are no out-and-out Nazis in positions of importance whose removal has not already been carried out."

The strange press conference proved totally unsatisfactory to Eisenhower. If anything, it deepened his conviction that Patton was not the right man to deal with the ex-Nazis or, indeed, to govern Bavaria. He instructed Smith to phone again, this time ordering Patton to report to Ike at Höchst, ostensibly to give a first-hand account of his stewardship of Bavaria.

The tragic confrontation took place on September 28th, behind closed doors in Eisenhower's office, while the entire press corps of Ike's headquarters was camping in the corridor awaiting the dénouement of the sensational affair. Bad weather had prevented Patton from flying to Frankfurt, so he arrived for the showdown late in the day, having covered the 300-mile trip from Bad Tölz in over six hours. Even more than the solemnity of his look, the uniform he was wearing showed that he himself regarded this as a grim and grave occasion. He was wearing plain GI trousers rather than his fancy riding breeches, and a simple Eisenhower jacket. And he had left his pistols behind.

He was closeted with Eisenhower for two hours, with Dr. Dorn and Major General Clarence Adcock in attendance during the first half hour of the meeting to confront Patton with the findings of their investigation and lay the groundwork for the action Ike was determined to take. When the meeting broke up shortly before 7 P.M., the friendship of the two men was on the rocks.

Ike had wielded the ax this time. He had taken the Third Army from Patton.

Patton left Ike's office pale and tense, his bitterness surging up in him like the acerbic taste of poison hemlock. By now he was totally blinded to the greater responsibilities Eisenhower had to shoulder; and he was deeply shocked by what he regarded as Ike's wanton ingratitude. In the gradual disintegration of their friendship, which had begun a quarter century before, Patton believed he saw the truth of Henry Adams' phrase that a friend in power is a friend lost.

His was, indeed, a strange set of rewards. In England, too, Montgomery was posing problems, for the Field Marshal was never altogether lost, as Moorehead phrased it, to the pleasures of making mischief. Yet whatever discomfort he caused with his eccentricities and brash pronouncements, it was obscured by the gratitude of his nation now showering

honors and gifts on him. But when on October 2nd Patton's
disgrace became official with the announcement that he had
been relieved of his duties as commander of Third Army
and Military Governor of Bavaria, he was left barren and
bare, and again the butt of the sharpest censure.

Eisenhower had no choice. If he had erred at all, it was
in having given Patton the job in Bavaria, but even that was
unavoidable. Patton's employment after the war was one
problem the War Department chose to dump into Eisenhower's lap. As early as May 1st he had begun work on the imminent redeployment of his forces to the Pacific. Hodges
and his staff were slated to go as soon as possible, and Ike
was making plans for Patton and his staff as well. It was
known at Supreme Headquarters that President Roosevelt
had promised Patton he would send him to the Pacific as
soon as the fighting was finished in Europe—but Roosevelt
was now dead, and the plans had changed.

While Eisenhower was not exactly anxious to rid himself
of Patton, he was not entirely unhappy about the prospect, if only because he realized that it would not be easy to
fit Patton into the new order in Europe after the war. By
June's end, however, Eisenhower was advised of the decision
to leave Patton with him, and that Bavaria had been set
aside as Patton's new domain of operations. It was with a
degree of compassion that Eisenhower now contemplated
Patton's uncertain future. "Don't know what will happen to
him now," Butcher wrote in the diary when Roosevelt's
death had canceled the old commitment. "He's always said
he wanted to die fighting."

He did, in the end. But it was not the kind of fighting he
craved or at which he was his warrior-best.

In the ambiguous words of the communiqué of October
2nd, so written as to save the face of the disavowed hero,
Patton was given command of something called the "Fifteenth United States Army." But it was an "army" only by
the most generous stretch of the imagination. It was the
rather grandiose name of a small group of "service troops"
—such as drivers, cooks and M.P.'s. They were serving a
good many officers whose function was solely to compile
from existing records a sort of military history of operations from D-Day to the German surrender.

Also called "Theater General Board" with headquarters
at Bad Nauheim, it produced a few dozen memoranda now

gathering dust on the shelves in the Office of the Chief of Military History. They have been outshone and superseded by the much better monographs prepared by the Army's brilliant staff of historians when all the data of the war became available.

Patton appeared to be through as a general. But he was still allowed to practice a profession he liked next best, that of the historian.

With his innate tact, Eisenhower granted him a last gesture of grace by asking Patton whom he wanted to be appointed as his successor in command of the Third Army and the new governor of Bavaria.

"Lucian Truscott," Patton said without a moment's hesitation.

On October 5th Patton summed up his feelings in a letter to his wife at this heartbreaking conclusion of his career: "My head is bloody but unbowed. All that I regret is that I have again worried you. I have been helping Lucian to get the hang of the show, and he feels rather depressed. I don't blame him. I was terribly hurt for a few days but I am normal again."

And two days later at Bad Tölz the Third Army reported to General George S. Patton Jr. for the last time, to listen to his farewell address.

"General Truscott," he began, "Officers and Men:

"All good things must come to an end. The best thing that has ever come to me thus far is the honor and privilege of having commanded the Third Army.

"The great successes we have achieved together have been due primarily to the fighting heart of America, but without the coordinating and supply activities of the General and Special Staffs, even American valor would have been impotent.

"You officers and men here represent the fighting, the administrative, and the supply elements of the Army. Please accept my heartfelt congratulations on your valor and devotion to duty, and my fervent gratitude for your unwavering loyalty.

"When I said that all good things must come to an end, I was referring to myself and not to you, because you will find in General Truscott every characteristic which will inspire in you the same loyalty and devotion which you have so generously afforded me.

"A man of General Truscott's achievements needs no introduction. His deeds speak for themselves. I know that you will not fail him.

"Good-bye—and God bless you."

Choking back tears shimmering in his eyes, he gave Truscott his proudest possession—the Third Army flag with its famed emblem of a big white letter "A" circled in red and blue.

The nation responded to Patton's punishment with compassion, for nothing he would do after the war could dim the glamour and glory of his wartime achievements. "Perhaps he himself will share the sense of relief his countrymen feel," wrote the *New York Times* on October 9th, in an editorial entitled *Patton, the Soldier,* "at so safe and quiet a transfer. He was obviously in a part which he was unfitted by temperament, training and experience to fill. It was mistake to suppose a free-swinging fighter could acquire overnight the capacities of a wise administrator. His removal by General Eisenhower was an acknowledgment of that mistake. . . . For all his showmanship he was a scientific soldier, a thorough military student. . . . He reaped no laurels from the peace, but those he won in war will remain green for a long time."

This was the general tone of editorial comment in the United States, with a single exception. Rumors had sprung up in the wake of his dismissal, and they burst into the open on October 3rd, with a strange column by John O'Donnell in the *New York Daily News.* Its style and innuendo were reminiscent of the vicious anti-Semitic diatribes Julius Streicher used to perpetrate in *Der Stürmer,* the Nazi newspaper Patton's own victory had silenced forever.

"Behind the successful drive to disgrace and remove General George S. Patton from his Army command in occupied Germany," O'Donnell wrote, "is the secret and astoundingly effective might of this republic's foreign-born political leaders—such as Justice of the Supreme Court Felix Frankfurter, of Vienna, White House administrative assistant Dave (Devious Dave) Niles, alias Neyhus, and the Latvian ex-rabbinical student now known as Sidney Hillman."

According to O'Donnell, Patton had been dismissed at the

urging of Henry Morgenthau Jr., the Secretary of the Treasury, because he had "used the word 'Jew' in reprimanding the reluctant warrior" Patton had slapped in the evacuation hospital in Sicily. O'Donnell rehashed the old incident, implying that the boy Patton had slapped was a Jewish soldier and claiming that "the racial issue in the story [had been] suppressed."

There was, of course, not an iota of truth in a single syllable of the vicious and cruel story, but it served its purpose—it lent respectability to the ugly rumors which it appeared to confirm. The new controversy came to Patton's attention in a letter he received at Bad Nauheim from Mrs. J. Borden Harriman, advising him that "certain ultra-nationalistic groups are seeking to exploit your high prestige for their own selfish purposes," and urging him to "disavow the implications read into your reported remarks."

Patton immediately denied that he had "ever made any statement contrary to the Jewish or any other religious faith." And he added with emphasis that he had "never interfered with or even examined into the religious or racial antecedents of the men" he had "the honor to command."

While he felt the full measure of the loss of the Third Army, he managed to adjust even to this grievous disappointment and overcome his grief. But he felt to the bitter end that those ruthless rumors which the *New York Daily News* had dignified by printing O'Donnell's column had compounded his disgrace. Discussing the malodorous aftermath of his professional loss, he felt like Leonato—done to death by slanderous tongues.

... AND A TIME TO DIE ...

On November 11, 1945, George Patton became 60 years old. It was a milestone, to be sure, but it came at a time of reckoning when his life was not entirely without qualms. He had had his adventure of discontent that had cost him command of the Third Army. However, this last in a long chain of disappointments no longer rankled him. And anyway, discontent always was a first step in his progress.

He was looking back on the bygone years without remorse, satisfied that he had lived a good and useful life. "It is rather sad to me to think," he wrote during those days, "that my last opportunity for earning my pay has passed. At least, I have done my best as God gave me the chance."

This willful and resolute man, whose flamboyant egotism was molded by his conscience, had forever flirted with destiny and frequently seduced fate. But it was worth the effort. The long pursuit had yielded its supreme reward. "General George Patton," wrote the *New York Times* in the wake of his latest incident, "has now passed from current controversy into history. There he will have an honored niche."

The immediate future seemed richly promising again. As his birthday approached, lavish gifts were showered on him by grateful people he had helped to liberate. Places in France and Belgium, whose names—like Verdun and St. Thierry—were hallowed by memories of battles old and new, were planning to make him their freeman. Belgium awarded him the Croix de Guerre and made him a Grand Officer of the Order of Leopold with Palm. Little Luxembourg, which literally adopted Patton, gave him the Grand Cross of the Order of Adolphe de Nassau and its own Croix de Guerre.

In his own country, the prodigal son was on the comeback trail. The city of New York was readying its traditional ticker tape parade for him. And on the very eve of his birthday it became known that Patton was slated to command all United States forces in Europe in the absence of General Eisenhower.

Patton himself viewed his exoneration with the becalmed philosophy of Seneca toward the end: *Non amittantur, sed praemittuntur*—nothing was lost, but all had gone before! In the privacy of his inner world, he was beginning to set his soul in order. He could be heard speaking of retirement but refused to let himself be pinned down. His personal plans for the future sounded vague, shrouding him in a mysterious aura of almost ethereal uncertainty.

In the immediate wake of the war, he had developed a strange premonition—in fact, something akin to a death wish—probably because he was so unsure of his prospects in a peaceful society of civilians. He always cherished what he used to call his credo, a romantic notion that smacked of the Samurai's edge of service. "The proper end for the professional soldier," he would say again and again, "is a quick death inflicted by the *last* bullet of the *last* battle.

Several times toward the end of the war it seemed that he would be granted his wish, even if not by the last bullet. On April 21, 1945, while flying to III Corps Headquarters at Reidfeld, his cub was attacked by what was taken for a German fighter but turned out to be a Spitfire flown by an inexperienced Polish volunteer serving with the RAF. On May 3rd he almost perished in a crash when an oxcart coming from a blind lane suddenly hit the road on which Patton's jeep was traveling at his customary fast clip. Sergeant Mims managed to avoid a collision, but the protruding pole to which the ox team was tied grazed the General's head.

"After all I've been through," he said to Colonel Codman, "think of being killed on the road by a team of oxen."

By the time he reached the States in June, his macabre preoccupation was filling him with acute premonitions. He spoke of death as a lovely and desirable alternative to the idle years he might have, and told his children that he never expected to see them again. They protested the gloomy prophecy but he dismissed them with the cryptic statement, "It is true. It has been revealed to me."

He spent the last day of the trip in blissful seclusion with Beatrice at their home in South Hamilton he loved so much but rarely had the leisure to enjoy. This was their quietest, most tender time together. They were just sitting on a sofa holding hands, looking out over the rolling fields of "Green Meadows"—Beatrice in devout silence, the General, with a rueful glance. To some, even to those closest to him, it seemed he was breaking with the past. In reality, he was solemnly liquidating this most exciting of his many lives.

On October 13th the accident-prone Patton was slightly hurt again in a minor automobile mishap. And then, on December 9th he embarked on his final journey.

It was a Sunday and Patton planned to spend it bird hunting around Speyer in the Rhenish Palatinate, where the woods were rich with pheasants. It was a quarter to noon.

He was riding south on Highway 38, the Frankfurt-Mannheim road, with Major General Hobart R. Gay, still his Chief of Staff, in a sedan driven by Private First Class Horace L. Woodring, a 23-year-old soldier attached to Patton's paper army. A sergeant named Joe Spruce followed in a quarter-ton truck.

Passing through the northern outskirts of Mannheim, crossing a maze of railroad tracks, Woodring slowed the car to 10 miles, then accelerated again on the open road, cruising at about 30 miles an hour. Traffic was relatively light. The weather was crisp.

On leaving the tracks, Sergeant Spruce passed the sedan to lead the way. He spotted a big truck coming up on the other lane at a speed of about 15 miles, apparently slowing down as it was approaching a driveway on the left side of the road.

Patton was carefree and genial, chatting easily with Gay, his curious little eyes darting from left to right as he surveyed the countryside. The litter of the recent war was piled high everywhere. It was now 11:48 A.M. The sedan was passing through a canyon of junk. Pointing to the right bank of the road, Patton said to Gay:

"How awful war is! Look at all those derelict vehicles, Hap!" Then he turned in the other direction, exlaiming, "And look at that heap of rubbish!"

Reacting automatically, Woodring also looked away from the road. Just then, T/5 Robert L. Thompson, the driver of the truck, who was alone in its cab, signaled that he was about to turn left, and took his vehicle at a 90° angle across the road. He was making for the half-hidden driveway leading to a roadside camp of his Quartermaster Corps unit.

Woodring had his eyes back on the road again. But it was too late. As the big truck seemed to bear down on him, Woodring jammed down the brake and swerved sharply, as did Thompson, but they could not avoid the collision. The sedan crashed into the truck's gasoline tank and had its front smashed in, yet it still appeared to be a minor accident. Gay, Woodring and Thompson were shaken up a bit but were otherwise unhurt.

It was different with Patton. Riding on the right-hand side of the back seat, he was thrown forward and was then hurled back, falling limply into General Gay's arms with his head to the left. He was bleeding profusely from cuts in his forehead and scalp, but was sitting up and was fully conscious. He was the first to speak. "Are you hurt?" he asked Gay.

"No, not a bit, sir," Gay said. "Are you, General?"

"I think I'm paralyzed," Patton said. "I'm having trouble in breathing. Work my fingers for me, Hap."

Gay tried it several times, until Patton said again, "Go ahead, Hap, work my fingers."

Gay now merely said, "I don't think it's advisable to move you, General."

A unit of the 8081st Military Police Company commanded by Lieutenant Peter Babalas arrived on the scene and Patton was driven to the 130th Station Hospital at Heidelberg, in the zone of the Seventh Army which was now commanded by General Geoffrey Keyes, his old friend and companion in arms. It was a small hospital the Germans had set up in a cavalry barracks toward the end of the war and which the Americans took over. Its medical staff was headed by Colonel Lawrence C. Ball. He had been advised of Patton's coming and was waiting downstairs with Lieutenant Colonel Paul S. Hill, the chief surgeon. Obviously in shock but lucid, Patton merely said, "My neck hurts," as he was taken to surgery.

News of the accident had been flashed to Frankfurt, and Major General Albert W. Kenner, Patton's Medical Officer in the Western Task Force, now the Theater Surgeon, arrived within hours to take charge. Then flying in from London, Brigadier Hugh Cairns, famed professor of neurosurgery at Oxford, joined the doctors. Before too long, X-ray pictures gave them the definitive clues they needed for their diagnosis.

"Fracture simple, third cervical vertebra," it read, "with posterior dislocation of fourth cervical. Complete paralysis below level of third cervical. Condition critical, prognosis guarded."

In the layman's language this meant that Patton had broken his neck and was paralyzed from the neck down.

As soon as Beatrice Patton received word of the accident, she prepared to fly to Heidelberg with the best neurosurgeon the U.S. Army's Medical Corps could spare for her husband. He turned out to be Colonel Roy Glen Spurling, senior consultant in neurosurgery, who had just returned to the States from duty in Europe and was traveling somewhere in Ohio. Intercepted on a train at Cincinnati, Dr. Spurling was flown to Washington, where he joined Mrs. Patton at the Air Transport Command for the flight to Germany. They left on a C-54 plane of the bucket-seat type, on its regular mail run. Also going with Mrs. Patton was Lieutenant Colonel Walter T. Kerwin of the General Staff Operations Division.

While Mrs. Patton was still in the air, her plane bucking strong head winds over the Azores, the doctors at Heidelberg issued another bulletin. The General's condition was still rated critical, but the dislocation of the vertebrae was, they said hopefully, responding satisfactorily to extension. The patient had spent a restful night, sleeping about five hours.

Patton was fairly comfortable and completely rational, even cheerful, lightening the gloom of his attendants with his good humor. When Lieutenant Bertha Hohle, his night nurse, gave him the glass tube for a sip of water, he shot back in mock irritation, "I won't drink the damn stuff unless it's whisky."

Captain Andrew J. White, a Catholic priest, was the first chaplain to see him. When he finished reading the ritual for the sick at Patton's bedside, Father White said, "Incidentally, General, your own chaplain has just arrived and will soon be in to see you." He was speaking of the Rev. William P. Price, an Episcopalian who was the hospital chaplain, but Patton asked eagerly, "You mean Father O'Neill?"— thinking of Colonel O'Neill, the Third Army Chaplain. "Well," he told Father White, "send him in and let him go to work."

Mrs. Patton arrived at 3:30 P.M. on December 11th and checked into a room at the hospital down the hall on the General's floor. When she was taken to her husband, she found him resting quietly and taking some nourishment. His condition had slightly improved. His temperature was 100, pulse 70, respiration 22. He greeted his wife with a grateful smile, but told her:

"I am afraid, Bea, this may be the last time we see each other."

By the 13th Patton had shown such improvement that his doctors began to weigh the possibility of flying him to Boston. The 130th was a small hospital, but it was as good as any in Europe, with all the facilities Patton needed, and he was enjoying the best of attention and care. But Mrs. Patton felt, and Colonel Spurling concurred, that hospitalization closer to "Green Meadows" would be an added boost to his recovery. As a matter of fact, the doctors expressed guarded optimism as his condition continued to improve, but feared that he might remain paralyzed for life.

Up to the afternoon of December 19th Patton had made what the bulletins described as "very satisfactory progress." But then, a crisis suddenly developed. He began to experience difficulty in raising the mucus that was accumulating in his bronchial tubes squeezed by fragments of the shattered vertebrae. Simultaneously, the pressure on the spinal cord increased.

At 2 P.M. on the 20th, he had an acute attack of breathlessness and pallor, lasting about an hour. The symptoms convinced Colonel Spurling that Patton had suffered a pulmonary embolism when a blood clot had gotten loose in his circulation and was pumped by the heart into his lungs, virtually destroying one. "When a man is older, in bed and paralyzed," Dr. Spurling explained, "he is likely to get such a clot in a vein of his leg or arm. It is always a great hazard in the illness of older people." It was strange to think and speak of Patton as an *old* man.

But he had a history of embolism—he had two embolisms when he was hospitalized with a broken leg eight years before in Boston—and survived them. This time, however, he has only a slight margin left for what the doctors called such compatibility.

He recovered satisfactorily from the initial shock, but then the symptoms of the embolism multiplied. He filled up with mucus more and more, and had increasing difficulty in raising it. His lungs became wetter and wetter. But he seemed to be bouncing back from hour to hour. The doctors did their best to halt this gradual deterioration of his condition but it was becoming evident that the General was now locked in his biggest battle, his struggle for survival itself.

Patton remained fully conscious all this time, never for a moment lapsing into coma. He was talking in a low whisper but he was still exchanging quips with Captain William Duane Jr., his young doctor, and Lieutenant Margery Rondell, his day nurse, who kept a constant vigil at his bedside. And he tried valiantly to reassure his apprehensive wife.

At 2 o'clock in the afternoon of December 21st he fell asleep and his wife tiptoed out of the room. At 3 P.M., Colonel Spurling looked in on him. Awake and cheerful, he told Spurling that he was feeling better and was comfortable. Then he fell asleep again. He was breathing heavily but showed no other outward signs that his struggle was nearing the end.

In actual fact, he was in a condition of acute danger the whole day. His heart had become affected by the increased load placed upon it, and, for the first time, he showed evidence of heart failure. But he kept up the good fight—until late in the afternoon.

Now it was eleven minutes to 6 o'clock.

Patton was sleeping comfortably but Lieutenant Rondell looked at him anyway, because she sensed that her patient had lost the fight. She beckoned to Captain Duane, who ran down the corridor at once to summon Beatrice. She came immediately. But Patton had breathed his last before she reached the bedside.

He died at 5:50 P.M. of acute heart failure when another embolism struck his remaining lung at the left side of his chest. "General Patton Dies Quietly in Sleep," the newspapers headlined the front-page story.

For Patton it was an incongruous death.

They buried him in the drizzle of a fog-shrouded December morning in the huge American Military Cemetery at Hamm in Luxembourg, where he joined 6,000 other dead heroes of the Third Army. For two days before the funeral, while he was lying in state in the Villa Reiner, one of the stately homes of Heidelberg, the GI's claimed him as one of their own. They came in seemingly endless procession to pay their last respects to the great soldier who, unlike themselves, would not be going home soon, or ever. Even in his grave he remained close to them. Nearest to him on the top of the gently sloping hillside was the grave of a private first class, John Hrzywarn of Detroit.

Patton was sent on his long journey with the Psalm David had sung in the wilderness of Judah . . . *O God, thou art my God; early will I seek thee; my soul thirsteth for thee, my flesh longeth for thee in a dry and thirsty land, so as I have seen thee in the sanctuary.*

It was Patton's own favorite Psalm, devout as well as defiant.

My soul followeth hard after thee; but those that seek my soul, to destroy it, shall go into the lower parts of the earth. They shall fall by the sword: they shall be a portion for foxes. But the king shall rejoice in God; every one that sweareth by him shall glory; but the mouth of them that speak lies shall be stopped.

In the final moment of the ceremony, Master Sergeant William George Meeks, the elderly Negro from Junction City, Kansas, who had served the General faithfully as his orderly for years, presented to Beatrice the flag that had draped the casket. There were tears in Meeks' eyes—his face was screwed up with strain.

He bowed slowly and handed the flag to Mrs. Patton. Then he saluted stiffly to her. For an instant their eyes met and held. Sergeant Meeks turned away. A 12-man firing squad raised its rifles and a three-round volley of salutes echoed into the Luxembourg hills.

Next morning the *New York Times* wrote in the most moving of the editorials with which the world press bade him farewell:

"History has reached out and embraced General George Patton. His place is secure. He will be ranked in the forefront of America's great military leaders. . . .

"Long before the war ended, Patton was a legend. Spectacular, swaggering, pistol-packing, deeply religious and violently profane, easily moved to anger because he was first of all a fighting man, easily moved to tears because underneath all his mannered irascibility he had a kind heart, he was a strange combination of fire and ice. Hot in battle and ruthless, too, he was icy in his inflexibility of purpose. He was no mere hell-for-leather tank commander but a profound and thoughtful military student.

"He has been compared with Jeb Stuart, Nathan Bedford Forrest and Phil Sheridan, but he fought his battles in a bigger field than any of them. He was not a man of peace. Perhaps he would have preferred to die at the height of his fame, when his men, whom he loved, were following him with devotion. His nation will accord his memory a full measure of that devotion."

He is identified by the barest inscription on the simple white cross that marks his grave—

GEO. S. PATTON JR.
GENERAL. 02605. 3D ARMY

But maybe his real epitaph was written in the anguished words that once echoed in the halls of a castle on Cyprus—

O, now for ever
Farewell the tranquil mind! farewell content!
Farewell the plumed troop and the big wars
That make ambition virtue! O, farewell,
Farewell the neighing steed and the shrill trump,
The spirit-stirring drum, the ear-piercing fife,
The royal banner and all quality,
Pride, pomp and circumstance of glorious war!
And, O you mortal engines, whose rude throats
The immortal Jove's dread clamours counterfeit,
Farewell! Othello's occupation's gone!

ACKNOWLEDGMENTS

In his introduction to *War As I Knew It,* the posthumously published collection of some of General Patton's wartime writings, Douglas Southall Freeman wrote: "He will be an ideal subject for a great biography." But the eminent biographer of Washington and Lee never got around to writing it himself. Others similarly well qualified and equipped also shied away from the task, for reasons best known to themselves. So where professional historians and biographers somehow feared to tread, I am walking rather boldly with this book about Patton.

It may be said that Patton did not get that great biography because he was not a truly great man. As Alexander Smith put it, great is the man who does a thing for the first time; and, according to Sydney Smith, the criterion of a man's greatness is his ability to lift up all who live in his time. In this sense, Patton was great only in what could be called a tactical meaning of history.

He was no dreamer of vast human schemes. His aspirations did not extend to the betterment of mankind. He was not what Henry James called the absolute genius from whose thoughts and deeds the future flows inexorably. If Patton had never lived, the world would not have missed him.

He was rather like Daniel Webster, a "steam-engine in pants"—a superb professional with a volcanic inner drive that pushed him on when others chose to halt. It was in this of his influence upon his time that he fills a special niche. He was a skilled, imaginative and dynamic practitioner of his craft, the executor of other people's grand designs or, for that matter, grand illusions. In this context, his enduring significance cannot be overstated.

General Patton died, suddenly and senselessly, before he,

too, could write his definitive memoirs. As a result, the Patton story has been presented in a number of biographies * which inevitably suffered from a variety of handicaps. Some of them were written far too soon after the war, when its comprehensive story was still buried in classified documents. Others were written by amateurs whose chief qualification was their friendship or kinship with the late General.

As a result, the picture of the man ran to extremes. At one end was General Semmes' effusive characterization of Patton as "the symbol of America . . . great soldier, great sportsman, great friend whose life has ushered in a new day in the affairs of man." At the other is the vulgar presentation of the General as the swashbuckling "Blood and Guts Patton."

The Patton that emerged from a cacophony of second-hand evidence was a complex and justly controversial figure. In the popular mind, in particular, he survives as a great captain of war, to be sure, but mostly as the general who had slapped an enlisted man, then redeemed himself by leading a dashing and dramatic campaign at the head of a competent and romantic army.

But Patton was not so simple as that. He was not so evil as the man seemed to be who had struck a nerve-racked soldier. And he was not quite so good as the legend.

This is part of the Patton mystique. Indeed, there is something acrane about him in death like a celestial mystery, something tantalizing like an unfinished sentence or a peremptorily slammed door. But even in his lifetime, he was elusive, difficult to place in any of the set personality slots. He was, to use a Freudian term, split in the ego—a confusing and confused man who pendulated between bravado and humility, between feelings of inferiority and superiority, in a subcutaneous torment that wrought havoc with the inner stability he so desperately sought.

It is not easy to draw the portrait of such a man—a mercurial human being, haphazard in his thoughts and impulsive in his acts—unless he is written up in a heroic poem.

---

* Patton: Fighting Man, by William Bancroft Mellor (1946); Patton and His Third Army, by Colonel Brenton Greene Wallace (1946); General George S. Patton Jr., by James Wellard (1946); George Patton: General in Spurs, by Alden Hatch (1950); Portrait of Patton, by Harry H. Semmes (1955); Patton and His Pistols, by Milton F. Perry and Barbara W. Parke (1957); Blood-and-Guts Patton, by Jack Pearl (1961); and Before the Colors Fade: Portrait of a Soldier, George S. Patton Jr., by Fred Ayer Jr. (1964).

This I never intended to do. Though I realized that, even with my best endeavor, I would be able only to hold a candle to the sun, I set myself the task of developing the Patton story by examining the legend with critical eyes and scrutinizing the man's life with clinical detachment.

It took me a dozen years (from 1952 to 1964) to gather the material for this book, covering as great a territory in my studies and researches as I could afford. It is, therefore, virtually impossible to acknowledge my indebtedness to all those who have aided me in assembling the stones for this mosaic. Only to often such formal acknowledgements are self-serving instruments anyway, calculated to gain an aura of respectability and authenticity for a book. However, I feel it is incumbent upon me and it gives me real pleasure to record my thanks to a number of generous people who helped me either with their own writings or by taking time out to give me access to their papers or share their memories with me.

First of all, I must mention my friend and collaborator, and my "source supreme," Mr. Joseph Daniel Rosevich, today a distinguished member of the New York City school system, who was General Patton's personal secretary throughout the war. It was characteristic of Patton that he permitted no barriers of caste or rank to quarantine him from even the humblest members of his entourage. As Mr. Rosevich put it, "I can say without qualifications that there was a disciplined but pleasant and dignified relationship—indeed, a kind of chumminess—between the commanding general and the enlisted men of his special staff—whatever our religions or the color of our skin."

As for his own association with the General, Mr. Rosevich wrote: "I was a private when I first joined him and only a non-com when I left him after the war. But this wasn't a relationship in which rank mattered. My official title was 'confidential secretary to the Commanding General,' and I enjoyed his confidence in full. It was to me that he dictated his general orders, combat narratives, reports to Eisenhower, comments on men and events. This long and intimate association with the most colorful and controversial general of the U.S. Army qualifies me, I feel, to describe the Patton apparently nobody knows and help in correcting a distorted picture."

However, Mr. Rosevich added with special emphasis: "I am conscious of my confidential relationship with him and draw only on my personal observations and recollections, careful never to trespass on his confidence."

The recollections of this remarkable tour of duty, which Mr. Rosevich has shared fully with me in the preparation of this book, enabled me to gain an exceptionally vivid and intimate picture of Patton. Just as important, Mr. Rosevich supplied detailed descriptions of certain major events in which he had a personal part at General Patton's side.

I have drawn on the General's own voluminous writings —the early ones published mostly in the old *Cavalry Journal* during the 1920's and 1930's; his later essays collected in *War As I Knew It* (Boston: Houghton Mifflin Company, 1947); and certain of his diary entries and letters reprinted in *Portrait of Patton,* by the late Brigadier General Harry H. Semmes (New York: Appleton-Century-Crofts, 1955). Permission of the copyright-owners and publishers to quote from these books is gratefully acknowledged.

All material quoted from General Patton's diary was taken from passages published in these books, and all references to his diary are to published entries. All material quoted from his personal letters was taken from passages heretofore published in one or the other of these books or in other works.

It is no secret that at one time during the evolution of my book, General Patton's heirs sought to enjoin its publication in a court action designed to clarify the use of certain privileged material the copyright of which is owned by them. In fairness to them and to my own independent efforts which produced the present book, I would like to affirm that at no time did they seek to suppress or censor my book. They undertook nothing in fact to limit or influence my presentation of this biography.

I am indebted in particular to two members of General Patton's staff whose own writings proved invaluable—to the late Charles R. Codman, author of *Drive* (Boston: Little, Brown & Company, 1957), a fact-studded, sensitive and delightful account of his devoted service as one of the General's aides; and to Robert S. Allen, as great a soldier as he is a newspaperman, whose *Lucky Forward* (New York: The Vanguard Press, 1947), written in the immediate wake of the war, endures as a remarkable historic document. I also benefited from William Bancroft Mellor's *Patton: Fighting Man* (New York: Putnam, 1946) and Harry C. Butcher's *My Three Years With Eisenhower* (New York: Simon & Schuster, 1946).

I had the honor of talking to others on Patton's staffs and to men who served under him at Fort Benning, at Indio, California, in the Western Task Force, the II U.S. Corps in Tunisia, and in the Seventh and Third U.S. Armies. Among them I would like to mention with gratitude Major General Robert W. Grow, wartime commander of the 6th Armored Division; Major Abraham L. Baum of the 4th Armored Division; Brigadier General Elton F. Hammond, called "Demon" by Patton for his uncanny skill as his Signal Officer throughout the war; Brigadier General Oscar W. Koch on whose knowledge and wisdom as his Assistant Chief of Staff for Intelligence the General had built some of his fascinating plans; Colonel John Boyd Coates, Jr., Surgeon of the Third Army; and others.

From abroad, I was aided in my quest by several distinguished participants in the events. My thanks go to Lieutenant General Sir Frederick E. Morgan, the great architect of the "Overlord" plan; Lieutenant General Kenneth W. H. Strong, General Eisenhower's Intelligence chief in North Africa and Europe; Major Lionel Frederick Ellis, custodian of the British records in the Cabinet Office in London; Major General Guenther Blumentritt, Field Marshal von Rundstedt's chief of staff and a military historian of the first rank; Lieutenant General Siegfried Westphal, who was chief of staff to both Rundstedt and Rommel; General of Panzer Troops Hermann Balck, commander of German Army Group G who opposed Patton on the Saar; Major General F. W. von Mellenthien, author of *Panzer Battles* (Norman: Oklahoma University Press, 1956), who was chief of staff to Balck; and Major General Wilhelm Russwurm, Chief German Signal Officer in the West in 1944.

I am especially grateful to Professor Percy Ernst Schramm of Goettingen University. The author and custodian of the German High Command's war diary, his *Kriegstagebuch des OKW: 1944-1945* (Frankfurt: Bernard & Graefe,

1961) was extremely helpful in the reconstruction of some of the operations in Western Europe from the viewpoint of General Patton's adversaries. I also had access to the interrogation-transcripts of Colonel General Heinz Guderian, Chief of Staff of the German Army, and Lieutenant General Walther Warilimont, who was General Jodl's deputy in and is the highest-ranking surviving member of Hitler's own *Fuehrungsstab.*

I pay tribute (for no other word would express the magnitude of my appreciation) to the Office of the Chief of Military History in the Department of the Army, for two major contributions—one, for their incomparable historical studies published in *U.S. Army in World War II* (Washington, D.C.: Government Printing Office, 1947-64) on which I drew and drew and drew; and, second, for their personal assistance in guiding me along my own path. I was allowed to pick the brains, either through their writings or in personal confrontations, of Mr. Charles B. MacDonald and Mr. Martin Blumenson, as well as other historians on the OCMH staff.

In the development of the Sicilian campaign's story I was materially aided by William Earl Brecher whose unpublished monograph, *Mission to Messina,* is by far the best account of "Husky" pending the publication of the official history. Mr. Brecher's correspondence with and interviews of eyewitnesses proved extremely helpful. I also thank Lieutenants Winston B. Lewis and John LaMont, USNR, whose brilliantly written combat narrative of the Sicilian campaign, prepared for the Office of Naval Intelligence, provided comprehensive coverage of the naval phase of the operation. In addition I had access to special memoranda prepared by Patton's adversaries in the campaign, including several written by Major General Walter Fries of the 29th Panzer Grenadier Division, General von Senger, Admiral Pietro Barone, and General Emilio Faldella. From the Historical Office of the Italian Army General Staff I received a copy of "Operazioni Juglio 1943 in Sicilia," General Guzzoni's after action report.

My friend John Toland, whose *Battle: The Story of the Bulge* (New York: Random House, 1959) is indubitably the best account of the Ardennes offensive, aided me with great generosity from his own seemingly inexhaustible files. I found the best account of the offensive's pre-history in OCMH, in the studies of Mr. Magna E. Bauer. The German version of the Bulge came from a paper prepared for me by the late General Fritz Bayerlein, and a study prepared for OCMH by the redoubtable General von Manteuffel.

The German version of the operations around Metz was supplied by General Walter Krause, commander of Division No. 462, intrepid defender of the fortress. For my account of Patton's tragic post-war experience in Bavaria I received valuable original material from Professor Saul Padover and Mr. Lewis Frederick Gittler, civil affairs specialists in Germany in the wake of her defeat.

The story of Patton's experiences in World War I was pieced together mostly from contemporary documents in the National Archives, including Major Brett's after action report in typescript. Additional original data was supplied by Mr. Gilbert Miller who served with Patton at General Pershing's Headquarters in France; Mr. Joseph Angelo, who was Patton's orderly in 1918; General Jean Houdemon of the French Army; and my friend and colleague Mr. Thomas M. Johnson, veteran war correspondent and distinguished military writer, who covered the 304th Tank Brigade at St. Mihiel and in the Argonne offensive.

For material on the operations in Czechoslovakia during the closing days of the war, I am grateful to Mr. Eugene Fodor who led a daring OSS team to Prague. Mr. Allen Dulles responded graciously to an inquiry about the mysterious "Alpine Redoubt" whose "inside story" from the German side was given me by Dr. Wilhelm Hoettl, a former high official of the Germans' wartime secret service apparatus.

I am grateful to the New York Public Library system for their many favors and services (and especially for access to a very rare edition of Mrs. Patton's privately published book about her father); the Henry E. Huntington Library of San Gabriel, California (Herbert C. Schultz, Curator of Manuscripts), and to Miss Haydee Noya of the Library's Department of Manuscripts, for material about the early history of the Patton family in California; to the Library in the Pentagon for permission to consult pertinent after actions reports, G-2 and G-3 Journals, and unit histories; and to the Library of the Navy Department for material on naval operations with a bearing on Patton's campaigns.

With apologies to those whose contributions remain unmentioned, I thank the following for help so generously given toward the completion of my work: Harold E. Adams (1st Division), Ken Anderson (9th Division), Admiral Walter Ansel (USS *Barnett*), George C. Appell (45th Division), Joseph D. Barry (45th Division), Dr. Harry Barsak (11th Field Hospital), Arthur L. Chaitt (1st Division), Timothy O. Daily (82nd Airborne Division), Edmund A. Drazga (82nd Airborne Division,) General Heinrich Eberbach, General Otto Elfeldt, James F. Ellis (II U.S. Corps), Frank Fazio (9th Division), Dr. Robert Franco (82nd Airborne Division), Rowland Gill of OCMH, Harwood Jackson (82nd Airborne Division), John G. Kimnit (2nd Armored Division), Thomas F. Lancer (1st Division), Bill Mauldin, Mrs. Hope Ridings Miller, Richard Ostrander (1st Division), Dr. Richard Paulovsky (11th Field Hospital), R. F. Perry (2nd Armored Division), Daniel Quinn (9th Division), Ralph Scoville (9th Division), Jack Scully (9th Divison), A. Lark Starr (45th Division), Marcus O. Stevenson, aide to the late General Theodore Roosevelt, Jr.; Dr. Leonard S. Thompson, Willis Thuma (2nd Armored Division), Robert P. Waters (3rd Division), Harry Wax (9th Division), Walter A. Wolford, City Clerk, San Gabriel, California, and Frank Wonneman (45th Division).

My special efforts to reconstruct the so-called "slapping incidents" with the greatest possible fairness and accuracy were substantially facilitated by the help I received from Colonel Coates, Dr. Ralph W. Nadell, Mr. Merril Mueller, Mr. John Charles Daly, and especially from Dr. Charles Barton Etter and the late Major General Frederick Arthur Blessé.

Last but not least, I record my gratitude to those who helped me physically in the preparation of this book, especially my friend and colleague Arthur Neuhauser, a veteran of the glorious 1st Division, whose editorial assistance proved an immense boon to the finished product; and to Mrs. Anna Walters and Miss Betty Ostrov who typed and retyped the manuscript until it hurt. I record with parental pride the very great help given me by my young son, John Michael Farago, in the preparation of our huge index.

Miss Jane Glaeser, associate editor of Ivan Obolensky, Inc., performed the herculean task of copy-editing and proof-reading the final draft and did it with infinite patience, unflagging good-will, an encyclopedic memory and a couple of blue eagle eyes.

Ruth Bornschlegel earned my heartfelt gratitude for the loving contribution she has made to the physical presentation of this book, drawing as she did on her reservoir of taste and skill as an accomplished artist in production.

Words are but empty thanks in expressing my sense of obligation to Ivan Obolensky and John G. Ledes whose contribution to this project far exceeded the help an author usually receives from his publishers. It needed courage to commission this book, stamina to stay with it and a sacrificial spirit bordering on philanthropy to see it through. We were all aided in our ups and downs, fiscal, legal and otherwise, by my friend and associate Joel H. Weinberg, whose indomitable optimism buoyed us in moments of crisis, and whose ingenuity and learning lifted us over some of the hurdles we found on the way blocking our path.

This final "thank you" to Liesel, my dear wife of three decades. She may seem to remind one of the little lady in Van Wyck Brooks' biography of Mark Twain, because she not only edits my works but edits me as well. But unlike poor Twain, to whom this represented an ordeal, I am quite pleased with the arrangement and full in heart for her devoted companionship in good days and bad.

SELECTED BIBLIOGRAPHY OF
GENERAL PATTON'S WRITINGS

War As I Knew It, Boston: Houghton Mifflin Company, 1947. Annotated by Colonel Paul D. Harkins, with an introduction by Douglas Southall Freeman: Part One: "Open Letters from Africa and Sicily;" Part Two: "Operation 'Overlord';" Part Three: "Retrospect. 1. Reflections and Suggestions. 2. Earning My Pay." Partially serialized in *Saturday Evening Post.*

    General Patton's Diary. Unpublished, in the family's possession.

"Address to the Third Army," October 6, 1945

ARTICLES:

    "Comments on 'Cavalry Tanks,'" *Cavalry Journal,* 1921, 251-252

    "The Army and the National Horse Show," *ibid.,* 1923, 66-68

    "Report of the Operations of the Army Polo Team," *ibid.,* 1923, 230-233

    "Mechanized Forces," *ibid.,* 1923, 5-8

    "The 1929 Cavalry Division Maneuvers," *ibid.,* 1930, 7-15

    "Mechanization and Cavalry," *ibid.,* 1930, 234-240

    "Motorization and Mechanization in the Cavalry," *ibid.,* 1930, 331-348

    "Success in War," *ibid.,* 1931, 26-30

    "Mechanized Forces," *ibid.,* 1933, 3-8

BOOK REVIEWS:

"The Remaking of Modern Armies, by Captain B. H. Liddell Hart," *Cavalry Journal*, 1929, 129-130

"Soldier, Artist, Sportsman, ed. by Major General Sir Frederick Maurice," *ibid.*, 1929, 130-131

"The Future of the British Army, by Major B. C. Dening," *ibid.*, 1929, 292-294

"History of the Third United States Cavalry, by Chaplain Ralph C. Deibert," *ibid.*, 1933, 49-50

"Case of Béthouart and His Adherents," Memorandum for General Dwight D. Eisenhower, November 14, 1942, in AFHQ AG, 336-62, Micro Job 24, Reel No. 78D

"Christmas Greetings to the Third Army," December 24, 1944

"Cooperation of French Authorities," Memorandum for General Eisenhower, November 15, 1942, in AFHQ AG, 336, Micro Job 24, Reel No. 78D

"Directive to General Haislip," August 17, 1944, in XV Corps G-3 Journal and File

"Directive to General Haislip," August 19, 1944, in XV Corps G-3 Journal and File

"Farewell Address to Units of Third Army," OWI File (on record)

"General Orders to Seventh U.S. Army," August 1, 1943

"General Orders to Third U.S. Army," May 9, 1945

"Letter of Instruction No. 1," March 6, 1944

"Letter of Instruction No. 2," April 3, 1944

"Letter of Instruction to XV Corps," August 8, 1944

"Letter of Instructions No. 4" September 25, 1944

LETTERS:

to his Father, March 13, 1905, in Semmes, p. 21

to Frederick Ayer, January 18, 1909, *ibid.*, 21-22

to his Wife, ibid., October 20, 1915, *ibid.*, 30-31

to his Wife, October 30, 1915, *ibid.*, 31-32

to his Wife, May 17, 1916, *ibid.*, 35-36

to his Wife, February 21, 1918, *ibid.*, 39

to his Wife, September 16, 1918, *ibid.*, 44-48

to his Wife, October 2, 1918, *ibid.*, 59

to his Wife, November 18, 1918, *ibid.*, 61

to Frederick Ayer, October 20, 1942, and throughout World War II, in *Atlantic Monthly*, November 1947

to his Wife, October 23, 1942, in Semmes, 91

to his Wife, October 29, 1942, in Patton, 5

to his Wife, November 2, 1942, *ibid.*, 5

to his Wife, November 6, 1942, *ibid.*, 8

to General Marshall, November 6, 1942, in OPD Exec 8, Book 7, Tab 5

to his Wife, November 8, 1942, in Patton, 8-9

to his Wife, November 11, 1942, *ibid.*, 9-10

to General Marshall, November 15, 1942, in OPD Exec 8, Book 7, Tab 5

to General Eisenhower, November 19, 1942, in AFHQ AG, Micro Job 24, Reel No. 136 D

to General Eisenhower, November 19, 1942, Semmes, 134-136

to General Eisenhower, November 21, 1942, in AFHQ G-3 OPS 77/3, Micro Job 10A, Reel No. 23C

to General Eisenhower, December 15, 1942, AFHQ G-3 77/1, Micro Job 10A, Reel No. 23C

to his Wife, December 21, 1942, in Semmes, 137-138

to his Wife, January 1, 1943, Patton, 27-30

to General McNair, March 26, 1943, in AGF Records, OCMH

to General Marshall, March 29, 1943, in WDCS 370 Africa 11, April 1943

to his Wife, April 13, 1943, in Semmes, 149-150.

to General Alvan C. Gillem Jr., May 21, 1943, in AGF Records with copy at OCMH

to his Wife, July 2, 1943, in Semmes, 158

to General Thomas T. Handy, July 5, 1943, in OPD File on A. C. Wedemeyer, Section 4, in Cline, 297

to his Wife, July 27, 1943, in Semmes, 164-165

to his Wife, August 9, 1943, *ibid.*, 166-167

to Mrs. George C. Marshall, no exact date, *ibid.*, 174

to his Wife, no date (1943), *ibid.*

to General Alexander, September 3, 1943, *ibid.*, 174-175

to his Wife, ibid., November 20, 1943, *ibid.*, 177

to his Wife, December 24, 1943, *ibid.*, 177-178

to General Walton H. Walker, August 11, 1944, in XV Corps G-3 Journal and File

to General Bradley, October 19, 1944, in 12th Army Group 371.3, Military Objective 2

to his Wife, December 29, 1944, in Semmes, 234-236

to his Wife, February 13, 1945, *ibid.*, 248

to General Bradley, February 20, 1945, in 12th A GP 371.3

Military Objective 6 (Gen. Bradley's answer, February 21, *ibid.*)

to his Wife, February 27, 1945, in Semmes, 250
to his Wife, February (no day), 1945, *ibid.*, 251
to his Wife, March 18, 1945, *ibid.*, 254
to his Wife, March 23, 1945, *ibid.*, 258-259
to his Wife, April 12, 1945, *ibid.*, 264
to General Middleton, April (no day), 1944, in OCMH
to his Wife, May 9, 1945, in Semmes, 268
to his Wife, May 20, 1945, *ibid.*, 276
to his Wife, July 21, 1945, *ibid.*, 277
to his Wife, August 18, 1945, *ibid.*, 280
to his Wife, September 11, 1945, *ibid.*, 281
to his Wife, October 5, 1945, *ibid.*, 284
to George S. Patton III, October 22, 1945, *ibid.*, 286-287
to his Wife, October 24, 1945 *ibid.*, 287
Memorandum for General Eisenhower, November 21, 1942, AFHQ SAC 000.2-2 NA Political, in AGO, Departmental Records Branch
Memorandum for General Gaffey, August (no day), in OCMH
Memorandum for General Gaffey, August 8, 1944, in XV Corps G-3 Journal and File
Memorandum for General Haislip, August 13, 1944, in OCMH
Message to the Western Task Force, November 7, 1942
Message to the Western Task Force, November 11, 1942
Message to Officers and Warrant Officers, 45th Division, June 27, 1943
Message to the Seventh U.S. Army, written June 27, delivered at sea, July 9, 1943
Message to General Grow, August 6, 1944, in OCMH
Message to General Walker, August 12, 1944, in XV Corps G-3 Journal and File
Notes on Bastogne, December 19, 1944, in TUSA AAR
"Outline Plan TORCH," October 8, 1942, in OCMH

POEMS:

"A Soldier's Burial," in Semmes, 271
"Bill," *ibid.*, 64-65
"Dead Pals," *ibid.*, 211-212
"Fear," *ibid.*, 226-227
"God of Battles," *ibid.*, 290-291
"The Moon and the Dead," *ibid.*, 256-257

"Through a Glass, Darkly," *ibid.,* 212-214

"To Our First Dead," *ibid.,* 63

"Valor," *ibid.,* 241-243

"Policy Toward French, Directive for Sub-Task Force and AAF Commanders," October 19, 1942, copy in OCMH

PRAYERS:

"A Soldier's Prayer," Semmes, 179

"Prayer," December 11, 1944, *ibid.,* 231

Record of Conference with General Bradley, August 19, 1944, ML-205, copy in OCMH

Report to General Pershing on the death of Colonel Cardenas, May 14, 1916, in Perry

Speech to divisions of Seventh U.S. Army, August 23, 1943, notes in Semmes, 170-172.

This list does not include General Patton's original writings in the After Action Reports of the Western Task Force, Seventh and Third U.S. Armies, and the Outline History of II Corps.

BIBLIOGRAPHY

(The following is a selection of the most important works among the more than 400 volumes consulted. It is followed by a listing of the primary documentary sources.)

Alexander, Harold R.L.G. (with John North), *The Alexander Memoirs 1940-1945,* New York, 1963.

Altieri, James J., *Darby's Rangers,* Durham, N.C., 1945.

Altieri, James J., *The Spearheaders,* Indianapolis, 1960.

Arnold, Henry H., *Global Mission,* New York, 1949.

Bajot, Pierre, *Le debarquement du 8 Novembre en Afrique du Nord,* Paris, 1948.

Baldwin, Hanson W., *Great Mistakes of the War,* New York, 1949.

Belden, Jack, *Still Time to Die,* New York, 1943.

Blumenson, Martin, *Breakout and Pursuit,* in U.S. Army in World War II, Washington, D.C., 1961.

Blumenson, Martin, *The Duel for France,* Boston, 1963.

Blumenson, Martin, *Anzio,* New York, 1963.

Blumentritt, Guenther, *Von Rundstedt, the Soldier and the Man,* London, 1952.

Bradley, Omar Nelson, *A Soldier's Story,* New York, 1951.

Bredin, A.E.C., *Three Assault Landings,* Washington, D.C., 1958.

Brereton, Lewis H., *The Brereton Diaries,* New York, 1946.

Brown, John Mason, *To All Hands: An Amphibious Adventure,* New York, 1943.

Bryant, Sir Arthur, *The Turn of the Tide: Study Based on the Diaries and Autobiographical Notes of Field Marshal The Viscount Alanbrooke,* London, 1957.

Bryant, Sir Arthur, *Triumph in the West: A History of the War Years Based on the Diaries of Field Marshal Alanbrooke,* Garden City, N.Y., 1959.

Carell, Paul, *Invasion: They're Coming! The German Account of the Allied Landings and the 80 Days' Battle for France*, New York, 1963.

Carew, Harold C., *History of Pasadena and the San Gabriel Valley*, 3 vols., Pasadena, California, 1930.

Cavallero, Ugo, *Commando Supremo, Diario 1940-1943 del Capo di S.M.G.*, Bologna, 1948.

Chambrun, Jacques de (with Charles de Marenches), *The American Army in the European Conflict*, New York, 1919.

Chronology of the Second World War, London, 1947.

Churchill, Winston S., *The World Crisis*, New York, 1924.

Churchill, Winston S., *The Second World War: Their Finest Hour*, Boston, 1949.

Churchill, Winston S., *The Second World War: The Hinge of Fate*, Boston, 1950.

Churchill, Winston S., *The Second World War: Closing the Ring*, Boston, 1951.

Clark, Mark W., *Calculated Risk*, New York, 1950.

Cline, Ray S., *Washington Command Post*, Washington, D. C., 1951.

Cole, Hugh M., *The Lorraine Campaign*, Washington, D.C., 1950.

Craven, Wesley Frank (with James Lea Cate), *Europe: Torch to Pointblank*, August 1942 to December 1943, in *The Army Air Forces in World War II*, vol. II, Chicago, Ill., 1949.

Craven, Wesley Frank (with James Lea Cate), *Argument to VE Day*, *ibid.*, vol. III, Chicago, Ill., 1951.

Critchell, Laurence, Four Stars of Hell, New York, 1947.

Cronologia della Seconda Guerra Mondiale, Rome, 1948.

Cunningham, Sir Andrew B., *A Soldier's Odyssey*, London, 1952.

Dupuy, R. Ernest, *The Compact History of the United States Army*, New York, 1956.

Ease, Charles (ed.), *Secret Session Speeches of the Right Hon. Winston S. Churchill*, London, 1946.

Ehrman, John, *Grand Strategy*, Vol. VI, October 1944-August 1945, in *History of Second World War*, United Kingdom Military Series, London, 1956, Vol. V, August 1943-September 1944, *ibid.*, London, 1956.

Eisenhower, Dwight D., *Crusade in Europe*, Garden City, N.Y., 1948.

Ellis, Lionel Frederic, *France and Flanders 1939-1940*, in *History of Second World War*, United Kingdom Military Series, London, 1956.

Ellis, Lionel Frederic (with G.R.G. Allen, A.E. Warhurst, Sir James Robb), *Victory in the West*, Vol. I, *The Battle of Normandy, ibid.*, London, 1962.

Esebeck, Hanns Gert von, *Afrikanische Schicksalsjahre. Geschichte des Deutschen Afrika-Korps unter Rommel*, Wiesbaden, 1949.

Farago, Ladislas (ed.), *Axis Grand Strategy*, New York, 1942.

Farago, Ladislas, *The Tenth Fleet*, New York, 1962.

Frye, William, *Marshall, Citizen Soldier*, Indianapolis, 1947.

Fuller, John Frederick Charles, *The Second World War: Its Strategy and Tactics*, London, 1948.

Funk, Arthur Layton, *Charles de Gaulle: The Crucial Years, 1943-1944*, Norman, Oklahoma, 1959.

Gallagher, Wes, *Back Door to Berlin. The Full Story of the American Coup in North Afrika*, Garden City, N.Y., 1942

Garth, David, *St. Lo*, Washington, D.C., 1946.

Gaulle, Charles de, *Memoires de guerre 1940-1944*, 3 vols., Paris, 1945-59.

Gibson, Hugh (ed.), *The Cicno Diaries, 1939-1943*, Garden City, N.Y., 1946.

Gilbert, Felix, *Hitler Directs His War*, New York, 1950.

Giraud, Henri, *Mes evasions*, Paris, 1946.

Giraud, Henri, *Un seul but, la victoire*, Paris, 1949.

Goerlitz, Walther, *History of the German General Staff 1657-1945*, New York, 1953.

Goerlitz, Walther, *Der zweite Weltkrieg, 1939-1945*, 2 vols., Stuttgart, 1951-52.

Greenfield, Kent Roberts (ed.), *Command Decisions*, Washington, D.C., 1960, with contributions by Martin Blumenson, Robert W. Coakley, Stetson Conn., Byron Fairchild, Richard M. Leighton, Charles V.P. von Luttichau, Charles B. MacDonald, Maurice Matloff, Ralph S. Mavrogordato, Leo J. Meyer, John Miller, Jr., Louis Morton, Forrest C. Pogue, Roland G. Ruppenthal, Robert Ross Smith, Earl F. Ziemke.

Greenfield, Kent Roberts (with Robert R. Palmer and Bell I. Wiley), *The Army Ground Forces: The Organization of Ground Combat Troops*, in U.S. Army in World War II series, Washington, D.C., 1947.

Greiner, H., *Die Oberste Wehrmachtfuehrung, 1939-1943*, Wiesbaden, 1951.

Grow, Robert W., *Brest to Bastogne. The Story of the Sixth Armored Division*, Paris, 1945.

Guderian, Heinz, *Achtung! Panzer!*, Berlin, 1938.

Guderian, Heinz, *Erinnerungen eines Soldaten*, Heidelberg, 1951.

Guderian, Heinz, *Panzer! Marsch!* Munich, 1956.

Guingand, Sir Francis de, *Operation Victory*, New York, 1947.

Gunther, John, *Eisenhower: The Man and the Symbol*, New York, 1952.

Gunther, John, *D-Day*, New York, 1943.

Harbord, James G., *Leaves from a War Diary*, New York, 1925.

Harbord, James G., *The American Army in France, 1917-1919*, Boston, 1936.

Harrison, Gordon A., *Cross-Channel Attack*, in *U.S. Army in World War II* series, Washington, D.C., 1951.

Hatch, Alden, *General Ike. A Biography of Dwight D. Eisenhower*, New York, 1944.

Hatch, Alden, *General Patton: General in Spurs*, New York, 1950.

Hayn, Friedrich, *Die Invasion: Von Cotentin bis Falaise*, Heidelberg, 1954.

Heiber, Helmut (ed.), *Hitlers Lagebesprechungen. Die Protokollfragmente seiner militaerischen Konferenzen, 1942-1945*, Stuttgart, 1962.

Heigl, Fritz, *Taschenbuch der Tanks*, 3 vols., Munich, 1926, 1939, 1938.

Herr, John K. (with Edward S. Wallace), *The Story of the United States Cavalry*, Boston, 1953.

Herre, Franz (with Hellmuth Auerbach), *Bibliographie zur Zeitgeschichte und zum zweiten Weltkrieg fuer die Jahre 1945-1950*, Munich, 1955.

Heusinger, Adolf, *Befehl im Widerstreit. Schicksalsstuden der deutschen Armee 1923-1945*, Tuebingen, 1957.

Horrocks, Sir Brian, *Escape to Action*, New York, 1960.

Howe, George F., *The Battle History of the 1st Armored Division*, Washington, D.C., 1954.

Howe, George F., *Northwest Africa: Seizing the Initiative in the West*, in *U.S. Army in World War II* series, Washington, D.C., 1957.

Hubatsch, Walther, *Hitlers Weisungen fuer die Kriegfueh-rung 1939-1945*, Frankfurt, 1962.

Hull, Cordell, *The Memoirs of Cordell Hull*, 2 vols., New York, 1948.

Hunt, Frazier, *The Untold Story of Douglas MacArthur*, New York, 1954.

Ingersoll, Ralph, *Top Secret*, New York, 1946.

Ismay, Sir Hastings L., *The Memoirs of General Lord Ismay*, New York, 1960.

Jacobsen, Hans-Adolf, *Der zweite Weltkrieg in Chronik und Dokumenten 1939-1945*, Darmstadt, 1961 (fifth rev. ed.)

Jewell, N.L.A., *Secret Mission Submarine*, New York, 1945.

Kahn, E.J., Jr., *McNair, Educator of an Army*, Washington, D.C., 1944.

Kammerer, Albert, *Du debarquement Africain au meurtre de Darlain*, Paris, 1949.

Kennedy, Sir John, *The Business of War*, New York, 1958.

Kesselring, Albert, *Soldat bis zum letzten Tag*, Bonn, 1953.

Kesselring, Albert, *Gedanken zum zweiten Weltkrieg*, Bonn, 1955.

Knickerbocker, H.R., *Danger Forward*, New York, 1945.

Koyen, Kenneth, *The Fourth Armored Division*, Munich, 1946.

Lambert, Arthur Lawrence, *The Ghosts of Patton's Third Army*. A History of Second U.S. Cavalry, Munich, 1946.

Langer, William L., *Our Vichy Gamble*, New York, 1947.

Leahy, William D., *I Was There*, New York, 1950.

Leighton, Richard M. (with Robert W. Coakley), *Global Logistics and Strategy, 1940-1943*, Washington, D.C., 1956.

Lemaigre-Dubreuil, Jacques ("Crusoe"), *Vicissitudes d'une victoire*, Paris, 1946.

Lochner, Louis P. (ed.), *The Goebbels Diaries*, Garden City, N.Y., 1948.

MacDonald, Charles B., *The Siegfried Line Campaign*, in *U.S. Army in World War II* series, Washington, D.C., 1964.

Macdonald, Dwight, *Memoirs of a Revolutionist*, New York, 1957.

Manstein, Erich von, *Verlorene Siege*, Bonn, 1955.

Marshall, George C., *The Winning of the War in Europe and the Pacific*. The Biennial Reports of the Chief of Staff for the Period July 1943 to June 1945, New York, 1945.

Marshall, Samuel Lyman Atwood, *Bastogne. The Story of the First Eight Days,* Washington, D.C., 1946.

Marshall, Samuel Lyman Atwood, *Night Drop,* Boston, 1962.

Matloff, Maurice (with Edwin M. Snell), *Strategic Planning for Coalition Warfare,* in *U.S. Army in World War II* series, Washington, D.C., 1953.

Mauldin, Bill, *Up Front,* New York, 1945.

Merriam, Robert E., *Dark December,* Chicago, Ill., 1947.

Millis, Walter (with E.B. Lippincott, eds.), *The War Reports of General Marshall, Admiral King and General Arnold,* New York, 1947.

Millis, Walter, *Arms and Men: A Study of American Military History,* New York, 1956.

Montagu, Ewen, *The Man Who Never Was,* New York, 1953.

Montgomery, Bernard L., *El Alamein to the River Sangro,* New York, 1949.

Montgomery, Bernard L., *Normandy to the Baltic,* New York, 1950.

Montgomery, Bernard L., *The Memoirs of Field Marshal Montgomery,* New York, 1958.

Montgomery, Bernard L., *The Path to Leadership,* New York, 1961.

Moorehead, Alan, *Montgomery: A Bibliography,* New York, 1946.

Moorehead, Alan, *Eclipse,* New York, 1945.

Mordal, Jacques, *La bataille de Casablanca,* Paris, 1952.

Morgan, Sir Frederick E., *Overture to Overlord,* New York, 1950.

Morison, Samuel Eliot, *Operations in North African Waters,* in *History of United States Naval Operations in World War II,* Boston, 1950.

Morison, Samuel Eliot, *Sicily, Salerno, Anzio, ibid.,* Boston, 1954.

Morison, Samuel Eliot, *The Invasion of France and Germany 1944-1945, ibid.,* Boston, 1945.

Norman, Albert, *Operation Overlord: Design and Reality,* Harrisburg, Pa., 1952.

North, John, *Northwest Europe, 1944-1945. The Achievement of Twenty-First Army Group,* London, 1953.

O'Connor, Richard, *Black Jack Pershing,* New York, 1961.

Palmer, Frederick, *John J. Pershing,* Harrisburg, Pa., 1948.

Patry, Robert, *St. Lo,* St. Lo, 1948.

Patton, Beatrice Ayer, *The Reminiscences of Frederick Ayer*, Boston, 1923.

Patton, Beatrice Ayer, *Blood of the Shark. A Romance of Early Hawaii*, Honolulu, 1936.

Payne, Robert, *The Marshall Story*, New York, 1951.

Pendar, Kenneth W., *Adventure in Diplomacy. Our French Dilemma*, New York, 1945.

Pershing, John J., *My Experiences in the World War*, 2 vols., New York, 1931.

Perry, Milton F. (with Barbara W. Parke), *Patton and His Pistols*, Harrisburg, Pa., 1957.

Pogue, Forrest C., *The Supreme Command*, in *U.S. Army in World War II* series, Washington, D.C., 1954.

Pogue, Forrest C., *George C. Marshall. Education of a General*, 1880-1939, New York, 1963 (first of a projected three-volume biography).

Pyle, Ernie, *Brave Men*, New York, 1943.

Repiton-Preneuf (ed.), *La 2e DB. General Leclerc: Combattants et combats en France*, Paris, 1945.

Rommel, Erwin, *Infantry in Angriff*, Berlin, 1938.

Rommel, Erwin, *Krieg ohne Hass*, Heidenheim, 1950.

Rousseau, Xavier, *La bataille de Normandie au pays d'Argentan*, Argentan, 1945-47.

Ruge, Friedrich, *Rommel und die Invasion. Erinnerungen*, Stuttgart, 1959.

Ruppenthal, Roland G., *Utah Beach to Cherbourg*, Washington, D.C., 1947.

Ruppenthal, Roland G., *Logistical Support of the Armies*, 2 vols., in *U.S. Army in World War II* series, Washington, D.C., 1953, 1958.

Schramm, Percy Ernst (with Hans O.H. Stange), *Geschichte des zweiten Weltkrieges*, Wuerzburg, 1956 (second rev. ed.)

Senger, V. (with Dr. F. Etterlin), *Taschenbuch der Panzer*, 1943-1954, Munich, 1954.

Sherwood, Robert E., *Roosevelt and Hopkins: An Intimate History*, New York, 1948.

Shulman, Milton, *Defeat in the West*, New York, 1948.

Smith, Walter Bedell, *Eisenhower's Six Great Decisions*, New York, 1946.

Speidel, Hans, *Invasion, 1944. Ein Beitrag zu Rommels und des Reiches Schicksal*, Tuebingen, 1949.

Stacey, C.P., *The Canadian Army 1939-1945*. An Official Historical Summary, Ottawa, 1948.

Stimson, Henry L. (with McGeorge Bundy), *On Active Service in Peace and War*, New York, 1947.

Strutten, William, *The Secret Invaders*, London, 1948.

Summersby, Kay, *Eisenhower Was My Boss*, New York, 1948.

Taggart, Donald G., *History of the Third Infantry Division in World War II*, Washington, D.C., 1947.

Terrett, Delany, *The Signal Corps: The Emergency* (to December 1941), in the *U.S. Army in World War II* series, Washington, D.C., 1956.

Thompson, George Raynor (with Dixie R. Harris, Pauline M. Oakes, Delany Terrett), *The Signal Corps: The Test* (December 1941 to July 1943), *ibid.*, Washington, D.C., 1957.

Thompson, R.W., *The Battle for the Rhineland*, London, 1958.

Tompkins, Frank B., *Chasing Villa. The Story Behind Pershing's Expedition into Mexico*, Harrisburg, Pa., 1934.

Toulmin, H.A., Jr., *With Pershing in Mexico*, Harrisburg, Pa., 1935.

Tregaskis, Richard, *Invasion Diary*, New York, 1944.

Truscott, Lucian K., Jr., *Command Mission. A Personal Story*, New York, 1954.

Vagts, Alfred, *Landing Operations*, New York, 1946.

Vagts, Alfred, *A History of Militarism* (rev. ed.), New York, 1959.

Vigneras, Marcel, *Rearming the French*, in *U.S. Army in World War II* series, Washington, D.C., 1957.

Wallace, Brenton Greene, *Patton and his Third Army*, Harrisburg, Pa., 1946.

Warlimont, Walther, *Erinnerungen*, Frankfurt, 1962.

Wedemeyer, Albert C., *Wedemeyer Reports*, New York, 1958.

Weinberg, Albert K. (with Harry L. Coles, Jr.), *Soldiers Become Governors*, Washington, D.C., 1963.

Westphal, Siegfried, *The German Army in the West*, London, 1952.

Whitehouse, Arch, *Tank. The Story of their Battles and the Men Who Drove them from their First Use in World War I to Korea*, New York, 1960.

Williams, Mary H., *Chronology 1941-1945*, in *U.S. Army in World War II* series, Washington, D.C., 1960.

Wilmot, Chester, *The Struggle for Europe*, London, 1952.

Wiltse, Dr. Charles M., *History of the U.S. Medical Corps in World War II*, Washington, D.C., 1963.

Woolcott, Alexander, *The Command of Forward*, New York, 1919.

Zanuck, Darryl F., *Tunis Expedition*, New York, 1943.

MAJOR DOCUMENTS CONSULTED

"Action Report Western Naval Task Force, The Sicilian Campaign," July-August 1943.

Alexander, H.R.L.G., "The African Campaign from El Alamein to Tunis, from 10 August 1942 to 13 May 1943," Supplement to the *London Gazette*, February 3, 1948.

Alexander, H.R.L.G., "Report to the War Office on Sicilian Operations," *ibid.*, February 10, 1948.

Army Ground Forces, "Report of Activities . . . to the Chief of Staff, by the Commanding General AGF," January 10, 1946.

"Bericht ueber die Vorgaenge in Franzoesisch-Morokko und Nordafrika, vom 8-11. XI. 1942," DWStK, Kontrollinspektion Afrika, IA, No. 150-42, November 15 1942.

Béthouart, Emile, "The Occurrences of 8 November in Morocco."

"Considerations on the Italian Campaign 1943-1944," transcript of the interrogation of Colonel Bogislaw von Bonin, 1947.

Eisenhower, Dwight D., "North African Campaign, 1942-1943."

Eisenhower, Dwight D., "General Order 128, HQ ETO, U.S. Army, June 17, 1945, as amended by General Order 182, August 7, 1945."

Eisenhower, Dwight D., "Report by the Supreme Commander to the Combined Chiefs of Staff on the Operations in Europe of the Allied Expeditionary Force," 1946.

Fifteenth (XV) Corps, "After Action Report," 1945.

Fifth (V) Corps, "Operations in ETO, After Action Report," 1945.

First (1st) Infantry Division, "G-2 Journal," "G-2 Operations Report," "G-3 Radio Log," May 15-September 15, 1943.

Fourth (4th) Armored Division, "After Action Report," 1945.

Forty-fifth (45th) Division, "Report on Operations, Sicily, July 10-August 22, 1943."

General Board Reports, a collection of 131 studies covering
all aspects of the war in ETO.

Gersdorf, Rudolf-Christoph Freiherr von, "The German
Counterattack against Avranches," Manuscript No. B-725.

"Geschichte des Oberbefehlshaber West," Manuscript No.
T-121, T-122.

"History of Allied Force Headquarters," AFQH, Mediterranean Theater of Operations.

"Landings in North Africa," *Combat Narrative,* U.S. Office
of Naval Intelligence.

Luttichau, C.V.P. von, "The Ardennes Offensive. Germany's
Situation in the Fall of 1944," *Manuscript* in OCMH.

Medicine Under Canvas. War Journal of the 77th Evacuation Hospital, 1949.

Meller, Sidney, "The Desert Training Center and California-
Arizona Maneuver Area," *Army Ground Forces Study
No. 15.*

"Minutes of General George C. Marshall's meeting with
General Béthouart," February 3, 1943, JRC Files, No.
902/II.

Montgomery, Bernard L., "Address to the officers in the
four field armies. Brief summary of Operation Overlord
as affecting the Army," April 7, 1944.

Montgomery, Bernard L., "Address to the General Officers
of the four field armies," London, May 15, 1944.

Montgomery, Bernard L., "Operations in North-West Europe from 6th June 1944 to 5th May 1944," Supplement,
London Gazette, September 3, 1946.

Ninetieth (90th) Division, "After Action Report."

Ninety-fifth (95th) Division, "After Action Report."

Oberkommando des Heeres (OKH), Gen.St.d.H/Organisa-
tions-Abteilung KTB, October 13, 1944, the German
Order of Battle in Western Europe.

"Post-Neptune Courses of Action after capture of Lodgment Area," May 3, 1944.

"Post-Neptune Planning Forecast, I," May 27, 1944.

"Prepartions for TORCH," Manuscript by William C.
Frierson.

"Report on the evacuation of Sicily," an essay prepared in
1946 for U.S. Navy by German Vice Admiral Friedrich
Ruge.

Second (II) U.S. Corps, "Chronology of Operations in Tunisia," May 1, 1943.

Second (II) U.S. Corps, "Outline of History," 1946.

Seventh U.S. Army, "Report of Operations . . . in the Sicilian Campaign," 1944.

Seventh U.S. Army, HQ Provisional Corps, "Report of Operations 15 July-20 August 1943," mimeographed, 1943.

Sicilian Campaign, information from German sources, Historical Section, Canadian Army Headquarters.

"Synopsis of Operations," 82nd Airborne Division, G-2, July 18-August 21, 1943.

Tenth (10th) Armored Division, "G-3 Journal" and "After Action Report."

Third U.S. Army, "After Action Report," 1945, 2 vols.

Twelfth Army Group, "Report of Operations," 14 vols., 1946.

Twelfth (XII) Corps, "Spearhead of Patton's Third Army," 1947.

Twelfth (XII) Corps, "Report of Operations," 1945.

Twentieth (XX) Corps, "G-3 Journal."

Twentieth (XX) Corps, "Operational Report," 1 September 6 December 1944.

Western Task Force, "Final Report," AGO, 1942.

"Verluste der Wehrmacht bis 1944," OKW/Allg. Wehrmachts-Amt, 1 December 1944.

(Post-war essays prepared for the U.S. Army by German Generals Kriepe, Knobelsdorff, Mellenthien, Blumentritt, Zimmermann, and others.)

INDEX

DON'T MISS THESE
BESTSELLERS FROM DELL

THE SHOES OF THE FISHERMAN
Morris L. West   75c

HARLOW Irving Shulman   95c

THE 480 Eugene Burdick   85c

PEYTON PLACE Grace Metalious   75c

THE CINCINNATI KID Richard Jessup   60c

THE DIAMOND SMUGGLERS Ian Fleming   50c

HERE GOES KITTEN Robert Gover   75c

SEX AND THE COLLEGE GIRL Gael Greene   75c

THE FEMININE MYSTIQUE Betty Friedan   75c

THE COLLECTOR John Fowles   75c

THE SPY WHO CAME IN FROM THE COLD
John Le Carré   75c

CATCH-22 Joseph Heller   75c